JOHNSON O'CONNOR
ENGLISH VOCABULARY
BUILDER

BOOKS BY
JOHNSON O'CONNOR

BORN THAT WAY
PSYCHOMETRICS

JOHNSON O'CONNOR

ENGLISH VOCABULARY

BUILDER

HOBOKEN

HUMAN ENGINEERING LABORATORY

1939

FIRST EDITION

First Printing, 5,000 copies, December 1937
Second Printing, 20,000 copies, October 1939

PRINTED IN THE UNITED STATES
BY GEORGE GRADY PRESS

ACKNOWLEDGMENTS

A study as extensive as that which has led to the present volume is practicable only because of the cooperation of many persons and organizations. The Research Corporation has each year since 1933 given the Human Engineering Laboratory funds for this research on English vocabulary. The General Education Board of the Rockefeller Foundation assisted the Laboratory in completing one portion of the work. The International Business Machines Corporation has enabled the Laboratory to have a set of data-handling machines for the accurate assembly of material. The Atwell Company of Boston has made it possible for the Laboratory to have Ediphone equipment which has contributed to the preparation of this volume. Without the aid which has been received from Stevens Institute of Technology as an organization, and from its president, Dr. Harvey N. Davis, and its vice president, Mr. James Creese, not only this volume but the Human Engineering Laboratory might never have existed.

COLLABORATORS .

Staff of the Human Engineering Laboratory, 1937

TEST ADMINISTRATORS

David Mack
O. S. Reimold II
Margaret E. Ferry
Charles R. Wilks
John M. Howe
Leonora Snow
William P. Baker
Jerome Salny
Alfred R. McWilliams, Jr.

RESEARCH ASSOCIATES

Samuel Pomeroy Horton
Mary E. Filley
Florence Hauck

STATISTICAL ASSISTANTS

Marie D. Alfano
Nelson Haflich

MECHANIC

Emile Monnier

SECRETARIAL STAFF

Elizabeth Hauck	Ann Pigari
Evelyn C. Wight	Angelina Cattaneo
Gertrude Engelking	Anne C. Hull
Louise W. Yawger	Virginia Whitehead
Ruth Felker	Barbara E. Armstrong

MIMEOGRAPH OPERATORS

Olive DeMan   Marguerite Corliss

VOCABULARY AND SUCCESS[1]

What is success? And how is it gained? Whether one thinks of success as financial reward, or as assured social position, or as satisfaction in able work accomplished and recognized, or as a combination of the three and something more, many factors contribute. Most of them elude our understanding and remain intangibly beyond definition. A vital force drives some persons over every obstacle. With others that great generalization, character, adds strength of a different sort. Neither may ever be restricted to a hard and fast formula; certainly, at the moment, neither can be measured. But other more concrete constituents of success have been isolated and studied in the laboratory. One of these is a large English vocabulary.

An extensive knowledge of the exact meanings of English words accompanies outstanding success in this country more often than any other single characteristic which the Human Engineering Laboratory has been able to isolate and measure.

What is meant by vocabulary? Just what the word signifies. Does ENERVATING mean SOOTHING, EXCITING, DISTRESSING, INVIGORATING, or WEAKENING? For most well-educated persons the choice is between INVIGORATING and WEAKENING. Fifty-two per cent of the college graduates measured by the Laboratory choose INVIGORATING as the synonym; only sixteen per cent choose WEAKENING, the dictionary definition. Does STILTED, in the phrase: 'His STILTED manner', mean IRRESOLUTE, IMPROPER, CORDIAL, STIFFLY FORMAL, or VICIOUS? A majority of educated persons mark STIFFLY FORMAL, but more than a third select IRRESOLUTE. Answers to the meaning of SCURRILOUS, in the phrase: 'SCURRILOUS rogue', divide themselves more or less evenly between HURRYING, DESPERATE, ABUSIVE, FRANTIC, and DISEASED, with DESPERATE the most popular. For PEREMPTORY, a majority mark DECISIVE, but many choose PERSUASIVE, UNCERTAIN, and ANGRY. PLEASANT, the fifth choice, is not so popular. LINGUIST and GLUTTON are

[1] This article, practically in the following form, first appeared in the Atlantic Monthly, February, 1934; and at that time was copyrighted, 1934, by the Atlantic Monthly Company, Boston, Massachusetts.

equally enticing as synonyms for POLYGLOT. For REFULGENT, in: 'A REFULGENT smile', REPELLENT is most alluring, and VERY BRIGHT next, with MISCHIEVOUS, FLATTERING, and SOUR, all following closely in popularity. For MONOGRAPH forty per cent choose SOLILOQUY and less than twenty per cent TREATISE and EPITAPH each.

The word VOCABULARY, as used in this book, signifies a knowledge of the dictionary meaning of just such words as ENERVATING, STILTED, SCURRILOUS, PEREMPTORY, POLYGLOT, REFULGENT, and MONOGRAPH. One may like the sound of a word and use it in a picturesque way without being accurate in its meaning. Not until one attempts to pick an exact synonym does one realize the difficulty.

I

To measure the vocabulary of an individual the Laboratory uses a list of one hundred and fifty test words. Each is printed in a short phrase and is followed by five choices, all of which fit the phrase but only one of which is a synonym of the test word. The instructions are: 'Underline that one of the five choices which is nearest in meaning to the word in the phrase'. The first selection of words to be defined was made by Alexander Inglis of the Graduate School of Education, Harvard University. His intention was to include words which appear once or twice in 100,000 words of printed matter; and to limit the selection to the general reader's vocabulary, excluding technical terms. Another selection has been made, by Mr. Bartlett Boyden of Deerfield Academy, of words encountered by the preparatory-school student.

The test words vary from some which are easy, such as UNTIDY in the item:

His UNTIDY room. BEAUTIFUL DISORDERLY NEAT GORGEOUS HIGH-CEILINGED

to others which are more difficult, such as ANFRACTUOUS in the item:

ANFRACTUOUS lines. CONTINUOUS DOTTED STRAIGHT DOUBLE WINDING

which only twenty per cent of college graduates mark correctly. Since one fifth, or twenty per cent, should guess the correct answer, the meaning of ANFRACTUOUS is practically unknown. The test measures knowledge of words one recognizes, not necessarily of those one uses. The words one uses accurately are, no doubt, fewer than those one recognizes, but there is probably a relation between the two.

Three hundred high-school freshmen average 76 errors in the list of 150 words. Seven hundred college freshmen average 42 errors. One thousand college graduates, from a wide variety of colleges, average 27 errors, and vary from one person in a thousand who achieves a perfect score to the one who knows less than 50 of the 150 items. College professors, measured by the Laboratory, average 8 errors; major executives average 7 errors.[1] Major executives score higher in this English vocabulary test than any other selected group with which the Laboratory has experimented.

By the term MAJOR EXECUTIVE is meant all persons who, for ten years or longer, have held the position of president or vice president in a business organization. Such a definition includes both successful and unsuccessful executives, provided only that they have survived ten years; it includes alike forceful personalities and figureheads; but it has the great advantage of excluding personal judgment from the process of selection. Major executives as thus defined average in the top ten per cent of college graduates.

Although it is impossible to define success rigidly, a large vocabulary seems to be typical, not exclusively of executives, but of successful persons. It happens that in the business world successful men and women are designated by this special appellation, EXECUTIVE. The successful lawyer or doctor is marked by no such name. But if, to the best of one's ability, one selects successful persons in the professions, they also score high in vocabulary.

For one meaning of success the Century dictionary gives: 'A high degree of worldly prosperity'. The measured English vocabularies of executives correlate with their salaries. This does not mean that every high-vocabulary person receives a large salary, but the relation is sufficiently close to

[1] One project, 'A Study of the English Vocabulary Scores of 75 Executives', appears in Technical Report Number Two issued by the Human Engineering Laboratory.

show that a large vocabulary is one element of success, and seemingly an important one.

Furthermore, the executive level which a man or woman reaches is determined to some extent by vocabulary. In many manufacturing organizations the first step in the executive ladder is the leading hand, called sometimes the working foreman. This man is in charge of half a dozen others. He works at the bench or at a machine as they do, but is the executive of the group. The next step is the foreman, who may be in charge of as many as a hundred or more workers. He does no bench work, he is not a producer, but devotes full time to his executive duties, to the keeping of records and to the handling of the personnel. The next step in many large organizations is the department head or superintendent or manager, who ordinarily does not come in direct contact with the workers, but handles them through his foremen. The final step is the major executive or official, the vice president or president.

These four executive ranks represent four degrees of success, in one sense in which that word is used. One is advanced from leading hand to foreman, from foreman to manager, from manager to president. As far as the Laboratory can determine by measurements, the leading hand and the official have much the same inherent aptitudes. They differ primarily in vocabulary. Typical non-college-graduate shop foremen average, as a group, about as high as college graduates. Department heads score higher, roughly fifteen errors, and major executives the highest of all, averaging only seven errors. Whether the word EXECUTIVE refers only to the major group or is used in the broader sense to mean anyone in charge of other workers, it is still true that the executive scores higher than those under him and higher than other persons of similar age and education.

II

An interesting sidelight on the high vocabulary scores of executives is that they were unforeseen. When a scientist expects a result and finally achieves it there is always the feeling that, regardless of the care he has taken, personal bias may have entered. Six or eight years ago the Human

Engineering Laboratory tested forty major executives of the Telephone Company who had offered themselves as victims to be experimented upon in a search for executive characteristics. At the same time the Laboratory was also revising the vocabulary test, not with the notion of using it with executives, but with the hope that it might prove of value in education. One day, with no thought of the consequences, it was given to an executive, and from then on was asked for regularly because of the interest it aroused. The Laboratory paid little heed to the results until one executive refused to take the test. He had been obliged by lack of money to leave school at fourteen. With no further formal education, he had worked his way to a major position. He had taken the aptitude tests without hesitation, but vocabulary seemed to him so directly the result of schooling that he knew in advance he would fail. His own words were that he had made his way without being found out and he was not willing to give himself away. But in scientific work one cannot test only those who think they will do well, and he was finally persuaded to try the vocabulary test. He made two errors where the average college graduate makes twenty-seven.

Was it luck? Or was it significant of something not recognized? The Laboratory listed the vocabulary scores of one hundred executives and, parallel with them, the scores of one hundred miscellaneous college graduates. The difference between the two arrays was striking. Only nine per cent of the college graduates scored as high as the average major executive.

Why do large vocabularies characterize executives and possibly outstanding men and women in other fields? The final answer seems to be that words are the instruments by means of which men and women grasp the thoughts of others and with which they do much of their own thinking. They are the tools of thought.

Before accepting so far-reaching a conclusion several more obvious explanations must be examined and excluded. The first and most natural supposition is that successful persons acquire words with age and with the experiences of life. Success does not usually occur early. The successful group were necessarily older in both years and experience than the general run of college graduates with whom they were compared; and their large vocabularies might be the inevitable result of age.

To probe this point a study of the growth of vocabulary with age was undertaken. From nine, the earliest age for which the Laboratory has a large number of measurements, to twenty-two or twenty-three vocabulary expands steadily and at a uniform rate. Through this school period the score on the vocabulary test of one hundred and fifty items improves five items a year. From twenty-five to fifty vocabulary continues to increase, but changes no more in these twenty-five years than in two school years, not enough to explain the high scores of executives. Normally, vocabulary is acquired early in life, before most men have made appreciable progress toward a responsible position. The large vocabularies of successful persons come before success rather than after. Age and the experiences of life may contribute new words, but certainly do not explain in full the high vocabulary scores of business executives.

The next thought is that effective schooling may be the source both of a wide vocabulary and of executive success. It is known, from the work which the American Telephone and Telegraph Company has undertaken, that there is a relationship between school success and business success later in life. Although not everyone who leads his class becomes a brilliant executive, and although not everyone who fails in school fails in life, in general school success preludes executive success. Schooling may be the vital factor of which the large vocabularies which the Laboratory is measuring are but by-products.

To obtain evidence bearing on this point, the Laboratory measured the vocabularies of twenty men who had left school at the age of fifteen and who had worked their way into major positions. They also averaged only seven errors. Their scores equaled those of the college-graduate executives. In the case of these twenty men it is their vocabularies which are important rather than their formal school education. Their large vocabularies are not the result of schooling and must, we therefore conclude, be significant for some other reason than as a by-product of an educational background.

Is, then, a college background of no importance? Has the non-college man the same chance of becoming an executive as has the college graduate? This fact seemed worth determining. Of the major executives in a large industrial organization, sixty per cent are college graduates, forty per cent non-college. At first glance, college would seem to have done little, for almost half are not college men. But, to be fair to education, there is another angle from which to view this result. Of the college graduates with this same company more than three quarters are in executive positions, whereas, of the non-college men, well under a tenth are in similar positions. College graduates, in general, average measurably higher in vocabulary than do non-college persons. Furthermore, of the college group a significantly larger percentage are executives.

One would like to conclude without further preamble that the vocabularies of the college group are large because of directed effort and that these purposefully gained vocabularies have contributed to executive success. Non-college executives, then, are those rare individuals who pick up words so easily that their vocabularies are large without effort. But there is one further possibility which must be investigated.

Although the vocabulary test was designed to measure knowledge which must have come through books or by word of mouth, a high score may reveal an underlying aptitude for language. It may be some flair for the meanings of words which is the contributing factor in both vocabulary and success later in life. The primary purpose of the Human Engineering Laboratory is the isolation and measurement of aptitudes in an attempt to aid each boy and girl in finding a type of work in which he or she has the best chance of success. The Laboratories, both at Stevens Institute of Technology and in Boston, are open to any boy or girl, from the age of nine on, interested in spending two hours or two hours and a half in going through a set of so-called sample jobs or worksamples and discussing his or her educational or vocational problems. Ten aptitudes have been isolated in this study, eight of which can be measured with some accuracy, and two others approximated. Yet that particular characteristic which contributes to a large vocabulary has not been found. For the time, we must leave the conclusion of this part of the research in abeyance and admit that the vocabularies of successful executives may reveal an aptitude.

III

Vocabularies may always be consciously increased regardless of the presence or absence of any gift. A knowledge of the meaning of each word at one's command must have been obtained by word of mouth or through reading, by some educational process.

Furthermore, with groups of persons of apparently similar aptitudes, the amount of vocabulary added in a given period varies with different educational techniques. At Stevens Institute of Technology the freshman class was at one time regularly divided alphabetically into four sections. Each of these studied freshman English under a different member of the faculty. Some years ago the entire class took the vocabulary test the first week of freshman year. The four sections averaged about the same in vocabulary, and there was no reason to suppose that, selected as they were, one would score higher than another or have more ability. Yet, when remeasured nine months later, two of the sections had improved more than average academic freshmen, one section had improved only half this amount, and the fourth had retrogressed slightly.

The improvement of one section may have been due to the fact that the instructor was interested in the vocabulary test and its implications. The important fact is that differences in vocabulary improvement were caused by differences in teaching techniques, that an improvement in vocabulary score can be produced by education.

Those boys and girls whom the Laboratory has measured and urged to better their vocabularies, and then remeasured at the end of two or three years, have shown more than average improvement. Here again vocabulary is induced independent of aptitude. There are available for school use nine forms of the English vocabulary tests. They vary from ones applicable to fifth grade to others designed for the college graduate, and are now administered annually by many schools.

We come now to the question of whether or not that increment of vocabulary directly due to educational stimulation contributes to success. The four sections of the freshman class at Stevens Institute of Technology to which reference has been made, which took freshman English with different members of the faculty and improved different amounts in vocabulary, were followed to see the effect of these new vocabularies on school work the next year. The four sections averaged nearly the same in school marks freshman year. Sophomore year the two sections which had enlarged their vocabularies the previous year showed general gain in all school subjects, not strikingly, not enough to prove the point once and for all time, but enough to suggest that a vocabulary acquired consciously reflects in general school improvement the next year.

It is always possible that the improvement in school work was due to inspired teaching, to added incentive, but if this were true it would seem as if the improvement in school work should appear immediately freshman year, whereas it did not appear until sophomore year after the vocabularies had been acquired. This seems to indicate that it is the additional words themselves which are the tools used the next year, that words are important in and for themselves.

IV

Granted that diction is important, and many would agree without elaborate proof of the point, how, from the standpoint of the school, can it best be given; and, from that of the individual, how best achieved? Is it a knowledge of Latin and Greek which lays a sound foundation for a real understanding of words? Or is it constant reading? Or the assiduous perusal of the dictionary? Probably all contribute.

In the search for a road to vocabulary, the Laboratory has unearthed three laws of learning.

First Law of Learning Vocabulary: It is possible to arrange the words of the dictionary in order of familiarity, in order of difficulty. The words HORSESHOER, SOAK, POST-PONE, and LAW, words 1, 2, 3, and 4, in this book, have been found by tests to be known to practically every grammar-school pupil. GIGANTIC, RUDE, and REMEDY, words 63, 64, and 65, are unknown to 11 per cent of grammar-school pupils but known to practically all adult readers. The meaning of IMMUNE, word 501 in this volume, was not recognized by 22 per cent of a group of one thousand adults; and TACIT, number 982, not recognized by 75 per cent.

Eleven hundred and eighteen words are here arranged in an order of difficulty which has been discovered as the result of measuring approximately twenty thousand persons. The percentage of this group which has misinterpreted each word can be followed by means of the running heading at the top of each page.

Why HORSESHOER (1) should be more familiar than FARRIER (895), SOAK (2) more familiar than SATURATE (139), POSTPONE (3) more familiar than PROCRASTINATE (679), is not known. The contributing factor is not always length, for CONFERENCE (11) is a longer but easier word than PARLEY (283), RUDIMENTARY (370) longer but easier than INCHOATE (1117). Yet length probably plays a part. Nor is it always the Anglo-Saxon word which is easiest; for HAPLESS (387), which can be traced back at least to Middle English, is more difficult than UNFORTUNATE (13), the body of which is Latin. A possible coincidence, which piques one's curiosity, is that ELUSORY (345), LUDICROUS (378), and ILLUSION (495), all from the same Latin *ludere*, to play, are not exactly but are of something the same order of difficulty. Perhaps a knowledge of the history of a word underlies a grasp of its meaning. No doubt many factors combine. Only a painstaking study of causes will ultimately disclose the reasons which contribute to the familiarity or difficulty of a word. Until this can be completed the arrangement of this book must be accepted as an empirical finding, one which will change slightly as additional data accumulates, but probably not materially.

Second Law of Learning: Each person knows most of the words which the Laboratory has studied up to those of a degree of difficulty at which his or her vocabulary stops, and knows but few words beyond that point. There is, of course, a region of uncertainty between the known and the unknown; but this does not invalidate the general finding. Most college graduates who open this volume will know intimately the first fifty or even one hundred words. Many will fail to know accurately and without hesitation the last hundred. Somewhere between lies the borderline of each person's vocabulary. For vocabulary advances with an almost unbroken front. The words at one's command are not a miscellany gathered from hither and yon. With a few exceptions they are all of the words in the dictionary up to those of an order of difficulty at which one's vocabulary stops, and almost no words beyond.

An exception to this rule is the foreign student who may know difficult words because of their similarity to those of his own language, but miss easier ones. Thus the Southern European often marks correctly such difficult words as CEPHALIC, GARRULITY, and PISCATORIAL, because of knowledge of Italian and French, but fails to know easier words of Anglo-Saxon origin.

Third Law of Learning: Rate of learning, to use an engineer's expression, is greatest for those words which are on or just beyond the boundary of one's vocabulary. For most persons, for the first few words at the beginning of this volume, rate of learning is zero for these words are already known. For all except those with exceptionally extensive vocabularies rate of learning for the last few words of the volume is also zero, for although they can be momentarily committed to memory they are soon forgotten. To learn new words at a maximum speed each reader should skip as many pages at the beginning of the book as contain words well known to him. He should start reading at a page where perhaps a quarter, perhaps a half, of the words are unknown or doubtful.

V

In the region where learning is taking place a common error is the confusion of a word with its exact opposite. Among seventh- and eighth-grade and first-year high-school pupils, nearly a third mark FOUND GUILTY as the correct meaning of ACQUITTED. UPRIGHT is the most popular misconception of the meaning of RECLINING; and, strange as it may seem, NEAT is the commonest misconception of UN-TIDY. The seventh-grade youngster berated for keeping an untidy room quite often evidently receives the impression that he is too orderly. The failing is not limited to the high-school group. For INCONTROVERTIBLE the correct answer INDISPUTABLE is usually marked by college men, but of the remaining four choices UNSOUND is by far most popular. In the phrase: 'You ALLAY my fears', where the five choices are JUSTIFY, CALM, AROUSE, INCREASE, and CONFIRM, CALM is usually answered by the educated group, but AROUSE is next most popular. In the phrase: 'He RETRACTS his criticism', WITHDRAWS is the correct answer and REPEATS is the most common delusion. In 'He VENTED his wrath', POURED FORTH is correct and RESTRAINED is the commonest misapprehension.

One need but turn to words of which one is not quite certain to see how difficult it is to distinguish opposites. One evening at dinner with a delightful dean of education, we fell to discussing this question. He recognized CATHODE and ANODE instantly as electrical terms designating the two poles, but hesitated a moment before saying which was which. PORT and STARBOARD he admitted he had never straightened out and resorted to some such phrase as: 'Jack left port'. GEE and HAW were beyond him. He surmised that they meant UP and DOWN, but said frankly he did not know the words. When told that they were used in plough-ing, he was instantly interested, but did not care at all which was right and which was left. He was taking the first step in the learning process, placing them in their correct en-vironment. The fifty-two per cent of adult readers who choose INVIGORATING as the meaning of ENERVATING are on the verge of knowing the word. The dictum of modern education, never to teach what a thing is not, has perhaps come from a realization of this confusion of opposites. The confusion seems, however, to be a natural step in the learn-ing process.

VI

In the study of human beings the factors involved are so numerous and so intertwined with one another that the experimenter, in unraveling the strands, must pause periodically to make certain that he is progressing. What then has been discovered? An exact and extensive vocabulary is an important concomitant of success. So much is known. Furthermore, such a vocabulary can be acquired. It increases as long as a person remains in school or college, but without conscious effort does not change materially thereafter.

There may be some subtle distinction between a natural vocabulary picked up at home, at meals, and in reading, and one gained by a study of the dictionary. The latter may not be so valuable as the former. But there is nothing to show that it is harmful and the balance of evidence at the moment suggests that such a consciously, even laboriously, achieved vocabulary is an active asset.

JOHNSON O'CONNOR

Director Human Engineering Laboratory
Stevens Institute of Technology
Hoboken, New Jersey

PRONUNCIATION

In this book no attempt has been made to give exact vowel sounds. In addition to the accent only two phonetic marks have been used, the long and the short. This book does not replace a dictionary; it is not primarily a reference book, but is an attempt to answer a few specific questions with which the general reader is frequently faced.

ă	CAP (kăp), FAT (făt), BLACK (blăk)
ā	MAKE (māk), CAGE (kāj), DAY (dā)
ĕ	MET (mĕt), TEN (tĕn), BELL (bĕl)
ē	DEEP (dēp), NEAT (nēt), SEEM (sēm)
ĭ	DIP (dĭp), IT (ĭt), THIS (thĭs)
ī	FIVE (fīv), LIKE (līk), FLY (flī)
ŏ	LOG (lŏg), ON (ŏn), TOP (tŏp)
ō	BONE (bōn), ROLL (rōl), NO (nō)
ŭ	UP (ŭp), SUN (sŭn), TUB (tŭb)
ū	TUNE (tūn), DUKE (dūk), USE (ūz)
ah	FAR (fahr), STAR (stahr), FATHER (fah'-ther)
aw	LAW (law), SAW (saw), CAUGHT (kawt)
er	HER (her), TURN (tern), DIRT (dert)
oo	SCHOOL (skool), FOOD (food), BOOT (boot)
o͝o	BOOK (bŏŏk), LOOK (lŏŏk), FOOT (fŏŏt)

Only one accent mark (') has been used; the secondary accent, when it occurs, having been omitted. LESSON (lĕs'-sŏn); RAILROAD (rāl'-rōd); ELEPHANT (ĕl'-ĕ-fănt); EVERLASTING (ĕv-er-lăs'-tĭng).

1. *HORSESHOER* (*hors'-shoo-er*) *n.* One who shoes horses or makes horseshoes, blacksmith, farrier (895).

HORSESHOE was once, in Anglo-Saxon, two separate words: *horsis sho.* It then passed through a stage in which the two words were hyphenated, *hors-scho.* But many years ago it became one word, *horscho*, now of course spelt HORSESHOE.

This is the history of many compound words. They start as separate words, are then hyphenated for the convenience of treating them as single words, and are finally written as one word. There is no rule by which one can tell infallibly whether a word is hyphenated or not. In general, words which have been in use for two or three hundred years have become single words with no hyphen. Thus: HORSEBACK, HORSEHAIR, HORSEMAN, HORSEMANSHIP, HORSEWHIP, HORSESHOE, and HORSE-SHOER, which go back to the fourteenth and fifteenth centuries, are all words of long standing and are all written as single words. On the other hand, more recent words such as HORSE-CAR and HORSE-POWER, both of which first appeared in the nineteenth century, are often hyphenated.

Perhaps in the future, with the gradual disappearance of horses from city streets, the word HORSESHOER may become less familiar; but today the word is known to practically every grammar-school pupil.

In this volume, about eleven hundred words are arranged in order of difficulty, as determined by the method which has been described in the introduction. This word, HORSE-SHOER, in the test phrase: 'The local HORSESHOER', is most familiar. A few pages over, such words as GIGANTIC, TOURNAMENT, and LOITER, are unknown to eleven per cent of grammar-school pupils, but are known to practically all adult readers. In the center of this volume are such words as IMMINENT, OBDURATE, and OSTRACIZE, which are unknown to nearly 25 per cent of adult readers. At the end of the volume are JEJUNE, ENERVATE, and GLABROUS, practically unknown to readers.

Thumb through the volume until you find where your vocabulary becomes doubtful. Do not waste time on the easy words in the first few pages, nor attempt to master the last one or two hundred, until you know those in the middle. Find a page of words which sound familiar, but where you are uncertain of the meaning; words which you might recognize by the context, but which you would hesitate to use. Start reading at that point and master a few words each day, in the order of their difficulty, in the order in which they appear in this book.

2. *SOAK* (*sōk*) *v.* To wet thoroughly, place in water, drench (23), saturate (139), immerse (256) in a liquid, steep (303), permeate with liquid.

SOAK and DRENCH both come from Anglo-Saxon. SOAK is from a word which meant to suck. DRENCH is the so-called causative form of a verb which meant to drink, and by derivation means to make something drink. One can today DRENCH cattle, that is make them drink. SOAK and DRENCH differ slightly in the way they are used. DRENCH means to wet thoroughly, suddenly, almost unexpectedly. The ground is DRENCHED by a short, hard rain. SOAK means to wet thoroughly for a longer time, often by placing in water, as: 'Clothes are SOAKED overnight'. The ground is SOAKED by several days of continuous rain.

The great majority of English words have come either from Anglo-Saxon or from Latin. Although there are many exceptions, formal and scientific words are Latin; while everyday words, such as SOAK and DRENCH, are Anglo-Saxon.

The proportions of the two elements differ with the manner in which words are counted. In the dictionary many, if not most, of the words are Latin; in every book an overwhelming percentage of the words are Anglo-Saxon. This is because FOR, HIS, IN, IS, OF, THE, each appears only once in the dictionary; but appears many times on every page of every book. Hardly a sentence is written without them.

The structure of English is Anglo-Saxon. Its grammar is Anglo-Saxon. Most of the words in constant use are Anglo-Saxon. Sentences, paragraphs, perhaps even chapters and books, could be written, almost every word of which would be of Anglo-Saxon origin. In the Lord's Prayer, in the Twenty-third Psalm, and in many parts of the King James version of the Bible, nearly 90 per cent of the words are of Anglo-Saxon origin. But only a few Anglo-Saxon words will be defined in this volume, for most of them, like HORSESHOER and SOAK, are known to most grammar-school pupils and to all adults.

3. *POSTPONE* (*pōs-pōn'*, not *pōst-pōn'*) *v.* To put off to a future time, delay (85), defer (305) to a later date.

POSTPONE comes from two Latin words, *post*, after; and *ponere*, to place, put; and by derivation means to put after. The Latin *post*, after, appears in other English words. Thus, the word POSTSCRIPT is a combination of *post*, after; and *scribere*, to write. A POSTSCRIPT (*pō'-skrĭpt*), abbreviated P.S., is written at the end of a letter, after the writer's signature. P.M., used after the hour of the day, as: '5 P.M.', stands for the Latin words *post meridiem*, after noon, now commonly written in English as one word ending in AN, POSTMERIDIAN. P.M. refers to the time of day when the sun has passed the MERIDIAN, its position at noon. POSTMERIDIAN is after noon; as A.M., *ante meridiem*, now written ANTEMERIDIAN, is before noon.

There is an obsolete word, ANTEPONE, which meant to set before, the opposite of POSTPONE, but it has dropped out of the language from lack of use. Things are evidently more frequently POSTPONED, put off, delayed.

POSTPONEMENT, as in the phrase: 'The POSTPONEMENT of their visit', is the noun which corresponds to the verb to POSTPONE, put off.

It is impossible not to use, occasionally, a word of Latin origin. Even in the quotations which are primarily Anglo-Saxon, the word which gives character to the whole is often from Latin. In the Lord's Prayer such words as: TEMPTATION, DELIVER, and GLORY, are Latin. English is a composite language. It is just as affected to select all words of Anglo-Saxon origin as it is stilted to use an overabundance of Latin.

4. *LAW* (*law*) *n.* A rule of conduct, regulation enforced by a community, principle, maxim, binding custom, commandment, prescribed procedure, formulated practice, order, decree, edict, statute (462), ordinance.

Law, which comes from Anglo-Saxon, is the source of several, frequently used, English words. Thus: a LAWYER is one whose profession is the interpretation of laws. LAWYER is a combination of the word LAW plus the familiar ending ER which is added to many words to designate the man, the agent. Thus: a FARMER is one who FARMS; a TEACHER, one who TEACHES. The Y in LAWYER stands for a G which was in the

Anglo-Saxon word from which LAW comes, and which still appears in the adjective LEGAL (35), a word directly from Latin but which comes originally probably from the same ultimate source as LAW. A similar Y occurs in two other words: a BOWYER (*bō'-yer*) is one who uses a BOW, an archer; a SAWYER (*saw'-yer*), one who uses a SAW.

Other words are made from LAW. A LAWFUL act is one permitted by law, in accordance with law. A LAWLESS person is by derivation one without law, one who does not obey the law, one who is literally unruly, not to be ruled. An OUTLAW is a fugitive from justice, one who is not protected by law. At one time anyone was allowed to shoot an OUTLAW on sight.

5. *SECRET* (*sē'-krĕt*) *adj.* Hidden, concealed, private, confidential, cryptic, kept from the knowledge of others.

A SECRET (*sē'-krĕt*) is the noun. To SECRETE (*sē-krēt'*), to hide, is the verb.

SECRET and PRIVATE are often given as synonyms of one another; both refer to matters which are not open to public inspection. The words differ in the manner by which freedom from inspection is obtained. PRIVATE matters are kept private because they are so labeled. A door is often marked PRIVATE in order to keep out the public. The PRIVACY of a private door depends upon everyone knowing that it is private. A SECRET door is never marked, but must be hidden in some way so that it can be found only by those who know the secret. The SECRECY of a secret door depends upon no one's knowing that it is there.

A SECRETARY is by derivation one who is intrusted with secret matters, a confidential officer; but this use of the word is unfortunately nearly obsolete and has been replaced by the redundant phrase: 'A PRIVATE SECRETARY'.

PRIVATE and PUBLIC; SECRET and OBVIOUS; are opposites.

6. *UNTIDY* (*ŭn-tī'-dĭ*) *adj.* Messy, disordered (16), disheveled (187), not neat, not kept in good order, slovenly, uncared for.

UNTIDY is a combination of the Anglo-Saxon prefix UN, not, and the word TIDY, neat, orderly, which is also of Anglo-Saxon origin. The prefix UN may be affixed to almost any Anglo-

Saxon adjective to give it a negative sense, thus: UNTRUE means not true; UNWISE, not wise; UNKIND, not kind; UNTIDY, not tidy.

UNTIDY does not mean dirty. An UNTIDY room may be perfectly clean, but is not in good order.

UNTIDY is known to practically all grammar-school pupils. When unknown, the popular misconception of the word is its exact opposite, NEAT.

7. *SINGLE* (*sĭng'-gl*) *adj.* Solitary, individual, separate, one and no more.

Many English words have various meanings. The word SINGLE may be used in at least five slightly different ways. It is used as a transitive verb in the phrase: 'To SINGLE out some person', to pick that person out from a group. It is used in baseball as an intransitive verb, to SINGLE, meaning to make a one-base hit. It is used as a noun, particularly in games and often in the plural, as: 'SINGLES in tennis', games in which only one person plays on a side.

SINGLE is used most often as an adjective, sometimes for emphasis when it is not needed for sense, as: 'He has not a SINGLE penny', which means he has not even one penny. Sometimes it means unmarried; a SINGLE man is one who has no wife. When used in the phrase: 'He fought in SINGLE combat', it means alone, with only one on a side.

SINGLE, although of Latin origin, comes to English through French, as do most words which are classified as Latin. Although Julius Caesar conquered England in 55 B.C. and although the Romans who remained spoke Latin in England for 500 years, they left few Latin words behind them. Not until after 1066, the date of the battle of Hastings, did such words as SINGLE, originally of Latin origin, begin to enter English, introduced by the Normans who spoke French, both the vocabulary and the structure of which are of Latin origin.

8. *CRIPPLED* (*krĭp'-pld*) *adj.* Deprived of the normal use of a limb, lame, maimed, deformed, injured, disabled.

A few English words, so few that they can be listed almost on a page, are of Scandinavian origin. These were added to the language by the Danes who settled in the north of England. These words are all short and serviceable and, although small in number, form an important part of everyday speech. Some of them are: BAG, BULL, CAKE, DAIRY, FELLOW, FOOL, KEG, KID, LEG, ROOT, SCREW, SKULL, SKY, WINDOW. CRIPPLE is another of these words of Danish origin.

CRIPPLED and LAME both mean deprived of the normal use of some part of the body. LAME usually means that the legs are not normal. A LAME person cannot walk normally. A CRIPPLED person may be deformed in any way.

9. *EARNINGS* (*er'-nĭngs*) *n.* Money earned, pay, wages, salary, compensation, fees, financial reward.

The verb to EARN means to deserve, acquire, obtain. The ending ING is added to many verbs to form nouns; thus, to BUILD plus ING makes a BUILDING; to EARN plus ING makes an EARNING. Although sometimes given in dictionaries in its singular form, this word is practically always used in the plural, EARNINGS, and is accompanied by a plural verb, as: 'His EARNINGS have increased'.

The meaning of EARNINGS is unknown to 4 per cent of grammar-school pupils.

When the Normans subdued England in 1066 they naturally tried to force the conquered tribes, the Angles and the Saxons, to speak French, the language of the conquerors. Officially the native language disappeared. Yet because the inhabitants never learned the new language, the Normans, in order to make their commands understood, used Saxon and Angle words. Like all foreigners learning a new language, they learned separate words but never fully grasped the grammar.

Before 1066 the languages which are now called collectively Anglo-Saxon had been grammatically very complicated. During the two hundred years which followed the Norman conquest many of these structural complications disappeared. Some such simplification would no doubt have taken place even had there been no conquest, for it has occurred in other languages and has continued to the present in English; but the Norman conquest hastened it so that English grammar is simpler today than French, German, or Italian. The ING which is added to EARN to make EARNING, and the s which makes the plural, are, with ED, which forms the past, almost the only endings which have survived from the Anglo-Saxon period.

10. *INJURY* (ĭn'-jū-rĭ) *n.* Harm, damage, hurt, wound, loss, mar, blemish, impairment, detriment (250).

INJURY comes from two Latin words, *in*, not; and *jus, juris*, right. This Latin *in*, meaning not, appears at the beginning of other English words of Latin origin, such as: INACCURATE, not accurate; INCORRECT, not correct; INVISIBLE, not visible. The plural of INJURY is INJURIES, made by adding ES to the singular, and changing the Y to an I. The Anglo-Saxon ending was originally ES and was added to all nouns to form the plural. In most cases the E has been dropped and appears now only in the few instances where it is needed for pronunciation, as: BUSHES, CHURCHES, BOXES; and in nouns ending with Y, INJURY, INJURIES.

11. *CONFERENCE* (kŏn'-fer-ĕns) *n.* A formal meeting for discussion, parley (283), official consultation. 'They called a CONFERENCE.'

CONFERENCE comes from two Latin words, *con*, which stands for *cum*, together; and *ferre*, to bring; and by derivation means a bringing together. Many English words start with the Latin *con*, together. To CONVENE, from *con*, together, and *venire*, to come, is literally to come together. CONVENTION is the corresponding noun, by derivation, a coming together. To CONTRACT is from *con*, together; and *trahere*, to draw; and means literally to draw together. To CONJOIN, to join together, and a CONJUNCTION, a word which joins other words or clauses, both come from *con*, together, and *jungere*, to join. The verb to CONFAB (kŏn-făb'), and the noun, a CONFAB (kŏn'-făb), a colloquial abbreviation of the more difficult word CONFABULATION, are from the Latin *con*, together, and *fabulari*, to talk. A CONFABULATION is an informal talk, chat, familiar conversation. Only occasionally however can *con* be translated so literally.

There are many words nearly synonymous with CONFERENCE. An ASSEMBLY is the general term for a number of persons gathered together for some common purpose. A CONCLAVE is a secret assembly, an assembly carried on behind locked doors. The word comes from the same *con*, together; and *clavis*, key.

The word CONVENTION may be used to mean an assembly, but specifically a CONVENTION is an assembly of delegates or representatives. A CONFERENCE is an assembly for the purpose of talking about something, of discussing something, for exchange of views.

12. *SHYNESS* (*shĭ'-nĕs*) *n.* Bashfulness, timidity, diffidence, coyness, reserve, keeping away from others through sensitiveness. 'She overcame her SHYNESS.'
The ending, or suffix, NESS is added to a number of adjectives to make nouns which name a quality. Thus: SHY is an adjective, as: 'A SHY person'; while SHYNESS is a noun, the quality or characteristic of being shy.

Affected shyness is called DEMURENESS; SHYNESS is the genuine quality. SHYNESS and BOLDNESS are opposites.

13. *UNFORTUNATE* (*ŭn-for'-tŭ-nāt*) *adj.* Not lucky, unsuccessful, hapless (387), ill-fated, disastrous, attended with misfortune. 'UNFORTUNATE occurrences.'
UNFORTUNATE comes from the Anglo-Saxon prefix *un* meaning not; and the Latin word *fortuna,* chance. There are two commonly used prefixes which mean not, the Anglo-Saxon UN, and the Latin IN. UN is used with Anglo-Saxon words, and IN with Latin words; but there are almost as many exceptions as there are words which follow the rule, and each UN and IN word must be learned and remembered. Thus, instead of *infortunate,* the logical negative, the Anglo-Saxon UN is placed in front of the Latin word FORTUNATE to make the English word UNFORTUNATE, not lucky.

14. *MIXTURE* (*mĭks'-tŭr*) *n.* A combination of different kinds of things, medley, miscellany, aggregate, blend (393). 'A good MIXTURE.'
MIXTURE is from the Latin *mixtus,* the past participle of *miscere,* to mix. From *miscere* comes also the English noun MISCELLANY, a collection of all kinds of things.

Both a MIXTURE and a COMPOUND are composed of two or more ingredients; but the words should be distinguished. In a COMPOUND the ingredients lose their own identity and unite. Water is a COMPOUND of oxygen and hydrogen. In a MIXTURE the original ingredients remain unchanged, do not unite chemically, and can usually be separated again mechanically.

15. *HOLY* (*hō'-lĭ*) *adj.* Partaking of the nature of God, of
   great goodness, consecrated, blessed, sacred, hallowed,
sacrosanct (752).
In the phrase: 'Three HOLY words', the meaning of HOLY is
unknown to 6 per cent of grammar-school pupils.
   HOLY, SACRED, and HALLOWED, are almost synonymous. HOLY
is however a higher word than SACRED; a person or thing is
HOLY by nature; whereas a thing may be made SACRED by a
declaration or by association with HOLINESS.
   HALLOWED is a more difficult word, with nearly the same
meaning. It lies between SACRED and HOLY in strength. To
HALLOW means to make sacred. HALLOW can be remembered
by association with HALLOWE'EN. HALLOW was once used as
a noun to mean a saint; and HALLOWE'EN is the evening before
All Saints' Day. HALLOWE'EN is spelt with an apostrophe to
show that the v of EVEN, meaning evening, has been left out.

16. *DISORDERED* (*dĭs-or'-derd*) *adj.* Fallen out of order,
   untidy (6), messy, slovenly, disarranged, confused, chaotic (*kā-ŏt'-ĭk*). 'DISORDERED clothes.'
The Latin prefix *dis*, like the Latin *in* and the Anglo-Saxon *un*,
is used at the beginning of many words to mean not. Thus:
DISHONEST means not honest; DISSIMILAR, not similar, not alike;
DISREPUTABLE, not reputable, not of good reputation; DISPLEAS-
ING, not pleasing, not attractive; and DISORDERED, not in order,
not tidy, messy.

17. *PILE* (*pīl*) *v.* To heap up, stack, cumulate, accumulate,
   assemble, amass, to mound, to lump, form a pile.
Although the verb, to PILE, can be used in reference to anything, as to PILE bricks, PILE wood, PILE dirt, when used of
guns it once meant to place them so that their butts rested
on the ground and their muzzles came together to form a
pyramid. In modern usage this is to STACK guns.

18. *LUKEWARM* (*lŭk'-wawrm*) *adj.* Moderately warm, neither cold nor hot, between cool and warm, tepid (422).
'LUKEWARM tea.'
Formerly there were two words, LUKE, which meant lukewarm; and LUKENESS, which meant lukewarmness. Both have

been dropped from the language. Luke remains only as a part of the word LUKEWARM.

TEPID, which means lukewarm, is used by the medical profession in place of the latter word, for it is of Latin derivation and therefore more scientific than LUKEWARM which is probably of German or Dutch ancestry.

19. *CROOKED* (*krook'-ĕd*) *adj.* Dishonest, deceitful, tricky, cunning (320), false, fraudulent, not straightforward.

Both CROOKED and STRAIGHT are used in figurative senses when applied to human beings. The word STRAIGHT means literally not bent, not curved, not crooked, as: 'A STRAIGHT road'; but when applied to human beings and their actions it means honest, straightforward. In the same way a CROOKED man does not mean bent over; but one who is dishonest, one who is not straightforward in his business dealings. CROOKED and STRAIGHT are opposites in both their literal and figurative senses.

Although the meaning of CROOKED in the phrase: 'A CROOKED stick', 'A CROOKED road', is probably known to every grammar-school pupil, when the word appears in the phrase: 'CROOKED in business', it is misinterpreted by 8 per cent.

CROOKED, as used in everyday speech, to mean either bent or dishonest, is pronounced with two syllables (*krook'-ĕd*). CROOKED (*krookt*), pronounced with one syllable, means with a crook, with a bend, usually at the end and there by design. The word is seldom used except in literature. The noun, a CROOK, is a bend or curve in anything, as a CROOK in the road; but the word is also used specifically to mean a shepherd's CROOK or a bishop's CROOK, a stick or staff with a crook or bend at the end.

Although CROOKED, meaning dishonest, is a good English word, the noun, a CROOK, meaning a dishonest person, is used in newspapers and in conversation but is still marked by dictionaries as slang and should not be used in writing.

20. *DAILY* (*dā'-lĭ*) *adj.* Happening every day, done day by day, everyday, diurnal. The word DAILY is also used as a noun to mean a journal, a newspaper issued every day.

Every grammar-school pupil knows the word DAY, and yet

8 per cent fail to recognize DAILY. When it is used in the phrase: 'She makes DAILY visits', 3 per cent believe it to mean FRIENDLY. Several adjectives are made by the addition of LY to nouns which express periods of time, as: HOUR, HOURLY, every hour; WEEK, WEEKLY, every week; MONTH, MONTHLY, every month; and YEAR, YEARLY, every year. The difference between these and the adjective DAILY is that the noun DAY ends in Y which is changed to I when LY is added.

DAILY, which comes from Anglo-Saxon, and DIURNAL, from Latin, show the difference in use between words of the same meaning from these two languages. Anglo-Saxon words, such as DAILY, are in constant use and form a large part of everyday speech. Latin words, such as DIURNAL, are often more scientific and belong to the vocabulary of the writer rather than the speaker.

21. *SUGGEST* (*sŭg-jĕst′*) *v.* To present, propose (182) for consideration, put forward. 'They SUGGEST a new member.'
To SUGGEST and to PROPOSE, although similar in meaning, differ slightly. To PROPOSE is more definite, more formal, and calls for action. To SUGGEST is less direct. It presents in an unobtrusive way, with a question, a hint, something for consideration. In dealing with one's elders, to SUGGEST is more respectful than to PROPOSE.

22. *APART* (*ă-pahrt′*) *adv.* To one side, aside, separately, aloof, at a distance, away from the group. 'They sat APART.'
In this use, APART, ASIDE, and ALOOF, although of different etymologies, are practically synonymous.

23. *DRENCH* (*drĕnch*) *v.* To wet thoroughly, soak (2), duck, douse (122), saturate (139), immerse (256) in liquid, steep (303).
DRENCH and DROWN come from the same Anglo-Saxon source. DROWN means suffocate by sinking in water or in any liquid, and implies destruction. DRENCH means dip quickly in water in the same way, so as to wet thoroughly, but DRENCH has no suggestion of suffocation.

DRENCH, SOAK, and STEEP, all mean wet thoroughly by immersion. STEEP usually implies some change taking place in

the substance soaked or in the liquid. STEEP and SOAK both
suggest a longer time than does DRENCH. DRENCH may even be
used in a figurative sense to mean wet thoroughly without
actual immersion in water.

When used in the phrase: 'His clothes are DRENCHED', the
word is believed by 4 per cent of grammar-school pupils to
mean WORN OUT; but there is no suggestion of destruction in
DRENCHED.

24. *CLUSTER* (*klŭs'-ter*) *n.* A group, bunch, collection of
things of the same kind, often a number of things of the
same kind growing together.

CLUSTER, from Anglo-Saxon, and COLLECTION, from Latin,
although sometimes used in place of one another, usually differ
in suggestion. COLLECTION often implies a number of unlike
things sometimes gathered together with difficulty from far
places. A COLLECTION may be of any size but is usually larger
than a CLUSTER. CLUSTER implies a number of similar things
grouped together naturally and often closely.

There are numerous words of this type each of which
has come to be used in its own particular sphere. Thus one
speaks of: 'A FLOCK of sheep', 'A HERD of cattle', 'A PACK of
wolves', 'A SCHOOL of fish', 'A SWARM of bees', 'A BEVY of girls',
'A BUNCH of bananas', 'A CLUSTER of trees', 'A CLUSTER of stars'.

25. *YOUTH* (*ūth*) *n.* A young man, boy older than a child
but younger than an adult, an adolescent (524).

The final TH of this word has a different pronunciation in the
singular and in the plural. In the singular, the final TH is like
TH in THIN. In the plural, the final s has the sound of z which
of necessity changes the sound of the TH almost to that in THE.

When the word YOUTH is used to mean the period of time
between childhood and maturity, as: 'In their YOUTH', it may
refer either to boys or girls; but when used to mean a person
it refers to a boy, never to a girl, as: 'YOUTHS and maidens'.

The meaning of the word, when it appears in the plural in
the test phrase: 'The YOUTHS passed by', is unknown to 9 per
cent of grammar-school pupils.

Legally, in the United States and Great Britain, every person
is called an INFANT until the age of 21. In conversation and

literature the word INFANT means either a boy or girl younger than about 7 years of age. The word is used in this way in such a phrase as: 'The INFANT CLASS in a school'. The word CHILD refers to a boy or girl older than an INFANT and younger than a YOUTH or MAIDEN. The word YOUTH refers to a boy between the ages of about 14 and 21. In its legal use the word ADULT refers to both men and women 21 years of age and over. In conversation and literature, it often refers to still older persons who have reached the age of perhaps 25.

26. *NATURAL* (*năt'-ū-răl*) *adj.* Inborn, normal, native, instinctive (200), inherent, intrinsic (912), innate, congenital. NATURAL comes from the Latin *natura*, nature, a derivative of *nasci*, to be born. The word may be used in two ways, which should be distinguished. It may mean simple, unaffected, easy; or it may mean inborn. Words are often easiest to remember when associated with their opposites. NATURAL in its first sense means not AFFECTED, not ARTIFICIAL (482); in its second sense it means not LEARNED, not ACQUIRED.

27. *ROUNDNESS* (*rownd'-něs*) *n.* Quality of being either round or spherical or circular in shape, rotundity, sphericity. 'This figure has ROUNDNESS.' ROUND and CIRCULAR, ROUNDNESS and CIRCULARITY, are in some senses interchangeable. CIRCULARITY comes from the Latin *circus*, ring. CIRCULAR must mean like a ring and cannot mean round like a ball. To convey specifically round like a ball, not flat, one must use the words SPHERICAL or GLOBULAR. ROUNDNESS comes from the Latin word *rota*, wheel, through the French *rond*, round. ROUND may mean shaped like a flat circle or like a ball.

It is said that King Arthur's ROUND TABLE had roundness so that there should be no head nor foot and therefore no order of precedence. A ROUND ROBIN is a letter or petition with the signatures in a circle so that it is impossible to tell which name was signed first.

28. *FLEXIBLE* (*flěk'-sĭ-bl*) *adj.* Easily bent without breaking, limber, lithe, pliable (117), pliant, supple, lissome, willowy, yielding, not stiff, not brittle, not rigid (504).

In the test phrase: 'FLEXIBLE willow twigs', the popular misconception of the word is FRAGILE. FRAGILE comes from the Latin *frangere*, to break, and means frail, delicate, easily broken. A FRAGILE thing breaks unless carefully handled. FLEXIBLE is from the Latin *flexus*, the past participle of *flectere*, to bend, and means literally capable of being bent. A FLEXIBLE thing may be bent without breaking.

BRITTLE, from an Anglo-Saxon word meaning to break, means, like FRAGILE, easily broken, but specifically easily broken if bent. A glass rod or even an iron casting may be quite strong but brittle.

STRONG is the opposite of FRAGILE; TOUGH the opposite of BRITTLE; STIFF the opposite of FLEXIBLE.

FLEXIBLE is a word which can be used both literally and figuratively. A FLEXIBLE stick or a FLEXIBLE wire is one which can be bent easily. A FLEXIBLE person is one who can be managed easily, one who yields to persuasion.

29. *SURRENDER* (*ser-rĕn'-der*) *v.* To give up, yield, renounce a claim to, concede, submit, relinquish, abandon (56), cede, give up possession of.

In the phrase: 'They SURRENDERED the fort', the word is probably known to every grammar-school pupil, but in the test phrase: 'He SURRENDERED his hat', it is unknown to 9 per cent.

SURRENDER comes from the Latin *super*, over, a prefix which, shortened to *sur*, plays a part in many English words. SURFACE is from the same *super,* over, and means literally the upper side, the top face. The word is now sometimes used to mean the outside. SURPRISE comes from the same *super*, and *prendere*, to seize, and means literally to seize upon, take unexpectedly. SURVEY comes from the same *super*, over; and *videre*, to see; and means to oversee, look over. SURRENDER is from *super* and the English word RENDER, which in turn comes from *re*, back, and *dare*, to give. To SURRENDER means literally to render over, give over.

30. *INDIVIDUALLY* (*in-dĭ-vĭd'-ū-ăl-lĭ*) *adv.* Each by himself, by itself, separately, one by one.

INDIVIDUAL, when used as a noun, is today employed too frequently to mean merely a person. The word should be re-

stricted to those instances where a person is to be contrasted
with a group. INDIVIDUAL, when used as an adjective, may
refer alike to a separate, isolated person or thing. INDIVIDUALLY
is the adverb.

31. *TOMBOY* (*tŏm'-boi*) *n.* A girl who behaves like a boy,
   romping and boisterous girl, a romp, hoyden.

In the test phrase: 'The TOMBOY next door', the word is
thought by 5 per cent of grammar-school pupils to mean
FLIRT, one who plays at love, pretends to make courtship.

TOM is short for THOMAS which comes through the Greek
from a Hebrew word meaning twin. THOMAS is the Greek
word Θωμᾶς, written in Roman letters. TOM is used in several
compounds and often has a contemptuous suggestion as in
the word TOMFOOL. It generally means boy, man, or male,
as for instance in TOMCAT which means male cat, a word
which is sometimes hyphenated, sometimes written as two
separate words, but which should probably be spelt as a
single word to agree with TOMBOY. TOMBOY originally meant
a rude, uncivil boy; but now a TOMBOY is always a boisterous,
romping girl who behaves like a boy.

32. *STALE* (*stāl*) *adj.* Old, threadbare, trite, commonplace,
   hackneyed, time-worn, worn-out by repetition, lacking in
   novelty.

STALE can be used with reference to almost anything which
has passed its best period. STALE bread is dry; STALE air is close,
foul, stagnant; an athlete is STALE who has overtrained; a STALE
joke is old, worn-out, uninteresting.

33. *BUSHY* (*boosh'-ĭ*) *adj.* Growing like a shrub or bush,
   shaggy, thick, spreading, overgrown.

BUSHY, when used in the phrase: 'He has BUSHY eyebrows',
is unknown to 10 per cent of grammar-school pupils, although
the word BUSH, from which it comes, is probably known to
every youngster.

Many adjectives are made from nouns by the addition of
Y. Some of these, such as HAIRY, mean having hair; others such
as FISHY, mean like a fish in some way. BUSHY may be used
in either sense. BUSHY hills are hills covered with bushes;

BUSHY eyebrows are eyebrows like bushes, shaggy, over-grown, thick.

The popular misconception of a word is often the exact opposite of its correct meaning. In this case, STRAIGHT-LINED and PLUCKED are the two most common misconceptions and are practically opposites of BUSHY, shaggy.

34. *FRAGRANT* (*frā'-grănt*) *adj.* Sweet smelling, pleas-antly scented, balmy (692), aromatic, odoriferous, agree-ably perfumed.

In the test phrase: 'A FRAGRANT flower', the word is thought by 4 per cent of grammar-school pupils to mean LOVELY, exquisitely beautiful, usually in appearance. Although FRAGRANT always means pleasing, delightful, and can never be used of anything disagreeable, it must refer to an odor, to something which appeals to the sense of smell, and not to an effect produced on any of the other senses.

DELICATE means pleasing to any of the senses, especially to the sense of taste, as in the noun, a DELICACY. MELODIOUS means pleasing to the ear. LOVELY means pleasing to the eye; and is also used in a more general sense to mean pleasing to the mind. FRAGRANT means pleasing to the nose.

35. *LEGAL* (*lē'-găl*) *adj.* Lawful, legitimate, licit, authorized, permitted by law, based on law, according to law.

LAW (4), known to 98 per cent of grammar-school pupils, LAWFUL, LAWLESS, and LAWYER, come from Anglo-Saxon, while LEGAL comes directly from the Latin word *lex, legis*. From this same Latin word *lex, legis*, comes LEGISLATURE, a body of persons which makes laws.

In the test phrase: 'A LEGAL right', the word is thought by 6 per cent of grammar-school pupils to mean PERFECT. PERFECT in this sense means complete, whereas LEGAL is narrowly limited to that which is in accord with formal law.

Although LEGAL and LAWFUL have almost the same meaning, they are used in different places. LAWFUL means permitted by law as: 'LAWFUL acts'. LAWFUL books are books which may be bought and sold according to law. LEGAL may mean lawful; or it may mean dealing with law, of the nature of law, as: 'LEGAL education'. LEGAL books deal with the subject of law.

36. *DISTRUST* (*dĭs-trŭst'*) *v.* To doubt, suspect (87), have no confidence in, put no reliance on. 'I DISTRUST him.'
DISTRUST is a combination of the Latin prefix *dis*, not; and the word TRUST, to rely on, reckon on, reveal one's secrets to, pin one's faith on. Although of Latin origin, *dis*, not, is used as a prefix for words of various derivations. TRUST is not of Latin origin but from the same Anglo-Saxon source as TRUE, and yet the negative verb has the Latin prefix; thus: to DISTRUST is not to trust.

37. *STICK* (*stĭk*) *v.* To hold fast, cling (351), remain fixed, adhere, stay, remain where placed.
In the phrase: 'Real knowledge STICKS', the word is unknown to 11 per cent of grammar-school pupils.

The noun, a STICK, a piece of wood, branch, is known to every youngster. There is a verb to STICK, which means to thrust a sharp point into something. It is familiar to everyone in the phrase: 'To STICK a pin into a cushion'. Although the verb to STICK, to cling, hold fast, is identical in spelling with the other, it comes from a different Anglo-Saxon word. There are other pairs of English words which have the same spelling but which come from different sources and have, therefore, different meanings. The verb to CLEAVE, for instance, comes from an Anglo-Saxon word and means to split, cut open, cut apart with a blow. But another word to CLEAVE, spelt the same in English but from a different Anglo-Saxon word, means to cling, adhere, stick fast.

38. *QUENCH* (*kwĕnch*) *v.* To put out, stifle, suppress, extinguish, make an end of, subdue, smother.
A popular misconception of this word is, as usual, an opposite of the correct meaning. To 3 per cent of grammar-school pupils, 'They QUENCHED the fire' incorrectly means they lit the fire. To LIGHT is to start a fire, set fire to, make burn, kindle, ignite. Both LIT and LIGHTED are correct forms of the past tense of to LIGHT. One can say: 'They LIT the fire' or 'They LIGHTED the fire'. If there is any choice between the two it is perhaps in favor of the first.

There was once an Anglo-Saxon word which meant to disappear, go out of sight. This word exists today only in what is called its causative form: 'To QUENCH', which means to make disappear, cause to disappear. Other words have causative forms. Thus, a tree FALLS down; but to FELL a tree, the causative form, means to make a tree fall down, to cause it to fall. In this same way 'To QUENCH one's thirst', to slake (317) it, means to make one's thirst disappear.

39. *CONTENT* (*kŏn-tĕnt'*) *adj.* Satisfied, appeased, gratified, at rest, resigned, contented.

CONTENT and SATISFIED, although almost synonymous, differ in their implications. One who is SATISFIED has all he wishes, without limiting his wants. CONTENT, which comes from the Latin *tenere*, to hold, the source of the English word CONTAIN, means, by derivation, held within limits. Its origin is thus the same as the noun CONTENT (*kŏn'tĕnt*) which means that which is contained. One who is CONTENT (*kŏn-tĕnt'*) holds his desires in check, limits his wants to what he has.

40. *OBJECT* (*ŏb-jĕkt'*) *v.* To say that one opposes something, announce opposition, state disapproval, deprecate (1081). In the test phrase: 'His parents OBJECTED', the word is thought by 3 per cent of grammar-school pupils to mean APPROVED, sanctioned, an exact opposite of the real meaning. By another 3 per cent the word is thought to mean OBSERVED. To OBSERVE means to see, take notice of, perceive, mark; but OBSERVE does not imply objecting, opposing, disapproving.

To OBJECT is from the Latin *ob*, before, against; and *jactus*, the past participle of the verb *jacere*, to throw. A large family of English words is built on this Latin word *jacere*, to throw. A PROJECTILE, cannon ball, shell, is, for instance, something which is thrown, *jacere*; forward, *pro*. A person who is DEJECTED is thrown, *jacere*; down, *de*; literally downcast, dispirited, unhappy, downhearted. To EJECT someone from a place is to throw, *jacere*, him out, *e*, expel him.

Whenever a word of this family exists as both a noun and a verb, the noun is accented on the first syllable and the verb on the second. Thus, the noun, a SUBJECT (*sŭb'-jĕkt*), one who is under the control or authority of another, is accented on the first syllable; while the corresponding verb, to SUBJECT (*sŭb-jĕkt'*), which by derivation means to throw, *jacere*;

under, *sub;* and which now has as one of its meanings to bring under power, put under compulsion, subdue, subordinate, is accented on the second syllable. The noun, an OBJECT (*ŏb'-jĕkt*), a thing, article, is accented on the first syllable; but the verb, to OBJECT (*ŏb-jĕkt'*), is accented on the second.

41. *TOURIST* (*toor'-ĭst*) *n.* A person who journeys for pleasure, holiday traveler, one who makes an excursion for sight-seeing.

The word TOUR and the noun a TURN, as: 'A TURN of the wheel', come from the same source, an old French word *tour*, meaning turn. In English, TURN is now the general word and TOUR is limited to a sight-seeing expedition, usually to one which returns to its starting place.

42. *GUESS* (*gĕs*) *n.* An opinion formed without knowledge, rough estimate, notion, conjecture, surmise, supposition based on insufficient evidence.

In the test phrase: 'A good GUESS', the word is thought by 5 per cent of grammar-school pupils to mean GESTURE, gesticulation, motion of the hand, movement of the head to emphasize an idea. The confusion may be due to a reading difficulty; or perhaps to some mistake in pronunciation. GESTURE is pronounced with a soft G (*jĕs'-chūr*), as in GIANT, GEM, GINGER. GUESS, on the other hand, is pronounced with a hard G (*gĕs*), as in GAME, GARDEN, GOOD. In most words beginning with GUE and GUI, the U is not pronounced but its presence makes the G hard, as in GUIDE, GUILD, GUILE, GUILT, GUITAR, and GUESS.

A GUESS, a CONJECTURE, and a SUPPOSITION, are three uncertain notions about what will happen in the future. A GUESS can be made by one who has few facts; and, if it proves to be correct, is largely luck. A CONJECTURE can be made only by one who has more facts and who considers them more carefully. A SUPPOSITION, although not necessarily accurate, has a still better chance of being true.

43. *ADOPT* (*ă-dŏpt'*) *v.* To accept, appropriate, receive as one's own, make one's own, take, follow, choose, embrace.

ADOPT comes from the Latin *ad*, to; and *optare*, to wish. From the same verb come also the English noun OPTION, choice; and the adjective, OPTIONAL, left to choice, dependent upon choice. ADOPT always suggests choosing to make one's own. He who ADOPTS a son wishes to make him his own.

44. *GIGGLE* (*gĭg'-gl*) *n.* A silly laugh, titter, snicker, affected laugh with short catches of the breath, nervous laughter.

GIGGLE and GIGGLING are both nouns and synonymous. In the test phrase: 'They heard the GIGGLE', the word is thought by 6 per cent of grammar-school pupils to mean CHATTERING, the popular misconception. CHATTER and CHATTERING both mean fast, foolish, and trivial talk, idle prattle. CHATTER and CHATTERING, GIGGLE and GIGGLING all suggest nervousness and foolishness; but CHATTER and CHATTERING are kinds of talk; while GIGGLE and GIGGLING are kinds of laughter.

45. *GROUCH* (*growch*) *n.* Fit of sulkiness, sullenness, moroseness, peevishness. The word GROUCH may also be used for the individual who is temporarily peevish.

GROUCH is a modern word. It did not appear at all in many dictionaries of thirty years ago and even today is usually marked colloquial. The word should probably rarely be used in writing, although its meaning is known to practically every adult reader.

46. *COPY* (*kŏp'-ĭ*) *n.* Something made like something else, an imitation, reproduction, duplicate, counterpart (461), transcript.

In the test phrase: 'Make a clear COPY', the word is thought by 6 per cent of grammar-school pupils to mean DESIGN, the popular misconception and almost an opposite of the correct meaning. A DESIGN is a plan or pattern made in advance. It is a record of the original idea and is not a copy.

COPY, DUPLICATE, and REPLICA, are three nouns which indicate something made like something else. A COPY is as nearly like the original as it can be made at a different time and by a different person. A DUPLICATE is an exact copy, made at the same time, or in the same way, as the original. A carbon copy is a DUPLICATE. The word REPLICA is sometimes used carelessly to mean a copy; but REPLICA is in reality a technical term in the field of art and means a copy made by the artist, or by the creator, of the original.

47. *ASSUME* (*ăs-sūm'*) *v.* To take in hand, undertake, accept, enter upon, invest one's self with.

A number of English words come from the Latin *sumere*, to take. RESUME starts with the Latin *re*, again, and is to take up again, as: 'He RESUMED his work'. PRESUME starts with the Latin *prae*, before, and is by derivation to take beforehand; the word now means to take for granted. ASSUME starts with the Latin *ad*, to, and means to take up, take in hand, as: 'He ASSUMED responsibility'.

48. *CHIMPANZEE* (*chĭm-păn-zē'*) *n.* A large monkey, an anthropoid ape, African orang-utan, a member of the family *Simiidae* (*sĭ-mī'-ĭ-dē*) from which comes the adjective SIMIAN, apish, like a monkey.

Four kinds of monkeys belong to the group called AN-THROPOID APES, the GORILLA, CHIMPANZEE, ORANG, and GIBBON. The GORILLA is the largest of the four, often more than five feet in height. The CHIMPANZEE is smaller, about four feet in height.

49. *PUBLIC* (*pŭb'-lĭk*) *n.* The people of a town, of a city, or of a country; mankind in general.

In the United States, a PUBLIC school is a school open to the PUBLIC, one to which anyone may go, a school for the people in general.

PUBLIC comes from the Latin word *populus*, the people. Both POPULATION and POPULAR come from the same source. POPULATION means the number of people in a given area, as the POPULATION of a city. POPULAR means approved, admired by the people in general, beloved by the PUBLIC.

In the test phrase: 'A notice to the PUBLIC', the word is unknown to 11 per cent of grammar-school pupils. The three common misconceptions, OFFENDERS, EMPLOYEES, and TRAVEL-ERS, describe specific groups of persons, while PUBLIC means people in general. The word is sometimes used in such phrases as: 'The reading PUBLIC', to mean all of the people who read newspapers, magazines, books; or 'The buying PUBLIC', to mean all of the people who buy things; but there is always something vague and intangible about the PUBLIC.

50. AUCTION (*awk'-shŭn*) *n.* A public sale to the highest bidder. In an AUCTION no article has a fixed price, but each person interested offers more than the previous bidder until a price is reached beyond which no one is willing to go. The article is then sold to the highest bidder.

AUCTION comes from the Latin *auctus*, the past participle of the verb *augere*, to increase, the source of the English verb to AUGMENT, to increase. In an AUCTION each bid augments, adds to, increases, the previous bid.

51. BEVERAGE (*bĕv'-er-āj*) *n.* Liquid meant for drinking, refreshing drink.

BEVERAGE comes from the Latin *bibere*, to drink, from the same source as the noun, a BIB, worn by children when drinking; and the verb, to IMBIBE, to drink. From the same Latin verb comes also the obsolete English word BEVER (*bē'-ver*), a collation, snack, a bit to eat given between meals to the students in some schools and colleges.

A BEVERAGE and LIQUOR are both refreshing liquids which are drunk. LIQUOR, as the word is ordinarily used, is alcoholic; a BEVERAGE is more often non-alcoholic.

52. CATHEDRAL (*kă-thē'-drăl*) *n.* A large church which contains the bishop's throne, usually the principal church of a diocese.

The word CATHEDRAL comes from the same source as the English word CATHEDRA (*kăth'-ē-dră*), the throne or seat of a bishop. The phrase EX CATHEDRA, literally from the chair, is used to mean with authority, as: 'He spoke EX CATHEDRA', he spoke from the bishop's throne or, more generally, from any position of authority. CATHEDRA, which is the Greek word καθέδρα rewritten in Roman letters, is a combination of the Greek κατά down, which appears directly in the English word CATASTROPHE, the down-turning of events, final disaster; and ἕδρα, a seat. From this word comes directly the unusual English word EXEDRA (*ĕks'-ē-dră*), an outdoor seat, a word used in architecture for a raised platform, out of doors, with seats.

A CATHEDRAL, the bishop's church, is built with its ground-plan usually in the form of a Latin cross. The NAVE, the main body of the church, is the long arm of the cross and always runs east and west. It is entered ordinarily at the west end; with the APSE, usually semi-circular, at the east end. The TRANSEPTS, which form the cross arm, run north and south.

53. *CONQUER* (*kŏng'-ker*) *v.* To beat, defeat, overthrow, crush, vanquish, rout, subjugate (291), acquire dominion over by fighting.

CONQUER, SUBJUGATE, and VANQUISH, all mean to overcome. The verb, to VANQUISH, suggests victory in a single struggle but does not imply that the victory is lasting or permanent. The verb, to SUBJUGATE, suggests not only that the victory is permanent but that the losers are entirely at the mercy of the victors. To CONQUER suggests more of a struggle than does the word VANQUISH, often a series of struggles, and also greater permanence to the victory, but CONQUER does not imply bringing the losers under subjection.

54. *CABLE* (*kā'-bl*) *n.* Large strong rope, wire rope, heavy chain, hawser (545), towline.

CABLE is from the Latin *capere*, to hold, from the same source as the English words, CAPTIVE, one held a prisoner; and CAPACIOUS, roomy, spacious, large enough to hold a considerable quantity.

Although the word CABLE is used in many ways, one meaning is large rope. In this sense a CORD, a ROPE, and a CABLE, are three degrees of size. All three may be made of hemp, manila, jute, flax, cotton, or coir (*kīr*), a fiber from the cocoanut shell. A CORD may be little more than a string, although it is usually stronger. A ROPE is a cord which is about an inch or more in circumference. A CABLE is a rope which is often three or more inches in circumference.

55. *VOLUNTARY* (*vŏl'-ŭn-tā-rĭ*) *adj.* Freely chosen, acting of one's own free will, not subject to compulsion.

In the test phrase: 'His VOLUNTARY action', the word is sometimes thought to mean COMPULSORY, an exact opposite of the correct meaning.

56. *ABANDON* (*ă-băn'-dŏn*) *v.* To give up, leave, withdraw from, surrender (29), forsake, desert.

A history of ABANDON shows the manner in which the meanings of words gradually change. A BAN, from the same source as ABANDON, originally meant a public proclamation, sometimes a call to arms. The BANS, which ought to be spelt with only one N, but which now usually has two, BANNS, is a public announcement, given in church, of an intended marriage. The word BAN always suggests public authority, public control.

ABANDONED originally meant under public control, under public jurisdiction, or under control of some type. The verb, to ABANDON, then came to mean to put under the control of someone. It then came to mean under the control of someone else; and, then, to give over the control to someone else, to surrender the control. Now the original meaning has almost disappeared, and to ABANDON no longer means to place the control in other hands, not even to give over the control, surrender it; but to give up the control, forsake, desert, as in the phrase: 'Do not ABANDON me'.

57. *INTACT* (*ĭn-tăkt'*) *adj.* Untouched, unchanged, whole, undisturbed, entire, without injury (10).
INTACT comes from the Latin *in*, not; and *tangere*, to touch; and means untouched. From the same source come: CONTACT, in touch with; and TACTILE, capable of being touched.

58. *BOULEVARD* (*boo'-lĕ-vahrd*) *n.* A broad street, highway, thoroughfare, an avenue often lined with trees.
In the test phrase: 'An attractive BOULEVARD', the popular misconception of the word is SIDEWALK. A SIDEWALK is a path for pedestrians at the side of a street or road. BOULEVARD may mean a broad walk for pedestrians, but never a walk which parallels a street and which is separated from it by a curb as is a SIDEWALK.

The word BOULEVARD is related to BULWARK (*bŏol'-wark*), perhaps through BOLE-WORK. The English word BOLE, although not frequently used, means the trunk of a tree, as: 'The BOLE of an elm'. It is a word with Icelandic ancestry and is perhaps distantly related to the words BOWL, a round, deep dish; and BALL. A BULWARK was originally a barrier, built of logs, to obstruct a passageway. The word BULWARK is now used for any embankment or mound of earth piled, for protection, around a fort or fortified town.

BOULEVARD originally meant bulwark, rampart. The word then came to be used for the public walk around the ramparts. It is now any important street often set aside for pleasure vehicles.

59. *CRAVE* (*krāv*) *v.* To long for, yearn for, desire. The verb CRAVE may also mean ask for urgently, beseech (324), beg, solicit (407), implore.
One may CRAVE a favor, one may CRAVE leave to speak. In this sense the word means ask with humility, entreat, and has almost the meaning of the Anglo-Saxon and Scandinavian words from which it comes. Although the verb, to CRAVE, and the adjective, CRAVEN, are so similar in appearance, they are probably unrelated etymologically. But the adjective seems to have influenced the meaning of the verb. For CRAVEN means cowardly; and when the verb is used in such a phrase as: 'He CRAVED tobacco', it always suggests yielding to a desire for something which is not good for one, yearning for something in order to satisfy one's appetite, as a means of gratification.

60. *STUPOR* (*stū'-por*, not *stoo'-por*) *n.* A daze, apathy, torpor, lethargy (433), state of insensibility. 'He fell into another STUPOR.'
STUPOR is from the Latin *stupere*, to be struck senseless, be stunned, amazed. It is from the same source as STUPID (*stū'-pĭd*), which is now used only in the sense of mentally dull, but which by derivation means to be stunned, benumbed.
STUPOR and TORPOR are interchangeable. Both are more extreme than INSENSIBILITY, the general term for loss of feeling from any cause.

61. *TRUCE* (*trūs*) *n.* Temporary peace, armistice, intermission in hostilities, respite (650).
There was once an English noun, TRUE, similar in spelling to

the present adjective. It first meant truth; then agreement; and then an intermission in war according to agreement. TRUE, as a noun, is now obsolete; but it has survived in the word TRUCE, which is the plural of TRUE, as DICE is the plural of DIE.

62. PROCEEDS (*prō'-sēdz*) *n.* Returns, results, an amount accruing from some business transaction as from a sale of goods.

The verb, to PROCEED (*prō-sēd'*), comes from the Latin *pro*, forth; and *cedere*, to go; and means literally to go forth, issue. The noun, PROCEED, now used only in its plural form PROCEEDS, means by derivation that which issues from a transaction.

63. GIGANTIC (*jī-găn'-tĭk*) *adj.* Very big, huge, immense, tremendous, enormous, titanic (226), colossal (249), like a giant.

Both GIGANTIC and GIANT come from the Latin word, *gigas*. GIGANTIC is the adjective; GIANT, the noun. GIGANTIC means, literally, like a giant.

When used in the test phrase: 'GIGANTIC figures', the word is thought by 4 per cent of grammar-school pupils to mean GORGEOUS. GORGEOUS is magnificent, richly colored, splendid, dazzling. While GORGEOUS and GIGANTIC are both extremes, GORGEOUS means extremely colorful; GIGANTIC, extremely big.

PYGMY, which should not be spelt *pigmy*, a small person, member of a diminutive race, dwarf, is the opposite of GIANT. There is an unusual adjective, PYGMEAN (*pĭg-mē'-ăn*), small, which is the real opposite of GIGANTIC, big, huge, immense. PUNY, small, undersized, weak, insignificant, a word which has no relation to PYGMY, is another opposite of GIGANTIC and in more frequent use.

64. RUDE (*rūd*) *adj.* Impolite, uncivil, discourteous, impertinent (211), coarse (411) in manner. This meaning is known to practically all readers. RUDE (288) also has a more unusual meaning, rough, crude, ill-fashioned, primitive (358), simple, and in this sense is unknown to 10 per cent of adult readers.

RUDE is from the Latin *rudis*, rough, raw, wild, untilled.

From this same word comes the adjective ERUDITE (*ĕr'-ŭ-dīt*), learned, educated, cultivated, from the Latin *e*, out, and *rudis*, rude, by derivation, therefore, free from rudeness. RUDE and ERUDITE are in some of their uses opposites of one another. Although RUDE is often used to mean uncivil, impolite, by derivation it should be used only in situations where incivility, impoliteness, spring from lack of knowledge.

65. *REMEDY* (*rĕm'-ĕ-dĭ*) *v.* To heal, repair (245), correct, make right, relieve, restore to soundness, help, aid, redress, cure. 'I can REMEDY that.'
REMEDY comes from the Latin *re*, again; and *mederi*, to heal; and by derivation means to heal again. It is from the same source as the word MEDICINE.

66. *REMEDY* (*rĕm'-ĕ-dĭ*) *n.* A cure for disease, healing medicine, restorative treatment, corrective, relief.
The noun has the same derivation as the verb and like the verb is unknown to 1 per cent of readers.

67. *TOURNAMENT* (*toor'-nă-mĕnt*) *n.* A contest of skill, encounter, tourney, often a series of contests in which a number of persons take part. 'He will enter the TOURNAMENT.'
TOURNAMENT, TOURNEY, TILT, and JOUST (*jŭst*), are all words dating from the Middle Ages and describe activities in existence as early as King Arthur's times, about the sixth century. All designate contests of men on horseback, armed with swords, lances, maces, and blunted weapons.
A JOUST was a duel on horseback, a single combat between two men, often a part of a tournament. The original English spelling of JOUST was *just*, and the word was pronounced (*jŭst*). Sir Walter Scott, in his novels, used the spelling JOUST and this is today generally accepted. When thus spelt it may be pronounced (*joost*), but the original pronunciation (*jŭst*) is preferable. The word should not be pronounced (*jowst*).
A TILT was a charge, usually on horseback, with a spear, against a single antagonist or against a mark.
TOURNEY and TOURNAMENT are practically synonymous. Both words come from the French verb *tourner*, to turn, from the same original source as the English word TURN.

TOURNEYS and TOURNAMENTS were both combats between groups, rather than between individuals; both comprised series of events. Today the word TOURNAMENT is used in a figurative sense to mean any trial of skill, not necessarily athletic, in which there is a series of contests, as: 'A tennis TOURNAMENT', 'A chess TOURNAMENT'.

68. *THRILLING* (*thrĭl'-lĭng*) *adj.* Exciting, stirring, moving, agitating, emotionally stimulating.

THRILLING is unknown to 1 per cent of readers. To this entire group it means UNUSUAL, out of the ordinary. Although the two words have something in common, they are not interchangeable. A book of UNUSUAL length is longer than average but is not necessarily thrilling, exciting. The opposites are more apt to be synonymous; a USUAL, everyday, occurrence is seldom thrilling, stirring.

THRILLING is from an Anglo-Saxon word which meant to penetrate, pierce; and in English the original meaning of the verb, to THRILL, was to drill, bore, pierce. This meaning is now obsolete; and the verb to THRILL, the noun a THRILL, and the participial adjective THRILLING, are all used in the figurative sense with reference to that which penetrates the emotions, pierces the sensations. The cause of the THRILL may be pleasure, wonder, even horror or pain.

69. *CARVED* (*kahrvd*) *adj.* Cut, sculptured, engraved, adorned with a cut pattern, decorated with figures in relief.

Almost everyone knows the verb, to CARVE, as: 'To CARVE meat'; but the adjective, CARVED, in the phrase: 'Made of CARVED wood', is unknown to 12 per cent of grammar-school pupils. CARVED comes directly from the verb to CARVE, and formerly meant cut in any sense. Today it usually implies cut artistically, but retains enough of its original meaning so that it is applied most frequently to those substances which can be cut with a knife.

70. *LOITER* (*loi'-ter*) *v.* To delay (85), dally, dawdle, lag, saunter (330), straggle (887), hang about, linger idly on the way, travel indolently, move lazily, trifle away time.

LOITER is probably of Dutch origin and is one of the few Dutch words in the English language. Most of these are nautical terms. Among them are: SCHOONER, a vessel with two or more masts rigged fore and aft; BLOCK, a pulley; BOOM, a horizontal pole to which a sail is attached; MARLIN, a cord used to bind the end of a rope; SKIPPER, a sailing master; SLOOP, a single masted sailing vessel rigged fore and aft; SMACK, a fishing sloop, a small sailing vessel; YACHT, a vessel for private cruising; and to LUFF, to sail nearer the wind. The word to LOITER was first used of a sail and meant to shiver, flap idly in the breeze, as does the sail of a boat which is making no headway.

LOITER, when applied to a human being, was originally used in a derogatory sense to mean to be a tramp, vagabond. The word is now coming back to this earlier use. To say that one LOITERS implies not only waste of time but almost general worthlessness.

71. *PROTRUDE* (*prō-trūd'*) *v.* To stick out, thrust out, project, jut out, extend forward beyond the main surface.

PROTRUDE is from the Latin *pro*, forward; and *trudere*, to push, the source of a large group of English words. To INTRUDE is to push one's way in; the word is applied to both persons and materials. To EXTRUDE is to push out, press out. Metal is EXTRUDED much as tooth paste is EXTRUDED from the tube. EXTRUDE is used exclusively of plastic materials. PROTRUDE is used of objects and means stick out.

72. *STURDY* (*ster'-dĭ*) *adj.* Strong, stout, hardy, lusty, vigorous, resolute, robust (560), standing firm.

STURDY, STOUT, and STRONG, are three simple words which denote strength. STURDY, ROBUST, and STALWART, are discussed under ROBUST (560).

73. *DAWN* (*dawn*) *n.* Beginning, start, commencement, origin, inception, incipience, first appearance. The word DAWN may also be used more specifically to mean daybreak, the first appearance of light in the morning.

In the test phrase: 'The DAWN of a great idea', the word is thought by 2 per cent of adult readers to mean DEVELOPMENT.

The DEVELOPMENT of an idea is its growth, slow unfolding, its evolution and consequences. The DAWN, the beginning, of an idea is its first appearance, often in a sketchy form.

74. *BUDGE* (*bŭdj*) *v.* Move slightly, stir, give way a little, change position by a small amount.

BUDGE is today used most frequently with the negative, and always suggests stubborn resistance to pressure, as: 'He did not BUDGE'.

75. *HUMID* (*hū'-mĭd*) *adj.* Moist, damp, watery, slightly wet, dank, containing moisture. 'A HUMID atmosphere.'

The corresponding noun, HUMIDITY, moisture, is probably more familiar. A HUMIDOR, another noun from the same source, is most frequently a box equipped with a moistened sponge or some such device, and in which tobacco is kept from drying out.

HUMID, SULTRY (335), and DANK, all mean wet, moist. DANK is wet and cold; SULTRY, wet and hot; HUMID, wet, moist, with no indication of cold or heat.

76. *INCREASE* (*ĭn-krēs'*) *v.* To become larger, swell, grow in amount, augment, multiply, expand, extend.

In the test phrase: 'The storm INCREASES', the word is thought by 5 per cent of grammar-school pupils to mean RAGES. To RAGE means to be furious, violent, madly angry, but does not mean to grow. INCREASE always signifies growth in amount, in intensity.

To INCREASE, grow in amount; and to DECREASE, diminish, lessen; are opposites.

77. *BLUNDER* (*blŭn'-der*) *n.* A stupid mistake, careless error, bungling act, bull, fault, omission.

BLUNDER is of Scandinavian origin. The French words *faux pas* (*fō pah'*), literally, false step, are used often to express exactly the kind of bungling, stupid error of judgment, statement, or action, implicit in the English word BLUNDER.

BLUNDER, MISTAKE, and ERROR, are similar. ERROR, from the Latin *errare*, to wander, is a wandering from the truth or from the right moral course. MISTAKE, a combination of

MIS and TAKE implies a false judgment. A BLUNDER is a gross error caused by clumsiness, either physical or intellectual.

78. *MATURE* (*mă-tūr'*) *v.* To develop fully, perfect, ripen, bring to completion, cause to reach maturity.

MATURE comes from the Latin *maturare*, to ripen. The noun MATURITY means complete development, as in the phrase: 'He reached MATURITY'. The transitive verb, in such a phrase as: 'He MATURED his plans', is probably less familiar.

79. *DRUDGERY* (*drŭj'-er-ĭ*) *n.* Wearisome toil, hard labor, ignoble work, disagreeable task, slavish exertion.

DRUDGERY is from an Irish word for slave. In the test phrase: 'This task is DRUDGERY', the only misconception is STIMULATING, exciting, arousing, animating. Although STIMULATING is an adjective and DRUDGERY a noun, the two words are opposed in idea.

80. *OCEANIC* (*ō-shē-ăn'-ĭk*) *adj.* Of or pertaining to the sea, marine, pelagic (1038), living in or by the ocean.

Every grammar-school pupil knows the noun OCEAN; and yet 12 per cent fail to recognize the adjective OCEANIC. Many adjectives are made from nouns by the addition of the suffix IC. Thus, the word ARTISTIC means of or pertaining to an artist; POETIC, of or pertaining to a poet; OCEANIC, of or pertaining to the ocean.

81. *PROHIBIT* (*prō-hĭb'-ĭt*) *v.* To forbid, stop, prevent, bar, hinder, preclude, ban, restrain, interdict.

In the test phrase: 'It was PROHIBITED', the word is thought by 2 per cent of adult readers to mean PASSED BY LAW. Although the word PASS can be used in more than a dozen different senses, in the phrase: 'PASSED by law', it probably means permitted, approved, authorized, sanctioned, an exact opposite of PROHIBITED.

To PROHIBIT is an official act, implying an attempt at enforcement by authority. To FORBID is less formal. An individual FORBIDS something; a government PROHIBITS it.

Originally both FORBID and PROHIBIT were used with the infinitive TO; and one is still FORBIDDEN TO do something, but with PROHIBIT the older form has disappeared and one is PROHIBITED FROM doing something.

82. *BRAWNY* (*braw'-nĭ*) *adj.* Large, strong, stout, fleshy, powerful, muscular, stalwart.

The original meaning of BRAWN, in English, is boar's flesh or pig's flesh which has been pressed in a mold in order to squeeze out the fat. The adjective BRAWNY has exactly this suggestion of large, fleshy, but not fat.

83. *REGION* (*rē'-jŭn*) *n.* Area, district, large piece of land, portion of territory, province, vicinity, sphere, tract.

REGION is from the Latin *regere*, to rule, from the same source as the English word REGENT, one who rules during the youth or absence of the ruler. Despite this derivation, the English word REGION, unlike such words as STATE, CITY, TOWN, is applied to a portion of territory which has no political organization, as: 'Mountainous REGIONS'. The corresponding adjective REGIONAL, as used in the phrase: 'REGIONAL planning', designates such projects as flood control and the building of through traffic routes, which do not fall within the confines of any one state.

84. *JEOPARDY* (*jĕp'-ahr-dĭ*) *n.* Danger, peril, harm, risk, hazard, insecurity, exposure to injury.

The corresponding verb, to JEOPARDIZE, is to endanger, imperil, expose to harm.

JEOPARDY is perhaps an attempt to pronounce in English the French words *jeu parti*, a divided game, even game, even chance; for the noun JEOPARDY in English originally meant a game evenly balanced. This meaning is now obsolete, and to place something in JEOPARDY is to place it in a position where its chances of failing are unnecessarily great.

85. *DELAY* (*dē-lā'*) *v.* To move slowly, waste time, be tardy, lag, linger, loiter (70), procrastinate (679).

In addition to this intransitive use, the word DELAY may be used as a transitive verb and mean to detain, hinder, obstruct the progress of, as: 'Heavy snow DELAYED the train'.

The meaning of DELAY, as an intransitive verb, is unknown

to 12 per cent of grammar-school pupils. In the test phrase: 'Do not DELAY', it is thought by 6 per cent to mean FORGET. One tends both to FORGET and to DELAY to do something which one does not want to do, but the words are not synonymous. To FORGET means to lose remembrance of, not remember, fail to recall. To DELAY means to put off doing something which one has not forgotten.

86. *OUST* (*owst*) *v.* To put out forcibly, turn out, drive out, eject, expel, evict, dislodge, supplant (274), dismiss. To 1 per cent of adult readers, to OUST incorrectly means to WARN, caution.

87. *SUSPECT* (*sŭs-pĕkt'*) *v.* To distrust (36), doubt, mistrust, imagine to be guilty, be suspicious of.
To SUSPECT is thought by 1 per cent of adult readers to mean RECOMMEND, speak well of, in connotation almost an opposite of the correct meaning.
    SUSPECT, EXPECT, INSPECT, RESPECT, and SPECTACLE, are all from the Latin *specere*, to look at. A SPECTACLE is a display, exhibition, public show, something to be looked at. RESPECT by derivation means to look back at, but the word is now used to mean look at with attention, regard as worthy of notice, esteem. INSPECT, by derivation to look into, means regard critically, examine. EXPECT, by derivation to look out for, means to await, anticipate. SUSPECT, from *sub*, under, and the Latin *spectare*, the frequentative of *specere*, means to look at again and again, regard with distrust, doubt.

88. *JEER* (*jēr*) *v.* To scoff (223), mock (240), taunt, deride, gibe at, sneer at, make fun of.
To 1 per cent of adult readers to JEER incorrectly means to APPLAUD. This is probably a confusion of JEER, to mock, with the verb to CHEER, which may mean to applaud.

89. *SEMBLANCE* (*sĕm'-blăns*) *n.* Likeness, image, guise, outward aspect, superficial appearance.
SEMBLANCE and RESEMBLANCE (*rē-zĕm'-blăns*), although so close in form, differ in use. RESEMBLANCE suggests an inherent similarity, a real likeness in nature. SEMBLANCE is used of that

which resembles something only on the surface, but differs from it fundamentally.

90. *ODD* (ŏd) *adj.* Unusual, strange, queer, peculiar, bizarre, quaint (382), curious, fantastic (401), not ordinary.

ODD, QUEER, and PECULIAR, mean strange, unusual, out of the ordinary. QUEER, which comes from a German word meaning slanting, awry, oblique, differs from the others in that it suggests slightly comical, laughable, ridiculous. PECULIAR comes from a Latin word *peculiaris*, one's own, which in turn comes from another Latin word *pecus*, cattle, and originally meant one's own cattle. PECULIAR means unusual because belonging to the individual. ODD, which comes from an Icelandic word meaning triangle, has no suggestion of amusement but means unmated, as: 'An ODD shoe', 'An ODD glove'. From this it has come to mean unusual, strange, as in the phrase: 'ODD arrangements'.

91. *APEX* (ā'-pĕks) *n.* Highest point, tip, peak, top, vertex, summit, pinnacle (398), apogee.

In the test phrase: 'The APEX of his career', the word is believed by 1 per cent of adult readers to mean AIM. The AIM is that point toward which one strives, but which one may never reach; the APEX, as used in this phrase, is the highest point actually reached.

92. *RETRIEVE* (rē-trēv') *v.* To regain, recover, get back; also: to remedy (65), repair (245), restore to a former good state after loss or injury, set right, as in the phrase: 'To RETRIEVE a mistake'.

RETRIEVE is from *re*, again; and the French word *trouver*, to find. The noun, a RETRIEVER, when used specifically, means a dog trained to seek and bring back to a sportsman a bird which has been shot.

93. *THUD* (thŭd) *n.* Thump, the dull non-resonant sound made by the fall of a heavy body, percussion.

The corresponding verb, to THUD, is perhaps in part imitative, like THUMP, but it is probably also related to an Anglo-Saxon word meaning to beat, strike. The past tense and the present participle of the verb are spelt THUDDED and THUDDING.

94. *TRASH* . (*trăsh*) *n.* Something broken, torn bits; hence: waste, refuse, rubbish, dross, worthless stuff, offal (865). The word TRASH is related to Scandinavian words which mean broken sticks, fallen leaves, heaps of twigs. By derivation the word means broken bits of wood, but is today used more generally as in the phrase: 'A collection of TRASH', to mean rubbish, refuse.

95. *STRESS* (*strĕs*) *v.* To emphasize, accent, utter forcefully, state positively, make distinctive by vivid language. In the phrase: 'They STRESSED the point', the word is thought by 2 per cent of adult readers to mean CRITICIZED. This is perhaps a misunderstanding of the word CRITICIZE. CRITICIZE means to judge fairly, impartially. The verb is sometimes used to mean find fault with, but the verbs to FIND FAULT WITH, to NAG, and to SCOLD, mean to stress the bad points; while the original meaning of CRITICIZE was to judge both the good and the bad points without stressing either one or the other. Or the confusion of CRITICIZE with STRESS may be caused by the vague similarity in appearance of CRITICIZE and EMPHASIZE, which means to stress, accent.

The words STRESS and STRAIN are constantly confused. The Oxford English Dictionary states that they are 'used variously by different writers'. There are two common phrases which differentiate sharply between their meanings. 'To STRESS the truth' means to emphasize it, urge it with force. 'To STRAIN the truth' means to warp it, distort it. In physics, STRAIN is the result of STRESS; STRESS is the action, force, push; STRAIN, the resulting bend, distortion.

96. *TRUSTWORTHINESS* (*trŭst'-wer-thĭ-nĕs*) *n.* Reliability (124), dependability, the quality of being worthy of confidence.
In the test phrase: 'I doubt his TRUSTWORTHINESS', the word is thought by 8 per cent of grammar-school pupils to mean ABILITY. Both ABILITY and TRUSTWORTHINESS inspire confidence, for however different reasons. The word ABILITY is a combination of the adjective ABLE, from the Latin *habere*, to have, plus the ending ITY which is added to many adjectives of Latin derivation to form abstract nouns, as: CIVIL,

CIVILITY. ABILITY is the power which makes one able; it is physical or mental capacity. An able, capable, person with ABILITY, may be untrustworthy, lacking in TRUSTWORTHINESS.

TRUSTWORTHINESS is from the same source as TRUE and characterizes one who can be trusted. The noun, TRUST, means confidence in a person, belief that a person or thing can be relied on. The suffix, WORTHY, is added to several words to represent worth, merit. TRUSTWORTHY is an adjective which means worthy of trust, capable of being trusted. The additional suffix, NESS, makes a noun of the adjective. TRUSTWORTHINESS is the quality of being worthy of trust.

97. *UNFAILING* (*ŭn-fāl'-ĭng*) *adj.* Dependable, reliable, trustworthy, sure, not likely to fall short.

In the test phrase: 'His UNFAILING friend', the word is thought by 2 per cent of adult readers to mean UNRELIABLE, not reliable, failing when wanted, an exact opposite of UNFAILING.

The word FAIL is used in many ways. The business man thinks instantly of an organization which has FAILED, become unable to meet its financial obligations. It is not in this sense that FAIL is used in UNFAILING. Nor is it used in the sense of FAILING in health, wasting away, declining. It returns more nearly to the meaning of the original Latin word *fallere*, to deceive, err, from which comes to FAIL, to disappoint, leave in the lurch, be wanting. One speaks of the steam FAILING on a cold day, of the water supply FAILING in an emergency. With this use of FAIL there is always the suggestion of FAILING when it is most needed. It is in this sense that the word is used in UNFAILING, not failing when needed, not disappointing one, not leaving one in the lurch.

98. *HEXAGON* (*hĕks'-ă-gŏn*) *n.* Six-sided figure, literally a figure with six angles, from the Greek ἕξ, six, and γωνία, which means angle, corner, not side.

To 1 per cent of adult readers HEXAGON incorrectly means MODEL, the common misconception. This may be a confusion of HEXAGON with the more unusual word PARAGON (589), a model, perfect example, a word which despite its similarity does not apparently come from the same Greek source as the large family of geometrical terms: PENTAGON, a figure with five angles; HEXAGON, one with six; HEPTAGON, one with seven; OCTAGON, one with eight; ENNEAGON (ĕn'-nē-ă-gŏn), one with nine; and DECAGON, one with ten angles. For a figure with three angles, which is more common than these, the Latin name TRIANGLE is used; for the commonest figure of all the Anglo-Saxon word SQUARE is used.

99. *ASK* (ăsk) *v.* To invite, bid, summon politely, request the presence of.

Although, in at least some of its senses, the word ASK is familiar to everyone, when used in the phrase: 'She was ASKED in advance', where it probably means invited, it is believed by 8 per cent of grammar-school pupils to mean HELD.

The verb to ASK, which is of Anglo-Saxon origin, has at least four different meanings. First, one may ASK a question which someone will ANSWER. Second, one may ASK help of someone. In this sense, to ASK and to OFFER, another Anglo-Saxon word, are opposites in suggestion. Third, a storekeeper may ASK so much a dozen. In this sense, to ASK and to DEMAND are synonymous, except that DEMAND, because it comes from Latin, through French, is more formal than the Anglo-Saxon ASK. Fourth, one may ASK someone to a party. In this sense, to ASK and to INVITE are synonymous, except that INVITE, again because it comes from the Latin *invitare*, to ask, invite, is more formal than ASK.

100. *BLEAK* (blēk) *adj.* Bare, exposed, barren, cold, wind-swept, desolate, dreary (346), cheerless. 'The shore looks BLEAK.'

The word BLEAK first appeared in the sixteenth century. Before that time, it may have been the same as BLEACH, to whiten, make white, remove the color from, a word five centuries older. BLEAK, when it first appeared in English, meant pale, wan, pallid, bleached, but this meaning is now obsolete.

BLEAK, BARREN, and BARE, are almost synonymous. BARE means without covering for any reason. A BARE hill may have been stripped of its trees. BARREN means incapable of producing, unproductive. A BARREN hill could never have grown trees. BLEAK, as it is most often used today, suggests not only

BARE, without covering; and sometimes BARREN, incapable of producing a cover; but also cold and wind-swept.

101. *APPRAISE* (*ăp-prāz'*) *v.* To evaluate justly, estimate the true value of, set a correct value on. 'He APPRAISED the estate.'

To APPRAISE, to PRAISE, to APPRECIATE, to PRIZE, and to PRICE, all come from the Latin word *pretium,* price, worth. All five verbs at one time or another in the past have meant to APPRAISE in its modern sense, to set a just value on; and all today mean to set a value on in some sense.

To PRICE (*prīs*), a business word, is to fix the selling price of. To PRIZE (*prīz*) is, by derivation, to price an object so highly that it will not be sold. Today, to PRIZE is to value highly, esteem. The word is in general literary use, and expresses an attitude toward one's own belongings.

To APPRAISE, APPRECIATE, and PRAISE, refer to others or to their belongings. To PRAISE is to laud, extol, tell another that one sets a high value on his services. To APPRECIATE may mean either to set a high value on, that is to praise, and so be an opposite of DEPRECIATE; or it may mean to set a just value on, and so be synonymous with APPRAISE, to evaluate correctly.

102. *TARNISH* (*tahr'-nĭsh*) *v.* To stain, sully (561), soil, dull, dim, discolor, destroy the luster of.

The word TARNISH is applied so frequently to the discoloration of a bright metal surface that when used figuratively it always implies the discoloration, darkening, loss, of something which has previously been bright; as: 'To TARNISH a reputation', 'To TARNISH a good name'.

103. *RUB* (*rŭb*) *v.* To chafe, abrade, scrape, scour, burnish, brighten, polish, are all synonyms of RUB when the word is used in one of its restricted senses. Thus: 'To RUB cloth' is to chafe it. 'To RUB a copper kettle' is to burnish it. But the word RUB may also be used in a general sense with reference to the action implied in all of the other verbs but without specifying the aim or result.

The verb to RUB must be known to every grammar-school pupil; but when it appears with two B's as in the phrase: 'The wheels RUBBED together', it is not recognized by 14 per cent. RUB is one of the words in which the B is doubled when an ending such as ER, ED, or ING, is added. The rule is: All simple, one-syllable words which end in B, double the B when a suffix is added which begins with a vowel. Thus: To DAB, which means to pat, has one B; but DABBED and DABBING have two. To MOB has one; but MOBBED and MOBBING have two. The same holds for all simple, one-syllable words, as, to FIB, FIBBER, FIBBED, FIBBING; LOB, LOBBED. The English language is, however, too much alive to be governed arbitrarily by any rule without exceptions. Thus, if the vowel in the one-syllable word is followed by R, the B is not doubled: CURB, CURBED, CURBING; BARB, BARBED. Furthermore, if the vowel in the one-syllable word is not a single vowel but a diphthong, a combination of two vowels, the B is not doubled: DAUB, DAUBER, DAUBED, DAUBING. RUB is a one-syllable word, without these complications, and the B therefore doubles: RUB, RUBBER, RUBBED, and RUBBING.

104. *ADMIRABLE* (ăd'-mĭr-ă-bl) *adj.* Excellent, highly pleasing, estimable, exciting approval and esteem, worthy of admiration.

ADMIRABLE comes from the verb to ADMIRE, to wonder at, from the same Latin source as MIRACLE, a wonder, and MIRACULOUS, wonderful. ADMIRE has now ceased to imply wonderment and means look upon with pleasure.

In the test phrase: 'ADMIRABLE persons', the word is thought by 1 per cent of adult readers to mean NAVAL, pertaining to the sea. This is perhaps because of some confusion between ADMIRABLE and ADMIRAL, a naval officer, the commander-in-chief of the navy, or the commander of a fleet.

ADMIRABLE as are all ADMIRALS, the latter word does not come from the former, but from one of the Arabic phrases, *amir-al-bahr*, commander of the sea, or *amir-al-ma*, commander of the water. AMIR (ah-mēr') is commander, and is sometimes spelt in English AMEER or EMIR; and *al* is the article, the, which appears at the beginning of other words from the Arabic as in ALGEBRA, ALCOVE, ALCOHOL, ALCHEMY, ALKALI, and ALMANAC. Despite the fact that ADMIRAL does not come from the same root as ADMIRABLE, the latter word may have contributed to the spelling of the former for there was no D in the Arabic *amir*, nor in *amiral*, the form in which ADMIRAL first appeared in English.

ADMIRABLE and ABOMINABLE, detestable, revolting, are opposites.

105. *SOLEMN* (*sŏl'-ĕm*) *adj.* SOLEMN is generally used in the sense of serious, grave, formal, earnest, deliberate, impressive, awe-inspiring; but it may also mean sacred, religious, reverent, ceremonial, devout.

In the test phrase: 'His manner was SOLEMN', the word is thought by 2 per cent of adult readers to mean INSOLENT, insulting, offensive, contemptuous.

SOLEMN, SEDATE, and SERIOUS, are all used of persons to mean the opposite of GAY, LIVELY, FRIVOLOUS. SERIOUS is the most general of the three words and is the opposite of GAY. SEDATE and the corresponding noun SEDATIVE, a medicine or in fact anything which soothes or calms, come from the Latin *sedere*, from the same source as the verb to SIT. SEDATE means quiet, calm, and is the opposite of LIVELY. SOLEMN, which comes from a Latin word meaning established, suggests ceremony, and is the opposite of FRIVOLOUS.

106. *TWIDDLE* (*twĭd'-dl*) *v.* To twirl idly, make one's thumbs rotate around each other, as: 'He TWIDDLED his thumbs'. The derivation of TWIDDLE is obscure, but the word is probably related to TWEEDLE, which means to handle lightly, fiddle with.

To FIDDLE, TWIDDLE, and TWEEDLE, are inconsequential English words, but are all in good standing.

107. *TRIFLE* (*trī'-fl*) *n.* A thing of little value, small article, something of no importance, anything of slight moment, insignificant object, bauble, gewgaw (*gū'-gaw*, not *jē'-jaw*). There is also a verb, to TRIFLE, to idle, waste time, dally, talk lightly, act frivolously; and an adjective TRIFLING, inconsequential, of small value.

108. *CATASTROPHE* (*kă-tăs'-trō-fē*) *n.* Disaster (231), calamity, great misfortune, mishap, cataclysm, accident, denouement, final event; originally, outcome of a Greek drama.

CATASTROPHE comes from two Greek words. The first, κατά, means down; and the second, στροφή, appearing directly in the English word STROPHE, means a turn, twist; a CATASTROPHE is the down-turning of events, the final twist.

To 1 per cent of adult readers CATASTROPHE incorrectly means EARTHQUAKE. An EARTHQUAKE may be no more than a tremor (trē'-mŏr, or sometimes trĕm'-ŏr), so slight as to be recorded only by scientific instruments. Such an EARTHQUAKE is not a catastrophe, either in the sense of calamity or final event. An EARTHQUAKE may shake a city and yet do no more than knock down a little plaster or crack a ceiling. Or an EARTHQUAKE may wipe out towns and destroy a hundred thousand lives as did the earthquake at Messina in Sicily in 1908, the most destructive earthquake on record and one of the great catastrophes of history.

A Greek drama, in the time of the ancients, was divided into four parts:

The PROTASIS (prŏt'-ā-sĭs), in Greek πρότασις, is an introduction.

The EPITASIS (ĕ-pĭt'-ā-sĭs), in Greek ἐπίτασις, is literally a stretching out, continuance, increase in intensity, from the same Greek source as the English word TENSION, strain. The EPITASIS appealed to the passions, the emotions.

The CATASTASIS (kă-tăs'-tă-sĭs), in Greek κατάστασις, is literally the settling down, heightening, that part of the drama which prepared one for the inevitableness of the catastrophe.

Finally, the CATASTROPHE is the end, sudden turn, development, final event. Originally, CATASTROPHE meant merely the unfolding of the plot, its winding up; but the word is used today almost exclusively to mean disastrous ending, calamitous conclusion. Whenever the word is used in this way, it must refer to a disaster which was inevitable. The word CALAMITY may be used for that which might have been avoided; but a Greek play failed unless it made one feel that the CATASTROPHE was inevitable.

109. *EXTIRPATE* (ĕks'-ter-pāt) v. To uproot, eradicate, get rid of, destroy, annihilate, root out, exterminate.

EXTIRPATE comes from the Latin *ex*, out; and *stirps*, the roots and lower trunk of a tree; and means literally to root out.

To 1 per cent of adult readers EXTIRPATE incorrectly means to PLANT, an opposite of the correct meaning.

110. *PETRIFY* (*pĕt'-rĭ-fī*) *v.* To turn to stone. The verb to PETRIFY is used in a figurative sense with reference to human beings to mean stupefy with amazement, paralyze with fear.

PETRIFY is from the Greek, πέτρα, rock; and the Latin, *facere*, to make. From the same Greek source come the words PETROLOGY (*pē-trŏl'-ō-jĭ*), the scientific study of rocks; and PETROGRAPHY (*pē-trŏg'-ră-fī*), the systematic description of rocks. To PETRIFY is literally to make into rock.

111. *TRIPLICATE* (*trĭp'-lĭ-kāt*) *adj.* Three-fold, triple, triplex (*trī'-plĕks*), three times as many, thrice repeated, composed of three units.

DUPLICATE means two-fold; and although QUADRUPLE is ordinarily used to mean four-fold, there is an unusual word QUADRUPLICATE, four-fold. To 2 per cent of adult readers TRIPLICATE incorrectly means TYPEWRITTEN.

TRIPLICATE is from the Latin *tres*, *tri*, three; and *plicare*, to fold; and means literally three-fold. From *plicare* come also PLY, which may mean a fold, thickness, twist, as in three-ply thread; PLIANT, easily folded, flexible, supple; and PLICATE (*plī'-kāt*), plaited, folded like a fan, used in botany of leaf structure.

Three other words from the same source as TRIPLICATE, and with much the same form, are: COMPLICATED, literally folded together, complex, involved, not simple, hard to unravel; EXPLICATED, unfolded, evolved, explained, expanded; and IMPLICATED, enfolded, involved, entangled. Although one speaks of a COMPLICATED situation, an EXPLICATED edition, an IMPLICATED person, the adjective TRIPLICATE ordinarily appears without the D, a TRIPLICATE copy.

112. *HISS* (*hĭs*) *v.* To make a sharp s sound expressing dislike or disapproval. 'The audience HISSED.'

To HISS and to CLAP express opposite emotions. An audience CLAPS when it likes or approves something; it HISSES when it dislikes or disapproves. HISS, HUM, and BUZZ, are believed to be man's attempts to imitate natural sounds which he has heard. The process is called ONOMATOPEIA (ŏn-ō-măt-ō-pē'-ă). All words may, according to some authorities, have started in this way. BUZZ is the sound of a bee, and the word appears in English both as a noun, a BUZZ, and as a verb, to BUZZ. HUM, which also appears as both noun and verb, is the sound of the humming bird. HISS is the sound made by an angry goose or by a snake. HISS is also both noun, a HISS, and verb, to HISS.

113. *UNFALTERING* (*ŭn-fawl'-ter-ĭng*) *adj.* Unwavering, unhesitating (191), unflinching, not stopping, not halting, not turning aside, progressing steadily, steadfastly pushing forward without stumbling.
UNFALTERING and UNFLAGGING are similar but differ in suggestion. UNFLAGGING implies pushing forward without loss of energy. UNFALTERING implies pushing forward without turning aside.

114. *UNFLAGGING* (*ŭn-flăg'-gĭng*) *adj.* Untiring, indefatigable (255), not failing, not drooping, sustained, assiduous (390), continuous, not diminished in energy.
The verb, to FLAG, which originally meant to hang loosely, is now employed most frequently to mean to droop, fail, tire, grow feeble, become languid, sink, decline, languish, slacken.
    Although the verb, to FLAG, to droop, tire, is spelt and pronounced like the more common noun, a FLAG, a banner, there is practically no historical relation between the two.
    The participial adjective, FLAGGING, from the verb to FLAG, means drooping, failing, languid, feeble, limp, as in the phrase: 'FLAGGING enthusiasm'. The Anglo-Saxon prefix, *un*, makes UNFLAGGING mean not flagging, not failing.

115. *SUBURB* (*sŭb'-erb*) *n.* A district adjacent to a city of which it may or may not be a political part. SUBURBS, in the plural, means outskirts, outlying parts of a metropolitan area.
SUBURB comes from two Latin words *sub*, near or under, as in SUBWAY; and *urbs*, city. The latter appears directly in the English word URBAN, of or pertaining to the city, in contrast to RURAL, of or pertaining to the country. The adjective SUB-

URBAN is between URBAN and RURAL, near the city, but not in the country.

116. *GASH* (*găsh*) *v.* To cut deeply, slash, slit, cleave, make a gaping wound.

In the test phrase: 'His leg was GASHED', the word is thought by 3 per cent of adult readers to mean CRUSHED. To CRUSH is to mash, squeeze, compress, press between hard bodies, bruise; whereas GASH is always to cut.

117. *PLIABLE* (*plī'-ă-bl*) *adj.* Flexible (28), easily bent, supple (*sŭp'-pl*, not *soop'-pl*) (397), limber, yielding, lithe, lissom, pliant.

PLIABLE, PLIANT, and FLEXIBLE, are near one another in meaning and sometimes interchangeable. FLEXIBLE comes from the Latin *flectere*, to bend; while PLIANT and PLIABLE come from *plicare*, to fold; and the difference between the first and the latter two is today much the same as the difference between BEND and FOLD. A twig may be bent slightly which could not be folded back upon itself without breaking. It would be FLEXIBLE, but not PLIANT. Soft metal which can be folded is PLIANT. That which is PLIABLE is workable at will into the form one desires.

118. *DISPLAY* (*dĭs-plā'*) *v.* To unfold, spread out, show, exhibit, present to view, arrange to be seen. 'He DISPLAYED the banner.'

The word DISPLAY has no relation to PLAY, despite the similarity. PLAY comes from Anglo-Saxon; while DISPLAY is from two Latin words, *dis*, apart; and *plicare*, to fold; and means literally unfold. The Latin verb *plicare* is the origin of a large family of English words. Among them are: TRIPLICATE (111), three-fold; and PLIABLE (117), flexible. The source of these words can be recognized by the *pli* of the Latin. To PLAIT (*plăt*), to make a flat fold in a piece of cloth, as: 'A PLAITED dress', sometimes spelt PLEAT and pronounced (*plēt*); and to DISPLAY, come from the same source but lack the *pli*.

Although to DISPLAY by derivation means to unfold, the word is used today almost exclusively to mean unfold in order to show, spread out in order to exhibit, present for inspection.

119. *GAPE* (*găp*) *v.* To yawn, open the mouth wide involuntarily. The verb to GAPE is also used figuratively to mean stare in astonishment, gaze in open-mouthed wonder. To GAPE and to YAWN are often synonymous. But YAWN should be reserved for the physical act of opening the mouth involuntarily because of hunger or fatigue; while GAPE is more general. There are two accepted pronunciations of the word GAPE. When used to mean yawn, open the mouth with fatigue or hunger, it is ordinarily pronounced (*gahp*) with the *a* as in FAR (*fahr*). This sound is often called the Italian *a*. It was the sound of the *a* in both Greek and Latin, and is the purest vowel sound, for it is the sound naturally sent forth when the mouth and throat are wide open as in a yawn. When the word GAPE is used to mean stand in open-mouthed astonishment, it more frequently has the long sound of TAKE (*tāk*), MAKE (*māk*), as: GAPE (*gāp*).

120. *TANTALIZE* (*tăn'-tă-līz*) *v.* To tease, plague, provoke, torment by showing a desired object but keeping it out of reach.

The corresponding participial adjective is TANTALIZING, annoying, vexing, teasing, exasperating, tormenting, as: 'TANTALIZING problems'.

TANTALIZE comes from the proper name, TANTALUS, son of Zeus and the nymph Pluto. TANTALUS was a mythical king of Lydia. Because he disclosed the secrets of the gods, he was condemned to fabled TARTARUS, the place of dire punishment of the gods, as far below Hades as Earth is below Heaven. His sentence was to stand up to his chin in water which drew back whenever he stooped to drink. Above his head, just out of reach, hung fruits which constantly eluded his grasp.

To TANTALIZE, to TORMENT, and to TEASE, all mean to vex in different ways. One is TEASED by petty annoyances, by trifles. One is TORMENTED by physical pain, bodily suffering. One is TANTALIZED by mental suffering.

TANTALIZE and GRATIFY are opposites.

121. *FEARLESSNESS* (*fēr'-lĕs-nĕs*) *n.* Bravery, boldness, daring, courage, intrepidity, valor, heroism, pluck.

In the test phrase: 'An act of FEARLESSNESS', the word is believed by 4 per cent of adult readers to mean TREACHERY, disloyalty, treason, betrayal of trust, in suggestion almost an opposite of FEARLESSNESS, for the man who is characterized by fearlessness, bravery, is ordinarily thought of as loyal, honest, trustworthy, all qualities which are opposites of treacherous.

The ending LESS may be added to many nouns to form adjectives. It means without, not having. Thus: CHILDLESS is without children; HATLESS, without a hat; FEARLESS, without fear.

As discussed under SHYNESS (12), the ending NESS makes a noun from the adjective to which it is added. FEARLESS is an adjective; FEARLESSNESS is a noun, the quality of being fearless, the characteristic of being without fear.

Other endings, suffixes, are added to the word FEAR. Thus: FEARFUL means full of fear, afraid, timid, the opposite of FEARLESS; FEARSOME means causing fear, inspiring fear, awful, terrible; FEARLESSNESS is bravery, the opposite of FEARFULNESS, timidity.

122. *DOUSE* (*dows*) *v.* To dip, duck, soak (2), drench (23), immerse (256), plunge into a fluid.

In the test phrase: 'They DOUSED the seniors', the word is thought by 2 per cent of adult readers to mean SERENADED. To SERENADE is to sing love songs under a window at night.

To DUCK is to douse and immediately withdraw, to plunge the head or whole body into water for a moment only. To DOUSE suggests no thought of withdrawal. To DIP is half way between the two. DUCK, DIP, DOUSE, is the order of length of time under water.

123. *SEVERE* (*sĕ-vēr'*) *adj.* Sedate, serious, austere (715), grave, as in the phrase: 'His manner is SEVERE'. SEVERE may also mean strict in discipline, harsh in judgment, exacting, rigid (504), rigorous, merciless, extreme, sharp, violent, cutting, keen, as: 'SEVERE pain'. Both meanings of the adjective are unknown to 4 per cent of adult readers.

SEVERE comes from the Latin *severus*, severe, serious, grave, probably from the same source as the English word SERIOUS.

The noun SEVERITY, like the adjective, has two senses. It

may mean seriousness, gravity, austerity; or violence, sharpness, intensity, as: 'The SEVERITY of an illness'. The adverb SEVERELY also has two meanings, although the meaning gravely, austerely, is seldom found except perhaps in the cliché: 'They left him SEVERELY alone'.

124. *RELIABILITY* (*rē-lĭ-ă-bĭl'-ĭ-tĭ*) *n.* Trustworthiness (96), dependability, responsibility, faithfulness, loyalty, stability, constancy, steadfastness, stanchness.

RELIABILITY is a combination of the verb to RELY, to trust, depend on, count on, plus ABLE, plus ITY. The suffix ABLE is added to many verbs to mean capable of, worthy of. Thus EATABLE means capable of being eaten; READABLE, capable of being read. Although the adjective RELIABLE differs slightly from these, it is similar to LAUGHABLE, capable of being laughed at. ITY is added to many adjectives to form corresponding nouns; as: RELIABLE, RELIABILITY.

125. *ADDRESS* (*ăd-drĕs'*) *v.* To speak to, lecture to, deliver a prepared speech.

ADDRESS comes from the Latin *ad*, to; and *directus*, direct, straight, which in turn comes probably from *di* and the Latin verb *regere*, to rule, direct, keep straight.

To ADDRESS, to HARANGUE, and to LECTURE, can all be used without the preposition TO. Thus, one can ADDRESS, HARANGUE, or LECTURE, a group. Of the three, only LECTURE can be used with the preposition TO. 'He LECTURED the group', without the preposition, means, as the phrase is usually employed, he took them to task, reproved, censured them. 'He LECTURED to the group', with the preposition TO, means, he delivered a lecture, addressed them.

To ADDRESS, and to LECTURE to, differ slightly. One LECTURES to an audience usually to instruct it; one ADDRESSES an audience more often to inspire it.

126. *THRIFTILY* (*thrĭf'-tĭ-lĭ*) *adv.* Frugally, carefully, prudently, economically. 'They managed THRIFTILY.'

THRIFTILY is an adverb formed from the noun THRIFT, careful management, economy, frugality. THRIFT in turn comes from the verb to THRIVE, in the same manner as the noun, a

RIFT, a split, fissure, cleft, comes from the verb to RIVE, to split, rend, cleave; and the noun DRIFT, as used in the phrase: 'A snow DRIFT', comes from the verb, to DRIVE.

THRIFT originally meant success, prosperity, a meaning which still survives in the phrase: 'The plant grows THRIFTILY', where the word means successfully. In the sixteenth century the word embraced the additional thought of the cause of thriving, industry, hard work, and, at the same time, economy, saving.

Of the three words THRIFTILY, ECONOMICALLY, and FRUGALLY, to manage FRUGALLY is to avoid both waste and unnecessary expense. To manage ECONOMICALLY is stronger, implying careful management. To manage THRIFTILY is still stronger, implying successful economy.

The exact meaning of THRIFTILY is unknown to 4 per cent of adult readers. SKILLFULLY is the common misconception and is not far from correct in implication, for THRIFT is skillful economy. But the word THRIFTILY adds to SKILLFULLY the additional implication of ECONOMICALLY.

THRIFTILY and WASTEFULLY are approximate opposites of each other.

127. *TOGGERY* (*tŏg'-ger-ĭ*) *n*. Clothes, dress, garments, togs, outfit, raiment, attire, habiliment, garb, apparel, costume. 'He chose his TOGGERY with care.'
Both TOGS and TOGGERY, which are synonymous, are marked by most dictionaries as slang. Both words may come from TOGA, the outer garment worn by a Roman citizen. The TOGA was usually of wool, and was a flowing mantle, wrapped loosely about the body in such a way as to leave the right arm free and uncovered.

128. *SENSES* (*sĕn'-sĕs*) *n*. Right mind, normal power of mind, sound judgment.
The word SENSE, from the Latin *sentire*, to feel, perceive, has many meanings. As a noun it may designate one of the five SENSES, as: 'The SENSE of touch', 'The SENSE of smell', 'The SENSE of taste, hearing, or feeling'. When thus used the plural means the five SENSES collectively. In such a phrase as: 'He came to his SENSES', the word has the specialized meaning of right mind.

129. *PREAMBLE* (*prē'-ăm-bl,* not *prē-ăm'-bl*) *n.* A preliminary statement, introduction, preface, prelude, prologue.
The word is used today specifically for the introductory part
of a statute. Thus used the PREAMBLE states the reasons for
and intent of what follows.
PREAMBLE comes from the Latin *prae,* before; and *ambulare,*
to walk; and by derivation means to walk before. From *ambulare* comes the English word AMBLE, to walk in a leisurely
and comfortable manner; but not the word RAMBLE, to roam,
wander about, despite the similarity in both sound and meaning. A horse in AMBLING lifts both feet on one side at the same
time, a gait which is easy for the rider. In this sense to AMBLE
and to PACE are synonymous. From the Latin *ambulare* come
also the English word AMBULANCE, originally, in French, *hô-
pital ambulant,* a walking hospital; and AMBULATORY, in architecture any passageway designed for walking, as for instance
the aisle around the choir and apse of a church.
  Both INTRODUCTION and PREFACE are more familiar words
than PREAMBLE. An INTRODUCTION should properly be a part
of what follows. It is from the Latin word *ducere,* to lead,
the source of CONDUCT, and means literally leading one in. A
PREFACE is not necessarily a part of what follows. Although
the PREFACE of a book is printed at the beginning, it may have
been written after the completion of the book itself. PREFACE,
from the Latin *fari,* to say, means by derivation a saying beforehand. A PREFACE may contain an apology for what follows,
or sometimes a history of the events which lead to what follows. A PREFACE can be read at any time, not necessarily at the
beginning. A PREAMBLE is, if one translates the Latin literally,
a delightful ambling about before undertaking the more serious business of what follows.

130. *RASHNESS* (*răsh'nĕs*) *n.* Haste, foolhardiness, impetu-
  osity, imprudence, action without thought, indiscretion,
recklessness, thoughtlessness, hurry without caution, heedless-
ness.
RASHNESS is a noun, the quality of being rash. The adjective
RASH once meant quick, active; and Dutch, German, and Scandinavian, words, which come from the same original source
as RASH, still mean quick, brisk, active. But this meaning is

obsolete in English, and RASH now always implies a tendency
to act too quickly, to act when it would be wiser to hesitate.

To 4 per cent of grammar-school pupils, RASHNESS incorrectly means COURAGE. Both COURAGE and RASHNESS are traits
of persons facing serious situations. COURAGE is calmness in
meeting a recognized danger. RASHNESS is a characteristic of
one who rushes into difficulties without stopping to think; it
is boldness without wisdom.

To another 3 per cent, RASHNESS incorrectly means FEAR;
and to still another 3 per cent it incorrectly means COWARDICE.
FEAR and COWARDICE are opposites of COURAGE, and in suggestion are opposites of RASHNESS, for one who is RASH does not
give himself time to feel fear or cowardice.

131. *RUDDY* (*rŭd'-dĭ*) *adj.* Red, rosy, rubicund, roseate,
(*rō'-zē-āt*), florid (410), having a healthy glow. 'She has
RUDDY cheeks.'

RUDDY, ROSY, and RUBY, all mean red, and are all applied to
complexions. RUBY is the deep, rich red of the precious stone,
the RUBY, and as an adjective is used only of RUBY lips. Because
it comes from the Latin, it is formal and appears more often
in writing than in conversation. Furthermore, it suggests beauty
rather than health.

ROSY, with both Anglo-Saxon and Latin ancestry, is lighter
in color than RUBY and is used most often of children; it suggests daintiness. RUDDY, sturdier and more homely than the
others, is used of healthy adults.

132. *CONTACT* (*kŏn'-tăkt*) *n.* Touch, connection, communication, proximity, a coming together, close union.
In the test phrase: 'In CONTACT with them', the word is thought
by 2 per cent of adult readers to mean: 'In BUSINESS with
them'. CONTACT comes from the Latin *con*, with, and *tangere*,
to touch; and the phrase means literally in touch with them.

133. *ENSUE* (*ĕn-sū'*) *v.* To follow, result, come afterwards,
occur as a consequence, succeed, supervene.

ENSUE and PURSUE are both from the Latin *sequi*, to follow.
To PURSUE, from *pro*, forth, in English means to follow, chase.
To ENSUE, from *in*, on, is literally to follow on as a result.

To ENSUE is to follow. To FOLLOW is the general word. To ENSUE is used only when that which follows has a close connection, is a part of a logical sequence. The phrase: 'A struggle ENSUED' means not merely that it happened later, but that it followed as a result.

134. *SECESSION* (sē-sĕsh'-ŭn) *n.* Act of resigning from an organized group, formal withdrawal, separation from association with others. 'The SECESSION of the states.'
The verb to SECEDE (sē-sēd'), which is unknown to 3 per cent of adult readers, and is therefore slightly more familiar than the noun, means to retire, go apart, withdraw formally from any organization. The word is applied to a group, which withdraws, rather than to an individual.

SECEDE comes from the Latin *se*, apart; and *cedere*, to go; and by derivation means to go apart from others. From *cedere* come also PROCEED, to go forward, originally spelt *procede*, but now PROCEED; and INTERCEDE, to go between. SECEDE is related to the noun SECESSION, the act of withdrawing, the act of going apart, much as the verb to PROCEED, to go forward, is related to the noun PROCESSION.

SECESSION originally meant withdrawal in general. The more difficult word RECESSION (580) is now reserved for physical retreat, for an actual going back. SECESSION is limited to the formal withdrawal, resignation, of a group from an association or organization.

135. *BOUNTIFUL* (bown'-tĭ-fŭl) *adj.* Abundant, plentiful, freely given, generous, ample, plenteous, unstinted.
BOUNTIFUL is from the Latin *bonus*, good. The exact meaning is unknown to 4 per cent of adult readers. In the phrase: 'BOUNTIFUL returns', the word is thought by 2 per cent to mean ADEQUATE. ADEQUATE means sufficient to meet the requirements, requisite for the purpose, enough; but the word does not suggest an abundance, great quantity, as does BOUNTIFUL, which implies more than enough.

136. *EXTREME* (ĕks-trēm') *n.* The furthest point, utmost limit, great length, ultimate.
The Latin word *exter*, outside, appears in the English adjec-

tive EXTERNAL, outer, outside. EXTERNAL remedies in medicine
are substances applied to the outside of the body; they are not
taken INTERNALLY. The Latin *exterior* is the comparative form
of *exter*, and by derivation means more outside; *extremus* is
the superlative, most outside. The comparative, *exterior*, is
today an English word, EXTERIOR, which may be used as either
a noun or an adjective to mean outer, outside. The Latin superlative, *extremus*, appears as the English EXTREME and means
the farthest point to which one can go, the utmost limit.

EXTREME is often used as an adjective in such phrases as:
'EXTREME views', 'EXTREME measures', to mean excessive, radical, drastic, extraordinary. When used as a noun the word
appears ordinarily in the plural, as: 'To go to EXTREMES', 'He
went to EXTREMES', and means he used extraordinary measures,
or he held radical views.

137. *RESOLVE* (*rē-zŏlv'*) *v*. To determine, purpose, design,
intend, decide, propose, conclude, make up one's mind,
form a resolution.

In the test phrase: 'He RESOLVES to succeed', the word is thought
by 2 per cent of adult readers to mean WISHES. To WISH is
weak; it may express only a passing fancy, momentary desire.
It has none of the determination to make the wish come true
which is embodied in the word RESOLVE.

To RESOLVE, PROPOSE, (*prō-pōz'*), PURPOSE, (*per'-pŭs*), DE-
CIDE, and DETERMINE, are closely related in meaning. To DETER-
MINE, from the same source as TERMINATION, end, is to set the
bounds within which one will act; the word applies more often
to the beginning than to the end. Thus, one may be DETER-
MINED to go. To DECIDE is to make up one's mind by stopping
further argument, by cutting short any further debate. It
applies even more to the beginning and has no conviction, no
thought of carrying through to the finish. To PURPOSE is again
to make up one's mind but does not imply having come to
that decision as the result of analysis, and also suggests no
conviction of accomplishment. To PROPOSE is most commonly
to state what one purposes to do.

RESOLVE is from the Latin *re*, again; and *solvere*, to loosen;
and suggests freeing, in the mind, some single act from others
which might interfere with its successful completion. It applies

to the end of an act, not to its start, and carries conviction of accomplishment; one RESOLVES to finish.

138. *MEND* (*mĕnd*) *v.* To improve, repair (245), set right, change for the better, reform, rectify, correct.

To MEND does not mean to SEW, as is often supposed. To MEND is to repair, patch up, restore to a sound condition. In this sense the word can be used literally, as: 'She MENDED her dress', 'He MENDED the vase', 'They MENDED the road'; or the word can be used figuratively as in the phrase: 'She MENDED her ways'. In this sense the word is unknown to 18 per cent of grammar-school pupils.

When used figuratively, MEND and AMEND are practically synonymous. AMEND was once used, as MEND is today, to mean repair, fix, in the physical sense, but this use is archaic. AMEND can now be used only in its more figurative senses; one may AMEND a resolution, AMEND a law, or still more figuratively, AMEND one's conduct. The verb to MEND may still be used in both senses. One can MEND a dress; or one can MEND one's ways.

139. *SATURATE* (*săt′-ū-rāt*) *v.* To soak (2), drench (23), douse (122), steep (303), fill with moisture, wet thoroughly, impregnate, permeate.

The verb to SATURATE is from the Latin *satur*, full, a word closely related to the Latin *satis*, enough. From *satis* come the English words SATISFY, to give enough to, gratify; and SATIATE (*sā′-shĭ-āt*) and SATE, both of which ordinarily mean to give too much to, surfeit, glut. SATURATE, and the corresponding participial adjective, SATURATED, both suggest filling that which is saturated with as much moisture as it is capable of containing.

140. *CATALOGUE* (*căt′-ă-lŏg*) *v.* To list, itemize, enumerate, arrange under headings either alphabetically or by subject matter so that separate items can be found easily.

In the test phrase: 'CATALOGUE those books', the word is thought by 2 per cent of adult readers to mean ADVERTISE.

CATALOGUE is from two Greek words κατά, down; and λέγειν, to tell, say. From the same Greek κατά, down, come many words: CATACLYSM, literally a down wash, a deluge;

CATACOMB, by derivation a down hollow, now an underground tomb; and CATASTROPHE (108), a down turning, the final turning point in a Greek drama.

To LIST books is to enumerate merely their names; to CATALOGUE them presupposes some descriptive material.

141. *PAWN* (*pawn*) *v.* To give as security, offer as pledge, deposit, leave as a gage for the fulfilment of an obligation. In the test phrase: 'He PAWNED his watch', the word is thought by 7 per cent of grammar-school pupils to mean REPAIRED. This is perhaps through a misunderstanding of the verb REPAIR (245), which is unknown to 8 per cent of adult readers and therefore more difficult. To REPAIR is literally to make ready again, mend, fix, restore to good condition.

To PAWN one's property is to give it as security in order to borrow money. There are several methods of borrowing which involve depositing something in order to guarantee repayment. The government borrows money and gives as security BONDS which are promises to repay. A house owner can borrow money by giving a MORTGAGE on his property as security. An individual can borrow a small amount of money, for a short time, by giving some actual object, such as a watch or a ring, as security.

'She PAWNED her jewels' means she gave her jewels temporarily as security, as a pledge that she would repay the money borrowed. Any article which is PAWNED is returned to the owner if the money is repaid within a specified time.

142. *UNFOUNDED* (*ŭn-fown'-dĕd*) *adj.* Groundless, idle, vain, unwarranted, having no foundation, not established. The verb to FOUND, although spelt like the preterit and past participle of FIND, has no etymological relation to that word. It comes from the Latin *fundare*, to lay the keel of, establish. The Latin *fundare* in turn comes from *fundus*, bottom, base, foundation, the source of the English word FUNDAMENTAL, basic, essential. To FOUND is to lay the base of, place, establish. FOUNDATION, basis, substructure, groundwork on which something rests, is the corresponding noun. UNFOUNDED, as in the phrase: 'The story was UNFOUNDED', means without basis in fact; hence: doubtful, uncertain, open to question.

143. *KNACK* (*năk*) *n.* Skill, facility, dexterity, adroitness, aptness in doing something, expertness, readiness.

To 2 per cent of adult readers KNACK incorrectly means BITE TO EAT. This is apparently a confusion of KNACK with SNACK, a bite to eat, hasty repast, light lunch, a word probably from the same source as SNATCH, grab, seize.

KNACK and FACILITY both suggest an ease and quickness in performance. FACILITY is an ease acquired by repetition. KNACK, which is a more informal word, suggests the same ease of performance resulting from a happy combination of natural aptitudes and acquired skill.

144. *POMP* (*pŏmp*) *n.* Great display, splendor, show of magnificence, parade of grandeur, ostentation.

When used in the test phrase: 'They came in POMP', the word is thought by 2 per cent of adult readers to mean GREAT HASTE. This is perhaps due to the verb ROMP which means to play boisterously, leap, frisk about, frolic, and which suggests a carefree running.

POMP is a noun; the corresponding adjective, POMPOUS, means ostentatious, boastful.

145. *POINT* (*point*) *n.* The main theme, important item, distinctive feature, that on which attention is fixed, the heart of the matter.

The word POINT is used in as many ways as probably any word in the language. The POINT of a needle is its sharp end. A POINT of land is a promontory, headland, extending into a body of water. The compass has 32 POINTS. Games are scored in POINTS.

In addition, the word POINT may refer to more intangible things, as: 'The POINTS to be considered', meaning the items to be considered; 'He gained his POINT', meaning his object, aim, end; and 'She spoke to the POINT', went to the heart of the matter, spoke of that on which attention was fixed.

146. *REVOLVE* (*rē-vŏlv′*) *v.* To rotate, move about an axis, circle, perform a revolution, move in a curved path around a center.

When used in the test phrase: 'A REVOLVING fan', the word is thought by 3 per cent of adult readers to mean ELECTRIC.

To REVOLVE and to ROTATE are constantly used as synonyms. When the terms are accurately employed, as in astronomy, the two are carefully differentiated. To ROTATE is to turn about an axis, as a planet ROTATES on its own axis. To REVOLVE is to move about a center, as a planet REVOLVES around the sun. Scientifically an electric fan ROTATES, but does not REVOLVE.

147. *CHASTISEMENT* (*chăs'-tĭz-mĕnt*, not *chăs-tĭz'-mĕnt*) *n.*
Infliction of punishment, authoritative correction, chastening, corporal punishment for the good of the sufferer, discipline, castigation.
The verb, CHASTISE, now pronounced (*chăs-tīz'*) had the accent originally on the first syllable, where it still exists in the case of the noun.
CHASTISEMENT is closely related to the verb CHASTEN, to purify by punishment, discipline, inflict pain. CHASTENING, PUNISHMENT, and CHASTISEMENT, vary slightly in meaning. CHASTENING is wholly corrective; PUNISHMENT is justly deserved; CHASTISEMENT is both corrective and deserved.

148. *SURVIVE* (*ser-vīv'*) *v.* To outlive, continue to live after an event, particularly after the death of another person.
In the test phrase: 'He SURVIVED his brother', the word is thought by 2 per cent of adult readers to mean FOLLOWED, the popular misconception. This misunderstanding may be due to some confusion of SURVIVE with *suivre*, a common French verb which means to follow. The French *suivre* and the English word ENSUE (133), to follow, are both from the Latin *sequi*, to follow; while SURVIVE is from the Latin *vivere*, to live, from the same source as VIVACIOUS, lively in action; VIVID, lively in appearance; and REVIVE, to make live again.
To SURVIVE biologically is to have children who live on after one's death; this is, however, an unusual and purely scientific meaning of SURVIVE which ordinarily means outlive.

149. *SCHEME* (*skēm*) *n.* Formulated plan, project, design, enterprise, program of something to be done.
SCHEME, as originally used in English, had the same meaning as the Greek word σχῆμα, figure, form, from which it comes, and was used dispassionately to mean diagram, organized plan,

methodical outline. In the eighteenth century, SCHEME came to have an unfavorable, underhand suggestion, and was used to mean a plot, self-seeking enterprise, underhand project, visionary plan, as: 'He has many SCHEMES'. Even though the parent Greek word had no such suggestion, SCHEME is today used popularly to mean WILD IDEA, and this must now be accepted as one meaning of the word. An architect still uses the word SCHEME, in the original meaning of design, formulated plan, to describe an architectural project.

150. *TRANSPARENT* (*trăns-pă'-rĕnt*) *adj.* Easy to see through, clear, sheer, gauzy, offering no obstacle to sight, pervious to light, pellucid (956), limpid, diaphanous (1076). Both TRANSPARENT and TRANSLUCENT objects allow light to pass through. TRANSLUCENT comes from the Latin *trans*, through; and *lucere*, to shine; and by derivation means shine through. Light shines through a TRANSLUCENT substance but in such a way that objects cannot be seen. Ground glass is TRANSLUCENT. TRANSPARENT comes from the same Latin *trans*, through; and *parere*, to appear; and by derivation means appear through. Objects appear clearly through a TRANSPARENT substance. Ordinary window glass is TRANSPARENT. OPAQUE, letting no light through and allowing no vision, is an opposite of TRANSPARENT in this literal sense.

TRANSPARENT can also be used figuratively of actions, intentions, to mean easily seen through, easily understood. In this figurative sense, when used in the phrase: 'His disguise was TRANSPARENT', the word is thought by 7 per cent of grammar-school pupils to mean CONCEALING, an exact opposite.

151. *ERODE* (*ē-rōd'*) *v.* To wear away, gnaw away, eat into, corrode, destroy by slow disintegration.
ERODE comes from the Latin *rodere*, to gnaw, from the same source as the English word RODENT, any gnawing animal.

By 2 per cent of adult readers ERODE is thought to mean DISCOLOR. This is perhaps due to the word CORRODE from the same Latin source and practically synonymous with ERODE. To CORRODE is to gnaw away, eat away, bit by bit; but the word is applied most frequently to wearing away by chemical reaction, a process which is usually accompanied by discoloration. To

ERODE is to wear away by mechanical means as by the rush of water.

ERODE and ABRADE are both to wear away. ABRADE, from the Latin *ab*, from; and *radere*, to scratch; is used of the wearing away caused by a moving glacier or by water containing sand. Clear, running water may ERODE; river valleys are deepened by EROSION, the corresponding noun.

152. *CRITICISM (krĭt'-ĭ-sĭsm) n.* Judgment of merit, opinion expressed after detailed examination, critical observation. The word CRITICISM is used in two ways. It may mean impartial judgment, either praise or blame, whichever is merited; or it may mean unfavorable judgment, fault-finding, censure, animadversion, stricture.

To 8 per cent of grammar-school pupils, CRITICISM incorrectly means PUNISHMENT. PUNISHMENT and CRITICISM have much in common but the two words differ in modern usage. Both are the result of a judgment made by a judge. PUNISHMENT, and CRITICISM in the sense of censure, follow as the result of some act which is thought to need correction. PUNISHMENT is pain, suffering, an actual penalty inflicted. It is imposed by someone in authority, and must be accepted by the offender. CRITICISM is given in words. It is made by someone who, as the result of careful study, has an opinion to express, but CRITICISM can be ignored by the one who is criticized.

A number of English words are built from the Greek word κριτής, judge. Thus, CRITIC, a connoisseur, one who is qualified to judge, especially in the fields of art and literature, is practically the Greek word written in English letters. CRITICISM is the judgment, expressed opinion of the CRITIC; and to CRITICIZE, to examine, judge, pass judgment upon, is the verb, a combination of CRITIC and the Greek ending IZE.

The verb, to CRITICIZE, is often incorrectly spelt with an s. In English about twenty words, which end with the sound (īz), must be spelt ISE. These must be memorized although some can be recognized as the ending ISE is not a suffix added, but an integral part of the verb. Thus: ADVERTISE, CHASTISE, COMPROMISE, DESPISE, DEVISE, DISGUISE, ENTERPRISE, EXERCISE, SURPRISE. Practically all others end in IZE, as: MEMORIZE, ORGANIZE, and SYMPATHIZE; BAPTIZE, RECOGNIZE, and CRITICIZE.

153. *ALLIED* (*ăl-līd'*) *adj.* Related, akin, associated, confederated, leagued, joined, united. 'The subjects are ALLIED.'
The adjective, ALLIED (*ăl-līd'*); the verb, to ALLY (*ăl-lī'*); and
the noun, an ALLY (*ăl-lī'*); are all accented on the last syllable.
The noun, an ALLY, is restricted usually to a government associated with another by treaty as: 'The ALLIES (*ăl'-līz'*) of the
Great War'. The verb, to ALLY, is more general and means to
unite by treaty, by marriage, or by friendly association, to
combine in any way. The adjective, ALLIED, is still more general and means united, joined.

154. *BULLETIN* (*bŏol'-lĕ-tĭn*) *n.* Announcement, short official statement, public notice, brief statement of news by
an acknowledged authority.
In the test phrase: 'Look at the BULLETIN', the word is thought
by 3 per cent of adult readers to mean PAPAL DECREE. A BULL is
a papal decree, an official proclamation issued by the Pope. It
derives its name from the Italian word *bulla*, the name of the
leaden seal attached to the document. BULLETIN comes from
bulletta, the diminutive of *bulla*. A BULLETIN is, in general, any
official statement.

155. *CONFER* (*cŏn-fer'*) *v.* To talk together, hold conference,
compare views, converse, discuss, consult with one another, deliberate together.
CONFER is from the Latin *con*, together; and *ferre*, to carry,
bear, bring.
Although the noun, CONFERENCE (11), is unknown to only 4
per cent of grammar-school pupils, this meaning of the verb, to
CONFER, is unknown to 19 per cent.
In the test phrase: 'I must CONFER with him', the word is
thought by 7 per cent of grammar-school pupils to mean
SYMPATHIZE. SYMPATHIZE comes from two Greek words, σύμ,
with; and πάθος, feeling; to which is added the Greek ending,
IZE, to form the verb. To SYMPATHIZE means by derivation to
feel with, be affected with feelings corresponding to those of
another. The confusion of SYMPATHIZE with CONFER is perhaps
due to the Latin *con* and the Greek σύμ, SYM, both of
which mean with.
To another 5 per cent, to CONFER incorrectly means to GO

OUT, the second most popular misconception. This is perhaps a confusion of CONFER with CONSORT. To CONSORT with means to associate with; to CONFER with means to talk with, consult with. Both verbs are followed by the preposition WITH.

To CONFER and to CONSULT both suggest a desire to obtain advice. One CONSULTS an authority, a dictionary, a lawyer, a physician, to obtain information. One CONFERS with one's equals, one's associates, to discuss a problem, exchange opinions.

156. *TERMINATION* (*ter-mǐ-nā'-shǔn*) *n.* End, ending, out-
     come, completion, conclusion, final cessation (254). 'A
dramatic TERMINATION.'
In Roman mythology, TERMINUS, spelt with a capital, was the god of landmarks and boundaries. A statue of TERMINUS, a human being without feet, who therefore never moved, was set up to designate important landmarks and to indicate boundaries. The English word, TERMINUS, is today a limit or boundary, and also, specifically, the last station on a rail-way. The word TERMINAL is the adjective, as: 'TERMINAL facilities'. It is occasionally used as a noun to mean the end; but, as a noun, is more exactly used to designate the clamp-ing screw at the end of an electric wire. The noun TERMI-NATION is today the general word for end, conclusion.

157. *SPACIOUS* (*spā'-shǔs*) *adj.* Roomy, ample, capacious,
     expansive, extensive, broad, vast in area, having a large
amount of space, not constricted, not cramped.
SPACIOUS and SPATIAL (*spā'-shǎl*) both come from the Latin *spatium*, room, space, distance, and both words were originally spelt with the T of the Latin. SPATIAL, which is the general adjective and means pertaining to space in any way, still retains the T, although it is occasionally spelt with a C. SPACIOUS, which means roomy, large, ample, has probably because of the pronunciation changed the T to C.

158. *TRAVERSE* (*trăv'-ers*, not *trăv-ers'*) *v.* To cross, pro-
     ceed through, pass from one side to the other of, go back
and forth. 'He often TRAVERSES the state.'
To TRAVERSE is from the Latin *trans*, across; and *vertere*, to turn; and by derivation means to turn across. The sense of

turning has, however, disappeared from the English word which means merely to cross, go across.

159. *TORTURE* (*tŏr'-tūr*, almost *tŏr'-chūr*) *n.* Extreme physical pain, intense mental suffering, anguish, agony, torment, excruciation.

TORTURE comes from the past participle, *tortus*, of a Latin verb *torquere*, which means to twist. Until the 19th century TORTURE was physical suffering inflicted, by law, with machines most of which twisted a person out of shape. From the same Latin verb come the words: TORSION, spelt with an s and not with a T; and TORMENT. TORSION is used most often with reference to physical objects, as: 'The TORSION produced in a steel rod'. The nouns, TORMENT and TORTURE, refer exclusively to the suffering of living things.

160. *MASTICATE* (*măs'-tĭ-kāt*) *v.* Chew, crush with the teeth, prepare for swallowing. 'MASTICATE your food carefully.' CRUNCH and CHAMP (800) are to masticate noisily.

To MASTICATE may originally have meant to chew mastic, a gum from the mastic tree. MASTIC (1104) is sometimes chewed in Asia, Indo-China, and other parts of the Far East, as spruce gum is chewed in this country.

161. *MUDDLE* (*mŭd'-dl*) *v.* To bewilder (185), perplex, becloud, befog, confuse, mix up, obfuscate (946). 'He was MUDDLED.'

The verb, to MUD, means to cover with mud, bedaub. The verb to MUDDLE is the frequentative of the verb to MUD; it expresses the repetition of the action. Other frequentatives of this same type are met. Thus, to WAG is to move from side to side; to WAGGLE is to do this again and again. To MUDDLE is by derivation to MUD again and again, to make foul, turbid; and so, figuratively, to mix up, becloud; and when applied to the mind, to bewilder, confuse.

162. *DAUNTLESS* (*dawnt'-lĕs*) *adj.* Fearless, brave, bold, intrepid, courageous, resolute, doughty, valiant, not to be frightened, not to be daunted.

To 2 per cent of adult readers DAUNTLESS incorrectly means

AGGRESSIVE, vigorously active, quick to attack. This confusion is no doubt due to the verb to DAUNT, which is still in good use and means to frighten, intimidate, dishearten. It comes from the Latin *domitare*, to tame, the direct source of the English word INDOMITABLE, not to be tamed, unconquerable. INDOMITABLE and DAUNTLESS are similar in suggestion. DAUNTLESS is passive. It does not suggest action but is defensive, and means not to be frightened, not to be intimidated, not to be daunted.

163. *PERFORATE* (*per'-fō-rāt*) *v.* To pierce, bore through, make holes in, punch openings in. To PERFORATE often suggests the making of a number of holes.

PERFORATE comes from the Latin *per*, through; and *forare*, to bore; and by derivation means to bore through.

Etymologically, to PERFORATE means to bore but the word is rarely used in this sense today. To BORE is to drill a hole of some size and suggests difficulty and labor. To PERFORATE is used most frequently of smaller holes which are pierced through some thin substance, as PERFORATIONS in paper or in a thin sheet of metal.

164. *RESPIRE* (*rē-spīr'*) *v.* To breathe in and out, inhale and exhale air successively.

RESPIRE, which is from the Latin *re*, again; and *spirare*, to breathe; is from the same source as the English words, SPIRIT, soul, life; EXPIRE; and INSPIRE. EXPIRE may mean to exhale, breathe out; or it may be used in a more figurative sense to mean stop breathing, die. INSPIRE may mean to inhale, breathe in; or it may be used more figuratively to mean breathe life into, animate, arouse, stimulate. RESPIRE can be used only in the specific sense of breathe in and out.

165. *TATTER* (*tăt'-ter*) *v.* To tear to pieces, rend, shred, make ragged, pull into bits.

TATTER is from an Icelandic word for rags. When used in the test phrase: 'A TATTERED suit', it is thought by 2 per cent of adult readers to mean PATCHED, clumsily mended. A PATCH, the noun, is a small piece of cloth sewed over a hole. The verb, to PATCH, is to mend by sewing on a patch. A TATTER, the noun, is a rag or piece of cloth, half torn from another, but still hanging to it. The participial adjective, TATTERED, means torn into rags in such a way that the pieces are left dangling. The noun, a TATTERDEMALION, is a ragamuffin, a ragged fellow.

166. *BLOOM* (*bloom*) *v.* To blossom, bear flowers, come into flower, effloresce. BUD, SPROUT, BURGEON, and GERMINATE, are related to BLOOM but not exact synonyms.

The nouns BLOOM and BLOSSOM, both from Anglo-Saxon, and the verbs, to BLOOM and to BLOSSOM, are close in meaning but differ slightly. BLOSSOM is applied to fruit trees, BLOOM to plants which are raised for flowers but not for fruit. Thus, an apple tree BLOSSOMS. 'Apple BLOSSOMS' is a familiar phrase; but a magnolia or dogwood BLOOMS.

The exact meaning of the verb, to BLOOM, is unknown to 20 per cent of grammar-school pupils. To 11 per cent it incorrectly means to BEAR FRUIT. The BLOSSOM comes before the fruit, and a BLOSSOMING tree gives promise of bearing fruit; but even the verb, to BLOSSOM, means to bear flowers, not to bear fruit. And the verb, to BLOOM, cannot correctly be used even of the BLOS-SOMS of a fruit tree.

167. *TOLERABLE* (*tŏl'-er-ā-bl*) *adj.* Bearable, supportable, endurable, moderately agreeable, passable, capable of being brooked, reasonably satisfactory.

TOLERABLE is from the Latin *tolerare*, to endure, and means literally capable of being endured.

In the test phrase: 'TOLERABLE conditions', the word is thought by 2 per cent of adult readers to mean INSUPPORTABLE (*ĭn-sŭp-pōr'-tă-bl*), unbearable, incapable of being borne, intolerable, the popular misconception and an exact opposite of the correct meaning.

168. *LOATHE* (*lōth*) *v.* To hate, detest, despise, abhor, abominate, dislike extremely, feel great disgust for.

The verb, to LOATHE, is pronounced (*lōth*) with the TH sound as in THE, THEN, THEIR. The adjective, LOATH, without the E, and pronounced (*lōth*) with the TH sound as in TEETH, BOTH, NORTH, is the same word, but has none of the strength of feeling of the verb, to LOATHE. 'I am LOATH to do it' means merely disinclined, reluctant, unwilling. This word is often spelt LOTH, but LOATH is preferable because it shows more clearly the connection with the verb, to LOATHE.

When used in the phrase: 'She LOATHED the child', the word is thought by 4 per cent of adult readers to mean NEGLECT, slight, leave undone, uncared for.

DESPISE, ABHOR, LOATHE, are degrees of dislike, in order of increasing intensity. DESPISE, from the Latin *de*, down; and the verb *specere*, to look; means, by derivation, to look down upon as a moral inferior. ABHOR, from the Latin *ab*, from; and *horrere*, to shudder; means, by derivation, to shrink from. LOATHE, from an Anglo-Saxon word meaning hateful, is the strongest of the three, first because of its meaning, and second because words of Anglo-Saxon origin are often more homely, plainer, more straightforward, than those from Latin.

169. *UNBRIDLED* (*ŭn-brī'-dld*) *adj*. Spirited, free, lively, active, unrestrained, unruly, uncurbed, unchecked, not controlled.

The source of UNBRIDLED is Anglo-Saxon and appears more directly in BRAID, which originally meant to jerk, make a sudden movement, and which is thought of today most often in the sense of BRAIDING one's hair, or BRAIDING rugs, twisting, intertwining with a jerking motion.

The ending, LE, of UNBRIDLE, indicates an instrument. Thus, a HANDLE is a mechanical device to be grasped by the hand. A BRIDLE is the instrument or headgear by which a horse is controlled, checked, or, if one uses the original meaning of the word, jerked. UNBRIDLED, used most often figuratively, is without a BRIDLE, unguided, uncontrolled, as in the phrase: 'Her UNBRIDLED tongue', 'His UNBRIDLED temper'.

170. *TWINGE* (*twĭnj*) *n*. Darting pain, annoying twitch, throe, sudden ache, sharp pang, crick, stitch, spasm, convulsive cramp.

To 2 per cent of adult readers TWINGE incorrectly means PUNCH, a blow with a fist. This may be a confusion of PUNCH, blow, with PINCH, a nip, squeezing flesh between thumb and finger. TWINGE comes from an Anglo-Saxon verb meaning to pinch, and in English a TWINGE was originally a pinch. This meaning is now rare and a TWINGE is ordinarily a pang, sudden pain.

171. *ADORE* (ă-dōr') *v.* To worship, reverence, love intensely, idolize, honor, admire, regard with fervent devotion. 'He ADORES her.'

ADORE is from the Latin *ad*, to; and *orare*, to pray, speak. It is from the same source as the adjective ORAL, which means spoken, not written. Although ADORE comes from a word meaning to speak, it has today the connotation of silent homage.

172. *CURB* (*kerb*) *v.* To restrain, hold back, check, keep in subjection, control, confine, bridle. 'CURB your speech.'

A CURB, the noun, is a chain added to an ordinary bridle to use with a spirited horse. It is fastened to the two ends of the bit in such a way as to hang below the lower jaw and to pull against it when the reins are tightened. To CURB, therefore, like the verb to BRIDLE, is to restrain, hold in check.

173. *KIN* (*kĭn*) *n.* One's relatives, kindred, kinsfolk, connections by birth or marriage, persons of the same family.

The phrase: 'KITH and KIN' originally meant friends and relatives; for KITH means friends, acquaintances, fellow-countrymen. But the phrase is now used loosely for KINSFOLK in general, family connections. With this lax use, KITH has become confused with KIN and is sometimes used as synonymous with it.

In the phrase: 'They are no KIN of mine', the word is thought by 4 per cent of adult readers to mean CHILDREN. The word KIN includes CHILDREN, as in the legal phrase: 'Next of KIN', but the word means relatives in general.

AKIN, literally of kin, means of the same kind, of the same nature, allied, as: 'AKIN to one another'. KIN; KINDRED, literally the condition or state of being kin; and KINSFOLK; are three words for those to whom one is related by blood or marriage.

174. *SEVER* (*sĕv'-er*) *v.* To separate, disjoin, sunder (839), divide, cut, part, disunite, dissociate, slash, rend apart, break open.

In the test phrase: 'He SEVERED the cord', the word is thought by 2 per cent of adult readers to mean TWISTED, the common misconception. As so often happens with popular misconceptions of words, there is historical reason for thinking of SEVER and TWIST as synonymous. TWISTED, in its intransitive sense, once meant divided, sundered, separated, severed; but this meaning is now obsolete, and to TWIST, when used in a transitive sense as in the phrase: 'He TWISTED the cord', means to wind, twine, intertwine.

SEVER and SEPARATE are doublets, that is they have the same etymology. The difference between the two words is largely in modern usage. To SEPARATE is deliberate. 'With care he SEPARATED the good from the bad', not SEVERED. To SEVER carries the implication of a sudden and final separation; 'He SEVERED the head from the body at a stroke'.

175. *INTRIGUE* (*ĭn-trēg′*, not *ĭn′-trēg*) *n.* Secret plotting, underhand scheming, stratagem, conspiracy, clandestine love affair.

In the phrase: 'He was fond of INTRIGUE', the word is thought by 2 per cent of adult readers to mean FORTUNE-TELLING.

INTRIGUE comes from the Latin *intricare*, to entangle, from the Latin word *tricae*, trifles. It is from the same source as the English word INTRICATE, involved, entangled, complicated.

The verb to INTRIGUE, and the participial adjective INTRIGU-ING, are often used to mean fascinating, piquing the curiosity, catching the interest. Until recently this meaning has either been labeled journalistic by dictionaries or not been given. It has, however, become so popular that it has established itself as good usage in the newer dictionaries. To forestall criticism by purists, it should perhaps be avoided in writing. The older, established, meaning of the verb, to INTRIGUE, is to plot, scheme; and of the participial adjective INTRIGUING, plotting, scheming, designing.

176. *MARTIAL* (*mahr′-shăl*) *adj.* Warlike, military, pertain-ing to war, belonging to an army, suited for military life, having the characteristics of a warrior.

The word, MARTIAL, is perhaps most frequently seen in the phrase: 'COURT MARTIAL', the military court which tries of-fenders against military law. COURT MARTIAL is spelt without a hyphen; but when used colloquially as a verb, to COURT-MAR-TIAL, it is hyphenated.

The original order of the words in the phrase was the logical

order: 'MARTIAL court', where MARTIAL is an adjective with its
correct meaning, military, so that a MARTIAL court was literally
a military court. But there seems to have been a confusion in
the sixteenth century between the two words MARTIAL, spelt
with a T and meaning military, and MARSHAL, spelt with SH
and meaning an official. Although pronounced alike, the two
words have no etymological connection. MARSHAL, with SH,
is from two German words. The first means horse and appears
in its feminine form in the English word MARE; the second
means servant. A MARSHAL was originally a groom in charge
of horses; but the word is today used by the army to designate
an official of high rank. A PROVOST MARSHAL is today the official
who carries out the sentence imposed by the military or
MARTIAL court. Through some confusion between the man, the
court MARSHAL, and the court, the MARTIAL court, the latter
has become known as the court MARTIAL and in the seventeenth
century was even sometimes incorrectly spelt COURT MARSHAL.
The spelling has been corrected but the inverted order of the
words has been retained and a military court is now called:
'A COURT MARTIAL'.

When used in the phrase: 'MARTIAL music', the word is
thought by 2 per cent of adult readers to mean CLASSICAL. This
confusion may arise from the fact that the adjective MARTIAL
comes from the proper name MARS, the ancient Roman god of
war. MARTIAL means by derivation Marslike, warlike.

177. *EXAMINATION* (*ĕks-ă-mĭ-nā'-shŭn*) *n.* Investigation,
    inspection, inquiry, test, scrutiny, the process of inquiring
into opinions and statements, asking questions of.
The three words EXAMINATION, INVESTIGATION, and DISCUSSION,
are fundamentally synonymous, but differ in usage. EXAMINA-
TION is from the Latin *ex*, out; and *agere*, to weigh; and means
by derivation a weighing out. EXAMINATION is the most general
of the three. INVESTIGATION is from the Latin *in*; and *vestigare*,
to follow a track; and means by derivation to track down. An
INVESTIGATION is a systematic, thorough, protracted examination. DISCUSSION comes indirectly from two Latin words *dis*,
apart; and *quatere*, to shake. A DISCUSSION is by derivation the
shaking apart of a subject, of a point of view, with the aim of
getting at the truth. In this sense, DISCUSSION is an exact synonym

of EXAMINATION. But the word DISCUSSION, as it is often used, suggests an argumentative rather than an impartial examination.

178. *ANNEX* (*ăn-nĕks'*) *v.* To take over, add, connect, append, attach, subjoin, affix.
ANNEX is from the Latin *ad*, and *nectare*, to fasten together. When used in the phrase: 'To ANNEX the country', the word is thought by 2 per cent of adult readers to mean RECOGNIZE, acknowledge, admit the existence of.
The noun, an ANNEX (*ăn'-nĕks*), is used in architecture to mean a subsidiary building, a smaller or less important building attached or adjacent to a large one. The verb, to ANNEX, means to join a smaller, less important, thing to a larger thing.

179. *OUTSTANDING* (*owt-stănd'-ĭng*) *adj.* Prominent, conspicuous, noticeable, striking, preeminent (339), distinguished, unique (494), salient.
To 11 per cent of grammar-school pupils OUTSTANDING incorrectly means DIFFICULT. The adjective DIFFICULT means hard to do, not easy, arduous, perplexing. OUTSTANDING implies none of these, but is a combination of the two simple Anglo-Saxon words OUT and STAND, and means literally standing out from the rest.

180. *ABDOMINAL* (*ăb-dŏm'-ĭ-năl*) *adj.* Pertaining to the belly, to the abdomen (*ăb-dō'-mĕn*, not *ăb'-dō-mĕn*), to the cavity of the body containing the stomach, bowels, etc., ventral (1019).
ABDOMINAL is of Latin origin. In the test phrase: 'ABDOMINAL operations', the word is thought by 5 per cent of grammar-school pupils to mean ABNORMAL, unusual, extraordinary. By another 5 per cent it is thought to mean DIFFICULT, hard to do; and by another 4 per cent to mean BAD. This last is perhaps a confusion of ABDOMINAL with ABOMINABLE, detestable, revolting. Despite the similarity there is no historical connection between the two words.

181. *EXCITING* (*ĕk-sīt'-ĭng*) *p. adj.* Stirring, rousing, thrilling, agitating, lively, stimulating, animating, elating.
The corresponding noun EXCITEMENT, commotion, disturb-

ance, retains the E after the T; the participial adjective EXCIT-
ING, does not.

EXCITING comes from two Latin words, *ex*, out; and *ciere*,
to rouse, call, summon; and means by derivation rousing,
calling into action, summoning.

182. *PROPOSE* (*prō-pōz'*) *v.* To suggest (21), nominate, pro-
    pound, offer for consideration, tender for acceptance.
In the test phrase: 'Whom do you PROPOSE?' the word is thought
by 2 per cent of adult readers to mean VOTE FOR. A law or the
name of a person must be proposed for acceptance or for membership before it can be voted upon.

PROPOSE is from the Latin *pro*, forward, and *ponere*, to put,
and means literally to put forward.

183. *STANDING* (*stănd'-ĭng*) *n.* Rank in society, reputation,
    repute (365), established position, place in public esteem,
imputed character, ascribed status.
When used in the phrase: 'His STANDING is low', the word is
thought by 9 per cent of grammar-school pupils to mean
STATURE. The word STATURE, tallness, refers to the physical
height of a person, usually, of a man; STANDING, which is
of Anglo-Saxon origin, refers to his place, position, rank, in
comparison with others, perhaps in school, in society, in a
profession. The verb, to STAND, may be used either in reference
to physical height, as: 'He STANDS five feet six', or in reference to social position, as: 'He STANDS well in his community';
but the noun STANDING always refers to position, never to
physical height.

To another 6 per cent STANDING means ALTITUDE. Both ALTI-
TUDE and STATURE refer to physical height; STATURE is used of
human beings, occasionally of animals; while ALTITUDE is used
of inanimate objects, usually of large ones, as: 'The ALTITUDE
of a mountain', 'The ALTITUDE of a star above the horizon'.
ALTITUDE cannot be used, as is STANDING, to mean reputation,
social position.

184. *AQUEOUS* (*ā'-kwē-ŭs*) *adj.* Watery, made from water,
    produced by water, pertaining to water. 'AQUEOUS vapor.'
AQUEOUS comes from the Latin word *aqua*, water, from the

same source as AQUEDUCT, a pipe or conduit to carry water from one place to another.

Although AQUEDUCT is pronounced with the short A, (ăk'-wē-dŭkt), AQUEOUS has the long A, (ā'-kwē-ŭs, not ăk'-wē-ŭs).

185. *BEWILDER* (*bē-wĭl'-der*) *v.* To muddle (161), confuse, perplex, mystify, puzzle, daze, obfuscate (946). 'A BEWILDERED expression.'

The adjective, WILD (*wĭld*), excited, distracted, crazy; the noun, WILDERNESS (*wĭl'-der-nĕs*), a tract of uncultivated land, a region uninhabited by human beings; the unusual verb, to WILDER (*wĭl'-der*), to cause to lose the way, to puzzle; and to BEWILDER, to confuse, muddle; all come from the same source. BEWILDERINGLY is the adverb; BEWILDERMENT is the noun.

186. *UNMOLESTED* (*ŭn-mō-lĕs'-tĕd*) *adj.* Undisturbed, untroubled, not annoyed, left alone, not vexed, not worried; tranquil, calm, peaceful, aloof.

To 2 per cent of adult readers UNMOLESTED incorrectly means UNAIDED, not helped, not assisted. UNAIDED suggests that one has asked for help which has not been given; UNMOLESTED, which is from the Latin *un*, and *molestare*, to annoy, vex, means literally not annoyed, not vexed, and implies that one prefers to be left alone.

187. *DISHEVELED* (*dĭ-shĕv'-ĕld*) *adj.* Untidy (6), disordered (16), unkempt, rumpled, disarranged, crumpled, tousled, mussed.

In the test phrase: 'His clothes are DISHEVELED', the word is thought by 3 per cent of adult readers to mean SOILED, dirtied. DISHEVELED clothes are out of order but need not be dirty, for DISHEVEL is from the same source as *cheveux*, the modern French word for hair. The English verb, to DISHEVEL, means by derivation to disarrange the hair, muss the hair, rumple the hair. The word has come to be used in a more general sense and can now be applied to clothes as well as hair.

188. *SEASONING* (*sē'-zŭn-ĭng*) *n.* Substance added to food to give it flavor, flavoring material, salt, spice.

The verb, to SEASON, may mean specifically to add spice to

food in order to give it greater relish, improve its taste. It may also mean to make fit for any use, ordinarily by some process which requires time. Thus, one SEASONS lumber by allowing it to dry out. To SEASON may also mean to soften, moderate, make gentler, less severe. One may SEASON justice with mercy. In this sense, to SEASON and to TEMPER are synonymous. It may be this similarity in the meaning of the two verbs, to SEASON and to TEMPER, which causes 11 per cent of grammar-school pupils to believe that SEASONINGS means TEMPERATURES, when it appears in the phrase: 'High SEASONINGS are harmful'. A TEMPERATURE was once a mixture, compound, the result of TEMPERING, mixing. But this meaning is now obsolete and the word TEMPERATURE has only its familiar sense, degree of heat.

The confusion between the words SEASONINGS and TEMPERA-TURES may be increased by some confusion between the nouns SEASONING and SEASON. Although both come from the same Latin verb *serere*, to sow, plant, they have today, in English, distinct meanings. A SEASON, originally planting time, is now a division of the year characterized, in the temperate zone, by a particular TEMPERATURE, as spring, summer, autumn, winter. The nouns, a SEASON, a part of the year, and SEASONING, added to food to give it flavor, should not be confused.

A SEASONING, a FLAVORING, a CONDIMENT, and a RELISH, are all added to food to improve its taste. A RELISH and a CONDI-MENT are eaten with food, as sauce; a RELISH is sometimes eaten before food as an appetizer. A RELISH and a CONDIMENT differ, if at all, in the fact that a CONDIMENT, from the Latin noun *condimentum*, spice, is spicier in taste, sharper, more pungent, than a RELISH; but the distinction does not always hold. SEA-SONING and FLAVORING are added to food usually during the cooking. FLAVORING may be sweet; SEASONING is spicy, sharp, pungent.

189. *BAFFLE* (*băf'-fl*) *v.* To foil, frustrate, avert (564), thwart, check by shifts and turns, to confound, defeat, balk, delude, confuse.
When the word is used in the phrase: 'They BAFFLED our plans', and is intended to mean foiled, it is incorrectly inter-preted by 4 per cent of readers as meaning RIDICULED. There is historical justification for this misinterpretation, for when

BAFFLE was first used in the sixteenth century it meant to treat with mockery, ridicule. This is today, however, an obsolete meaning.

To BAFFLE, FRUSTRATE, THWART, and BALK, are all to prevent action but in different ways. To BALK is to prevent action in one direction, and is annoying rather than confusing. To THWART is to prevent action by placing a barrier in the way. To FRUSTRATE is not to prevent action, but to counteract it so that the result is of no avail, to nullify, bring to naught. To BAFFLE is to stop completely, confuse so as to prevent action in any direction.

190. *SHUFFLE* (*shŭf'-fl*) *v.* To walk without lifting the feet from the ground, move with a dragging gait, walk awkwardly, clumsily.

The same verb, to SHUFFLE, is used in a figurative sense to mean to be shifty, evasive (464).

The word SHUFFLE was not used until the end of the sixteenth century, during the reign of Queen Elizabeth. To SHOVE, to push along, and to SHOVEL, are earlier words, probably from the same source as SHUFFLE, but dating back to the tenth or eleventh century, before the Norman conquest.

When used in the test phrase: 'He SHUFFLED along', the word is thought by 5 per cent of adult readers to mean SCAMPERED. To SCAMPER is to caper, run about nimbly, lightly. To SHUFFLE is to walk heavily without lifting the feet.

191. *UNHESITATING* (*ŭn-hĕz'-ĭ-tā-tĭng*) *adj.* Prompt, ready, showing no reluctance, decided, not wavering, unfaltering (113).

UNHESITATING is a combination of the Anglo-Saxon prefix *un*, not, which reverses the action; and the verb, to HESITATE, to waver, be doubtful, be uncertain.

When used in the test phrase: 'UNHESITATING courage', the word is thought by 6 per cent of grammar-school pupils to mean UNNECESSARY, not needed, not required; and by another 6 per cent to mean CARELESS. The two positive nouns, HESITATION and CARE, both suggest a desire to avoid mistakes. They differ, however, in manner. One who proceeds with care does not pause but advances thoughtfully and accurately. CARE is a desirable quality. One who proceeds with hesitation pauses at each step. HESITATION is not desirable because it suggests the possibility of stopping short of accomplishment.

The two negative adjectives, CARELESS, without care, and UNHESITATING, without hesitation, are in the reverse order of desirability. One who is CARELESS lacks the desirable quality of care, and may be slovenly, slipshod. One who is UNHESITAT-ING lacks the undesirable quality of hesitation, and is prompt, ready to face only those difficulties which he believes unavoid-able, necessary.

192. *ACCOMPLICE* (ăk-kŏm'-plĭs) *n.* A partner, ally, coop-erator. ACCOMPLICE is also used specifically to mean an associate (302) in guilt, confederate, abettor, accessory, co-adjutor (kō-ăd-jū'-tŏr, not kō-ăd'-jū-tŏr).

To 2 per cent of adult readers ACCOMPLICE incorrectly means SKILL, dexterity in execution, expertness. This is no doubt a confusion of ACCOMPLICE, associate, with some form of the verb, to ACCOMPLISH, to finish, succeed in doing. The par-ticipial adjective, ACCOMPLISHED, means skilled, adept; and ACCOMPLISHMENTS, the noun, are skills acquired.

ACCOMPLICE is from the Latin *ad* and COMPLEX, interwoven, a word which in turn comes from the Latin *plicare*, to fold. An ACCOMPLICE is anyone with whom one is closely connected in some undertaking. The word is used most frequently, how-ever, for a companion in crime, an associate in an unlawful, nefarious enterprise.

193. *BOUILLON* (bool-yŏgn') *n.* A clear soup, broth made from meat or vegetables cooked in water and strained.

To 3 per cent of adult readers BOUILLON incorrectly means NUGGET, a word which may have come from the phrase, AN INGOT, shortened to *ningot*, now NUGGET. An INGOT, from Anglo-Saxon words meaning to pour in, is a mass of metal poured and cast in a mold. NUGGET is synonymous with INGOT except that the metal is more apt to be precious. This confusion is no doubt one between BOUILLON, soup, and BULLION (869), gold or silver in bulk before it is coined.

BOUILLON, the soup, is a French word adopted by English. It is often pronounced as is the French word ending with a

French nasal N, and sometimes even without the L (*boo-yogn'*); but when completely anglicized it is indistinguishable in pronunciation from BULLION (*bool'-yŭn*), an ingot of gold or silver.

BOUILLON, from the French verb *bouillir*, to boil, comes ultimately from the Latin *bullire*, to bubble, the source of the unusual English word EBULLITION, boiling, often used figuratively to mean a sudden overflowing of feeling. BOUILLON is always a clear soup, usually made by simmering meat, boiling it slowly in water.

194. *TEDIOUS* (*tē'-dǐ-ŭs*, not *tē'-jŭs*) *adj.* Tiresome, wearisome, irksome, boring, fatiguing, burdensome, monotonous, humdrum.

TEDIOUS, and the corresponding noun TEDIUM, wearisomeness, come from the Latin *taedium*, irksomeness. There is today no verb which corresponds to the adjective TEDIOUS.

TEDIOUS and IRKSOME, TEDIUM and the awkward noun IRKSOMENESS, and the verb to IRK (513), all mean wearying, fatiguing. A task is IRKSOME because of its nature; it is possible to know in advance whether or not a task will be IRKSOME. For this reason an IRKSOME task is sometimes never started. A task becomes TEDIOUS by the time required for its accomplishment, and cannot be TEDIOUS until it has been pursued for some time.

195. *ASCERTAIN* (*ăs-ser-tān'*) *v.* To find out, make certain, make sure of, establish, determine, fix conclusively, reach a conclusion as a result of an investigation.

ASCERTAIN, a combination of the Latin *a*, to; and the English word CERTAIN, sure; when used in the test phrase: 'To ASCERTAIN the weight of a substance', is thought by 4 per cent of adult readers to mean to STATE. This is perhaps a confusion of ASCERTAIN with one or both of the words ASSERT and MAINTAIN. To ASSERT is to declare, state as true, affirm, aver. To MAINTAIN, in this sense, is to assert as true, uphold by argument.

To ASCERTAIN was at one time similar in meaning to the verb to VERIFY, and suggested, as does VERIFY today, some doubt in the mind of the investigator. To ASCERTAIN now means merely to find out; but because of Latin origin, it suggests more exactness, more of the scientific approach, than does FIND OUT.

196. *LENIENT* (*lē'-nĭ-ĕnt*) *adj.* Mild, indulgent, forbearing, clement, benignant (717), merciful, compassionate, not strict, not severe. 'The LENIENT law.'

Several adjectives, which like LENIENT, end in ENT, have corresponding nouns which may end in either CE or CY, as: LENIENCE or LENIENCY both of which are correct. In some cases only one of the two is in use today, the other having become archaic. Thus, from COINCIDENT, corresponding, agreeing in time or in place, comes COINCIDENCE, not coincidency; from INTELLIGENT, capable of comprehending, understanding, comes INTELLIGENCE, not intelligency; from MAGNIFICENT, splendid, brilliant, comes MAGNIFICENCE, not magnificency. But from CLEMENT, kind, gentle, comes the noun CLEMENCY (596), not clemence; from COGENT, potent, convincing, comes COGENCY, not cogence; and from DECENT, respectable, becoming, comes DECENCY, not decence. With some words both endings are possible. In general, the endings used are:

CE for long words		CY for short words	
COINCIDENT	COINCIDENCE	COGENT	COGENCY
INTELLIGENT	INTELLIGENCE	CLEMENT	CLEMENCY
MAGNIFICENT	MAGNIFICENCE	DECENT	DECENCY

Although LENIENCY is preferable to LENIENCE, neither is wrong and either may be used to make a sentence more agreeable in sound.

LENIENT and CLEMENT are both expressions for mildness. CLEMENCY is the lightening of a penalty for a criminal offense, and only one in high authority can be CLEMENT. LENIENCY is not restricted to criminal offenses nor is the display of LENIENCY limited to those in authority; anyone may be LENIENT in excusing any offense.

197. *PERFECTION* (*per-fĕk'-shŭn*) *n.* Highest development, completion, highest pitch, consummation. PERFECTION is often used specifically to mean the highest possible degree of excellence.

PERFECTION comes from two Latin words *per*, through; and *facere*, to do; and means, by derivation, a carrying through, finishing, completing. In the phrase: 'The PERFECTION of art', the word incorrectly means BEAUTY to 19 per cent of grammar-school pupils. BEAUTY is often defined as perfection of form, but the word PERFECTION may be applied to the highest development of any quality, as: 'The PERFECTION of bad taste'.

198. *ADORN* (*ă-dōrn'*) *v.* To decorate, embellish (537), set off, render beautiful, ornament, enrich, garnish, bedeck, emblazon, add to the attractiveness of.

In the test phrase: 'She ADORNED herself', the word is thought by 3 per cent of adult readers to mean ADMIRED. This is perhaps a confusion of ADORNED, decorated, with ADORED, loved.

ADORN comes from the Latin *ad*, to; and *ornare*, to deck, the source of the English word ORNATE, richly ornamented, highly decorated, embellished. The verb, to ADORN, means to ornament, decorate.

199. *VENDER* (*vĕn'-der*) *n.* A peddler, hawker, seller usually of small articles, barterer, trader, trafficker (737), one who transfers something to another for a price.

VENDER is from the Latin *vendere*, to sell. There is an unusual English verb to VEND, to sell, from the same source.

In legal use, as in: 'The VENDOR and Purchaser Act', the word is spelt VENDOR. But in popular use, as in the phrase: 'A news-VENDER', the word ends with ER.

200. *INSTINCTIVE* (*ĭn-stĭnk'-tĭv*) *adj.* Natural (26), intuitive, involuntary, spontaneous, innate, acting without reasoning, determined by natural impulse.

When used in the test phrase: 'INSTINCTIVE fear', the word is thought by 2 per cent of adult readers to mean DEADLY. To another 1 per cent, INSTINCTIVE incorrectly means ACQUIRED, an exact opposite of the correct meaning.

201. *INCESSANT* (*ĭn-sĕs'-sănt*) *adj.* Continual, repeated, unceasing, uninterrupted, constant, perpetual (550), continuing without interruption.

INCESSANT is from the Latin *in*, not; and *cessare*, to cease, stop, leave off, desist; and means by derivation not stopping. From the same verb come the unusual English adjective, CESSANT, which means resting, dormant, inactive; the more familiar noun, CESSATION (254), discontinuance, stopping, pause, rest; and UNCEASING, practically synonymous with INCESSANT, a combination of the Anglo-Saxon prefix *un*, with the familiar verb, to CEASE.

In the test phrase: 'The footsteps were INCESSANT', the word is thought by 1 per cent of preparatory-school juniors to mean IMAGINARY, fancied, unreal.

INCESSANT and CONTINUOUS both mean going on without interruption. CONTINUOUS is passive. It may describe a static condition or an unbroken line. INCESSANT is more active, and suggests the effort expended. It is often applied to that which constantly stops and starts again immediately, as: 'An INCESSANT ticking'. Perhaps, because of its similarity to INSISTENT, pressing for attention, demanding notice, INCESSANT is apt to be used of that which is continually forced upon one's attention.

202. *BESTOW* (*bē-stō'*) *v.* To confer, deposit, impart, donate, present, give, grant, award, accord (238), make a gift to.

BESTOW is a combination of the Anglo-Saxon prefix BE, which has various meanings and appears in such words as BEGRUDGE (446), grant reluctantly; BEGUILE (784), delude, deceive; and BEDIZEN (948), dress gaudily, adorn, bedeck, where the prefix is discussed; and the verb to STOW, which means to place, as in the phrase: 'STOW the cargo of the ship'.

GRANT, CONFER, PROFFER, AWARD, BESTOW, are all to give in various ways. Of the group, BESTOW implies giving gratuitously, regardless of merit, often where there is no need.

To 2 per cent of adult readers BESTOW incorrectly means RECEIVE, an opposite of the correct meaning.

203. *BRAVE* (*brāv*) *v.* To dare, defy, challenge, encounter with courage, meet a hostile foe with boldness.

To BRAVE, to DEFY, and to CHALLENGE, are three degrees of seeking danger. To CHALLENGE is active, to invite a contest, call to account, as: 'He CHALLENGED the foe'. To DEFY is provocative, to provoke to combat, probe to strife. To BRAVE is passive compared with the others; it is to meet with courage a situation forced upon one, as: 'He BRAVED the storm'.

204. *ECONOMIZE* (*ē-kŏn'-ō-mīz*) *v.* To spend sparingly, be frugal, avoid expense, save, use to the best advantage, manage with thrift, husband one's resources, retrench.

When used in the test phrase: 'He refused to ECONOMIZE', the word is believed by 8 per cent of grammar-school pupils to mean ANSWER, to reply, respond.

ECONOMIZE comes from two Greek words, οἶκος, house; and νέμειν, to manage; and means by derivation to manage a house. The modern phrase, HOME ECONOMICS, might be said to be tautological, for the noun ECONOMICS originally meant the science of household management. This meaning is however obsolete, and ECONOMICS is today synonymous with POLITICAL ECONOMY, the study of wealth, its production and distribution.

ECONOMY, from the same source, means either good management or care in spending; but the verb, to ECONOMIZE, always suggests the latter notion, careful spending, avoiding expense, saving.

205. *REPULSIVE* (rē-pŭl'-sĭv) *adj.* Disgusting, loathsome, repellent, forbidding, revolting, offensive, odious, abhorrent, detestable, execrable, arousing aversion.
In the test phrase: 'The REPULSIVE sight', INTERESTING, holding the attention, almost an exact opposite of REPULSIVE, is the common misconception.

REPULSIVE is from the Latin *re*, back; and *pulsus*, the past participle of *pellere*, to drive, push. Directly from the verb come also REPEL, to drive back, and the adjective REPELLENT.

In modern usage, a REPELLENT object prevents one's approach. REPULSIVE is more offensive; a REPULSIVE object drives one away.

206. *DENUDE* (dē-nūd') *v.* Strip, lay bare, unclothe, divest of covering, make naked, despoil.
The verb, to DENUDE, is from the same Latin source as the adjective NUDE, bare, uncovered, naked.

To 4 per cent of adult readers DENUDE incorrectly means to PLANT, in one sense an exact opposite of the correct meaning. 'To PLANT a garden' means to provide it with seeds, bulbs, roots, in such a way that plants will grow; while 'To DENUDE a garden' is to strip it of flowers, plants, vegetation. Although DENUDE is most frequently used in this way with reference to vegetation it may be used to mean strip of any covering.

207. *RIGOR* (rĭg'-ŏr) *n.* Severity, inclemency, inflexibility, rigidness, exactitude, harshness, sternness, strictness, cruelty, oppression, austerity.

RIGOR and RIGIDITY come from the same Latin word, *rigere*, to be stiff, and in some uses are exactly synonymous. Both may be applied figuratively to the inflexibility of a rule or law. RIGIDITY is, however, applied more often than RIGOR to physical stiffness, inflexibility; whereas RIGOR is used, as RIGIDITY never is, to mean, as applied to weather, inclemency, harsh extremity of cold, as: 'The RIGORS of a northern climate'.

208. *AUDACITY* (aw-dăs'-ĭ-tĭ) *n.* Boldness, recklessness, daring, effrontery, presumptuous impudence, venturesomeness, confidence.

When used in the test phrase: 'He wins by sheer AUDACITY', the word is believed by 3 per cent of adult readers to mean ABILITY. ABILITY is power to act, might, the combination of skill and capacity, capability. Both ABILITY and AUDACITY may lead to action and accomplishment. But ABILITY is capacity; whereas the word AUDACITY suggests recklessness, attempting that which is beyond one's ability. Many persons of ability, with both inherent capacity and acquired skill, fail of accomplishment through lack of daring, venturesomeness, audacity. On the other hand, it is because of those who lack ability but have audacity, that AUDACITY has acquired its disagreeable sense of presumptuous impudence, effrontery.

209. *TRANSVERSE* (trăns-vers') *adj.* Lying across, athwart, extending crosswise as distinguished from longitudinal.

TRANSVERSE is believed by 4 per cent of adult readers to mean STRAIGHT, not crooked, not curved, direct.

The adjective, TRANSVERSE, crosswise, and the verb, to TRAVERSE (trăv'-ers) (158), to cross, both come from the Latin *trans*, across, and *vertere*, to turn. The verb comes to English through French and has lost the NS; the adjective comes directly from the Latin and, like the Latin, is spelt TRANSVERSE.

210. *FASTNESS* (făst'-nĕs) *n.* Stronghold, fortress, fort, secure retreat, fortified place.

The adjective FAST may mean firmly fixed; or it may mean

strong against attack or even fortified, as: 'A FAST place'; or, when used more figuratively, steadfast, as: 'A FAST friend'. FASTNESS is the corresponding noun, and means a place strong against attack.

When used in the test phrase: 'A mountain FASTNESS', it is believed by 3 per cent of adult readers to mean CAVE. A CAVE is any hollow place in the earth, a natural or artificial cavern, subterranean den, usually a hollow which extends horizontally into a hill. A CAVE is not necessarily either inaccessible or fortified; a FASTNESS is usually both.

211. *IMPERTINENT (ĭm-per'-tĭ-nĕnt) adj.* Impudent, saucy, pert, uncivil, bold, insolent, rude (64), unmannerly, disrespectful, unfitting.

The word PERTINENT comes from the Latin, *per*, through; and *tenere*, to hold; and means closely connected to the matter in hand, appropriate, to the point, suitable, as: 'A PERTINENT remark', 'A PERTINENT suggestion'.

IMPERTINENT is a combination of PERTINENT and the negative prefix IN, which usually becomes IM before B, P, and M. IMPERTINENT is used in two ways: first, to mean not PERTINENT in the general sense, not to the point, not connected; and second, with reference to conduct which is not suitable to the occasion, inappropriate, as: 'An IMPERTINENT child'.

Three closely related adjectives, all of which refer to disagreeable conduct, are IMPROPER, IMPERTINENT, and IMPUDENT. IMPROPER is the most general of the three and means ordinarily not proper, not fitting to the time or occasion. IMPERTINENT is more specific and usually applies to improper behavior of the young toward their elders. IMPUDENT, which comes from the Latin *in*, not, and *pudere*, to be ashamed, is still stronger and means, by derivation, shamelessly impertinent. SAUCINESS and PERTNESS, a word which has no connection with IMPERTINENCE, are liveliness and sprightliness overdone; both are often keen and vivid. IMPERTINENCE and IMPUDENCE are usually gross and stupid.

212. *FICTITIOUS (fĭk-tĭ'-shŭs) adj.* Imaginary (440), made-up, false, feigned (487), counterfeit, invented, fabricated, assumed, unreal, sham, fabulous, factitious (1064), not genuine.

FICTITIOUS is from the Latin *fingere*, to feign, pretend. It is from the same source as the English noun FICTION, an imaginative story, novel. It is probably this relationship which leads 3 per cent of adult readers to believe that FICTITIOUS means LITERARY.

213. SANCTIFY (*sănk'-tĭ-fī*) *v.* To make holy, consecrate, bless, devote, dedicate, free from sin, purify, hallow, set apart for religious use.

When used in the test phrase: 'He was SANCTIFIED', the word is thought by 2 per cent of adult readers to mean CONDEMNED, pronounced guilty; and by another 2 per cent to mean CRUCIFIED, nailed to the cross. This last may be a confusion of SANCTIFIED, made holy, with SACRIFICED. To SACRIFICE comes from the Latin *sacer*, sacred; and *facere*, to make; and by derivation means to make sacred. The word is, however, never used in exactly this literal sense but means either to offer to God in worship or to give up something. SANCTIFY, from the Latin *sanctus*, holy, sacred; and *facere*, to make; means by derivation to make holy and today has exactly this literal meaning.

214. ENTHRALL (*ĕn-thrawl'*) *v.* To hold spellbound, enslave, captivate, subjugate, enchant, fascinate, bewitch, charm, enrapture.

ENTHRALL is a combination of the causal EN, as used in the word ENCIRCLE, and the Anglo-Saxon word THRALL, which may mean either a slave, bondsman, or slavery, servitude. To ENTHRALL means by derivation to make a slave of, hold in bondage; but the word is always used in the figurative sense with reference to the mind, emotions, attention.

In the test phrase: 'ENTHRALLED by the music', the word is thought by 4 per cent of adult readers to mean ATTRACTED. The words are similar in suggestion. To ATTRACT means to get the attention of, engage the interest of. To ENTHRALL is stronger; it is to hold one spellbound after one's attention has been attracted.

215. TRANSGRESS (*trăns-grĕs'*) *v.* Violate, break, overstep, infringe upon, profane, disregard, fail to obey.

When used in the test phrase: 'He TRANSGRESSED the law', the word is believed by 4 per cent of adult readers to mean EXPLAINED. EXPLAIN is to make plain, interpret, clear up, make intelligible. To TRANSLATE the law may mean to explain it in other words, express it in different terms, interpret it; but TRANSGRESS means violate.

TRANSGRESS is one of a large family of words from the Latin *gradi*, step, walk. Thus, to PROGRESS is to go forward; to REGRESS is to go back; to DIGRESS (451) is to go off in another direction; to TRANSGRESS means by derivation to go across, and in modern usage to overstep, infringe, violate.

216. *CONTRABAND* (*kŏn'-tră-bănd*) *adj.* Prohibited, illicit, smuggled, interdicted, forbidden by law to be imported or exported.

CONTRABAND comes from the Latin *contra*, against; and *bandum*, proclamation, summons; and by derivation means proclaimed against. From this same source comes the English word, a BAN, a proclamation, specifically in the plural BANNS, notice given in church of an intended marriage.

When used in the test phrase: 'CONTRABAND goods', the word is thought by 1 per cent of preparatory-school juniors to mean LAWFUL, the popular misconception, and an exact opposite of the correct meaning.

217. *PREJUDICE* (*prĕj'-ŭ-dĭs*) *n.* Prejudgment, partiality, predilection, prepossession, unreasonable bias, preconceived opinion, unfavorable inclination.

In the test phrase: 'I have no PREJUDICE', the word is thought by 3 per cent of adult readers to mean FEAR.

PREJUDICE is from the Latin *prae*, before; and *judicium*, judgment; and means by derivation prejudgment, an opinion formed without due investigation of the facts.

218. *SPRY* (*sprī*) *adj.* Active, brisk, lively, agile, vigorous, nimble, sprightly, spirited, quick in movement, as: 'A SPRY youngster'.

Of the few short words which end in Y, such as: DRY, SHY, and SPRY, the Y of DRY is always changed to I when ED, ER, or EST, is added to the word. Thus: DRIED, DRIER, and DRIEST. SHY and SPRY may retain their Y and be spelt SHYER and SPRYER, but are now more frequently spelt with ɪ, as SHIER, SPRIER, in order to make them agree with the more common word DRY. SPRY is an inconsequential word and is often marked as colloquial or provincial.

219. *ADEPT* (*ă-dĕpt'*) *adj.* Accomplished, proficient, skilled, well-versed, clever, dexterous, facile, expert, adroit, apt, masterly. In the test phrase: 'ADEPT players', the word is thought by 3 per cent of adult readers to mean MATURE. This is perhaps a confusion of ADEPT, accomplished, with ADULT (*ă-dŭlt'*), mature, grown-up.

ADEPT is from the Latin *ad*, to; and some form of the verb *apisci*, to reach, arrive at, attain; and is used in English to mean having arrived at a degree of skill, having attained proficiency.

220. *BLOTCH* (*blŏtch*) *v.* To blemish, spot, cover with spots, dab with ink, blot, blur, bedaub, maculate. When used in the test phrase: 'He BLOTCHED his work', the word is thought by 3 per cent of adult readers to mean CURSED, swore at. This is perhaps a confusion of BLOTCH, spot, with the verb to BLAST, which may mean to curse.

BLOTCH is apparently unconnected historically with BOTCH, to bungle, spoil by poor work, patch, mend in a clumsy manner. It comes probably from the same source, perhaps Dutch, perhaps Scandinavian, as BLOT. A BLOT is a spot, ink stain, or sometimes a blemish. To BLOTCH, to daub with ink, is the verb.

221. *COMPOSE* (*kŏm-pōz'*) *v.* To calm, quiet, tranquilize, rally, soothe, pacify, make serene. COMPOSE shows the queer way in which languages grow. An obsolete word COMPONE, which came directly from the Latin *con*, together, and *ponere*, to put, place, has disappeared; and COMPOSE has replaced it. COMPOSE, although etymologically from another source, has exactly the form and meaning to have come from *con*, together, and *positus*, the past participle of *ponere*. Other words, the meanings of which have come from *ponere*, to put, are: PROPOSE (182), put forward; OPPOSE, put against; IMPOSE, put on; and COMPOSE, put together. To COMPOSE a poem is by derivation to put it together. The phrase:

'COMPOSE yourself' means put yourself together, and is used in English as synonymous with the idiomatic phrase: 'Pull yourself together'.

222. *MUSTY* (*mŭs'-tĭ*) *adj.* Moldy, fusty, frowzy, stale (32), sourish, fetid (933), rancid, rank, having an offensive smell, spoiled by dampness; close, moist, and stuffy.

When used in the test phrase: 'A MUSTY odor', the word is thought by 2 per cent of adult readers to mean PENETRATING, piercing, sharp. This is perhaps a confusion of MUSTY, moldy, with MUSKY, smelling like MUSK, the most persistent and penetrating of odors.

MUSTY, moldy, is from the Latin word *mustum*, new wine. The English noun MUST may today be used to mean unfermented grape juice, new wine; or it may mean mold. From the same Latin source, *mustum*, new wine, come the English words MOIST, wet, and MUSTARD, a condiment, seasoning.

The adjective MUSTY suggests the dampness of MOIST, and the sourness of MUST, new wine.

223. *SCOFF* (*skŏf*) *v.* To deride, sneer, flout, rail, jeer (88), mock (240), gibe, ridicule, contemn, taunt, speak derisively, express contempt for.

SCOFF is found in Middle English, but does not go back to Anglo-Saxon.

When used in the test phrase: 'They SCOFFED mercilessly', the word is thought by 4 per cent of adult readers to mean SCOLDED. To SCOLD is to find fault with in a noisy manner; while to SCOFF is to sneer, jeer.

Of the three words SCOFF, SNEER, and JEER, all of which may be used with the preposition AT, the last is the noisiest for one JEERS at a person in words. SNEERING need involve no language. One may SNEER by gesture or facial expression, as with a grin or grimace. SCOFF is the strongest of the three, for it involves both words and expression.

224. *STEAD* (*stĕd*) *n.* Place, use, service, advantage, lieu (699). STEAD appears in many compounds but seldom as a word by itself in modern writing.

INSTEAD is understood by almost everyone. Once it was written as two words, IN STEAD, and is a contraction of: 'In his STEAD', in his place. HOMESTEAD, literally the home-place, refers usually to both house and grounds, the whole environment of the home. ROADSTEAD is a place near the shore in which ships can anchor. A HARBOR is sheltered from the open sea; a ROADSTEAD is not. STEADFAST means firmly in place, fixed, unwavering.

The only two familiar phrases in which STEAD is used alone are: 'In his STEAD' where it means place, and 'It stood him in good STEAD', where it means advantage.

225. *STANCH* (*stănch*) *adj.* Seaworthy, water-tight, strong, sound, firm, as in the phrase: 'A STANCH boat'. STANCH is also used in the more figurative sense of loyal, true, reliable, trusty, faithful, constant, steadfast, unswerving, as: 'A STANCH ally'.

STANCH is from the Latin *stagnum*, a pool, standing water. From the same source come the English words, STAGNANT, not flowing, motionless, standing; and STANCHION, a pillar, post, used for a support.

STANCH may also be spelt STAUNCH and pronounced (*stawnch*); STANCH is usually, however, given the preference in dictionaries.

226. *TITANIC* (*tī-tăn'-ĭk*) *adj.* Big, gigantic (63), huge, enormous, great, colossal (249), vast, super-human, tremendous, of immense power. 'A TITANIC force.'

The TITANS, from whose name comes the adjective TITANIC, were a race of mythological beings. According to one legend they were twelve in number, six males and six females. They were of great strength and gigantic size, children of Heaven and Earth. In their wars, which were numerous, they piled mountains upon one another in order to reach Heaven.

ATLAS, who carried the Earth on his shoulders, was one of the Titans, probably today the best known. From his name comes the modern word ATLAS, a book of maps. This was first used by Mercator for his collection of maps, in which a picture of Atlas, holding the world on his shoulders, appeared on the title page.

TITANIC and the adjective LILLIPUTIAN, spelt with a capital, are opposites. LILLIPUTIAN, which means tiny, very small, is from the proper name, LILLIPUTIAN, one of a diminutive race of people described by Swift in his Voyage to Lilliput.

NAVAL is the popular misconception of the word TITANIC, perhaps because of the association of the name of the steamship, TITANIC, with an ocean disaster; or perhaps because Oceanus was one of the male Titans. Whatever the cause of the confusion the adjective TITANIC, usually spelt with a small letter, can mean only big, huge, gigantic.

227. *AMIABLE* (*ā'-mĭ-ā-bl*) *adj.* Friendly, charming, pleasing, attractive, lovable, sweet-tempered, agreeable, pleasant, kindly, kindhearted.

The word AMIABLE, from the Latin *amare*, to love, is thought by 3 per cent of adult readers to mean POLITE, well-bred, urbane, refined in behavior, courtly. AMIABLE and POLITE both refer to attractive personalities; but they differ in that POLITENESS is largely an acquired, social skill; whereas AMIABILITY is inherent lovableness.

228. *TRANSPORT* (*trăns'-pōrt*) *n.* Troopship, ship conveying military stores; carriage, vessel, conveyance.

TRANSPORT is from the Latin *trans*, across; and *portare*, to carry; and the verb to TRANSPORT (*trăns-pōrt'*), accented on the second syllable, is literally to carry across from one place to another. The noun a TRANSPORT, accented on the first syllable, may be used for any conveyance, carriage, automobile, ship, or airplane; or more specifically for a ship used by a government to carry soldiers in time of war.

229. *HARP* (*hahrp*) *v.* To dwell tediously on one subject, speak so often of something as to become tiresome, write with monotonous reiteration. This is the same word as to HARP, to play upon a harp.

DILATE, EXPAND, and REITERATE, are three words similar in implication to but not exactly synonymous with HARP. To REITERATE, from the Latin *re*, again; and *iterare*, to repeat, do again; is by derivation to repeat again. The word emphasizes the repetition. To EXPAND and to DILATE are practically synonymous. EXPAND is from the Latin *ex*, out; and *pandere*, to spread; and means literally to spread out. DILATE is from the

Latin *dis*, apart; and *latus*, the past participle of the verb *ferre*, to carry; and by derivation means to carry apart and so again to spread out. To HARP, because of its Anglo-Saxon origin, is more direct, more homely, than the others. To HARP, meaning to talk constantly about one subject, is used with either ON or UPON, as: 'To HARP ON or UPON one subject'.

230. *CONVERSANT* (*kŏn'-ver-sănt*, not *kŏn-ver'-sănt*) *adj.*
Versed, thoroughly familiar with, well-acquainted with, having intimate knowledge of.
CONVERSANT comes from the Latin *conversari*, to live, dwell, live with, keep company with. The English word CONVERSATION, which comes from the same source, once meant acquaintance, intercourse; and CONVERSANT still carries this original meaning of being acquainted with.
VERSED in, SKILLED in, and PROFICIENT in, are other words for acquainted with. SKILL is that increased facility which comes with repeating a performance. PROFICIENCY implies knowledge added to skill. One is seldom PROFICIENT in more than a single subject; one may be CONVERSANT with many.
In the test phrase: 'I am CONVERSANT with art', the word is thought by 4 per cent of adult readers to mean GIFTED. To be GIFTED with a characteristic is to be endowed with it naturally, to possess it instinctively; to be CONVERSANT with a subject is to have acquired knowledge about it.
To another 2 per cent CONVERSANT WITH incorrectly means UNACQUAINTED WITH, ignorant of, an exact opposite of the correct meaning.

231. *DISASTER* (*dĭz-ăs'-ter*, not *dĭs-ăs'-ter*) *n.* An unfortunate event, blow, mishap, terrible accident, mischance, misadventure, affliction, adversity, sudden misfortune, calamity, catastrophe (108).
DISASTER comes from the Latin *dis*, a negative prefix; and *astrum*, a star, a word which in turn comes from the Greek ἄστρον, a star, the source of the word ASTRONOMY, a study of the stars; and ASTROLOGY, a system of predicting events by the position of the heavenly bodies. DISASTER means by derivation ill fate, misfortune, due to an unfavorable aspect of the planets.
To 8 per cent of grammar-school pupils, DISASTER incorrectly

means EXCITEMENT. EXCITEMENT may be the mental state of being excited, agitated, stirred up; or it may be the event which causes the excitement. A DISASTER always stirs the emotions and is therefore an excitement in the second sense; but an EXCITEMENT may be a party, an unexpected pleasure; it need not necessarily be a DISASTER, a calamity.

232. *SUCCEED* (*sŭk-sēd'*) *v.* To follow, come after, take the place of, be subsequent to, step into the shoes of.

This meaning is unknown to 8 per cent of adult readers. To 4 per cent SUCCEED incorrectly means OUTDO, surpass, excel. The verb, to SUCCEED, from the Latin *sub*, and *cedere*, to go along, may be used either transitively or intransitively. Intransitively, in such a phrase as: 'He SUCCEEDED', it means he gained his end, obtained the desired object, prospered, a sense which does not mean, but may suggest, outdo. The transitive verb, however, in the phrase: 'He SUCCEEDED his father', cannot be used in this way and can mean only followed, came after.

233. *SUSTENANCE* (*sŭs'-tĕ-nănce*) *n.* Food, nourishment, provisions, victuals (*vĭt'-ls*), means of subsistence.

To 4 per cent of adult readers SUSTENANCE incorrectly means OPPORTUNITY, convenient occasion, fit time. SUSTENANCE is the noun corresponding to the verb to SUSTAIN, support, keep alive. SUSTENANCE, food, is that which sustains life, keeps one alive.

Of the two words SUSTENANCE and SUBSISTENCE (*sŭb-sĭs'-tĕns*), the latter includes food, clothing, and even financial income; whereas SUSTENANCE is more often limited to food, victuals, nutriment.

234. *CONCOCT* (*kŏn-kŏkt'*) *v.* To prepare by combining, mix. In this sense the word is ordinarily used in cookery; but it may also be used more generally to mean to plan, devise, make up, contrive, as: 'To CONCOCT a story'.

In the test phrase: 'CONCOCTING the punch', the word is thought by 3 per cent of preparatory-school juniors to mean CONSUMING, using up, drinking up, eating up, in suggestion an opposite of the correct meaning.

CONCOCT is from the Latin *com*, together; and *coquere*, to cook; and often today has this literal meaning of cook together.

235. *TOUCH* (*tŭch*) *v.* To concern, interest, be a matter of importance to, affect the welfare of, relate to, make a difference to.

TOUCH goes back to Middle English, and is directly related to the French word *toucher*, to touch, feel, and probably to the German *ziehen*, to pull, draw, tug.

Although to TOUCH, in its physical sense, as: 'His hand TOUCHED the glass', is probably known to every grammar-school pupil, the same verb used figuratively: 'The dispute TOUCHES him', is unknown to 25 per cent. To 10 per cent it incorrectly means FRIGHTENS; and to 7 per cent PLEASES. Every event which TOUCHES one affects one emotionally; it may frighten, please, or disturb, one in a number of ways. But the verb to TOUCH does not designate the manner in which one is moved, but means merely to concern, affect, be of consequence, significance, moment, to.

236. *CONDUCTOR* (*kŏn-dŭk'-tor*) *n.* Leader, guide, manager, director, pilot, impresario (884), entrepreneur.

CONDUCTOR is from the Latin *con;* and *ductum*, the past participle of *ducere*, to lead.

In the test phrase: 'CONDUCTOR of a tourist party', the word is thought by 6 per cent of adult readers to mean ADVISOR. An ADVISOR is a counselor, consultant, one who gives advice; whereas a CONDUCTOR is primarily a leader, manager, executive.

237. *SUBSTANTIATE* (*sŭb-stăn'-shē-āt*) *v.* To verify, confirm, bear out by evidence, establish, prove to be true, authenticate, corroborate, validate.

SUBSTANTIATE is unknown to slightly more than 8 per cent of adult readers. In the phrase: 'My statement was SUBSTANTIATED', the word is incorrectly interpreted by this entire group to mean: 'My statement was UNDERSTOOD'. The literal translation of SUBSTANTIATE is UNDERSTAND; for the first part of the word is the Latin prefix *sub*, under; and the second part is from *stare*, to stand. But this has never been the meaning of the English word SUBSTANTIATE.

SUBSTANTIATE is the verb which corresponds to the noun SUBSTANCE, tangible material. To SUBSTANTIATE may mean to put into concrete form, make real, cause to exist in actuality.

But the word is more frequently used today in the sense of verify.

Although SUBSTANTIATE and VERIFY are similar, one SUBSTANTIATES evidence, testimony, one SUBSTANTIATES a claim, an assertion, one SUBSTANTIATES that which is not capable of rigorous proof; but one VERIFIES a mathematical result, a scientific finding. CORROBORATE, another word of this same general meaning, is to strengthen, give support to a belief. SUBSTANTIATE is to make that belief real and so to establish it.

238. *ACCORD* (ăk-kord′) *v.* To grant, give, bestow (202), award, concede, confer, present, vouchsafe, proffer.

In the test phrase: 'He was ACCORDED privileges', the word is thought by 3 per cent of adult readers to mean ASSURED, promised, made confident of. To ACCORD one privileges is not merely to promise, assure, but actually to give one privileges.

ACCORD is from the same Latin source, *cor, cordis,* heart, as CORDIAL, hearty, and CORDIALITY, heartiness, and by derivation means heart to heart. To ACCORD originally meant to bring to ACCORD, to bring to agreement. It then came to mean to agree; and then apparently to agree to give. Now the verb usually means to give, grant, bestow, without the implication of agreement. The noun, ACCORD, used in the phrase: 'In ACCORD with one another', still means harmony, agreement, concurrence, the opposite of DISCORD.

The verb, to GIVE, is general in its significance. To GRANT is to give as the result of a request. To PRESENT is to give formally a gift of importance and value. To ACCORD is applied to intangibles, as: 'He was ACCORDED merit', 'He was ACCORDED honor'.

239. *INSINUATION* (ĭn-sĭn-ū-ā′-shŭn) *n.* A subtle suggestion, innuendo, derogatory intimation, covert allusion, indirect hint. INSINUATION may also be the act of gaining favor by gentle or artful means.

In the test phrase: 'His base INSINUATION', the word is believed by 3 per cent of preparatory-school juniors to mean THOUGHT.

INSINUATION comes from the Latin *in;* and *sinus,* a bend, winding, the source of the English word SINUOUS, winding, tortuous, full of curves, serpentine. An INSINUATION is, by derivation, a creeping in; and the word can be used in English in this sense, to mean a stealthy passage into anything, as for instance the worming of one's way into favor.

When INSINUATION is used to mean a suggestion, it always connotes a suggestion made in an indirect, roundabout manner. The word has come to be used most frequently in an unpleasant sense in place of INNUENDO which is always a mean and crafty hint. This is perhaps because of the similarity in appearance between INSINUATION and the adjective INSIDIOUS which always means sly, deceitful, treacherous. There is, however, nothing in the derivation of INSINUATION to suggest this disagreeableness, and the word can be applied equally well to a suggestion made with delicacy and skill.

240. *MOCK* (*mŏk*) *v.* To make fun of, ridicule, jeer at (88), mimic, scoff at (223), deride, taunt, flout (*flowt*).

The verb, to MOCK, may be used to mean imitate, simulate, mimic, as: 'Sleep which MOCKED death'. When the verb is used to mean make fun of, it is apt to imply making fun of by mimicking.

241. *INFLEXIBLE* (*ĭn-flĕk'-sĭ-bl*) *adj.* Stiff, unbending, unyielding (392), firm, rigid (504), not flexible (28).

INFLEXIBLE is a combination of the Latin prefix *in*, not; and FLEXIBLE, and like that word can be used either literally of a stick which cannot be bent, or figuratively of behavior or of a disposition which is rigid, unyielding.

To 2 per cent of adult readers INFLEXIBLE incorrectly means PLIABLE (117), flexible, easy to bend, the common misconception and an exact opposite of the correct meaning.

242. *CLAMOR* (*klăm'-or*) *n.* Shouting, loud and continuous noise, hullabaloo, hubbub, uproar, din, much ado, tumult, turbulence.

Many words with the same ending as CLAMOR, among them ARDOR, COLOR, FAVOR, HONOR, HUMOR, LABOR, and VALOR, are spelt in Great Britain with the ending OUR, as *clamour*. Many other words, which once ended in OUR, as: *actour, authour, censour, confessour,* and *doctour,* are now spelt without the U even in Great Britain, ACTOR, AUTHOR, DOCTOR, etc. The United

States has dropped the U from both sets of words; and the tendency in Great Britain seems to be in the same direction. CLAMOR, without the U, is more like the original Latin than is *clamour*, and is always used today in the United States. If the tendency to drop the U continues in Great Britain, CLAMOR may some day be accepted there.

CLAMOR is from the Latin *clamare*, to call out. In the test phrase: 'The CLAMOR ceased', it is thought by 4 per cent of adult readers to mean FIGHTING. Fighting and noise are naturally associated; but the word CLAMOR alone does not include the idea of fighting.

CLAMOR, UPROAR, HUBBUB, and DIN, are loud, continuous noises, slightly different in character. DIN is a rattling, clattering, booming, banging, plangent noise, as: 'The DIN of battle'. DIN is incorrect when applied to voices. HUBBUB is a confused sound of voices, and should never be applied to sounds produced by mechanical contrivances. UPROAR suggests the cause of the noise rather than its character. The word has nothing to do with ROAR; but comes from UP, and the Dutch word *roeren*, to stir. An UPROAR is by derivation a stirring up; and the word designates noise produced by a group which is stirred up. CLAMOR, which comes from the same source as the English word CLAIM, has an inherent sense of demand for attention.

243. *SUPREME* (*sū-prēm'*) *adj.* Highest in rank, of the utmost importance, greatest possible, absolute, ultimate, final, sovereign (277).

The Latin *superus* means high. From this comes the Latin *superior*, the comparative form, which means higher, of greater excellence, preferable, finer, the source of the English word SUPERIOR, better, of greater excellence. That which is SUPERIOR to something else is higher in quality.

From *superus*, high, comes also the Latin *supremus*, the superlative, highest, of greatest excellence, finest, the source of the English word SUPREME. That which is SUPREME is of highest quality.

When used in the test phrase: 'SUPREME commands', the word is believed by 8 per cent of grammar-school pupils to mean POLITICAL. POLITICAL, from the Greek πόλις, a city, means either pertaining to the administration of the government, belonging to the science of government; or, in a more limited sense, pertaining to some group of persons interested in controlling the government. In neither sense does it mean SUPREME, highest, absolute.

244. *ALBEIT* (*awl-bē'-ĭt*) *conj.* Although, even if, notwithstanding, though, be it so, even so, in spite of, however. When used in the test phrase: 'Pleasant, ALBEIT wild', the word is thought by 3 per cent of preparatory-school juniors to mean SOMEWHAT, rather, a little.

ALBEIT goes back to Middle English and is a combination of the three words, ALL, BE, and IT. The same AL appears in the more common word ALTHOUGH, and when thus used means even. ALTHOUGH means literally even though; and ALBEIT means literally even be it, but should seldom be used in writing of modern affairs.

245. *REPAIR* (*rē-pār'*) *v.* To mend, fix, remedy (65), renew, retrieve (92), renovate, set right, make sound, restore to good condition.

When used in the test phrase: 'It was REPAIRED', the word is believed by 3 per cent of adult readers to mean LOST.

To REPAIR and to PREPARE, despite the difference in spelling, both come from the Latin word *parare*, to make ready. To PREPARE, from the Latin *prae*, before, is literally to make ready ahead of time, get ready in advance; to REPAIR, from the Latin *re*, again, is literally to make ready again. In Middle English, REPAIR was spelt *repare*, like PREPARE of today; and there are still two adjectives, REPAIRABLE (*rē-pār'-ă-bl*) and REPARABLE (*rĕp'-ă-ră-bl*) (989), one with and the other without the ɪ; but the verb, to REPAIR, is always today spelt with the ɪ.

It may be the word IMPAIR (*ĭm-pār'*) which has led to this spelling. To IMPAIR is to make worse, damage, injure, mar; and is therefore practically an opposite of REPAIR, to mend. IMPAIR is not from *parare*, to make ready, but from the Latin *in* and *pejorare*, to make worse, a word which in turn comes from *pejor*, worse. IMPAIR must, because of its derivation, be spelt with ɪ, which stands for the J of the Latin. Since, in the learning process, words are most frequently associated with their oppo-

sites, it is perhaps to be expected that REPAIR should acquire the
I to match its opposite.

246. *BREED* (*brēd*) *v.* To bring up, raise, generate, rear,
nourish, nurture (405), procreate, produce, propagate.
BREED may also be used in a more figurative sense to mean
cause to exist, engender, excite, as: 'To BREED strife', 'To BREED
discontent'.
BREED is of Anglo-Saxon origin. The past tense is BRED (*brĕd*),
as in the phrase: 'They were BRED artificially'.

247. *DIVULGE* (*dĭ-vŭlj'*) *v.* Reveal, disclose, impart, uncover,
expose, betray, tell, make public, communicate.
In the test phrase: 'They DIVULGED the information', the
word is thought by 2 per cent of adult readers to mean
CONCEALED. To CONCEAL is to hide, keep secret, an exact opposite of DIVULGE, to make known.
To another 2 per cent DIVULGE incorrectly means OBTAIN,
get. When applied to information, to OBTAIN means to hear, be
told. To OBTAIN is to get, to DIVULGE is to give information,
usually information which is supposed to be kept secret.

248. *LUBRICATE* (*lŭ'-brĭ-kāt*) *v.* Make smooth, make slippery. The verb, to LUBRICATE, is used most frequently
today in its more technical sense, to grease, oil, apply a lubri-
cant to.
In the test phrase: 'LUBRICATE the machines', the word is
thought by 5 per cent of adult readers to mean STOP, the
common misconception, and almost an opposite of the correct meaning.

249. *COLOSSAL* (*cō-lŏs'-săl*) *adj.* Very big, gigantic (63),
huge, tremendous, enormous, monstrous, stupendous,
titanic (226), elephantine. Other words which mean big are:
BROBDINGNAGIAN (*brŏb-dĭng-năg'-ĭ-ăn*), a word invented by
Swift in Gulliver's Travels; and GARGANTUAN (*gahr-găn'-tū-
ăn*), from Rabelais' satire.
To 2 per cent of adult readers COLOSSAL incorrectly means
MYTHICAL, imaginary, fabulous, the common misconception.
This is perhaps because of the derivation of the word COLOSSAL,

which comes from the word COLOSSUS. The COLOSSUS of RHODES was a huge bronze statue of Apollo, said to be 70 cubits, just over 100 feet in height. It was built by the sculptor Chares (*kā'-rēz*), finished in 280 B.C., and stood for fifty-six years at one side of the entrance to the harbor at Rhodes. It was destroyed by an earthquake in 224 B.C. and the fragments lay where they fell for a thousand years. Although the Colossus of Rhodes was a real statue, an exaggerated story has been handed down that it stood astride the mouth of the port and that ships sailed between its legs. Because of the untruth of this version, the statue itself is often thought of as mythical, fabulous.

From COLOSSUS come the words: COLOSSEUM, the great amphitheater at Rome, begun by Vespasian (*vĕs-pā'-zhĭ-ăn*) in 75 A.D. and which, when completed, seated 87,000 persons; and the adjective COLOSSAL, big, huge.

250. *DETRIMENT* (*dĕt'-rĭ-mĕnt*) *n.* A damage, harm done, injury (10), mischief, disadvantage, hurt, loss, diminution, decrement.

DETRIMENT is from the Latin *de*, away; and *terere*, to rub; and is by derivation a rubbing away, a loss, damage. Although DETRIMENT is ordinarily used in the figurative sense to mean an injury, harm; it may mean, more literally, a diminution, a loss, that which is rubbed off.

When the word is used in the test phrase: 'A DETRIMENT to his reputation', it is thought by 3 per cent of preparatory-school juniors to mean an ADDITION. This may be a confusion of DETRI-MENT, damage, with INCREMENT, an increase, something added, an exact opposite of DETRIMENT in its unusual sense, decrement. Ordinarily INCREMENT means that which is added in a physical sense or, in mathematics, any quantity added to something else. A DECREMENT is the exact opposite of an increment. The word DETRIMENT is seldom used in this concrete sense of diminution, decrement, but more often means an injury, damage.

251. *AUDIBLE* (*aw'-dĭ-bl*) *adj.* Perceptible to the ear, loud enough to be heard, some dictionaries add 'distinctly heard'.

AUDIBLE is from the same source as the more familiar words: AUDIENCE, a group or assembly of hearers; AUDITOR, one who hears; and AUDITORIUM, a room or hall planned for auditors, hearers, listeners.

In the test phrase: 'Little was AUDIBLE', the word is thought by 4 per cent of preparatory-school juniors to mean VISIBLE, apparent, easily seen. It is thought by 5 per cent of adult readers to mean INDISTINCT, not clearly distinguishable, dim, vague, obscure, the popular misconception, and a word which, when applied to sounds, is nearly an opposite of AUDIBLE, loud enough to be heard more or less distinctly.

252. AVERSE (ă-vers') adj. Disinclined, reluctant, opposed, unwilling, disliking, antipathetic, loath, indisposed.

AVERSE comes from the Latin *ab*, from, away; and *vertere*, to turn; and by derivation means turned away from. From the same source come ADVERSE, by derivation, turned against, unfavorable, hostile, as: 'ADVERSE criticism'; CONVERSE, by derivation, turned around, opposite, as: 'CONVERSE statements'; DIVERSE (dī-vers'), by derivation, turned apart, of differing kinds, dissimilar, varied, as: 'DIVERSE amusements'; and REVERSE, by derivation, turned back, opposite, as: 'The REVERSE direction'.

AVERSE, when it means disinclined, is always used with the preposition TO, as: 'AVERSE to study'. In this it differs from all other adjectives from *vertere*, for they are never used in this way.

The noun, AVERSION, fixed dislike, antipathy, repugnance, is probably more familiar than the adjective AVERSE. It also may be used with the preposition TO, as: 'An AVERSION to disorder'. The verb, to AVERT, comes from the same source and may have the literal meaning, to turn away, as: 'She AVERTED her eyes'.

AVERSE and RELUCTANT both mean disinclined. RELUCTANT suggests an impelling force against which one struggles; one who is RELUCTANT to exercise is being pushed to exercise either by his own conscience or by someone else and may ultimately accede. AVERSE, on the other hand, implies no urgency, merely a habitual and usually mild disinclination.

253. IMPENETRABLE (ĭm-pĕn'-ĕ-tră-bl) adj. Incapable of being pierced, not possible to get into or through, that cannot be entered, impermeable, impervious. IMPENETRABLE may also at times mean dense, compact, obtuse, unfathomable, inscrutable.

The verb, to PENETRATE, from the Latin *penes*, within; and *trare*, to enter; means by derivation to enter into; but the word suggests today entering with difficulty. PENETRABLE, the adjective, means capable of being entered. Before words which begin with P, B, or M, the Latin prefix *in*, not, becomes *im*. Thus, IMPENETRABLE means not PENETRABLE, not capable of being entered.

To 9 per cent of grammar-school pupils, IMPENETRABLE incorrectly means UNKNOWN; and to another 6 per cent, DANGEROUS. IMPENETRABLE regions, IMPENETRABLE forests, IMPENETRABLE swamps, may be both unknown and dangerous; but the word IMPENETRABLE, not capable of being entered into, can be used in phrases where both UNKNOWN and DANGEROUS are inapplicable, as: 'IMPENETRABLE armor', armor which cannot be pierced; and 'Rock IMPENETRABLE to light', rock which light cannot enter.

IMPENETRABLE and IMPASSABLE both suggest difficulties in the way of progress. IMPASSABLE means literally that which cannot be passed, gone by and left behind. An IMPASSABLE forest cannot be passed through. IMPENETRABLE means impossible to get within, into the interior of. An IMPENETRABLE forest cannot be entered.

254. *CESSATION* (*sĕs-sā'-shŭn*) *n.* End, close, rest, stop, ceasing, discontinuance, termination (156), conclusion, respite (650), surcease (1006).

When used in the test phrase: 'She talks without CESSATION', the word is thought by 4 per cent of adult readers to mean VARIETY, change, alteration, diversity. A change, VARIETY, may be caused by an interruption, for an interruption may be no more than an obstacle, hindrance, which causes a change of course; but a CESSATION is a complete, although perhaps temporary, stopping.

CESSATION, TERMINATION, and INTERMISSION, are three words which indicate the stopping of some activity. An INTERMISSION is a stopping in the middle of an activity which continues after the intermission, as: 'The INTERMISSION between the acts of a play'. A TERMINATION is the final end, beyond which an activity will not continue. The word CESSATION is used for the stopping of an activity which may or may not begin again.

255. *INDEFATIGABLE* (*ĭn-dē-făt'-ĭ-gă-bl*) *adj.* Tireless, unremitting, unwearying, unflagging (114), persevering, persistent, assiduous (390), sedulous. 'INDEFATIGABLE exertions.' INDEFATIGABLE comes from the Latin *fatigare*, to tire, from the same source as the English verb to FATIGUE, to tire, weary, exhaust. INDEFATIGABLE is by derivation untiring.

256. *IMMERSE* (*ĭm-mers'*) *v.* To dip under the surface of a liquid, submerge, sink, plunge, douse (122). IMMERSE may also be used figuratively, as in the phrase: 'IMMERSED in his work', to mean engrossed, absorbed.

IMMERSE, in its literal sense, dip, is unknown to 9 per cent of adult readers. To 4 per cent it incorrectly means CONCEAL, hide from sight, withdraw from view. Both to CONCEAL and to IMMERSE mean to cover; but the method of covering and the purpose differ with the two verbs. To CONCEAL is to cover with anything so that what is concealed cannot be seen, or sometimes so that it cannot be found. The purpose of concealing is hiding, secreting. To IMMERSE, except in its figurative sense, is specifically to cover with liquid. The purpose of IMMERSING is to treat, affect in some way, that which is immersed, so that it is soaked, saturated, impregnated with liquid.

IMMERSION, the noun, the act of immersing, is thought by 5 per cent of preparatory-school juniors to mean APPEARANCE. This is no doubt a confusion of IMMERSION (*ĭm-mer'-shŭn*, not *ĭm-mer'-zhŭn*) with EMERSION (*ē-mer'-shŭn*), appearance, coming into view, emergence. The word IMMERSION is used in astronomy to mean disappearance and in this sense is an exact opposite of EMERSION; but ordinarily IMMERSION means the act of plunging into a liquid, and the verb, to IMMERSE, is to plunge, dip.

257. *DEITY* (*dē'-ĭ-tĭ*) *n.* A god, goddess, divine person, divinity, supreme being, godhead, divine nature.

The word DEITY, from the Latin *deus*, god, is thought by 2 per cent of adult readers to mean LAW, rule of conduct.

The word DEITY, when used to mean a divine person, is not

capitalized. The DEITY, spelt with a capital, means God, Jehovah, the Creator.

258. *APERTURE* (*ăp'-er-tūr*) *n*. Opening, hole, gap, passage, open space, perforation, breach (443), interval, orifice.
The word APERTURE, from the Latin *apertus*, the past participle of *aperire*, to open, is also used in optics to mean the diameter of the exposed part of the object glass.

259. *STAY* (*stā*) *v*. To stop, check (399), restrain, arrest, halt, withhold, as: 'He STAYED his hand'. The verb, to STAY, may also mean put off, postpone (3), delay (85), as: 'To STAY judgment'.

260. *APPROPRIATE* (*ăp-prō'-prĭ-āt*) *adj*. Fit, proper, suitable, befitting the place, well adapted to the occasion.
APPROPRIATE is from the Latin *ad*, to; and *proprius*, one's own, special. The verb, to APPROPRIATE, is to make a thing one's own, take possession of, make it one's own property.
The adjective, APPROPRIATE, in the test phrase: 'With APPROPRIATE gestures', is unknown to 26 per cent of grammar-school pupils.

261. *COGITATE* (*kŏj'-ĭ-tāt*) *v*. To ponder, think deeply, reflect, muse, engage in continuous thinking, meditate, ruminate (868), cerebrate.
In the test phrase: 'He sat and COGITATED', the word is believed by 3 per cent of preparatory-school juniors to mean CHEWED. This confusion may be due to the word RUMINATE which has two separate meanings. To RUMINATE originally meant to chew the cud, and may still be used in this way. To RUMINATE may also mean to meditate, ponder, think over again. But COGITATE has no such double meaning, and can mean only ponder, think deeply.

262. *REPUDIATE* (*rē-pū'-dĭ-āt*) *v*. To refuse to acknowledge, disdain, disavow, disown, renounce (636), abjure, disclaim, recant (848).
In the test phrase: 'REPUDIATE a statement', the word is thought by 3 per cent of college seniors to mean APPROVE,

think well of, in concept an opposite of the correct meaning. REPUDIATE is from the Latin *re*, again; and *pudiare*, to be ashamed; and means by derivation to be ashamed of. It is from the same source as IMPUDENCE, by derivation lack of shame, shamelessness, immodesty; and the unusual English word PUDENCY, shame, bashfulness, modesty.

To REPUDIATE was formerly limited to the one sense, to divorce, as: 'He REPUDIATED his wife'. Today it has the general meaning of refusing to acknowledge anything; one may REPUDIATE a friend, a debt, a statement.

To REPUDIATE and to ACKNOWLEDGE are opposites.

263. *OVERWHELM* (*ō-ver-hwĕlm'*) *v.* To crush, submerge, overpower, overcome, defeat, vanquish.

In the test phrase: 'An OVERWHELMING force', the word is believed by 5 per cent of adult readers to mean SUPERNATURAL. This is probably because of the suggestion embodied in the word OVERWHELM. OVERWHELM and OVERPOWER both express the idea of suppression by superior force. That which OVERPOWERS has been fought against and overpowers only after a struggle. That which OVERWHELMS is so vast as to crush without resistance; and is perhaps for this reason thought of as SUPERNATURAL, miraculous, outside of the laws of nature.

The two verbs, OVERWHELM and WHELM, are similar in meaning. To WHELM, with counterparts in most of the Scandinavian and Germanic languages, is to submerge, ruin, crush, destroy, overpower. OVER adds action and intensity.

264. *INCUR* (*ĭn-ker'*) *v.* Bring upon one's self, become liable for, contract, acquire.

In the test phrase: To INCUR a debt', the word is thought by 3 per cent of adult readers to mean REPUDIATE (262), refuse to accept, disavow, disclaim. REPUDIATION is a second step. One cannot REPUDIATE a debt until one has acquired, INCURRED it.

265. *CRAFTINESS* (*krăf'-tĭ-nĕs*) *n.* Cunning, guile, artifice, wiliness, trickiness, stratagem, sly skill in effecting a purpose.

To 5 per cent of adult readers CRAFTINESS incorrectly means HANDIWORK. This is probably a confusion of CRAFTINESS, cunning, with CRAFTSMANSHIP, manual skill, ability to handle a tool well, workmanship, skilled handiwork.

The adjective CRAFTY was used in about 1370 in Piers Plowman to mean having manual skill. This meaning is now archaic and today CRAFTY always means too skillful in devising underhand schemes, wily, sly, cunning (320). The corresponding noun CRAFTINESS can now have only this last meaning sly skill, stratagem, trickiness.

266. *STUBBORN* (*stŭb'-born*) *adj*. Obstinate, fixed in purpose, inflexible (241), unyielding (392), wilful, mulish, intractable, resolutely perverse (1049).

STUBBORN is, perhaps, from the same Anglo-Saxon source as STUB, a word which originally meant the stump of a tree, but which is used today for any blunt projection. STUBBORN certainly suggests rooted in one's opinions, as firmly fixed as the stump of a tree.

In the test phrase: 'The fellow is STUBBORN', the word is thought by 14 per cent of grammar-school pupils to mean STUPID. Both STUPID and STUBBORN mean slow but for different reasons. The STUPID person is slow because he does not understand. He is dull, slow-witted. The STUBBORN person may understand, but is slow because he does not wish to move.

STUBBORN and OBSTINATE both apply to a person who will not change. OBSTINATE is active; the OBSTINATE person goes ahead with his plans without listening to advice. STUBBORN is negative; the STUBBORN person is immovable and will not listen to suggestions for action.

267. *POLLUTE* (*pŏl-lūt'*) *v*. To contaminate, foul, befoul, soil, taint, defile, thoroughly permeate with an undesirable constituent.

In the test phrase: 'POLLUTING the air', the word is thought by 5 per cent of preparatory-school juniors to mean FILLING.

POLLUTE and DEFILE are both stronger than CONTAMINATE and TAINT. Both mean to make foul at the source.

268. *PULSATE* (*pŭl'-sāt*) *v*. To throb, beat, vibrate, quiver, palpitate, flutter, expand and contract rhythmically.

In the test phrase: 'PULSATING with excitement', the word is

thought by 4 per cent of adult readers to mean SHOUTING,
crying out. PULSATING is from the same Latin word as PULSE,
the heart beat, and means throbbing, beating.

269. *VEER* (*vēr*) *v.* To swerve, tack, change direction, turn
     aside, shift, deviate from a course.

VEER comes from the French *virer*, to tack, change direction,
the source also of the English word ENVIRONS, surroundings.

    In the test phrase: 'The boat VEERED', the word is thought by
3 per cent of adult readers to mean ROLLED. To ROLL and to
VEER are both to turn, but in different ways. To ROLL, as
applied to a boat, is to rock from side to side, turn about a
longitudinal axis. To VEER is to turn from the course, change
direction, turn about a vertical axis.

270. *BOOTY* (*boo'-tĭ*) *n.* Plunder, spoil, pillage, loot, gain,
     prize, that which is taken from another by force.

In the test phrase: 'He escaped with his BOOTY', the word is
thought by 4 per cent of adult readers to mean FOOT-COVERING,
the common misconception. This comes, of course, from a confusion of BOOTY with BOOT, a foot-covering, or perhaps with
BOOTEE, a diminutive of BOOT and a trade name used in various
ways, sometimes for a lady's light boot, or a baby's shoe.
BOOTEE is, however, accented on the last syllable (*boo-tē'*);
while BOOTY, spoil, plunder, is accented on the first syllable
(*boo'-tĭ*).

    BOOTY, PLUNDER, PILLAGE, SPOIL, are words for goods taken
by force. SPOIL and PILLAGE imply heavy loss to the owner.
PLUNDER emphasizes the value of the goods taken. BOOTY is
most often goods taken in a raid.

271. *PLACIDITY* (*plă-sĭd'-ĭ-tĭ*) *n.* Calmness, tranquillity,
     serenity, peacefulness, quietness, state of being unruffled,
undisturbed.

PLACIDITY is from the Latin adjective *placidus*, which in turn
comes from the verb *placere*, to please, the source of the
English word PLEASE; and the more difficult verb to PLACATE,
to quiet, calm, appease, pacify.

    In the test phrase: 'She inquired with PLACIDITY', the word
is thought by 5 per cent of preparatory-school juniors to mean

GENTILITY, fashionableness, stylishness, upper-class habits, the manner of polite society.

PLACIDITY and CALMNESS, although practically synonymous, differ slightly. CALMNESS can be an assumed attitude. CALMNESS in the face of danger may be tense repression. PLACIDITY cannot be used in this way. PLACIDITY is an inherent characteristic, almost an inability to be moved, disturbed.

The second most common misconception of the word is SHARPNESS, abruptness, brusqueness, practically an opposite of PLACIDITY, quietness.

272. *CANDID* (*kăn'-dĭd*) *adj.* Frank, open, sincere, straightforward, outspoken, blunt.

CANDID comes from the Latin *candere*, to shine, glitter, be white, from the same source as the English word CANDLE. CANDID, originally in English, meant white, bright. This meaning is obsolete, and CANDID is now used only in the figurative sense of honest, frank.

To 3 per cent of adult readers CANDID incorrectly means FLATTERING. The verb, to FLATTER, differs from to PRAISE because it includes the idea of undue praise, overpraise. In this respect, the participial adjective, FLATTERING, praising unduly, is an opposite of CANDID, honest.

273. *GIRD* (*gerd*) *v.* To bind, encircle, confine by encircling, secure with a belt, surround with a flexible band.

The verb, to GIRD, is from the same source as the noun, a GIRDLE, a band or sash around the waist; and GIRTH, the measure around a person's body, or any band, especially the band which is passed under a horse's body to hold the saddle in place. The word GIRDER, used today in construction work to mean a beam of steel or wood, is from the same source. A GIRDER is by derivation something which girds, binds a building together.

274. *SUPPLANT* (*sŭp-plănt'*) *v.* To replace, take the place of, displace, oust (86), supersede, especially by strategy, craft, or scheming.

The original English meaning of the word SUPPLANT was the same as that of the Latin word from which it comes, to trip up and so to undermine, overthrow. This meaning is now obsolete, but the word still has the connotation of displacing by underhand methods. It should be reserved for this use.

In the test phrase: 'He SUPPLANTED his friend', the word is thought by 3 per cent of adult readers to mean ASSISTED, the common misconception, and practically an opposite of the original meaning of SUPPLANT.

SUPPLANT, DISPLACE, and REPLACE, may all be used to mean take the place of. To REPLACE may mean substitute a more satisfactory object or person; and, even when REPLACE is used to mean merely put in the place of, it suggests improvement. To DISPLACE may mean remove; and, when used to mean put in the place of, emphasizes the removal of the incumbent without commenting on its advisability. To SUPPLANT is to displace by strategy, scheming, and underhand methods.

275. *TYPICAL* (*tĭp'-ĭ-kl*) *adj.* Representative, regular, normal, usual, characteristic, true to type, emblematic, symbolic, exemplary. The corresponding verb is to TYPIFY (394). To 7 per cent of adult readers TYPICAL incorrectly means SIMILAR, resembling, nearly corresponding, possessing a general likeness. A SIMILAR case is only partly like a group of others with which it is compared. A TYPICAL case is like a group of others in all important respects.

276. *SECLUSION* (*sē-klū'-zhŭn*) *n.* Retirement, solitude, privacy, retreat, withdrawal from society.

SECLUSION is from the Latin *se*, aside; and *claudere*, to shut. To 3 per cent of adult readers the word incorrectly means FREEDOM, liberty, exemption from control.

277. *SOVEREIGN* (*sŏv'-er-ĭn*) *adj.* Supreme (243), chief, paramount, highest, most excellent, preeminent (339).

The word SOVEREIGN is also used as a noun to mean supreme ruler, monarch, potentate (353), person having supreme power, and in this sense is more familiar than the adjective for it is unknown to only 1 per cent of adult readers.

The end of the modern word SOVEREIGN is spelt like the verb to REIGN. Although a SOVEREIGN is one who reigns over others, the word does not come from the same source as REIGN, but is probably from the Latin *super*, above, over. There is no etymological justification for the present spelling; the G is a modern insertion, added no doubt because of a notion that the word should be spelt like the verb to REIGN.

When SOVEREIGN is used as an adjective it is thought by 4 per cent of adult readers to mean POLITICAL. Both words, POLITICAL and SOVEREIGN, may refer to government. POLITICAL applies specifically to the policies of a government or to a party attempting to gain control of a government. SOVEREIGN when used in reference to a government applies only to those in supreme power. The adjective SOVEREIGN may also be used in a more general sense to mean supreme in any situation.

278. *PRECISE* (*prē-sīs'*) *adj.* Exact, accurate, right, correct, definite, distinct, punctilious (533), scrupulous (604), explicit, strictly worded, not vague.

The word PRECISE, as used in the test phrase: 'A PRECISE statement', is believed by 10 per cent of grammar-school pupils to mean BROAD. A BROAD statement is comprehensive, not limited, general. In this sense BROAD is almost an opposite of PRECISE, strictly worded. The same word, BROAD, is applied with a slightly different meaning to a person. A BROAD person is not reserved, he is sometimes even unrestrained. In this sense, when applied to conduct, BROAD and PRECISE are exact opposites, for a PRECISE person is strict, formal, prim, apt to be overexact in behavior. In such a phrase as: 'A BROAD hint', the word BROAD has still a third meaning, plain, clear, not ambiguous, unmistakable. In this sense BROAD and PRECISE are almost synonymous.

To another 7 per cent PRECISE means PRECIOUS. An obsolete meaning of PRECIOUS is PRECISE; and, although PRECIOUS, as used today, ordinarily means costly, of great price, expensive, valuable, in the phrase: 'A PRECIOUS statement', it means overnice, fastidious, scrupulous, affectedly refined, exaggeratedly precise.

Three words, ACCURATE, EXACT, and PRECISE, are so close as to be almost indistinguishable.

279. *RUDIMENT* (*rū'-dĭ-mĕnt*) *n.* Undeveloped beginning, first crude principle, germ, embryo, elementary idea.

RUDIMENTARY (370) is the corresponding adjective.

In the test phrase: 'He does not know the RUDIMENTS', the word is thought by 3 per cent of adult readers to mean DETAILS,

minute points, particulars, in suggestion almost an opposite of
the correct meaning, for the DETAILS of a subject, its minute
points, are not studied until long after the RUDIMENTS, the
elementary principles, have been mastered.

A RUDIMENT, or more frequently the plural form RUDIMENTS,
as: 'The RUDIMENTS of a subject', is so often defined as its first
principles, that the word has come to be used in two different
senses. The first principles of a subject may be its most important, chief, fundamental, basic principles. RUDIMENTS should
never be used in this sense, for the word comes from the Latin
rudis, rude, crude, raw, and by derivation means something
in a rough, crude, unfinished state. The RUDIMENTS of a subject are its early aspects, its crude beginnings.

280. *INDICTMENT* (*in-dīt'-mĕnt*) *n.* An accusation espe-
      cially by a legal process, formal complaint, grand jury
charge.

INDICTMENT comes from the Latin *dicere*, to say, the source of
the English word DICTIONARY.

The two nouns INDICTMENT and IMPEACHMENT are specific;
ACCUSATION and CHARGE are more general. Legally, the House
of Representatives in the United States and the House of Com-
mons in Great Britain, make an IMPEACHMENT; a grand jury
may make an INDICTMENT.

281. *SCRUTINY* (*skrŭ'-tĭ-nĭ*) *n.* Careful examination, search-
      ing look, critical inspection, perusal (763), minute inquiry,
close investigation.

To 3 per cent of adult readers SCRUTINY incorrectly means
SCORN, contempt, disdain, derision.

282. *NEAT* (*nēt*) *adj.* To the point, well expressed, nice, pre-
      cise (278), adroit, cleverly put, skillfully phrased.

NEAT can be traced back to Middle English, with similar words
in almost every language; but the word comes originally from
the Latin *nitere*, to shine.

NEAT, when used in the test phrase: 'A NEAT answer', is unknown to 29 per cent of grammar-school pupils. To 16 per cent
it incorrectly means AFFIRMATIVE; and to 5 per cent, NEGATIVE.
These words are opposites of each other. An AFFIRMATIVE an-

swer is one which gives consent, says: 'Yes'. A NEGATIVE answer is one which refuses, denies, says: 'No'.

NEAT and NICE are synonymous. Colloquially NICE means agreeable, pleasant, but more accurately it means NEAT with an added suggestion of delicacy, fastidiousness, subtlety. From the same source as NEAT comes the adjective NET (*nĕt*), a more recent word which means free from everything extraneous, clear of all that is unnecessary. NET weight is the weight not counting wrappings, box, package, or container. NET price is the price after all deductions have been made.

This same idea of free from all that is superfluous is contained in the word NEAT. A NEAT room is clean and tidy, but not showy. Brandy taken NEAT is clear, unadulterated, not mixed with anything. 'A NEAT answer', 'A NEAT stroke', 'A NEAT turn', contain nothing superfluous, fit the situation exactly.

NET and GROSS are opposites. NEAT and SLOVENLY are opposites, in both their literal and figurative senses.

283. *PARLEY* (*pahr'-lĭ*) *n.* Mutual discourse, discussion, conversation; specifically a conference (11) between enemies, meeting of opposing leaders.

PARLEY is probably from the French *parler*, to speak. To 3 per cent of adult readers PARLEY incorrectly means TRUCE, a suspension of hostilities, armistice. The terms of a TRUCE, may be discussed in a PARLEY, conference between enemies.

284. *HAMLET* (*hăm'-lĕt*) *n.* A cluster of houses, little village, very small town.

HAMLET comes from the Anglo-Saxon *ham*, a home. HAM appears in such proper names as: BIRMINGHAM, NOTTINGHAM, WAREHAM.

In the test phrase: 'A restful HAMLET', the word is thought by 5 per cent of adult readers to mean COUCH, a bed, the popular misconception. Some association comes perhaps through the word COT, which means either a small house, a hut, cottage; or a small, portable bed.

HAMLET, VILLAGE, TOWN, and CITY, are arranged roughly in order of size. Originally a CITY contained a cathedral and was the seat of a bishop. Now a CITY can be incorporated as such after it reaches some specified population, usually about 10,000 inhabitants. Although today a small CITY and a large TOWN are indistinguishable in outward appearance, originally in England a TOWN was carefully defined as possessing both a church and public market but not a cathedral. Today, especially in the United States, the chief difference between a CITY and a TOWN is in the organization of their governments. A TOWN may remain a TOWN no matter how large it grows; but TOWNS are, in general, smaller than CITIES. A VILLAGE is still smaller and technically, in England, possesses a church but no market. In the United States, a VILLAGE is any small community, for the word HAMLET is seldom used. Technically, in England, a HAMLET is smaller than a village and possesses no church.

285. *DENIAL* (*dē-nī'-ăl*) *n.* Refusal, rejection, negation, refutation, disavowal, contradiction of a statement.
In the test phrase: 'A firm DENIAL', the word is believed by 13 per cent of grammar-school pupils to mean FOUNDATION, basis, groundwork, that on which anything rests.

The verb, to DENY (*dē-nī'*), to declare something to be untrue, refuse to admit, say: 'No', is from the Latin *de* and *negare*, to deny, the source of the English word NEGATIVE, no, as in the phrase: 'A NEGATIVE answer'. Ordinarily the ending AL is added to a Latin noun to make an adjective. Thus: a CLASSIC, a book, writing, production, of the highest rank, first-class, becomes the adjective, CLASSICAL, of the highest rank, first-class. The same ending is sometimes added to a verb to make a noun. Thus: the verb, to TRY, to attempt, becomes a noun, TRIAL, an attempt, effort, the Y changing to I with the addition of the AL. In the same way the verb, to DENY, to say: 'No', becomes the noun, DENIAL, refusal, the act of denying.

286. *TERRESTRIAL* (*tĕr-rĕs'-trĭ-ăl*) *adj.* Earthly, pertaining to the earth, sublunary, terrene, mundane (815).
TERRESTRIAL comes from the Latin *terra*, earth, a word which is familiar in the phrase: 'TERRA FIRMA', dry land. TERRA is the source of TERRIER, a small dog so named because he routs out of the ground, animals, such as badgers, which burrow.

To 4 per cent of adult readers TERRESTRIAL incorrectly means CELESTIAL, heavenly, the popular misconception, and practically the reverse of the correct meaning.

287. *EXACT* (*ĕgz-ăkt'*) *v.* To extort, demand, claim, enforce, insist upon, wrest from, wring from, force to be paid, require peremptorily.

In spelling and pronunciation the verb, to EXACT, is like the more familiar adjective, EXACT, accurate, precise, definite. Both come from the Latin *ex*, out; and *actus*, the past participle of the verb *agere*, to drive.

288. *RUDE* (*rūd*) *adj.* Simple, crude, rough, rugged, primitive (358), rudimentary (370). RUDE (64) may also mean impolite, uncivil; and in this more familiar sense is known to practically all adult readers.

In the test phrase: 'A RUDE hut', the word is believed by 4 per cent of adult readers to mean LOG. A LOG hut is a specific type of hut built of trunks of trees. A RUDE hut may be any type of primitive structure whether built of logs, straw, mud, or stone.

289. *GRIMACE* (*grĭ-mās'*, not *grĭm'-ās*) *n.* Wry face, distorted countenance made from pain, disgust, or in jest.

By 6 per cent of preparatory-school juniors a GRIMACE is thought to be an OGLE, an amorous glance, coquettish look.

GRIMACE is from the French word, *grimace*, a wry face, and has exactly this meaning in English.

290. *USABLE* (*ūz'-ă-bl*) *adj.* Capable of use, useful, such as can be used, practicable (484), workable, feasible, utilitarian, serviceable, applicable.

In the test phrase: 'USABLE plans', the word is thought by 11 per cent of grammar-school pupils to mean IMPRACTICAL, not based on experience, nearly but not exactly an opposite of the correct meaning; for IMPRACTICABLE is the exact opposite of USABLE, workable.

291. *SUBJUGATE* (*sŭb'-jŭ-gāt*) *v.* To conquer (53), defeat, overcome, compel to submit to authority, subdue, vanquish, enslave, obtain dominion over.

In the test phrase: 'SUBJUGATED nations', the word is thought by 3 per cent of adult readers to mean WARRING. When applied to nations, WARRING means fighting, contending, striving. A

SUBJUGATED, subdued, conquered, nation has ordinarily given up, and is past the point of striving.

SUBJUGATE is from the Latin *sub*, under; and *jugar*, yoke; and by derivation means to place under the yoke. The word is used today both in a material and in a moral sense. One may SUBJUGATE a nation or an appetite.

292. *POOL* (*pool*) *v*. To combine, unite, consolidate, amalgamate, contribute with others to a common venture, put into a common fund.

In the test phrase: 'They POOLED their resources', the word is thought by 3 per cent of adult readers to mean LIQUIDATED. To LIQUIDATE is to settle, pay, turn every asset into cash.

POOL is from the French word *poule*, hen, and has come to mean contribute, perhaps because of a French game, in which hens' eggs are the stakes and are placed together in the center of the table and called the POT or POOL.

293. *DISUSE* (*dĭs-ūs'*) *n*. Neglect, unemployment, obsolescence, desuetude (925), condition of being no longer in use. 'Fallen into DISUSE.'

The verb, to USE (*ūz*), as: 'USE your pencil', is undoubtedly known to every grammar-school pupil. The corresponding noun USE (*ūs*), employment, application, as: 'The USE of gas for cooking', is spelt the same but pronounced differently. DISUSE is a combination of the Latin prefix *dis*, not, and the noun USE.

294. *MAIM* (*mām*) *v*. To cripple, disable, injure, mangle, mutilate, deprive of the use of a limb.

To 4 per cent of adult readers MAIM incorrectly means PUNISH, chastise, discipline. Although to PUNISH severely may cripple, disable, maim the person so punished, to MAIM has no implication of the retribution inherent in PUNISH, but is to injure, mutilate in any way.

295. *STIMULATE* (*stĭm'-ū-lāt*) *v*. To excite, rouse, spur to action, enliven, incite, impel (475), animate, invigorate, energize, exhilarate, give vitality to.

To 3 per cent of adult readers STIMULATE incorrectly means

BIND UP. The verb, to STIMULATE, is from the Latin *stimulus*, a goad, which appears as the more difficult English noun STIMULUS (669), an incentive, a spur to action. STIMULATE is by derivation to spur the mind to activity, rouse to action.

296. *EPOCH* (*ĕp'-ŏk*) *n.* The beginning of an era in history, fixed date, point of time from which succeeding years are numbered; also a period of time.

EPOCH is thought by 5 per cent of preparatory-school juniors to mean HEIGHT in the sense of highest point, zenith, culmination. EPOCH is from a Greek word which means pause, stop, check. It was used at one time for the highest point reached by a star in moving across the sky, the point at which it seemed to pause. In this obsolete sense, HEIGHT is nearly a synonym of EPOCH. By derivation EPOCH can be used only for the point from which a period of time is counted. This point is always an important date, but is not necessarily the height, culmination, of a civilization.

In English, the word EPOCH has come to be used for a period of time, elapsed time, rather than for the date from which a period is counted. In this an EPOCH differs from an ERA, for an ERA is correctly a period of time, a length of time. When the word EPOCH is used to designate a period of time, it should be used only for a period during which some single important event has taken place, from which an ERA or period of time can be computed.

297. *EFFIGY* (*ĕf'-fĭ-jĭ*) *n.* An image, representation, semblance in sculpture particularly on a tomb. EFFIGY is sometimes popularly used for a stuffed figure representing an obnoxious person.

When used in the simple phrase: 'His EFFIGY', the word is thought by 4 per cent of adult readers to mean ASSISTANT.

The word EFFIGY is from the Latin *ex*, from; and *figere*, to fashion; from the same source as the English verb to FEIGN, to pretend, relate falsely; and the noun FICTION, a fabrication, invented narrative. As used in English, EFFIGY has the same suggestion of falsehood, untruth, as do these two words.

An EFFIGY and a STATUE are both representations, a STATUE may be a true likeness of a living person; while an EFFIGY, although the semblance of a person, does not portray his living personality. Thus, the word EFFIGY is often used for the recumbent figure on a tomb. It is also used occasionally for a crude portrayal, which bears no real likeness, but merely stands for the original.

298. *DIE* (*dī*) *n.* A stamp for imprinting a design on metal; steel form used in a press for shaping metal, leather, paper, or other substance. A DIE is used in making, among other things, coins, medals, and soles of shoes.

In the test phrase: 'Made with a special DIE', the word is thought by 7 per cent of adult readers to mean FORMULA, rule.

DIE is also the singular of DICE (*dīs*), a small cube with the numbers one to six on its six faces. The only common use of the singular DIE, in this sense, is in the phrase: 'The DIE is cast'. When the word DIE is used to mean a stamp or knife the plural is DIES (*dīz*).

299. *CACHE* (*kăsh*) *v.* To store underground for future use, hide, secrete, deposit in a protected place, put away for safe keeping.

A CACHE, the noun, may be a hiding place; or it may be that which is put away for safety, usually food stored and left by explorers for future use.

CACHE is a French word, related to the French word *cacher* (*kă-shā'*), to hide. It was introduced into English by the French Canadians, at the time of the Hudson Bay Colony; but the word has never been completely anglicized, and still retains its French pronunciation.

In the test phrase: 'He CACHED his supplies', the verb is thought by 6 per cent of adult readers to mean COLLECTED. To COLLECT is to gather together; but COLLECT does not have the significance of storing safely for future use, implicit in CACHE.

300. *GANDER* (*găn'-der*) *n.* The male goose, a web-footed flat-billed bird with a large body.

In the test phrase: 'He shot the GANDER', the word is thought by 6 per cent of adult readers to mean DUCK, the popular misconception. The words DRAKE, male duck, and GANDER, male goose, come from the same ultimate source, another instance of the popular misconception revealing some actual historical connection.

Although ornithologists might shudder at the classification, a GOOSE may be distinguished from a DUCK by the fact that he has a longer neck; and distinguished from a SWAN by having a shorter one.

301. *SULKINESS* (*sŭl'-kĭ-nĕs*) *n.* Sullenness, moodiness, moroseness; the state of being sulky, ill-humoredly keeping aloof from others, stubbornly cross, doggedly refusing to speak or act. 'Her SULKINESS was evident.'

The noun, SULKINESS, sullenness; the verb, to SULK, to refuse to speak; the adjective, SULKY, sullen; and even the more unusual noun, a SULKY; all come from the same Anglo-Saxon source and all suggest the desire to be alone. The last, a SULKY, is a light two-wheeled, horse-drawn vehicle with only one seat, in which the driver sits alone.

The noun SULLENNESS and the adjective SULLEN have by derivation a similar suggestion, for both come from the Latin *solus*, alone. The adjective SULLEN, when it first appeared in English, meant solitary, with no unpleasant suggestion.

SULKINESS and SULLENNESS are close in meaning. Both are temporary states, not habitual dispositions; both suggest silence and this differentiates them from other words expressing disagreeableness, such as MOROSENESS, which implies meeting advances with rude words. They differ in that SULLENNESS is an adult characteristic; whereas SULKINESS is more youthful, more whimsical.

302. *ASSOCIATE* (*ăs-sō'-shĭ-āt*, not *ăs-sō'-sĭ-āt*) *n.* Colleague, ally, partner, comrade, companion, compeer, confrere, fellow-member, accomplice (192), confederate.

ASSOCIATE is from the same Latin source as the adjective, SOCIAL, friendly, and the noun SOCIETY, companionship.

Although ASSOCIATION is pronounced either (*shĭ* or *sĭ*) (*ăs-sō-shĭ-ā'-shŭn* or *ăs-sō-sĭ-ā'-shŭn*), the latter is preferred by some, in order to avoid the double SH sound. The repetition of the s, however, is almost as unpleasant. In words which have no other s sound, as ANNUNCIATION and PRONUNCIATION, the ending is pronounced (*sĭ-ā-shŭn*, not *shĭ-ā-shŭn*). But in words where there must be a repetition either of the s or of the sh, either is allowable.

Although fundamentally the word ASSOCIATE means a companion of equal rank, it is now used by learned societies and clubs in general to signify a person without full privileges of membership. Perhaps from this use the word is coming to suggest not quite an equal, so that in referring to an equal one is apt to use COMRADE in the military world, or COLLEAGUE in the business world, rather than ASSOCIATE.

303. *STEEP* (*stēp*) *v.* To soak (2), drench (23), impregnate, infuse, saturate (139), immerse (256) in liquid, macerate (*măs′-ĕ-rāt*).

The verb, to STEEP, goes back to Middle English, perhaps to Icelandic. There are today in the Scandinavian languages words which can be traced back to the same source.

In the test phrase: 'STEEP his towels anew', the word is thought by 5 per cent of preparatory-school juniors to mean WRING OUT. To WRING is to twist, squeeze tightly. To WRING OUT a cloth is to press water out by twisting or squeezing. To WRING OUT is, in suggestion, an opposite of to STEEP, to soak.

STEEP, DRENCH, and SOAK, are similar in meaning. Things SOAKED or DRENCHED may however be injured in the process. That which is STEEPED is immersed in liquid for a specified time to bring about some desired change, such as to clean, to soften, or more frequently to extract a flavor.

304. *PARRY* (*păr′-rĭ*) *v.* To turn aside, ward off, avert (564), evade, foil, thwart, frustrate.

In the test phrase: 'He PARRIED the blow', the word is thought by 6 per cent of adult readers to mean RETURNED. To RETURN, in this sense, is to assume the offensive. To PARRY is to act on the defensive. To PARRY comes from the Latin *parare*, to prepare, get ready, and, therefore, guard against.

To PARRY and to AVERT are practically synonymous. AVERT is a literal translation of the Latin *a*, away; and *vertere*, to turn; and means to ward off in any sense, as: 'He AVERTED a disaster'. To PARRY is a technical term in fencing, and means to turn aside a thrust. When the word is used figuratively it retains this sense of turning aside an imaginary thrust. Thus: 'One PARRIES an impertinence'.

305. *DEFER* (*dē-fer'*) *v.* To postpone (3), delay (85), put off to another time, stay (259), adjourn, prorogue. To 5 per cent of adult readers DEFER incorrectly means PREVENT. This is perhaps a confusion of DEFER, postpone, with the word DETER, prevent, hinder. DEFER and DELAY are both from the Latin *dis*, away; and *ferre*, to carry. DELAY is from *latus*, the past participle of the verb *ferre*; while DEFER, directly from the verb, and by derivation to carry away, now means put off, postpone.

306. *ABASH* (*ă-băsh'*) *v.* To confuse, embarrass, confound, fluster, discompose, disconcert, put out of countenance. When used in the test phrase: 'He seemed ABASHED', the word, which is probably of Anglo-Saxon origin, is thought by 4 per cent of adult readers to mean SELF-POSSESSED, an exact opposite of the correct meaning.

To CONFUSE, ABASH, and CONFOUND, are three degrees of loss of self-possession. To CONFUSE is the mildest, to CONFOUND is the strongest of the three.

307. *SUPPRESSION* (*sŭp-prĕ'-shŭn*) *n.* Putting down, crushing, subduing, quelling, overpowering, restraint, destruction, putting an end to the activity of. SUPPRESSION is from the Latin *sub*, under; and *pressus*, the past participle of *premere*, to press.

To 3 per cent of adult readers SUPPRESSION incorrectly means MISERY, great unhappiness, extreme pain, anguish. SUPPRESSION is an act. The SUPPRESSION of an individual may cause misery; but the SUPPRESSION of crime, the SUPPRESSION of a nuisance, may be desirable and increase happiness.

SUPPRESSION and REPRESSION, literally a pressing back, differ only slightly. REPRESSION is usually a partial restraining, and may be temporary; while SUPPRESSION is more nearly complete.

308. *OBLIGING* (*ō-blī'-jĭng*) *p. adj.* Accommodating, courteous, kindly, pleasing, compliant (418), complaisant (*kŏm-plā-zănt'*), ready to serve, willing to do favors.

In the test phrase: 'An OBLIGING friend', the word is thought by 15 per cent of grammar-school pupils to mean FAITHFUL; and by another 6 per cent to mean TRUE. Both FAITHFUL and TRUE, as used in this sense, mean loyal, steadfast, firm in holding to friends. Both words express a more lasting devotion than OBLIGING and neither implies specifically the willingness to do small favors inherent in OBLIGING.

309. *FUROR* (*fū'-rŏr*) *n.* Craze, great enthusiasm, mania for something, fuss, ado, overmastering passion for anything, enthusiastic popular admiration.

FUROR comes from the Latin *furere*, to rage, the source of the English words FURY, anger, frenzy, any violent emotion; and FURIOUS, mad, angry, agitated.

Of the three words: FUROR, FURY, and RAGE, the last, RAGE, may be used to mean either angry outburst or temporary enthusiasm. FURY can have only the first meaning, angry outburst, wrath; FUROR can have only the second, temporary enthusiasm.

A FUROR and a CRAZE are practically identical. Both are temporary enthusiasms for something unusual which catches the popular fancy. The word CRAZE is used more often for an enthusiasm displayed by people of fashion, as: 'A CRAZE for old furniture'; FUROR is used of the masses, as: 'The FUROR over a popular hero'.

In the test phrase: 'A sudden FUROR', the word is thought by 3 per cent of college seniors to mean CALM, quiet, stillness, tranquillity, the popular misconception, and an opposite of FUROR, great enthusiasm.

310. *FRICTION* (*frĭk'-shŭn*) *n.* Rubbing, attrition, abrasion, frication, chafing. The word FRICTION is used in mechanics to mean resistance to the relative motion of two surfaces in contact with one another.

FRICTION is from the Latin *frictus*, the past participle of the verb *fricare*, to rub, rub down.

The English word FRICTION may be used in a literal sense to mean resistance, or in a figurative sense with reference to human beings to mean mutual irritation, difficulty, lack of harmony, chafing, fretting.

311. *AGILE* (ă'-jĭl) *adj.* Active, nimble, quick to move,
     lively, alert, brisk, sprightly.
The adjective AGILE, quick and easy in motion, and the corresponding noun AGILITY, nimbleness, are both from the Latin
verb *agere*, to do, act.

312. *ENGROSS* (ĕn-grōs') *v.* To absorb, monopolize, engulf,
     interest deeply, engage completely, occupy wholly, hold
the attention of.
When used as a participial adjective, in the test phrase: 'An
ENGROSSING terror', the word is believed by 5 per cent of
preparatory-school juniors to mean MANY-SIDED.
    ENGROSS is from the same source as the English word
GROSS (745), whole, total, and by derivation means to take
as a whole, entirely.
    ENGROSSING and ABSORBING are practically synonymous. One
is, however, ABSORBED when one is passive, as: 'ABSORBED in
one's thoughts'. One is ENGROSSED when one is active, as:
'ENGROSSED in a pursuit'.

313. *MOROSE* (mō-rōs') *adj.* Sullen, ill-humored, crabbed,
     crusty, surly, gloomy, bitter, unsociable, of sour temper.
To 4 per cent of adult readers MOROSE incorrectly means
SUSPICIOUS, distrustful, fearful, suspecting.
    MOROSE comes from the Latin word, *morosus*, scrupulous,
fastidious; and the word MOROSE once had exactly this meaning
in English. Although this sense is now obsolete, MOROSE, sullen,
suggests the fastidious person who has become soured against
the world.

314. *INCOMMODIOUS* (ĭn-kŏm-mō'-dĭ-ŭs) *adj.* Annoying,
     inconvenient, troublesome, impeding, disadvantageous,
not fitted for easy use.
To 5 per cent of preparatory-school juniors INCOMMODIOUS
incorrectly means DIRTY.
    INCOMMODIOUS and INCONVENIENT are practically synony-
mous. INCONVENIENT, however, comes from the Latin *venire*,
to come, and applies to that which happens at the wrong time,
as: 'An INCONVENIENT caller', one who comes at the wrong
moment. When INCONVENIENT is applied to an object, as: 'An

INCONVENIENT room', it suggests that things are not at hand when wanted. INCOMMODIOUS comes from the Latin *modus*, measure, and by derivation means that which is made to the wrong measure. INCOMMODIOUS is applied, therefore, exclusively to objects, as: 'An INCOMMODIOUS house'.

The difference between the two positive words, CONVENIENT and COMMODIOUS, can be seen clearly in the two phrases: 'A CONVENIENT harbor', one which is at hand when wanted, and 'A COMMODIOUS harbor', one suited to the purposes for which it was designed.

COMMODIOUS has come to be used to mean large, spacious. It can, however, be applied equally well to that which is small but fits its purpose. The negative, INCOMMODIOUS, is used only in this last sense with reference to that which does not fit its purpose.

315. *PREVALENT* (*prĕv'-ā-lĕnt*) *adj.* Widespread, generally seen, in vogue, current, prevailing, predominating, existing widely.

In the test phrase: 'This disease is PREVALENT', the word is thought by 5 per cent of adult readers to mean CHRONIC. CHRONIC comes from the Greek word χρόνος, time, from the same source as CHRONOMETER, an accurate timepiece, watch; and CHRONICLE, a record of events in order of time. CHRONIC means lasting in time, extending in time; PREVALENT, which corresponds to the verb PREVAIL, is from the Latin *prae*, before; and *valere*, to be strong, powerful, able; and now means extending in space, widespread.

PREVALENT and COMMON both mean generally seen; but, correctly used, COMMON should modify persons and things, while PREVALENT should modify opinions, diseases, and intangibles.

In medicine, CHRONIC, lasting, and ACUTE, coming quickly to a crisis, are opposites. In everyday usage, COMMON and RARE are opposites. PREVALENT and LOCAL are opposites. PREVALENT and PROVINCIAL are a pair of contrasting words which can perhaps be remembered more easily because of their similarity in sound. PROVINCIAL means restricted to a particular region or province, local, and in this sense is an opposite of PREVALENT, widespread.

316. *REGENERATION* (rē-jĕn-er-ā'-shŭn) *n.* Rebirth, renewal, reformation, renovation, the act of being born anew, condition of being made over.

The verb, to GENERATE, is from the Latin *generare*, to produce, beget, which in turn comes from the Latin *genus*, a kind, race, family. To GENERATE means to produce, bring into life, cause to exist. To REGENERATE is to give new life to. REGENERATION is the corresponding noun.

317. *SLAKE* (slāk) *v.* To quench (38), assuage, extinguish, gratify, appease, relieve (349), allay (607), abate (664), satisfy, mitigate, ameliorate (792).

In the test phrase: 'He SLAKED his thirst', the word is thought by 5 per cent of adult readers to mean ENDURED. To ENDURE is to put up with, tolerate, practically an opposite of the correct meaning.

The words SLAKE and SLACK are from the same source. To SLAKE is by derivation to make SLACK, slow, sluggish, loose. SLAKE once meant to loosen, slacken, but is now used most frequently to mean render inactive, quench, extinguish, assuage.

318. *TEEM* (tēm) *v.* To abound, swarm, throng, be full, prolific, replete, stocked to overflowing.

In the test phrase: 'TEEMING with ideas', the verb, which is of Anglo-Saxon origin, is thought by 5 per cent of preparatory-school juniors to mean SPEAKING.

TEEMING WITH, REPLETE WITH, and FULL OF, are similar in suggestion. FULL OF is colorless, noncommittal. REPLETE WITH sometimes suggests surfeited, gorged with food. Although the word need not necessarily have this disagreeable suggestion, it always implies completely full. To TEEM originally meant to bring forth young, to bear; and TEEMING WITH always has the suggestion of abundance, prolific with, full of that which has been produced.

319. *CUMBERSOME* (kŭm'-ber-sŭm) *adj.* Burdensome, unwieldy, hampering, unmanageable, cumbrous, clumsy, inconveniently large or heavy.

CUMBERSOME is probably from the Latin *cumulus*, a heap, from the same source as the noun, an ENCUMBRANCE, a burden, impediment; and the verb, to CUMBER, to obstruct the movements of, be an inconvenience to.

The common misconception of CUMBERSOME, held by 4 per cent of adult readers, is FRAGILE, easily broken, brittle, weak; sometimes delicate, slight. A FRAGILE, easily broken, package may be an ENCUMBRANCE, an awkward burden, impediment to progress; the same package may CUMBER one, be an inconvenience. Neither of the words, ENCUMBRANCE nor CUMBER, necessarily implies size. But the word CUMBERSOME always means large; a CUMBERSOME package must be big.

TINY, thought by another 3 per cent to be a synonym of CUMBERSOME, is an exact opposite.

320. *CUNNING* (*kŭn'-nĭng*) *adj.* Tricky, crooked (19), wily, sly, deceiving, crafty, artful, shrewd, astute (746), guileful. 'The foe is CUNNING.'

CUNNING, SLY, and SUBTLE, were all once complimentary words; but all three now suggest concealment in achieving one's ends. Words often tend to become disagreeable in suggestion. The process can be seen underway today. SHARP, for instance, means keen-witted, acute of mind, quick; but a SHARPER is a cheat, tricky gambler. Even the adjective, SHARP, although still used most frequently in the good sense, may mean barely honest, unscrupulous, dishonest.

Of the three words, CUNNING, SLY, and SUBTLE, the last is the least unpleasant. It most frequently modifies human beings, and implies the operation of superior intelligence. The other two, although they may also modify human beings, are used ordinarily in reference to animals. SLY comes from a Scandinavian word meaning wise, knowing; but it has lost entirely this original sense and now suggests meanly crafty, wily. In the United States, CUNNING is applied to a child in a pleasant sense to mean attractive; but ordinarily the word means tricky, crafty, artful.

321. *ECCENTRICITY* (*ĕk-sĕn-trĭs'-ĭ-tĭ*) *n.* A peculiarity, irregularity, oddity, whimsicality, idiosyncrasy (447), crotchet, anomaly (1012).

To 4 per cent of preparatory-school juniors ECCENTRICITY incorrectly means MAGNETISM, the property of attracting certain substances. This is perhaps due to some confusion of ECCEN-TRICITY, peculiarity, with ELECTRICITY, a word which in modern physics is closely associated with magnetism.

ECCENTRICITY is from two Greek words ἐκ, out, and κέντρον, center. The English adjective, CONCENTRIC, is from the same source and means having the same center. An ECCENTRICITY is by derivation a deviation from the center; but the word is always used in the figurative sense to mean a peculiarity.

322. *ANNALS* (*ăn'-năls*) *n.* Chronicles, records, register, history of events arranged by years.

Although the word, ANNALS, is ordinarily used in the plural, the singular, an ANNAL, may be used to mean the record of a single year.

In the test phrase: 'The ANNALS of Rome', the word is thought by 7 per cent of adult readers to mean CALENDAR. The association of the two words is not so remote as one might at first think, for the word CALENDAR may be used for a list of events as in the phrase: 'A court CALENDAR'.

A CALENDAR, an ALMANAC, and an ANNAL, are all arranged on a yearly basis. A CALENDAR is usually a mere list of months and days, but may show holidays, religious festivals, astronomical data such as the phases of the moon, and even important events in various professions. An ALMANAC is a more elaborate list, giving more complete astronomical data, lists of events, and various statistics. An ANNAL is still more complete, but is arranged in much the same manner. The major distinction between the words is that a CALENDAR and an ALMANAC are made up in advance, sometimes many years in advance; while an ANNAL is a record of past events.

ANNALS, CHRONICLES, and HISTORIES, are more nearly akin. The first two are practically identical. A CHRONICLE, which comes from the Greek χρόνος, time, is a record arranged in order of time. ANNALS, which comes from the Latin *annus*, a year, is a record of events arranged by years.

323. *PERJURE* (*per'-jŭr*) *v.* To swear falsely, lie under oath, forswear, bear false witness.

PERJURE is from the Latin *per*, and *jurare*, to swear, the source of the English word JURY, a body of men sworn to give a true verdict; and the more unusual verb to ADJURE, to beseech, beg, entreat, charge earnestly, bind solemnly by oath; and ADJURATION (995), the corresponding noun.

Of the two words, to PERJURE and to FORSWEAR, the last is general. To PERJURE is technical and means to be guilty of swearing falsely to an oath in judicial proceedings. The word is ordinarily used reflexively as: 'The witness PERJURED himself'.

324. BESEECH (bē-sēch') v. To entreat, crave (59), ask (99), implore, solicit (407), beg for, plead, supplicate (872), importune.

The verb, to ASK, is general and conveys no special implications. To BESEECH, to ENTREAT, and to IMPORTUNE, are to ASK with increasing degrees of wearying repetition. One who BESEECHES has need of help, but makes no claims on the one approached. Thus, 'One BESEECHES a favor', 'One BESEECHES aid'. One who ENTREATS, beseeches continuously and pictures the need of help to move the one approached. One who IMPORTUNES is still more persistent, and with less humility.

BESEECH, which is from the same source as the verb to SEEK, is unknown to 12 per cent of adult readers. To OFFER and to SPURN are the two common misconceptions, each held by 4 per cent. Both are opposites of BESEECH. OFFER and BESEECH are opposites in the sense of give and receive; one OFFERS aid with the expectation of giving, one BESEECHES aid with the hope of receiving. SPURN, to reject with disdain, and BESEECH are opposites in the sense of refuse and ask.

325. WEAR (wār) v. To last, hold out, endure, withstand use, resist the waste of time.

The verb, to WEAR, can be used in many ways. One WEARS a coat after putting it on. One WEARS out a coat by using it, uses it up, rubs off its surface, destroys its value. One WEARS a hole through the elbow, makes a hole by rubbing. These phrases are so familiar that one forgets that in them the verb to WEAR has three different senses, each one of which must be learned as if it were a different word.

One intransitive use of the verb is almost an opposite of WEAR out, for to WEAR may mean to last, endure. In this sense, WEAR is generally used in such a phrase as: 'It WEARS well', 'It WEARS badly'. This use of WEAR is unknown to 30 per cent of grammar-school pupils.

In the test phrase: 'The coat WEARS well', the word is thought by 19 per cent to mean FITS. To FIT has as many meanings as to WEAR. Thus, to FIT may mean to make suitable, adapt, adjust, as: 'A tailor FITS a coat to a customer'. In this sense, it is the tailor who FITS, and the customer who WEARS the coat. Another use of to FIT means to be suitable in size and form, be correctly adjusted, commodious, as: 'A coat FITS a person'. In this sense, to FIT well means to be of the right size. To WEAR well means to last, endure.

326. *REPAIR* (rē-pār') v. To go to a place, betake one's self, resort to, have recourse to especially in numbers.

This verb to REPAIR, as: 'They REPAIRED to the house', and the more familiar REPAIR (245), to mend, although spelt and pronounced alike, have perhaps different derivations. REPAIR, meaning to go, is probably from the Latin *re*, back; and *patria*, native land.

327. *VENT* (vĕnt) v. To pour forth, emit, utter, give utterance to, give free expression to, relieve by speech.

A VENT, the noun, is any small hole, usually one through which air may pass. Thus, in a barrel, the hole which allows air in, as liquid is poured out, is a VENT; the fingerholes in wood-wind instruments are VENTS; in foundry practice the holes through which air escapes, as metal is poured into a mold, are VENTS.

To VENT, the verb, is literally to make a hole so that something, which would otherwise be under pressure, can escape. The verb is often used figuratively as: 'They VENTED their rage', 'She VENTED her anger'.

In the test phrase: 'He VENTED his wrath', the word is believed by 6 per cent of adult readers to mean RESTRAINED. VENT and RESTRAIN are practically opposites; although VENT and REPRESS are perhaps more exact opposites.

328. *UTTER* (ŭt'-ter) adj. Extreme, total, complete, final, entire, perfect, unqualified, absolute.

Although at first glance there seems little relation between the adjective UTTER, absolute, and the verb, to UTTER, to say, both come from an Anglo-Saxon word meaning out, outside. The verb to UTTER meant originally to put out, put forth, expel, emit. The adjective UTTER originally meant on the outside, then beyond the limits, and from this has come to mean complete, entire, total, absolute.

329. *RETRACT* (*rē-trăkt'*) *v.* To withdraw, take back, recall, recant (848), revoke.

RETRACT is from the Latin *re*, back; and *trahere*, to draw. From the latter come the words TRACTOR, TRACTION, the act of drawing or pulling, and ATTRACTION.

In the test phrase: 'He RETRACTS his criticism', the word is believed by 4 per cent of adult readers to mean REPEATS, says again, an opposite of the correct meaning.

To another 4 per cent RETRACT means REPENT, regret, sorrow over some past act. The actions of REPENTING and RETRACTING often accompany one another, but the two words are not synonymous. The word REPENT describes a mental act, a silent process within one's own mind, a wishing one had not done something; RETRACT describes an outward act, a verbal process of taking back either in speech or writing. RETRACT may even be used in a purely physical sense as: 'A cat RETRACTS her claws'.

RETRACT, ABJURE, RENOUNCE, and RECANT, all mean to take back, give up something. To RECANT is to take back an opinion or belief, admitting error; it implies the acceptance of the opposite viewpoint. One RECANTS an erroneous belief. To RENOUNCE is to give up publicly, without necessarily changing one's private views. One RENOUNCES one's claims to property. To ABJURE is to forswear, to give up or abandon upon oath. To RETRACT is to take back, give up, but not upon oath.

330. *SAUNTER* (*sawn'-ter*) *v.* To loiter (70), amble, walk idly, wander in a leisurely manner, stroll aimlessly, ramble. The exact derivation of SAUNTER is unknown. There are apparently no other closely related English words.

To SAUNTER and to RAMBLE are both to move without aim. To RAMBLE is to go here and there, in various directions. SAUNTERING is more apt to be in one direction, but slowly.

To 4 per cent of adult readers SAUNTER incorrectly means to STUMBLE, to trip in walking, almost fall; to another 3 per cent it incorrectly means to SKIP, to leap lightly, bound, hop, caper; and to another 2 per cent, to SPEED, an exact opposite of the correct meaning.

331. *PETTY* (*pĕt'-tĭ*) *adj.* Trifling, of small importance, of little worth, trivial, insignificant.

PETTY, in derivation, is closely related to the French word, *petit*, small; and if accented on the second syllable is not very different in pronunciation.

In the test phrase: 'PETTY affairs', the word is thought by 10 per cent of grammar-school pupils to mean IMPORTANT, an exact opposite of the correct meaning.

332. *SINISTER* (*sĭn'-ĭs-ter*) *adj.* Ill-looking, of malignant aspect, wicked, threatening, of evil omen, malicious (549), base, baleful (992).

SINISTER comes from the Latin *sinister*, left, on the left hand. Both SINISTER and DEXTER are still used in heraldry in their literal senses of left and right, as: 'The SINISTER part of a shield', as opposed to the DEXTER, right-hand part. DEXTER has retained some of this literal meaning in the word DEXTEROUS, which originally meant right-handed, but which now means generally clever in the use of the hands.

The literal meaning of SINISTER, left, has practically disappeared, except in heraldry. But the left has, for some reason, always been thought of as unlucky, and it is in this sense that the word, SINISTER, is used most frequently in English to mean ill-omened, malign (598), unlucky.

SINISTER, ill-omened, and AUSPICIOUS, lucky, of good omen, are opposites; for there is no word from DEXTER which means lucky.

333. *UNCOMPROMISING* (*ŭn-kŏm'-prō-mī-zĭng*) *adj.* Inflexible (241), stubborn (266), unyielding (392), decided, obstinate, perverse (1049), not agreeing to terms, giving no concession.

To 5 per cent of adult readers UNCOMPROMISING incorrectly means DISAGREEABLE. This is perhaps a confusion of the words DISAGREEABLE, unpleasant, and DISAGREEING, not agreeing, for an UNCOMPROMISING person refuses to agree to terms.

The noun, a COMPROMISE, is a combination of the Latin *com*, together, and the word PROMISE (*prŏm'-ĭs*), and is by derivation a mutual promise to abide by the decision of an arbiter. UNCOMPROMISING is the opposite and suggests so strong a belief in the rightness of one's cause that one is not willing to compromise.

334. *ANXIOUS* (*ănk'-shŭs*) *adj.* Troubled, uneasy in mind, disturbed, worried, solicitous, concerned, fearful, apprehensive (396). 'He was ANXIOUS.'

ANXIOUS, from the Latin *angere*, to distress, the source of the English words ANGUISH, severe mental pain, and ANGER, applies to a mental, not to a physical, state.

ANXIOUS and APPREHENSIVE both imply uncertainty as to the future. APPREHENSIVE suggests impending evil. ANXIOUS can be used only if there is some hopeful possibility.

APPREHENSIVE and HOPEFUL; ANXIOUS and UNCONCERNED; are opposites.

335. *SULTRY* (*sŭl'-trĭ*) *adj.* Oppressively warm and damp, close, swelteringly hot and moist.

To 3 per cent of adult readers SULTRY incorrectly means DISCOURAGING, disheartening; and to another 3 per cent CLOUDY.

SULTRY, like HUMID and TORRID, is a word used of climate and means at the same time hot and moist, as in the phrase: 'SULTRY air before a storm'. TORRID (485) means hot; HUMID (75) means wet, damp; SULTRY means hot and wet, hot and damp.

336. *UNGAINLY* (*ŭn-gān'-lĭ*) *adj.* Clumsy, awkward, uncouth (710), ill-made, lumbering, not dexterous.

In the test phrase: 'Her UNGAINLY figure', the word is thought by 5 per cent of adult readers to mean LARGE. Although a LARGE person is sometimes UNGAINLY, there is nothing in the word UNGAINLY to suggest size. UNGAINLY is a combination of the Anglo-Saxon *un*, not, and the English word GAINLY, well-formed, shapely, graceful. GAINLY in turn is from an Icelandic word meaning ready, convenient, serviceable. UNGAINLY by derivation means inconvenient, incommodious, not serviceable, the original English meaning of the word. This meaning is obsolete and UNGAINLY now means uncouth, awkward.

337. *GRUDGE* (*grŭdj*) *n.* Ill will, malice (391), rancor (693), animosity (764), spite, long-standing dislike, secret enmity. The verb to GRUDGE, also written BEGRUDGE (446), may mean to envy one the possession of.

In the test phrase: 'An ancient GRUDGE', the word is thought by 6 per cent of adult readers to mean WRONG, hurt, harm, injury. WRONG and GRUDGE may be associated as cause and effect. A WRONG done is often the cause of a GRUDGE, ill feeling.

338. *SUPERCILIOUS* (*sū-per-sĭl′-ĭ-ŭs*) *adj.* Arrogant, overbearing, haughty, disdainful (454), insolently superior, contemptuously indifferent.

SUPERCILIOUS is from the Latin *supercilium*, eyebrow, which in turn comes from *super*, over, and *cilium*, eyelid. SUPERCILIOUS by derivation suggests the lifted eyebrow.

339. *PREEMINENT* (*prē-ĕm′-ĭ-nĕnt*) *adj.* Outstanding (179), supreme (243), unique (494), surpassing others, superior in excellence, eminent beyond all others.

PREEMINENT is a combination of the Latin *prae*, before, and EMINENT. EMINENT in turn is from the Latin *e*, out; and *minere*, to project, jut, the source of the words IMMINENT (521), threatening, impending, and PROMINENT, outstanding. PREEMINENT is strikingly eminent.

340. *CULINARY* (*kū′-lĭ-nā-rĭ*) *adj.* Of cooking, pertaining to the kitchen, to the preparation of food by heat.

CULINARY is probably from a Latin word *culina*, kitchen; but, with the possible exception of KILN (*kĭl*), a furnace for baking, there are no other common English words from the same source.

In the test phrase: 'Imparting CULINARY mysteries', the word is thought by 4 per cent of preparatory-school juniors to mean DEEP; and by another 3 per cent to mean UNMENTIONABLE. CULINARY is always used in a pleasant sense. 'The CULINARY art' is the art of good cooking; 'CULINARY secrets' are the secrets of good cooking.

341. *SACERDOTAL* (*săs-er-dō′-tăl*, not *săk-er-dŏt′-ăl*) *adj.* Priestly, holy (15), pertaining to priests or to the priesthood, presbyterial, pertaining to one who offers sacrifice.

The first part of the word SACERDOTAL comes from the same source as SACRIFICE (359) and SACRED, hallowed, made holy, consecrated to religious use. The second part comes from the Latin *dare*, to give, the source of the English word DOT (*dŏt*, not *dōt*), a marriage gift, dowry. SACERDOTAL by derivation means bestowing a sacred gift.

In the test phrase: 'SACERDOTAL rites', the word is thought by 4 per cent of adult readers to mean BLASPHEMOUS (*blăs'-fē-mŭs*), the popular misconception. BLASPHEMOUS means irreverent, impious (*ĭm'-pĭ-ŭs*), using profane language. BLAS-PHEMOUS, which comes from a Greek word meaning to speak, utter, applies only to that which is spoken, to profane language, but in suggestion is an opposite of SACERDOTAL, priestly.

A PRIEST, a DIVINE, a MINISTER, and a CLERGYMAN, are all religious workers. The word CLERGYMAN is general, generic, and includes all persons in holy orders. A MINISTER or PASTOR looks after the spiritual welfare of his congregation. A DIVINE is learned in the Scriptures. A PRIEST is appointed to offer sacrifice, the distinguishing rite of the priesthood. Properly used, SACERDOTAL applies only to priestly functions, and not to any pastoral or intellectual activities of the clergy.

342. *RECURRENT* (*rē-ker'-rĕnt*) *adj.* Reappearing, fre-
    quently used, returning from time to time, repeating
itself.

To 6 per cent of adult readers RECURRENT incorrectly means WELL-KNOWN. This is probably a confusion of RECURRENT, oft-repeated, with CURRENT, in general use, common, prevalent (315), a word which comes from the Latin *currere*, to run. The noun, a CURRENT, as applied to electricity, means the flow of electricity through a conducting body. The CURRENT of a stream is its flow, running. CURRENT, the adjective, once meant literally running, flowing, but is now used only in the figura-tive sense with reference to something which is running from one person to another, and is, therefore, widely used, general, prevalent.

RECURRENT, from the Latin *re*, back; and the same *currere*, to run; by derivation means running back. The word is used today, however, in a more figurative sense to mean returning from time to time, reappearing after an interval, recurring.

343. *BARRISTER* (*băr'-rĭs-ter*) *n.* A lawyer, advocate, counselor entitled to plead at the bar.

To 8 per cent of preparatory-school juniors the word BARRISTER incorrectly means GUARD, perhaps a confusion of BARRISTER, lawyer, with BARRIER, an obstacle, rail, bar placed across an opening to stop progress.

A BARRISTER is always a lawyer of some sort, but the exact technical significance of the word varies in different countries. The word is seldom used in the United States. In England, a SOLICITOR prepares a case, but he is not admitted to plead it. It is the BARRISTER, especially in the higher courts, who pleads it at the bar.

344. *DETONATION* (*dĕt-ō-nă'-shŭn*) *n.* Violent explosion, loud and sudden report.

To 4 per cent of adult readers DETONATION incorrectly means ACCENT, stress, emphasis. This is probably a confusion of DETONATION, explosion, with INTONATION, mode of enunciation, modulation of the voice in speaking. Both INTONATION and DETONATION come from the Latin *tonare*, to thunder. The DE of the latter intensifies the meaning.

An EXPLOSION may be a relatively slow expansion, as the explosion which pushes the piston in the cylinder of an automobile engine. A DETONATION is an explosion of the first order, so violent that it shatters.

345. *ELUSORY* (*ē-lū'-sō-rĭ*, not *ē-lū'-zō-rĭ*) *adj.* Deceitful, fallacious, baffling, illusive, artfully deceptive.

The verbs, ALLUDE, DELUDE, ELUDE, and ILLUDE, all from the Latin verb *ludere*, to play, are difficult to differentiate clearly. To ALLUDE, by derivation to play at, is to refer to casually, indirectly, incidentally, to play at referring to something rather than to cite it directly. 'He ALLUDED to the incident.' To DELUDE is to deceive the mind of another, mislead the judgment, beguile, and is closely associated with the noun DELUSION. ELUDE, by derivation to play out of, is to evade, dodge, escape, keep clear of, avoid by artifice, as: 'He ELUDED pursuit'. The verb ILLUDE, by derivation to play on, is seldom used but means to play upon, play tricks on, mock, cheat, trick, to deceive with false appearance. ILLUDE differs from DELUDE much as an ILLUsion (495), a momentary false conception, differs from a DELUSION, a fixed false conception.

The adjectives are almost impossible to keep clear. ELUSIVE is evasive (464), tending to slip away. ELUSORY on the other hand is synonymous with ILLUSIVE, deceitful.

346. *DREARY* (*drēr'-ĭ*) *adj.* Gloomy, dismal, cheerless, forlorn, desolate, lonely. DREARY may also mean tiresomely monotonous, although this sense is rare.

DREAR is a poetical abbreviation of DREARY, with the same meanings.

DREARY is from an Anglo-Saxon word meaning sad, mournful. It is interesting that in the test phrase: 'A DREARY prospect', the word is interpreted by 9 per cent of adult readers as meaning FATIGUING, tiring, wearying, exhausting, monotonous, tedious, the unusual sense; rather than gloomy, dismal, the more common meaning.

To 4 per cent of adult readers the poetical form DREAR incorrectly means INTERMINABLE, endless, unceasing, continuing for a long time, limitless. This is probably a misinterpretation of the word INTERMINABLE, so often used with reference to a tiresomely monotonous task. INTERMINABLE, however, comes from the Latin *terminus*, end, limit, and means literally without end. Both INTERMINABLE and DREAR may be applied, with something of the same suggestion, to an unpleasant task. But DREAR may also be used of situations to which INTERMINABLE is inapplicable, as: 'A DREAR house', 'A DREAR scene'.

347. *PECUNIARY* (*pē-kū'-nĭ-ā-rĭ*) *adj.* Of money, financial, relating to money, monetary.

To 4 per cent of preparatory-school juniors PECUNIARY incorrectly means STRANGE. This is probably a confusion of PECUNIARY, financial, with PECULIAR, a word which may mean strange, queer, odd, singular. Both PECULIAR and PECUNIARY come probably from the same Latin word *pecus*, a herd of cattle. The word PECULIAR comes from the fact that a herd of cattle was one's own private property; and the fundamental meaning of the word PECULIAR in English today is one's own, personal, individual. From this it has come to mean singular, individual, different from others, queer, odd, strange. The word PECUNI-

ARY has developed from the fact that a herd of cattle represented wealth, money. PECUNIARY comes directly from the Latin word *pecunia*, money, riches, wealth, a word which originally meant wealth in cattle.

PECUNIARY and FINANCIAL are synonymous but differ slightly in their implications. A FINANCIAL interest is merely one which involves money. The word PECUNIARY, in such a phrase as: 'A PECUNIARY interest', implies that one is interested in personal gain.

348. *INCONGRUOUS* (*ĭn-kŏn'-grū-ŭs*) *adj.* Unsuitable, inappropriate, inconsistent, conflicting, clashing, absurd, not in harmony.

The three words, INCONGRUOUS, INCONSISTENT, and INCOMPATIBLE, all mean not agreeing, not in harmony. The last is used with reference to personalities, as: 'INCOMPATIBLE temperaments'. INCONSISTENT is used with reference to that which does not come up to a standard, as: 'An action INCONSISTENT with one's position'. INCONGRUOUS, a combination of the Latin *in*, not, and *congruere*, to agree, differs in suggesting a lack of agreement apt to produce an unexpected, absurd, ridiculous effect. It is probably this aspect of the word which leads 5 per cent of college seniors to believe that INCONGRUOUS means SILLY, foolish, fatuous.

COMPATIBLE and INCOMPATIBLE; CONSISTENT and INCONSISTENT; CONGRUOUS and INCONGRUOUS; are opposites.

349. *RELIEVE* (*rē-lēv'*) *v.* To lessen, lighten, ease, mitigate, slake (317), alleviate (575), allay (607), abate (664), ameliorate (792), render less burdensome.

RELIEVE is from two Latin words, *re*, again; and *levis*, light; and by derivation means to lighten again. It is from the same source as LEVITY (954), lightness of spirit.

In the test phrase: 'It RELIEVES pain', the word is thought by 9 per cent of grammar-school pupils to mean PREVENTS. PREVENT is from two Latin words, *prae*, before; and *venire*, to come; and by derivation means to come before. It was once used in English in this literal sense to mean precede. To PREVENT now means to stop beforehand, hinder from happening. 'To PREVENT suffering' is to take steps in advance in order to avoid it, forestall it. 'To RELIEVE suffering' is to reduce, lessen, that which already exists.

350. *COPE* (*kōp*) *v.* To strive, contend adequately, match, equal, oppose on equal terms.

The derivation of COPE is difficult to follow, but the word can be traced back at least to Middle English.

When used in the test phrase: 'He can COPE with his enemies', the word is thought by 4 per cent of adult readers to mean WORK. To WORK WITH, in this sense, implies cooperating with, getting along with. To COPE WITH is to struggle with successfully, contend with adequately, succeed in resisting, to some extent an opposite of WORK WITH.

351. *CLING* (*klĭng*) *v.* To hold fast, maintain a grasp, adhere closely, cleave.

CLING is from Anglo-Saxon words meaning to hold in, surround, and is perhaps ultimately from the same source as CLIMB and CLAMBER. ADHERE is from an Anglo-Saxon word meaning to stick. This difference in derivation still distinguishes the present-day use of these two words. Something fastened by glue may be said to ADHERE. ADHESIVE tape is sticky, glutinous. That which CLINGS does so by wrapping itself about something else, as: 'A CLINGING vine'.

352. *PROBATIONARY* (*prō-bā'-shŭn-ā-rĭ*) *adj.* Trial, proving, serving for a test, pertaining to probation. The noun, PROBATION, means a trial period, any procedure which tests one's character or ability, a trial, test, act of proving, as: 'A boy freed on PROBATION', on trial. PROBATIONARY is the corresponding adjective.

By 5 per cent of adult readers, PROBATIONARY is thought to mean HONORARY, in suggestion an opposite of the correct meaning. An HONORARY member is one upon whom membership has been conferred in recognition of distinguished attainments. A PROBATIONARY member has been accepted on trial only.

353. *POTENTATE* (*pō'-těn-tāt*) *n.* A ruler, sovereign (277), monarch, person who possesses great power.

To 5 per cent of preparatory-school juniors POTENTATE incorrectly means POWER-HOUSE. This misconception can perhaps be traced back to the Latin word *potent*, powerful, the source of both POTENTATE and POTENT. The English word POTENT means either powerful in the sense of physically strong, or powerful in the sense of having great authority. The English word POTENTATE can be used only in the last sense to mean one who has great authority.

A POTENTATE, a MONARCH, and a SOVEREIGN, are all rulers. Of the three, a SOVEREIGN is the only one who necessarily inherits his power; a SOVEREIGN is always an hereditary ruler. The word MONARCH by derivation means ruling alone; a MONARCH must have undivided power. The word POTENTATE suggests, more than the others, the relation of the ruler to other nations or powers.

354. *INVULNERABLE* (*ĭn-vŭl'-ner-ā-bl*) *adj.* Unassailable, safe, secure, protected, unimpeachable (476), incapable of being wounded, not open to injury or criticism.
INVULNERABLE is from the Latin *in*, not; and *vulnerare*, to wound, hurt. The word is perhaps distantly related etymologically to VULTURE, a bird of prey.

355. *SCOPE* (*skōp*) *n.* Extent, range of view, outlook, sweep, field, latitude (751), sphere of action, reach, capacity.
SCOPE is from the Greek σκοπός, a mark to aim at; and is related to the Latin *specere*, to see. In English the word originally had the literal meaning of the Greek, a mark to shoot at, but this meaning is now obsolete. The word then came to mean an end or aim kept in mind; and from this, by a slight shift in meaning, it came to mean outlook, intellectual range of view, as in the phrase: 'A mind of great SCOPE'.
In the test phrase: 'Of wide SCOPE', the word is thought by 5 per cent of adult readers to mean INFLUENCE, ability to sway others, power to produce effects. A man's INFLUENCE, power, may be great, but of limited SCOPE, range.

356. *DIVERS* (*dī'-verz*) *adj.* More than one or two, a few, several, sundry (735). DIVERS can modify only a plural noun, as in the phrases: 'DIVERS opinions', 'DIVERS ways'. DIVERS and DIVERSE (*dī-vers'*) were once synonymous. They

are perhaps different spellings of the same word. DIVERSE now means different in kind, various, essentially different. This meaning of DIVERS is obsolete; and DIVERS can now mean only several in number without implying different in kind.

357. *ASTRAL* (*ăs'-trăl*) *adj.* Stellar, starry, siderial, pertaining to the stars.

To 5 per cent of adult readers ASTRAL incorrectly means FLORAL, pertaining to flowers. The common botanical name ASTER, an autumn flower, a plant which blooms in the late fall; and ASTRAL, starry, both come directly from the Greek ἀστήρ, star. ASTRAL means literally of the stars, pertaining to the stars. From the same Greek word comes the English word ASTRONOMY, a study of the stars.

To another 4 per cent ASTRAL incorrectly means PECULIAR, strange, odd. This is perhaps because of the use of the word ASTRAL in occult studies to characterize ethereal, spiritual bodies, as in the phrase: 'An ASTRAL body'. In this use, ASTRAL has almost a scientific exactness. Ordinarily, ASTRAL means merely pertaining to the stars.

358. *PRIMITIVE* (*prĭm'-ĭ-tĭv*) *adj.* Pertaining to early times, ancient, original, primeval, first, rudimentary (370), pristine, primordial.

In the test phrase: 'PRIMITIVE tribes', the word is thought by 10 per cent of grammar-school pupils to mean WARLIKE, hostile; and by another 7 per cent to mean FRIENDLY, amicable, the opposite of WARLIKE, the two popular misconceptions.

PRIMITIVE and PRIMEVAL both come from the same Latin word, *primus*, the superlative of *pro*, before. PRIMEVAL means early in time, belonging to the first ages. A PRIMEVAL civilization dates from an early time, is of an early era. A PRIMITIVE civilization may exist today; but it must have the characteristics of early times.

359. *SACRIFICE* (*săk'-rĭ-fīs*) *n.* A self-denial, immolation, offering, the giving up of something, a loss incurred by devotion to some interest; more specifically an offering made to a deity, oblation.

In the test phrase: 'He made SACRIFICES', the word is thought by 6 per cent of adult readers to mean AMENDS, restitution, compensation, repayment.

Although the noun, and the verb to SACRIFICE, to give up, are spelt alike, the verb is usually pronounced (*săk'-rĭ-fīz*), with a z sound, while the noun is pronounced with an s sound.

360. *MEDIOCRE* (*mē-dĭ-ō'-ker*) *adj.* Ordinary, indifferent, commonplace, having only a moderate degree of excellence, middling, second-rate.

By 4 per cent of college seniors, MEDIOCRE is thought to mean BACKWARD, dull, slow to understand. The word MEDIOCRE suggests inferiority, but it is an inferiority due to the lack of any distinguishing characteristic. BACKWARDNESS, lack of intelligence, keeps one from being MEDIOCRE.

MEDIOCRE and the corresponding noun MEDIOCRITY come from the Latin *medius*, middle, from the same source as the English word MEDIUM, lying in the middle. One can, however, say: 'A man of MEDIUM height', meaning average, with no suggestion of disparagement, of detraction, of belittling him; while the word MEDIOCRE always has the suggestion of ordinary, commonplace, second-rate.

361. *SUBSTRATUM* (*sŭb-strā'-tŭm*, not *sŭb-străt'-ŭm*) *n.* The lower layer, something spread under, an under stratum.

To 5 per cent of preparatory-school juniors, SUBSTRATUM incorrectly means SUBSTITUTE, an understudy, a person or thing performing a function in place of another.

SUBSTRATUM comes from the Latin *sub*, under; and *sternere*, to spread, extend. In Latin, the word *stratum* means a spread for a bed, quilt, blanket, coverlet. In English, a STRATUM is a layer of any material; the word is used largely in the sciences, in geology and zoology.

362. *PRECARIOUS* (*prē-kā'-rĭ-ŭs*) *adj.* Uncertain, insecure, unstable, risky, perilous, hazardous, depending upon the will of another, of doubtful issue.

In the test phrase: 'His situation was PRECARIOUS', the word is thought by 6 per cent of adult readers to mean UNPLEASANT.

The adjective, PRECARIOUS; the adverb, PRECARIOUSLY; and the noun, PRECARIOUSNESS; all come from the Latin *precari*, to pray. PRECARIOUS means by derivation dependent upon prayer, and therefore liable to be withdrawn.

PRECARIOUS and HAZARDOUS both mean uncertain. HAZARDOUS means dangerous, risky, perilous, because dependent upon the laws of chance; PRECARIOUS means uncertain, insecure, because dependent upon the will of another.

PRECARIOUS and SECURE are opposites.

363. *PLEDGE* (*plĕdj*) *v.* To pawn, mortgage, deposit as security. To PLEDGE may also mean to promise, plight (860), undertake to give, guarantee.

When the verb to PLEDGE is used to mean give as security, as in the phrase: 'He PLEDGED it', it is thought by 6 per cent of adult readers to mean EXCHANGED. To PLEDGE and to EXCHANGE both mean to give something in return for something else. The word EXCHANGE suggests a permanent transfer of ownership, as: 'One may EXCHANGE one article for another'. The word to PLEDGE suggests a temporary transfer of ownership, as: 'One may PLEDGE an article as security that what one has taken in exchange will be returned'.

To another 5 per cent of adult readers, to PLEDGE means to SECURE, to make safe, ensure the payment of. A banker SECURES his loan, that is, makes it safe by demanding a PLEDGE.

The original meaning of the verb to PLEDGE is to give a pledge, to promise; but even in this sense to PLEDGE is generally used with the underlying suggestion of offering something as security, as in the phrases: 'I PLEDGE my vow', 'I PLEDGE myself'.

364. *ECCLESIASTIC* (*ĕk-klē-zĭ-ăs'-tĭk*) *n.* Clergyman, person in holy orders, priest; any dignitary who performs a function of the church service.

ECCLESIASTIC is from the Greek word ἐκκλησιάζειν, meaning to sit in the assembly. It is from the same source as ECCLESIA, which means an assembly, specifically the great assembly of the people at Athens in ancient Greece in which every free citizen had a right to vote.

An ECCLESIASTIC is thought by 5 per cent of preparatory-school juniors to be a FANATIC. FANATIC is from the Latin *fanum*, a temple, and a FANATIC is an enthusiast, a zealot, bigot. The word was originally applied, as its derivation indicates, to zeal in religion, but the word has come to be used more generally and is applied to anyone with extreme ideas on any subject. The word ECCLESIASTIC means merely a clergyman, not necessarily one with wild or extravagant ideas.

365. *REPUTE* (*rē-pūt'*) *n.* Standing (183), reputation, character, established position, character attributed; sometimes specifically good character.

REPUTE comes from the Latin *putare*, a word which originally meant to clean, but which later came to mean to think.

When used in the test phrase: 'A man of REPUTE', the word is believed by 6 per cent of adult readers to mean POWER, strength. REPUTE may mean reputation, either good or bad; or it may mean specifically good reputation, when DISREPUTE is its opposite.

366. *CONDOLE* (*kŏn-dōl'*) *v.* To sympathize, lament with, commiserate (851), speak compassionately, express sorrow for the misfortune of another.

In the test phrase: 'CONDOLE with them', the word is thought by 5 per cent of preparatory-school juniors to mean PLAN; and by another 5 per cent to mean DISCUSS. These confusions may be due to the prefix CON, with, which appears at the beginning of such words as, CONFER, CONSULT, CONVERSE, all of which mean, loosely, talk together, discuss, plan.

CONDOLE is from the Latin *con*, with; and *dolere*, to grieve. It is from the same source as a large group of English words implying sorrow, such as: DOLEFUL (*dōl'-fŭl*), sorrowful; DOLOROUS (*dŏl'-er-ŭs*), dismal, arousing sorrow, mournful; and the more unusual word DOLE, grief, lamentation, a word now used only poetically. To CONDOLE and to SYMPATHIZE are sometimes synonymous. To SYMPATHIZE is general and by derivation is to feel with, occasionally even to agree with. To CONDOLE is literally to grieve with.

367. *STEALTHY* (*stĕl'-thĭ*) *adj.* Furtive, sly, secret (5), clandestine (455), covert, surreptitious.

STEALTHY is of Anglo-Saxon origin. To 5 per cent of adult readers the word incorrectly means RAPID, quick, speedy. Although STEALTHY does not actually mean slow, it suggests movement which is gradual, quiet, imperceptible; and in this sense is almost an opposite of RAPID.

368. *RETENTION* (*rē-tĕn'-shŭn*) *n*. Keeping in one's possession, retaining, keeping in mind, memory.
RETENTION is from the Latin *re*, back; and *tenere*, to hold. It is the noun which corresponds to the verb to RETAIN, to keep. To 3 per cent of preparatory-school juniors, RETENTION incorrectly means DISCARDING, an exact opposite.

369. *TITTER* (*tĭt'-ter*) *n*. A foolish hysterical giggle (44), snicker, silly half-suppressed laugh.
TITTER is thought by 7 per cent of adult readers to mean CHATTERING. Although the word comes from a Middle English word which meant to chatter, a TITTER is today always a laugh.

370. *RUDIMENTARY* (*rū-dĭ-mĕn'-tā-rĭ*) *adj*. Undeveloped, elementary, embryonic, initial, incipient, primitive (358), inchoate (1117).
RUDIMENTARY is the adjective which corresponds to the slightly more familiar noun RUDIMENT (279). In the test phrase: 'A RUDIMENTARY tale', meaning an undeveloped one, the word is thought by 6 per cent of adult readers to mean ARTIFICIAL (482), produced by art rather than by nature.
The adjectives RUDIMENTARY and PRIMITIVE have much in common. Both PRIMITIVE and RUDIMENTARY ideas exist today. PRIMITIVE ones are those which might have characterized early man. RUDIMENTARY ones are in process of formation. The first concepts of a new science are RUDIMENTARY, crude.

371. *EQUIVALENT* (*ē-kwĭv'-ā-lĕnt*) *adj*. Same in effect, equal in value, alike in meaning.
In the test phrase: 'EQUIVALENT to success', the word is thought by 12 per cent of grammar-school pupils to mean RELATED, connected, allied, akin.
EQUIVALENT comes from two Latin words, *aequus*, equal; and *valere*, to be strong, have power; and by derivation means having equal power.
EQUIVALENT, IDENTICAL, and ALIKE, refer to things which are the same. ALIKE is the general term and may refer to things

which are exactly alike; or to things which are only partially alike; or alike in some respect. IDENTICAL can be used only in reference to things which are exactly alike. The word EQUIVALENT implies that the things to which it refers are not identical, are not alike in every respect, but are alike in effect, in significance, in force, or in power.

372. *BASIC* (*bā'-sĭk*) *adj.* Fundamental, elementary, essential, primary, cardinal, relating to the starting point. 'The BASIC truth.'

BASIC is derived from the Greek word βάσις, a pedestal, base. OBVIOUS, easily understood, is the popular misconception. BASIC, fundamental, principles are not necessarily OBVIOUS, easily understood. This confusion of the BASIC, fundamental, with the OBVIOUS, is similar to that which will later be found in the case of the word SIGNIFICANT (748), meaningful, weighty, important, momentous, which is thought by 18 per cent of readers to mean CONSPICUOUS, obvious.

373. *DEBATABLE* (*dē-bā'-tă-bl*) *adj.* Questionable, controvertible, unsettled, moot, open to dispute, capable of being discussed, subject to controversy. 'DEBATABLE statements.'

The adjective, DEBATABLE, and the verb, to DEBATE, come from the Latin *de*, down; and *batuere*, to beat. To DEBATE, to argue, discuss, is by derivation to beat down.

The noun, a DEBATE, is an argument for and against, a discussion usually of an abstract subject. DEBATABLE is the adjective, and means capable of being discussed, subject to argument.

DEBATABLE and INCONTROVERTIBLE (416) are opposites.

374. *MALADY* (*măl'-ă-dĭ*) *n.* Disease, ailment, sickness, illness, indisposition, infirmity (622), complaint.

MALADY, which is from the Latin *malus*, bad, is used especially of a deep-seated, lingering, physical disorder.

375. *INSIPID* (*ĭn-sĭp'-ĭd*) *adj.* Tasteless, flavorless, without savor, flat, uninteresting.

INSIPID is from the Latin *in*, not; and *sapidus*, having savor.

SAPID (*săp'-ĭd*), savory, having taste or flavor, is an unusual
English word but in good repute.

In the test phrase: 'The tea is INSIPID', the word is thought
by 5 per cent of adult readers to mean SWEET, the popular
misconception. Although one ordinarily thinks of SWEET as
meaning sugary, the word comes from the Greek ἥδεσθαι,
pleasant, to be pleased. One need only think of the word
SWEET as applied to sounds, sights, odors, or manners, to realize
that it does not always mean sugary. SWEET, meaning pleasant,
is almost an opposite of INSIPID, especially when, as occasionally
happens, INSIPID suggests slightly disagreeable.

376. *PILFERER* (*pĭl'-fer-er*) *n.* A thief, one who practices
     petty theft, one who steals in small quantities, purloiner,
peculator.

The verb, to PILFER, and the noun, a PILFERER, are from the
same Old French source as PELF (918), an English word which
means riches, money, 'filthy lucre'.

To 7 per cent of preparatory-school juniors PILFERER incorrectly means BEGGAR. This confusion may perhaps be due to
the familiar line: 'Rich man, poor man, beggar man, thief', in
which BEGGAR and THIEF, pilferer, are closely associated. There
is nothing in the word BEGGAR which implies robbing, stealing,
pilfering.

A PILFERER, a ROBBER, and a THIEF, all take other people's
property; a THIEF takes it without their knowledge; a ROBBER
takes it openly; a PILFERER takes it in small amounts by stealth.

377. *ANTEDILUVIAN* (*ăn-tē-dĭ-lū'-vĭ-ăn*) *adj.* Existing be-
     fore the flood. ANTEDILUVIAN is also used figuratively to
mean very old, ancient, primitive (358).

ANTEDILUVIAN comes from the Latin *ante*, before; and *dilu-
vium*, flood; and means literally before the flood, specifically
before the flood in Noah's time, described in the first book
of the Old Testament, Genesis. ANTEDILUVIAN is also used
to mean before any great flood, deluge.

378. *LUDICROUS* (*lū'-dĭ-krŭs*) *adj.* Comical, absurd, laugh-
     able, droll, ridiculous, burlesque, risible (*rĭz'-ĭ-bl*) (1031).
To 4 per cent of preparatory-school juniors LUDICROUS incor-

rectly means SENSELESS. NONSENSE is senseless talk, words without meaning, absurd language, twaddle; and the adjective NONSENSICAL means absurd, foolish, ridiculous, and is a synonym of LUDICROUS. But the word SENSELESS, although it also means without sense, is used only with an unpleasant connotation to mean incapable of sensation, without understanding, foolishly stupid, unwise, ill-judged.

LUDICROUS is a delightful word. It comes from the Latin *ludere*, to play; and has not even the unpleasant suggestion of such a word as RIDICULOUS, apt to imply a contemptuous, derisive (*dē-rĭ'-sĭv*), attitude. In this respect, LUDICROUS is like FUNNY and COMICAL, but stronger than either.

379. *AGGRESSION* (*ăg-grĕsh'-ŭn*) *n.* Assault, invasion, unprovoked attack, unwarranted encroachment upon the rights of others.

The corresponding adjective, AGGRESSIVE, has come to mean self-assertive, pushing, almost enterprising; but the noun AGGRESSION has kept its original meaning of unprovoked attack.

To 6 per cent of adult readers, AGGRESSION incorrectly means GREED, great hunger, covetous desire, acquisitiveness, avarice, cupidity.

To another 4 per cent AGGRESSION means MARCH, a literal translation of the Latin *ad*, to; and *gradi*, to walk; the source of the word AGGRESSION. The English word PROGRESSION, from the Latin *pro*, forward; and the same *gradi*, to walk; means advance, moving forward; but AGGRESSION always means an unprovoked attack, assault, invasion.

380. *LEPROSY* (*lĕp'-rō-sĭ*) *n.* A chronic infectious incurable skin disease.

To 4 per cent of preparatory-school juniors LEPROSY incorrectly means APPEARANCE. This is perhaps because one of the manifestations of the disease is an abnormal white appearance of the skin, caused by scales from which the disease derives its name; for it comes from the Greek word λέπος, scale.

381. *AFFIDAVIT* (*ăf-fĭ-dā'-vĭt*) *n.* A sworn statement, written declaration made on oath for use as judicial proof.

AFFIDAVIT comes from the Latin *affidare*, to make oath, the source of the English verb, to AFFIANCE (*ăf-fī'-ăns*), to betroth, to bind by promise of marriage. The Latin *affidare* comes in turn from *fides*, the source of the English word FIDELITY, faithfulness, truth, veracity. An AFFIDAVIT is a written statement which is sworn to be true.

382. *QUAINT* (*kwānt*) *adj.* Odd (90), unusual in a pleasing way, curious, antique and dainty, attractively old-fashioned.

To 8 per cent of adult readers QUAINT incorrectly means SIMPLE. In the complexities of modern life that which is SIMPLE often seems old-fashioned, curious, quaint; but there is nothing inherent in the word QUAINT to suggest simplicity.

383. *QUAIL* (*kwāl*) *v.* To cower, cringe, flinch, tremble, shrink, lose heart, give way through fear.

In the test phrase: 'They QUAIL before the enemy', the word is thought by 11 per cent of adult readers to mean RETREAT. To RETREAT is to retire, withdraw, give way in the physical sense of turning around and marching or running back. To QUAIL is to give way to fear, lose courage. To QUAIL does not imply physical retreat. On the other hand, an obsolete meaning of QUAIL is to yield, fail, give way, in a sense very close to retreat. Surprisingly often the popular misconception of a word can be justified historically. Why this should be is a moot question. Perhaps obsolete meanings survive in popular speech after they have been discarded by dictionaries. Certainly most of those who believe QUAIL to mean RETREAT do not know the historical connection between the words.

The word QUAIL was popular in the 16th century and was then not used for two hundred years. It was called obsolete in dictionaries until revived in the 19th century.

384. *REQUISITION* (*rĕk-wĭ-zĭ'-shŭn*) *n.* A demand, the act of requiring, usually a formal, written demand; especially an authoritative order for supplies.

REQUISITION is from the Latin *re*, again; and *quaerere*, to ask, seek; the source of the English word QUESTION. From *quaerere* come also the noun a REQUISITE, a necessity, something which is indispensable; and the verbs to REQUEST and to REQUIRE.

To REQUIRE may mean to need, want, but may also mean to demand, claim, ask for, insist on having. REQUISITION is the noun, a formal demand.

385. *CHASTITY* (*chăs'-tĭ-tĭ*) *n.* Purity (601), chasteness, virtue, immaculateness, continence, freedom from depravity, moral cleanliness.

CHASTITY is thought by 7 per cent of adult readers to mean EMBELLISHMENT; and the corresponding, but more difficult, adjective CHASTE (789), pure, virtuous, simple, is thought by 21 per cent of preparatory-school juniors to mean EXTRAVAGANT. This confusion between the idea of CHASTITY, purity, and that of decoration may be due to some confusion of CHASTE, pure, with the word CHASED, decorated, which is discussed under CHASTE (789); or it may be due to a confusion of a word with its opposite. An EMBELLISHMENT is an ornament, decoration; or an EMBELLISHMENT may be an enrichment, adornment. The adjective, CHASTE, is employed in art and literature to mean simple, free from elaborate ornaments. Although in this sense the noun is usually CHASTENESS, CHASTITY may be used in the same way to mean simplicity, refinement of style, freedom from excessive ornamentation. In this sense CHASTE and EMBELLISHED are opposites; while CHASTITY and the plural, EMBELLISHMENTS, are practically opposites, as in the phrases: 'The EMBELLISHMENTS of his style', 'The CHASTITY or CHASTENESS of his style'.

This use of CHASTITY with reference to style in art or writing is, however, figurative and rare. Ordinarily CHASTITY means moral cleanliness, sexual purity, virtue.

CHASTITY and WANTONNESS are opposites.

386. *IMMACULATE* (*ĭm-măk'-ū-lāt*) *adj.* Unspotted, pure, clean, chaste (789), without blemish.

The corresponding noun, IMMACULATENESS (*ĭm-măk'-ū-lāt-nĕs*), is synonymous with CHASTITY (385).

IMMACULATE comes from the Latin *in*, not; and *macula*, a spot; and means by derivation spotless. The word MACULA is used today in various sciences to mean a spot, blotch, fleck. It is probably the source of the word MACKEREL, a kind of fish, even though the common mackerel is striped rather than spotted. IMMACULATE means literally not spotted, not blotched, not stained.

387. *HAPLESS* (*hăp′-lĕs*) *adj.* Unfortunate (13), unlucky, unhappy, disastrous, ill-starred, unsuccessful, ill-fated. In the test phrase: 'HAPLESS lot', the word is thought by 5 per cent of adult readers to mean ODD. ODD may mean strange, peculiar; or it may mean casual, incidental. This is perhaps a confusion of HAPLESS, unlucky, with HAPHAZARD, casual, random, accidental.

HAP, although rarely met, is an English word which can be traced back to Middle English and which can be used today as either a noun, to mean luck, chance; or as a verb, to mean occur by chance, befall, happen. It is familiar in the compounds: PERHAPS, by chance, possibly, it may be, perchance; and MISHAP, an unlucky chance, misfortune, disaster. HAPLESS means by derivation without luck, without good luck.

388. *ACCOST* (*ăk-kŏst′*) *v.* To address, greet, hail, salute, speak to first, make overtures to.
ACCOST is from the Latin *ad*, to; and *costa*, which may mean side, the source probably of the English word COAST. The word COSTAL (*kŏs′-tăl*) is used today in the sciences to mean pertaining to the ribs, to the side of the body. To ACCOST originally meant in English to come along side of; and, although this meaning is obsolete, ACCOST, to speak to, is used only for speaking to a person whom one has just approached.

By 7 per cent of adult readers ACCOST is believed to mean REBUKE, chide (506), reprove, reprimand. This may be a confusion of ACCOST with ACCUSE, blame, charge, indict. Or it may be due to the frequent appearance of such a phrase as: 'ACCOSTED by an officer of the law', a correct use of the word so long as one thinks of it as meaning approached, addressed, spoken to by an officer, for even in this phrase it does not mean REBUKED, reproved, reprimanded.

To 14 per cent of preparatory-school juniors ACCOST incorrectly means EVALUATE, appraise, set a just value on. This is probably some confusion of the verb, to ACCOST, address, with the word COST. COST comes from the Latin *constare*, to stand; and when used in the phrase: 'It COSTS a dollar', means literally it stands at a dollar. Although the verb, to COST, cannot mean EVALUATE, appraise, price, the ideas are closely associated.

To another 9 per cent of preparatory-school juniors ACCOST incorrectly means AVOID, to evade, shun, an opposite of the correct meaning, address, speak to.

To ACCOST and to GREET are practically synonymous but differ radically in use. GREET comes directly from Anglo-Saxon and is used for the friendly meeting with an equal. ACCOST, because of its Latin origin, is more formal. One ACCOSTS a stranger for the purpose of asking information.

389. *TIMOROUS* (*tĭm'-ō-rŭs*) *adj.* Shrinking, fearful, timid, apprehensive (396), cowering, quailing, easily alarmed, shy with timidity.

TIMOROUS and TIMID both come from the Latin *timere*, to fear. They are often synonymous. TIMID, however, can refer to a temporary state. One may be TIMID in the dark. One may be TIMID as a child, but not so when grown up. TIMOROUS refers to a permanent characteristic, as: 'A TIMOROUS disposition'.

TIMOROUS and ADVENTUROUS are opposites.

390. *ASSIDUOUS* (*ăs-sĭd'-ū-ŭs*) *adj.* Persistent, persevering, zealous, sedulous, diligent, unflagging (114), indefatigable (255), unremitting, constant in application.

ASSIDUOUS comes from the Latin verb *sedere*, to sit. From the same source come the English words SEDATE, quiet, composed, placid, as: 'A SEDATE person'; SEDENTARY, done sitting down, as: 'A SEDENTARY occupation'; and the adjective, SEDATIVE, soothing, calming, tranquilizing.

ASSIDUOUS, INDUSTRIOUS, and DILIGENT, all suggest sticking to work. DILIGENT, from the Latin *legere*, to choose, means by derivation sticking to work which one has chosen, working constantly at that which one loves. INDUSTRIOUS suggests leaving no idle time, but the word does not necessarily imply accomplishing much. ASSIDUOUS implies sticking quietly, placidly, sedately, to a task until it is finished.

391. *MALICE* (*măl'-ĭs*) *n.* Enmity, hatred, rancor (693), spite, animosity (764), malignity (893), malevolence.

The corresponding adjective, MALICIOUS (549), is less familiar.

Both MALICE and MALICIOUS are from the Latin *malus*, bad.

When used in the phrase: 'She bore him no MALICE', the word is thought by 1 per cent of preparatory-school juniors to mean MALE CHILDREN.

In the test phrase: 'It may be due to MALICE', the word is thought by 6 per cent of adult readers to mean CUNNING (320). The words MALICE and CUNNING are sometimes nearly synonymous, but often widely apart. Thus, the noun CUNNING may be used in a pleasant sense to mean skill, dexterity, even knowledge. When the word is used unpleasantly to mean shrewdness, deceit, craftiness, it has most of the unpleasant suggestions of MALICE. CUNNING is however the means, the ability, by which an underhand act is accomplished; while MALICE is the disposition, ill will, hatred, which leads to the desire to accomplish such an act.

Although MALICE and MALIGNITY are both dispositions to do harm, MALIGNITY is the more intense, the more deep-rooted of the two.

392. *UNYIELDING* (*ŭn-yēld'-ĭng*) *adj.* Firm, obstinate, inflexible (241), stubborn (266), resisting, unbending, headstrong, perverse (1049).

In the test phrase: 'An UNYIELDING attitude', the word, which is of Anglo-Saxon origin, is thought by 13 per cent of grammar-school pupils to mean UNUSUAL. Both UNUSUAL and UNYIELDING start with the Anglo-Saxon negative *un*, not; but, except for this similarity, it is difficult to see why the two words should be confused. UNUSUAL means uncommon, rare, odd, strange, not usual.

One of the meanings of the verb, to YIELD, is to give way to an argument, agree to a request, assent, comply with an entreaty. Although the participial adjective, YIELDING, is seldom used, the negative is more common, and means not giving way, not agreeing, not complying.

UNYIELDING and COMPLIANT (418) are practically opposites.

393. *BLEND* (*blĕnd*) *n.* Mixture (14), mingling of various
sorts, merging, combination, amalgamation of several elements to make a whole.

By 8 per cent of adult readers BLEND is believed to mean

FLAVOR, taste, savor, relish. This confusion probably arises from the use of the word BLEND in cases where a mixture is made to gain flavor, as: 'A BLEND of tea', 'A BLEND of whiskey', 'A BLEND of tobacco'. A BLEND is, however, any mixture.

394. *TYPIFY* (*tĭp'-ĭ-fī*) *v.* To stand for, represent, signify, exemplify, show the qualities of, serve as a specimen, be typical (275) of.
In the test phrase: 'How TYPIFY the subject', the word is thought by 7 per cent of adult readers to mean CARICATURE. To CARICATURE is to represent in a ridiculous or exaggerated manner, to travesty, burlesque, parody. CARICATURE necessitates exaggeration. To TYPIFY is to represent accurately, truly.

395. *TENSION* (*tĕn'-shŭn*) *n.* Mental strain, intensity of feeling, taut condition of nerves, severe mental effort.
TENSION comes from the Latin word *tendere*, to stretch. From this come a large family of English words: the verb, to EXTEND, by derivation to stretch out, enlarge, lengthen; the noun, a TENT, a shelter made of a cloth, supported in the center and stretched by cords fastened to pegs in the ground; and many others, in which it is more difficult to see the original meaning of stretch, such as: to ATTEND, to be present; to CONTEND, to strive, struggle; to PORTEND, to indicate in advance, betoken; and to PRETEND, to make-believe. Notice that TENSION, mental strain, EXTENSION, enlargement, and PRETENSION, claim, are spelt with s; whereas ATTENTION, thought, concentration, and CONTENTION, strife, although of similar origin, are spelt with T.
The word TENSION may also be used literally, as: 'The TENSION of a rope', to mean the state of being stretched as the result of pulling. When used figuratively, as: 'The TENSION in a situation', it means the feeling of strain, mental stress.

396. *APPREHENSIVE* (*ăp-prē-hĕn'-sĭv*) *adj.* Anxious (334), fearful, timorous (389), afraid, worried, concerned, disquieted, alarmed, suspicious.
To 4 per cent of adult readers APPREHENSIVE incorrectly means GUILTY, not innocent, culpable, delinquent. A GUILTY conscience may make one apprehensive of detection, of punishment; but strictly a GUILTY conscience is one which troubles its possessor,

not because he fears detection or punishment, but because he sincerely regrets having done wrong. APPREHENSION is a fear of detection, of punishment; but the line between the two is fine. Both the noun, APPREHENSION, and the adjective, APPRE-HENSIVE, may be used in situations where there is no feeling of guilt. One may be: 'APPREHENSIVE of an approaching storm', or 'APPREHENSIVE of not being understood', or 'APPREHENSIVE of not understanding'.

397. *SUPPLE* (*sŭp'-pl*, not *soop'-pl*) *adj.* Flexible (28), limber, lithe, pliable (117), lissom, pliant, bending easily.

In the test phrase: 'A SUPPLE branch', the word is thought by 4 per cent of adult readers to mean WITHERED, dried-up, faded.

SUPPLE, LISSOM, and LITHE, are practically synonymous. They may all be used to describe a well-coordinated human figure the muscles of which are elastic and on which there is no superfluous flesh. SUPPLE, which comes from the Latin *sub*, under; and *plicare*, to fold; may be applied, however, to other things, to trees, and to materials of various sorts, to mean pliable, bending easily.

398. *PINNACLE* (*pĭn'-nă-kl*) *n.* A peak, mountain top, summit, apex (91), topmost point, acme, culmination, highest elevation.

PIN, the common pin; PEN; perhaps PENCIL; and PINNACLE; are probably related. Although the exact relationship is in dispute, they all seem to come, directly or indirectly, from the Latin word *pinna* or *penna*, feather, wing, point. The Latin *pinna* appears in English with its meaning of feather in PINNATE (*pĭn'-nāt*), resembling a feather, a word which is used in botany to describe the leaves of a flower, shrub, or tree. PEN and FEATHER are still closely connected. It was only a few years ago that one wrote with a QUILL, one of the large feathers of a goose. A PENKNIFE is so called because it was used to sharpen the quill or pen; and the French word for pen is still *la plume*, which is also the French word for feather.

In the test phrase: 'The lofty PINNACLE', the word is thought by 5 per cent of adult readers to mean TEMPLE. This is perhaps a confusion of PINNACLE, peak, with TABERNACLE, by derivation a tent, hut, shed. In Jewish history the TABERNACLE was a tent which was used for religious worship during the wandering of the Jews before their settlement in Palestine.

Another word similar in appearance to PINNACLE, but which does not come from the same source and should not be confused with it, is PINNACE (*pĭn'-năs*), a light boat, sometimes two-masted and schooner-rigged, often used in conjunction with a larger vessel.

Although a PINNACLE is any sharp point rising into the air, as for instance a sharp point of rock or a pointed mountain top, a PINNACLE is also in Gothic architecture any one of the stone points projecting upward like small spires.

399. *CHECK* (*chĕk*) *v*. To stop, stay (259), hold back, arrest, inhibit, put a sudden restraint upon, retard, hinder, impede (532). 'They CHECKED the enemy.'
The verb, to CHECK, was first used in the game of chess and meant to attack, to threaten, the king. The word can be traced back, as can also the word CHESS, to the Persian word for king. All of the modern meanings of the word CHECK have developed from its use in the game of CHESS.

400. *OLFACTORY* (*ŏl-făk'-tō-rĭ*) *adj*. Pertaining to smelling, having the sense of smell.
OLFACTORY comes from the Latin *olere*, to smell; and *facere*, to make. GUSTATORY, pertaining to taste; AUDITORY, pertaining to hearing; TACTILE, pertaining to touch; VISUAL, pertaining to sight; and OLFACTORY, pertaining to smell; are adjectives which correspond to the five senses.

401. *FANTASTIC* (*făn-tăs'-tĭk*) *adj*. Fanciful, odd (90), imaginative, imaginary (440), visionary, capricious, unreal, illusive (*ĭl-lū'-sĭv*), bizarre, wild, whimsical, chimerical (822). In the test phrase: 'FANTASTIC proposals', the word is thought by 9 per cent of adult readers to mean FAR-REACHING. The hyphenated phrase FAR-REACHING means influential, of wide application, continuing to produce an effect for a long time. FAR-REACHING is always used in a commendatory sense; whereas FANTASTIC, of the nature of a phantom, is like VISIONARY, always used in an unfavorable sense.

FANCIFUL, FANTASTIC, and GROTESQUE (*grō-tĕsk'*), are three

degrees of oddity. FANCIFUL is unusual but not unpleasing. FANTASTIC is fanciful carried to a greater degree of unreality. GROTESQUE is still more extreme and distinctly unpleasant.

402. *TENET* (*tĕn'-ĕt*) *n.* A belief, principle, dogma, doctrine, precept (1054), an opinion maintained as true.

TENET comes from the Latin *tenere*, to hold, the source also of TENACIOUS, holding fast.

A TENET and a DOGMA are both opinions held. A DOGMA is an authoritative opinion, often formulated by some sect or school, and pressed energetically for acceptance. A TENET is milder. It is little stronger than opinion, and may be held either by a school or by an individual.

403. *PEASANT* (*pĕz'-ănt*) *n.* Rustic laborer, farmer, farm worker, farmhand, uneducated countryman.

In the test phrase: 'They are PEASANTS', the word is thought by 7 per cent of adult readers to mean CITIZENS. The word CITIZEN has been used in at least three different ways. In modern usage it means one who has the rights, privileges, and responsibilities, which belong to a member of the state or nation. It has in the past been used to mean a person engaged in trade as opposed to one of noble birth and breeding. It has also been used to mean one who lives in a city. In all three senses a CITIZEN and a PEASANT are almost diametrically opposed. A CITIZEN has the full rights of the state; and although the political rights of the PEASANT have varied at different times, in different countries, they have usually been restricted in some way. In the second sense in which the word CITIZEN is used, both a CITIZEN and a PEASANT are of low birth compared with a noble, but a CITIZEN, as thus defined, is engaged in trade, while a PEASANT works on the land. In the third sense, a CITIZEN is one who lives in a city, while a PEASANT lives in the country.

Both a PEASANT and a SERF are farm laborers. A SERF cannot own land; he belongs to the soil, and is sold with it. A PEASANT, on the contrary, may own and work his own land.

The word PEASANT is not used of Americans, FARMHAND being the nearest substitute. An American college boy could take a job on a farm for the summer and would then be a FARMHAND; but he could not, in a like manner, be a PEASANT.

404. *BLUDGEON* (*blŭj'-ŏn*) *n.* A club, heavy-headed stick,
       bat used as a weapon.

In the test phrase: 'They fought with BLUDGEONS', the word
is believed by 9 per cent of adult readers to mean BLOODY
DAGGERS. A DAGGER is a short, sharp-pointed weapon for stab-
bing. The origin of the word BLUDGEON is unknown, but there
is apparently no etymological connection between BLOOD and
BLUDGEON. The word BLUDGEON, although it begins with BL,
has no suggestion of blood. The word BLOOD goes far back in
Anglo-Saxon and has counterparts in Old German, Icelandic,
and the Scandinavian languages. BLUDGEON did not appear in
English until after 1700, and may at first have been slang.

405. *NURTURE* (*ner'-tūr*) *v.* To foster, nourish, breed (246),
       bring up, train, cherish, promote, develop.

NURTURE, NOURISH, and NURSE, are all from the same Latin
nutrire, to feed, foster, cherish. Of the three words, to NURSE
more often implies physical care, to NURTURE, moral, spiritual
care.

In the test phrase: 'An affection thus NURTURED', the word
is thought by 5 per cent of preparatory-school juniors to mean
SUPPRESSED. To SUPPRESS is to crush, restrain, in connotation
almost an opposite of NURTURE, to nourish.

406. *PRETENTIOUS* (*prē-tĕn'-shŭs*) *adj.* Boastful, ostenta-
       tious (428), showy (442), gaudy (492), vainglorious, claim-
       ing unmerited superiority, pretending to possess more than
       one does.

PRETENTIOUS is the adjective which corresponds to the verb
PRETEND, which may mean to make a false show, as: 'To PRE-
TEND friendship'. It comes from the past participle, *tentus*, of
the Latin verb *tendere*, to stretch, and by derivation means
stretching out that which one has in order to make it appear
more than it is.

407. *SOLICIT* (*sō-lĭs'-ĭt*) *v.* To crave (59), ask (99) for, en-
       treat, plead for, request, petition, beseech (324), suppli-
       cate, beg, implore, importune.

SOLICIT is from the Latin *ciere*, to excite, the source of the
English word SOLICITOUS, anxious, concerned. To 9 per cent

of adult readers SOLICIT incorrectly means GRANT, give, bestow (202), practically an opposite of the correct meaning.

408. DISMAY (dĭs-mā') n. Consternation, terror, dejection, discouragement, state of embarrassment, loss of mental resource.

When used in the test phrase: 'Fresh tidings brought DISMAY', the word is thought by 12 per cent of adult readers to mean DISCORD. This may be due to a misunderstanding of the word DISCORD, which comes from the Latin dis, without; and cor, heart; and which translated literally might mean the condition of being without heart, and therefore dejection. The word DISCORD, despite its derivation, is not used in this way, but means disagreement, lack of harmony, strife. It is the opposite of CONCORD, harmony, agreement. The English word DISCOURAGEMENT, from the same Latin cor, is used today to mean the state of being deprived of heart, disheartened, dispirited, depressed.

DISMAY is from the simple verb MAY which is known to everyone. The phrase: 'MAY I?' today means, am I permitted?, but originally meant, can I?, am I able?, have I the power?. DISMAY is a combination of the Latin prefix dis, deprived of; and the Anglo-Saxon MAY; and suggests deprived of power, without the ability to do. The word is used today for that state in which one is rendered inactive by fear, terror, shock.

409. YAWNING (yawn'-ĭng) p. adj. Wide-open, gaping, broad, vast. The verb to YAWN, in its literal sense, means to open the mouth wide, involuntarily, because of drowsiness, boredom, or hunger.

In the test phrase: 'The YAWNING chasm', the word is thought by 11 per cent of grammar-school pupils to mean DEEP. A YAWNING chasm is wide, wide-open, rather than merely deep.

By another 10 per cent YAWNING is thought to mean TERRIFYING, frightening. A YAWNING chasm may be terrifying; but intrinsically there is nothing in the word YAWNING which suggests terrifying. Furthermore, there are many situations where TERRIFYING can be used, where YAWNING is inappropriate, as: 'A TERRIFYING scene'. YAWNING, which is of Anglo-Saxon origin, means wide-open.

410. *FLORID* (*flŏr'-ĭd*) *adj.* Flushed with red, high-colored, red, ruddy (131), rubicund.

FLORID is from the same source as FLOWER, a word with relations in many languages. It goes back probably to Anglo-Saxon; and is related to the Latin *florere*, to bloom, blossom, flourish. The adjective FLORID, by derivation flowery, can be used of architecture to mean loaded with decoration, ornamented, embellished, ornate. Or it can be used more figuratively, but with the same sense, of musical compositions or of literary style. When used of a person, with reference to face, countenance, it is from the same source, but has a different meaning, for here it means bright in color, flushed, red.

Whether used with reference to artistic style or personal appearance, FLORID always has a slightly unpleasant suggestion. A FLORID style is too flowery, over-embellished; a FLORID countenance is too red to be healthy. Pleasanter words, which suggest the red of health, are: BLOOMING, glowing with the freshness of youth; and RUDDY, red with health.

In the test phrase: 'A FLORID countenance', the word is thought by 4 per cent of preparatory-school juniors to mean FULL. A FULL countenance is round, filled out, rounded out, ample. FULL, in this use, refers to the shape, as: 'The FULL moon', which is round. FLORID, thus used, refers to color and means red.

411. *COARSE* (*kŏrs*) *adj.* Vulgar, common, mean, indelicate, crude, rude (64), gross (745), of inferior quality, showing lack of refinement.

COARSE can be traced back to the 16th century, but its exact origin is unknown.

In the test phrase: 'Several COARSE fellows', the word is thought by 13 per cent of grammar-school pupils to mean CRUEL, hardhearted, pitiless. CRUEL, hardhearted, and CRUDE, unrefined, are closely related etymologically for both come from the same Latin source, *crudus*, rough, raw. As CRUDE, unrefined, is almost a synonym of COARSE, there is historical justification for the misconception. Today, neither COARSE nor CRUDE has any suggestion of CRUEL, hardhearted, pitiless.

COARSE and CRUDE, although almost synonymous, differ slightly. CRUDE means unrefined, unpolished, rough, not necessarily vulgar. COARSE, when it refers to manners, to words, or to a person, always suggests vulgarity.

412. CUMULATIVE (*kū'-mū-lā-tǐv*) *adj.* Piling (17) up, heaping up, amassing, gradually increasing, being made up of parts added one after the other, accumulating, collecting, as: 'CUMULATIVE evidence', 'A CUMULATIVE effect'. CUMULATIVE is thought by 6 per cent of adult readers to mean SATISFACTORY, perhaps because of the use of the word CUMULATIVE in the business world to designate interest which if not withdrawn is added to the principal.

CUMULATIVE is from the Latin *cumulus*, a heap, from the same source as the verb to ACCUMULATE, to heap up, pile up. CUMULUS is today an English noun in good usage, and is the name for the heaps of white summer clouds, piled up on a horizontal base, like a snowy mountain range. The word appears usually in the plural, CUMULI (*kū'-mū-lī*).

Of the two practically synonymous verbs, to CUMULATE and to ACCUMULATE, the latter is more frequently seen; of the two adjectives, CUMULATIVE and ACCUMULATIVE, the former is more frequent.

413. OBSOLETE (*ŏb'-sō-lēt*) *adj.* Fallen into disuse (293), out of use, no longer accepted, antiquated, discarded, outworn.

To 5 per cent of adult readers OBSOLETE incorrectly means MISUSED. This is perhaps a confusion of DISUSED, out of use, obsolete, with MISUSED, wrong, incorrectly used.

OBSOLETE, ARCHAIC, and OLD, differ in their technical use when applied to language. Many OLD words are still in use. The word FATHER was used as early as the 9th century, but is neither ARCHAIC nor OBSOLETE. ARCHAIC words are those in the process of being discarded. OBSOLETE words are those which have been out of use perhaps a hundred years. OBSOLETE words have a way of coming back into good and common parlance. In 1816 such useful words as ATHIRST, thirsty; GARNER, gather; JEOPARDY (84), danger; LACK, having none; PASSION, emotion; STRAIGHTWAY, at once; and QUAIL (383), to cower, cringe; were classed as OBSOLETE, antiquated. All are today heard in conversation and seen in modern literature.

414. *VOGUE* (*vōg*) *n.* Fashion, accepted mode, popular favor, current style.

VOGUE, FASHION, and STYLE, are almost synonymous. STYLE is a higher type of word than either of the others. STYLE in writing is that mode of expression which gives individuality. STYLE in art is the distinctive manner which gives character. STYLE, as thus defined, is permanent and in this differs from both FASHION and VOGUE.

FASHION is the general word for the style which is popular at the moment. VOGUE, a word which has been taken directly from the French, is synonymous with FASHION, but is applied more frequently to that which is in fashion in exclusive society. The word often appears in the phrase: 'In VOGUE'.

415. *ELUCIDATE* (*ē-lū'-sǐ-dāt*) *v.* To explain, illustrate, explicate, make clear, throw light upon.

ELUCIDATE is from the same Latin source, *lucidus*, light, as the English word LUCID, clear, transparent, and means literally make clear, make transparent.

When used in the test phrase: 'ELUCIDATE that statement', the word is thought by 5 per cent of adult readers to mean CONDENSE, to make briefer, shorten, compress, concentrate. To CONDENSE and the word to ELABORATE, enlarge upon, develop in detail, are practically opposites; but ELUCIDATE does not specify whether or not the clarifying is done by greater length.

To ELUCIDATE, to EXPOUND, and to EXPLAIN, are all similar in meaning. To EXPLAIN is the generic term. To EXPOUND is to explain in a formal and long-drawn-out manner. To ELUCIDATE suggests some formality but does not mean long-drawn-out; it means specifically to explain through the use of illustrations.

416. *INCONTROVERTIBLE* (*ǐn-kǒn-trō-vert'-ǐ-bl*) *adj.* Indisputable, too clear to admit of argument, too certain to question, impossible to disprove, not debatable (373), not moot.

INCONTROVERTIBLE is from the Latin *in*, not; and CONTROVERTIBLE, a word which in turn comes from *contra*, against, and *vertere*, to turn. From the same source come the verb, to

CONTROVERT (*kŏn'-trō-vert*), to dispute, deny, oppose by argument; and the noun, a CONTROVERSY, a debate, dispute.

A CONTROVERSY differs from a DISPUTE in that a CONTROVERSY is usually written, may be participated in by many persons, and may last for a long time. A DISPUTE is oral, undignified, and of short duration. The difference between a CONTROVERSY and a DISPUTE distinguishes the adjective INCONTROVERTIBLE from INDISPUTABLE. INCONTROVERTIBLE expresses a more formal and more final conclusion than INDISPUTABLE.

Why should INCONTROVERTIBLE end in -IBLE and INDISPUTABLE in -ABLE? The normal, most-frequently-met ending is -ABLE, as: APPLICABLE, DEBATABLE, DISTINGUISHABLE, FAVORABLE, REMARKABLE, and many others. All words ending in -IBLE are exceptions and should be memorized. The only -IBLE words which apply to arguments are: ADMISSIBLE, CONTROVERTIBLE, CONVINCIBLE, CREDIBLE, DEDUCIBLE, DEFENSIBLE, DISCERNIBLE, FALLIBLE, INCOMPREHENSIBLE, INCONTROVERTIBLE, INDEFEASIBLE, INVINCIBLE, IRRESISTIBLE, OSTENSIBLE, PERCEPTIBLE, and PLAUSIBLE.

When used in the test phrase: 'His argument is INCONTROVERTIBLE', the word is thought by 11 per cent of adult readers to mean UNSOUND, erroneous, fallacious, ill-founded, questionable, all opposites of INCONTROVERTIBLE, too certain to be debated.

417. *DEXTEROUSLY* (*dĕks'-ter-ŭs-lĭ*) *adv*. Skillfully, expertly, aptly, handily, adroitly, cleverly, artfully, adeptly, proficiently, competently, capably, facilely, efficiently, with finesse, in a callid manner.

In the test phrase: 'They combated it DEXTEROUSLY', the word is thought by 6 per cent of preparatory-school juniors to mean RIGHTLY. The Latin *dexter* means right, at the right side, on the right hand; and the word DEXTER is used in heraldry today with this original meaning. DEXTERITY once meant right handedness; and the two unusual adverbs, DEXTRAD and DEXTRALLY, synonyms of one another, mean toward the right side, in a right-handed manner, as opposed to SINISTRAD, on the left side. The English word, DEXTEROUSLY, has lost entirely the significance of the right side; and today can mean only cleverly, skillfully. It can be applied either to skill in using the hands, manual cleverness; or skill in using the mind, mental cleverness.

DEXTER and SINISTER (332); RIGHTLY and WRONGLY; DEXTEROUSLY and AWKWARDLY; are opposites.

418. *COMPLIANT* (kŏm-plī'-ănt) *adj.* Obliging (308), yielding, complaisant, acquiescing, submitting willingly, ready to consent.

COMPLIANT and PLIANT, in its figurative sense of easily influenced, are nearly synonymous; and yet, despite their similarity in meaning and form, they do not seem to have come from the same source. PLIANT is from the Latin *plicare*, to fold; while COMPLIANT is an adjective made from the verb to COMPLY, to yield, act in accordance with another's wishes, a word which may come from the same source as the adjective COMPLETE, the Latin *com*, and *plere*, to fill.

To 6 per cent of adult readers COMPLIANT incorrectly means DISCONTENTED, not satisfied. One who YIELDS may be discontented, unsatisfied with the result; for the verb, to YIELD, suggests giving in after a struggle, submitting because of external pressure. To COMPLY has not the same suggestion; one may COMPLY instantly with the request of a friend and take pleasure in so doing. The corresponding adjective, COMPLIANT, may even signify a little too ready to oblige. It never has the suggestion of yielding under pressure.

YIELDING and OBSTINATE; PLIANT and OBDURATE; COMPLIANT and HEADSTRONG; are practically opposites.

419. *EGOISM* (ē'-gō-ĭzm) *n.* Self-love, self-interest, conceit, self-esteem, amour-propre (ah-moor-prŏ'-pr).

EGOISM, which is from the Latin *ego*, I, may be pronounced either (ē'-gō-ĭzm), with the long E (ē), such as appears in EKE (ēk), or (ĕ'-gō-ĭzm), with the short E (ĕ), as in EGG (ĕg).

EGOISM and EGOTISM (ē'-gō-tĭzm) are often confused. EGOTISM, from the same Latin *ego*, I, is the too-frequent use of the word I, the vice of thinking too much of one's self. An EGOTIST is one who talks and thinks constantly about himself. The word EGOTISM is slighter than EGOISM, for the latter is dignified by representing systems of philosophy and ethics.

An EGOIST is one who makes regard for his own interest the guiding principle of conduct.

In metaphysics, EGOISM is the belief that nothing exists except in one's own mind, or at least that there is no proof to the contrary. In ethics, EGOISM is the belief that self-interest is the basis of morality. In ordinary usage, EGOISM is the habit of looking upon all questions in their relation to one's self, the excessive exaltation of one's own opinion, self-opinionatedness. EGOISM and ALTRUISM are opposite in suggestion.

420. *ENVIRON* (ĕn-vī'-rŏn) *v.* To surround, encompass, encircle, gird (273), form a ring around.

The verb, to ENVIRON, is thought by 7 per cent of preparatory-school juniors to mean CONFRONT, to face, challenge.

Both the verb, to ENVIRON, and the noun, the ENVIRONS, a word which is always used in the plural and which means the surroundings of a place, come directly from the French *environ*, around.

421. *FIGURE* (fĭg'-ūr) *n.* Appearance, external shape, outline, presence (569), visible form.

FIGURE, which comes from the Latin *fingere*, to form, has more than a dozen English meanings. It may refer to an image in the likeness of a man and so be synonymous with STATUE, image, as: 'A marble FIGURE'. Or the word FIGURE may refer to any one of the Arabic numerals from 1 to 9, as: 'The FIGURE 8'. When the word is used in the phrase: 'He made a fine FIGURE', it is the general term for the outward appearance of a human being.

422. *TEPID* (tĕp'-ĭd) *adj.* Lukewarm (18), moderately warm, neither hot nor cold.

TEPID comes from the Latin *tepere*, to be lukewarm. In ancient Rome, the TEPIDARIUM was the warmed room in the public baths, which the bather entered in preparation for the hot or vapor baths.

423. *COMPORT* (kŏm-pōrt') *v.* To conduct, behave, carry, manage, bear, demean (dē-mēn'), deport.

In the test phrase: 'COMPORT yourself properly', the word is thought by 4 per cent of adult readers to mean CALM, soothe, quiet, tranquilize, bring into repose. This is perhaps a confusion of COMPORT, conduct, with COMPOSE (221), to calm, tranquilize, bring into a state of repose, a word which is frequently used in the admonition: 'COMPOSE yourself'.

424. *HILARITY* (*hĭl-ăr′-ĭ-tĭ*) *n.* Jollity, joyousness, glee, gaiety, jubilance, jubilation, boisterous mirth, noisy merriment.

In the test phrase: 'A burst of HILARITY', the word is thought by 7 per cent of adult readers to mean CHEERS. HILARITY is cheer, good spirits, mirth, gaiety; but the plural CHEERS, substituted in this phrase, can mean only shouts, applause, sometimes an expression of HILARITY, but not a synonym of the word.

HILARITY and JOVIALITY are demonstrations of joy. The word JOVIALITY is from JOVE, a name for the Roman god JUPITER. In theory, the planet JUPITER endows those born under its sign with a mirthful disposition. JOVIALITY is therefore an inherent characteristic; and, perhaps because the word comes from JOVE, is applied most aptly to mature men. HILARITY, from the Greek word ἱλαρός, cheerful, gay, is social merriment. The word refers to actions, to occasions, as: 'The HILARITY of the evening', rather than to dispositions; and to the young more often than to the mature.

425. *SILHOUETTE* (*sĭl-oo-ĕt′*) *n.* Shadow picture, profile, representation of a head, figure in solid black.

SILHOUETTE is from the name ETIENNE SILHOUETTE, the minister of finance of France in 1737, a man who was scrupulously economical. The implication is that a SILHOUETTE, a solid black profile, is the simplest, most economical means of representing a head.

426. *SOLIDARITY* (*sŏl-ĭ-dăr′-ĭ-tĭ*) *n.* Unity, community of objectives, mutual responsibility, fellowship in gain and loss, single-mindedness of purpose.

In the test phrase: 'The SOLIDARITY of our citizens', the word is thought by 7 per cent of adult readers to mean WELFARE, well-being, exemption from misfortune. SOLIDARITY is often thought to mean fellowship under good conditions only. In reality it means communion not only of interests but of responsibilities.

SOLIDARITY comes directly from the French *solidarité*, joint liability, mutual responsibility, introduced to the world by the French communists, in 1871, to signify the unity which they wished each French commune to possess. SOLIDARITY today means unity in gain and loss, in victory and defeat, in honor and dishonor.

427. *OPPRESSIVE* (*ŏp-prĕs'-sĭv*) *adj.* Burdensome, unreasonably severe (123), depressing, overpowering, overwhelming (263), unjustly harsh.

OPPRESSIVE is from the Latin *ob*, against; and *premere*, to press; and by derivation means pressing against. From *premere* come COMPRESS, to press together; DEPRESS, to press down; REPRESS, to press back; and SUPPRESS, to press under.

In the test phrase: 'The taxes were OPPRESSIVE', the word is believed by 13 per cent of grammar-school pupils to mean OPPOSED. The verbs, to OPPOSE and to OPPRESS in its original sense, are close but not identical. To OPPOSE is to stand in the way of, place something in the way; the word suggests stolid inaction. One who OPPOSES progress contributes nothing, but merely places himself in the way of progress. To OPPRESS is by derivation to push against, press against actively. The word is used today not so much to mean push against as press down upon heavily, weigh down, overburden; and the adjective OPPRESSIVE can be used only in this last way. The taxes were OPPRESSIVE does not mean that they were fought against; but that they were unreasonably heavy, weighty, unjustly burdensome.

428. *OSTENTATIOUS* (*ŏs-tĕn-tā'-shŭs*) *adj.* Vainglorious, pretentious (406), showy (442), meretricious, making a display from vanity or love of admiration.

OSTENTATIOUS, like PRETENTIOUS, comes from the Latin *tendere*, to stretch, and by derivation suggests stretching one's possessions to the limit in order to make a display. OSTENTATIOUS and PRETENTIOUS are practically synonymous but differ in purpose. One who is PRETENTIOUS wishes to give a false,

exaggerated, impression of his possessions. One who is OSTENTA-
TIOUS wishes because of pride, vanity, to parade, display (118),
show off, what he possesses.

OSTENTATIOUS and SHOWY are similar in suggestion. SHOWY
is applied most often to showing off with inexpensive materials, to the display made by a person of moderate means. The
word SHOWY may also be used in a not unpleasant sense to
mean gay, brilliant, gorgeous, striking in appearance. OSTEN-
TATIOUS is applied most often to the display made by a
wealthy person, with expensive materials; and it can be used
only in the disagreeable sense of a boastful, vain, showing-off
of wealth.

429. *DILATE* (*dī-lāt'*) *v.* To distend, expand, enlarge, spread
out, extend.

DILATE is from the Latin *di;* and *latus,* the past participle of
the irregular Latin verb *ferre,* to carry. From the same source
comes the word ABLATIVE, the grammatical name for the case
which denotes separation, removal.

To 9 per cent of preparatory-school juniors DILATE incorrectly means SHRINK, an exact opposite of the correct meaning.

430. *VERACITY* (*vē-răs'-ĭ-tĭ*) *n.* Truth, truthfulness, conformity with actuality, habitual regard for truth.

VERACITY, from the Latin *veritas,* truth, is unknown to 18 per
cent of adult readers. To 5 per cent it incorrectly means
EAGERNESS. This is perhaps a confusion of VERACITY, truthfulness, with VIVACITY, animation, liveliness, from the Latin word
vivere, to live.

431. *RECLINING* (*rē-klī'-nĭng*) *p. adj.* Leaning back, lying
down, recumbent (591), resting, reposing, supine.

RECLINING comes from the Latin *re,* back; and *clinare,* to
lean; and means literally leaning back. From the Latin *clinare*
come also the English nouns, an INCLINE (*ĭn-klīn'*), literally
something which leans, a slope; and a DECLINE (*dē-klīn'*), by
derivation a leaning downward, now most frequently a going
downward, descent.

Three participial adjectives, LYING, RECLINING, and LEANING,
all suggest resting. A LEANING position is almost upright, as:

'The LEANING tower of Pisa'. A RECLINING position is more nearly lying down.

To 11 per cent of grammar-school pupils RECLINING incorrectly means UPRIGHT, practically an opposite of the correct meaning.

432. *OPAQUE* (*ō-pāk'*) *adj.* Impervious to light, letting no light through, allowing no vision, not transparent (150). OPAQUE is from the Latin *opacus*, darkened, shady. It is thought by 6 per cent of adult readers to mean SHIMMERING, opalescent, shining with a tremulous light. OPAQUE and TRANSPARENT are opposites.

433. *LETHARGIC* (*lē-thahr'-jik*) *adj.* Drowsy, languid, dull, heavy, apathetic, morbidly sluggish, torpid, inert.

To 4 per cent of adult readers LETHARGIC incorrectly means SORROWFUL, sad, dismal.

LETHARGIC and the corresponding noun LETHARGY (*lĕth'-ăr-ji*), stupor (60), lack of interest, apathy, both come directly from the Greek word λήθη, forgetfulness, oblivion. From the same word comes LETHE (*lē'-thē*), in Greek mythology, the river of oblivion, one of the rivers of Hades. Those who drank of the waters of LETHE forgot their former existence.

LETHARGIC should not be confused with LETHAL (*lē'-thăl*), which comes from a different source and means deadly, fatal. LETHARGIC means dull, inert, listless, inactive.

434. *ELICIT* (*ē-lĭs'-ĭt*) *v.* To draw forth, evoke (614), educe, extract, extort, wring from.

In the test phrase: 'ELICITING a response', the word is thought by 9 per cent of preparatory-school juniors to mean PROHIBITING. This may be due to some confusion of the verb to ELICIT, to draw forth, with the adjective ILLICIT, forbidden, prohibited. ILLICIT is from the Latin *licitus*, lawful, the past participle of *licere*, to be lawful, the source of the English word LICENSE, a legal permit. ELICIT is from the Latin *e*, out; and *lacere*, to entice, allure; the ultimate source of the English words LACE, which originally meant a loop, and LASSO (*lăs'-sō*), a lariat. ELICIT by derivation means to entice out, draw forth.

435. *AFFIRM* (*ăf-ferm'*) *v.* To assert positively, declare, aver, allege, pronounce, maintain to be true, tell with confidence, state with definiteness.

AFFIRM is from the Latin *ad*, to; and *firmare*, to make firm. The Latin *firmare* is the source also of the adjective, INFIRM, literally not firm, weak, decrepit, feeble, usually because of old age.

ASSERT, AFFIRM, and SWEAR TO, all mean to state positively. To ASSERT is to state with a self-confidence which borders on egotism, often with no actual proof. To AFFIRM is to state more solemnly; but the word does not suggest invoking the name of God as does to SWEAR TO.

To 13 per cent of grammar-school pupils to AFFIRM incorrectly means to DENY, declare not to be true, the exact opposite of the correct meaning, declare to be true.

436. *UNWITTING* (*ŭn-wĭt'-tĭng*) *adj.* Ignorant, not knowing, unconscious, unaware.

In the test phrase: 'UNWITTING of his danger', the word is thought by 5 per cent of adult readers to mean FORGETFUL. In order to forget a fact one must once have known it; to be UNWITTING of a fact is to be ignorant of it.

To another 5 per cent, UNWITTING incorrectly means CARELESS, having no concern, heedless.

The verb, to WIT, to know, is of Anglo-Saxon origin, but has practically disappeared from English, except in the phrase: 'To WIT', which is used to mean namely. From the verb come the noun WITNESS, by derivation one who knows; the adverb WITTINGLY, knowingly, consciously; and the adjective UNWITTING, ignorant, unconscious, unaware.

437. *SYNTHETIC* (*sĭn-thĕt'-ĭk*) *adj.* Artificial (482), put together, manufactured, factitious (1064), made in the laboratory, produced by combining, not natural (26).

The corresponding noun, SYNTHESIS (*sĭn'-thĕ-sĭs*) (592), a putting together of different things, is less familiar for it is unknown to 28 per cent of adult readers.

In the phrase: 'SYNTHETIC rubber', the word is thought by 6 per cent of adult readers to mean ELASTIC, springy, yielding, tending to resume natural shape after stretching.

SYNTHETIC is a combination of the Greek σύν, together; and τιθέναι, to place; and by derivation means placed together, put together.

438. BUXOM (bŭk'-sŭm) adj. Sturdy (72), robust (560), vigorous, healthy, jolly, frolicsome.

BUXOM once meant amorous, enamored, easily falling in love; and, although this meaning is marked by dictionaries as obsolete, BUXOM is still thought by 5 per cent of adult readers to mean FLIRTATIOUS, amorous.

In the test phrase: 'The BUXOM widow', the word is thought by another 3 per cent to mean FORLORN, deserted, pitiful, practically an opposite of the correct meaning.

439. RAVAGE (răv'-āj) v. To lay waste, plunder, pillage, spoil, sack, destroy, devastate, make havoc of.

To RAVAGE the land is thought by 8 per cent of preparatory-school juniors to mean ROAR THROUGH the land, slang and picturesque, but almost an exact definition of RAVAGE. Although the English word, to ROAR, does not mean to destroy, as does RAVAGE, to ROAR once meant, in slang, to riot; and a ROARING time is still a riotous, disorderly occasion. Thus: 'To ROAR THROUGH the land' means in slang usage to go through riotously.

The two verbs, RAVAGE and DEVASTATE, are practically synonymous. DEVASTATE comes from the Latin vastare, to lay waste, destroy, the source of the English word WASTE; and the word DEVASTATE suggests the wastefulness of the destroying process. RAVAGE comes from the Latin rapare, to snatch, seize, the source of the English words: RAPID, quick; to RAPE, to seize by force; and RAVISH, to carry away violently, a RAVISHING beauty sweeps one suddenly off one's feet. The word RAVAGE suggests the suddenness of the destroying process.

440. IMAGINARY (ĭ-măj'-ĭn-ā-rĭ) adj. Fancied, unreal, fanciful, fictitious (212), visionary, fantastic (401), unfounded, feigned (487), whimsical, chimerical (822), existing only in the imagination.

IMAGINARY, from the Latin imago, a likeness, copy, image, is thought by 13 per cent of grammar-school pupils to mean VISIBLE, the popular misconception. This may be a confusion of VISIBLE, capable of being seen by the physical eye, with VISIONARY, seen only by the mind, a synonym of IMAGINARY. Or it may be the fact that VISIBLE, perceptible, is an opposite of IMAGINARY, which means existing only in the imagination.

441. *FRETFUL (frĕt'-fŭl) adj.* Irritable, peevish, impatient, querulous, petulant, easily vexed. 'FRETFUL patients.'
DISCOURAGED, disheartened, dejected, is the common misconception, not apparently because of any etymological connection, perhaps only because DISCOURAGED, dejected, persons become FRETFUL, peevish.

FRETFUL, PEEVISH, PETULANT, and PETTISH, all mean impatient in different ways. PETTISH is impatient over small, petty things. PETULANT is quickly, capriciously impatient. PEEVISH is more permanent. FRETFUL is the only one of these words which implies a just cause for impatience.

442. *SHOWY (shō'-ĭ) adj.* Gay, brilliant, of striking appearance, pretentious (406), ostentatious (428), gaudy (492), attracting attention.
SHOWY, which is of Anglo-Saxon origin, is thought by 20 per cent of grammar-school pupils to mean NEW. NEW clothes are fresh, just made, not worn out; but they may be dark, quiet, and attract no attention. The word NEW is sometimes used to mean novel, strange, unexpected, striking; and in this sense it is not far from SHOWY. But there is a difference which can be seen most clearly from their opposites. NEW and OLD; NOVEL and FAMILIAR; SHOWY and QUIET; are opposites.

443. *BREACH (brēch) n.* An opening broken through a wall, rent, rift, break, gap, aperture (258), fissure, split.
The word BREACH is also used to mean a split in friendship, schism (987), breaking off of friendly relations.
In the test phrase: 'They rushed into the BREACH', the word is thought by 10 per cent of adult readers to mean FRAY, a brawl, mêlée, riot, public fight. This is not far from BREACH

when the word means a quarrel, break in friendship. A FRAY, however, necessitates an exchange of blows in public; whereas a BREACH may involve an exchange of words but never blows. In the strict sense, the exchange of words is a QUARREL; the break, split, for whatever reason, is a BREACH.

444. *INEFFICIENT* (*ĭn-ĕf-fĭsh'-ĕnt*) *adj.* Lacking skill, incapable, incompetent, ineffective, ineffectual, not efficacious, not producing the desired result. 'An INEFFICIENT executive.'
INEFFICIENT is a combination of the Latin *in*, not; and *efficere*, to effect, accomplish. *Efficere* in turn comes from *ex*, out; and *facere*, to do.
INEFFICIENT and INEFFECTIVE are practically synonymous. Both may modify persons. The word INEFFECTIVE is applied most aptly to a person from whom nothing is expected at the moment, but who would probably be incapable of contributing if something were expected. INEFFICIENT is applied to one who attempts to contribute, to be helpful, but who does not succeed, is not equal to the demand. An INEFFICIENT person may be willing, but is awkward, clumsy, stupid.

445. *SCAVENGER* (*skăv'-ĕn-jer*) *n.* A person employed to remove refuse from the street, street-cleaner.
To 10 per cent of adult readers SCAVENGER incorrectly means PEASANT. A PEASANT is a rustic, country laborer. A PEASANT is a person of inferior rank; but, except for this, he has no other characteristic in common with a SCAVENGER.
To another 3 per cent SCAVENGER incorrectly means MESSENGER. This is perhaps because of the similarity in pronunciation, for there are only a few words in English in which an N before a G is pronounced as a distinct letter, as: PASSENGER, MESSENGER, HARBINGER, SCAVENGER.
Although a SCAVENGER is literally a street-cleaner, the word has come to be used in a more general sense to characterize any creature which eats carrion, as the SCAVENGER-CRAB, a crab which feeds on dead animals.
A SCAVAGE, a noun now obsolete, was a duty paid on goods in a given location, by a foreigner, stranger. A SCAVENGER was the officer who collected the SCAVAGE, duty; he was the

customs inspector. Later these customs inspectors took over the responsibility of seeing that the streets were kept clean; and from this the word SCAVENGER has come to mean street-cleaner, street-sweeper, 'white-wing', the name given at one time, because of their white uniforms, to the street-cleaners of New York City.

446. *BEGRUDGE* (*bē-grŭdj'*) *v.* To grant with reluctance, give unwillingly, part with ungraciously. BEGRUDGE may also mean envy the possession of.

BEGRUDGE is a combination of the Anglo-Saxon prefix BE and the word GRUDGE (337), which can be traced back to Middle English and is of French origin. It is from the same source as the English word GROWL, snarl, grumble, and suggests growling about every favor which must be granted.

In the test phrase: 'He BEGRUDGED each penny', the word is thought by 11 per cent of adult readers to mean HOARDED. To HOARD is to store, lay up, collect, treasure; it is, specifically, not to part with. To BEGRUDGE, in this sentence, is to part with unwillingly.

447. *IDIOSYNCRASY* (*ĭd-ĭ-ō-sĭn'-kră-sĭ*) *n.* An eccentricity (321), whimsy, mental habit belonging to an individual, constitutional peculiarity, distinctive characteristic, singularity, idiasm.

IDIOSYNCRASY comes from two Greek words ἴδιος, one's own; and σύγκρασις, mixture; and by derivation means one's own mixture, one's own temperament. From the same source comes the word IDIOM, by derivation a personal peculiarity, now a mode of expression peculiar to a language.

To 8 per cent of college seniors IDIOSYNCRASY incorrectly means FANATICISM, excessive enthusiasm, wild and extravagant notions especially in religion. FANATICISM, wild enthusiasm, may be the idiosyncrasy, the eccentricity, of a particular person; but the word IDIOSYNCRASY is a general term for any peculiarity.

448. *SLOTH* (*slōth*) *n.* Laziness, slowness, tardiness, sluggishness, indolence, disinclination to work.

To 5 per cent of adult readers SLOTH incorrectly means

DRINKING. SLOTH is one of the seven MORTAL, deadly, SINS: PRIDE, COVETOUSNESS, LUST, ANGER, GLUTTONY, ENVY, and SLOTH.

449. *NETTLE* (*nĕt'-tl*) *v.* To irritate, vex, fret, pique, provoke, rankle (754), stir the wrath of.

In the test phrase: 'Do not be NETTLED', the word is thought by 7 per cent of preparatory-school juniors to mean DECEIVED, misled, deluded; and by another 5 per cent CAUGHT. Although the exact derivation of the word, NETTLE, is unknown, it can be traced back to Anglo-Saxon and may come from the same source as the word NET. The verb, to NET, may mean to capture, catch; and it may be this etymological relationship which has led to the confusion of the verb to NETTLE, irritate, with to CATCH. Perhaps the similarity of NET and NETTLE has led also to the confusion of NETTLE with DECEIVE; for to NET may mean to entangle, entrap by stratagem, ensnare by wiles, beguile, a sense not far from DECEIVE.

Almost everyone knows the common NETTLE, a plant with stinging hairs. The verb, to NETTLE, comes from the name of the plant, and means to sting, irritate, as do the spines of the nettle.

450. *SIDLE* (*sī'-dl*) *v.* To move sidewise, edge along unobtrusively, go obliquely, walk side foremost.
SIDLE comes from the word SIDE, which is of Anglo-Saxon origin.

In the test phrase: 'He SIDLED up to the speaker', the word is thought by 9 per cent of adult readers to mean BUSTLED. To BUSTLE is to hurry, hustle, move quickly and energetically, stir, be active, move in haste with a certain amount of fuss and noise. To BUSTLE is to move straight ahead, noisily and quickly, in such a way as to attract attention. To SIDLE is to move quietly, unobtrusively, and to the side in an effort to remain unnoticed.

451. *DIGRESS* (*dī-grĕs'*) *v.* To deviate (654), diverge, swerve, wander, stray, aberrate, turn aside from the main theme of a discourse. A DIGRESSION is the corresponding noun.
DIGRESS is from the Latin *dis*, apart; and *gradi*, to go; from

the same source as the verb to TRANSGRESS (215), to over-step.

In the test phrase: 'He DIGRESSES amazingly', the word is thought by 8 per cent of adult readers to mean FIBS. This confusion may be due to the frequent use of the phrase: 'To DIGRESS from the truth', to wander from the truth, fib; or it may be due to the similarity of the words DIGRESS, deviate, and TRANSGRESS, literally to pass over, go beyond, a word which has come to mean overstep a rule, infringe upon a law, violate. To DIGRESS almost invariably means to turn aside from the main issue, wander from the point.

452. *DESTINY* (dĕs'-tĭ-nĭ) *n.* One's appointed lot, fore-ordained fate, predetermined doom, fortune, kismet (955). The words DESTINY and FATE are almost synonymous. FATE comes from the Latin *fari*, to speak, and the word may be used with reference to the outcome of, for instance, a legal trial. The Fates, in Greek mythology, were the three goddesses, Clotho (klō'-thō), who spun the thread of life; Lachesis (lăk'-ĕ-sĭs), who measured the thread; and Atropos (ăt'-rō-pŏs), who severed it. DESTINY, which can be traced back to Middle English, may come from a Latin word meaning to ordain, settle, and designates a foreordained condition beyond human control.

453. *INCREDULITY* (ĭn-krĕ-dū'-lĭ-tĭ) *n.* Unbelief, skepticism, doubt, distrust (36), amazed disbelief.

To 7 per cent of preparatory-school juniors INCREDULITY incorrectly means UNREST, uneasiness, lack of repose, disquietude.

INCREDULITY comes from the Latin *in*, not; and *credere*, to believe; and by derivation means the characteristic of not believing. The Latin *credo*, I believe, the first person singular of the verb *credere*, is familiar as the first word of the Latin version of the Apostles' Creed. From *credere* come also the English words: CREED, a statement of belief; CREDIT, to believe, trust; and CREDULITY. CREDULITY has come to mean not merely belief, but readiness to believe without proof, a disposition to believe too easily, tendency to believe in the impossible and absurd, gullibility. In much this same way,

INCREDULITY is a tendency not to believe easily, to require overwhelming proof, to be skeptical.

INCREDULITY and DISBELIEF, the second of Anglo-Saxon origin, are practically synonymous, but differ in use. One may express DISBELIEF in a single fact; but INCREDULITY is a general characteristic. Thus, one speaks of an INCREDULOUS person, one characterized by INCREDULITY.

454. *DISDAINFUL* (*dĭs-dān'-fŭl*) *adj.* Scornful, contemptuous, haughtily superior, supercilious (338), proud, lofty, arrogant.

DISDAINFUL comes from the Latin *dis*, not; and *dignus*, worthy. In the test phrase: 'DISDAINFUL of our kindness', the word is thought by 13 per cent of adult readers to mean UNWORTHY, wanting merit, a literal translation of the Latin, and the common misconception of the word. DISDAINFUL, as the word is used in English, does not mean unworthy, but means regarding another as unworthy, and therefore being scornful, contemptuous, DISDAINFUL of him.

CONTEMPTUOUS is the general term. SCORNFUL is passionately contemptuous. DISDAINFUL is high-mindedly, proudly, indignantly, contemptuous.

455. *CLANDESTINE* (*klăn-dĕs'-tĭn*) *adj.* Secret (5), illicitly covert, furtive, stealthy (367), surreptitious, concealed for an underhand purpose.

To 4 per cent of adult readers CLANDESTINE incorrectly means RIOTOUS, tumultuous, wild, disorderly, wanton. This may be due to a confusion of the Latin word *clam*, secretly, the immediate source of CLANDESTINE, with the English word CLANG, a loud metallic sound, or with CLAMOR (242), shouting, hubbub, uproar. CLANDESTINE is probably from the same ultimate source as the Latin word *celare*, to hide, from which comes more directly the English word to CONCEAL, hide, secrete. CLANDESTINE means hidden, concealed.

456. *CRITERION* (*krĭ-tē'-rĭ-ŏn*) *n.* Standard, rule, measure, test, touchstone, principle held as a standard in judgment, as: 'A CRITERION of beauty'.

CRITERION comes from a Greek word κρίνειν, judge, from

the same source as the English word CRITIC, one who judges, expresses a reasoned opinion.

457. *SUPPOSITIOUS* (*sŭp-pō-zĭ'-shŭs*) *adj.* Spurious (683), counterfeit, false, not genuine, substituted fraudulently, assuming the character of another.
SUPPOSITIOUS comes from the Latin *sub*, under; and *ponere*, to place, put; and means put in place of another.

In the test phrase: 'SUPPOSITIOUS remedies', the word is thought by 7 per cent of adult readers to mean LAXATIVE, having a tendency to loosen, relaxing, the popular misconception. This is no doubt a confusion of the adjective SUPPOSITIOUS, false, with the noun SUPPOSITORY (*sŭp-pŏz'-ĭ-tō-rĭ*), a cone or cylinder introduced into the body as a laxative.

SUPPOSITIOUS (*sŭp-pō-zĭ'-shŭs*) and SUPPOSITITIOUS (*sŭp-pŏz-ĭ-tĭ'-shŭs*) are two forms of the same adjective; both mean spurious. The second, SUPPOSITITIOUS, is the more desirable; SUPPOSITIOUS is often marked as archaic.

458. *ACOUSTICAL* (*ă-koos'-tĭ-kăl*) *adj.* Auditory, pertaining to the sense of hearing, pertaining to the science of sounds. ACOUSTICAL and ACOUSTIC are both adjectives and synonymous. ACOUSTIC is the more usual of the two.
In the test phrase: 'ACOUSTICAL properties', the word is thought by 6 per cent of preparatory-school juniors to mean ADDRESSING. The word ADDRESS (*ăd-drĕs'*) may be either noun or verb. Both have many meanings. An ADDRESS, the noun, may be a lecture, oration; as: 'He delivered an ADDRESS'. To ADDRESS (125), the verb, may mean to lecture, speak to formally, as: 'He ADDRESSED the audience'. The ADDRESSING properties of a hall might therefore conceivably be its ACOUSTICAL properties; but the participial adjective, ADDRESSING, is never used in this way. An ADDRESSING machine is one which stamps or prints ADDRESSES, house number, street, and city; but it is difficult to imagine a situation in which the participial adjective, ADDRESSING, could be used to mean speaking, lecturing.

By another 5 per cent ACOUSTICAL is thought to mean GHOSTLY, emaciated, pale.

Both ACOUSTICAL and AUDITORY come originally from Greek words, and are practically synonymous. They are however used differently. AUDITORY is more familiar, and is from the same source as such common words as AUDIENCE, a group of hearers; and AUDITORIUM, a place for hearing. ACOUSTICAL is associated with science. The noun, ACOUSTICS, is the science of sound.

459. *MIRAGE* (*mǐr-ahj'*) *n.* Misleading image, optical illusion (495) produced by atmospheric conditions.
MIRAGE comes ultimately from the Latin *mirus*, wonderful, the source of the English words MIRROR, looking glass; ADMIRE, by derivation to wonder at; and MIRACLE, a wonder.

To 13 per cent of preparatory-school juniors MIRAGE incorrectly means a CONCEPTION, a word which may mean an original idea, also the act of conceiving. This is perhaps due to a confusion of the word CONCEPTION with DECEPTION, that which deceives, a cheat, fraud; for the word MIRAGE, in its general sense, means any deceptive appearance, illusion.

460. *PERENNIAL* (*pĕr-ĕn'-nĭ-ăl*) *adj.* Perpetual (550), unceasing, continuing from year to year, recurring yearly, lasting for a long time.
To 7 per cent of adult readers PERENNIAL incorrectly means EARLY, in good season, betimes. The three words PERENNIAL, BIENNIAL, and ANNUAL, are used in botany as both adjectives and nouns. An ANNUAL is a plant which lives for only a single season, which grows from seed each year. A BIENNIAL lives for two years. A PERENNIAL continues to grow from the same roots year after year.

461. *COUNTERPART* (*kown'-ter-pahrt*) *n.* A double, duplicate, copy (46), a thing so like another as to be mistaken for it, correlative (*kŏr-rĕl'-ă-tĭv*) of another.
In the test phrase: 'Standing with your COUNTERPART', the word is thought by 13 per cent of preparatory-school juniors to mean FELLOW MEMBER.
The prefix, COUNTER, is used in many English words to mean opposite, opposing, contrary, antagonistic. Thus: to COUNTERACT is to act in opposition to; to COUNTERBALANCE is to neutralize by contrary power. The prefix, COUNTER, may also mean corresponding, as in the word COUNTERFEIT, to

copy, imitate. The word COUNTERPART may mean either an opposing part, complement; or an exactly similar part.

462. *STATUTE* (*stăt'-ūt*) *n.* Law (4), enactment, permanent rule, act of a legislative body; in Great Britain an act of Parliament.

To 8 per cent of adult readers STATUTE incorrectly means MONUMENT. This is probably a confusion of STATUTE, law, with STATUE (*stăt'ū*), a sculptured figure. To another 4 per cent STATUTE incorrectly means PHYSIQUE. This is undoubtedly a confusion of STATUTE, law, with STATURE (*stăt'-ūr*), bodily height.

A STATUTE and an ORDINANCE are both laws. An ORDINANCE is a local city law. A STATUTE is a more general law, one which may apply to a state or a country, and which is usually enacted by a legislature.

463. *STINT* (*stĭnt*) *v.* To restrict to a scant allowance, restrain within fixed limits, confine, limit.

The corresponding noun STINT means allotted amount of work, limitation of effort; and sometimes limit, restraint, as: 'They drank without STINT'.

In the test phrase: 'She did not STINT herself', the word is thought by 5 per cent of adult readers to mean BLAME, find fault with; and by another 5 per cent to mean FLATTER, seek to please, overpraise.

464. *EVASIVE* (*ē-vā'-sĭv*) *adj.* Avoiding the point, not straightforward, shuffling (190), elusory (345), quibbling, prevaricating (653), equivocal (958).

Evasive is from the Latin *e*, out; and *vasus*, the past participle of the verb *vadere*, to go, probably from the same ultimate source as the English words, to WADE and to WADDLE.

EVASIVE, EQUIVOCAL, and PREVARICATING, all apply to speech, and describe increasingly dishonorable attempts to avoid being found out.

465. *CORROBORATION* (*kŏr-rŏb-ō-rā'-shŭn*) *n.* Confirmation, supporting fact, verification, additional assurance.

To 12 per cent of preparatory-school juniors CORROBORATION

incorrectly means THOUGHT, the act of thinking. This may be a confusion of CORROBORATION, verification, with CEREBRATION, the act of thinking.

CORROBORATION is from the Latin *con*, together; and *robarare*, to strengthen, a verb which in turn comes from *robur*, strength, the source of the English word ROBUST; and, by derivation, CORROBORATION is the act of giving strength, robustness, to a belief.

466. *OBITUARY* (*ō-bĭt'-ū-ā-rĭ*) *adj.* Relating to the death of a person, necrological (*nĕk-rō-lŏj'-ĭ-kăl*).

OBITUARY is from the Latin *obire*, to die. The Latin *obire* in turn is a combination of *ob* and *ire*, to go, and by derivation means to go to meet.

In the test phrase: 'An OBITUARY column', the word is thought by 6 per cent of adult readers to mean CIRCULAR. This may be due to a confusion of the word OBIT, death, decease, funeral solemnities, the root of OBITUARY, with ORBIT, the nearly circular course of a heavenly body moving about another, the path of a planet about the sun.

The noun, an OBITUARY, is a biographical notice of a person recently deceased. The adjective is more general and means relating to death.

467. *PENANCE* (*pĕn'-ăns*) *n.* An atonement, outward act by which sorrow for sins is shown, punishment voluntarily submitted to as an expression of penitence.

In the test phrase: 'He gloried in his PENANCE', the word is thought by 14 per cent of adult readers to mean POVERTY. This is perhaps a confusion of the word PENANCE, atonement, with PENURY, extreme poorness, severe poverty. PENANCE is suffering submitted to as a punishment for faults.

468. *PONDEROSITY* (*pŏn-der-ŏs'-ĭ-tĭ*) *n.* Heaviness, weightiness, cumbersomeness, bulkiness, massiveness.

When used in the test phrase: 'The PONDEROSITY of his style', the word is believed by 13 per cent of adult readers to mean THOUGHTFULNESS. The word THOUGHTFULNESS, in this phrase, has its original meaning, reflectiveness, contemplativeness, studiousness, serious meditation. THOUGHTFULNESS and PONDEROSITY, weightiness, are so closely associated that a rare meaning of PONDEROSITY is actually THOUGHTFULNESS. But PONDEROSITY as the word is ordinarily used today does not necessarily imply THOUGHTFULNESS, studiousness, but means heaviness.

469. *INFRACTION* (*ĭn-frăk'-shŭn*) *n.* Violation, infringement, transgression, breaking, breach (443).

INFRACTION is from the Latin *in;* and *frangere,* to break, the source of the English word FRACTURE, a break; and REFRACTION, the breaking up of a light ray as it passes through a substance.

To 7 per cent of preparatory-school juniors INFRACTION incorrectly means LIKENESS, resemblance. This confusion may be due to the similarity of the three words REFLECTION, an image, likeness produced by the turning back of light rays; REFRACTION; and INFRACTION, a violation, infringement.

470. *EXUDE* (*ĕks-ūd'*) *v.* To give forth, ooze, discharge slowly, emit, trickle out, issue gradually, excrete, perspire, as: 'A pine EXUDES resin', or 'Resin EXUDES'.

To 7 per cent of preparatory-school juniors EXUDE incorrectly means DEMAND, require, ask. This is perhaps due to a confusion of EXUDE, ooze out, with EXACT, to demand, require.

EXUDE and the corresponding noun EXUDATION, which may also still be spelt EXSUDATION, are from the Latin *ex,* out; and *sudare,* to sweat. To EXUDE by derivation means to ooze out as does sweat through the pores of the skin. From *sudare* come also the unusual English words SUDORIFIC, causing sweating, inducing perspiration; and TRANSUDE (*trăn-sūd'*), to ooze through the pores of a membrane.

EXUDE, TRANSUDE, and TRANSPIRE, are practically synonymous. The word TRANSPIRE is so frequently used incorrectly to mean happen, take place, that its misuse is finding its way even into dictionaries. Although language must grow in order to keep pace with modern science and with the increasing complexities of civilization, the incorrect application of an exact word to convey an idea already correctly conveyed by other words is not growth. TRANSPIRE is from the Latin *trans*, through; and *spirare*, to breathe; and means to pass out through pores, pass off invisibly from the body as vapor. TRANSPIRE may also be correctly used figuratively to mean leak out, emerge gradually from secrecy into public knowledge. 'It TRANSPIRED' does not mean it happened but that it gradually became public knowledge. TRANSUDE is used most frequently of fluids passing gradually through pores from one place to another. EXUDE is used of anything which escapes gradually through pores, oozes out.

471. *LONGEVITY* (*lŏn-jĕv'-ĭ-tĭ*) *n.* The characteristic of living to a great age, a predisposition to a long life, great length of life.

To 6 per cent of preparatory-school juniors LONGEVITY incorrectly means HEIGHT. LONGEVITY comes from two Latin words *longus*, long; and *aetas*, age; and means specifically long life.

472. *RANDOM* (*răn'-dŏm*) *adj.* Aimless, haphazard, casual, stray, incidental, fortuitous (953), left to chance, having no definite purpose.

RANDOM can be traced back through Middle English to Old French.

In the test phrase: 'RANDOM remarks', the word is thought by 29 per cent of grammar-school pupils to mean OFT-REPEATED. This misunderstanding may be due to some survival of the obsolete noun, a RANDOM, which meant originally in English a rushing as of a torrent, a violent force; and then later a continuous flow of words, harangue, a meaning which might easily lead to OFT-REPEATED. But the noun has practically disappeared from the language, except in the phrase: 'At RANDOM', aimlessly, without direction. The present adjective, RANDOM, has come by ellipsis from the phrase: 'At RANDOM', and means aimless, casual, haphazard.

To another 20 per cent, the word incorrectly means SILLY. Both SILLY remarks and RANDOM remarks fail to fit the situation. A SILLY remark fails because it is foolish, stupid, unwise, and lacks common sense. A RANDOM remark fails because it is aimless, casual, and probably has nothing to do with the subject in hand.

473. *EXCHEQUER* (*ĕks-chĕk'-er*) *n.* Money supply, treasury, cash, funds, finances, pecuniary (347) resources.

An EXCHEQUER was originally the checkered board used in the games of chess and checkers; the word CHECK (399), an attack on the king in the game of chess, comes from the same source. Then EXCHEQUER was applied to the checkered cloth used in court, on which accounts were calculated by means of counters. From this came the name COURT OF EXCHEQUER, which dealt with cases involving money and accounts due the Crown. The EXCHEQUER, spelt with a capital, is in England the department of income, revenue, with the Chancellor of the Exchequer at its head; all from the fact that an EXCHEQUER was a checkered board. EXCHEQUER, to mean one's own money supply, is more or less colloquial and should be used, if at all, only jocosely.

VITALITY, power, energy, is the popular misconception, perhaps because to some persons money is so much the vital force of life that VITALITY, power, and EXCHEQUER, money supply, are inseparable.

474. *SANCTITY* (*sănk'-tĭ-tĭ*) *n.* Holiness, godliness, saintliness. From this, SANCTITY has come to mean sacredness, solemnity, inviolability.

SANCTITY is from the Latin *sanctus*, holy, the source of the English words: SAINT, holy person; and SANCTION, originally the act of making sacred. Today in international law a SANCTION is a provision for securing obedience to an agreement by the enactment of penalties or rewards, in effect a threat to enforce obedience.

475. *IMPEL* (*ĭm-pĕl'*) *v.* To drive on, actuate, instigate, incite, stimulate (295), excite to action, urge forward.

IMPEL is from the Latin *in*, on; and *pellere*, to drive; and means literally to drive on. It is from the same source as the English verbs, to EXPEL, to drive out; to REPEL, to drive back; and to PROPEL, to drive forward; and the corresponding nouns EXPULSION, REPULSION, and PROPULSION, all of which come from *pulsus*, the past participle of *pellere*.

IMPEL and PROPEL are practically synonymous, except that commonly PROPEL is used of mechanical motions, and IMPEL of mental and spiritual forces. Thus: 'A propeller PROPELS a boat'; but, 'Ambition IMPELS one to action'.

476. *UNIMPEACHABLE* (*ŭn-ĭm-pēch'-ā-bl*) *adj.* Blameless, free from guilt, irreproachable, invulnerable (354), giving no opening to censure.

In the test phrase: 'An UNIMPEACHABLE patriot', the word is thought by 10 per cent of preparatory-school juniors to mean ARDENT, burning, fiery, passionate, eager.

To IMPEACH comes from the Latin word *pes*, foot, and originally meant to fetter, entangle, hinder. It is from the same ultimate source as the verb to IMPEDE. IMPEDE (532) has, however, kept its original meaning of hinder, obstruct; while IMPEACH has lost this and means either to accuse in general or specifically to accuse a public official. UNIMPEACH-ABLE is used ordinarily in the general sense of incapable of being accused.

477. *LAGGARD* (*lăg'-gahrd*) *n.* A loiterer, procrastinator, one who moves slowly, falls behind, a lazy person, slack fellow, one who lags.

LAGGARD comes from the Latin *laxus*, lax, loose, from the same source as the English words LAX, loose, slack; and LANGUID, drooping.

To 8 per cent of college seniors LAGGARD incorrectly means a TRAMP, a vagrant. LAGGARDS and TRAMPS are both lazy and may both move aimlessly. But a TRAMP can be only a professional beggar who wanders from place to place; while a LAGGARD is any person who falls behind others.

A LAGGARD, a LOITERER, and a LINGERER, all move slowly. A LINGERER remains too long in one place while on the way somewhere else; a LOITERER wastes time on the way; a LAGGARD remains behind others.

478. *ABSOLUTION* (*ăb-sō-lū'-shŭn*) *n.* The forgiveness of sins, acquittance, exoneration, exculpation; loosely, the release from obligations or penalties; specifically, release from the consequences of sin, remission of sins.

In its earliest use, ABSOLUTION meant forgiveness granted by the Church and, although the word has come to mean forgiveness in general, it is still used primarily in its ecclesiastical sense to mean an official declaration by a clergyman assuring a penitent that his sins are forgiven.

ABSOLUTION is the noun which corresponds to the verb, to ABSOLVE (516), to free from sin, release from obligation. It is from the same source as the verb, to SOLVE, literally to loosen, free from difficulties, a word which is more familiar as used in mathematics to mean obtain the answer; and the nouns SOLUTION; RESOLUTION, the process of separation, also today more commonly steadfastness of purpose, determination; and DISSOLUTION, disintegration.

In the test phrase: 'He was granted ABSOLUTION', the word is believed by 7 per cent of adult readers to mean AUTHORITY, power, command, dominion.

To another 6 per cent ABSOLUTION means PERMISSION. This may be due to a confusion of PERMISSION, formal consent, with REMISSION, pardon, forgiveness, release, a synonym of ABSOLUTION.

An ABSOLUTION and a PARDON both recognize guilt. The word PARDON is used most frequently for the forgiveness of a crime against society; a PARDON reinstates an individual in society. An ABSOLUTION is granted for a sin committed by an individual against himself and reinstates him in his own opinion.

479. *TEMPERAMENT* (*tĕm'-pĕr-ă-mĕnt*) *n.* Characteristic nature, disposition, temper, natural make-up, mood, humor, character, total personality.

TEMPERAMENT is from the Latin *temperare*, to mix in due proportion, moderate, qualify, mingle. TEMPERAMENT is the blending of all of one's qualities and characteristics.

To 5 per cent of adult readers TEMPERAMENT incorrectly means PASSION, emotion, feeling, or sometimes rage, wrath. This may be a confusion of TEMPERAMENT with one meaning of TEMPER; for TEMPER and PASSION may be synonymous as in the phrases: 'In a TEMPER' and 'In a PASSION', where both words are used to mean fit of anger. TEMPER and TEMPERAMENT may also be synonymous. Thus: 'To lose one's TEMPER' is to lose that nice balance between one's conflicting tendencies which enables one to act intelligently. Although the word TEMPER can be used to mean fit of anger, passion, and that adjustment of one's conflicts which keeps one from flying into a passion, the word TEMPERAMENT can be used only in the last sense.

To another 5 per cent TEMPERAMENT incorrectly means ABILITY. ABILITY is that combination of inherent aptitudes, acquired skill, and knowledge, which enables an individual to achieve results when the circumstances are right and the opportunity presents itself. But there are many persons of ABILITY who are kept by circumstances from accomplishing as much as they should. This mingling of ability and the effects of environment, which makes the individual, has been called TEMPERAMENT.

480. *DISCIPLINARIAN* (*dĭs-ĭ-plĭ-nā'-rĭ-ăn*) *n.* A strict teacher, martinet (905), one who maintains order, one who enforces obedience.

Three words, DISCIPLINARIAN, DISCIPLINE, and DISCIPLE (*dĭs-sĭ'-pl*), all come from the Latin word *discere*, to learn. A DISCIPLE is one who learns, who receives instruction, especially one who believes wholeheartedly in the teachings of his master, as: 'The DISCIPLES of Christ'. The verb, to DISCIPLINE, may mean to teach, train, drill, educate, to impart that which a DISCIPLE receives. Or it may mean to punish, chastise. The noun, a DISCIPLINARIAN, is used only in this last sense to mean one who disciplines, one who maintains order, a strict teacher. DISCIPLINARIAN is never used to mean merely a teacher, instructor.

To 23 per cent of grammar-school pupils DISCIPLINARIAN incorrectly means POLITICIAN, one skilled in the science of government. There is a remote connection between the nouns POLITICIAN and DISCIPLINARIAN through the verb, to GOVERN. A POLITICIAN is interested in government, and would often like to govern, but may be entirely without authority; a DISCIPLINARIAN actually governs those under him, but may be indifferent to public affairs.

481. *FLURRY* (*fler'-rĭ*) *n.* Commotion, flutter, fluster (509), momentary agitation, excited movement. FLURRY is also used specifically to mean a gust of wind, squall.

The exact etymology of FLURRY is unknown. There are, however, similar words in the Scandinavian languages.

To 10 per cent of adult readers FLURRY incorrectly means UPHEAVAL. An UPHEAVAL and a FLURRY are both agitated movements. An UPHEAVAL is violent and leaves in its wake a permanent change in conditions. UPHEAVAL is, for instance, applied in geology to that raising of the earth's crust which forms mountain ranges. UPHEAVAL is also applied to a social or political agitation which is violent enough to cause a permanent change. A FLURRY is lighter, slighter, and its effect only momentary.

482. *ARTIFICIAL (ahr-tĭ-fĭsh'-ăl) adj.* Manufactured, synthetic (437), factitious (1064), produced by art rather than by nature.

ARTIFICIAL is from two Latin words, *ars, artis,* art, the source of the English words ART, ARTIST, and ARTISAN, handicraftsman, mechanic, one skilled in any trade; and *facere,* to make, the source of MANUFACTURED, literally hand-made, made by hand. ARTIFICIAL is by derivation art-made, made by art.

ARTIFICIAL may mean imitation, made to imitate nature, and so suggest poor in quality. In this sense ARTIFICIAL and REAL are opposites. Or the word may mean manufactured, not necessarily of inferior quality, as in the phrase: 'ARTIFICIAL ice'. In this sense ARTIFICIAL and NATURAL (26) are opposites.

483. *ALIENATE (ā'-lĭ-ĕn-āt) v.* To estrange, disaffect, create a repugnance to, turn away in feeling, make hostile.

The adjective, ALIEN, from the Latin *alius,* another, has two meanings. It may mean foreign, belonging to another country; or it may mean hostile, adverse, estranged. The verb, to ALIENATE, has this last meaning, to estrange, make hostile, turn away.

484. *PRACTICABLE (prăk'-tĭk-ă-bl) adj.* Usable (290), feasible, workable, capable of being put into practice.

PRACTICABLE and PRACTICAL are often used interchangeably without regard to the difference in their meanings. PRACTICAL means pertaining to use, derived from experience. PRACTICABLE means capable of being used or accomplished. PRACTICABLE is, therefore, a synonym of USABLE; and IMPRACTICABLE is an exact opposite.

It is probably the confusion of PRACTICAL with PRACTICABLE which leads to the common misconception of the word THEORETICAL. THEORETICAL means pertaining to pure knowledge, arrived at by reasoning. It is an exact opposite of PRACTICAL, pertaining to experience. It does not mean, as is often supposed, incapable of being used, not workable, impracticable. Thus: PRACTICAL and THEORETICAL; PRACTICABLE and UNUSABLE, impracticable, are opposites.

485. *TORRID* (*tŏr'-rĭd*) *adj*. Hot, arid, parching, dry with heat, searing (687), scorching, adust (1052).

Both TORRID and ARID are used to mean at the same time hot and dry; ARID is, however, primarily dry; TORRID is primarily hot. That TORRID means hot may perhaps be remembered by the fact that the earth's surface is divided into three temperature zones: the FRIGID, cold, zone; the TEMPERATE, moderate, zone; and the TORRID, hot, zone. TORRID, hot, is therefore the opposite of FRIGID, cold.

In the test phrase: 'The TORRID day', the common misconception of the word is HUMID, damp, moist, wet. HUMID (75) does not refer to temperature; it does not mean either hot or cold, but means damp, moist.

HUMID and DRY; TORRID and FRIGID; are opposites.

486. *TRANSCRIBE* (*trăn-skrīb'*) *v*. To copy in writing, make a written or typewritten copy (46) of shorthand notes. TRANSCRIPT and TRANSCRIPTION are corresponding nouns. TRANSCRIBE, TRANSLITERATE, and TRANSLATE, are all from the Latin *trans*, over. TRANSLATE, from *latus*, the past participle of the Latin verb *ferre*, to carry, originally meant to carry from one place to another. TRANSFER, directly from the Latin *ferre*, is now used more frequently in this sense; and TRANSLATE, when applied to writing, means to express in another language, change from one language into another. TRANSLITERATE, from the Latin *litera*, letter, is to rewrite in the letters, in the alphabet, of another language, as when a

Greek word is rewritten in Roman letters. TRANSCRIBE, from the Latin *scribere*, is by derivation to write over, rewrite. The word is used today specifically to mean type in full from notes taken in shorthand.

487. *FEIGN* (*fān*) *v*. To pretend, profess, make believe, dissemble, romance, invent.

In the test phrase: 'He FEIGNED to go', the word is thought by 13 per cent of preparatory-school juniors to mean CONDESCENDED. This is no doubt a confusion of FEIGN, pretend, profess, with DEIGN (898), condescend.

The noun, a FEINT, is a word used in fencing and boxing for a pretended blow, often for an open attack from one direction made with the purpose of covering up a real attack from another direction. Although a FEINT is spelt without the G, it is the noun which corresponds to the verb to FEIGN. Both FEINT and FEIGN come originally probably from the Latin *fingere*, touch, handle, a word which later came to mean devise, and then imagine. Once in English both verb and noun were spelt without the G; the G of the present English verb is apparently a recent addition.

488. *VERSATILE* (*ver'-să-tĭl*) *adj*. Many-sided, having many aptitudes, turning with ease from one subject to another.

In the test phrase: 'VERSATILE persons', the word is thought by 6 per cent of adult readers to mean LIKEABLE. This may be due to a confusion of VERSATILE, many-sided, with some form of the verb AVERSE, disinclined, or the noun AVERSION. As AVERSION means dislike, *version* should mean liking, and VERSATILE should mean likeable. This analogy does not always follow in English. Although VERSATILE and AVERSION both come from the Latin *vertere*, to turn, and although the words were once used in their literal senses, their figurative meanings are widely different. An AVERSION was originally a physical turning away; but this meaning is now obsolete and an AVERSION is a fixed dislike, habitual antipathy, repugnance. VERSATILE, from the Latin *versare*, to turn again and again, the frequentative form of *vertere*, to turn, originally meant capable of being turned, and the word may still be used in this way; but its ordinary meaning is turning often and with ease from one thing to another.

489. *TABLET* (*tăb'-lĕt*) *n.* Flat slab, panel usually of stone or bronze and bearing an inscription.

TABLET is from the Latin *tabula*, a board, tablet, painting. A TABLET and a PLAQUE (*plahk*) are both flat slabs. A PLAQUE is decorated, ordinarily by sculpture in low relief. A TABLET bears an inscription, a written record.

490. *REHABILITATE* (*rē-hă-bĭl'-ĭ-tāt*) *v.* To reinstate, reestablish, restore to a former rank.

To 8 per cent of adult readers REHABILITATE incorrectly means INSPECT, examine, view critically.

REHABILITATE is a combination of the prefix RE, and the word ABLE, and means by derivation to make able again, reinstate.

491. *SEGREGATE* (*sĕg'-rē-gāt*) *v.* To set apart, separate, isolate, make a separate group.

In the test phrase: 'SEGREGATE these plants', the word is thought by 8 per cent of adult readers to mean TRANSPLANT, plant in another place.

SEGREGATE is from the Latin *segregare*, to separate from the flock; a combination of *se*, apart; and *grex*, *gregis*, flock, the source of the English word GREGARIOUS, flocking together. To SEGREGATE is literally to separate from others.

492. *GAUDY* (*gaw'-dĭ*) *adj.* Gay, garish, dressy, glittering, pretentious (406), tawdry, flashy, ostentatiously fine, tastelessly showy (442).

GAUDY and the noun a GAUD, a worthless trinket, come from the Latin, *gaudium*, joy.

To 9 per cent of adult readers GAUDY incorrectly means STYLISH, fashionable, modish, in suggestion almost an opposite of GAUDY, showy but without taste.

493. *TERSE* (*ters*) *adj.* Brief, concise, neat, short and to the point, succinct, laconic (629), pithy (1009), sententious. Formerly the word TERSE was used to describe any-

thing which was clean, smooth, rubbed to a polish, even a person who was polished, refined. Today TERSE applies only to literary style, to language.

In the test phrase: 'TERSE style', the word is believed by 8 per cent of college seniors to mean MINCING. 'A MINCING style' or 'A MINCING manner' is overnice, affectedly refined. This is however a derived meaning of the word. The verb to MINCE means to cut, chop into small pieces, as in the word MINCEMEAT, literally minced meat; and in such a phrase as: 'With no MINCING of words', MINCING means cutting short, stopping without finishing. A MINCING style is cut short because one is too prim to continue, it leaves much unsaid. A TERSE style gives the entire thought, with elegant completeness, in the fewest possible words.

494. *UNIQUE* (*ū-nēk'*) *adj.* Unrivaled, outstanding (179), peerless, preeminent (339), exceptional, paramount, singular, matchless, unparalleled (529), without an equal, not like anything else.

In the test phrase: 'UNIQUE events', the word is thought by 9 per cent of adult readers to mean AUSPICIOUS, favorable, propitious.

UNIQUE is from the Latin *unus*, one, from the same source as the English words, UNIT, a single thing; UNITE, to combine into one; and UNITY, state of being combined into one. UNIQUE means being the only one of its kind.

495. *ILLUSION* (*ĭl-lū'-zhŭn*) *n.* A deceptive appearance, hallucination, mistaken perception, unreality, unreal image, mirage (459), momentary false conception which is soon corrected.

ILLUSION is from the Latin *in*, on; and *ludere*, to play; and suggests a playing on, playing tricks upon.

In the test phrase: 'An optical ILLUSION', the word is believed by 16 per cent of adult readers to mean VIEW. This may be due to some confusion of ILLUSION, deceptive appearance, with ILLUSTRATION, for the word VIEW may be used to mean a picture, sketch.

The words ILLUSION and DELUSION are from the same source. A DELUSION is a fixed false conception, a permanent mental misconception, as: 'The DELUSIONS of insanity'. One acts on a DELUSION, for a DELUSION is not dispelled by the ordinary processes of reasoning. An ILLUSION is a momentary, harmless mistake of the senses; one usually recognizes an ILLUSION before acting.

496. *TRIAL* (*trī'-ăl*) *n.* An affliction, trouble, tribulation, cross, hardship, ordeal, trying circumstance, test of one's endurance.

To 16 per cent of grammar-school pupils TRIAL incorrectly means TYRANT. TYRANT comes from τύραννος, a Greek word which originally meant master, sovereign, ruler, but which came, about 700 years before Christ, to be applied to rulers who got their power by force. At that time the so-called TYRANTS were often excellent administrators, governing with the approval of the people. But in the course of the next 300 years power was often seized by unscrupulous men and as a result the word TYRANT came to have its present meaning of cruel oppressor.

TRIAL comes from the Latin verb *terere*, to thresh grain, from the same source as the English word to TRY. To TRY originally meant to refine, assay, separate the good from the bad as in threshing; but the word is now rarely used in this sense, except in cooking, where one TRIES fat in order to purify it. To TRY more often means to make an effort, attempt, as: 'TRY to do something'. To TRY may also mean to put to the test, subject to experimental treatment, as: 'To TRY a new automobile'. Or, to TRY may mean to examine judicially, as: 'To TRY a case in court'. To TRY is also to afflict, as: 'To be sorely TRIED'.

The noun, a TRY, means the act of trying in its second sense, an effort, attempt.

The participial adjective, TRYING, is used only in the fifth sense of the verb. TRYING always means severe, difficult, as: 'A TRYING experience'.

The noun TRIAL may be used in all but the original sense of the verb to TRY. A TRIAL may mean an attempt, effort, as: 'He succeeded on the third TRIAL'. Or a TRIAL may be a judicial proceeding, as: 'The TRIAL of a case'. Or the word TRIAL may be used in the sense in which the participial adjective, TRYING, is always used, to mean affliction, hardship, trouble, as: 'It is a great TRIAL'.

497. *RECONCILE* (*rĕk'-ŏn-sīl*) *v.* To adjust, harmonize, mediate, appease, intercede successfully, make consistent, settle a quarrel, bring into agreement.
To 7 per cent of preparatory-school juniors to RECONCILE incorrectly means TAKE NOTICE OF. This is perhaps a confusion of RECONCILE, adjust, with RECOGNIZE, take notice of.
RECONCILE comes from the Latin *re*, again; and *conciliare*, to unite, bring together, the source of the English word CONCILIATE. To CONCILIATE may mean to gain the good will of, make friendly, propitiate; or it may be a synonym of RECONCILE. Because of the RE, RECONCILE is used more accurately to signify readjusting differences between persons who have temporarily fallen out; it is by derivation to conciliate again.

498. *PURGE* (*perj*) *v.* To cleanse by washing away waste matter, purify, rid of whatever is foul. PURGE may also be used in a figurative sense to mean make spiritually clean, clear from accusation.
PURGE comes from the Latin *purus*, pure, clean; and *agere*, to make; and means literally to make clean. It is from the same source as the noun PURGATORY, the temporary stopping-place where souls are purged, spiritually cleansed, on the way to heaven; the word PURGATORY comes directly from a Latin word which means wash-house, laundry.
By 6 per cent of adult readers, to PURGE is thought to mean to ACCUSE, to charge with guilt, blame, reproach, censure, practically an opposite of the verb PURGE, which may be used to mean to free from accusation. Opposites of PURGE are: CONTAMINATE, CORRUPT, DEBASE, DEFILE, DEPRAVE, INFECT, POISON, SOIL, SPOIL, TAINT, VITIATE.

499. *SUBTLETY* (*sŭt'-l-tĭ*) *n.* Fine point, nicety, delicacy, refinement, niceness of discrimination, fine-drawn distinction.
SUBTLETY comes from the Latin *subtilis*, thin, fine, delicate. In the test phrase: 'The SUBTLETIES of speech', the word is

thought by 6 per cent of adult readers to mean ERRORS, mistakes, faults. The noun SUBTLETY may be used to mean slyness, cunning (320), artifice, and so suggest conscious departure from the truth. An ERROR is, however, an unconscious, unintentional, departure from the truth. There have been two forms of the adjective, SUBTLE and SUBTILE. The one now in good use is SUBTLE, pronounced (*sŭt'-l*) without the B. When SUBTILE is encountered it should be pronounced, like SUBTLE, without the B (*sŭt'-l*). SUBTILE is sometimes pronounced (*sŭb'-tĭl*), with the B, in an attempt to distinguish it from SUBTLE. But all of the modern meanings of the two words are identical and there is no point in distinguishing them. The two corresponding nouns are SUBTLETY and SUBTILITY (*sŭ-tĭl'-ĭ-tĭ*), the first the only one in good use.

500. *ACQUIT* (*ăk-kwĭt'*) *v.* To declare innocent, exonerate, absolve (516), exculpate (903), free from blame, release from accusation, pronounce not guilty.
ACQUIT and the corresponding nouns ACQUITTAL and QUITTANCE (512) are from the Latin *ad*, to; and *quietare*, to quiet. To ACQUIT by derivation means to quiet, set at rest. The word is used today only in the limited sense of quieting an accusation.
In the test phrase: 'He was ACQUITTED', the word is thought by 29 per cent of grammar-school pupils to mean FOUND GUILTY, an exact opposite of the correct meaning. This may be a confusion of ACQUIT, declare innocent, with ACCUSE, charge with guilt. It is almost certain that a proportion of jurymen, in voting to ACQUIT a culprit, believe that they are finding him guilty.

501. *IMMUNE* (*ĭm-mūn'*) *adj.* Exempt, secure, free, having nothing to fear, not susceptible, not liable to contagion.
To 13 per cent of adult readers, IMMUNE incorrectly means WEARY, tired, exhausted. This may possibly be a confusion of IMMUNE, exempt, with the French word ENNUI (*ŏn-nwē'*), boredom, weariness.
IMMUNE is from the Latin *in*, not; and *munus*, service, obligation, duty; and by derivation means exempt from pub-

lic service, free from obligation. IMMUNE is from the same source as the verbs to COMMUNE (*kŏm-mūn'*), to talk together, converse, exchange ideas; and COMMUNICATE, to give to another, impart. Both COMMUNICATE and IMMUNE are used specifically of diseases. To COMMUNICATE a disease is to hand it to another, impart it. To be IMMUNE, applied to a disease, is to be free from the possibility of contagion.

Although IMMUNE and EXEMPT are practically synonymous, the words differ slightly in modern usage. EXEMPT is used most frequently to mean free from legal obligation. One is declared EXEMPT by a legal decree. One is EXEMPT from military service. IMMUNE, despite its derivation, is used most often for inherent physical freedom from a natural liability.

502. *POLTROON* (*pŏl-troon'*) *n.* Coward, sluggard, recreant, dastard (707), craven, wretch, caitiff, mean-spirited fellow.

To 12 per cent of preparatory-school juniors, POLTROON incorrectly means FOOL. This is probably a confusion of POLTROON, coward, with BUFFOON, fool.

POLTROON comes directly from the French word *poltron*, a coward.

503. *POTION* (*pō'-shŭn*) *n.* A drink, draught, dose of medicine in liquid form, definite quantity of a liquid carefully measured. 'A pleasant POTION.'

A POTION and a DRAUGHT (*drăft*) are both an amount drunk. The word DRAUGHT is today the more general of the two. POTION is often reserved for a drink of medicine. The Oxford English Dictionary goes to the extreme of limiting POTION to this specific use and of designating as obsolete the general meaning, any drink. DRINK is, however, accepted as the meaning of POTION by 78 per cent of adult readers.

504. *RIGID* (*rĭj'-ĭd*) *adj.* Strict, severe (123), inflexible (241), inexorable, rigorous, unyielding (392), exacting, harsh, Draconic, not indulgent, not lax.

RIGID comes from the Latin *rigere*, to be stiff, from the same source as the noun RIGOR (*rĭg'-ŏr*) (207), stiffness, rigidity, a word also used figuratively to mean sternness, harshness, cruelty.

When RIGID is applied to physical objects in its literal sense to mean stiff, not easily bent, RIGID and FLEXIBLE (28) are opposites. When it is used figuratively, as in the phrases: 'RIGID criticism', 'A RIGID disciplinarian', 'RIGID rules', RIGID and LAX are opposites.

505. *DEMOCRACY* (dē-mŏk'-rā-sĭ) *n.* Government by the people, the principle that all citizens have equal political rights. 'He believes in DEMOCRACY.' DEMOCRACY may also mean 'the people' in a collective sense.

The word ARISTOCRACY, literally government by the best people, is etymologically almost an opposite of the word DEMOCRACY, government by all the people.

506. *CHIDE* (chīd) *v.* To rebuke, reprimand, reprove (565), upbraid (573), admonish (670), censure, reproach, scold, find fault with.

To 7 per cent of adult readers CHIDE, which is of Anglo-Saxon origin, incorrectly means to FLATTER, to praise unduly, soothe by praise, practically an opposite of CHIDE, to reproach, rebuke.

507. *CATECHIST* (kăt'-ĕ-kĭst) *n.* One who teaches by questions and answers, questioner, instructor.

CATECHIST is from the Greek word, κατά, down; and ἠχεῖν, to sound; from the same source as the English word ECHO.

In the test phrase: 'A pupil and his CATECHIST', the word is thought by 13 per cent of preparatory-school juniors to mean TEXTBOOK. This is probably a confusion of CATECHIST, one who questions, with CATECHISM, a word from the same source, which may mean either instruction by questions and answers; or more specifically a textbook for elementary religious instruction. The first important CATECHISM of this type was arranged by Martin Luther in 1529.

508. *CAJOLE* (kă-jōl') *v.* To coax, wheedle, flatter, blandish, inveigle (544), beguile (784), delude by flattery.

When used in the test phrase: 'A CAJOLING speech', the participial adjective is thought by 5 per cent of adult readers to mean SCORNFUL, contemptuous, disdainful, in connotation an opposite of the correct meaning.

CAJOLE comes from the Latin *cavea*, cage; from the same source as the English word CAGE. To CAJOLE is to gain one's own way by flattery, by empty promises, literally by chattering like a bird in a cage. To CAJOLE, to WHEEDLE, and to COAX, are all ways of leading a person into doing something against his better judgment. To COAX is, by derivation, related to the word COXCOMB, the cap worn formerly by a licensed fool; and today COAXING is a simple-minded process of pleading which offers no inducements. A child COAXES. To WHEEDLE and to CAJOLE are similar except that WHEEDLING tends to suggest more artful cunning than is possessed by the chattering CAJOLER.

509. *FLUSTER* (*flŭs'-ter*) *n.* An agitation, excitement, flurry (481), confusion, disturbance, disorder, stir, commotion.

In the test phrase: 'An unusual FLUSTER', the word is thought by 10 per cent of adult readers to mean CELEBRATION, a festival, festivity, ceremony in honor of an event, an observance to distinguish some occurrence. This may be a confusion of FLUSTER, excitement, with either of the two words FESTIVAL or FESTIVITY, both of which mean CELEBRATION; or it may be merely because a celebration is an exciting event and stirs up a FLUSTER, a commotion, excitement.

510. *DIVISION* (*dĭ-vĭ'-zhŭn*) *n.* A part separated from the rest, portion, branch, section, faction (645).

DIVISION is from the Latin *divisus*, the past participle of *dividere*, to divide, the source of DIVIDEND and also of DIVISOR by which the DIVIDEND is divided to obtain a QUOTIENT.

The word DIVISION may mean the act, process, of dividing. In this sense it is an opposite of MULTIPLICATION. A DIVISION may be a dividing line, a partition, as the DIVISION, partition, between two rooms. Or the word may refer to the condition of being divided, and so mean disagreement, difference of opinion, schism. It may also refer to some part which has been divided from the rest, to a portion, branch, section.

This last meaning of the word is unknown to 54 per cent of grammar-school pupils.

511. *LATENT* (*lā'-tĕnt*) *adj.* Dormant, embryonic, potential, quiescent (788), invisible, unawakened, hidden, concealed, existing but not apparent.

In the test phrase: 'A LATENT desire', the word is thought by 8 per cent of adult readers to mean BELATED, delayed past the proper time, retarded, backward, slow. The participial adjective BELATED, literally BE-LATE, is of Anglo-Saxon origin. Despite the apparent similarity, the adjective LATENT is from the Latin *latere*, to lurk, lie hidden, and by derivation means hidden, dormant.

512. *QUITTANCE* (*kwĭt'-tăns*) *n.* A discharge from a debt, release, receipt, the document which is the evidence of a release.

QUITTANCE, and the more familiar word ACQUITTAL, are from the same Latin word *quietare*, to quiet.

In the test phrase: 'The QUITTANCE was delayed', the word is thought by 8 per cent of adult readers to mean ALLOWANCE, an amount granted for some purpose, limited portion. This may be a confusion of QUITTANCE, release, with PITTANCE, originally an allowance of food or drink, now any small allowance, dole.

By another 9 per cent QUITTANCE is thought to mean SENTENCE. The verb to SENTENCE means to condemn, judge, pass judgment on, doom to punishment, and is the opposite of ACQUIT (500), declare innocent. In court procedure, a SENTENCE is a condemnation, judgment pronounced upon a criminal. A SENTENCE dooms him to punishment. An ACQUITTAL frees him from punishment. A QUITTANCE frees him from debt or financial obligation.

513. *IRK* (*erk*) *v.* To annoy, tire, bore, fatigue, irritate, vex, weary, displease, exasperate, provoke, harass.

The corresponding adjective IRKSOME means wearisome, tedious (194).

To 13 per cent of adult readers IRK incorrectly means to URGE, force one on, impel, incite. Although IRK comes from the Latin *urgere*, to urge, through a Swedish word meaning to urge, to IRK, in English, means to weary, bore, tire.

514. *TUMBREL* (*tŭm'-brĕl*) *n.* A tip-cart especially for manure, a farmer's cart consisting of two wheels and a removable box called a WHICH. The TUMBREL is supposed to be the type of cart in which victims of the French Revolution were conveyed to the guillotine. The word is now used for the two-wheeled, covered, cart in which the artillery carries its ammunition.

To 17 per cent of preparatory-school juniors TUMBREL incorrectly means FORERUNNER, harbinger (*hahr'-bĭn-jer*), precursor, omen.

TUMBREL comes from the same source as the English word TUMBLE, and as the French word *tomber*, to fall. A TUMBREL is a cart which tumbles its load.

515. *VANTAGE* (*văn'-tāj*) *n.* Advantage, benefit, gain, profit, superiority, favorable opportunity.

VANTAGE is a clipped, shortened, form of ADVANTAGE. The loss of an unaccented syllable or letter from the beginning of a word is called APHERESIS (*ă-fĕr'-ĕ-sĭs*). It seems odd when encountered, as in this instance, in process of taking place, when both words still exist; but APHERESIS has already shortened words which are accepted without question. Thus: DOWN comes from ADOWN; BACK, the adverb, as used in the phrase: 'He moved BACK', comes from ABACK; WAYWARD from AWAYWARD; SPECIAL from ESPECIAL; SQUIRE from ESQUIRE.

In the test phrase: 'A position of VANTAGE', the word is thought by 12 per cent of adult readers to mean RESPONSIBILITY, accountability, the likelihood of being called to account, the only frequent misconception of VANTAGE, advantage, superiority.

516. *ABSOLVE* (*ăb-sŏlv'*) *v.* To acquit (500), exonerate, exculpate (903), free from blame.

ABSOLUTION (478), forgiveness, is the corresponding noun.

In the test phrase: 'He was ABSOLVED', the word is thought by 7 per cent of adult readers to mean BANKRUPT. This is perhaps because of some confusion of the verb, to ABSOLVE, to acquit, with the adjective, INSOLVENT, not sound financially, unable to pay one's debts, bankrupt. SOLVENT, INSOLVENT, and ABSOLVE, are all from the Latin *solvere*, to loosen, a word which in turn comes from *se*, apart; and *luere*, to loosen. SOLVENT, as the word is used in English, means able to pay one's debts as they come due. INSOLVENT is the opposite, unable to pay one's debts. To ABSOLVE is to free from a feeling of guilt.

517. *ABDICATE* (*ăb'-dĭ-kāt*) *v.* To resign, surrender (29), quit, abandon (56), relinquish, renounce (636), withdraw from, give up claim to.

This word is familiar because of the recent abdication of Edward VIII of Great Britain. An earlier abdication was that of Charles V, Emperor of the Holy Roman Empire. Charles V was born in Ghent, Flanders, in 1500, a grandson of Maximilian I. He became king of Spain under the title of Charles I in 1516, and was elected Emperor of the Holy Roman Empire in 1519, and crowned at Aix-la-Chapelle, in 1520. He abdicated the government of the Netherlands in 1555, that of Spain in 1556 in favor of his son Philip II, and that of Germany in 1556 in favor of his brother Ferdinand I. He himself retired to the monastery of Yuste, in Spain.

ABDICATE is from the Latin *ab*, from; and *dicere*, to say. To 8 per cent of adult readers the word incorrectly means to CLAIM, to demand as a right, an exact opposite of ABDICATE, to give up claim to.

518. *PACIFIC* (*pă-sĭf'-ĭk*) *adj.* Peaceful, calm, still, smooth, tranquil, conciliatory, mollifying, mild, peaceable, not belligerent, not stormy.

To PACIFY (*păs'-ĭ-fī*), to calm, quiet, is the corresponding verb.

To 11 per cent of adult readers the word incorrectly means EXACT, accurate. This is no doubt a confusion of PACIFIC, peaceful, with SPECIFIC, definite, precise.

This same word PACIFIC, spelt with a capital, is the name of the ocean which lies west of America. It was named by

Magellan in 1520 because he found it quiet and peaceful after the storms of the Atlantic. Magellan had been given five ships and sent on his expedition by Charles V, Emperor of the Holy Roman Empire, who later abdicated (517). PA-CIFIC is from the Latin *pax, pacis,* peace; and means peaceful.

519. *OBDURATE* (*ŏb'-dū-rāt*) *adj.* Stubborn (266), un-yielding (392), firm, unbending, harsh, callous, inexo-rable, not to be moved by appeals to the feelings.
OBDURATE comes from the Latin *ob,* to; and *durare,* to harden; the source of the English word DURABLE, lasting.
OBDURATE, HARDENED (588), and CALLOUS, all have some suggestion of resisting good influences. OBDURATE is the strongest of the three and may even mean actively, wick-edly resisting.

520. *VILLAIN* (*vĭl'-lān*) *n.* A deliberate scoundrel, miscre-ant, rogue, rascal, knave, caitiff, bravo, depraved man capable of crime, one guilty of gross wickedness.
VILLAIN comes from the Latin *villa,* a country house, coun-try seat, farm; the source also of the English word VILLAGE. Originally, a VILLAIN was a servant of the villa, a farm la-borer, feudal serf of the lowest class. He was not a slave, could not be bought or sold; but he belonged to the land and went with it when it was transferred or inherited. VIL-LAIN then lost this technical meaning and came to designate any person of low birth; now the word is used almost ex-clusively to mean a rascal, scoundrel.

521. *IMMINENT* (*ĭm'-mĭ-něnt*) *adj.* Impending, threaten-ing, close at hand, about to occur, likely to happen immediately.
In the test phrase: 'The discovery was IMMINENT', the word is thought by 8 per cent of adult readers to mean FAMED, well-known. This is no doubt a confusion of IMMINENT, impending, about to happen, with EMINENT, notable.
IMMINENT, EMINENT, and PROMINENT, all come from the same Latin word *minere,* to project, jut out, stick out. PROMINENT is used of both objects and persons to mean outstanding. PROMINENT cheek bones are those which liter-

ally project, stand out. A PROMINENT person is one who stands out from the multitude. EMINENT was once used of anything which stood out above other things, much as is PROMINENT today. But EMINENT is now used most frequently of persons, and usually in a good sense to mean distinguished. IMMINENT has apparently departed furthest from the original meaning of the Latin *minere*, to jut out; but its meanderings are easy to follow. IMMINENT first meant literally jutting out. Then it came to have the sinister suggestion of hanging over one's head, of jutting out too far and of being about to fall. Now it has lost entirely its literal meaning of jutting out, and means only hanging over one's head in a figurative sense, about to happen.

522. *PERFIDY* (*per'-fi-dĭ*) *n.* Treachery, untrustworthiness, falseness, faithlessness, disloyalty, breach of allegiance, violation of trust.

PERFIDY is from the Latin *fides*, faith, the name also of the Roman goddess who personified faith, honor, loyalty. From *fides* comes the English word FIDELITY, loyalty; and from this in turn comes PERFIDY, in which the prefix PER means turned away from.

The Latin *per* can usually be translated as through or by. But it has many other meanings, of which two are almost diametrically opposed. PER at times intensifies the meaning of the word to which it is prefixed, as in PERTINACIOUS, literally very tenacious; and PERACUTE, very acute. The same PER may also have a negative suggestion, as in the two words: to PERJURE, to swear falsely, from *per*, in the negative sense; and *jurare*, to swear; and PERFIDY, treachery, faithlessness.

523. *CURATE* (*kū'-rāt*) *n.* Clergyman, minister, one who has the care of souls, deputy of a parish priest, assistant to a rector or vicar.

In the test phrase: 'An unpopular CURATE', the word is thought by 9 per cent of adult readers to mean REMEDY (66), that which cures, medicine, restorative, cure. The words CURATE and CURE, both from the same Latin *cura*, cure, care, are closely related. The noun, CURE, once meant care, a meaning now obsolete; and the task of the CURATE was the cure of souls, that is their care. CURE is the office, task, subject, of the CURATE, much as LAW is the subject, profession, of the LAWYER.

To another 6 per cent CURATE means DOCTOR. DOCTOR, from the Latin *docere*, to teach, designates today specifically one who cures diseases, one who cares for those who are physically, or, as the word is sometimes used today, mentally sick. The modern doctor is often not far from a CURATE in the original sense, except that a CURATE is always connected with the Church, employed by some church organization.

524. *ADOLESCENCE* (*ăd-ō-lĕs'-sĕns*) *n.* Youth (25), period between puberty and maturity.

ADOLESCENCE is thought by 6 per cent of adult readers to mean OLD AGE, almost an opposite of the correct meaning.

PUBERTY, ADOLESCENCE, MATURITY, and SENILITY, are four phases of physical development. SENILITY, the last of the four, often used to mean the weakness of old age, even its imbecility, may mean old with no derogatory suggestion, for it is from the same Latin word *senex*, an old man, as is the English word SENATE, literally a council of elders.

ADOLESCENCE is from the Latin, *adolescere*, to grow up. From this same source comes the English word ADULT (*ă-dŭlt'*, not *ăd'-ŭlt*), a fully grown person, one who has reached maturity. An ADOLESCENT is one who approaches maturity. ADOLESCENCE is the period of life just before maturity.

525. *CONGRUENCE* (*kŏn'-groo-ĕns*) *n.* Harmony, agreement, correspondence, consistency, concordance, appropriateness.

CONGRUENCE comes from the Latin *con*, together; and *gruere*, a word of obscure origin which appears only in one or two Latin compounds such as *congruere*, to agree, accord.

In the test phrase: 'CONGRUENCE of materials', the word is believed by 6 per cent of adult readers to mean SHORTAGE, the opposite of abundance, affluence.

By another 6 per cent CONGRUENCE is believed to mean POOR TASTE. This is perhaps due to a confusion of CONGRU-

ENCE, harmony, with INCONGRUOUSNESS, inappropriateness, a word which may suggest POOR TASTE and is an exact opposite of CONGRUENCE, harmony.

To still another 5 per cent CONGRUENCE incorrectly means CONSPICUOUSNESS, obviousness.

The adjective INCONGRUOUS is familiar to many. From this come the nouns, INCONGRUOUSNESS, INCONGRUITY, and INCONGRUENCE, which are practically synonymous with one another and all of which mean lack of agreement. The three less familiar positive nouns, CONGRUOUSNESS, CONGRUITY, and CONGRUENCE, mean agreement, much as the three negative nouns mean disagreement.

526. OVERSIGHT (ō′-ver-sīt) *n.* Something overlooked, inadvertence, unintentional omission, mistake due to inattention, error due to failure to see something.

This meaning of OVERSIGHT is unknown to 54 per cent of grammar-school pupils. The fact that, to 24 per cent, OVERSIGHT means LOVELY VIEW is an interesting comment on the specialized meanings which words acquire. 'To LOOK OVER a piece of property' is to view it, examine, survey, inspect it. But to OVERLOOK it is to neglect it, not notice it; and the noun, an OVERSIGHT, corresponds to this meaning of OVERLOOK.

527. SOMNIFEROUS (sŏm-nĭf′-ĕ-rŭs) *adj.* Sleep-producing, soporific (sō-pō-rĭf′-ĭk), tending to induce drowsiness, as: 'A SOMNIFEROUS potion', 'A SOMNIFEROUS drink'.

SOMNIFEROUS comes from the Latin *somnus*, sleep; the source of SOMNOLENT, sleepy, drowsy; and of the more familiar INSOMNIA, sleeplessness, wakefulness, inability to sleep.

To 8 per cent of adult readers SOMNIFEROUS incorrectly means STIMULATING (295), exciting, animating, rousing, an exact opposite of the correct meaning.

528. UNISON (ū′-nĭ-sŏn) *n.* Agreement, accord, concord, union, concordance, concurrence, harmony.

UNISON is from the Latin words *unus*, one; and *sonus*, sound. Both appear in other English words; *unus* in UNITE, UNIT, UNITY, and UNIQUE (494); and *sonus* in SONOROUS (sō-nō′-rŭs) (916), giving off sound when struck; DISSONANCE (dĭs′-sō-

năns), a mingling of discordant sounds; and CONSONANCE, (*kŏn'-sō-năns*), a mingling of harmonious sounds.

UNISON by derivation means one sound. The word is used primarily in music, of voices, tones, or strings, of the same pitch. Although often figurative, it should be used only where sounds are implied. Thus, one speaks of individuals or committees being in UNISON, with the suggestion that their voiced opinions are in UNISON; but one never speaks of colors or materials as being in UNISON.

In the test phrase: 'They were in UNISON', SEQUENCE is the popular misconception, and is believed by 12 per cent of adult readers to be a synonym of UNISON. SEQUENCE, in the phrase: 'In SEQUENCE', means in order, succession, one following the other in orderly arrangement. Notes may follow one another, in SEQUENCE, without being of the same pitch, in UNISON; and, on the other hand, several notes may sound simultaneously as one sound, in UNISON.

529. *UNPARALLELED* (*ŭn-păr'-ăl-lĕld*) *adj*. Matchless, unrivaled, peerless, paramount, exceptional, superior, singular, unique (494), having no equal.

UNPARALLELED is a combination of the Anglo-Saxon prefix *un*, not; and two Greek words, παρά, beside, and ἄλλος, another. A large number of English words begin with the Greek PARA, beside, as: PARABLE, fable, short story from which a moral is drawn; PARAGRAPH; PARASITE, literally someone who lives constantly beside another. All of these words are spelt, like PARALLEL, with only one R.

When used as technical terms in mathematics, PARALLEL and EQUAL have different meanings. EQUAL numbers have the same magnitude. PARALLEL lines run side by side but never meet. When, however, EQUAL and PARALLEL are used figuratively, to modify situations, and especially when they are appended to the negative prefix UN, they are practically synonymous. An UNPARALLELED situation is UNEQUALED.

530. *BICAMERAL* (*bī-kăm'-ĕr-ăl*) *adj*. Two-chambered, having two legislative chambers.

To 6 per cent of adult readers BICAMERAL incorrectly means QUARRELSOME, belligerent.

The word is a direct transference into English of the Latin *bi*, two; and *camera*, a chamber, vault, the source of the English words CAMERA, the photographic instrument; and CHAMBER, a room.

531. *SKITTISH* (*skĭt'-tĭsh*) *adj.* Nervous, lively, active, sprightly, volatile, capricious, spirited, high-strung.

In the test phrase: 'The SKITTISH mare', the word is believed by 16 per cent of adult readers to mean BALKY, the popular misconception. BALKY means stopping, refusing to go on, refusing to leap. BALKY is, therefore, in suggestion, almost an opposite of SKITTISH, nervous, lively, active.

532. *IMPEDE* (*ĭm-pēd'*) *v.* To stand in the way of, hinder, check (399), clog, fetter, hamper, obstruct, be an obstacle to.

When used in the test phrase: 'That IMPEDES progress', the word is believed by 16 per cent of grammar-school pupils to mean AIDS, an exact opposite of the correct meaning. This may be a confusion of IMPEDE, hinder, with IMPEL (475), drive on.

To another 11 per cent to IMPEDE incorrectly means to ASSURE, to give certainty to, an opposite by suggestion.

IMPEDE comes from the Latin *in*, in, on; and *pes, pedis*, foot; and implies holding the foot and so slowing down progress.

533. *PUNCTILIOUS* (*pŭnk-tĭl'-ĭ-ŭs*) *adj.* Precise (278), particular, ceremonious, strict, scrupulously exact, laying stress on nice points, minutely observant of formalities.

PUNCTILIOUS is from the Latin *punctum*, point, through the Spanish *puntillo*, a small point, and means literally attentive to nice points. From the same source come the English words PUNCTURE, to prick; and PUNCTUAL, a synonym of PUNCTILIOUS, but a word which is used most frequently today to mean punctilious as to time, arriving exactly at the appointed time.

In the test phrase: 'PUNCTILIOUS behavior', the word is thought by 7 per cent of adult readers to mean DISCOURTEOUS, impolite, uncivil, rude. PUNCTILIOUS means in general exact as to details, scrupulous (604), nice; but the word is often applied to conduct to mean carefully observant of ceremonious forms. In this sense DISCOURTEOUS is an opposite in suggestion, although NEGLIGENT is perhaps a more exact opposite.

534. *BALD* (*bawld*) *adj.* Plain, bare, unadorned, too literal, meagerly simple, without appropriate ornament.
The word BALD can be traced back to Middle English, but its complete history is unknown.

In such a phrase as: 'His BALD head', where it means without hair, the word is undoubtedly known to every grammar-school pupil; but when used figuratively to mean bare, plain, without ornament, as: 'A BALD statement', it is unknown to 55 per cent. To 19 per cent it incorrectly means RASH, hasty, venturesome, impetuous, too quick in action, precipitate, foolhardy. This is, perhaps, due to some confusion of BALD, plain, with BOLD, fearless, courageous, daring, not an exact synonym of RASH, but a word with something of the same suggestion. A BOLD statement is made with courage. A RASH statement is made too quickly, without thought. A BALD statement is plain, meager, unadorned, too bare.

To another 15 per cent of grammar-school pupils BALD incorrectly means BROAD. Although BROAD has many senses, when used in the phrase: 'A BROAD statement', it may mean comprehensive, inclusive, not narrow, liberal. It is possible that this confusion is due to the two words LIBERAL and LITERAL, almost opposites in suggestion. A BROAD statement is LIBERAL; a BALD statement is LITERAL, often too literal.

535. *OSTRACIZE* (*ŏs'-tră-sīz*) *v.* To banish, exile, expel, deport, bar from public good will, exclude from favor by popular consent, send to Coventry.
In ancient Greece OSTRACISM and PETALISM were both methods of banishing undesirable citizens. PETALISM was practiced in Syracuse. The word comes from the Greek πέταλον , a leaf, the source of the English word PETAL. PETALISM was so called because the name of the person to be banished was written on an olive leaf. Banishment was for a period of five years. OSTRACISM was practiced in Athens.

The word is from the Greek ὄστρακον, potsherd (*pŏt'-shĕrd*), any ceramic fragment, piece of earthenware. In the vote which determined the banishment the name of the undesirable citizen was written on a potsherd. From the same Greek source come os, which is today medical terminology for bone; and OYSTER, named from its hard shell. OSTRACISM was for a period of ten years. The word PETALISM has disappeared except in its historical significance. The noun OSTRACISM, and the corresponding verb, to OSTRACIZE, have survived and are used today with reference to any exclusion from popular favor.

In the test phrase: 'He was OSTRACIZED', the word is thought by 12 per cent of adult readers to mean CRITICIZED. To CRITICIZE is to pass judgment upon. OSTRACISM, banishment, follows upon the heels of CRITICISM; but the word to OSTRACIZE means definitely to banish, and not merely to CRITICIZE, pass judgment upon.

536. *DIABOLICAL* (*dĭ-ă-bŏl'-ĭ-kăl*) *adj.* Fiendish, infernal, satanic, perfidious, impious, extremely malicious (549), outrageously wicked, demoniac (*dē-mō'-nĭ-ăk*).

DIABOLICAL comes from the Greek prefix διά, across; and βάλλειν, to throw; and originally, in Greek, the combination διάβαλλειν meant to slander, to throw false reports about. From this the corresponding Greek noun came to mean devil; and it is in this last sense that it appears in the adjective DIABOLICAL.

To 14 per cent of college seniors DIABOLICAL incorrectly means TWO-FACED, deceitful, hypocritical, insincere; and to 7 per cent of preparatory-school juniors the word means TWO-FOLD. These misinterpretations may come from a confusion between the two prefixes, DI, two, two-fold, double, as in DICHROMATIC, two colored, and DIPTEROUS, having two wings; and DIA, through, across. DIABOLICAL comes from DIA, through, across; and has no suggestion of DI, two, two-fold. The confusion of DIABOLICAL with TWO-FACED may be augmented by the fact that TWO-FACED means deceitful, insincere, double-dealing, which is not unlike DIABOLICAL in connotation. DIABOLICAL is, however, much stronger and means treacherous, atrociously wicked.

537. *EMBELLISH* (*ĕm-bĕl'-lĭsh*) *v.* To beautify, decorate, adorn (198), ornament, elaborate, bedeck, chase.

In the test phrase: 'They EMBELLISHED the narrative', the word is thought by 13 per cent of adult readers to mean CONDENSED. To CONDENSE is to abridge, reduce, compress, shorten, consolidate, make briefer, practically an antonym of the verb, to EMBELLISH, to adorn, decorate, elaborate.

EMBELLISH is a combination of the Latin *in;* and *bellus,* beautiful, the source of the modern French word *belle,* beautiful; and of the English words, BEAUTY; BEAU, a dandy, a society man particular about his dress; and BELLE, a beautiful society woman. To EMBELLISH is by derivation to beautify.

538. *FILCHING* (*filch'-ĭng*) *p.adj.* Thieving in a small way, pilfering, petty stealing, cribbing, purloining, peculating.

In the test phrase: 'A FILCHING expedition', the word is thought by 8 per cent of adult readers to mean EXPLORING, searching.

539. *TART* (*tahrt*) *adj.* Sharp to the taste, sour, subacid, acrid, pungent, piquant, caustic, acidulous.

TART, the adjective, is of Anglo-Saxon origin. In the test phrase: 'A TART apple', the word is unknown to 56 per cent of grammar-school pupils. To 18 per cent it incorrectly means SWEET, an exact opposite of the correct meaning.

TART may also be used figuratively to mean sharp, severe, cutting, as in the phrase: 'A TART reply'. In this sense, the word is unknown to 26 per cent of adult readers. To 9 per cent it incorrectly means OBSCENE, indecent, impure, indelicate, lewd. This is perhaps because of some confusion with the slang use of the noun, a TART, to mean an immoral woman. The adjective TART cannot be used in this way.

540. *THROTTLE* (*thrŏt'-tl*) *v.* To choke, suffocate, strangle, stifle, compress the throat of.

In the test phrase: 'THROTTLE the umpire', the word is thought by 6 per cent of adult readers to mean KILL. The verb STRANGLE may mean to choke to death; but THROTTLE is never used in this way. To THROTTLE is to choke, strangle, but not to kill.

The verb to THROTTLE is perhaps best known today as used in connection with the automobile. The THROTTLE is the device which cuts off the flow of gasoline. To THROTTLE is to reduce or shut off the flow.

541. PAIN (pān) n. Penalty, fine, punishment, suffering inflicted for an offense.

PAIN comes from the Greek ποινή, a fine, penalty, punishment. Although the English word PAIN can be used in several ways, in the phrase: 'On PAIN of death', the word returns to its original Greek meaning, punishment. This use of PAIN is unknown to 58 per cent of grammar-school pupils. To 31 per cent it incorrectly means EXPECTATION. To EXPECT is to look forward to, usually with pleasure. The noun EXPECTATION implies awaiting with anticipation and, in suggestion, is almost an opposite of PAIN in the sense of penalty, punishment.

542. TOXIC (tŏk'-sĭk) adj. Poisonous, noxious, baneful (857), deleterious, virulent (1097), venomous, pertaining to poisons.

TOXIC comes from a Greek word τοξικόν, the poison which was used on the tip of an arrow.

To 6 per cent of adult readers TOXIC incorrectly means ACOUSTIC (458), pertaining to sound, to the science of sound. This may be a confusion of TOXIC, poisonous, with TONIC, a word which may mean pertaining to tones or sounds, but which is more familiar today in the figurative sense of giving tone to, strengthening, bracing.

To another 6 per cent TOXIC incorrectly means FATAL, causing death, lethal. TOXIC means poisonous, pertaining to poisons; but not necessarily deadly, fatal.

543. SAVANT (să-vŏgn') n. A learned person, scholar, philosopher, scientist, erudite individual, one renowned for his wisdom, man of high literary or scientific attainments.

SAVANT is a French word, which has been incorporated in the English language, but which still keeps its French pronunciation. The T is not pronounced and the word is accented

on the last syllable. The word has been slow in being anglicized, perhaps because it refers only to learned individuals.

In the test phrase: 'The arrival of the SAVANT', the word
is thought by 10 per cent of adult readers to mean WAITER,
perhaps a confusion of SERVANT with SAVANT, a scholar.

SAVANT is a doublet of SAPIENT, sage, wise, possessing deep
sagacity; for both SAPIENT and SAVANT come from the same
Latin word, *sapere*, to know. A SAVANT is by derivation one
who knows.

544. *INVEIGLE* (ĭn-vē'-gl, not ĭn-vā'-gl) *v.* To lead astray
by blinding to the proper course, decoy, allure, seduce,
wheedle, cajole (508), beguile (784), entice into action against
one's better judgment.

INVEIGLE is from the same source as the modern French word
aveugle, blind; originally from the Latin *ob*, from; and *oculus*,
eye, the source also of the English noun OCULIST, a physician
skilled in the treatment of the eyes. INVEIGLE is by derivation
to blind.

In the phrase: 'I was INVEIGLED into doing it', the word
is thought by 9 per cent of adult readers to mean BRIBED.
To BRIBE and to INVEIGLE are both to tempt a person into
doing something against his better judgment. To BRIBE is to
do this by offering money or a gift. To INVEIGLE is to offer
no inducement, but is to blind one to the proper course.

By another 8 per cent to INVEIGLE is thought to mean to
FORCE, almost an opposite of the correct meaning, for IN-
VEIGLING is getting one's way without force.

INVEIGLE, CAJOLE, BEGUILE, and ALLURE, all mean to tempt,
to coax, to wheedle, by different methods. ALLURE tempts
by offering attractive bait; a LURE was originally a decoy
used in falconry (faw'-k'n-rĭ) to draw a hawk back to its
owner. BEGUILE tempts by deception, and is related to GUILE,
trickery. CAJOLE tempts by flattering phrases and empty
promises; a CAJOLING person chatters like a bird, the original
meaning. INVEIGLE tempts by blinding.

545. *HAWSER* (haw'-zer) *n.* Large rope, small cable (54),
anchor line, cable used in towing ships.

To 11 per cent of adult readers HAWSER incorrectly means

SAILOR. The only apparent connection is that HAWSER is a nautical term.

HAWSER probably comes directly from the obsolete English verb to HAWSE, to lift, raise.

546. *RAMPANT* (*răm'-pănt*) *adj.* Unrestrained, unchecked, extravagant, arrant, aggressive, exuberant, unrestricted, unbridled (169).

RAMPANT is from the French *ramper*, to climb, creep, crawl; and, by derivation, means climbing unchecked. From the same source comes the noun, a RAMP, a gradually rising walk, road, plane, which leads to a higher level.

When used in the test phrase: 'RAMPANT socialists', the word is thought by 9 per cent of adult readers to mean DANGEROUS, harmful, ready to do injury. RAMPANT is used in heraldry, as in the phrase: 'A lion RAMPANT', to mean standing on its hind legs, rearing. This is a threatening position and in consequence the word RAMPANT is sometimes incorrectly used to mean menacing; but correctly used it means unrestrained, exuberant.

547. *MAGNANIMOUS* (*măg-năn'-ĭ-mŭs*) *adj.* Unselfish, generous, liberal in judging others, high-minded, elevated in soul.

The corresponding noun MAGNANIMITY (677) is less familiar for it is unknown to 35 per cent of adult readers.

MAGNANIMOUS comes from two Latin words, *magnus*, great; and *anima*, soul, breath; and means, literally, great in soul. From *anima* come such English words as ANIMAL; and ANIMATE, to make alive.

To 11 per cent of college seniors, MAGNANIMOUS incorrectly means ENORMOUS. ENORMOUS, in the sense of gigantic, mammoth, very great, huge, is an exact translation of the Latin word *magnus*, the first part of MAGNANIMOUS. But ENORMOUS may also mean very wicked, atrocious, heinous; and so be an opposite of MAGNANIMOUS, high-minded.

The words MAGNANIMOUS and GENEROUS differ in intensity. A GENEROUS person may be honorable, high-minded, noble; or may merely wish good, instead of evil, for others. A MAGNANIMOUS person must be generous in the face of an injury;

to be MAGNANIMOUS one's GENEROSITY must rise above an insult to one's self.

548. *JAUNTY (jŏn'-tĭ) adj.* Gay, sprightly, airy, showy (442), natty (804), affectedly elegant.
This word was first used in the seventeenth century and was apparently an attempt to pronounce in English the French word *gentil (zhŏn-tē')*. Other English words which come from the same source are: GENTEEL *(jĕn-tēl')*, refined, well-bred, elegant, fashionable; and GENTLE, quiet, mild, docile, moderate. Each one of the words GENTLE, GENTEEL, and JAUNTY, expresses one aspect of the French word *gentil.*
In the test phrase: 'His JAUNTY appearance', the word is believed by 13 per cent of adult readers to mean STURDY, stout, robust, strong, the popular misconception, and, in suggestion, almost an opposite of the correct meaning.

549. *MALICIOUS (mă-lĭsh'-ŭs) adj.* Spiteful, ill-disposed, evil minded, venomous, malevolent, malignant, harboring enmity. MALICIOUS is the adjective which corresponds to the more familiar noun MALICE (391).
MALICIOUS, MALIGNANT, and MALEVOLENT, three words from the Latin *malus*, bad, all express badness of heart, delight in harm to others, often for its own sake. MALEVOLENT may be used of a casual wish to do harm; while disagreeable enough, it is often more temporary than the others. MALEVOLENT and BENEVOLENT are opposites, both implying wishing rather than acting. MALIGNANT is the most intense; it designates an active hate, destructive desire. MALIGNANT and BENIGNANT (717), kind, gentle, tender, are opposites. MALICIOUS is between the two in intensity and duration. GOOD-NATURED is perhaps its nearest opposite.
In the test phrase: 'A MALICIOUS jest', the word is thought by 17 per cent of grammar-school pupils to mean MERRY; and by another 14 per cent to mean FRIENDLY, an exact opposite of the correct meaning.

550. *PERPETUAL (pĕr-pĕt'-ū-ăl) adj.* Continuous, unfailing (97), uninterrupted, incessant (201), never ceasing, constant, going on without a break; also: everlasting, im-

mortal, eternal, interminable, going on without end, of infinite duration.

The Latin word *petere* went through many changes and can now be translated by a number of English words. In PERPETUAL it has its fundamental suggestion of motion. PERPETUAL means literally moving continuously, going on without stopping.

PERPETUAL, ETERNAL, and EVERLASTING, are nearly synonymous. EVERLASTING means without end, continuing from the present into an endless future. ETERNAL means without either beginning or end. PERPETUAL is general and is used more freely than the others of anything which lasts a long time.

551. *AGGLOMERATION* (*ăg-glŏm-ĕr-ā'-shŭn*) *n.* Cluster (24), heap, accumulation, aggregation, assemblage, haphazard collection, confused mass of similar things.

AGGLOMERATION is from the Latin *ad*, and *glomerare*, to gather into a ball, a verb which in turn comes from *glomus*, ball, the source of the English word GLOBE.

To 9 per cent of adult readers AGGLOMERATION incorrectly means FERTILIZATION, enrichment, making fruitful.

To another 8 per cent it incorrectly means CONCOCTION, a mixture, a word applied usually to foods.

AGGLOMERATION and CONGLOMERATION are nearly synonymous. A CONGLOMERATION is a collection of different things. The word emphasizes the heterogeneity of the mass. An AGGLOMERATION is more often a cluster, collection, mass of similar things.

552. *UNFAVORABLE* (*ŭn-fā'-vŏr-ā-bl*) *adj.* Not friendly, adverse, contrary, opposing, antagonistic, discouraging, unpropitious, not favorable.

UNFAVORABLE is a combination of the Anglo-Saxon *un*, not; and the Latin *favere*, to be well disposed toward, befriend. This Latin verb is the source of a large group of English words. To FAVOR has the meaning of the Latin word, to be friendly toward, well disposed toward, inclined toward. A FAVORITE is a person with whom one is friendly, toward whom one is well disposed. To be in DISFAVOR means that others are not friendly, not well disposed toward one. FAVOR-

ABLE means friendly, well disposed. UNFAVORABLE means not friendly, not well disposed.

To 29 per cent of grammar-school pupils UNFAVORABLE incorrectly means DANGEROUS. DANGEROUS may mean unsafe, perilous, hazardous, full of risk. DANGEROUS weather conditions are UNFAVORABLE, not friendly; but DANGEROUS and UN-FAVORABLE are not synonymous, for it is possible to use UNFAVORABLE in many places where DANGEROUS would not apply, as: 'An UNFAVORABLE answer', 'An UNFAVORABLE opinion', 'UNFAVORABLE criticism'.

553. *UNSOPHISTICATED* (ŭn-sō-fĭs'-tĭ-kā-tĕd) *adj.* Simple, natural (26), naive, unaffected, ingenuous (1099), artless, unassuming, inexperienced in worldly ways.

In the test phrase: 'The UNSOPHISTICATED youth', the word is thought by 9 per cent of adult readers to mean SPOILED, the common misconception. To SPOIL, as applied to a child, means to injure the character of, impair the disposition of, render less obedient.

The noun, a SOPHIST (sŏf'ĭst), the source of UNSOPHISTI-CATED, comes directly from a Greek word σοφός, skilled, learned, the source also of the English word, PHILOSOPHER, one devoted to a search for truth. A SOPHIST, however, differed from a PHILOSOPHER in that a SOPHIST imparted his knowledge for money, while a PHILOSOPHER devoted himself exclusively to the search for truth for the pure love of learning. The word SOPHIST has always had a disparaging note; it has been tainted by the fact that a SOPHIST accepted money. The adjective, SOPHISTICATED, in its mildest sense, means deprived of simplicity, not genuine; and the word may even mean false, obscured with fallacies, corrupt, debased.

UNSOPHISTICATED, although it means not SOPHISTICATED, is nevertheless not particularly complimentary. It means, by derivation, unlearned, without knowledge.

554. *PRIMARY* (prī'-mā-rĭ) *adj.* First, chief, highest, principal, paramount, supreme (243).

PRIMARY and PRIME, both from the same Latin source, *primus,* first, are identical in meaning but differ in usage. Thus, one writes: 'PRIME minister', not PRIMARY, to mean one of first rank, although PRIME in this phrase has exactly the meaning of PRIMARY in the phrase: 'Of PRIMARY importance'.

555. *HOWBEIT* (*how-bē′-ĭt*) *adv.* and *conj.* Nevertheless, notwithstanding, be it as it may.

In the test phrase: 'HOWBEIT it is correct', the word is believed by 10 per cent of adult readers to mean PERHAPS.

HOWBEIT is obsolete, except when it is used to mean nevertheless, in which sense it is archaic. It should never be used in a sentence dealing with modern affairs, and should be avoided altogether by the inexperienced writer.

556. *QUANDARY* (*kwŏn′-dă-rĭ*) *n.* Dilemma, predicament, difficulty, plight, state of perplexity, position of uncertainty, condition of indecision.

Although its exact derivation is uncertain, it has been suggested that QUANDARY may have come from the same ultimate source as the word HYPOCHONDRIA, exaggerated anxiety about one's health. This association of QUANDARY with a morbid state is perhaps the reason for 17 per cent of adult readers believing that QUANDARY means FRENZY, delirium, madness, distraction. Or the misinterpretation may be due to some confusion between the words DILEMMA, a synonym of QUANDARY, and DELIRIUM, a synonym of FRENZY.

A QUANDARY and a DILEMMA are both states of indecision. DILEMMA is from the Greek $\delta\iota$, two; and $\lambda\tilde{\eta}\mu\mu\alpha$, anything taken for granted, the source of the English word LEMMA (*lĕm′-mă*), in logic, a premise. A DILEMMA was originally a form of argument depending upon two equally possible premises. The word is now used figuratively for any situation in which one of two unattractive alternatives must be accepted. A QUANDARY is a state of perplexity presenting several equally desirable possibilities.

557. *VASSAL* (*văs′-săl*) *n.* Dependent, subject, serf, retainer, slave, bondsman, henchman.

VASSAL can be traced back to the French; but there are similar words in Spanish, Italian, and the Scandinavian languages.

To 14 per cent of adult readers VASSAL incorrectly means ADVISOR, one who gives advice.

The word VASSAL is intimately associated with the feudal system. During the Middle Ages in Europe land was not bought and sold, but was granted by the king to overlords and in turn by them to others on condition that the owners gave military service when required. One who held land under these conditions was called a VASSAL. He might be a prince, lord, or minor person. VASSAL later came to mean any slave, bondsman.

558. ROOTED (*roo'-těd*) *adj.* Fixed by the roots, firmly implanted, imbedded, established.

A ROOT, a word of Anglo-Saxon origin, is, as every grammar-school pupil knows, that part of a plant which grows downward into the ground and holds the plant firmly fixed. ROOTED is an adjective, made from the noun, ROOT, and means firmly fixed.

559. PLEXIFORM (*plěks'-ĭ-fōrm*) *adj.* Complicated, elaborate, intricate, involved, complex, having the form of a network.

PLEXIFORM comes from the Latin *plexus*, a word used in English today to mean network, an interlacing, as: 'A PLEXUS of leaves'. From *plexus* come also such English words as COMPLEX and COMPLEXION, a word which now means the color of the skin, especially of the face; but which originally meant the state of being complex, complexity.

PLEXIFORM, complicated, and UNIFORM, unvarying, literally of one form, are almost opposites; although MULTIFORM, literally of many forms, and UNIFORM, are more exact opposites. UNIFORM has been generally adopted and appears in everyday conversational English; while MULTIFORM and especially PLEXIFORM have a marked technical flavor.

560. ROBUST (*rō-bŭst'*) *adj.* Strong, sturdy (72), muscular, sound, vigorous, lusty, hardy, stoutly built. 'A ROBUST child.'

ROBUST comes from an Old Latin word meaning oak tree and suggests having the strength of the oak.

ROBUST, STURDY, and STALWART, differ only slightly from one another for all imply strength. STALWART, by derivation, means having a firm foundation, well-based, firmly set. Both STURDY and ROBUST mean strong, but STURDY can be used of a small person, as in the phrase: 'The STURDY little fellow', while ROBUST implies size.

To 25 per cent of grammar-school pupils ROBUST incorrectly means FAT. Although the word suggests size, ROBUST means primarily strong, muscular; while FAT means merely large in size and often suggests lack of muscle.

561. *SULLY* (*sŭl'-lĭ*) *v.* To stain, soil, dirty, spot, tarnish (102), discolor, defile, maculate, blemish.

In the test phrase: 'It SULLIES your reputation', the word is thought by 10 per cent of adult readers to mean DIMINISHES, reduces in amount, lessens; and by another 5 per cent to mean DESTROYS. That which SULLIES, stains, dirties, one's reputation may diminish or destroy it; but the word SULLY always implies dirtying, soiling, tarnishing, an idea not conveyed by either DIMINISH or DESTROY.

562. *ADAPT* (*ă-dăpt'*) *v.* To fit by alteration, make suitable, remodel, modify, attune, adjust, change for new use.

ADAPT is from the Latin *aptus*, fit, fitted. From this same word comes the adjective APT, having the qualities necessary for a given purpose; and the noun APTITUDE, natural capacity for a particular task.

In the test phrase: 'ADAPT it to your needs', the word is thought by 20 per cent of adult readers to mean APPLY, to put to use, devote to a particular purpose. The word APPLY does not suggest change or alteration in the object applied, put to use. The misunderstanding may perhaps be due to some confusion of ADAPT with ADOPT. To ADOPT is to choose, select, take to one's self, take into one's family, as: 'To ADOPT a name', 'To ADOPT a child'. To ADAPT is to modify an object in such a manner that it can be APPLIED. To ADAPT a name for instance is to change it to suit one's self.

To ADAPT and to FIT are in some senses synonymous. To FIT, from Anglo-Saxon, may however at times be passive, as in the phrase: 'To FIT a pair of shoes', where no actual change in the object is implied. To ADAPT is always active, to change, adjust, modify.

563. *RECOURSE* (*rē-cōrs'*) *n.* Resort, appeal for aid, application for help when in difficulty.

In the test phrase: 'He had RECOURSE to the library', the word is believed by 35 per cent of grammar-school pupils to be a verb, and to mean RETURNED. RECOURSE comes from the Latin *re*, back; and *currere*, to run; and by derivation means to run back, return. RECOURSE was once used in this sense, as an intransitive verb, to mean recur, return, but this use is now obsolete. Today, the word RECOURSE appears only as a noun and implies the need for help, advice, assistance.

564. *AVERT* (*ă-vert'*) *v.* To ward off, turn aside, foil, hinder, obstruct, baffle (189), frustrate, parry (304).

AVERT is from the Latin *ab*, from; and *vertere*, to turn, from the same source as VERSATILE (488), turning often and with ease from one thing to another. To 19 per cent of adult readers AVERT incorrectly means ESCAPE. This may be a confusion of AVERT, to ward off, parry, with EVADE. To EVADE is to elude, escape, slip away from, but does not, as does AVERT, suggest changing the course of the impending blow or disaster.

565. *REPROVE* (*rē-proov'*) *v.* To rebuke, chide (506), reproach, upbraid (573), reprimand, admonish (670), censure, blame openly. 'She REPROVED him.'

REPROVE is from the Latin *re*, again; and *probare*, to prove. REPROVE does not, however, mean to prove again, the literal meaning, but rather to censure, disapprove.

REPROVE, REBUKE, and CENSURE, all express open disapproval of an error which has already been made. To CENSURE is the most formal of the three and presupposes an offense of some seriousness. A CENSURE is, in part, punishment in itself and is administered by a superior or by one who has the right to censure. REBUKE and REPROVE are not so formal and apply to matters of less weight. A REBUKE is administered on the spur of the moment, in language which is sharp and outspoken. To REPROVE, and the noun REPROOF, lie between the other two in formality. Although the verb to REPROVE does not suggest spontaneity, one may REPROVE by a gesture or in a few words, without the need of formal language.

To 25 per cent of grammar-school pupils REPROVE incorrectly means UPHOLD. To UPHOLD may mean to sanction, countenance, approve, and in this sense is an exact opposite of the correct meaning.

566. *RETROGRADE* (*rĕt'-rō-grād*) *adj.* Deteriorating, backward, contrary, receding, declining from a better to a worse state, reversing progress. 'A RETROGRADE tendency.' RETROGRADE is from the Latin *retro*, backward; and *gradere*, to go. The prefix RETRO appears in the words: RETROACTIVE, applicable to past events; RETROSPECTIVE, looking backward; and RETROGRESSIVE. RETROGRESSIVE and RETROGRADE are practically synonymous. Of the two RETROGRESSIVE has a slightly stronger suggestion of deterioration.

To 8 per cent of adult readers RETROGRADE incorrectly means VICIOUS, evil, bad, depraved, wicked, abandoned. VICIOUS defines a static, unchanging condition. RETROGRADE, when it is occasionally used in the sense of moral deterioration, always implies an active reversion from a better state and describes the motion rather than the condition.

567. *SPIRITUAL* (*spĭr'-ĭ-tū-ăl*, almost *spĭr'-ĭ-chū-ăl*) *adj.* Of the spirit as distinguished from matter, pertaining to the soul, non-physical, incorporeal (*ĭn-kōr-pō'-rē-ăl*). SPIRITUAL is from the Latin *spiritus*, breath, air. SPIRIT is by derivation the breath of life, the essence of existence.

SPIRITUAL and INCORPOREAL are practically synonymous. INCORPOREAL means non-physical, immaterial, intangible, much as does SPIRITUAL; but INCORPOREAL has none of the nobler connotations of the word SPIRITUAL.

In the test phrase: 'SPIRITUAL beings', the word is thought by 8 per cent of adult readers to mean DREAMY, given to dreaming, visionary; and by another group to mean LANGUID, listless, sluggish, drooping, dragging, the two popular misconceptions. Both words suggest lack of interest in the tangible world; but neither contains the breath-giving qualities of SPIRITUAL.

Some opposites of SPIRITUAL are BODILY, CORPOREAL, TEMPORAL, limited by time, pertaining to this life, MATERIAL, SECULAR, WORLDLY.

568. *REMAINS* (*rē-mānz'*) *n.* Corpse, dead body, cadaver (*kă-dăv'-er*, not *kăd'-ă-ver*), that which is left of a human being after life is gone.

The verb, to REMAIN, is from the Latin *re*, back, behind; and *manere*, to remain; and means literally to remain behind. The verb to REMAIN, to be left, is doubtless known to everyone. From the verb come two nouns, REMAINDER and REMAINS. REMAINDER is general and refers to anything which is left. REMAINS, used in the plural, is limited ordinarily to specific usages: (1) to that which is left of a human being after life is gone; (2) to the literary works which an author leaves unpublished at his death; and (3) more generally to that which is left of any concrete thing which has been partially destroyed, as: 'The REMAINS of a picnic', 'The REMAINS of a house', 'The REMAINS of a city'. It is, perhaps, this last use of the word which leads 36 per cent of grammar-school pupils to believe it to mean SURROUNDINGS. Both SURROUND-INGS and REMAINS are used in the plural. The SURROUNDINGS of a house are its environs, its lawns, its gardens, or its neighborhood. The REMAINS of a house are those parts of the house itself which are left after the house has been partially destroyed.

569. *PRESENCE* (*prĕz'-ĕns*) *n.* Bearing, carriage, demeanor, figure (421), appearance, mien (879), aspect, deportment. The word PRESENCE is used especially of a person who is stately, dignified, impressive in appearance.

When used in the test phrase: 'A man of fine PRESENCE', the word is believed by 16 per cent of adult readers to mean IDEALS, the common misconception. IDEALS are mental standards, inner aspirations; PRESENCE is outward appearance. It is however the existence of IDEALS which distinguishes the words PRESENCE and FIGURE. FIGURE means physical appearance. PRESENCE, although it is primarily outward appearance, suggests also the spiritual aura of a person with ideals.

570. *AMENITY* (*ă-mĕn'-ĭ-tĭ*) *n.* Agreeableness of situation, civility, pleasantness, geniality, suavity, urbanity, complaisance, attractiveness, delightfulness, charm. AMENITY comes directly from the French word *aménité*;

and carries with it all the implications of agreeableness, politeness, characteristic of a polished French civilization.

To 7 per cent of college seniors AMENITY incorrectly means DISCORD, dissension, differences. This may be a confusion of AMENITY, agreeableness, with ENMITY, rancor, hatred, hostility, ill will, in suggestion nearly an opposite of AMENITY, civility.

The word, AMENITY, is often used in the plural, as in the title of Edward Newton's delightful book: 'The AMENITIES of Book Collecting', that is, its pleasures, attractions. In this sense, the plurals, AMENITIES and DRAWBACKS, are opposites.

571. *COERCION* (*kō-er'-zhŭn*) *n*. Compulsion, constraint, forcible restraint, control by force.

COERCION comes from the Latin *co*, together; and *arcere*, to confine, inclose, the source of the English words ARK, the boat on which Noah was saved from the flood; and ARCADE, a series of arches supported by columns.

COERCION and COMPULSION are similar in suggestion but the words are used in different situations. COMPULSION is the general term for force which makes one act against one's will. COERCION is the compulsion of a presumably free agent. COERCION is used most often of social situations, of social acts, of forcing one into conformity. Legally, COERCION is that degree of force, whether physical or moral, which renders invalid any acts which result from the coercion. INTIMIDATION is one form of COERCION.

572. *VACUOUS* (*văk'-ū-ŭs*) *adj*. Empty, vacant, stupid, dull, unintelligent, blank, expressionless, fatuous (837), inane (1047).

In the test phrase: 'VACUOUS remarks', the word is believed by 10 per cent of adult readers to mean BITTER, biting, caustic, acrimonious; and by another 6 per cent to mean MISLEADING, deceiving, deluding.

VACUOUS comes from the Latin *vacuus*, empty, from the same source as the English word VACUUM, an empty space, specifically in physics, a space from which the air has been removed by a VACUUM PUMP. Although VACUOUS, empty, is the adjective which corresponds to the scientific noun VACUUM,

the word is used most frequently today in its figurative sense
to mean unintelligent, stupid.

573. *UPBRAID* (*ŭp-brād'*) *v.* To reproach, chide (506), reprove (565) severely, blame, censure, admonish (670),
condemn.

The three words: BRAID, ABRAID, and UPBRAID, are all of Anglo-
Saxon origin. Although the verb to BRAID now means to
weave three strands together, it originally meant to pull,
snatch, and also to brandish. Something of this notion of
brandishing remains in the verb UPBRAID. ABRAID is obsolete,
but should not be confused in spelling with ABRADE, wear
away, scrape off, which is of Latin origin.

UPBRAID differs from such words as: DERIDE, FLOUT, MOCK,
and TAUNT, by having as a purpose a desire to make the
culprit feel his shortcomings and mend his ways. It differs
from such words as: CENSURE, CRITICIZE, and REPROVE, in
being slightly less dignified, noisier, and more apt to express
the personal feelings of the one who UPBRAIDS.

In the test phrase: 'She UPBRAIDED him', the word is thought
by 8 per cent of adult readers to mean PRAISED, an exact
opposite of the correct meaning.

574. *METAMORPHOSE* (*mĕt-ă-mŏr'-fōz*) *v.* To transform,
change from one form into another, transmute, cause
to assume a different character.

To 8 per cent of adult readers the verb, to METAMORPHOSE,
incorrectly means to WEAKEN, to make weak, faint.

To another 7 per cent, to METAMORPHOSE incorrectly means
to UNDERMINE, to work against secretly, insidiously.

METAMORPHOSE, and the corresponding noun METAMOR-
PHOSIS, complete change of form, are from two Greek words,
μετά, over; and μορφή, shape, form. By derivation to META-
MORPHOSE means to form over again, reshape.

575. *ALLEVIATE* (*ăl-lē'-vĭ-āt*) *v.* To lessen, lighten, moderate, soften, mollify, relieve (349), mitigate, allay (607),
make easier to be endured.

By 16 per cent of adult readers ALLEVIATE is thought to mean
to REMOVE, take away, not far from correct in connotation.

ALLEVIATE suggests permanency and in this differs from
ALLAY which denotes the temporary lessening of an effect.
ALLEVIATE is from the Latin *ad*, to; and *levare*, to lift, ultimately from *levis*, light; and denotes a lessening of an effect
by a change in the conditions causing it.

ALLEVIATE and AMELIORATE (792) are practically synonymous. One AMELIORATES conditions; one ALLEVIATES pain by
removing its cause.

576. *SAGACIOUS* (*să-gā'-shŭs*) *adj*. Wise, knowing, shrewd,
        astute (746), acute, perspicacious, sapient, having insight.
SAGACIOUS and SAGE are used only as complimentary terms.
Despite their similarity in appearance they come from different sources. SAGE comes from the Latin *sapere*, to be
wise, discerning; the source of the words SAPIENT, wise; and
SAPID, tasteful, savory; and means wise, judicious, prudent,
farseeing; and recently learned, profound. SAGACIOUS comes
from the Latin *sagire*, to perceive by the senses; and means
discerning, perceptive.

In the test phrase: 'SAGACIOUS comments', the word is
thought by 8 per cent of adult readers to mean ABSURD,
foolish, preposterous, obviously inconsistent with reason, the
common misconception and an opposite of SAGACIOUS, wise.

577. *CAMEO* (*kăm'-ē-ō*) *n*. Carved gem. Although a CAMEO
        may be any carved gem in which the design rises above
the surface, a type of CAMEO often seen is carved from ONYX,
a stone which is a kind of quartz composed of layers of different colors usually red, brown, or black. A CAMEO is cut
in such a way that the design and the background come from
different layers and are, therefore, of different colors.

To 8 per cent of adult readers CAMEO incorrectly means
SILHOUETTE, a head in profile. This confusion is probably due
to the fact that the design on a CAMEO is often a head in
profile, a SILHOUETTE, but it may equally well be flowers or
any conventional design.

A CAMEO and an INTAGLIO (*ĭn-tăl'-yō*) are both carved
gems. In an INTAGLIO the design sinks below the surface, is
a depression cut into the stone. In a CAMEO the carving rises
above the surface in low relief.

578. *GLOAMING* (*glō'-mĭng*) *n.* Twilight, dusk, crepuscle (*krĕ-pŭs'-l*), partial light just after sunset.
To 15 per cent of adult readers GLOAMING incorrectly means ENVIRONMENT, surroundings.

GLOAMING is of Anglo-Saxon origin, from the same source as the English word GLOOM, darkness, obscurity.

579. *HUMMOCK* (*hŭm'-mŏk*) *n.* Mound, rounded knoll, hillock, ridge, copple (1094), crest of land.
In the test phrase: 'He stood on the HUMMOCK', the word is thought by 14 per cent of adult readers to mean SWING. This is perhaps a confusion of HUMMOCK, mound, with HAMMOCK, a swinging couch made of net or of canvas.

A HUMMOCK may be a bump, protuberance in an ice field; or it may be a small rounded mass of earth rising above a swamp; or it may be a hillock, a small mound covered with trees. In the last use HUMMOCK and SAVANNAH are associated. A SAVANNAH (*să-văn'-nah*), as the word is used in the Southern States, is a level plain without trees. A HUMMOCK is a small hill, often covered with trees, which rises in the plain.

580. *RECESSION* (*rē-sĕsh'-ŭn*) *n.* Receding, the act of moving back, withdrawal, retirement, retreat.
To 8 per cent of adult readers RECESSION incorrectly means SURRENDER, probably a confusion of RECESSION, withdrawal, with CONCESSION, yielding, surrender. The corresponding verbs are more familiar. To CONCEDE is to give in, yield, admit, grant. To RECEDE is to withdraw, retreat, retire, move back.

The adjective RECESSIONAL is perhaps most familiar when used as a noun to designate the hymn sung while the clergy, choir, and sometimes the congregation, leave the church.

The words RECESSION and SECESSION should not be confused. SECESSION (134) is the resignation of a group from an association, the withdrawal of a state from a union. RECESSION may be an actual, physical marching back; or it may be retirement from a position in an argument.

581. *STILTED* (*stĭlt'-ĕd*) *adj.* Stiffly formal, lofty, bombastic, pompous, pedantic (838), artificially elevated.
Everyone is familiar with the wooden STILTS which boys make

for themselves and with which they walk, raised a foot or two above the ground. STILTED, by derivation, means equipped with STILTS; and although the word is used figuratively, usually in reference to language, it suggests not only the elevation which stilts give, but the stiff, artificial, unnatural, manner in which one must walk on stilts.

In the phrase: 'His STILTED manner', IRRESOLUTE, hesitating; and IMPROPER, unseemly, unfit; are equally popular misconceptions, each held by 8 per cent of adult readers. IRRESOLUTE suggests the stepping back and forth which one must occasionally do on stilts in order to keep one's balance, but the word conveys none of the superior feeling of STILTED.

582. *ABANDON* (ă-băn'-dŏn) *n.* Unrestraint (609), freedom, liberty, license, without inhibitions, absence of conventionality, careless ease.

This meaning of ABANDON is unknown to 28 per cent of adult readers. When used in the test phrase: 'They play with ABANDON', it is thought by 12 per cent to mean LISTLESSNESS, indifference, spiritlessness, practically an opposite of the correct meaning. To do anything with ABANDON is to give one's self up entirely to the task in hand, to ABANDON one's self entirely to it.

583. *STRIFE* (strīf) *n.* Conflict, discord, rivalry, contention, quarreling, competition, struggle for victory, exertion for superiority.

In the test phrase: 'Constant STRIFE', the word is thought by 13 per cent of adult readers to mean EFFORT. The verb, to STRIVE, has two meanings. It may mean to struggle, contend; or to make an effort, try hard, endeavor earnestly. STRIFE is the corresponding noun; and once meant effort, earnest endeavor. This meaning is now archaic; and STRIFE means struggle, contention, quarrel, specifically a struggle for superiority.

STRIFE and CONTENTION are practically synonymous. CONTENTION, from the Latin *tendere*, to stretch, originally meant, like STRIFE, a reaching out, earnest effort to obtain a desired object. STRIFE, which is related to German, Icelandic, and Scandinavian words, is perhaps the stronger of the two.

584. *AUTOPSY* (*aw'-tŏp-sĭ*) *n.* Examination, dissection of a
dead body often for the purpose of discovering the
cause of death, post-mortem examination.
AUTOPSY is from two Greek words, αὐτός, self; and ὀπτός,
seen. An AUTOPSY is, therefore, by derivation, seeing for
one's self.
To 15 per cent of adult readers AUTOPSY incorrectly
means INQUEST. An INQUEST may be an official investigation
into the cause of death, in which evidence is presented to a
jury and in which the findings of an AUTOPSY play a part.
An INQUEST is primarily a legal proceeding; an AUTOPSY is
conducted by a doctor.

585. *OGLE* (*ō'-gl*) *v.* To make eyes, glance amorously, look
at in an overfamiliar manner, cast flirtatious glances.
In the test phrase: 'Horror of being OGLED', the word is
thought by 9 per cent of preparatory-school juniors to mean
HAUNTED. This is probably a confusion of OGLE, to make
eyes, with the noun OGRE, an evil giant, hideous monster.
OGLE comes from the same source as the word EYE, and
is similar in form to both Dutch and German words for
EYE. It means, however, specifically to cast flirtatious, overfamiliar, glances; and only a man can OGLE.

586. *REMINISCENCE* (*rĕm-ĭ-nĭs'-sĕns*) *n.* Recollection, retrospection, remembrance, power of recalling to mind
past experiences. A REMINISCENCE may also be that which is
recalled; especially an incident remembered and narrated.
REMINISCENCE is from the Latin *reminisci*, to recall, recol-
lect. To 11 per cent of adult readers it incorrectly means
RECRIMINATION, the returning of one accusation with another, retort.
REMINISCENCE, RECOLLECTION, and REMEMBRANCE, are three
methods of recalling to mind. REMEMBRANCE applies to those
things which remain in the memory even though they may
not be consciously present. RECOLLECTION is the act of
bringing into consciousness things present in the memory.
RECOLLECTION requires effort and is often the recalling of
intangible facts, of one's opinions and thoughts. REMINIS-
CENCE, like RECOLLECTION, is the act of bringing into con-

sciousness but is less energetic and is specifically the recalling of past experiences with the intention of recounting them.

587. *LATERAL* (*lăt'-er-ăl*) *adj.* Sidewise, pertaining to the side, directed toward the side, proceeding from the side, at a right angle to the main axis.

In the test phrase: 'LATERAL motion', the word is thought by 17 per cent of adult readers to mean PARALLEL, continuously equidistant, extending in the same direction, side by side. The noun, a LATERAL, from the same Latin *latus, lateris*, side, is a branch, an off-shoot.

588. *HARDENED* (*hahr'-dĕnd*) *p. adj.* Unfeeling, toughened, confirmed in vice, callous, harsh, impenitent, obdurate (519).

The adjectives HARDENED and CALLOUS are similar in many respects. Each can be used of both physical and moral states. The adjective, CALLOUS, which is always spelt ous, means physically hard-skinned, thick-skinned, hardened by continuous rubbing; the noun, a CALLUS, spelt us, is a thick, hard place on the skin. In the moral sense, the adjective, CALLOUS, suggests a person made insensitive by hard treatment. HARDENED, from the verb to HARDEN, which is of Anglo-Saxon origin, appears in its physical sense in the phrase: 'His muscles were HARDENED by exercise'. In the moral sense, HARDENED may be used either of a person who has been made hard by external conditions or of one who has HARDENED himself against better feelings.

589. *PARAGON* (*păr'-ă-gŏn*) *n.* A model or pattern of special excellence, perfect example. PARAGON is generally used of a supremely excellent person.

In the test phrase: 'Another PARAGON of beauty', the word is thought by 12 per cent of adult readers to mean GEOMETRIC FIGURE, the popular misconception. This is presumably because of some association of PARAGON, model, with such words as: PENTAGON, a figure of five angles; HEXAGON (98), a figure of six angles; and POLYGON, a figure of many angles; all directly from Greek. PARAGON does not seem to come from the same source as these words. It first appeared in its present form in the fourteenth century in Italian, and in the sixteenth century in English. Although numerous attempts have been made, it has been impossible to trace its origin back with certainty to either Latin or Greek.

590. *BUMPER* (*bŭm'-per*) *n.* A full glass, cup filled to the brim, overflowing cup used in drinking a toast.

BUMPER is probably from the same source as BUM, used colloquially, as a noun, to mean a drunken loafer; and BUMMER, an idle, worthless person who sponges on others.

In the test phrase: 'Refreshed himself with a BUMPER', the word is believed by 13 per cent of preparatory-school juniors to mean COCKTAIL. This is not far from correct, for, although a BUMPER is literally a full glass, the word is used especially of a full glass drunk as a toast.

591. *RECUMBENT* (*rē-kŭm'-bĕnt*) *adj.* Reclining (431), lying down, supine, leaning back, reposing, prostrate, flat on one's back.

To 7 per cent of adult readers RECUMBENT incorrectly means UNTENABLE, indefensible, incapable of being held.

RECUMBENT is from the Latin *re*, back; and *cubare*, to lie; from the same source as the English word INCUMBENT (807), office-holder; and the more unusual word CUBICLE (1022), a small bedroom.

592. *SYNTHESIS* (*sĭn'-thĕ-sĭs*) *n.* The putting of different things together, composition, construction, integration, combination of separate parts.

The corresponding adjective, SYNTHETIC (*sĭn-thĕt'-ĭk*) (437), artificial, manufactured, is more familiar for it is unknown to only 18 per cent of adult readers.

To 13 per cent of college seniors SYNTHESIS incorrectly means ANALYSIS. As ordinarily used in English, an ANALYSIS is the breaking down of a whole into its parts, the resolution of a compound into its elements, the exact opposite of a SYNTHESIS.

SYNTHESIS comes from two Greek words σύν, together; and τιθέναι, to place; and by derivation means to place together.

ANTITHESIS, from the Greek prefix ἀντί, against, and the same word to place, means placing against, contrasting, and by derivation ought to be an exact opposite of SYNTHESIS. But the word, ANTITHESIS, although it means a direct contrary, a strong contrast, can be used only in such a phrase as: 'Evil is the ANTITHESIS of good'. One cannot say the ANTITHESIS of good and evil, the ANTITHESIS of two ideas, as one can say the SYNTHESIS of them.

In logic, SYNTHESIS and INDUCTION are practically synonymous; for INDUCTION is that method of reasoning which arrives at a general conclusion from a number of isolated cases; and SYNTHESIS is the process of drawing a conclusion from a number of separate facts, reasoning from the parts to the whole.

593. *IMPETUOUS* (ĭm-pĕt'-ū-ŭs) *adj.* Impulsive, vehement, rash, precipitant, headlong, hasty, excitable, reckless, foolhardy, acting with sudden energy.

To 19 per cent of adult readers IMPETUOUS incorrectly means INSOLENT, offensive to others, overbearing. This may be a confusion of IMPETUOUS, rash, either with IMPERTINENT, rude, saucy, insolent, or with IMPUDENT, brazen, audacious, insolent.

IMPETUOUS is from the Latin *in*, upon, and *petere*, to fall upon, attack, assault. The verb *petere* is also the source of PETULANT, impatient, peevish, fretful, and IMPETUS, a word which may mean energy of motion, or more figuratively, stimulus. IMPETUOUS means acting with sudden energy.

594. *CANDIDACY* (kăn'-dĭd-ā-sĭ) *n.* Nomination, seeking election, aspiration to office, condition of being a candidate.

By a Roman custom, seekers for office wore a white robe or toga. The Latin word *candidatus*, from which comes directly the English word CANDIDATE, means a person dressed in white, and therefore a seeker for office. It is from the Latin word *candere*, to be white, glisten, the source of the English word CANDLE.

In the test phrase: 'His CANDIDACY is popular', the word is thought by 12 per cent of adult readers to mean PLATFORM.

A PLATFORM, in this sense, is a formulated policy, plan, declaration of principles issued by a political party. Both a PLATFORM and a CANDIDACY may be announced before an election; but a PLATFORM is a policy; while a CANDIDACY is a seeking for office, by an individual.

By another 11 per cent CANDIDACY is thought to mean SINCERITY. This is probably a confusion of CANDIDACY with CANDIDNESS, frankness, sincerity, the state of being candid. CANDID comes from the same Latin source *candere*, to be white, and once meant pure, clean, stainless. It may now mean impartial, just, free from bias; but more often means frank, open, straightforward, fair, ingenuous.

CANDIDATESHIP and CANDIDATURE are both exactly synonymous with CANDIDACY, and are sometimes thought to be preferable forms.

595. *TROOP* (*troop*) *v.* To flock, herd, move in a crowd, swarm, throng, march in company, pass in order. 'The men TROOPED by.'
TROOP comes from the French *troupe*, a word which has been adopted by English with no change of spelling, TROUPE (*troop*), to mean a band of actors, a group of performers.

The noun, TROOP, with its revised English spelling, may mean any band, multitude, collection of people; but is used specifically of a body of soldiers. The verb, to TROOP, may mean to gather together, assemble, flock together; or, more frequently, to march, move in a body.

596. *CLEMENCY* (*klĕm'-ĕn-sĭ*) *n.* Mildness, mercy, compassion, gentleness, tenderness, merciful treatment, the quality of being lenient (196).
In the test phrase: 'The CLEMENCY of the law', the word is thought by 11 per cent of adult readers to mean JUSTICE, impartiality, fairness, justness, reasonableness, equity. JUSTICE may also mean vindictive retribution, merited punishment. In this sense it is almost an opposite of CLEMENCY, mercy. CLEMENCY is from the Latin *clemens*, *clementis*, mild, gentle, calm, a word used of weather. The English word CLEMENCY may still be used of weather to mean mildness, but it is also used figuratively of human behavior to mean forbearance,

mercy, compassion. In both senses INCLEMENCY and SEVERITY are opposites.

597. *PREDOMINATE* (prē-dŏm'-ĭ-nāt) v. To prevail, rule, preponderate, surpass in strength, be most influential. PREDOMINATE is from the Latin *prae*; and *dominari*, to rule. In the test phrase: 'Making it PREDOMINATE everywhere', the word is thought by 12 per cent of preparatory-school juniors to mean POPULAR. That which is POPULAR enjoys the favor of the people, is pleasing. That which PREDOMINATES may do so by undue influence, intrigue, or physical force, in opposition to the will of the majority.

598. *MALIGN* (mă-līn') v. To speak evil of, slander, defame, disparage, calumniate, traduce, vilify (vĭl'-ĭ-fī). In the short test phrase: 'He was MALIGNED', the word is thought by 10 per cent of adult readers to mean SWINDLED. To SWINDLE and to MALIGN are both to injure. To SWINDLE a person is to cheat him financially, defraud him; to MALIGN him is to speak evil against him, defame him. The confusion may be augmented by the similarity of DEFRAUD, a synonym of SWINDLE, and DEFAME, a synonym of MALIGN.

To 14 per cent of preparatory-school juniors 'He was MALIGNED', incorrectly means he was COMPLAINED OF. To COMPLAIN OF is to find fault with, grumble about, criticize. To MALIGN is much stronger; it is to run down, blacken the reputation of, injure. The action of MALIGNING is malicious, evil.

The verb, to MALIGN, to speak evil of; the adjective, MALIGN, by derivation born bad; the noun MALICE (391), ill will; and the adjectives, MALICIOUS (549), spiteful, and MALIGNANT, exceedingly malicious; all come from the Latin, *malus*, bad.

The adjectives, MALIGN, possessed of an evil disposition, and BENIGN, kindly, gentle, are opposites. The verbs to MALIGN and to PRAISE are practically opposites.

599. *OPTION* (ŏp'-shŭn) n. Right of choice, alternative, preference, wish, election. OPTION is from the Latin *optare*, to choose, and means right

of choice. From the same source comes the adjective OP-TIONAL, elective, left to choice, depending upon preference.

In the test phrase: 'He had no OPTION', the word is thought by 11 per cent of adult readers to mean TITLE. Both an OPTION ON and a TITLE TO property may be bought; but a TITLE is the legal right of possession, right of ownership. Legally, an OPTION is the privilege of executing or relinquishing a commercial transaction on fixed terms; it is the right of choosing whether or not one will acquire TITLE, ownership.

600. *INTERMENT* (*ĭn-ter'-mĕnt*) *n.* Burial, inhumation, sepulture, act of entombing, ceremony of burying the dead.

To 9 per cent of preparatory-school juniors INTERMENT incorrectly means MEDDLING DISPOSITION. This may be due to some confusion of DISPOSITION, temperament, nature, with DEPOSITION, a word which has many uses. A DEPOSITION may be specifically the burial of a saint's body. The DEPOSITION from the cross was the removal of Christ's body from the cross.

To another 7 per cent INTERMENT means IMPRISONMENT. This is no doubt a confusion of INTERMENT, burial, with INTERNMENT, originally the confinement of soldiers in the interior of a country; sometimes, more generally, imprisonment, detention.

The verb, to INTER, is to bury, deposit in the earth, inhume. It is from the Latin *in*, and *terra*, the earth. INTERMENT is the noun, the act of interring.

601. *PURITY* (*pū'-rĭ-tĭ*) *n.* Cleanliness, innocence, virtue, chastity (385), freedom from guilt, absence of moral corruption.

When used figuratively, of a human being, PURITY is thought by 34 per cent of grammar-school pupils to mean CHRISTIAN-ITY. This may be due to a confusion of CHASTITY, purity, with CHARITY, Christian love, good will, one of the three Christian virtues: faith, hope, and charity.

PURITY, from the Latin *purus*, clean, pure, may be used of material things, to mean free from any foreign substance,

as: 'The PURITY of water', 'The PURITY of a metal'; or in
a figurative sense to mean innocence, chastity.

602. *CAPILLARY* (*căp'-ĭl-lā-rĭ*) *adj.* Hairlike, slender, fine,
    capillaceous. CAPILLARY is used specifically of a tube
with a minute, hairlike, bore.
CAPILLARY is from the Latin *capillus*, hair. This, in turn,
comes from *caput*, head. From *caput* comes CAPITAL, the
large initial letter of a sentence, the first letter of a proper
name; also the chief city of a country, the first city of a
State, the seat of government. From the Latin *caput*, head,
comes also CAPITOL, which begins with a large letter and
ends in OL. CAPITOL is the name of the temple of Jupiter
in Rome, so named, tradition says, because those who dug
the foundations came upon a human head. The same word
CAPITOL is used for the building in Washington occupied
by Congress and for the chief governmental building in
many states, sometimes called a state-house or, as in Massachusetts, the State House.
   In the test phrase: 'These are CAPILLARY tubes', the word
is thought by 11 per cent of adult readers to mean INNER,
the common misconception.
   CAPILLARY is exclusively a scientific term. It is used in such
an expression as: 'CAPILLARY attraction' to mean that force
which causes a liquid to climb up in a capillary, hairlike,
tube.

603. *DIRGE* (*derj*) *n.* Funeral song, song of mourning,
    piece of mournful music, elegy, requiem, exequy.
DIRGE is a contraction of the first word of a Latin hymn
which is sung at funerals and which begins: '*Dirige, Domine,
Deus meus*'. The Latin *dirige* is the imperative of *dirigere*, to
direct; and the translation is: 'Direct, O Lord, my God'.
   PLACEBO (*plă-sē'-bō*), a responsive chant sung for the dead,
comes also from the initial word of a Latin hymn beginning:
'*Placebo Domino*', 'I shall be acceptable to the Lord'. The
word PLACEBO is still used in music; but may also mean a
medicine given because it is pleasing to the patient rather
than because it is effective.
   To 11 per cent of adult readers DIRGE incorrectly means

PROPHECY, inspired foretelling, prediction, prognostication. To another 7 per cent DIRGE means KNELL. A DIRGE and a KNELL (606) are both sounds associated with a funeral. A KNELL is, however, always the sound of a bell; a DIRGE is specifically a song.

604. *SCRUPULOUS* (*skrū'-pū-lŭs*) *adj.* Conscientious, precise (278), overnice in small matters, punctilious (533). 'SCRUPULOUS in all things.'
SCRUPULOUS and PUNCTILIOUS are nearly synonymous, for both mean observant of minute details. PUNCTILIOUS, attentive to PUNCTILIOS, minute details, nice points, is from the Spanish *puntillo*, which in turn is the diminutive of *punto*, point. PUNCTILIOUS is therefore attentive to nice points.

SCRUPULOUS comes from the Latin *scrupulus*, a tiny pebble, a diminutive of *scrupus*, a rough, sharp stone. In English a SCRUPLE is a doubt, uncertainty. SCRUPULOUS is troubled by scruples, minutely exact. SCRUPULOUS has the connotation of an uncomfortable pebble in the shoe and is used most often of matters bothersome to the conscience.

605. *MERCENARY* (*mer'-sĕn-ā-rĭ*) *adj.* Working for money only, hired, sordid, intent on gain, influenced by selfish advantage, not disinterested.
In the test phrase: 'MERCENARY crimes', the word is thought by 12 per cent of preparatory-school juniors to mean ORDINARY. This misconception has, as so frequently happens, some historical justification. Although today the word ORDINARY means commonplace, usual, it was defined by Samuel Johnson, in his dictionary of 1770, as ugly, coarse, and at that time had the same disagreeable suggestion as MERCENARY.

MERCENARY comes from the Latin word, *merces*, pay, reward, wages. It is from the same source as MERCANTILE, commercial, trading. MERCANTILE has kept an agreeable meaning; whereas MERCENARY means not only working for money, but has come to mean sordid, ready to accept dishonorable gain.

Both MERCENARY and VENAL (*vē'-năl*) imply holding the value of money above almost everything else. VENAL is the stronger of the two, and means ready to sell anything, including one's principles and honor, for money. MERCENARY means acting with money as a motive, considering the financial return of every action.

606. *KNELL* (*nĕl*) *v.* To toll, sound a bell, ring; specifically to toll a bell at a funeral; also ring a bell as a warning, or as a summons for help. The noun, a KNELL, is often a sound of ill omen.

To KNELL, which is of Anglo-Saxon origin and comes from a word meaning the sound of a bell, is thought by 16 per cent of adult readers to mean to SWING, oscillate, move to and fro. The verb, to SWING, is general. One may SWING one's arms, SWING a club. A bell which SWINGS does not necessarily make a sound, does not necessarily ring. The word KNELL always specifies sound. A bell which KNELLS gives forth a sound, usually a mournful, ill-omened, warning, sound.

607. *ALLAY* (*ăl-lā'*) *v.* To quiet down, calm, relieve (349), soothe, lessen, assuage, alleviate (575), abate (664).

ALLAY has, in the past, been closely associated with the word ALLEGE. In the fifteenth century ALLEGE, like ALLAY, meant to soothe, relieve. Today, ALLAY and ALLEGE have no meanings in common for to ALLEGE signifies to affirm, assert, declare, as: 'He ALLEGED its truth'.

In the test phrase: 'You ALLAY my fears', the word is thought by 10 per cent of adult readers to mean AROUSE, stir up, an exact opposite of ALLAY, soothe, quiet down. By another 7 per cent ALLAY is thought to mean CONFIRM, another opposite, at least in suggestion.

Of the two similar words ALLAY and ALLEVIATE, the latter should be used to suggest permanent improvement. ALLAY, which at one time meant ALLOY, to mix a baser metal with another and so make it go further, now denotes a lessening of the effect without changing the fundamental conditions. ALLAY suggests temporariness. One ALLAYS suffering, perhaps by the use of drugs, without removing the cause.

608. *AUGURY* (*aw'-gŭ-rĭ*) *n.* Art of foretelling events, prophecy, divination; also any indication of the future, sign, portent, omen, foretoken, prognostic.

To 8 per cent of college seniors, AUGURY incorrectly means GUESS, estimate, supposition, conjecture. Both a GUESS and an AUGURY are judgments made with insufficient data. A GUESS is acknowledged to be based upon almost no data, and can be made about an existent fact, as: 'A GUESS at the height of a tree', 'A GUESS at the right answer'. An AUGURY is based upon signs and omens, which may be real or imaginary; and an AUGURY must be of the future. An AUGURY is a guess about future events.

AUGURY, PORTENT, and PRESAGE, are all indications of future events. A PRESAGE (*prĕs'-āj*) is a foreboding, presentiment, intuition, impression, felt by some person. A PORTENT is an indication of the future shown by some physical sign or condition. An AUGURY may be either something felt by a person as likely to happen; or a prediction based on physical conditions.

609. *UNRESTRAINT* (*ŭn-rē-strānt'*) *n.* Freedom, license, liberty, abandon (582), lack of reserve. 'They showed UNRESTRAINT.'

RESTRAINT means repression, restriction, confinement, the state of being hindered, of being held back. The prefix UN is the negative; UNRESTRAINT is the state of not being repressed, hindered, confined.

610. *LUCRATIVE* (*lū'-krā-tĭv*) *adj.* Profitable, gainful, remunerative, yielding money, giving considerable profit. In the test phrase: 'A LUCRATIVE practice', the word is believed by 8 per cent of preparatory-school juniors to mean LAUGHABLE, probably a confusion of LUCRATIVE, profitable, with LUDICROUS, funny, comic, nonsensical.

The word LUCRE (*lū'-ker*) can be traced back in many languages. It is probably related to the Latin *lucrum*, gain, profit; to the Greek word λεία, booty, spoils; and perhaps to an Anglo-Saxon word for reward, pay. In English LUCRE means money, profit as measured in money, gain in money. The word usually suggests the disagreeable aspects of money; and in place of the hackneyed phrase: 'FILTHY LUCRE', one may with the same implication use merely the word LUCRE.

LUCRATIVE means yielding lucre, producing lucre, profit-

able in terms of money. The word is not so pleasant as
PROFITABLE, and yet not so disagreeable as LUCRE.

611. *COY* (*koi*) *adj.* Shy, bashful, diffident, distant, modest,
    slow to respond to advances, shrinking demurely from
familiarity.
COY is a doublet of QUIET; etymologically it is the same
word. QUIET may mean undisturbed by emotion; and COY
has something of this same suggestion.

In the phrase: 'The COY maiden', DECEITFUL is the common
misconception, and in the minds of many persons there is a
mistaken notion that COY has a come-hither implication. But
there is no such thought in the adjective COY. The unusual
verb, to COY, may mean to allure, decoy, lead into danger
by strategy; but the adjective COY is free from this suggestion.

COY, DIFFIDENT, and BASHFUL, are practically synonymous.
BASHFUL, very modest, easily put to confusion, is applied to
either sex. DIFFIDENT, literally without faith, wanting in self-
confidence, is used of men; COY, exclusively of women.

612. *HUMOR* (*hū'-mōr*) *v.* To make content, please, soothe,
    spoil, gratify, indulge, satisfy, yield to the mood of.
In the test phrase: 'She HUMORED the child', the word is
thought by 32 per cent of grammar-school pupils to mean
CARESSED. Both HUMOR and CARESS imply a fondness for the
person humored or caressed, but the method of expressing
the fondness differs with the two. To CARESS is to fondle,
stroke, pat with the hand, or, in general, treat with fondness,
with affection. To HUMOR is specifically to express fondness
by complying with a person's desires.

The noun HUMOR, from the same source as HUMID, moist,
wet, originally meant moisture and was used by early physi-
cians for the important fluids of the body. The four CARDINAL
HUMORS determine one's temperament; and to HUMOR is to
comply with one's temperament.

To HUMOR, INDULGE, and GRATIFY, all convey the idea of
pleasing, satisfying, making content. To GRATIFY is used in
a good sense, as: 'To GRATIFY a child's curiosity', by supply-
ing facts, offering an explanation. To INDULGE often implies
a bad result. 'To INDULGE a child' suggests giving something

which he would be better off without. 'To HUMOR a child'
may be to satisfy his curiosity with knowledge; or it may
be to spoil him.

613. *ARROGANCE* (ăr'-rō-găns) *n.* Haughty pride, assumed
    dignity, disdain, presumption, self-importance, overcon-
    fidence, egotism (419), conceit.

In the test phrase: 'He is noted for ARROGANCE', the word is
thought by 10 per cent of adult readers to mean INDIF-
FERENCE, the popular misconception. An indifference to the
rights of others is one aspect of ARROGANCE, but the word
INDIFFERENCE has no suggestion of haughty pride, assumed
dignity, as has ARROGANCE.

ARROGANCE and HAUGHTINESS are similar characteristics; and
are related to one another much as are PRIDE and VANITY.
VANITY demands the adulation of others; PRIDE is self-
sufficient. HAUGHTINESS is generally a feminine quality. The
word implies height, and therefore a comparison with others,
a looking down upon others. ARROGANCE is masculine; it is
dignity assumed with little thought of comparison.

614. *EVOKE* (ē-vōk') *v.* To call out, summon forth, call
    up, arouse, excite.

In the test phrase: 'To EVOKE this condition', the word is
believed by 8 per cent of preparatory-school juniors to
mean MAKE. By another 8 per cent it is thought to mean
REPEAL. This is probably a confusion of EVOKE, call out, with
REVOKE, call back, repeal.

EVOKE is one of the many words from the Latin *vocare*, to
call; thus: REVOKE, to call back; CONVOKE, to call together;
INVOKE, call upon, to ask earnestly, address in prayer; and
EVOKE, to call forth.

615. *REPLENISH* (rē-plĕn'-ĭsh) *v.* To renew, fill again,
    refill; also to fill completely, stock.

REPLENISH, from the Latin *re*, again; and *plenus*, full; means
literally fill again. REPLENISH is from the same source as the
English word, PLENTY, abundance, fullness, adequate supply.

To 11 per cent of adult readers REPLENISH incorrectly
means to INCREASE. To INCREASE is to add to something

already there, augment, intensify. One can INCREASE the supply on hand. The word presupposes the presence of something to which to add. Furthermore, the word does not imply filling to the brim. One can INCREASE one's stock by a small amount.

REPLENISH has two meanings. It may mean to fill again something already empty. In this sense the word presupposes an empty glass, an empty cupboard. REPLENISH may also mean to fill completely, fill to the brim; for the verb comes from the same source as the adjective, REPLETE, full to capacity, surfeited, lacking nothing, and the noun REPLETION, fullness, surfeit.

To another 9 per cent REPLENISH incorrectly means DIMINISH, in suggestion an opposite of the correct meaning.

When used in the phrase: 'He kept his glass REPLENISHED', the word is believed by 1 per cent of preparatory-school juniors to mean EMPTIED, an opposite of the correct meaning.

616. *GOURMAND* (*goor'-mănd*); also spelt GORMAND (*gŏr'-mănd*) *n.* Glutton, ravenous eater, greedy person, one who is intemperate in eating.

To 8 per cent of college seniors GOURMAND incorrectly means BRAGGART, boaster.

GOURMAND and GOURMET (*goor-mā'*) should be distinguished. A GOURMET is an epicure, connoisseur of food and drink, one of discriminating taste. Although GOURMAND is sometimes incorrectly used to mean GOURMET, epicure, GOURMAND correctly used is a greedy, ravenous eater, a voracious fellow.

The word GOURMET was once used, in French, to mean a judge of wine, and GOURMAND to mean a judge of food. But now, in French as in English, a GOURMET is a judge of food and wine; a GOURMAND is a glutton.

617. *FRUGAL* (*froo'-găl*) *adj.* Avoiding waste, sparing, economical, thrifty, prudent, parsimonious (961), careful in expenditure, saving expense.

The corresponding adverb is FRUGALLY, thriftily (126).

To 7 per cent of adult readers FRUGAL incorrectly means EXTRAVAGANT, an exact opposite of the correct meaning.

618. *LURK* (*lerk*) *v.* To lie hidden, keep out of sight, exist unobserved, lie in wait.

The derivation of the verb, to LURK, is uncertain. It goes back to Middle English, and there are similar words in Dutch, German, Icelandic, and in the Scandinavian languages. There are apparently no other common English words from the same source.

In the test phrase: 'A doubt still LURKS', the word is thought by 10 per cent of preparatory-school juniors to mean PREYS. To PREY (*prā*) originally meant to pillage, spoil, rob. The word is now used with reference to animals which habitually seize and devour others. Both to PREY UPON and to LURK IN are also used figuratively. A doubt which PREYS upon the mind is ever present, wasting its energy, destroying it. A doubt which LURKS in the mind lies hidden.

To LURK and to SKULK are practically synonymous. To SKULK often suggests lying hidden from shame, slinking into a corner for fear of detection, sneaking away from work. To LURK is more apt to be aggressive, and suggests lying hidden with the aim of preying upon what passes.

619. *ABSTEMIOUS* (*ăb-stē'-mĭ-ŭs*) *adj.* Self-denying, sparing in the use of food and drink, temperate, moderate, abstinent.

ABSTEMIOUS is from the Latin *abs*, from; and *temetum*, wine, strong drink. By derivation and in its early use ABSTEMIOUS was limited to abstaining from drink; but the word is now applied generally to moderation in any form.

ABSTEMIOUS and ABSTINENT (*ăb'-stĭ-něnt*) are close in meaning, except that ABSTINENT may be applied to a single act, while ABSTEMIOUS is used to describe an habitually moderate, self-denying person. It is curious that ABSTINENT, the adjective of ABSTAIN, from the Latin *abs*, from, and *tenere*, to hold, with no suggestion of drink in its origin, is now most often applied to refraining from drink; while ABSTEMIOUS, which comes directly from a word meaning wine or strong drink, has today no such special connotation but can be used for abstaining from anything.

In the test phrase: 'His ABSTEMIOUS wife', the word is thought by 11 per cent of adult readers to mean GLUTTONOUS, given to overeating, voracious, crapulous, an opposite of the correct meaning of ABSTEMIOUS, self-denying.

620. *BOON* (*boon*) *n.* A favor, blessing, benefit, gift, something to be thankful for.

In the test phrase: 'A great BOON', the word is thought by 22 per cent of grammar-school pupils to mean ACHIEVEMENT. An ACHIEVEMENT and a BOON differ in that an ACHIEVEMENT is gained by boldness, valor, exertion, or is the result of superior ability; a BOON, favor, gift, is obtained without effort.

To another 20 per cent BOON incorrectly means SUCCESS. This is perhaps a confusion of BOON with BOOM. A BOOM may be a rush, sudden increase in activity; and the verb to BOOM may mean to be prosperous, flourish.

BOON is from Anglo-Saxon and Icelandic words which mean prayer, petition; and the English word BOON may today mean that which is prayed for, something desired, a favor asked. BOON, however, more often means something received, a favor granted.

621. *EXTEMPORIZE* (*ĕks-tĕm'-pō-rīz*) *v.* To improvise, produce without preparation, make on the spur of the moment.

EXTEMPORIZE comes probably from the Latin phrase *ex tempore*, on the spur of the moment, from the Latin *ex*, out of, and *tempus*, time.

In the test phrase: 'EXTEMPORIZED strong-rooms', the word is thought by 12 per cent of preparatory-school juniors to mean VERY AGED; and by another 8 per cent to mean TIME HONORED. Either might be an incorrect translation of the Latin *ex tempore*.

The adjective, EXTEMPORANEOUS, unprepared, off-hand; and the corresponding adverb, EXTEMPORANEOUSLY, as: 'He spoke EXTEMPORANEOUSLY'; are more familiar than the verb to EXTEMPORIZE, to improvise.

622. *INFIRMITY* (*ĭn-fĕrm'-ĭ-tĭ*) *n.* A weakness, malady (374), defect, imperfection, feebleness, frailty, debility, illness, foible (858).

INFIRMITY is from the Latin *in*, not; and *firmus*, strong, steadfast, stable; and means, by derivation, not strong, not firm.

INFIRMITY, IMBECILITY, and DEBILITY, are three types of weakness. DEBILITY is general physical weakness. IMBECILITY is mental weakness. An INFIRMITY may be either mental, as: 'The INFIRMITY of noble minds', or physical. When used in the physical sense an INFIRMITY is usually specific and localized. Deafness, blindness, and lameness, are specific infirmities. But the word may also be used in such a phrase as: 'The INFIRMITY of age', to mean a general weakness, lack of strength.

623. *FIDGET* (*fĭj'-ĕt*) *v.* To make someone nervous, make him restless, worry him, exasperate, annoy, make him uneasy. 'It FIDGETS me.'

This is a transitive use of the verb to FIDGET which is more common in its intransitive use as: 'Stop FIDGETING'. In this sense FIDGET means to move restlessly, stir about nervously.

624. *COQUETRY* (*kŏ'-kĕt-rĭ*) *n.* Flirtation, trifling in love, philandering, affectation of amorous advances, playing with men's affections, seeking to attract attention by pretense. To 15 per cent of adult readers COQUETRY incorrectly means FLATTERY, compliment, adulation, obsequiousness.

A COQUETTE is a vain woman who endeavors to attract admiration by pretending to make love. The word is the diminutive of *coq*, the French word for COCK, and suggests strutting like a rooster. The English word is, however, applied exclusively to women. PHILANDERER (1078) is the corresponding word applied to men.

625. *TALISMAN* (*tăl'-ĭs-măn*) *n.* A charm, amulet, phylactery, mezuzah (*mĕ-zoo'-zah*).

A TALISMAN was originally a figure carved under circumstances which gave it the power of averting evil. From this the word came to be used to signify any magic charm.

When used in the test phrase: 'An unfailing TALISMAN', the word is thought by 10 per cent of preparatory-school juniors to mean OLD SERVANT. This is perhaps a confusion of TALISMAN, charm, with PARTISAN, not a personal attendant,

but one who is devoted to a cause, an adherent, often one
whose judgment gives way to his zeal. TALISMAN is related
to Dutch, German, and Scandinavian words, and comes to
English perhaps through Arabic, although it is originally
from Greek. A TALISMAN is not a man, but a charm, amulet.

626. *GAMUT* (*găm′-ŭt*) *n.* Complete range, whole scale,
    diapason (*dī-ă-pā′-sŭn*).
The musical scale of seven notes is said to have been devised
by Guido d'Arezzo, who was born about 990. The first
note of his scale he called UT, the first two letters of a hymn
to St. John. From this UT come apparently the last two
letters of the word GAMUT which combines GAMMA, the
name of the Greek letter γ, the last note of the musical
scale, with UT the first note. GAMUT means therefore from
the last note to the first, the whole scale.

627. *SEDIMENT* (*sĕd′-ĭ-mĕnt*) *n.* Dregs, lees, settlings,
    matter that settles to the bottom of a liquid.
SEDIMENT comes from the Latin *sedere*, to sit. From the
same source come many English words, such as: SEDENTARY,
used frequently in the phrase: 'A SEDENTARY occupation',
one which can be performed sitting down; SEDATE, quiet,
composed, free from agitation, by derivation settled down;
and SEDATIVE, tending to soothe, that which calms.

SEDIMENT is thought by 10 per cent of preparatory-school
juniors to mean SKIMMING. SKIMMINGS, a word which usually
appears in the plural, means that which is removed from the
surface. SKIMMINGS may be either valuable or worthless.
Cream, for instance, is SKIMMED from the top of the milk.
SCUM, a word practically synonymous with SKIMMINGS, is
always used in a bad sense, to mean refuse which floats to
the top. SCUM and SEDIMENT both suggest refuse; but SCUM
rises, while SEDIMENT sinks.

628. *OBVIOUSLY* (*ŏb′-vĭ-ŭs-lĭ*) *adv.* Clearly, patently, evi-
    dently, plainly, unmistakably, indubitably, manifestly,
apparently, without doubt.
In the test phrase: 'He is OBVIOUSLY right', the word is
thought by 12 per cent of adult readers to mean OFFEN-

SIVELY, unpleasantly. This may perhaps be a confusion of OBVIOUSLY with OBNOXIOUSLY, offensively, objectionably.

OBVIOUSLY is from the Latin *ob;* and *via,* way; and by derivation means lying in the way, and therefore impossible to avoid seeing.

629. *LACONIC (lă-kŏn'-ĭk) adj.* Concise, brief, using few words, succinct, sententious, terse (493), pithy (1009). Previous to the Peloponnesian War, which lasted from 431 B.C. to 404 B.C., the PELOPONNESUS, the southern peninsula of Greece, was divided into seven or eight countries. The inhabitants of one of these countries, LACONIA, were noted for their brevity of speech. The adjective, LACONIC, now spelt with a small letter, means like a LACONIAN in speech, of few words, brief, sententious.

LACONIA was captured by the SPARTANS and became known as SPARTA. The Spartans were noted for their rigid discipline and the adjective SPARTAN, still spelt with a capital, means extreme, rigid, great, as: 'SPARTAN endurance', 'SPARTAN simplicity'.

Another adjective from the Peloponnesus is ARCADIAN. ARCADIA was a mountainous country in the center of the Peloponnesus. Its inhabitants were simple, rustic folk; and ARCADIAN, also spelt with a capital, now means simple, rustic, pastoral.

In the test phrase: 'A LACONIC answer', the word is thought by 6 per cent of preparatory-school juniors to mean JOKING, perhaps because of some confusion with COMIC, funny, facetious.

By another 5 per cent LACONIC is thought to mean COMPLETE, an idea embodied in the word LACONIC, for although such words as MEAGER, PERFUNCTORY, SKETCHY, suggest short and incomplete, LACONIC suggests short and complete, at least sufficient.

630. *AVENGE (ă-věnj') v.* To retaliate, revenge, vindicate, inflict punishment on behalf of, require satisfaction for injury.
In the test phrase: 'I shall AVENGE myself', the word is believed by 10 per cent of adult readers to mean PUNISH.

To PUNISH a person is to inflict punishment upon him. To
PUNISH one's self is to inflict punishment upon one's self.
To AVENGE a person is to PUNISH someone else who has done
the person an injury. To AVENGE one's self is to inflict punishment upon someone else who has done one an injury.

AVENGE and REVENGE are practically synonymous. Both
come from the same Latin source as the noun VENGEANCE. The
word to REVENGE always suggests personal bitterness, a desire
to injure another in return for some harm done. AVENGE
suggests a just return, more nearly equitable punishment.

631. *ORGY* (*awr'-ji̇̆*) *n.* A carousal, nocturnal revelry,
      drunken revel, noisy drinking bout.

The word ORGIES was originally the name of the ceremonies
connected with the worship of DIONYSUS, specifically the
festival in his honor celebrated by song and dance, and with
wild unrestraint. In this sense the word is always used in
the plural, for there was no singular form for the corresponding Greek word.

BACCHANALIA (*băk-kă-nā'-lĭ-ă*), and the more familiar adjective, BACCHANALIAN, come from the same festival, from the
word BACCHUS, the Latin name for the god Dionysus. BAC-
CHANALIA, drunken revelry, unbounded licentious carousing,
a word which exists only in the plural, is exactly synonymous
with ORGIES.

Today an ORGY is any wild revel, nocturnal carousal,
drunken revelry; and in this sense the word can be used
either in the singular or in the plural.

632. *SERVILE* (*ser'-vı̆l*) *adj.* Slavish, cringing, fawning,
      ignoble, menial, meanly submissive, lacking independ-
ence, like a servant.

SERVILE comes from the Latin *servire*, to serve, from the
same source as SERVANT and the verb to SERVE.

The correct meaning of SERVILE is unknown to 86 per
cent of grammar-school pupils. In the test phrase: 'He was
of SERVILE rank', the two common misconceptions are IM-
PORTANT and NOBLE. NOBLE is an exact opposite of SERVILE
which may mean IGNOBLE; and IMPORTANT is an opposite at
least in suggestion.

633. *PRATE* (*prāt*) *v.* To talk idly, babble, chatter, prattle, be foolishly loquacious, speak to little purpose.

To 10 per cent of college seniors PRATE incorrectly means to ARGUE, debate.

PRATE and PRATTLE, both from the same Dutch source, mean to talk without knowledge and to little purpose. Children PRATTLE; elders PRATE.

634. *SHAMBLING* (*shăm'-blĭng*) *adj.* Shuffling (190), weak-kneed, awkward, clumsy, walking with a dragging gait.

To 23 per cent of adult readers SHAMBLING incorrectly means AIMLESS, without purpose. In suggestion the two words have much in common, but they differ in their exact meanings. One may speak of an AIMLESS existence, one without aim, with no purpose; also of AIMLESS running about. The word AIMLESS describes the intent of one's actions or thoughts. SHAMBLING characterizes specifically physical gait. One would never apply SHAMBLING to running, for one who SHAMBLES would ordinarily be too weak-kneed to run.

635. *RESCIND* (*rē-sĭnd'*) *v.* To cut off, revoke, annul, repeal, vacate, void, abrogate, destroy, take back, abolish, do away with utterly.

In the test phrase: 'He RESCINDED the order', the meaning is unknown to 32 per cent of adult readers. RESCIND means take back in the figurative sense of withdraw, as: 'To TAKE BACK a promise'. It does not mean take back in the physical sense of carry back. Some confusion with this latter idea probably leads to the commonest misconception, SEND BACK, which is thought by 15 per cent of adult readers to be the meaning of RESCIND.

RESCIND is from the Latin *re*, back; and *scindere*, to cut, from the same source as INCISION, a cut; and perhaps the word SCISSORS; and by derivation means to cut off.

636. *RENOUNCE* (*rē-nowns'*) *v.* To disclaim, declare against, give up, abandon (56), quit, reject, relinquish, repudiate (262), recant (848), abjure, forswear.

In the test phrase: 'RENOUNCING the works of darkness', the word is thought by 14 per cent of preparatory-school juniors

to mean PROCLAIMING. This may be a confusion of the verb
RENOUNCE, to declare against, disclaim, with ANNOUNCE, to
proclaim, give notice of, make known; or it may be remotely
due to a confusion of DECLAIM, to recite, with DISCLAIM, a
synonym of RENOUNCE.

RENOUNCE is from the Latin *re*, back; and *nuntius*, messenger, the source of the English words: ANNOUNCE, to make
known; DENOUNCE, to accuse, condemn; and PRONOUNCE, to
utter, speak.

637. *CONDUCE* (*kŏn-dūs'*) *v.* To lead, contribute, further,
    promote, tend toward, aid in bringing about.

The adjective, CONDUCIVE, contributing to, leading to, as:
'CONDUCIVE to health', is met more frequently than the verb,
to CONDUCE, to aid in bringing about, which, in the test
phrase: 'It CONDUCES to success', is unknown to 31 per cent
of adult readers.

638. *ATHEISTICAL* (*ă-thē-ĭs'-tĭ-kl*) *adj.* Disbelieving in
    God, godless, impious. There are two forms of the
adjective: ATHEISTIC and ATHEISTICAL.

To 11 per cent of preparatory-school juniors ATHEISTICAL
incorrectly means RELIGIOUS, pious, godly, devout, an opposite of the correct meaning.

ATHEISTICAL, IRRELIGIOUS, and IMPIOUS (*ĭm'-pĭ-ŭs*, not
ĭm-pī'-ŭs), all deny the existence of God. One who is
IMPIOUS is wanton and defiant in his contempt of God. The
word IRRELIGIOUS is not so strong; one who is IRRELIGIOUS
is without religion and usually unchecked by its restraints.
One who is ATHEISTICAL believes in the doctrine that there
is no God; but such a person is not necessarily actively
defiant or unrestrained.

639. *VERDANT* (*ver'-dănt*) *adj.* Green in color, grass-
    covered, covered with fresh vegetation, abounding in
green foliage.

VERDANT is from the Latin *viridis*, green; this in turn comes
from the verb *virere*, to be green, be fresh. From this same
source come the French word *vert*, green; and the English
words VERDURE, greenness, especially the green of fresh

vegetation; VIRIDESCENT, greenish; and VERDIGRIS (ver'-dĭ-grēs, not ver'-dĭ-grē), the greenish acetate of copper which forms when copper is exposed to acetic acid.

To 13 per cent of adult readers VERDANT incorrectly means THICKLY-WOODED, densely grown with trees. THICKLY-WOODED does not necessarily suggest either fresh vegetation or green, both of which are implied by VERDANT.

640. FORAY (fŏr'-ā) n. A raid, pillaging expedition, foraging incursion, predatory excursion.

In the test phrase: 'Engaged in making FORAYS', the word is thought by 8 per cent of preparatory-school juniors to mean TRIPS. TRIP is a general word for any excursion, any expedition. A FORAY is an expedition the purpose of which is always robbery.

FORAY, FORAGE, and FODDER, all come from the same Anglo-Saxon source. FODDER is food for cattle. FORAGE may be food for cattle; and in this sense the word is synonymous with FODDER. Or a FORAGE may be the act of searching for provisions. A FORAGING expedition may be conducted peacefully or with the aim of stealing, but always has food as its objective. A FORAY is always a stealing, pillaging, predatory expedition; and may be for food or any other booty.

641. GRUFF (grŭf) adj. Surly, stern, harsh, coarse, rough-mannered, brusque.

In derivation GRUFF is closely connected with Scandinavian words which mean coarse, rude, gross.

In the test phrase: 'A GRUFF rejoinder', the word is thought by 9 per cent of adult readers to mean THREATENING, menacing; and by another 10 per cent to mean ENGAGING, winning, attractive, almost an opposite of the correct meaning.

642. AMENDS (ă-mĕndz') n. Reparation, satisfaction, restitution, return, restoration, recompense, compensation, redress (728), requital (1070).

In the test phrase: 'I shall make AMENDS', the word is believed by 16 per cent of adult readers to mean REFORMS, changes for the better. This is perhaps a confusion of AMENDS with AMENDMENT, from the same Latin e, out; and mendum, fault; literally the smoothing out of a fault, the elimination of a fault. An AMENDMENT is a change, usually a change for the better, a reform. AMENDS, always written in the plural, with the s, means compensation, something done in order to make right again a past injury, recompense.

643. *BERSERK* (*ber'-serk*, not *ber-serk'*) *adj.* Extremely wild, fierce, ferocious, savage, violent, frenzied, furious. In Norse legend, a BERSERK or a BERSERKER (*ber'-serk-er*) was a warrior who fought with a frenzied fury and who could assume the form and ferocity of a wild beast. Today a BERSERKER is anyone given to violence and fury. The word BERSERK has come to be used in English as an adjective to mean extremely wild, ferocious.

To 10 per cent of college seniors BERSERK incorrectly means UNUSUAL, rare, uncommon. This is perhaps a confusion of BERSERK with BIZARRE (*bĭ-zahr'*), a word of French origin. The Italian word *bizarro*, which corresponds to the English BIZARRE, means irascible, choleric, not far from BERSERK; and the French word *bizarre* once meant angry. Both BIZARRE and BERSERK may even today mean violent, wild; each, however, in its own fashion. A BIZARRE effect is often gained by a violent contrast; it is wild in the sense of extravagant, weird. BERSERK means physically violent, wild in the sense of ferocious, savage.

644. *COMPLACENT* (*kŏm-plā'-sĕnt*) *adj.* Tranquilly self-satisfied, content (39), gratified, in a pleasant mood, pleased with one's self.

CIVIL, KINDLY, and BENEVOLENT, are given by many dictionaries as definitions of COMPLACENT. Properly speaking there are two words: COMPLACENT (*kŏm-plā'-sĕnt*), self-satisfied; and COMPLAISANT (*kŏm-plĭ-zănt'*), civil, kindly, benevolent. The two words should be distinguished in spelling, pronunciation, and meaning.

In the test phrase: 'A COMPLACENT smile', the word is thought by 12 per cent of adult readers to mean ATTRACTIVE. The misconception is not so remote from the correct meaning as one might suppose. ATTRACTIVE means agreeable, charming, and therefore pleasing to others; and the literal translation of the Latin word *complacens* is very pleasing. COMPLACENT in English, however, has not the meaning of pleasing to others; but of being pleased, satisfied, pleased with one's self.

645. *FACTION* (*făk'-shŭn*) *n.* A group formed to accomplish a purpose, an insistent clique, political coterie, cabal (996), combination of persons belonging to a community or to an association, a small party organized to effect its own ends often by underhand methods and usually in opposition to the government.

FACTION is from the Latin *facere*, to do; and a FACTION is a group of persons combined for the purpose of doing something.

In the test phrase: 'A powerful FACTION', the word is thought by 30 per cent of grammar-school pupils to mean ADDITION, an increment, part which has been added. This may be due to some confusion of FACTION, small political party, with FRACTION. A FRACTION and an ADDITION are parts of a whole. FRACTION is the general word for any part, as: 'A FRACTION of an apple', 'A FRACTION of the receipts'. A FACTION may be a group of persons within a larger organization, within a party, and, in this sense, is a fraction of the organization; but neither the word FRACTION nor ADDITION need apply to a political party as does FACTION.

A FACTION and a PARTY are both combinations of persons united for a common purpose. The word PARTY is used in a reputable sense; while the word FACTION refers to a section of a party the aims of which are usually selfish and the means employed irregular and underhand.

646. *SYNCHRONOUS* (*sĭn'-krō-nŭs*) *adj.* Happening at the same time, simultaneous, concurrent, coincident.

SYNCHRONOUS is from two Greek words σύν, together; and χρόνος, time; which, translated literally, mean together in time. The first part, SYN, together, enters other more usual words. Thus: a SYNAGOGUE, which by derivation means together-lead, is now an assembly of Jews for religious worship, or more often the building in which they meet. A SYNONYM, by derivation together-name, was originally a word with the same meaning as another. With the increased complexities of civilization has come a need for differentiating fine shades of meaning. There are today almost no exact SYNONYMS. A SYNONYM is now a word with the same general significance as another, but with its own connotation, implication, suggestion.

The combining form CHRON, pertaining to time, appears in the English words: CHRONIC, continuing a long time; and CHRONOLOGICAL, in order of time. The significance of this Greek word is so well known that TIMELY, happening at the right time, seasonable, opportune, is the common misconception of SYNCHRONOUS, happening at the same time.

SYNCHRONOUS and CONTEMPORANEOUS are exactly synonymous, but differ in modern usage. CONTEMPORANEOUS is from the Latin con, together; and tempus, time. By derivation the word means together in time, exactly as does SYNCHRONOUS. But because a word from Latin can be used more freely, more popularly, and with less chance of a stilted effect, than one from Greek, CONTEMPORANEOUS, and the similar word, CONTEMPORARY, are more general and nontechnical. The first applies to events which happen at the same time; the second to persons who live at the same time.

SYNCHRONOUS is primarily a technical term and should be used sparingly and only when a technical connotation is needed. It may, for instance, be used of mechanical motions, as: 'SYNCHRONOUS motors'; but is never used of persons or historical events.

647. *INFAMOUS* (ĭn'-fă-mŭs) *adj.* Of ill fame, odious, detestable, notorious, shameful, vile.

To 15 per cent of preparatory-school juniors INFAMOUS incorrectly means WELL-KNOWN. This is probably a confusion of INFAMOUS with FAMOUS. FAMOUS is today used most frequently to mean well-known in a good sense, celebrated. It may, however, mean well-known in any sense, as in the phrase: 'A FAMOUS criminal'. INFAMOUS, which is a combination of the Latin *in*, not; and the word FAMOUS; means by derivation not famous in the first sense of that word. INFAMOUS characterizes those actions which deserve a complete loss of fame; it means ill-famed, known to be detestable.

648. *RESPONSIVE* (*rē-spŏn'-sĭv*) *adj.* Answering, reacting, inclined to reply, responding readily. 'RESPONSIVE to treatment.'

RESPONSIVE is from the Latin *re*, again; and *spondere*, to promise.

To 29 per cent of grammar-school pupils RESPONSIVE incorrectly means DEVOTED, attached, addicted, wholly given up to. The confusion may be due to the fact that the words DEVOTED and RESPONSIVE are closely associated when used in reference to an attachment between persons. One may be DEVOTED, attached, to another; while the other may be RESPONSIVE, inclined to reply, to such devotion.

649. *MENACE* (*mĕn'-ās*) *n.* A threat, portent, indication of coming danger, prophecy of approaching evil.

In the test phrase: 'The MENACE of war', the word is thought by 12 per cent of adult readers to mean FEAR. The sensation of fear is often aroused by a menace. FEAR is, however, the result; while the MENACE, the threat, is the cause.

By another 11 per cent, MENACE is thought to mean RESULT. A RESULT follows, is the outcome; a MENACE precedes, foreshadows, a disaster.

MENACE and THREAT are synonymous, but differ much as do Latin and Anglo-Saxon words in general. A THREAT, of Anglo-Saxon origin, is obvious, open, may even be expressed in words. THREAT often applies to an everyday occurrence, to any unpleasantness great or small. A MENACE, of Latin origin, is more intangible, is seldom expressed verbally; and the word applies more often to impending danger of considerable moment.

650. *RESPITE* (*rĕs'-pĭt*) *n.* Reprieve, postponement, delay, temporary intermission of labor, pause, cessation (254), stay, rest, suspension of activity.

In the test phrase: 'A brief RESPITE', the common misconception of the word is REVIEW, thought by 9 per cent of adult readers to be a synonym of RESPITE. RESPITE comes from the Latin *re*, back; and *specere*, to look, see; and by derivation means therefore to look back, reconsider, review. REVIEW, a looking back on, reconsideration, is an exact translation of the Latin from which RESPITE comes; but, although a RESPITE may be granted for the purpose of reviewing a case, the English word RESPITE signifies specifically the delay, postponement, not the review.

RESPITE, REPRIEVE, PAUSE, and INTERMISSION, are similar in suggestion. PAUSE and INTERMISSION are general words for a break in any activity, as, the INTERMISSION between acts in the theatre. RESPITE and REPRIEVE are limited to breaks in unpleasant activities. RESPITE has come to be used as the general word for an intermission in work or for the postponement of something burdensome. REPRIEVE, although occasionally used in this general way, now usually appears in the limited technical sense to mean the postponement of an execution for murder.

651. *INEPT* (*ĭn-ĕpt'*) *adj.* Unsuitable, unfit, inappropriate, awkward, out of place.

INEPT comes from the Latin *in*, not; and *aptus*, the past participle of the verb *apere*, to fit, the source of the English word APT, fit, suitable.

In the test phrase: 'INEPT for our purpose', the word is thought by 10 per cent of adult readers to mean EXCELLENT; and by another 9 per cent to mean FIT; both opposites of the correct meaning.

652. *FERVENT* (*fer'-vĕnt*) *adj.* Hot, glowing, ardent, intense, earnest, vehement, animated, warm in feeling, eager, fervid, zealous, impassioned.

FERVENT and ARDENT are similar in meaning. ARDENT comes from the Latin *ardere*, to burn, and is more intense than FERVENT which comes from *fervere*, to boil. ARDENT is used of actions; FERVENT of feelings.

653. *PREVARICATE* (*prē-văr'-ĭ-kāt*) *v.* To quibble, equivocate, misrepresent, speak evasively, deviate from the truth, evade the issue.

The Latin word *praevaricator* was used in Roman law for an advocate who, because of the office he held, should have prosecuted a charge but who did it so half-heartedly, so faintly, that the accused was freed. The Latin *praevaricator* is in turn from the verb *varicare*, to straddle; and the noun by derivation referred to a lawyer with one foot on each side of the case. From *varicare*, to straddle, comes also the Latin verb *praevaricari*, to walk crookedly. It is perhaps this Latin word which leads 12 per cent of adult readers to believe that the English word PREVARICATE, in the test phrase: 'She likes to PREVARICATE', means to SHOP, to visit shops for purchasing goods. PREVARICATE is always used in the figurative sense of evading the truth, equivocating, quibbling.

654. *DEVIATE* (*dē'-vǐ-āt*) *v.* To depart, digress (451), swerve, deflect, turn aside from the course, leave the beaten track.

The corresponding adjective DEVIOUS, roundabout, winding, circuitous, is of the same order of difficulty. DEVIOUS is thought by 20 per cent of college seniors to mean DOUBTFUL. This is probably a confusion of DEVIOUS, roundabout, with DUBIOUS, doubtful. DOUBTFUL and CERTAIN; DEVIOUS and STRAIGHTFORWARD; are opposites.

Both DEVIATE and DEVIOUS come from the Latin *de*, from; and *via*, way. To DEVIATE is literally to turn from the way, swerve from the road.

655. *THROE* (*thrō*) *n.* Pang, agony, spasm, violent pain, extreme anguish.

THROE is from Anglo-Saxon and was once spelt THROW, but is now always THROE.

The phrase: 'In the THROES of death' is thought by 18 per cent of adult readers to mean in the PATH of death. The noun THROW is sometimes used to mean distance traveled, as in the familiar phrase: 'A stone's THROW'. THROW is also used in engineering to designate the distance which, for instance, a piston rod travels from its mean position. THROE, although pronounced like THROW, is never used in this way. THROE usually appears in the plural, THROES, and always means pains, agonies, anguish.

656. *AUGMENT* (*awg-měnt'*) *v.* To increase, enlarge, expand, extend, swell, add to, make bigger.

AUGMENT is from the Latin *augere*, to increase. In the test phrase: 'His fortune was AUGMENTED', the word is thought by 7 per cent of adult readers to mean LOST. In this sense to LOSE and to AUGMENT are practically opposites.

657. *APPELLATION* (*ăp-pĕl-lā'-shŭn*) *n.* Name, title, designation, epithet, term by which a person is known.

The three words APPELLATION, DESIGNATION, and NAME, are almost synonymous. NAME is the general word. CHARLES is a NAME. A DESIGNATION is that which specifically distinguishes a person or thing from others. Every use of both the noun, DESIGNATION, and the verb, to DESIGNATE, calls attention to exactness. A successor is, for instance, DESIGNATED. CHARLES THE BOLD OF BURGUNDY is a DESIGNATION, because it points out incisively a particular individual. In naming an individual, the word DESIGNATION is, however, used less frequently than is APPELLATION. The word APPELLATION, except for the fact that its obvious Latin origin gives it a certain preciseness, is almost as general as NAME. To indicate that CHARLES THE BOLD designates a particular person one must call it a SPECIAL APPELLATION.

658. *DEFRAY* (*dē-frā'*) *v.* To pay, settle, meet, discharge, bear the expense of, provide the money for.

To 15 per cent of adult readers DEFRAY incorrectly means DELAY, put off, postpone; perhaps because of the similarity in appearance of DEFRAY and DELAY; or perhaps because of a confusion of DEFRAY, pay, with DEFER, put off, postpone, delay.

DEFRAY and AFFRAY come probably through French, although they can be traced back to both Anglo-Saxon and Latin. The Anglo-Saxon word from which FRAY comes means peace. An AFFRAY, now sometimes abbreviated FRAY, is literally a breaking of the peace, a brawl, public fight. To DEFRAY was once to pay a fine imposed upon one for breaking the peace. Today the word is used in a more general sense and means to pay, carry the cost of.

659. *DISPROVE* (*dĭs-proov'*) *v.* Show to be untrue, refute, confute, prove false, convict of error.

DISPROVE is from the Latin *dis;* and *probare*, to test; and means literally to prove to be false.

To 55 per cent of grammar-school pupils DISPROVE incorrectly means REJECT, discard, refuse, decline. This may be a confusion of DISPROVE, prove to be false, with DISAPPROVE. DISAPPROVE means to be unfriendly toward, not approve, refuse to sanction, reject. The confusion may be augmented by the similarity of REFUSE, a synonym of REJECT, with REFUTE, a synonym of DISPROVE.

660. *COHERENTLY* (*kō-hē'-rĕnt-lĭ*) *adv.* Connectedly, in a well-knit manner, consistently, logically, sequaciously. In the test phrase: 'They spoke COHERENTLY', the word is thought by 11 per cent of preparatory-school juniors to mean WITH HESITATION, a misconception which seems absurd to one who knows the correct meaning of COHERENTLY. But there is historical justification, for both to HESITATE and to COHERE come from the Latin verb, *haerere*, to stick, cleave, adhere. To HESITATE is to stick fast where one is, when one ought to go ahead, to delay indecisively, hold back with uncertainty. To COHERE has the literal meaning of the Latin and means to stick together.

COHERENTLY and CONSISTENTLY are closely allied. CONSISTENTLY applies ordinarily to subject matter. That which is CONSISTENT contains no fact in disagreement with the rest. COHERENTLY applies to treatment, to the manner of presentation, to the order, sequence, in which facts are presented. That which is COHERENT is well-organized.

661. *DEFALCATION* (*dē-făl-kā'-shŭn*) *n.* An embezzlement, fraudulent shortage, deficiency in trust funds. 'His DEFALCATION was detected.'
DEFALCATION comes from the Latin *de*, away; and *falcare*, to cut with a sickle, from *falx*, sickle, the source of the English word FALCON, a hawk trained for hunting, so called because of its curved claws. A DEFALCATION is by derivation a cutting off of any part, diminution. From the same Latin source as DEFALCATION come the two unusual English verbs, to DEFALCATE (*dē-făl'-kāt*) and to DEFALK (*dē-fawlk'*), both of which mean to deduct, take away. DEFALCATION is not related to the verb to DEFAULT (*dē-fawlt'*), which means to fail in carrying out an obligation; for to DEFAULT comes from the Latin *de*, away; and *fallere*, to fail, the source of

the English word FAILURE. The noun, a DEFAULT, is spelt
and pronounced like the verb.

DEFALCATION and EMBEZZLEMENT are practically synonymous. An EMBEZZLEMENT is, however, always fraudulent. It
is the dishonest use, for one's own purposes, of money with
which one has been entrusted. A DEFALCATION need not
necessarily be fraudulent; for both by derivation and in
modern English a DEFALCATION may be any curtailment,
abatement, as for instance a reduction of expenses. The
word is, however, used most frequently to mean a fraudulent shortage, a deficiency in trust funds due either to
dishonesty or mismanagement.

662. *LEWD* (*lūd*) *adj.* Indecent, immodest, impure, dis-
    solute, lustful, not chaste (789).
LEWD is from an Anglo-Saxon word meaning ignorant,
unlearned. In the test phrase: 'LEWD remarks', the word is
practically unknown to grammar-school pupils.

663. *ABSTINENCE* (*ăb'-stĭ-nĕns*) *n.* Refraining, complete
    abstemiousness, active abstaining, self-denial.
To 19 per cent of adult readers, ABSTINENCE incorrectly
means INDIFFERENCE, unconcern, apathy, absence of interest,
neutrality. ABSTINENCE means specifically denying one's self
voluntarily something which one wants, something to which
one is not indifferent.

The two nouns, ABSTINENCE and ABSTEMIOUSNESS, differ
from each other much as do the two adjectives, ABSTINENT
and ABSTEMIOUS (619). ABSTEMIOUSNESS is temperance, self-
restraint, and is applied to moderation in anything. ABSTI-
NENCE means complete refraining, self-denial, and is more apt
to be applied to drinking.

664. *ABATE* (*ā-bāt'*) *v.* To reduce, diminish, decrease,
    mitigate, moderate, curtail, lessen in amount.
ABATE is from the Latin *ab;* and *batuere,* to beat; and by
derivation means to beat down.

The phrase: 'The taxes were ABATED', is thought by 22
per cent of adult readers to mean the taxes were SUPPRESSED.
This is an unusual but correct interpretation of the word

for, although to ABATE is ordinarily to lessen, reduce, in legal phraseology to ABATE may mean to remove, stop, put an end to, subdue, suppress.

By another 3 per cent of adult readers to ABATE is thought to mean INCREASE, an exact opposite of the usual meaning, to reduce.

To 8 per cent of preparatory-school juniors ABATE means to STRENGTHEN, another opposite of the correct meaning.

665. CURSORY (ker'-sō-rĭ) adj. Hasty, hurried, slight, superficial, carelessly passing over a subject, without close attention.

CURSORY is practically unknown to grammar-school pupils. To 36 per cent it incorrectly means ANGRY. This is perhaps a confusion of CURSORY with some form of the word CURSE. To CURSE, directly from Anglo-Saxon but probably originally from the same source as CURSORY, is to wish evil upon, to call down evil upon someone with whom one is angry. CURSED (ker'-sĕd) means under a curse, afflicted, tormented; or deserving of a curse, hateful, abominable, detestable. An obsolete form of the word, which was spelt and pronounced CURST, means ill-tempered, snarling. CURSORY comes more directly from the Latin cursor, runner, racer, which in turn is from the verb currere, to run. From the same source come such words as: a CURRENT, the flow of a stream; and EXCURSION, by derivation a running out, running forth.

To another 19 per cent CURSORY incorrectly means PENETRATING, discerning, comprehending, almost an opposite of CURSORY, superficial.

666. HETEROGENEOUS (hĕt-ĕ-rō-jē'-nē-ŭs) adj. Miscellaneous, varied, dissimilar, diversified, having unlike qualities, differing in kind.

HETEROGENEOUS is from two Greek words. The first, ἕτερος, means different; and the second, γένος, means kind, sort. From the last word comes directly the English word GENUS, a kind, sort, class. HETEROGENEOUS, translated literally, means differing in kind, of different sorts.

In the test phrase: 'A HETEROGENEOUS collection', the word

is believed by 11 per cent of adult readers to mean BOTANICAL, the common misconception, perhaps from the frequent use of the word GENUS, sort, class, in botany. BOTANICAL means connected with the study of plants, and is the adjective formed from the noun BOTANY. Both BOTANY and HETEROGENEOUS come from Greek. Although BOTANY today means the science which deals with plants, it comes from a Greek word meaning to feed and originally meant the science of things to be eaten.

To another 8 per cent of adult readers, HETEROGENEOUS incorrectly means QUEER. QUEER may mean incongruous, inharmonious, ill-sorted; and in this sense is not far from HETEROGENEOUS, miscellaneous. But QUEER, by derivation, means slanting, out of the ordinary, stray, odd, and usually has the suggestion of something slightly comical, whimsical. A QUEER collection might contain a number of stray objects all of the same general kind. HETEROGENEOUS has no suggestion of the unusual or the comical, but means consisting of different kinds.

The Greek HETERO, different, and its opposite HOMO, same, appear at the beginning of many English words, most of them scientific terms. The adjective, HETERODOX, means holding an opinion which differs from the accepted, ORTHODOX, view. A HETERONYM is a word which differs from another in both sound and meaning but not in spelling. A HOMONYM is a word the same as another in both sound and spelling but not in meaning. HOMOGENEOUS, all of similar kind, is the opposite of HETEROGENEOUS, of different kinds.

667. *PROTRACT* (*prō-trăkt'*) *v.* To prolong, continue, extend, stretch out, draw out, lengthen in time.

PROTRACT is from the Latin *pro*, forth; and *trahere*, to draw; and by derivation means to draw forth, prolong. RETRACT, to draw back, take back a statement; and CONTRACT, to draw together; are from the same *trahere*, to draw.

In the test phrase: 'To PROTRACT the conference', the word is thought by 17 per cent of adult readers to mean POSTPONE, put off, delay. This is an unusual but correct interpretation of PROTRACT, which may mean postpone, but which ordinarily means prolong, lengthen in time, drag out.

668. *ERST* (*erst*) *adv.* Formerly, once, at first, long ago, hitherto, whilom (*hwĭ'-lŏm*).

In the test phrase: 'ERST a poet', the word is believed by 12 per cent of adult readers to mean WHEN.

ERST is a short and poetic form of ERSTWHILE. Both ERST and ERSTWHILE are archaic and should rarely be used today.

669. *STIMULUS* (*stĭm'-ū-lŭs*) *n.* An incentive, goad, spur, motive, urge, something which rouses the mind to activity. 'He needs added STIMULUS.'

STIMULUS and the corresponding verb, to STIMULATE, come directly from the Latin word *stimulus*, a goad, sharp pin at the end of a stick used in driving oxen. The English word, STIMULUS, now means anything which spurs one to action. STIMULUS and STIMULANT are sometimes given as synonymous with one another. STIMULANT is, however, used more often of a drug which has a physical effect; for example, alcohol is a STIMULANT. The word STIMULUS is occasionally used by the medical profession in this same sense, but the word commonly refers to a spiritual or mental incentive.

In the test phrase: 'He needs added STIMULUS', the word is believed by 57 per cent of grammar-school pupils to mean NOURISHMENT, food, sustenance, nutriment, that which sustains life and makes possible normal growth; and is believed by another 25 per cent to mean STRENGTH. One need but go back to the meaning of the Latin word *stimulus*, goad, sharp pointed stick, to realize that a STIMULUS supplies neither nourishment nor strength, but is that which makes a person use his strength to the full.

670. *ADMONISH* (*ăd-mŏn'-ĭsh*) *v.* To exhort, counsel, warn, advise, remind, chide (506), censure, reprove (565), rebuke, caution.

To 12 per cent of preparatory-school juniors to ADMONISH incorrectly means to REQUEST POLITELY. Although an ADMONITION, the corresponding noun, is the gentlest form of a reproof, it is stronger than a polite request.

To ADMONISH comes from the Latin *ad*, to; and *monere*, to remind, sometimes to warn, a word which in turn comes from the Latin *mens*, mind. To ADMONISH is, therefore, by derivation to remind or to warn. From the same source comes the English word MONITOR, instructor, a word first used to mean one who warns, an ADMONISHER. The word is now used to designate a senior school boy who is appointed to instruct a junior class or to keep a record of attendance.

The verb to ADMONISH, in English, is stronger than to REMIND. Although it can apply either to past acts like REPROVE, or to possible future acts like WARN, it is not quite so strong as either.

671. *DOFF* (*dŏf*) *v*. To take off, remove, the opposite of DON, to put on.

In the test phrase: 'He DOFFS his overcoat', the word is thought by 23 per cent of adult readers to mean PUTS ON. This is perhaps a confusion of DOFF, to take off, with DON, to put on. DOFF, and its opposite DON, are apparently contractions of DO OFF and DO ON. Both words belong to literature rather than to conversation.

672. *SUMPTUOUS* (*sŭmp'-tū-ŭs*) *adj*. Magnificent, lavish, luxurious, expensive, costly, splendid, regal.

To 19 per cent of adult readers SUMPTUOUS incorrectly means LARGE. One can instantly think of any number of things which are LARGE but not SUMPTUOUS, as, for instance: 'A LARGE barn', 'A LARGE factory'.

SUMPTUOUS and LUXURIOUS are similar in meaning. LUXURIOUS and the corresponding noun LUXURY come from the Latin *luxus*, extravagance, and suggest excess, rankness, almost wantonness. SUMPTUOUS comes from the Latin *sumptus*, cost, expense; and means primarily expensive, costly.

673. *IMPLACABLE* (*ĭm-plā'-kā-bl*) *adj*. Relentless, unforgiving, inexorable, merciless, severe (123), irreconcilable, unyielding (392), pitiless, not to be appeased.

In the test phrase: 'With IMPLACABLE hatred', the word is thought by 15 per cent of adult readers to mean UNJUSTIFIED, not legitimate, unfair, not conforming to standards of justice. IMPLACABLE comes from the Latin *placare*, to pacify, satisfy, from the same source as the English verb, to PLACATE, to appease, pacify. IMPLACABLE, by derivation, means not to be satisfied, appeased, pacified, in any way.

674. *REPELLENT* (rē-pĕl'-lĕnt) *adj.* Forbidding, uninviting, formidable, repulsive (205), bristling.

In the test phrase: 'Her REPELLENT manner', the word is thought by 12 per cent of adult readers to mean INEFFABLE, unutterable, unspeakable, inexpressible. INEFFABLE, which comes from the Latin *fabulare*, to speak, talk, the source of the English word FABLE, a story, tale, may be applied to that which is either so beautiful or so ugly as to be indescribable, as: 'INEFFABLE joy', or 'INEFFABLE loathing'.

REPELLENT comes from the Latin *re*, back; and *pellere*, to drive. From the same source comes the noun, PROPELLER, that which drives anything forward, specifically the device which drives ships and airplanes. REPELLENT by derivation means driving back, and always characterizes something unpleasant.

675. *EULOGISTIC* (ū-lō-jĭs'-tĭk) *adj.* Laudatory, extolling, panegyrical, commendatory, encomiastic, highly complimentary, expressing extravagant praise.

EULOGISTIC and the noun, EULOGY, are from the Greek εὐ, well; and λέγειν, to speak. EULOGISTIC is therefore speaking well of. There are two Greek prefixes meaning bad, κακός and δυσ-. The opposite of EULOGISTIC should therefore be either CACOLOGISTIC or DYSLOGISTIC. A CACOLOGY was once a speaking evil of a person, the exact opposite of a EULOGY. This meaning is, however, obsolete, and a CACOLOGY is today either the misuse of words or their faulty pronunciation. DYSLOGISTIC, disapproving, censorious, opprobrious, is today the opposite of EULOGISTIC, but is rarely used.

To 9 per cent of college seniors EULOGISTIC incorrectly means DISPARAGING, depreciating, undervaluing, an opposite of EULOGISTIC, complimentary.

Both a EULOGY and an ENCOMIUM are expressions of praise. An ENCOMIUM may be in a few words and may refer to a policy, an act, or a work of art. A EULOGY is more formal, more eloquent, and is always in praise of a person. The corresponding adjectives are ENCOMIASTIC, which is unusual; and EULOGISTIC.

676. *GLINT* (*glĭnt*) *n.* Glitter, glimmer, gleam, flash, sparkle, glisten, something which appears and disappears quickly, as: 'The fatal GLINT of gold'.

The verbs to GLIMMER, GLIMPSE, GLEAM, GLITTER, GLISTEN, and GLINT, are probably all related etymologically.

677. *MAGNANIMITY* (*măg-nă-nĭm'-ĭ-tĭ*) *n.* Noble generosity, dignity of soul, intrinsic nobility, greatness of heart, high-mindedness, the quality of being magnanimous. The corresponding adjective MAGNANIMOUS (547) is more familiar for it is unknown to only 26 per cent of adult readers.

MAGNANIMITY is from the Latin, *magnus*, great; and *animus*, soul, mind; and means literally greatness of soul. In the test phrase: 'It shows MAGNANIMITY', the word is thought by 10 per cent of adult readers to mean EFFICIENCY, effectiveness, competency, capability.

Of the three words, MAGNANIMITY, GENEROSITY, and NOBILITY, only the last has kept the full strength of its original meaning and is applied exclusively to those of high birth. GENEROSITY was originally synonymous with NOBILITY, but the word is now used for one characteristic of NOBILITY, liberality, nobility in giving. MAGNANIMITY refers primarily to the same characteristic, GENEROSITY, but retains in addition the exalted qualities of NOBILITY. MAGNANIMITY is between NOBILITY and GENEROSITY, with the best of both.

The awkward and unusual noun, PUSILLANIMITY (*pū-sĭl-lă-nĭm'-ĭ-tĭ*), is the opposite of MAGNANIMITY; the more common adjective, PUSILLANIMOUS (*pū-sĭl-lăn'-ĭ-mŭs*), faint-hearted, low-spirited, is the opposite of the adjective, MAGNANIMOUS, noble, generous.

678. *STATURE* (*stăt'-ūr*, almost *stă'-chūr*) *n.* Physical height, tallness of a human body.

In the test phrase: 'His STATURE is noteworthy', the word is thought by 16 per cent of adult readers to mean POSITION, the popular misconception. This is no doubt because of the similarity of STATURE (*stăt'-ūr*) and STATUS (*stā'-tŭs*, not *stă'-tŭs*), both from the same Latin word *stare*, to stand. The STATUS of an individual is his position in society, his standing in a profession.

IMAGE, held by another 12 per cent to be a synonym of STATURE, is a second popular misconception, due no doubt to the confusion of STATURE with STATUE, another word from the same Latin source. A STATUE is an image, monument, often in marble or bronze. STATURE is bodily, physical, height.

679. *PROCRASTINATE* (*prō-krăs'-tĭ-nāt*) *v.* To put off from day to day, postpone (3), delay (85), defer to a future time, leave undone as long as possible.

PROCRASTINATE comes from the Latin *pro*, for; and *cras*, tomorrow; and means literally to put off for tomorrow. The Latin *cras* appears in no other common English word.

To 12 per cent of college seniors PROCRASTINATE incorrectly means DECEIVE, to mislead, cheat. This may be a confusion of PROCRASTINATE, to postpone action, with PREVARICATE, to evade telling the truth, equivocate.

To another 9 per cent PROCRASTINATE means DENOUNCE. This may be a confusion of PROCRASTINATE with EXECRATE, to express abhorrence for, curse because of personal hatred; or perhaps of PROCRASTINATE with IMPRECATE, to curse in a milder way.

To still another 14 per cent to PROCRASTINATE incorrectly means to ANTICIPATE. To ANTICIPATE, from the Latin *ante*, before; and *capere*, to take; may mean to foresee, expect, look forward to; or it may mean to do before the proper time, forestall, take up in advance. In this last sense to ANTICIPATE is an exact opposite of PROCRASTINATE, to put off.

680. *TRANSCEND* (*trăn-sĕnd'*) *v.* To surpass, exceed, go beyond, outstrip, excel, surmount.

In the test phrase: 'It TRANSCENDS description', the two words, to LACK and to REQUIRE, are each held by 10 per cent of adult readers to be synonymous with TRANSCEND. To LACK and to REQUIRE are practically synonymous; both mean to need, want, be destitute of. Both suggest insufficiency, falling short, and in this sense are opposites, at least in suggestion, of TRANSCEND which means to surpass, exceed.

TRANSCEND is from the Latin *trans*, over; and *scandere*, to climb; from the same source as ASCEND, to go up, climb up; and DESCEND, to go down. Originally, to TRANSCEND meant literally to climb over, just as ASCEND and DESCEND mean to climb up and down. But TRANSCEND is now used only figuratively, as: 'It TRANSCENDS experience', 'It TRANSCENDS understanding', to mean surpasses, goes beyond.

681. *EMANATE* (*ĕm'-ă-nāt*) *v*. To proceed from, flow from, originate, take rise, issue from.

EMANATE FROM is thought by 13 per cent of adult readers to mean ARE COPIED FROM.

EMANATE is from the Latin *e*, out; and *manare*, to flow, trickle; and by derivation means to flow out from. The corresponding noun is EMANATION familiar today as that which issues forth from a radioactive substance.

682. *SUBLIME* (*sŭb-līm'*) *adj*. Surpassing, exalted, lofty, preeminent (339), high in excellence, so impressive as to inspire awe.

To 13 per cent of adult readers SUBLIME incorrectly means UNDERLYING. This is perhaps because SUBLIME begins with the same Latin *sub*, under, as such words as: SUBWAY, by derivation under the street; SUBTERRANEAN, underground, under the surface of the earth; SUBCUTANEOUS, under the skin; and SUBJACENT, underneath, lying below but not directly under. Why SUBLIME, and the corresponding Latin word, *sublimis*, which start with the Latin *sub*, should both mean raised on high, lofty, an exact opposite of under, is one of the queer twists of language which has not yet been explained.

By another 12 per cent, SUBLIME is thought to mean RARE. RARE may mean uncommon, infrequent, unusual; or it may mean uncommonly good, of an excellence seldom encountered, and so suggest unusually delightful. In this last sense, RARE has much in common with SUBLIME. SUBLIME, however, always connotes height; that which is SUBLIME is so high in character that it inspires awe rather than delight.

683. *SPURIOUS* (*spū'-rĭ-ŭs*) *adj.* Counterfeit, pretended, supposititious (457), sham, bogus, fraudulent, not genuine, having no right to the name.

SPURIOUS is from the Latin *spurius*, of illegitimate birth. In the test phrase: 'SPURIOUS documents', the word is thought by 13 per cent of adult readers to mean HERALDIC (*hĕ-răl'-dĭk*), having to do with coats of arms, pertaining to heraldry. A HERALD, in the Middle Ages, was the messenger of a sovereign, or of some other person of high rank. He was protected from injury or capture by his costume, which bore the coat of arms of his chief. Because of the importance of this insignia to the herald, he was later given supervision over the granting and recording of such coats of arms; and, as a result, HERALDRY is today the science of armorial bearings. Because HERALDIC symbols descend from father to son, and because the history of a family can be traced through its armorial bearings, the word HERALDRY is often used to mean the study of genealogy. It is, perhaps, some association of the idea of HERALDRY in its connection with genealogy, and the Latin word *spurius*, of illegitimate birth, which leads so large a percentage to believe that HERALDIC is a synonym of the English word SPURIOUS, false, bastard, counterfeit, not genuine, having no right to the name.

684. *NUGATORY* (*nū'-gă-tō-rĭ*) *adj.* Ineffectual, inoperative, futile, null, without force, not valid.

When NUGATORY is used in the test phrase: 'The law was NUGATORY', it is interpreted by 15 per cent of adult readers to mean ANNULLED. To ANNUL is to abolish, destroy the force of, render nugatory, inoperative. A law may be NUGATORY, ineffectual, without force, because it has been ANNULLED, formally abolished; or it may have become NUGATORY, without force, through disuse or lack of popular support, without having been formally ANNULLED, set aside. In this sense ANNULLED and NUGATORY are not synonymous.

An ANNULMENT need not, however, necessarily be formal; disuse may be thought of as having ANNULLED a law. In this sense ANNULLED and NUGATORY are so close in meaning as to be practically synonymous. Ordinarily, however, ANNULLED means abolished, set aside; while NUGATORY means ineffectual, inoperative.

685. *IGNOMINIOUS* (*ĭg-nō-mĭn'-ĭ-ŭs*) *adj.* Shameful, scandalous, infamous (647), dishonorable, disgraceful, opprobrious (1046).

IGNOMINIOUS comes from the Latin *in*, not; and *nomen*, name, fame; and means, literally, of ill name. From *nomen* comes also the English word COGNOMEN (*kŏg-nō'-mĕn*), a surname, last name, the name common to all members of a family. To 16 per cent of college seniors IGNOMINIOUS incorrectly means FOOLISH, absurd, unwise, silly. This may be due to a confusion of IGNOMINIOUS, disgraceful, with IGNORANT, foolish. IGNOMINIOUS and INFAMOUS are practically synonymous. Of the two, INFAMOUS is the stronger. INFAMY, the noun, is public disgrace which is almost certain to be based on facts; IGNOMINY (*ĭg'-nō-mĭn-ĭ*) is disgrace which may be the result of gossip, opinion, or expressed feelings. IGNOMINIOUS, shameful, is the corresponding adjective.

686. *SPASMODIC* (*spăz-mŏd'-ĭk*) *adj.* Fitful, jerky, convulsive, violent, acting by fits and starts but soon exhausted. A SPASM, from the Greek word σπᾶν, to draw, pluck, pull, is an involuntary and abnormal muscular contraction. SPASMODIC is the corresponding adjective in literary use.

SPASTIC and TETANIC, used in medicine, are almost synonymous with SPASMODIC. SPASTIC is apt to be used for the contraction of a muscle which remains taut. TETANIC (*tē-tăn'-ĭk*) corresponds to the noun TETANUS (*tĕt'-ă-nŭs*), a disease characterized by a violent spasm of the muscles. To 22 per cent of adult readers SPASMODIC incorrectly means REPEATED. Both REPEATED and SPASMODIC efforts are intermittent, not continuous; but REPEATED efforts are likely to be fruitful; whereas SPASMODIC efforts are almost invariably fruitless, they are sudden, violent, and ineffective.

687. *SEAR* (*sēr*) *v.* To scorch, singe, wither, parch, blast, cauterize, brand, make callous. SEARED, the participial adjective, is thought by 22 per cent of preparatory-school juniors to mean WRINKLED. To SEAR is to

wither by heat, an action which often causes wrinkles; but wrinkles may be formed without heat as when a cloth is thrown down in a rumpled heap.

To SEAR, SCORCH, and SINGE, are all to burn. SINGEING is the most external, the least destructive, of the three. It usually suggests no vital injury. Thus, a chicken is SINGED in order to burn off the downy feathers which cannot be plucked; cloth is SINGED in order to burn off threads projecting unevenly above the surface; hair is SINGED. To SCORCH is to burn more deeply, usually in such a way as to discolor the surface. To SEAR is to heat so as to dry up, wither.

688. *EXTRICATE* (*ĕks'-trĭ-kāt*) *v.* To free, liberate, release, disentangle, disengage, rid of hindrances.

In the test phrase: 'He was EXTRICATED', the word is believed by 19 per cent of adult readers to mean DISPOSED OF. This is probably a confusion of EXTRICATE, to free, with EXTIRPATE, to pull up by the roots, stamp out, eradicate, destroy. Or it may be a confusion of EXTRICATE, to free, with EXTERMINATE, to put an end to, eradicate, extirpate, drive out.

EXTRICATE is from the Latin *ex*, from; and *tricae*, hindrances, trifles; and means literally to free from hindrances, clear of entanglements.

689. *RAZE* (*rāz*) *v.* To level to the ground, tear down, demolish, destroy, obliterate, efface, wipe out.

To RAZE is from the same source as ERASE; RAZOR; and RASCAL, a word which by derivation suggests a scraping, offscouring of society. Originally the word could be spelt in only one way, RASE (*rāz*), and meant to erase, efface, cancel, obliterate. When spelt RASE today it means to shave, graze, scratch. When spelt RAZE it means to tear down, level to the ground.

In the test phrase: 'The village was RAZED', the two popular misconceptions of the word are: BURNED, held by 12 per cent of adult readers; and PLUNDERED, held by 11 per cent. Both imply destruction. A village may be RAZED by fire or by a plundering expedition, but neither BURNED nor PLUNDERED specifies RAZED, leveled to the ground.

To RAZE and to DEMOLISH both mean to destroy, but in slightly different senses. To DEMOLISH is, by derivation, to build down, destroy the structure. A building may be DE-MOLISHED even though parts of its walls still stand. To RAZE is literally to level to the ground.

690. *COPSE* (*kŏps*) *n.* A thicket, coppice, grove, plantation of trees, woods of small growth.

In the test phrase: 'He did not see the COPSE', the word is thought by 23 per cent of adult readers to mean BODY. This is clearly a confusion of COPSE, small wood, with CORPSE, a dead body.

COPSE is a contraction of the more familiar word COPPICE (*kŏp'-pĭs*). The two words, COPPICE and COPSE, can be used interchangeably.

691. *DILAPIDATION* (*dĭl-ăp-ĭ-dā'-shŭn*) *n.* Decay, deterioration, impairment, gradual ruin from neglect, state of bad repair. 'DILAPIDATION was apparent.'

DILAPIDATION is from the Latin *di*, apart; and *lapidare*, to throw stones at, a verb which in turn comes from the Latin *lapis*, *lapidis*, a stone. There is an unusual English word LAPIDATION which means the act of throwing stones at a person, execution by stoning; and a more familiar word LAPIDARY, a stonecutter. DILAPIDATION is by derivation the throwing apart of stones; but the word has come to be used in a more general sense to mean any gradual ruin, decay, disorder, impairment.

692. *BALMY* (*bahm'-ĭ*) *adj.* Mild, soothing, fragrant (34), aromatic, refreshing like balm.

In the test phrase: 'A BALMY spring day', the word is thought by 13 per cent of adult readers to mean BREEZY, airy; and by another 12 per cent to mean CLEAR, transparent.

BALM is a fragrant, healing, ointment. BALMY, the adjective, is used to mean either fragrant, aromatic, smelling like balm; or refreshing, soothing, healing like balm.

693. *RANCOR* (*răng'-kōr*) *n.* Nourished grudge (337), rankling malice (391), spitefulness, ill will, bitter animosity (764), inveterate ill feeling.

To 11 per cent of adult readers RANCOR incorrectly means

ZEAL, enthusiasm, ardor, eagerness, intense interest. To another 8 per cent, RANCOR incorrectly means PASSION. PASSION, ZEAL, and RANCOR, all express a warmth of feeling; but, of the three, RANCOR is the only one which suggests hatred, animosity, ill will.

RANCOR is from the Latin *rancere*, to be sour, from the same source as RANCID, sour, offensive. RANCOR originally meant sourness, bitterness, but this meaning is obsolete and RANCOR is now a sour disposition, a bitter attitude toward life.

694. *DESCRY* (*dē-skrī'*) *v.* To perceive, see faintly, make out with difficulty, discern, detect, espy, catch sight of. In the test phrase: 'He DESCRIED other faces', the word is thought by 10 per cent of preparatory-school juniors to mean PORTRAYED. This is perhaps a confusion of DESCRY, perceive, with DESCRIBE, give an account of, portray. Both words come from the same Latin *de*, and *scribere*, to write. DESCRIBE means to depict, represent in words; DESCRY means see faintly.

695. *ESCUTCHEON* (*ĕs-kŭt'-shŭn*) *n.* A shield, the shield of a family, the field on which a coat of arms is presented. ESCUTCHEON is from the Latin *scutum*, a shield; and, although in HERALDRY, the two words ESCUTCHEON and SHIELD are sometimes synonymous, they differ technically. A SHIELD, in heraldry, is always shield-shaped, usually flat across the top, with bulging, curved sides which come together to form a point at the bottom. An ESCUTCHEON is any surface on which appear the arms, armorial bearings, of a family. Although the surface is usually a shield in shape, the ESCUTCHEON of a widow or spinster is lozenge-shaped, diamond-shaped.

696. *SAVOR* (*sā'-vor*) *n.* Flavor, odor, appetizing taste and smell, relish, nidor (*nī'-dor*), that quality of a substance which affects the sense of taste and smell.

To 17 per cent of adult readers SAVOR incorrectly means RESCUER. This is obviously a confusion of SAVOR, flavor, taste, with SAVIOR, rescuer; or perhaps with the more awkward SAVER, one who saves. Despite the similarity there is no etymological connection between SAVOR, taste, and SAVER, one who saves; for SAFE, SAVE, SAVER, and SAVIOR, all come from the Latin *salvus*, whole, safe; while SAVOR is from the Latin *sapere*, to taste.

697. *PROVENDER* (*prŏv'-ĕn-der*) *n.* Food for animals, fodder, dry feed, mixture of meal and cut straw or hay.
To 8 per cent of preparatory-school juniors PROVENDER incorrectly means MEMORANDUM, reminder.
There are three words which designate food for farm animals. FEED is general. FODDER is any feed except PASTURAGE, growing grass. PROVENDER is dry feed.

698. *SHADE* (*shād*) *n.* A trace, slight difference, minute amount, one hardly perceptible, vestige (744), soupçon (*soop-sŏgn'*).
The exact meaning of SHADE is unknown to 38 per cent of adult readers. To 22 per cent it incorrectly means AMOUNT. A SHADE is specifically a very small amount, a trace.

699. *LIEU* (*lū*) *n.* Place, stead (224), room. LIEU appears in English only in the phrase: 'In LIEU of' which means instead of.
In the test phrase: 'In LIEU of', the word is thought by 10 per cent of preparatory-school juniors to mean FEAR. This may be due to a confusion of the two French words, *peur*, fear, with *lieu*, place, the direct source of the English word LIEU, place.

700. *GLIB* (*glĭb*) *adj.* Talkative, fluent, loquacious, chattering, garrulous, plausible, more voluble than sincere.
In the test phrase: 'A GLIB speaker', the word is thought by 12 per cent of adult readers to mean HASTY. Although the original meaning of HASTY is quick, speedy, when the word is applied to a speaker it ordinarily means rash, impulsive, inconsiderate, precipitate, superficial, showing lack of thought.
GLIB, LOQUACIOUS, and GARRULOUS, all mean talkative, emitting a flow of words. GARRULOUS implies rambling, especially about trivial things. LOQUACIOUS implies incessant, without stop. GLIB implies smooth, too smooth, for the word carries a note of contempt, of untrustworthiness.
GLIB is thought by 12 per cent of preparatory-school juniors

to mean SLIPPERY, an unusual but correct meaning of the word. GLIB may come from the same source as the verb to GLIDE, to slip, slide, and originally meant smooth, slippery. One may today speak of GLIB ice. When the word is used of a speaker, it means talkative and implies slippery, smooth, untrustworthy, not easily caught.

To another 10 per cent of preparatory-school juniors GLIB means SILENT, an exact opposite of the correct meaning.

701. *REDOUBTABLE* (*rē-dowt'-ā-bl*) *adj.* Dreadful, tremendous, fearful, formidable, to be dreaded, terrible to face.

To 14 per cent of college seniors REDOUBTABLE incorrectly means UNRELIABLE, untrustworthy, not to be relied upon. This may be a confusion of REDOUBTABLE, formidable, with DOUBTFUL, uncertain, unreliable.

REDOUBTABLE, perhaps originally from the Latin *dubitare*, to doubt, is from the same source as the French *douter*, to fear, and means literally capable of being feared.

702. *INUNDATE* (*ĭn'-ŭn-dāt*) *v.* To flood, deluge, overflow, swamp, overwhelm (263).

In the test phrase: 'INUNDATED with letters', the word is thought by 10 per cent of adult readers to mean INDICATED. To INDICATE is to show, point out, make known, state briefly, intimate.

INUNDATE, and the corresponding noun, INUNDATION, are from the Latin *in*; and *undare*, to rise in waves, overflow. From the same source comes the English verb, to UNDULATE, to move with a wavelike motion, vibrate. To INUNDATE is, by derivation, to flood; but the word may be used figuratively to mean overwhelm.

703. *PALLID* (*păl'-lĭd*) *adj.* Wan (*wawn*), colorless, pale, whitish, ghastly, bloodless, ashen, deficient in color.

PALLID is from the Latin *pallere*, to be pale. PALLID and PALE are doublets.

PALLID, WAN, and PALE, all imply lack of color. PALE is applied to a normal lightness, as: 'A PALE color'; or, with a human being, to a temporary condition, as: 'You look PALE this morning'. WAN, like PALE, may be used of both objects and persons; but the word suggests a cold, dreary, eerie, ghostly lightness. PALLID is used more often in relation to persons; and suggests a chronic, sickly condition.

704. *INTEGRITY* (*ĭn-tĕg'-rĭ-tĭ*) *n.* Uprightness, justice, honor, moral soundness, virtue, probity, rectitude (790), righteousness, honesty.

In the test phrase: 'The INTEGRITY of our citizens', the word is thought by 12 per cent of adult readers to mean JUDGMENT, good sense, sagacity, discernment.

By another 11 per cent it is thought to mean INTELLIGENCE, intellect, quickness of understanding. INTEGRITY does not necessarily imply either INTELLIGENCE or JUDGMENT, but means honesty, uprightness. INTEGRITY comes from the same source as the English word INTEGER, a whole number, from the Latin *in*, not; and *tangere*, to touch. INTEGRITY means by derivation the state of being untouched, intact, unhurt, whole, entire, pure, uncorrupted.

705. *STIPULATE* (*stĭp'-ū-lāt*) *v.* To specify, insist upon, demand, require, make an agreement.

In the test phrase: 'He STIPULATED imported beer', the word is thought by 14 per cent of adult readers to mean HANDLED.

The corresponding noun STIPULATION (706) is of the same order of difficulty.

706. *STIPULATION* (*stĭp-ū-lā'-shŭn*) *n.* An essential condition, arrangement, covenant, a demand stated as a condition of consent to an agreement.

In the test phrase: 'He STIPULATED imported beer', the word thought by 16 per cent of preparatory-school juniors to mean FALSE CHARGES; and by another 12 per cent to mean PROPHECIES, predictions.

STIPULATION, and the corresponding verb to STIPULATE, come from the Latin *stipulare*, to bargain for. A STIPULATION is a condition essential to a bargain.

707. *DASTARD* (*dăs'-tărd*) *n.* A contemptible coward, craven, recreant, poltroon (502), faint-hearted wretch.

In the test phrase: 'They are DASTARDS', the word is thought

by 13 per cent of adult readers to mean BOASTERS, braggarts.
By another 7 per cent a DASTARD is thought to be an ILLE-
GITIMATE CHILD, one born out of wedlock. This is of course
a confusion of DASTARD, a coward, with BASTARD, a child born
out of wedlock. There is no historical connection between
these two words despite their similarity of form.
DASTARDS, POLTROONS, CRAVENS, and COWARDS, are all pusillanimous, weak, feeble, faint hearted. A COWARD is anyone
who shows fear. A COWARD who has already accepted defeat
is a CRAVEN. An obsolete meaning of the adjective, CRAVEN,
is beaten, defeated; and the noun, a CRAVEN, carries this connotation. A COWARD who is base, mean, despicable, is a POL-
TROON or DASTARD. Of the two, DASTARD is the stronger word.

708. *PROGNOSIS* (*prŏg-nō'-sĭs*) *n.* A prediction, forecast,
 judgment in advance, act of foretelling.
PROGNOSIS, and the corresponding verb, to PROGNOSTICATE (801),
to foretell, come from two Greek words πρό, before; and
γνῶναι, to know.
To 17 per cent of college seniors PROGNOSIS incorrectly
means WARNING, a caution against danger, a notice of danger
to come. A WARNING is always the foretelling of a future
danger. A PROGNOSIS is the foretelling of any future happening.
PROGNOSIS, PROGNOSTIC, and PROGNOSTICATION, are all nouns.
A PROGNOSTICATION is either the sign which makes possible a
prediction, or it is the act of predicting. A PROGNOSTIC is
the sign; a PROGNOSIS is ordinarily the act of predicting.

709. *PROPENSITY* (*prō-pĕn'-sĭ-tĭ*) *n.* A tendency, predisposition, permanent inclination, penchant (824), natural
proclivity (952), bias, proneness.
PROPENSITY comes from the Latin *pro*, forward; and *pendere*,
to hang. From the same source comes a large group of English words: the noun, PENDANT, anything hanging for ornamentation; the adjective, PENDENT, hanging; the noun, a PEN-
DULUM; and ultimately a PENT-HOUSE. A PROPENSITY is a
leaning, natural inclination, tendency toward something.
A PROPENSITY, an INCLINATION, and an APTITUDE, are all
natural tendencies. An APTITUDE is a gift for a particular
activity. An INCLINATION is a liking for, attraction toward a

particular activity. A PROPENSITY, like an INCLINATION, is an attraction toward but usually is reserved for situations involving a question of morals.

PRONENESS is another word associated with leaning, bending, which may be used figuratively to mean PROPENSITY. PRONENESS is from the Latin *pro*, forward, and may mean lying face down; or, figuratively, natural tendency, generally for something harmful. One has a PRONENESS for mischief, for overdrinking, for overindulgence.

In the test phrase: 'A PROPENSITY for drinking', the word is thought by 12 per cent of preparatory-school juniors to mean DISLIKE, antipathy, the popular misconception, and practically an opposite of PROPENSITY, inclination, proneness.

710. UNCOUTH (*ŭn-kooth'*) adj. Awkward, ungainly (336), outlandish, clownish, boorish, unmannerly, lacking in polish, not graceful in bearing.
In the test phrase: 'His manner is UNCOUTH', the word is thought by 29 per cent of adult readers to mean INSIPID (375), tasteless, dull, uninteresting, vapid. Although INSIPID sometimes has the suggestion of slightly disagreeable, it is never so strong as UNCOUTH, which means not merely uninteresting, or slightly unpleasant, but manifestly awkward, ungainly.

711. PENURIOUS (*pĕ-nū'-rĭ-ŭs*) adj. Niggardly, miserly, parsimonious to a fault, excessively sparing in the use of money.
PENURIOUS, and the corresponding noun PENURY, come from the Latin *penuria*, and the French *penurie*, both of which mean having to do with poverty.
The three words, PENURIOUS, NIGGARDLY, and MISERLY, all suggest dislike of spending money. MISERLY lays stress on the love of the gold which is saved by not spending; the typical MISER stores his money. NIGGARDLY lays stress on the effect, on other people, of not spending; a NIGGARD begrudges spending for others. PENURIOUS lays stress on the abject, sordid, state due to not spending.
To 10 per cent of college seniors PENURIOUS incorrectly means WEALTHY, rich. A MISER always possesses money, may even be wealthy. A NIGGARD may or may not have money.

A PENURIOUS person must have some money which he does not spend; but the word PENURIOUS does not suggest WEALTH. The noun, PENURY, means poverty in its most abject state; and is the opposite of WEALTH. The adjective PENURIOUS has come to mean not so much actual poverty as living in an abject state.

POOR and WEALTHY; NIGGARDLY and GENEROUS; PENURIOUS and LAVISH; are opposites.

712. *GAINSAY* (gān-sā') *v.* To deny, impugn, contradict, oppose in words, declare to be untrue.

The Anglo-Saxon prefix, GAIN, against, has survived in only a few words. GAINSAY, to say against, is the only common one; and even this is almost never used in conversation, and rarely in modern writing.

To GAINSAY, to DISPUTE, and to CONTROVERT, are often given as synonyms. DISPUTE and CONTROVERT, however, both suggest entering into an argument, giving reasons for one's disagreement. The word GAINSAY means merely contradict, deny, without argument.

In the test phrase: 'Do not GAINSAY it', the word is thought by 9 per cent of preparatory-school juniors to mean AGREE TO, an exact opposite of the correct meaning.

713. *PRIVY* (prĭv'-ĭ) *adj.* Private, one's own, individual, of personal ownership, not for public use.

In the test phrase: 'His PRIVY purse', the word is believed by 24 per cent of adult readers to mean GENEROUS, liberal, free in giving.

PRIVY is a doublet of PRIVATE, has the same etymology. PRIVATE was used little before the fifteenth century, PRIVY being the early word, the one used in the thirteenth and fourteenth centuries. The shift from PRIVY, now obsolete in this early sense, to the present word PRIVATE, occurred because PRIVY, through use in the phrase: 'A PRIVY place', had acquired what were considered objectionable connotations. PRIVATE for PRIVY is therefore a EUPHEMISM, an agreeable and sometimes less accurate word used in place of an offensive one. PRIVY is today used to mean PRIVATE only in phrases which have enough official dignity to give it standing, despite its history, as: 'PRIVY chamber', private room in a royal residence; 'PRIVY council'; 'PRIVY councilor'; 'PRIVY seal'.

714. *PREGNANT* (*prĕg'-nănt*) *adj.* Full of meaning, weighty, significant (748), suggestive, teeming with ideas.

In the short test phrase: 'PREGNANT thoughts', the word is believed by 15 per cent of adult readers to mean VIRGINAL, pure, maidenly, unsullied, an exact opposite of the literal meaning of PREGNANT, being with child, with young.

To another 9 per cent PREGNANT means IMPROPER. PREGNANT, from the Latin *prae*, before, and *nasci*, to be born, when used figuratively means full of meaning, weighty, and is a literary word in good standing.

715. *AUSTERE* (*aws-tēr'*) *adj.* Severe (123), harsh in judgment, strict, rigorous, rigid (504), inflexibly stern.

AUSTERE is from the Greek word αὐος, dry, withered. In the test phrase: 'An AUSTERE manner', the word is thought by 13 per cent of college seniors to mean SMOOTH. SMOOTH, as applied to manner, means bland, mild, soothing, flattering, almost an opposite of AUSTERE, harsh.

AUSTERE, SEVERE, and STERN, are practically synonymous but differ in duration. STERN characterizes a temporary state. SEVERE is more permanent, but is not habitual, as is AUSTERE.

716. *MARMOT* (*mahr'-mŏt*) *n.* A type of rodent, a burrowing animal of the same genus as the woodchuck.

To 10 per cent of college seniors MARMOT incorrectly means LIZARD. A LIZARD belongs to the REPTILE family and is therefore cold blooded and OVIPAROUS (*ō-vĭp'-ă-rŭs*), lays eggs from which the young are hatched. A MARMOT is a MAMMAL and is therefore warm blooded, and VIVIPAROUS (*vĭ-vĭp'-ă-rŭs*), produces its young alive.

A MARMOT has thick, short fur and a sharp tail. The animal lives in a burrow, in cold and snowy regions, and hibernates in winter, after laying in a supply of dried grass for use until torpid. The typical MARMOT is found in the Alps, the Pyrenees, and the Carpathian mountains. MARMOT is the name of a subdivision of the larger group RODENT. A RODENT, from the Latin *rodere*, to gnaw, is any gnawing animal. The group

includes rats, moles, mice, beavers, and woodchucks. MAR-
MOTS are rodents which burrow and hibernate. The group
includes prairie dogs and woodchucks.

717. *BENIGNANT* (*bē-nĭg'-nănt*) *adj.* Amiable, kindly, hu-
mane, merciful, graciously condescending.
To 21 per cent of college seniors BENIGNANT incorrectly
means RADIANT, refulgent, beaming with brightness. This
confusion may be due to the fact that a BENIGNANT, kindly,
person is often thought of as having a countenance beaming
with amiability, radiant with a kindly expression. Or it may
be due to the adjective, BENIGN. The two adjectives BENIG-
NANT and BENIGN (*bē-nīn'*) are both combinations of an early
form of the Latin *bonus*, good; and *genitus*, born. BENIGN
characterizes an outward appearance which implies kindness,
as: 'A BENIGN expression', 'A BENIGN smile'. In this respect
BENIGN and RADIANT are similar. BENIGNANT is more apt to
modify disposition.
The adjectives BENIGNANT and MALIGNANT, ill willed; and
the nouns BENIGNITY and MALIGNITY (893); are opposites.

718. *DECOROUS* (*dē-kō'-rŭs*, sometimes *dĕk'-ō-rŭs*) *adj.*
Proper, seemly, becoming, orderly, suitable for the occasion, marked by propriety (1042).
To 18 per cent of college seniors DECOROUS incorrectly means
BOISTEROUS, noisy, impetuous, tumultuous, an opposite, in
connotation, of DECOROUS, orderly.
DECOROUS and DECENT, from the same Latin word *decus*,
honor, fame, differ in modern usage. DECENT means respectable; the opposite, INDECENT, means immodest, immoral, gross,
obscene, filthy, not fit to be seen, unfit to be heard. Everyone
is expected to be DECENT. DECOROUS defines a characteristic
not taken for granted. It is an instinctive feeling for doing
the right thing at the right time.

719. *FERRET* (*fĕr'-rĕt*) *v.* To search carefully, rout (*rowt*),
rummage, drive out of a hiding place.
In the test phrase: 'FERRET out the scheme', the word is
thought by 10 per cent of preparatory-school juniors to
mean CARRY. This is no doubt a confusion of FERRET, to

search out, with the verb to FERRY, to carry, transport over a narrow body of water.

The verb, to FERRET, comes from the noun, a FERRET, the name of a small weasellike animal raised for the purpose of killing rats and other vermin. To FERRET may mean either to work one's way in as a ferret works its way into a rat-hole; or it may mean drive out as a ferret drives out the occupant.

720. *PRELUSORY* (*prē-lū'-sō-rĭ*) *adj.* Introductory, previous, prelusive, preliminary, preparatory.

PRELUSORY is from the Latin *pre*, before; and *ludere*, to play; and, by derivation, means played ahead of time. PRELUSORY and PRELUSIVE are synonymous. They are formed from the verb to PRELUDE (*prē-lūd'* or *prĕl'-ūd*), exactly as the adjective ELUSORY is formed from the verb, to ELUDE, to evade, avoid by artifice; and DELUSIVE from DELUDE, mislead, deceive.

To 14 per cent of college seniors PRELUSORY incorrectly means EXPLANATORY, serving to elucidate, define. This is perhaps a remote confusion of PRELUSORY, introductory, with ELUCIDATE, to explain.

A PRELUDE (*prē'-lūd* or *prĕl'-ŭd*) and a PREFACE are similar. A PREFACE, discussed more fully under PREAMBLE (129), is usually written or spoken, and is designed to explain or to prepare one for what follows. A PRELUDE may consist of any act or occurrence which happens to precede something else. The adjectives PREFATORY, from PREFACE, and PRELUSORY, from PRELUDE, differ as do the nouns.

721. *SLEAZY* (*slē'-zĭ*) *adj.* Flimsy, thin, open meshed, without firmness, insubstantial, composed of poor material. To 22 per cent of adult readers SLEAZY incorrectly means SMOOTH. This is perhaps a confusion of SLEAZY, flimsy, with SLEEK (*slēk*), smooth.

Both SLEAZY and FLIMSY imply poor quality. FLIMSY is applied to structures which are slight, too light, and apt to give way; SLEAZY most often to thin fabrics, textiles.

GOSSAMER (*gŏs'-să-mer*), like SLEAZY, means thin and is applied to fabrics. That which is GOSSAMER, although thin, may be relatively strong and of excellent quality. That which is SLEAZY is weak and unsatisfactory.

722. *FINICAL (fĭn'-ĭ-kăl) adj.* Overprecise, overnice, fastidious, foppish, affectedly refined, unduly particular.

In the test phrase: 'A FINICAL scientist', the word is believed by 12 per cent of adult readers to mean EXPERIENCED. FINICAL and FINIKIN are synonymous and are both words of long standing. They have recently been largely replaced by FINICKY, a word which twenty years ago was called colloquial but which is today in good standing and means overnice, unduly particular.

723. *PUNITIVE (pū'-nĭ-tĭv) adj.* Disciplinary, involving punishment, retributive, that which punishes. To 29 per cent of adult readers PUNITIVE incorrectly means INSIGNIFICANT. This is perhaps a confusion of PUNITIVE, disciplinary, with PUNY, tiny, small, weak, insignificant. PUNITIVE is an adjective from the Latin *punire*, to punish; it is from the same source as the noun PUNISHMENT; and the verb, to PUNISH, to chasten, chastise, castigate.

724. *PROSTRATE (prŏs'-trāt) v.* To bow down in humble reverence, do obeisance (ō-bā'-săns) to, throw one's self flat on the ground.

The word PROSTRATE is from the Latin *pro*, before; and *stratus*, the past participle of the verb *sternere*, to spread out, strew. The Latin *stratus* is the source also of the English words: STRATUS, a horizontal layer of summer clouds; STRATUM, a word used in science for a layer of rock; and SUBSTRATUM (361).

The verb to PROSTRATE may have at least three distinct meanings. It may mean to throw down, lay flat, in the literal sense as: 'To PROSTRATE the body'. Or it may mean to throw down in the sense of overthrow, demolish, ruin, as: 'To PROSTRATE a monarchy'. It is probably this meaning which leads 19 per cent of preparatory-school juniors to believe that PROSTRATE means OPPRESS, burden, crush, weigh down, even when the context indicates that the word is used in its third sense. For when used reflexively as: 'To PROSTRATE one's self', the word means to bow down in reverence, throw one's self humbly upon the ground.

PROSTRATE may also be used as an adjective with three corresponding meanings. A PROSTRATE person is one lying down either supine, face up, or prone, face down. A PROSTRATE monarchy has been overthrown. A PROSTRATE position may be one of reverence, homage, veneration.

725. *RESPLENDENT* (rē-splĕn′-dĕnt) *adj.* Very bright, brilliant, dazzling, glittering, splendid, refulgent, shining, lustrous, gorgeous, radiant, vivid.

RESPLENDENT is from the Latin *splendere*, to shine, the source of the English word SPLENDID.

To 14 per cent of adult readers RESPLENDENT incorrectly means TAWDRY, trumpery, showy but without taste. TAWDRY is apparently a contraction of ST. AUDRY, the name of an English town in which a fair was held where imitation laces and gay toys could be bought. TAWDRY means gay, bright colored, but at the same time cheap, without elegance. RESPLENDENT means bright, gay, with no suggestion of cheapness, shoddiness.

726. *PILASTER* (pĭ-lăs′-ter) *n.* A column of rectangular instead of circular section attached to a wall and projecting a third to a fourth of its breadth.

To 13 per cent of college seniors PILASTER incorrectly means CHANDELIER, a lighting fixture suspended from the ceiling; perhaps a confusion of PILASTER, rectangular wall column, with LUSTER, a chandelier ornamented with glass prisms. To another 12 per cent PILASTER incorrectly means MOLD.

Both a PILASTER and an ENGAGED COLUMN are attached to the wall. An ENGAGED COLUMN is circular; and a PILASTER is always rectangular. Both have the same parts as a free-standing column, BASE, SHAFT, and CAPITAL.

727. *VAGRANT* (vă′-grănt) *adj.* Wandering, unsettled, aimless, roving, roaming, stray, moving with uncertain direction.

VAGRANT is from the Latin *vagari*, to wander; the source of VAGUE, undetermined, unsettled, indefinite; and VAGABOND, a wanderer.

In the test phrase: 'VAGRANT breezes', the word is thought by 18 per cent of adult readers to mean BALMY. This is

obviously a confusion of VAGRANT, wandering, with FRA-
GRANT, sweet-smelling, aromatic, balmy.

The noun, a VAGRANT, meaning a tramp, idle wanderer,
beggar, vagabond, is perhaps more familiar than the adjective,
VAGRANT, wandering.

728. *REDRESS* (*rē-drĕs'*) *n.* Reparation, remedy (66), satisfaction, amends (642), requital (1070), restitution, in-
demnification, compensation for wrong.

REDRESS comes from the Latin *re*, again; and *directus*, direct,
straight. The verb REDRESS meant originally, in English, to
put in order again, set right, straighten again. To DRESS,
when used of soldiers, still means to arrange in a straight line,
the original meaning of the word.

In the test phrase: 'He sought REDRESS', the noun is thought
by 22 per cent of adult readers to mean CONSOLATION. This
may be a misunderstanding of the word CONSOLATION, which
means that which soothes distress; or it may be a confusion
of CONSOLATION, comfort, with COMPENSATION, a synonym of
REDRESS.

729. *INGRATIATE* (*ĭn-grā'-shĭ-āt*) *v.* To gain favor for,
establish in the good graces of another, commend to
another's favor, insinuate.

In the test phrase: 'He INGRATIATED himself', the word is
believed· by 19 per cent of adult readers to mean FAVORED.
The verb, to FAVOR, in the phrase: 'He FAVORED himself',
means to spare, refrain from exerting. One may FAVOR one's
eyes by not using them constantly, literally by treating them
kindly. To FAVOR ordinarily means look kindly upon, show
favor to, treat kindly, incline to, indulge, aid, support. The
action of INGRATIATING one's self is to acquire FAVOR for one's
self; to gain aid, support, indulgence, for one's self.

Practically synonymous with the verb to INGRATIATE one's
self is the phrase: 'To CURRY FAVOR'. This idiomatic expression comes probably from the obsolete word FAVEL, which
once meant a dun horse, one dark brown, chestnut, in color.
To CURRY FAVEL was originally to smooth down a dun horse.
This phrase apparently came to mean to flatter and was then
corrupted into the modern phrase: 'To CURRY FAVOR'. To

CURRY FAVOR is most frequently used for the process by which one INGRATIATES one's self, gains favor for one's self.

730. *ENSANGUINE* (*ĕn-săng'-gwĭn*) *v.* To stain with blood, make blood-red, cover with gore.

To 15 per cent of adult readers the verb, to ENSANGUINE, incorrectly means to CONCEAL; and to another 8 per cent to SHADE, to screen, hide in part, obscure, a word with something of the same suggestion as CONCEAL. These misconceptions are perhaps due to the prefix EN which is sometimes affixed to a noun to form a corresponding verb and which suggests put into, cover with, almost conceal. Thus: to ENCIRCLE is to make a circle about; to ENCASE is to put in a case; to ENCLOSE is to shut in, shut up; to ENSANGUINE is to cover with blood.

731. *HIBERNAL* (*hĭ-ber'-năl*) *adj.* Wintry, hiemal (*hĭ'-ĕ-măl*), pertaining to winter, the coldest season of the year.

To 12 per cent of adult readers HIBERNAL incorrectly means WARM, in suggestion an opposite of HIBERNAL, wintry.

To another large group HIBERNAL means IRISH. This is no doubt a confusion of HIBERNAL with HIBERNIAN, Irish. Despite the similarity, there is no etymological connection. HIBERNIAN is from *Hibernia*, the Latin name for Ireland; *Hibernia* in turn comes from an old Greek word, Ἰέρνη, from which ERIN, another name for Ireland, may have come more directly.

HIBERNAL is from the Latin *hibernare*, to pass the winter; from the same source as the French word *l'hiver*, the winter; and the English verb, to HIBERNATE, to pass the winter in a torpid condition as does the bear.

VERNAL means pertaining to the spring; ESTIVAL (*ĕs'-tĭ-vahl*), pertaining to the summer; AUTUMNAL, pertaining to autumn; HIBERNAL, pertaining to winter.

732. *EXTRANEOUS* (*ĕks-trā'-nē-ŭs*) *adj.* Foreign, alien, outward, external, irrelevant, unessential, remote, extrinsic, impertinent, not appertaining to.
In the test phrase: 'EXTRANEOUS matter', the word is thought

by 23 per cent of adult readers to mean WORTHLESS, of no value, without merit, useless. There are many phrases in which WORTHLESS and EXTRANEOUS can be used practically interchangeably, as: 'EXTRANEOUS information', 'EXTRANEOUS data', information and data which have no essential relation to the subject and are therefore worthless. But fundamentally the two words are not synonymous, for EXTRANEOUS pressure, foreign pressure, pressure from the outside, and EXTRANEOUS influences, influences from without, may be momentous and not worthless.

733. *IMPLICIT* (*ĭm-plĭs'-ĭt*) *adj.* Unquestioning, complete, trusting absolutely, without reserve.
IMPLICIT is from the Latin *in;* and *plicare*, to fold. In the test phrase: 'Her confidence was IMPLICIT', the word is thought by 20 per cent of adult readers to mean INCREDIBLE, too extraordinary to be believed.
   The word IMPLICIT has at least two distinct meanings. It may mean implied, tacit (982), understood although not directly expressed, as: 'A meaning IMPLICIT in the words'. In this sense IMPLICIT and EXPLICIT, outspoken, are opposites. Or IMPLICIT may mean complete, absolute, blind, as: 'IMPLICIT faith', 'IMPLICIT confidence'.

734. *CRASS* (*krăs*) *adj.* Crude, stupid, dull, dense, gross (745), coarse, obtuse (984), lacking in refinement.
To 18 per cent of adult readers CRASS incorrectly means DECEITFUL, insincere, tricky. This is perhaps a confusion of CRASS, crude, with CRAFTY, cunning, artful, deceitful.
   CRASS is from the Latin *crassus*, thick, dense, solid; and the English word CRASS may still be used in the physical sense of thick, as: 'A CRASS fabric'. But the word is most frequently used figuratively to mean stupid, dull, gross, as: 'CRASS ignorance', 'A CRASS remark'.

735. *SUNDRY* (*sŭn'-drĭ*) *adj.* Various, divers (356), several, a small number, more than one or two.
SUNDRY is of Anglo-Saxon origin. In the test phrase: 'In SUNDRY places', the word is thought by 21 per cent of adult readers to mean ARID, parched by heat, dry. This may be a

confusion of SUNDRY, various, with SULTRY, oppressively hot; or it may be due to the spelling of SUNDRY which does not mean sun-dry, but which means several, various.

736. REGIMEN (*rĕj'-ĭ-mĕn*) *n.* Prescribed course, regime (*rā-zhēm'*), orderly system.

REGIMEN is from the Latin *regere*, to rule. To 14 per cent of adult readers the word incorrectly means LESSON, exercise, assigned reading. This confusion may perhaps be due to the word COURSE, for a COURSE may consist of a series of lessons. A REGIMEN is not a course in this sense but a course of conduct, rule of life, series of prescribed practices.

REGIMEN, like the word DIET, may be used of food. A DIET prescribes only the kinds of food to be eaten; while a REGIMEN may prescribe not only kinds and amounts, but even the hours at which food is to be taken.

The words REGIMEN and REGIME are practically identical. REGIME is the French word and is more apt to be used of a social order, political system, government rule. REGIMEN, more directly from the Latin, is used for a systematized course of living.

737. TRAFFICKER (*trăf'-fĭk-ĕr*) *n.* Dealer, trader, barterer, bargainer, negotiator, merchant, vender (199), one who buys and sells.

To 9 per cent of preparatory-school juniors a TRAFFICKER incorrectly means a TRAITOR. This may be a confusion of TRAITOR, one who betrays a trust, commits treason, with TRADER, one who buys and sells. Or it may be due to the word TRAFFICKER, for although there is nothing in the derivation to suggest such an interpretation, the word sometimes implies one who trades in a mean way.

To another 8 per cent, TRAFFICKER incorrectly means a TRAVELER. The noun, TRAFFIC, originally meant trade, commerce, exchange of goods. It then came to mean in addition goods carried over a route; or persons moving along the route. This is the first thought which the word TRAFFIC arouses in the mind today. The noun TRAFFICKER never means one who travels, but is used only in the sense of one who traffics, one who exchanges goods, a merchant, trader.

738. *BAROUCHE* (*bă-roosh'*) *n.* Four-wheeled carriage having a folding top, a driver's seat on the outside, and inside two seats which face each other.

To 13 per cent of college seniors BAROUCHE incorrectly means BEER-GARDEN.

Although BAROUCHE comes originally from the two Latin words *bi*, two; and *rota*, wheel; and by derivation means two-wheeled; the word BAROUCHE today can mean only a four-wheeled vehicle.

739. *ACCOUTRE* (*ăk-koo'-ter*) *v.* To equip, attire, array, dress for parade, furnish with equipment for military service.

ACCOUTRE is directly from the French *accoutrer*, to dress, clothe. The corresponding noun ACCOUTREMENTS (854), equipment, apparel, trappings, is less familiar for it is unknown to 60 per cent of adult readers.

740. *CONVIVIAL* (*kŏn-vĭv'-ĭ-ăl*) *adj.* Festive, festal, jovial, social, devoted to feasting, characterized by good fellowship in eating and drinking.

To 14 per cent of preparatory-school juniors CONVIVIAL incorrectly means DANGEROUS, perilous.

CONVIVIAL comes from the Latin *com*, together; and *vivere*, to live, the source of the English words: VIVID, bright; VITAL, essential to life; and VICTUAL (*vĭt'-l*), food. CONVIVIAL, which by derivation means living together, is not exactly synonymous with SOCIAL, inclined to friendly intercourse, or SOCIABLE, friendly, companionable, but applies specifically to the enjoyment of feasting and drinking.

741. *TRANSIENT* (*trăn'-shĕnt*) *adj.* Fleeting, quickly passing away, transitory, momentary, hasty, evanescent (846), of short duration.

TRANSIENT is from the Latin *trans*, across; and *ire*, to go; and suggests passing across the scene and then disappearing.

In the test phrase: 'TRANSIENT views', the word is thought by 14 per cent of adult readers to mean THOUGHTFUL, a word which in this sense may mean either kind, considerate, solicitous; or careful, well thought out. In this last sense,

THOUGHTFUL is almost an opposite of TRANSIENT, hasty, momentary.

742. *TRIDENT* (*trī'-dĕnt*) *n.* Three pronged fish-spear, any forklike instrument with three tines.

TRIDENT comes from the Latin *tri*, three, which appears in the common word TRIANGLE, a figure with three angles; and *dens, dentis*, tooth, the source of DENTIST, DENTAL, and DENTISTRY; and means by derivation three-toothed.

In the test phrase: 'Her shield and TRIDENT', the word is thought by 13 per cent of preparatory-school juniors to mean SYMBOL, emblem, sign. The confusion may perhaps arise from the fact that the symbol, emblem, attribute, of Neptune, God of the Sea in Roman mythology, is a TRIDENT, a three-toothed fork.

743. *FIGMENT* (*fĭg'-mĕnt*) *n.* Fabrication, invention, fiction, contrivance, concoction, something imagined.

To 14 per cent of adult readers FIGMENT incorrectly means TENDENCY, proclivity, leaning, disposition.

FIGMENT is from the Latin *fingere*, to make, the source of the English words FICTION and FEIGN (487), to invent, pretend. A FIGMENT is anything which has been invented. The hackneyed phrase: 'FIGMENT of the imagination' is tautological, for the word FIGMENT alone means an invention of the imagination.

744. *VESTIGE* (*vĕs'-tĭj*) *n.* Trace of something which has disappeared, remaining bit, shade (698), evidence, impression left, soupçon, speck, jot, particle, iota, scintilla.

In the test phrase: 'Every VESTIGE of a garment', the word is thought by 16 per cent of preparatory-school juniors to mean TEXTURE, woven fabric, textile. This may be a confusion of VESTIGE, trace, with VESTURE, clothing, garments in general.

VESTIGE comes from the Latin *vestigium*, a footprint, trace, mark. VESTIGE may still have in English its literal meaning, footprint; but the word is ordinarily used in the broader sense to mean any trace, sign, impression.

VESTIGE and TRACE are practically synonymous. The word

TRACE implies continuity, perhaps a series of footprints. A TRACE is more apparent than a VESTIGE, which may be insignificant in amount.

745. *GROSS* (*grōs*) *adj.* Big, large, great, bulky; flagrant, enormous, crass (734), glaring, palpable.

GROSS is the same as the French word *gros* (*grō*) which means thick. The feminine form of the French word, *gros*, is *grosse*, pronounced like the English GROSS.

The word GROCER, formerly spelt *grosser*, is from the same source and originally meant a wholesaler, one dealing in large, gross, quantities. The use of GROCER, to mean one who deals in foodstuffs, first appeared in the nineteenth century.

In the test phrase: 'Her GROSS error', the word is thought by 24 per cent of adult readers to mean EXPENSIVE, costly, the most common misconception. This may be merely because GROSS errors are costly, expensive. Or it may be due to the fact that EXPENSIVE comes from a source meaning weighty, heavy; and there is an obvious connection between great, GROSS, and heavy, the source of EXPENSIVE.

SLIGHT, a second misconception of GROSS, held by 6 per cent, is an opposite of the correct meaning.

GROSS, HEINOUS (*hā'-nŭs*), and FLAGRANT, may all be used to describe offenses. FLAGRANT is literally flaming and therefore striking, glaring; HEINOUS is hateful and therefore odious; GROSS is characterized by size, either literal or figurative.

The adverb GROSSLY (*grōs'-lĭ*) may mean either entirely, in a big way; or shamefully, indecently, vulgarly, coarsely, flagrantly.

746. *ASTUTE* (*ăs-tūt'*) *adj.* Shrewd, keen, acute, crafty, cunning (320), discerning, penetrating, subtle (*sŭt'-l*), sagacious. 'Her ASTUTE answer.'

The corresponding adverb ASTUTELY, shrewdly, sagaciously, is thought by 8 per cent of adult readers to mean LONG-WINDEDLY, tediously, wearisomely, tiresomely.

ASTUTE and ASTUTELY come from the Latin *astus*, cunning, craft, and, with the noun ASTUTENESS, are the only common English words from this source.

ASTUTE and SAGACIOUS both mean knowing. SAGACIOUS

is always used in a good sense and suggests the wisdom of age and experience. ASTUTE may be used in the same sense or it may imply shrewdness, craftiness, cunning. ASTUTE, in this last sense, differs from ACUTE and KEEN which suggest merely sharpness. The ASTUTE mind adds to acuteness and keenness an element of cunning, finesse (*fē-nĕs'*).

747. *ROISTERER* (*rois'-ter-er*) *n.* A jovial swaggerer, bold blusterer, noisy reveler, turbulent fellow.
To 13 per cent of college seniors ROISTERER incorrectly means HAWKER, peddler who sells his wares by crying them out, huckster. Both a ROISTERER and a HAWKER are noisy, but there is little else in common between the two.

ROISTERER is from the Latin *rusticus,* a rustic; the source of the English words RUSTIC, a farmer, one who lives in the country; and RURAL, of the country, not living in the city.

BOISTEROUS, noisy, uproarious, from a Welsh word meaning ferocity, is an adjective with something of the same suggestion as the noun ROISTERER. Both words suggest noise; but they differ in that BOISTEROUS actions are the results of animal spirits. Thus one speaks of: 'A BOISTEROUS boy'. A ROISTERER is primarily a reveler.

748. *SIGNIFICANT* (*sĭg-nĭf'-ĭ-kănt*) *adj.* Meaningful, noteworthy, suggestive, consequential, expressive, weighty, important, momentous, signifying something.
In the test phrase: 'A SIGNIFICANT fact', the word is thought by 18 per cent of adult readers to mean CONSPICUOUS. CONSPICUOUS and OBVIOUS are practically synonymous. Both mean clear, manifest, distinct, noticeable, apparent, striking. Facts which are OBVIOUS, CONSPICUOUS, easily seen, are not necessarily SIGNIFICANT, important; and facts which are important, SIGNIFICANT, are often difficult to discover and are not obvious, conspicuous.

749. *VAUNT* (*vŏnt*) *n.* A boast, brag, boastful assertion, vain display, parade, gasconade.
In the test phrase: 'A remarkable VAUNT', the word is thought by 23 per cent of adult readers to mean JUMP, leap. This is no doubt a confusion of VAUNT, boast, with the word

VAULT, which means a springing leap made by resting the hand upon a support or with the aid of a pole, as: 'A VAULT over a fence', or 'A pole VAULT'. VAULT is from the Latin *volvere*, to turn; while VAUNT is from the Latin *vanus*, empty, the source of the English word VAIN, conceited. A VAUNT is a boast, an empty assertion.

750. *GARRULITY* (*găr-rool'-ĭ-tĭ*) *n.* Talkativeness, chatter, loquacity, fluency, glibness, volubility. GARRULOUS, gabbling, jabbering, talkative, is the corresponding adjective and is probably more familiar than the noun.

GARRULITY is from the Latin *garrire*, to prattle, chatter. In the test phrase: 'The GARRULITY of age', the word is thought by 15 per cent of adult readers to mean FEEBLENESS, weakness. This may perhaps be due to a remote confusion of GARRULITY, talkativeness, with SENILITY, infirmity, weakness.

GARRULITY, LOQUACITY (*lō-kwăs'-ĭ-tĭ*), and TALKATIVENESS, all suggest a flow of words. Of the three, GARRULITY is the only one which suggests the minute repetition of unimportant trivialities.

751. *LATITUDE* (*lăt'-ĭ-tūd*) *n.* Scope (355), range, extent, breadth, amplitude, extent of deviation from a standard. In the test phrase: 'He was given LATITUDE', the word is thought by 19 per cent of adult readers to mean ADVICE, suggestion, counsel.

In geography, LATITUDE means specifically the distance north and south from the equator, in contrast to LONGITUDE which is measured east and west from Greenwich in England, near London. LONGITUDE is from the Latin *longus*, long, while LATITUDE is from the Latin *latus*, broad. LATITUDE is often used in literature to mean scope, range.

752. *SACROSANCT* (*săk'-rō-săngkt*) *adj.* Sacred, holy (15), hallowed, consecrated, blessed, inviolable, of great goodness, as: 'A SACROSANCT volume'.

To 15 per cent of adult readers SACROSANCT incorrectly means PROHIBITIVE, forbidding, impossible. To another 13 per cent SACROSANCT incorrectly means OUT-OF-PRINT.

SACROSANCT is from the two Latin words *sacer* and *sanctus*, both of which mean holy, sacred, so that SACROSANCT is literally doubly sacred, extremely holy.

753. *ALTERCATION* (*awl-ter-kă'-shŭn*) *n.* Quarrel, stormy controversy, wrangle, noisy dispute, angry debate, row, hot argument, warm contention in words. ALTERCATION is from the Latin *alter*, another, and suggests speaking alternately one after another.

To 44 per cent of preparatory-school juniors ALTERCATION incorrectly means CONVERSATION, talk, interchange of thoughts in spoken words. Although an ALTERCATION is necessarily in words it is always a dispute, argument, disagreement and always heated, angry, and usually unpleasant.

754. *RANKLE* (*răng'-kl*) *v.* To give pain, gnaw, fester, nettle (449), provoke, inflame, enrage, exasperate, cause continuous irritation.

In the test phrase: 'Criticism RANKLES', the word is thought by 20 per cent of adult readers to mean INCREASES. The adjective RANK, in the phrase: 'RANK vegetation', means vigorous, strong; and the noun RANKNESS means rapid increase, vigorous growth. But the verb to RANKLE is never used in this way. The adjective RANK may also mean sour, rancid, and it is in something of this last sense that RANKLE is used, for to RANKLE is to fester, remain inflamed; or, in a transitive sense, to cause inflammation, irritate.

755. *INCAPACITATE* (*ĭn-kă-păs'-ĭ-tāt*) *v.* To disable, disqualify, make unfit, deprive of power, render incapable. In the test phrase: 'He was INCAPACITATED', the word is thought by 10 per cent of adult readers to mean INJURED, hurt; and by another 9 per cent to mean BEHEADED. This is probably a confusion of INCAPACITATE, deprive of power, with DECAPITATE, behead. Despite the similarity of the two words in both sound and spelling, there is no etymological connection between them. DECAPITATE comes from the Latin word *caput*, head, and means literally deprive of the head, behead. INCAPACITATE has no connection with *caput;* it comes from the Latin *capere*, to hold, seize, take, the source of the English words, CAPACITY and CAPABLE. The unusual verb, to

UNKNOWN TO 45 PER CENT

CAPACITATE, means to make capable, to enable. To INCAPACI-
TATE is to make incapable, to disable.

756. *MODICUM* (*mŏd'-ĭ-kŭm*) *n*. A small bit, moderate
quantity, little piece, scanty allowance, meager amount,
trace, shade (698), vestige (744), barely enough.
MODICUM is from the Latin *modus*, measure, manner, kind,
way, a word which has as many meanings as the English
word MODE, one of the many which come from it and which
may mean method, fashion, style.
  To 16 per cent of college seniors MODICUM incorrectly
means GROUP, an assemblage of persons, cluster, crowd,
throng.
  In the test phrase: 'A MODICUM of wood', the word is
thought by 18 per cent of preparatory-school juniors to
mean a SUPPLY. Substituted in this phrase, a SUPPLY would
mean a quantity on hand, amount, store, stock, enough for
use, practically an opposite of MODICUM, hardly sufficient.
  Both a MODICUM and a MOIETY (*moi'-ĕ-tĭ*) are parts of
the whole. A MOIETY is literally a half, one of two equal
parts; a MODICUM is so small as to be barely enough.

757. *CAUDAL* (*caw'-dăl*) *adj*. Taillike; of, pertaining to, or
near the tail, the hindmost part of an animal.
In the test phrase: 'A CAUDAL appendage', the word is
thought by 13 per cent of adult readers to mean INFLAMED.
This is perhaps due to some confusion of CAUDAL, taillike,
with CAUSTIC, burning, corrosive, destructive; or perhaps
with CAUTERIZE, to burn, sear.
  CAUDAL is directly from the Latin *cauda*, tail; and means,
literally, taillike.

758. *ASSEVERATION* (*ăs-sĕv-er-ā'-shŭn*) *n*. An earnest
declaration, positive assertion, solemn affirmation.
ASSEVERATION comes from the Latin *ad*, to; and *severus*,
severe, the source of the English word SEVERE. An ASSEVERA-
TION is a severe, serious, grave, assertion.
  To 16 per cent of preparatory-school juniors ASSEVERATION
incorrectly means a DIVISION. This is probably a confusion
of ASSEVERATION, an assertion, with the verb, to SEVER, to

separate, divide; or with the noun, a SEVERANCE, a separation, division. Despite the similarity of the two words there is no etymological connection.

To another 14 per cent an ASSEVERATION incorrectly means a DENIAL. An ASSEVERATION is often a positive affirmation and in this sense is practically the opposite of a DENIAL. Both an ASSEVERATION and a DECLARATION are assertions. A DECLARATION is emphatic. An ASSEVERATION is solemn.

759. *VIRILE* (vĭr'-ĭl) *adj.* Manly, masculine, forceful, masterful, not effeminate.

To 13 per cent of adult readers VIRILE incorrectly means NOBLE, illustrious, excellent. This may be a confusion of VIRILE with the noun VIRTUE. VIRTUE is from the Latin *virtus*, strength, bravery, which in turn comes from the Latin *vir*, man. VIRTUE once meant in English strength, bravery, courage. The word is now used most frequently to mean moral goodness, moral excellence, uprightness, rectitude; although it may also mean any excellence, as in the phrase: 'One of his VIRTUES'.

VIRILE, from the same Latin word *vir*, man, is more specific and means definitely manly, having the characteristics of an adult man.

VIRAGO (vĭ-rā'-gō, not vĭr'-ă-gō), a woman of great strength, a female warrior, is from the same source. VIRAGO is now used most frequently to mean a termagant, bold impudent woman.

VIRILE and EFFEMINATE are opposites.

760. *QUARTER* (kwaw'-ter) *n.* Mercy, indulgence, forbearance, pity, clemency (596) in sparing the life of a captive. 'He begged for QUARTER.'

The noun QUARTER is best known when used to mean a fourth part. The same word with the same derivation may mean a section of a city, as: 'The Latin QUARTER'. The noun QUARTER to mean mercy has apparently a different history. It has been suggested that it comes from demanding a quarter of a soldier's pay for his release; or it may come from the word QUARTER used to mean a building or abode in which soldiers were lodged before being ransomed; but the exact history of the word is uncertain.

761. *EXPUNGE* (*ĕks-pŭnj'*) *v.* Erase, rub out, obliterate, cancel, blot out, remove, efface, strike out.

EXPUNGE, wipe out, is not from SPONGE, as might be supposed, but from the same source as PUNGENT, piercing, sharp, biting. To EXPUNGE is, by derivation, to prick out, punch out, in the sense in which the value of a railroad ticket is wiped out when the ticket is punched.

In the test phrase: 'EXPUNGE that sentence', the word is thought by 24 per cent of adult readers to mean EXPLAIN, make clear, show the meaning of, make intelligible, explicate. This is perhaps because of the frequent occurrence of the phrase: 'EXPLAIN away', which means remove, and in a loose sense, EXPUNGE, efface. Or it may be due to a confusion of EXPUNGE, erase, with EXPOUND, explain, set forth, make clear.

EXPUNGE, OBLITERATE (*ŏb-lĭt'-er-āt*), ERASE, and CANCEL, are varying degrees of blotting out. To CANCEL is to cross out, strike out, with no attempt at removing the original impression. The CANCELLI (*kăn-sĕl'-lī*) are the cross-bars of a latticed window, or of a screen or grating; and to CANCEL is to make such cross lines through that which is to be canceled. To ERASE is to rub out the original in such a manner that something else may be written in its place; but even a careful ERASURE usually leaves some trace of the original. To OBLITERATE is to remove in such a way as to leave no trace either of the original or of the fact that something has been removed. To EXPUNGE is to cut out, often leaving no trace of the original, but making no attempt to cover up the fact that something has been cut out.

762. *IMPERTURBABLE* (*ĭm-per-ter'-bă-bl*) *adj.* Calm, serene, unruffled, placid, tranquil, unmoved, composed (221), self-contained, cool, not perturbed.

IMPERTURBABLE, the negative of PERTURBABLE, excitable, is from the same source, the Latin *perturbare*, to disturb, as the verbs to PERTURB, to agitate, and to DISTURB, to perplex, discompose; and the adjectives TURBID, roiled, stirred up, and TURBULENT, in violent commotion.

In the test phrase: 'IMPERTURBABLE officials', the word is thought by 12 per cent of adult readers to mean RELIABLE, trustworthy, the common misconception. The next most common misconception is EXCITABLE, an opposite of the correct meaning.

763. *PERUSAL* (*pĕ-rooz'-ăl*) *n.* Careful reading, inspection, scrutiny (281), examination, thoughtful survey.
PERUSAL is the noun formed from the verb, to PERUSE (*pĕ-rooz'*). The verb, in turn, is a combination of the Latin *per*, through; and the verb to USE. To PERUSE is, by derivation, to use through to the end, make complete use of; to PERUSE a book is to get all that is possible out of it.

In the test phrase: 'The PERUSAL gave pleasure', the word is believed by 24 per cent of adult readers to mean GLANCE. A GLANCE is a hasty look, rapid view, momentary glimpse; the word GLANCE always suggests speed, rapidity. A PERUSAL is either leisurely, or careful, or both. In suggestion, therefore, the PERUSAL of a book is the opposite of a GLANCE at it.

764. *ANIMOSITY* (*ăn-ĭ-mŏs'-ĭ-tĭ*) *n.* Hostility, active enmity, antagonism, ill will, violent hatred, malevolence, rancor (693), malignity (893).
To 16 per cent of adult readers ANIMOSITY incorrectly means REBELLION, insurrection, mutiny, resistance.

By another 14 per cent ANIMOSITY is thought to mean ENTHUSIASM, animated interest, zeal, ardor. This is perhaps a confusion of ANIMOSITY, enmity, with ANIMATION, vivacity, life, liveliness, a word from the same Latin source. Or it may be a survival of the original meaning, for ANIMOSITY is from the Latin *animus*, spirit, mind, courage; and the word originally meant courage, animation. This meaning is now obsolete; and ANIMOSITY has come to mean active hatred.

To 27 per cent of preparatory-school juniors, ANIMOSITY incorrectly means FEELING. The word FEELING is general; it may be almost any sensation, pleasurable or disagreeable. ANIMOSITY is specifically violent hatred, hostility.

ANIMOSITY, HOSTILITY, and ENMITY, all imply ill will between persons. ENMITY is the most enduring and determined of the three, but it is not necessarily active, apparent. HOSTILITY is always active, apparent. ANIMOSITY has the characteristics of both; it is determined, accompanied by passion; and also active, apparent, overt. It differs from GRUDGE (337),

HATE, HATRED, MALICE (391), and SPITE, in being more active than any of them.

765. *INSENSATE* (*ĭn-sĕn'-sāt*) *adj.* Unfeeling, without sensibility. INSENSATE may also mean stupid, senseless, destitute of sense, foolish.

INSENSATE does not mean unfeeling in the sense of hardhearted, unsympathetic; but means literally without feeling, without sensibility, as: 'INSENSATE things'. INSENSATE and INSENSIBLE are often synonymous. The word, INSENSIBLE, may mean either without sense, destitute of the power of sensation; or it may mean unfeeling, indifferent, hard, callous, lacking tenderness. INSENSATE should be reserved for the first of these two meanings. It should be used only to mean not endowed with the power of sensation. This lack of sense may be carried to such an extreme that under some conditions INSENSATE may mean stupid, dull, foolish, senseless, or even irrational, insane.

766. *ACRIMONIOUS* (*ăk-rĭ-mō'-nĭ-ŭs*) *adj.* Sharp, bitter, sarcastic, biting, tart (539), stinging, caustic, mordant.
ACRIMONIOUS, VIRULENT, MALIGNANT, CAUSTIC, TAUNTING, SARCASTIC, and SEVERE, are all sharp, biting, but in different senses. SEVERE (123) is unsparing but without scorn, malice, or anger. SARCASTIC is scornful; TAUNTING is still stronger, bitterly sarcastic. CAUSTIC is burning. MALIGNANT, intent upon doing harm, and VIRULENT (1097), poisonous, are both more extreme than ACRIMONIOUS. ACRIMONIOUS is from the Latin *acer, acris,* sharp, from the same source as ACID, sour, sharp; ACUTE, sharp, intense; and ACRID, sharp, bitter, pungent; and the more unusual words ACERBITY, sharpness, literally of unripe fruit and figuratively of temperament; and ACERBATE, to embitter. ACRIMONIOUS means, in a figurative sense, sharp, bitter, as in the phrase: 'His ACRIMONIOUS answer'.

767. *FEALTY* (*fē'-ăl-tĭ*) *n.* Loyalty, fidelity, faithfulness, homage, reverence, allegiance.
FEALTY is from the Latin *fides,* faith. To 15 per cent of adult readers the word incorrectly means PRIVILEGE, immunity, peculiar benefit, prerogative, liberty. To another 9 per

cent it incorrectly means INFIDELITY, faithlessness, an exact
opposite of the correct meaning.

768. *MYRIAD* (*mĭr'-ĭ-ăd*) *n*. A great number, multitude,
    throng, vast quantity, specifically ten thousand.
MYRIAD can be employed either as a noun, as: 'MYRIADS of
small creatures'; or as an adjective: 'MYRIAD leaves'.
MYRIAD is from the Greek μυρίος, numberless, countless,
a word which was used in its plural form, μύριοι, for the
definite numeral ten thousand.
To 25 per cent of preparatory-school juniors MYRIAD incorrectly means GROUP. A GROUP is a number of persons or
things; but the word GROUP does not designate specifically
a great number, as does the word MYRIAD.

769. *CONSUMMATE* (*kŏn'-sŭm-māt*) *v*. To perfect, achieve,
    complete, finish, accomplish, bring to final excellence.
CONSUMMATE is from *con*, together; and the Latin word,
summa, sum, chief part. From the same word come the noun,
a SUMMARY, a summation, formed into a sum, reduced to a
few words, summed up; and the verb, to SUMMARIZE, to
sum up.
In the test phrase: 'His plan was CONSUMMATED', the word
is thought by 18 per cent of adult readers to mean APPROVED,
commended, thought well of.
By another 14 per cent, to CONSUMMATE is thought to
mean BRING TO NAUGHT, an exact opposite of the correct
meaning, bring to completion.

770. *PREJUDICE* (*prĕj'-ū-dĭs*) *v*. To bias, influence unduly,
    inspire with feelings against a person, cause to form
an opinion before examination of the facts.
In the test phrase: 'I shall not PREJUDICE you', the word is
thought by 24 per cent of adult readers to mean FAVOR. To
FAVOR may mean to treat tenderly, show partiality for, as:
'To FAVOR a sore arm', and in this sense is an exact opposite
of one meaning of PREJUDICE, to injure, hurt, damage, impair, as: 'To PREJUDICE a cause'.
The noun PREJUDICE is from the Latin, *prae*, before; and
judicium, a judgment; and means literally a judgment formed

in advance, without due consideration of the facts. The verb to PREJUDICE is to make such a judgment in advance. To PREJUDICE is to cause someone else to make such a judgment.

771. *SPECULATE* (*spĕk'-ū-lāt*) *v.* To meditate, conjecture, wonder, guess, ponder over, indulge in thought, cogitate (261), ruminate. This is the same word which is so widely used at present to mean deal in financial transactions of uncertain outcome, gamble.

In the test phrase: 'SPECULATE upon the outcome', the word is thought by 25 per cent of preparatory-school juniors to mean LOOK. SPECULATE comes from the Latin word *specula*, a watchtower, a word which in turn comes from *specere*, to see, the source of the English words: SPECTACLES, glasses to look through; and SPECTATOR, an onlooker, observer. To SPECULATE originally meant in English to observe, to view as from a watchtower. This meaning is, however, obsolete; and SPECULATE now means to think as if viewing a subject from a mental watch tower, to note various aspects, relationships, and possibilities.

772. *PANACEA* (*păn-ă-sē'-ă*) *n.* Cure-all, that which corrects all evil, remedy for all ills, universal curative, catholicon (*kă-thŏl'-ĭ-kŏn*).

To 15 per cent of college seniors PANACEA incorrectly means NEMESIS, vengeance, retribution, retributive justice. A NEMESIS and a PANACEA are, by connotation, opposites; for NEMESIS suggests punishment, destruction; while PANACEA means cure, remedy. NEMESIS and PANACEA both come from Greek words. NEMESIS, spelt with a capital, was the name of a female divinity, a personification of the righteous anger of the gods, the goddess of vengeance. PANACEA comes from the Greek πᾶς, παντός, all, a word familiar today in the adjective Pan-American, all-American; and ἄκος, cure; and means, literally, a cure-all.

773. *HARRY* (*hăr'-rĭ*) *v.* To lay waste, plunder, pillage, ravage (439); also worry, torment, harass (*hăr'-ăs*).

HARRY is of Anglo-Saxon origin. To 27 per cent of adult readers the word incorrectly means SCATTER, disperse, drive

away in disorder. This is perhaps due to a confusion of
HARRY with HURRY, a verb which can be used transitively to
mean urge to great haste.

774. *SPRITE* (*sprīt*) *n.* Fairy, elf, pixie, hobgoblin, brownie,
sylph, imp, fay, kobold, banshee, nymph, nixie, jinn.
To 20 per cent of adult readers SPRITE incorrectly means
CHILD. This may be a confusion of SPRITE, fairy, with MITE,
originally a coin of little value, but now a word which is
used to designate anything small, often specifically a small
person, a child. The word ELF may mean a diminutive person, dwarf, urchin, small child; but SPRITE is not used in
this way.

SPRITE and SPIRIT come from the same Latin word, *spiritus,*
spirit; and the two words were once synonymous. SPIRIT is
now used to mean vital principle, breath of life; while SPRITE,
which once had this sense, now means elf, fairy, goblin.

775. *ALLOCATE* (*ăl'-lō-kāt*) *v.* To apportion, allot, assign,
destine, give, award, distribute.
In the test phrase: 'He ALLOCATED the funds', the word is
thought by 14 per cent of adult readers to mean RAISED,
probably in the sense of collected, brought together, in suggestion almost an opposite of ALLOCATE, distribute, allot.
To LOCATE, DISLOCATE, and ALLOCATE, all come from the
Latin *locare,* to place. To LOCATE today means to place,
establish in a particular spot. To DISLOCATE is by derivation
to displace, but the word is used precisely to mean throw
out of joint. To ALLOCATE is from the Latin *ad,* to; and *locatus,*
the past participle of *locare,* to place, the source also of the
noun LOCATION, place, position, site. To ALLOCATE is by derivation to locate, but the word is used only in its acquired
sense to mean allot shares, assign funds, apportion.

776. *REFRACTORY* (*rē-frăk'-tō-rĭ*) *adj.* Obstinate, stubborn (266), unmanageable, unyielding (392), sullen in
disobedience, perverse (1049) in opposition.
In the test phrase: 'REFRACTORY members', the word is
thought by 23 per cent of preparatory-school juniors to
mean DISSENTING. DISSENTING means disagreeing, differing in

opinion; but the word suggests none of the stubbornness, obstinacy, implicit in REFRACTORY.

Although REFRACTORY and FRACTIOUS are similar in appearance and close in meaning, they are etymologically distinct words. FRACTIOUS (*frăk'-shŭs*) is probably connected with the obsolete English word *fratch*, a quarrel, brawl. FRACTIOUS has apparently acquired its c only to be like REFRACTORY in spelling. In meaning it still retains the suggestion of being quarrelsome, snappish, fretful, cross.

REFRACTORY is from the Latin *re*, back; and *fractus*, the past participle of *frangere*, to break. The verb to REFRACT is by derivation to break back, and from this has come to mean turn back abruptly, bend back sharply. One who is REFRACTORY turns sharply aside from the course which others would like him to follow, he literally breaks away. He is not amenable, not easily led.

777. *OPULENT* (*ŏp'-ū-lĕnt*) *adj.* Rich, wealthy, affluent, prosperous, possessing large means or property.

To 20 per cent of college seniors OPULENT incorrectly means TALKATIVE, chatty, garrulous, loquacious, fluent, ready in the use of words. The confusion between OPULENT, wealthy, affluent, and TALKATIVE, chatty, fluent, may be due to a confusion of AFFLUENT, rich, with FLUENT, talkative.

OPULENT, AFFLUENT, and WEALTHY, can be used almost interchangeably. WEALTHY is the general word for the possession of money. AFFLUENT, which comes from the Latin *affluere*, to flow towards, characterizes one with a large income. It suggests money coming in. It is often a more temporary state than WEALTHY. OPULENT suggests the enjoyment of wealth. It characterizes one who lives in the midst of abundant possessions. One who hoards his money cannot be OPULENT. The corresponding nouns are WEALTH, AFFLUENCE, and OPULENCE.

WEALTHY and POOR; AFFLUENT and BROKE; OPULENT and DESTITUTE; are opposites.

778. *PURLOIN* (*per-loin'*) *v.* To steal, appropriate, filch, pilfer, peculate, make off with.

In the test phrase: 'The PURLOINED letter', the word is

thought by 15 per cent of adult readers to mean FORGED, counterfeited, falsified, feigned, fabricated.

In the phrase: 'The PURLOINER of forty shillings', the noun is thought by 3 per cent of preparatory-school juniors to mean MAKER. This is probably a confusion of PURLOINER, a stealer of money, pilferer (376), with COINER, a maker of money, one who coins, mints, money. A PURLOINER is a thief, stealer, pilferer, one who makes away with something; and the verb, to PURLOIN, is to steal.

779. EFFUSION (ĕf-fū'-zhŭn) n. Unrestrained utterance, outpouring, gushing writing, outpour of thought in writing or speech, literary effort.

EFFUSION is from the Latin *ex*, out, forth; and *fundere*, to pour; and means literally a pouring forth. The Latin verb *fundere*, to flow, appears in a number of English words. A CONFUSION, a disorder, jumble, turmoil, is by derivation a flowing together; a DIFFUSION, spread, dispersion, is a flowing apart; a TRANSFUSION, transference, is a flowing across.

To 15 per cent of adult readers EFFUSION incorrectly means DREAM. This may be due to the similarity of EFFUSION, unrestrained utterance, and ILLUSION, an unreal vision.

To another 14 per cent, EFFUSION incorrectly means FOOLISH AMBITION. This misconception is perhaps due to the word FOOLISH, for an EFFUSION, in speech or writing, is extravagant, often foolish; but the word EFFUSION means literally a gushing forth. The adjective, EFFUSIVE, gushing, is perhaps better known.

780. ESCHEW (ĕs-chū') v. To shun, avoid, refuse, reject, evade, abstain from, stand aloof from.

To ESCHEW and to SHY are from the same ultimate source. SHY, in this sense, is always intransitive. Thus: 'A horse SHIES at a post', recoils from it, shrinks back. He cannot, however, SHY the post. ESCHEW has the transitive meaning of shun, avoid; but is used largely of human beings and of such intangibles as conduct.

To ESCHEW and to SHUN differ slightly in implication. An obsolete meaning of SHUN is abhor, detest, shrink from; and SHUN has the suggestion of avoiding because of abhorrence.

ESCHEW, which is related to German words meaning afraid, frighten, suggests avoiding through fear, through shyness. One ESCHEWS a task which is too big for one; one ESCHEWS responsibility which one hesitates to assume.

To 27 per cent of college seniors ESCHEW incorrectly means COVET, to long for, desire, wish to possess, an opposite of ESCHEW.

To another 10 per cent ESCHEW incorrectly means ANNEX. To ANNEX land is to take possession of it, and in this sense to ANNEX is an opposite of to ESCHEW.

In the test phrase: 'ESCHEW such conduct', the word is thought by 7 per cent of adult readers to mean ENCOURAGE, foster, promote, in suggestion another opposite of ESCHEW.

781. *CONTRAVENE* (kŏn-tră-vēn') v. To oppose in principle, obstruct in operation, contradict, conflict with. When used in such a phrase as: 'To CONTRAVENE the law', the word may mean to infringe upon, violate, transgress.

To 13 per cent of college seniors CONTRAVENE incorrectly means to SUBORDINATE, to consider of less value, place in a lower rank, make of less importance.

To another 10 per cent, to CONTRAVENE incorrectly means to ARBITRATE, to settle a dispute, mediate. This may perhaps come from some confusion of CONTRAVENE, obstruct, with INTERVENE, to come between, interpose; for one who ARBITRATES a dispute comes between the disputants.

CONTRAVENE, and the corresponding noun, CONTRAVENTION, opposition, contradiction, come from two Latin words *contra*, against; and *venire*, to come. To CONTRAVENE is, by derivation, to come up against. The Latin verb *venire* is the source also of INTERVENE, to come between; and CONVENE, to come together, meet, assemble.

To CONTRAVENE and to CONTROVERT are often defined in identical terms but differ slightly. To CONTROVERT is to oppose by argument, contend against in discussion, attempt to disprove in words. To CONTRAVENE is to come into actual conflict with, impede the operation of, oppose in action, not merely in words.

Only one word, CONTROVERSY, discussion; and its near relations, CONTROVERSIAL, open to discussion; and CONTROVERT; are

spelt with o, CONTRO. All others are spelt with A, as: CONTRA-
BAND (216); CONTRADICT, by derivation to say against; and
CONTRAVENE.

782. *SEETHE* (*sēth*) *v.* This verb is usually intransitive, and
means to boil, be agitated by heat, bubble, be in a state
of ebullition as the result of heat, literal or figurative. Thus,
a liquid may SEETHE; or a nation may SEETHE with discontent
because of internal friction.

In the test phrase: 'The water SEETHES', the word is thought
by 14 per cent of adult readers to mean FLOWS RAPIDLY; and
by another 8 per cent to mean TUMBLES, the two popular
misconceptions. A rapidly flowing river, striking an obstacle,
does not SEETHE; nor does a tumbling waterfall.

There are words for this bubbling action due to causes
other than heat. One is the unusual noun EBULLITION, which
has no verb in good standing. EBULLITION is the same agitated
state, which may or may not be caused by heat. A torrent
which bubbles is, if one wishes to be perfectly correct, in
a state of EBULLITION.

To EFFERVESCE is another verb for this same bubbling action. It is to be in a state of natural EBULLITION, bubbling.
EFFERVESCENCE, the noun, the act of bubbling, is never the
result of heat, as: 'The EFFERVESCENCE of new wine'. To
EFFERVESCE and to FERMENT are similar; except that to FER-
MENT is to decompose by bubbling invisibly, so slowly that
the bubbles are not apparent; to EFFERVESCE is to bubble
visibly.

The verb to SEETHE is also used occasionally in a transitive
sense, to boil, cook by boiling, as: 'To SEETHE food', to
prepare food by boiling. In this sense, the word is related
to DECOCT, which means to boil down or to extract the essence of a thing by boiling. A DECOCTION is the liquid in
which something has been boiled and which has become
impregnated with its essence.

SEETHE is derived from words all of which are connected
with the idea of burning. It is related to Icelandic and
Danish words meaning to burn, singe; to a Gothic word
meaning burnt offering; and to the Anglo-Saxon word for
smoke. SEETHING, correctly used, must be caused by heat.

783. *NEFARIOUS* (nē-fā'-rĭ-ŭs) *adj.* Wicked, heinous, execrable, abominable, flagitious.

Seven words for extreme wickedness are: HORRIBLE, shocking, exciting horror, mental agitation, shrinking; ABOMINABLE, loathsome, object of religious detestation; VILLAINOUS, capable of great crimes; ENORMOUS, sometimes used to mean wicked beyond common measure; FLAGITIOUS (flă-jĭ'-shŭs), grossly wicked, vile, proceeding from burning desire, lust; EXECRABLE, utterly hateful, worthy of being cursed; NEFARIOUS, unspeakably wicked, impious (ĭm'-pĭ-ŭs, not ĭm-pĭ'-ŭs).

In the test phrase: 'A NEFARIOUS crime', the word is thought by 23 per cent of adult readers to mean NOTORIOUS, publicly known usually to disadvantage, not favorably known. NEFARIOUS and NOTORIOUS may both apply to the disagreeable. NOTORIOUS means known to deserve an ill name; the emphasis is on the publicity rather than on the ill name. NEFARIOUS designates the inherent wickedness of the person; but the word does not suggest that this wickedness is publicly recognized.

784. *BEGUILE* (bē-gīl') *v.* To cause time to pass by easily, deceive, delude, tempt, mislead, while away, divert, amuse, charm, entertain.

The word GUILE means trickery, deceit, craft, cunning, a disposition to cheat. The verb, to GUILE, to deceive, is now obsolete; it has been replaced by BEGUILE. To BEGUILE fundamentally means to delude, deceive. It has come, however, to be used in the phrase: 'BEGUILE the time' to mean while away the time. Even when thus used it has the idea of cheating time by making it pass quickly and unnoticed. From this, to BEGUILE has come to mean to charm, divert, amuse, in such a manner as to make time pass quickly.

785. *IMPUTE* (ĭm-pūt') *v.* To ascribe, attribute, charge, refer, assign, set down.

The corresponding noun IMPUTATION (ĭm-pū-tā'-shŭn) means insinuation, charge of evil, censure, reproach.

The verb to IMPUTE and the noun IMPUTATION come directly from the Latin verb *imputare*, a word used in the conduct of business to mean charge to the account of, assign to, ascribe to. The Latin *imputare*, in turn, comes from an earlier word, *putare*, which meant to clean, clear, a word originally from the Sanscrit root *pu*, clean. The transformation from the original meaning, clean, to the derived meaning, charge to the account of, is circuitous. The Latin *putare*, with its original meaning, to clean, was combined with *rationes*, an account, and used in the Latin phrase: '*Putare rationes*', to mean literally clean up an account, settle an account. As so often happens even today, the two-word phrase was, in time, shortened, without losing its meaning, to the one word, *putare*. Thus, *putare*, to clean, came to mean to clean up an account, settle an account; thence came *imputare*, charge to the account of, enter in the account of, assign to; and from this comes the English verb, to IMPUTE, to charge to the account of, but which is now used almost always in the figurative sense of ascribe to, attribute to.

All English words from the Latin *putare* came after it had been adopted by the business world, after it had ceased to mean to clean and had come to mean clean up an account; as for instance to COMPUTE which means to reckon, figure up an amount.

The English words which come more or less directly from the Sanscrit root *pu* all have the fundamental meaning clean. Thus: PURE means clean; a PURITAN is, by derivation, one who is morally clean; the verb, to PURGE, means to clean, cleanse; and to EXPURGATE, by derivation, means to clean, but the word is often used with reference to books to mean to make pure by removing the objectionable parts.

In the test phrase: 'Do not IMPUTE faults to him', the word is thought by 23 per cent of adult readers to mean REVEAL, disclose, divulge, make known, expose, by far the most common misconception. By another 7 per cent, it is thought to mean IMPUGN, gainsay, call in question, challenge in words, attack in argument, question the truth of.

In the test phrase: 'No IMPUTATION on him', the noun is thought by 6 per cent of preparatory-school juniors to mean HARPING, a word which in this phrase probably means talking about tediously, dwelling on monotonously.

IMPUTE, ASCRIBE, and ATTRIBUTE, all mean to assign a

quality to something or someone. To ATTRIBUTE may refer to either good or bad qualities; and the word often implies judgment on the part of the one who does the attributing. Thus: 'One ATTRIBUTES his success to his work' is the expression of an opinion. To ASCRIBE refers usually to good qualities, and seldom to bad ones; and the word implies knowledge, rather than judgment or prejudice, as: 'One ASCRIBES a certain quotation to an author'. To IMPUTE refers only to bad qualities; and the word usually implies moral responsibility.

786. *PERNICIOUS (per-nĭsh'-ŭs) adj.* Destructive, injurious, hurtful, harmful, ruinous, destroying, noxious, deadly, baneful (857), deleterious (866).

PERNICIOUS comes from the Latin *per*, which intensifies the meaning; and *necare*, to kill, from the same source as NECROLOGY, a list of persons who have died during the previous year or during any specified interval.

In the test phrase: 'PERNICIOUS tendencies', the word is thought by 21 per cent of preparatory-school juniors to mean MYSTERIOUS, unexplained, incomprehensible.

PERNICIOUS and DESTRUCTIVE are synonymous. DESTRUCTIVE, which comes from the Latin *de*, down; and *struere*, to build; means by derivation building down, pulling down, demolishing. It is an opposite of CONSTRUCTIVE, and is applied most frequently, although not always, to that which affects physical things, as: 'A DESTRUCTIVE wind', 'A DESTRUCTIVE earthquake'. PERNICIOUS, by derivation deadly, is used more frequently of that which affects the intangible, as: 'A PERNICIOUS influence'.

787. *INCARCERATE (ĭn-kahr'-sĕ-rāt) v.* To jail, imprison, shut up, confine, immure, immew, detain in custody.

To 14 per cent of college seniors INCARCERATE incorrectly means to THRASH, whip. The three words, CASTIGATE, LACERATE, and INCARCERATE, all mean to inflict suffering and are apt to be confused. CASTIGATE is from the Latin *castus*, pure, the source of the English word CHASTE (789), pure, unsullied; and *agere*, to make. To CASTIGATE is by derivation to punish in order to purify; but the word is often used to mean punish by whipping. LACERATE (lăs'-ĕ-rāt) is from the Latin *lacer*, torn to pieces, mangled. To LACERATE is to tear, rend, and is often used figuratively as in the phrase: 'LACERATE one's feelings'. INCARCERATE is from the Latin *in*; and *carcer*, a prison; and is literally to imprison.

788. *QUIESCENT* (kwī-ĕs'-ĕnt, not kwĭ-ĕs'-ĕnt) *adj.* Inactive, dormant, inert, passive, resting, tranquil, serene, placid, still, calm.

QUIESCENT is from the same source as ACQUIESCENT (ăk-kwĭ-ĕs'-ĕnt), unresisting, submissive, a word which by derivation means disposed to come to rest. ACQUIESCENT, QUIESCENT, and QUIET, are all from the Latin *quiescere*, to keep quiet.

In the test phrase: 'The QUIESCENT crowd', the word is thought by 14 per cent of adult readers to mean REVERENT. REVERENT is from the Latin *vereri*, to be afraid; and means awestruck, humble, respectful. One of the outward manifestations of REVERENCE, awe, is a quiescent, quiet, attitude; but QUIESCENT means quiet, inactive, for any reason, not necessarily as the result of fear, reverence, awe.

By another 7 per cent of adult readers, QUIESCENT is thought to mean NOISY, an exact opposite of QUIESCENT in one of its uses; for QUIESCENT may be applied to a letter which is not sounded in a word and may mean silent, mute. QUIESCENT, when applied to a person, means quiet, not only in the sense of silent, but also motionless, inactive, and usually also at rest mentally.

789. *CHASTE* (chāst) *adj.* Pure, virtuous, modest, simple, clean, immaculate (386), continent.

In the test phrase: 'A noble and CHASTE fashion', the word is thought by 21 per cent of preparatory-school juniors to mean EXTRAVAGANT, needlessly lavish, excessive in expenditure. This may be remotely due to a confusion of CHASTE, pure, with CHASED, pronounced the same but a word which means decorated and is applied most frequently to metal which has been decorated with lines cut into the surface. A confusion of this same nature occurs with the more familiar noun CHASTITY (385), purity, which is thought by 7 per cent of adult readers to mean EMBELLISHMENT, ornamentation, decoration, elaboration. The verb, to CHASE, to engrave, decorate by engraving, is from the Latin *capsa*, chest; while the adjective, CHASTE, is from the Latin *castus*, pure, and means pure, clean, free from defilement.

790. *RECTITUDE* (*rĕk'-tĭ-tūd*) *n.* Righteousness, moral uprightness, goodness, honesty, integrity (704), probity. RECTITUDE is from the same Latin word, *rectus*, straight, as are the English words, RECTIFY, to straighten, make straight, make right; and ERECT, upright.

RECTITUDE is misinterpreted by 50 per cent of adult readers. In the test phrase: 'Commendable RECTITUDE', it is thought by 12 per cent to mean PROMPTNESS. PROMPTNESS, which comes from a Latin word *promere*, to produce, bring forth, means readiness of action, quickness of decision, alacrity. The word is used colloquially today to mean arriving at the right time; and it may be this suggestion of rightness which leads to the connection in so many minds between PROMPTNESS, quickness of decision, readiness, and RECTITUDE, righteousness, honesty.

By another 12 per cent RECTITUDE is thought to mean PREACHING. The connection is perhaps through the word RECTOR, a clergyman in charge of a parish. RECTOR and RECTITUDE come probably from the same original Sanscrit source, or at least from two closely related Sanscrit roots; but even in Latin they were separate words. RECTOR is from *rectus*, the past participle of the verb *regere*, to rule. A RECTOR is by derivation a ruler. RECTITUDE is from the Latin adjective *rectus*, straight, direct, right.

The words RECTITUDE and UPRIGHTNESS, the first from Latin, the second from Anglo-Saxon, have similar meanings. UPRIGHTNESS, because of its native origin, is stronger, more direct, than RECTITUDE, which sometimes suggests a quality not quite sincere.

791. *ELEGIACAL* (*ĕl-ē-jī'-ă-kal*) *adj.* Plaintive, mournful, sad, doleful, dolorous, lamentable (*lăm'-ĕn-tă-bl*), pertaining to a funeral song, of the nature of an elegy.

To 14 per cent of college seniors ELEGIACAL incorrectly means ELEGANT, polished, refined, having good taste. An

ELEGY is a lament, dirge (603), song of lamentation, especially for the dead. ELEGIACAL is the adjective.

792. *AMELIORATE* (*ă-mēl'-yō-rāt*) *v.* To better, improve, rectify, correct, reform, amend, mitigate, meliorate. AMELIORATE and MELIORATE are synonymous. With most such pairs, the word without the A is a later and abbreviated form. In this case, MELIORATE is the older word; and AMELIORATE, by derivation, to meliorate, is more recent, of eighteenth century origin.

AMELIORATE and ALLEVIATE (575) are practically synonymous but are used in different contexts and are difficult to keep sharply differentiated. ALLEVIATE is from the Latin *levis*, light, from the same source as the English word LEVITY, light humor; ELEVATE, to lift, raise; and ELEVATOR, a lift. Wherever the word LIGHTEN can be substituted, ALLEVIATE is correct. Thus, suffering can be LIGHTENED and can therefore be ALLEVIATED. Conditions cannot be LIGHTENED or ALLEVIATED. AMELIORATE comes from the Latin *melior*, better. Wherever the word BETTER can be substituted AMELIORATE is correct. Conditions can be BETTERED, and can therefore be AMELIORATED; but suffering cannot.

793. *JOCUND* (*jŏk'-ŭnd*) *adj.* Jovial, jolly, merry, blithe, sprightly, lively, sportive, gleeful, mirthful, gay, frolicky, rollicking, full of fun.
To 20 per cent of adult readers JOCUND incorrectly means MUSCULAR, brawny, powerful, strong, possibly a confusion of JOCULAR, joking, with MUSCULAR. JOCUND, JOCULAR, and JOCOSE, are discussed under JOCOSE (794).

794. *JOCOSE* (*jō-kōs'*) *adj.* Given to joking and jesting, jocular, waggish, humorous, witty, droll, facetious, of the nature of a joke or jest.
JOCOSE and JOCULAR are practically synonymous. JOCOSE may however be used disparagingly; while JOCULAR, from the Latin *joculus*, a diminutive of *jocus*, joke, the source of JOCOSE, has a pleasanter, more playful connotation. Both words apply to joking and jesting and differ in this respect from JOCUND (793) which comes from the Latin *jocundus*,

pleasant. JOCUND has no suggestion of joking, but means gay, merry, sprightly, lively.

In the test phrase: 'She was unusually JOCOSE', TALKATIVE is the popular misconception. This may be a confusion of JOCOSE, waggish, with VERBOSE (797), wordy; or it may be due to the fact that TALKATIVE is not far from the correct meaning of JOCOSE. One cannot be JOCOSE without talking; but one may be fond of talking, of chattering, without ever joking or jesting.

795. *CANDOR* (*kăn'-dor*) *n.* Frankness, candidness, sincerity, freedom from affectation, naïveté (*nah-ēv-tā'*), ingenuousness, bluntness, outspokenness.

CANDOR and the corresponding adjective CANDID, frank, open, sincere, come from the Latin *candere*, to be bright. While CANDID (272), the adjective, is a familiar word unknown to only 9 per cent of adult readers, CANDOR, the noun, is unknown to 50 per cent.

In the test phrase: 'He spoke with CANDOR', the word is thought by 17 per cent of adult readers to mean FERVOR, zeal, ardor, enthusiasm, warmth, earnestness.

CANDOR and GUILE are opposites.

796. *TOKEN* (*tō'-kĕn*) *n.* Symbol, sign, mark, evidence, guarantee, souvenir, memento, keepsake, pledge, indication of love or friendship.

The word TOKEN may be used in almost a dozen different ways. It may mean a symbol, something which represents something else, as: 'A TOKEN of kindness'. It may be used more concretely to mean a keepsake, souvenir. Or it may be used commercially for a small piece of metal which stands for a coin, has the appearance of a coin, but is of little intrinsic value.

This last use of the word TOKEN goes back at least to Queen Elizabeth. There are several historic TOKENS. The HARRINGTON TOKEN had the value of a farthing, was issued by Lord Harrington in England in 1613, and was used during the reigns of JAMES I and CHARLES I. It is often abbreviated to the single word HARRINGTON. Other TOKENS were the SEVENTEENTH-CENTURY TOKEN; the EIGHTEENTH-CEN-

TURY TOKEN; the BANK TOKEN; and the TAVERN-TOKEN. In more recent times TOKENS have been issued by many street railway lines for trolley-car fares.

Despite this commercial use the word TOKEN, because of its Anglo-Saxon origin, has retained a homely significance and is perhaps most frequently used to mean a sign of friendship, symbol of affection.

797. *VERBOSE* (*ver-bōs'*) *adj.* Wordy, prolix (906), pleo-
nastic (1053), redundant, tautological, abounding in words, tedious by reason of multiplicity of words.

In the test phrase: 'Her speech was VERBOSE', FLOWERY, ornate, overwrought, enriched with highly elaborate expressions, adorned with figurative language, is the most popular misconception.

VERBOSE comes from the Latin *verbum*, word, from the same source as the English word VERB, that part of speech which expresses action.

VERBOSE refers to wordy writings just as GARRULOUS, talkative, refers to trivial conversation. VERBOSE is a contemptu-
ous word and differs from REDUNDANT, which has the same meaning but is without the implication of contempt.

798. *TACITURNITY* (*tăs-ĭ-ter'-nĭ-tĭ*) *n.* A disinclination to
talk, reserve, reticence, uncommunicativeness, habitual silence.

TACITURNITY comes from the Latin *tacere*, to be silent; it is from the same source as the adjective TACIT (982), silent, understood but not spoken.

To 12 per cent of adult readers TACITURNITY incorrectly means MELANCHOLY, despondency, depression, sadness.

To another 10 per cent TACITURNITY, disinclination to talk, means GARRULITY (750), an inclination to talk much and idly about trivial things, an exact opposite of the correct meaning.

799. *INGRESS* (*ĭn'-grĕs*) *n.* Entrance, entry, access, liberty
of access, right of entrance; the word INGRESS may be used either for the act of entering or for the place of entrance.

INGRESS comes from the Latin *in*, in; and *gressus*, the past participle of the verb *gradi*, to walk, the source of the English verbs: to PROGRESS, to go forward; to REGRESS, to go backward; and to TRANSGRESS, to go across.

In the test phrase: 'No means of INGRESS', the word is thought by 17 per cent of adult readers to mean ATONEMENT, reparation, giving an equivalent in return for an injury, compensation, expiation for sin. This may be due to some confusion of INGRESS, entrance, with TRANSGRESS, a word which is often used figuratively to mean overstep a rule, violate a law, sin.

To another 15 per cent INGRESS incorrectly means REVENGE, retaliation.

INGRESS and EGRESS are opposites.

800. *CHAMP* (*chămp*) *v.* To munch, chew noisily, crunch, bite into small pieces impatiently, bite repeatedly.

When the phrase: 'To CHAMP at the bit' is so familiar, it is strange that the meaning of CHAMP should be unknown to so large a percentage of preparatory-school juniors. In the test phrase: 'CHAMPING the fragments', the word is thought by 12 per cent to mean LICKING, lapping; by another 8 per cent to mean COLLECTING, gathering together, perhaps because of some association with the word STAMP; and by still another 8 per cent to mean TREADING UPON, stepping on, perhaps because of the word TRAMP.

The origin of CHAMP is uncertain. It is perhaps from a Scandinavian word meaning to chew with difficulty.

801. *PROGNOSTICATE* (*prŏg-nŏs'-tĭ-kāt*) *v.* To predict, foretell, foreshadow, prophesy, tell beforehand by means of signs or symptoms, make a prognosis (708).

To 16 per cent of college seniors PROGNOSTICATE incorrectly means to PROLONG, drag out, continue, lengthen the duration of. This may be due to a confusion of PROGNOSTICATE, to predict, foretell, with PROCRASTINATE, to put off, leave undone as long as possible.

To another 14 per cent, PROGNOSTICATE incorrectly means to CAUSE, to produce, bring about. This is perhaps a confusion of PROGNOSTICATE with PRECIPITATE which may mean to hasten, cause to happen in advance.

There are two unusual English words of Greek origin, GNOSIS (*nō'-sĭs*), which means knowledge, science, mystical wisdom; and the adjective, GNOSTIC (*nŏs'-tĭk*), pertaining to knowledge. From them come a number of more common words. An AGNOSTIC, which starts with the Greek privative *a*, by derivation one who does not know, is today one who believes that mankind does not know the ultimate nature of things, one who neither believes nor disbelieves in God. A DIAGNOSIS is by derivation a thorough knowledge; a PROGNOSIS, a preknowledge, a foreknowledge.

To PROGNOSTICATE, to PREDICT, and to PROPHESY, are all to foretell important future events in different ways. One PROPHESIES on pure inspiration. One PREDICTS on the basis of vague and uncertain facts and some ability to interpret them. One can PROGNOSTICATE only by sound reasoning based on known facts.

802. *GRUELLING* (*groo'-ĕl-lĭng*) *n.* Punishment in the sense of belaboring, mauling, severe handling; defeat, especially in an athletic contest. The verb, to GRUEL, in a transitive use, means to punish, exhaust, use up, disable.
Both the verb, to GRUEL, and the noun, a GRUELLING, have been marked by most dictionaries as slang. Both words are, however, making their way into accepted English.

803. *RIMOSE* (*rī-mōs'*) *adj.* Chinky, creviced, fissured, cracked, cleft like the bark of a tree, full of rimes.
To 16 per cent of adult readers RIMOSE incorrectly means FROSTED. This confusion is probably due to the dual meaning of the noun RIME. RIME, derived from Icelandic, through Anglo-Saxon, means hoarfrost, white frost, the coating of tiny crystals which forms on a window pane in the winter. The corresponding adjective is RIMY, frosty, frosted, covered with hoarfrost. RIME, derived from the Latin *rima*, means crack, chink, fissure. The adjective is RIMOSE, fissured.
RIMOSE and SMOOTH are practically opposites.

804. *NATTY* (*năt'-tĭ*) *adj.* Neatly trim, spruce, smart, dapper. NATTY is probably a diminutive of NEAT and is usually marked as colloquial.

In the test phrase: 'A NATTY coat', the word is thought by 14 per cent of adult readers to mean CONSPICUOUS, showy. The words NEAT and NATTY both suggest the absence of anything superfluous as in the phrase: 'A NEAT stroke'. CONSPICUOUS is therefore in suggestion almost an opposite of NATTY, neat, trim.

By another 14 per cent of adult readers NATTY is thought to mean MUCH WORN. A WORN coat might be neat, clean, but could hardly be NATTY for this word suggests spruceness, smartness, in addition to neatness.

There is a list of words: CLEAN, ORDERLY, TIDY, PRIM, SPRUCE, TRIM, and DAPPER, which differ slightly in shades of meaning. The first three are simple words with no sophisticated implications. PRIM is consciously formal and a bit stiff. SPRUCE is more dandified. Both PRIM and SPRUCE are used somewhat contemptuously, the former of women, the latter of men. TRIM is attractively neat. DAPPER and NATTY are flattering, and usually applied to small persons.

805. *ANTITHESIS* (*ăn-tĭth'-ĕ-sĭs*) *n.* A contrast, the direct contrary, opposition of words, a figure of speech in which contrasted words oppose one another.

In the test phrase: 'A marked ANTITHESIS', the word is thought by 13 per cent of adult readers to mean DISLIKE, the popular misconception. This is probably a confusion of ANTITHESIS, contrast, with ANTIPATHY, dislike.

ANTITHESIS is from the Latin *anti*, against, opposite; and the word THESIS. *Anti* often appears as a prefix. Thus, an ANTIDOTE is a medicine which counteracts or acts against a poison; an ANTIPATHY is a dislike, a feeling against something; and ANTISEPTIC is counteracting, acting against decay or putrefaction.

Anti, against, should not be confused with the similar Latin prefix *ante*, before, which appears in ANTEROOM, a room entered before another, or used as an entrance to another; in ANTEDILUVIAN, before the flood; in ANTECEDENT, someone who precedes another or something which happens before something else; and ANTEMERIDIAN, before noon.

A THESIS, the second part of the word ANTITHESIS, is a proposition one is prepared to uphold. A THESIS and a THEME differ slightly. A THEME is a subject on which one writes or converses without taking sides. A written THEME, a school exercise, may discuss any subject. A THESIS, on the other hand, takes a definite stand. A written THESIS, such as is required for an advanced academic degree, should uphold a specified point of view.

The words ANTITHESIS and CONTRAST are synonymous but differ in use. A CONTRAST refers to the balancing of two things against one another, as: 'The CONTRAST of virtue and vice'. ANTITHESIS, properly used, refers to the setting of one against the other, as: 'Virtue is the ANTITHESIS of vice'.

806. *CARRION* (kăr'-rĭ-ŏn) *n.* Dead putrefying flesh, decaying animal carcass, garbage, offal (865).

In the test phrase: 'In search of other CARRION', the word is thought by 21 per cent of preparatory-school juniors to mean VICTIMS, a word which originally meant a living being, usually a beast, sacrificed in a religious ceremony, but which is now used in a more general sense to mean any person or thing injured or destroyed.

CARRION comes from the Latin *caro*, flesh; from the same source as CARNIVOROUS, flesh eating; and CARNAL, pertaining to flesh, bodily. CARRION is literally dead flesh.

807. *INCUMBENT* (ĭn-kŭm'-bĕnt) *adj.* Obligatory, morally binding, resting upon one as a duty. INCUMBENT is also used as a noun in such a phrase as: 'They welcomed the INCUMBENT', to mean an officeholder.

INCUMBENT comes from the Latin verb *cubare*, to lie, the source of the English word RECUMBENT, lying down, reclining, a word which retains the original Latin meaning.

The verb, to ENCUMBER, which may also be spelt INCUMBER, means to burden, overload, obstruct, perplex, embarrass, weigh down. The noun, an ENCUMBRANCE, or an INCUMBRANCE, may also mean a burden, clog, impediment, obstruction, embarrassment. The adjective, INCUMBENT, can be spelt only IN, not EN, and by derivation means lying upon, resting upon, but is often used figuratively to mean pressing upon one as a duty, resting upon one as an obligation, obligatory, as in the phrase: 'He felt it INCUMBENT upon him'.

808. *MUGGY* (*mŭg′-gĭ*) *adj.* Moist, damp, close, warm and humid (75), sultry (335), oppressive. The word MUGGY may be used of hay or straw to mean moldy.

MUGGY is of Scandinavian origin, and is related to words used for fog and drizzle. To 27 per cent of adult readers it incorrectly means ILL-SMELLING. This may be a confusion of MUGGY with MUSTY (222), sour, stale, foul, fetid. MUGGY means moist, damp.

MUGGY and SULTRY are practically synonymous. Both mean at the same time hot and damp. SULTRY emphasizes the heat. MUGGY emphasizes the moisture.

809. *CHICANERY* (*shĭ-kā′-nĕ-rĭ*) *n.* Trickery, quibbling, stratagem, caviling, sharp practice, using unfair means in a contest or discussion.

To 12 per cent of college seniors CHICANERY incorrectly means BUFFOONERY, low jests, ridiculous pranks, vulgar tricks. Both BUFFOONERY and CHICANERY are a kind of trickery. BUFFOONERY is physical; it is the practice of ridiculous tricks with the idea of being amusing. CHICANERY is mental trickery with the idea of deceiving by mean, unfair, artifice.

810. *AUTONOMOUS* (*aw-tŏn′-ō-mŭs*) *adj.* Self-governing, independent in government. AUTONOMOUS may also be used of an individual acting of his own free will and of an organism subject to its own laws.

AUTONOMOUS is a combination of AUTO, self, from the Greek αὐτός, self; and the Greek word νέμειν, to govern, hold sway. AUTO is found in other English words. An AUTOGRAPH, by derivation self-writing, is one's own signature; an AUTO-CRAT, by derivation self-strength, is an undisputed ruler; an AUTOPSY (584), by derivation self-seeing, seeing with one's own eyes, is now a post-mortem examination.

In the test phrase: 'An AUTONOMOUS people', the word is thought by 19 per cent of adult readers to mean MECHANI-CAL, the popular misconception. This is probably due to the word AUTOMOBILE, and to the knowledge that it is mechanical. MECHANICAL is the adjective which corresponds to the noun, MACHINE, a device, contrivance. There is nothing in either of the words MECHANICAL or MACHINE which suggests self-acting or self-propelling. The word AUTOMOBILE comes from AUTO, self; and by derivation means self-moving. AUTONOMOUS is an adjective and means self-governing.

811. ENGENDER (ĕn-jĕn'-der) v. To give rise to, produce, cause, bring forth, excite, create, stir up, occasion.

In the test phrase: 'A mass so ENGENDERED', the word is thought by 18 per cent of preparatory-school juniors to mean ODOROUS, fragrant, perfumed.

ENGENDER is from the Latin in; and generare, to beget, produce, a word which, in turn, comes from genus, family, kind, race. From the same source comes the English verb, to GENERATE, to produce, cause, give origin to. To ENGENDER and to GENERATE are almost synonymous. To GENERATE is used of physical forces, as: 'To GENERATE steam', 'To GENERATE power'. To ENGENDER is used of intangible forces, often of those which are destructive, as: 'To ENGENDER hatred', 'To ENGENDER strife'.

812. ARGOT (ahr-gō', or ahr'-gŏt) n. Slang, cant, jargon, lingo, flash, the peculiar phraseology of any class, language intended to conceal from the uninitiated the real import of what is said.

ARGOT is a French word, adopted by English with no change in spelling. The pronunciation (ahr-gō') follows the French; but the word is sometimes anglicized (ahr'-gŏt).

To 14 per cent of college seniors ARGOT incorrectly means a SWAGGER, insolent air, blustering strut, boastfulness, noisy bragging.

To another 13 per cent ARGOT incorrectly means PURSE. The word PURSE may be used for a sum of money offered as a prize. The confusion between ARGOT and PURSE may perhaps be caused by a confusion between the two French words argot, slang, and argent, silver, money.

ARGOT, CANT, and SLANG, all refer to a language peculiar to a group. SLANG, which perhaps comes from the Norse and by derivation suggests slinging insulting words, has departed from the original meaning, and is used most frequently today for the language peculiar to the young. It is often a picturesque rebellion against the bonds of conservative grammar. CANT, as the word is used in this connection, and ARGOT were both originally the language of thieves, rogues, and beggars. CANT is today used most often for religious phraseology. ARGOT is almost synonymous with SLANG, although it has kept more of its original unpleasant character.

813. *MIMETIC* (*mĭ-mĕt'-ĭk*) *adj.* Imitative (*ĭm'-ĭ-tā-tĭv*), given to mimicry, mocking, aping, shamming, copying the action of, simulating the real.

To 22 per cent of adult readers MIMETIC incorrectly means SICKENING. This is no doubt a confusion of MIMETIC, imitative, with EMETIC, causing vomiting.

MIMETIC comes from the Greek word μῖμος, an imitator, actor. A MIME (*mĭm*) is an actor who takes part in a farce portraying real characters. MIMETIC is the adjective.

814. *NICETY* (*nī'-sĭ-tĭ*) *n.* Precision, subtle quality, minute distinction, fastidiousness, delicacy of perception, daintiness, delicate management.

NICETY comes from the Latin *ne*, not; and *scire*, to know, the source of the English word, SCIENCE, knowledge. NICETY originally meant ignorance, foolishness, folly, a meaning now obsolete. From this it came to mean foolishness in regard to trivial things, squeamishness, fastidiousness, a meaning which is still in use. With this meaning it acquired for the first time a commendatory significance, and came to imply real discrimination, acuteness, another meaning still in use. From this developed the meaning of precision, exactness, accuracy, a meaning far from the original.

815. *MUNDANE* (*mŭn'-dān*, not *mŭn-dān'*) *adj.* Earthly, terrestrial. MUNDANE may also be used to mean worldly, secular, temporal, belonging to this world.

MUNDANE comes from the Latin *mundus*, world. To 15 per cent of college seniors MUNDANE incorrectly means LUNAR. LUNAR is pertaining to the moon, much as MUNDANE is pertaining to the earth.

MUNDANE, WORLDLY, TEMPORAL, and SECULAR, are similar in suggestion. TEMPORAL, from the Latin *tempus*, and SECULAR, from the Latin *saeculum*, age, generation, the source of the

French word *siècle*, century, both by derivation mean pertaining to time, to things which are not eternal, not of the spirit. SECULAR and ECCLESIASTICAL; TEMPORAL and SPIRITUAL; are opposites. MUNDANE means pertaining to the world.

816. BEATIFIC (*bē-ă-tĭf'-ĭk*) *adj.* Blissful, exaltedly happy, ecstatic, rapturous, bringing happiness, making blessed. BEATIFIC is from the Latin *beatus*, happy; and *facere*, to make; and means literally creating happiness.

To 18 per cent of adult readers BEATIFIC incorrectly means GENTLE, mild, soothing, soft, not rough, not rude. Even in the sense of soothing, which approaches nearest to BEATIFIC, GENTLE means quieting, comforting in a mild manner; BEATIFIC means producing great happiness, making exaltedly happy.

817. CAPITULATE (*kă-pĭt'-ū-lāt*) *v.* To surrender on stipulated (705) conditions, give up on stated terms, yield conditionally.

The Latin verb *capitulare* means to arrange in chapters, under headings. The Latin noun *capitulum* is a chapter; it is the diminutive of the word *caput*, head. In English, to CAPITULATE may mean to draw up in writing under chapter headings; but the word has come to be used almost exclusively to mean draw up an agreement. From this sense, it has come to mean surrender under conditions which have been agreed upon.

In the test phrase: 'The workers CAPITULATED', the word is thought by 19 per cent of preparatory-school juniors to mean RUSHED HEADLONG. This is perhaps because CAPITULATE comes from the Latin *caput*, head; or it may be due to some confusion of CAPITULATE, surrender, with the verb to CATAPULT, to hurl. The suggestion of the verb, to CAPITULATE, is almost the reverse of a headlong rush, for although CAPITULATE is to surrender, it is to do so under accurately prescribed conditions, agreed to in advance by all parties.

818. AFFRONT (*ăf-frŭnt'*) *v.* To treat with indignity, insult, displease, slight intentionally, offend openly by discourtesy. 'He AFFRONTED me.'

There was once a verb EFFRONT. It is now out of use but survives in the word EFFRONTERY, saucy boldness, impudence, shameless assurance, audacity. Although it is from the same source as AFFRONT, the two should not be confused. To face is the literal meaning of AFFRONT and is today an unusual but correct use of the word. An AFFRONT is a public indignity, an INSULT a private affair. AFFRONT, INSULT, INDIGNITY, OUTRAGE, PROVOCATION, IMPERTINENCE, OFFENCE, and RUDENESS, are all words for disrespect expressed openly and in a galling manner.

819. *AGHAST* (ă-găst') *adj.* Appalled, horrified, astounded, terrified, filled with dismay (408), struck with sudden fright. 'AGHAST at his expression.'
AGHAST is from an Anglo-Saxon word meaning to terrify. Although both GHASTLY, hideous, having a deathlike appearance; AGHAST; as well as GHOST, specter, apparition, disembodied spirit; and the corresponding adjective, GHOSTLY, spectral; are today always spelt with the H and are incorrect without it, there is no etymological reason for its use.
AGHAST, APPALLED, and DISMAYED, although similar in effect, differ in cause. DISMAY means by derivation rendered incapable. One may be DISMAYED by a bit of gossip, by a surprising occurrence, by anything which renders one momentarily speechless. APPALLED means by derivation turned pale. One may be APPALLED by a horrible sight. AGHAST means terrified.

820. *CHARLATANIC* (shahr-lă-tăn'-ĭk) *adj.* Pretending to a knowledge and skill not possessed, tricky, fraudulent, sham, swindling, dissembling, hypocritical.
A CHARLATAN (shahr'-lă-tăn) is an impostor, quack, mountebank.
CHARLATAN, although directly from the French word *charlatan*, quack, comes originally from an Italian word meaning to prate, talk foolishly. To 17 per cent of college seniors CHARLATANIC incorrectly means FIERY, impetuous, vehement, passionate.
A CHARLATAN, a MOUNTEBANK, and a QUACK, are all pretenders. A QUACK is an impostor who tries to sell remedies which he knows to be of no value. The word is a shortened

form of QUACKSALVER (*kwăk'-săl-ver*), one who sells SALVE (*sahv*), ointment, balm. A MOUNTEBANK, from an Italian word meaning to mount on a bench, may be a quack or a charlatan, or even a juggler. He differs from the others in being noisier and more demonstrative, proclaiming his wares loudly in public, often literally from a bench. A CHARLATAN is one who has nothing to offer except his own pretence to a skill and knowledge which he does not possess. He is the most self-assured of the three.

821. *INSCRUTABLE* (*in-skroo'-tă-bl*) *adj.* Mysterious, impenetrable (253), incomprehensible, cryptic, occult, recondite, abstruse, incapable of being understood.

INSCRUTABLE is from the Latin *scrutari*, to search, the source of the English word SCRUTINY. SCRUTINY is critical inquiry, minute examination, close investigation; and that which is INSCRUTABLE does not yield to such scrutiny.

INSCRUTABLE, MYSTIC, and MYSTERIOUS, all baffle the understanding. Both the MYSTERIOUS and the MYSTIC arouse one's curiosity, excite wonder, invite inquiry. The MYSTERIOUS is darkly silent. The MYSTIC may have a double meaning, signifies more than it shows. The INSCRUTABLE is more remote; it must be accepted as too baffling to be understood.

822. *CHIMERICAL* (*kĭ-měr'-ĭ-kal*, not *kĭ-měr'-ĭ-kal*) *adj.* Visionary, fantastic (401), merely imaginary, wildly conceived, that which has or can have no existence except in the imagination.

In the test phrase: 'CHIMERICAL projects', the word is thought by 19 per cent of adult readers to mean WEIGHTY, important, momentous, the popular misconception. This is perhaps due to some confusion between the proper names CHIMERA, the source of the adjective CHIMERICAL, and COLOSSUS. The CHIMERA (*kĭ-mē'-ră*), according to Greek mythology, was a fire-breathing monster, with the body of a lion, a goat's head in the middle of its back, and a snake for a tail. The COLOSSUS was a gigantic statue of Apollo erected at Rhodes about 280 B.C. The adjective, COLOSSAL (249), big, is from COLOSSUS; while CHIMERICAL comes from CHIMERA, and means as wildly conceived as was that animal.

823. *DEBAUCH* (*dē-bawch'*) v. To corrupt in morals, make disloyal, seduce from duty, pervert, deprave (826), lead into dishonest practices.
DEBAUCH is of French origin. In the test phrase: 'He DE-BAUCHED the voters', the word is thought by 29 per cent of adult readers to mean DECEIVED, misled. DECEIVE and DEBAUCH have the common element of dishonesty. To DECEIVE is to mislead by falsehood, but not necessarily to affect the morals of the person deceived. To DEBAUCH is to lead a person into dishonest practices, corrupt his principles.

824. *PENCHANT* (*pŏgn-shŏgn'*) n. Strong inclination, propensity (709), leaning, decided taste, aptitude, bias, bent, proclivity (952).
PENCHANT is a French word, which retains its French pronunciation. To 24 per cent of adult readers it incorrectly means DISLIKE, almost an opposite of the correct meaning.

825. *OSTENSIBLE* (*ŏs-tĕn'-sĭ-bl*) adj. Apparent, manifest, avowed, specious, professed, shown on the surface.
OSTENSIBLE is from the Latin *ob*; and *tendere*, to stretch.
In the test phrase: 'Pursuing his OSTENSIBLE calling', the word is thought by 24 per cent of preparatory-school juniors to mean SHOWY, gaudy. This is probably a confusion of OSTENSIBLE, apparent, with OSTENTATIOUS, a word from the same source, which means showy, gaudy, pretentious, fond of excessive display. Both words suggest stretching the truth, for although OSTENSIBLE means apparent, it has in it the suggestion of being not necessarily real.

826. *DEPRAVED* (*dē-prāvd'*) adj. Morally debased, lacking in principle, degenerate, debauched (823), perverted, corrupt.
DEPRAVED comes from the Latin *de*, thoroughly; and *pravus*, crooked, depraved, debased; and means thoroughly debased.

827. *PEREMPTORY* (*per-ĕmp'-tō-rĭ*) adj. Decisive, positive, dictatorial, imperious, arbitrary, assertive, dogmatic, overbearing, absolute.
In the test phrase: 'PEREMPTORY tones', the word is thought

by 14 per cent of adult readers to mean PERSUASIVE, convincing, winning, the most popular misconception and nearly an opposite of PEREMPTORY. To 11 per cent PEREMPTORY incorrectly means UNCERTAIN, even a closer opposite than PERSUASIVE. To another 11 per cent PEREMPTORY means ANGRY. PEREMPTORY is from the Latin *peremptus*, destroyed, extinguished, annihilated; and PEREMPTORY means decisive, not in the sense of angry or sharp, but in the sense of destroying further debate, annihilating further discussion, precluding further consideration.

828. *MATRICIDE* (*măt'-rĭ-sīd*) *n.* A mother killer; or the act of killing a mother.

To 17 per cent of adult readers MATRICIDE incorrectly means INSECT EXTERMINATOR. This is no doubt a confusion of MATRICIDE, mother killer, with INSECTICIDE, a poison for killing bugs, a word which comes from the same Latin word *caedere*, to kill.

A PARRICIDE, another word from the same source and unknown to the same percentage of adult readers, is a parent killer. To 17 per cent it incorrectly means VAGRANT, an idle wanderer, vagabond; and to another 16 per cent, BEGGAR, mendicant. These may both be due to a confusion of PARRICIDE, parent murderer, with PARASITE, a hanger-on. PARASITE is from the Greek παρά, beside; and σῖτος, food; and by derivation means one who lives at the table of another.

From the Latin *caedere*, to kill, come such English words as SUICIDE, the killing of one's self; HOMICIDE, the killing of a man; PATRICIDE, the killing of a father; and MATRICIDE, the killing of a mother.

829. *APOCRYPHAL* (*ă-pŏk'-rĭ-făl*) *adj.* Fictitious (212), doubtfully authentic, sham, spurious (683).

APOCRYPHAL comes from the Greek ἀπό away; and κρύπτειν, to hide. It is from the same source as the English word CRYPT (*krĭpt*), an underground vault. The word is thought by 26 per cent of preparatory-school juniors to mean MYSTERIOUS, secret, occult, obscure, enigmatical (*ē-nĭg-măt'-ĭ-kăl*). This is no doubt a confusion of APOCRYPHAL, spurious, with CRYPTIC, a word from the same Greek source, which has kept the original meaning hidden, secret.

APOCRYPHAL is an adjective from the noun APOCRYPHA. An APOCRYPHA is any writing of doubtful authenticity. Spelt with a capital APOCRYPHA refers to 14 books which do not appear in the Hebrew Bible but which occurred in the Septuagint (*sĕp'-tū-ă-jĭnt*) and Vulgate versions of the Old Testament. They are now usually omitted. APOCRYPHAL means of doubtful authenticity.

830. *TREPIDATION* (*trĕp-ĭ-dă'-shŭn*) *n.* Nervous alarm, perturbation, agitation, fear mingled with uncertainty. TREPIDATION is from the Latin *trepidus*, alarmed, anxious, shaken, from the same source as the more familiar word INTREPID (*ĭn-trĕp'-ĭd*), undaunted, free from alarm, courageous. TREPIDATION and TREMBLING are associated. TREMBLING is the outward, physical action. TREPIDATION is the state of mind which causes trembling.

831. *NEBULOUS* (*nĕb'-ū-lŭs*) *adj.* Misty, hazy, indistinct, cloudy, vague, diaphanous (1076), indefinite, formless. NEBULOUS is from the Latin *nebula*, a cloud, mist, vapor. To 16 per cent of adult readers it incorrectly means IMAGINARY, unreal, fancied, not real. NEBULOUS and IMAGINARY (440), when used figuratively with reference to thoughts, ideas, are difficult to separate sharply from one another. When used with reference to tangible objects they are, however, easily differentiated. Thus, an IMAGINARY cloud is one which does not exist; a NEBULOUS cloud exists but is hazy, misty, indistinct.

832. *FRIEZE* (*frēz*) *n.* Longitudinal decorated band, any decorative horizontal border often on a wall.
In architectural terminology, à FRIEZE is the middle division of an ENTABLATURE (*ĕn-tăb'-lă-tūr*). ENTABLATURE, from an Italian word for ceiling, is the upper part of a wall. An ENTABLATURE rests usually upon columns or pilasters, and consists of three parts: the ARCHITRAVE (*ahr'-kĭ-trāv*) which rests directly on the columns; the FRIEZE, middle division; and the CORNICE above. A FRIEZE, as thus defined, may be flat and plain, as in the Roman Tuscan order; ornamented, as in the

Greek Doric; or highly enriched with sculpture as in the Corinthian order.

833. *CLAVICLE* (*klăv'-ĭ-kl*) *n.* Collar bone, the bone between the SCAPULA, the shoulder bone, shoulder blade, and the STERNUM, the breast bone.
CLAVICLE comes ultimately from the Latin *clavis*, a key. To 18 per cent of adult readers it incorrectly means HIP BONE. In the human skeleton there are two CLAVICLES, one on each side. In birds the two are replaced by a single forked bone, the WISH BONE.

834. *OVERT* (*ō'-vert*) *adj.* Patent, openly done, unconcealed, obvious, apparent, clear, manifest, unobstructed, plain, evident, not covert.
OVERT is from the French *ouvert*, open, from the verb *ouvrir*, to open. By 22 per cent of adult readers OVERT is thought to mean UNLAWFUL, not legal. In legal phraseology 'An OVERT act' is one which can be proved clearly to have been committed and from which criminal intent can be inferred. Except in this particular phrase, the word OVERT means evident, plain, open, apparent, with no suggestion of unlawful or of criminal intent.
OVERT and COVERT are opposites.

835. *PROVISIONAL* (*prō-vĭzh'-ŏn-ăl*) *adj.* Tentative, temporary, provided for the occasion only, for present needs.
PROVISIONAL is from the Latin *pro*, before; and *videre*, to see. To 20 per cent of adult readers it incorrectly means EARLY. This may be due to some confusion of PROVISIONAL, temporary, with PREVIOUS, happening before, prior, preceding in time.
To another 11 per cent, PROVISIONAL, temporary, incorrectly means PERMANENT, fixed, lasting, an exact opposite of the correct meaning.

836. *EXPEDITIOUSLY* (*ĕks-pĕ-dĭsh'-ŭs-lĭ*) *adv.* Speedily, quickly, hastily, promptly, summarily, with dispatch.
The adverb, EXPEDITIOUSLY, and the adjective, EXPEDITIOUS, quick, nimble, speedy, are both formed from the verb, to

EXPEDITE (*ĕks'-pē-dīt*). This, in turn, comes from the Latin *ex*, out; and *pes, pedis*, foot; and means literally to free the feet from a snare, hence disengage, dispatch. EXPEDITE has practically this literal meaning in English today for it means to remove the impediments to the progress of, accelerate the progress of, and so to hasten, quicken. The noun, EXPEDITION, originally had the corresponding meaning, quickness, dispatch, haste, speed, promptness, and is still used in this way, as in the phrase: 'He moved with EXPEDITION'. From this it acquired the specialized, developed meaning, voyage, journey for a definite purpose.

In the test phrase: 'He EXPEDITIOUSLY hid his watch', the word is thought by 32 per cent of preparatory-school juniors to mean CAREFULLY, cautiously, attentively, watchfully, almost an opposite of EXPEDITIOUSLY, quickly.

Of the three adverbs which imply speed, EXPEDITIOUSLY, RAPIDLY, and QUICKLY, the first is applied exclusively to the progress made in the undertakings, enterprises, of intelligent beings. A mechanical contrivance, such as a tram, moves QUICKLY, RAPIDLY. An undertaking, an enterprise, moves EXPEDITIOUSLY, with celerity, with dispatch.

837. *FATUOUS* (*făt'-ū-ŭs*) *adj.* Foolish, vain, senseless, stupid, unconsciously silly, idiotic, imbecile (*ĭm'-bĕ-sĭl*), inane (1047), foolishly conceited.
In the test phrase: 'FATUOUS schemes', the word is thought by 17 per cent of adult readers to mean PERILOUS, risky, precarious, hazardous, dangerous. This is perhaps due to some confusion with the word FATE (*fāt*), doom, destiny, in one of its forms. Thus: FATAL (*fā'-tăl*) may mean deadly, disastrous; FATEFUL may mean charged with destructive possibilities; and the noun FATALITY is occasionally used to mean a dangerous, hazardous, perilous tendency. FATUOUS, foolish, is not connected with the word FATE, but comes from the Latin *fatuus* which, as an adjective, meant foolish, silly, and, as a noun, meant a professional fool, jester. From the same source come the noun FATUITY, silliness, unconscious foolishness, stupidity; and the unusual adjective FATUITOUS (*fă-tū'-ĭ-tŭs*), foolish, fatuous.
To another 15 per cent FATUOUS incorrectly means WELL-

CONSIDERED, well thought out, the exact opposite of the correct meaning, foolish.

838. *PEDANTIC* (*pĕ-dăn'-tĭc*) *adj.* Ostentatiously learned, full of misplaced erudition, using far-fetched words or expressions, characterized by learning without common sense. To 14 per cent of college seniors PEDANTIC incorrectly means IMPETUOUS, hasty, rash, impulsive, acting with sudden energy. To another 13 per cent PEDANTIC incorrectly means VERY ABLE. This is perhaps a confusion of PEDANTIC, pretentiously learned, with PEDAGOGIC (*pĕd-ă-gŏj'-ĭk*). A PEDAGOGUE (*pĕd'-ă-gŏg*), from the two Greek words, παῖς, παιδός, a boy; and ἄγειν, to lead, was originally the slave who led the boys to school. From this, the word came to mean a tutor; and is now used to mean a school teacher. PEDANTIC, which comes from the same original source but through the Italian, is used in an exaggerated sense of one who makes a display of his learning.

839. *SUNDER* (*sŭn'-der*) *v.* To part, sever (174), break, separate, dissolve, destroy the connection between; disunite in almost any manner as by rending, cutting, or breaking. SUNDER, and the corresponding adverb, ASUNDER, apart, are of Anglo-Saxon origin. In the test phrase: 'Do not SUNDER them', the word is thought by 23 per cent of adult readers to mean DESTROY. To SUNDER does not mean to tear down, demolish, bring to ruin, annihilate, exterminate, nullify, all of which are synonyms of DESTROY; but instead SUNDER means destroy the connection between.

840. *OBLIVION* (*ŏb-lĭv'-ĭ-ŏn*) *n.* State of being forgotten, permanently lost to memory. OBLIVION comes from the Latin *ob*, over; and probably *livere*, to grow dark, the source of the English word LIVID, black and blue, bluish, leaden in color.

In the test phrase: 'The OBLIVION of a prison', the word is thought by 32 per cent of preparatory-school juniors to mean DARKNESS. This may be because OBLIVION comes from the verb to grow dark; or it may be a confusion of OBLIVION with OBSCURITY. OBSCURITY comes from the Latin *ob*, over; and *scurus*, covered; and by derivation means covered over. The word can be used either in the literal sense, to mean darkness, dimness, dismalness, murkiness, gloominess; or, in the figurative sense, to mean the condition of being unknown to fame, unnoticed. In this last sense, OBSCURITY may be a temporary state. One who falls into OBSCURITY may be unknown for the moment only. The word OBLIVION can be used only in the figurative sense to mean the state or condition into which something falls when it has been forever forgotten.

841. *PERVIOUS* (*per'-vĭ-ŭs*) *adj.* Penetrable, permeable, passable, capable of being passed through.

PERVIOUS is from the Latin *per*, through; and *via, way*; from the same source as DEVIOUS, from the way, indirect, out of the straight line.

To 19 per cent of adult readers PERVIOUS incorrectly means HARD, almost an opposite of the correct meaning. This may be a confusion of PERVIOUS, penetrable, with its opposite IMPERVIOUS, impenetrable.

To another 10 per cent PERVIOUS incorrectly means EARLIER. This is obviously a confusion of PERVIOUS, penetrable, with PREVIOUS, earlier, before in time, from *pre*, before; and the same Latin *via*, way.

PERVIOUS and PASSABLE both mean capable of being penetrated. PASSABLE is used of the movements of a human being, as: 'A PASSABLE road'. The word PERVIOUS is used of inanimate things, as: 'A substance PERVIOUS to liquid'. PERVIOUS, and its opposite, IMPERVIOUS, are used also of human beings in a figurative sense, as: 'He is IMPERVIOUS to reason', meaning that reasoning cannot penetrate his mind.

842. *RELEVANCY* (*rĕl'-ĕv-ăn-sĭ*) *n.* Applicability, pertinency, fitness, appositeness, suitability, patness, quality of bearing on the matter in hand.

In the test phrase: 'The argument lacks RELEVANCY', the word is thought by 19 per cent of adult readers to mean SUPPORT, aid, the popular misconception. This is practically the meaning of the Latin from which RELEVANCY comes. RELEVANCY, and the verb to RELIEVE, are both from the Latin *re*, again; and *levare*, to lift. RELIEVE has been used as an English word

since the fourteenth century and has today the original meaning, lift, help, assist, aid. RELEVANCY, the noun, and RELEVANT,
the adjective, although both recent words, have departed more
from the original meaning. RELEVANT means helpful in the
situation; and so, as the word is used today, fitting the situation. RELEVANCY is the corresponding noun.

IMPORTANCE, the second most common misconception, is
close to the correct meaning and is in fact given in some dictionaries as a synonym of RELEVANCY. An argument may
however be RELEVANT, applicable, suitable to the situation,
without being of IMPORTANCE, of moment. To be of IMPOR-
TANCE an argument must be both RELEVANT and weighty.

Opposites of RELEVANCY are: IRRELEVANCY, INAPPLICABILITY,
IMPERTINENCE.

843. *DEPILATE* (*dĕp'-ĭ-lāt*) *v.* To deprive of hair, remove
hair from a person's body.

In the test phrase: 'He was DEPILATED', the word is thought
by 23 per cent of adult readers to mean DENOUNCED, informed
against. This may be a confusion of DEPILATE, deprive of hair,
with DEPRECATE, to express disapproval of, plead earnestly
against.

DEPILATE is from the Latin *de*, from; and *pilus*, hair. From
the same source comes the English word PILE, the hairlike
surface of a fabric.

The noun, a DEPILATORY (*dĕ-pĭl'-ă-tō-rĭ*), a chemical used
to remove hair, is probably more generally known than the
verb, to DEPILATE.

844. *IMMEMORIAL* (*ĭm-mĕ-mō'-rĭ-ăl*) *adj.* Ancient beyond
memory, of unknown age, not within the bounds of
memory, extending back beyond record.

IMMEMORIAL is a combination of the Latin prefix *in*, not; and
MEMORIAL, which comes from the Latin *memorare*, to remember. The English word MEMORIAL can be used to mean
within the memory of men and so be an exact opposite of
IMMEMORIAL; but this use is rare. MEMORIAL, when used as
an adjective, ordinarily means serving to perpetuate the memory, as: 'A MEMORIAL window'.

In the test phrase: 'IMMEMORIAL usage', the word is thought

by 27 per cent of preparatory-school juniors to mean REMEM-
BERABLE, capable of being remembered, almost an opposite
of IMMEMORIAL, so ancient that its beginning cannot be
remembered.

845. *CALUMNY* (*kăl'-ŭm-nĭ*) *n.* Slander, defamation, aspersion, false and malicious misrepresentation with the intention of injury to a reputation. 'He was a victim of CALUMNY.'
ASPERSIONS, SLANDERS, and CALUMNIES, are all false statements
made behind one's back with intent to injure; all are deliberate assaults upon one's reputation. ASPERSION, literally a
sprinkling with false accusations, is the weakest of the three
disagreeable words. SLANDER, which is closely related to
SCANDAL, is the repetition of gossip, tales, or reports. CAL-
UMNY is the dissemination of falsehoods which have been
invented.

846. *EVANESCENT* (*ĕv-ă-nĕs'-sĕnt*) *adj.* Vanishing, fleeting,
transitory, transient, fading, passing away gradually like
vapor, as: 'An EVANESCENT glow'.
To 18 per cent of adult readers EVANESCENT incorrectly means
BRILLIANT, sparkling, glittering, shining, lustrous, effulgent.
A similar confusion appeared in a group of preparatory-school
juniors where the noun, EVANESCENCE, was thought by 18
per cent to mean BRIGHTNESS.
The three words, EVANESCENT, PHOSPHORESCENT, and EFFLO-
RESCENT, are easily confused. EFFLORESCENT means blossoming forth, blooming. PHOSPHORESCENT means faintly luminous
in the dark. EVANESCENT, which comes from the Latin *e;* and
vanescere, to vanish; from the same source as the English verb,
to VANISH; means fleeting, transient, vanishing, transitory.
The terminations ESCE, of verbs; ESCENCE of nouns; and
ESCENT, of adjectives; often suggest beginning. To CONVALESCE
is to begin to get well. To EFFLORESCE is to begin to bloom;
PHOSPHORESCE, begin to shine; EVANESCE, begin to vanish. The
noun and adjective are EVANESCENCE and EVANESCENT.

847. *OBESE* (*ō-bēs'*) *adj.* Fat, fleshy, excessively plump,
pursy, adipose, portly, stout, corpulent.
OBESE is from the Latin *ob;* and *edere*, to eat. It is believed

by 26 per cent of adult readers to mean STUPID. This is perhaps a confusion of OBESE, fat, with OBTUSE, dull-witted, stupid.

848. *RECANT* (*rē-kănt'*) *v.* To withdraw, recall, renounce, forswear, repudiate (262), retract (329), disavow, abjure, rescind (*rē-sĭnd'*), repeal, abrogate.
RECANT comes from the Latin *re*, again; and *cantare*, to sing; and by derivation means to sing again, repeat in song. There are other English words from *cantare*. A CANTATA is a musical composition, a short oratorio, a story set to music and recited but not acted. To CANT is to speak in a singing, whining, manner; also to talk in a jargon peculiar to some sect or religious group. To CANT has today only unpleasant associations suggesting the voice of a beggar whining for alms or the hypocritical phrases of affected piety. To CHANT, from the same source, has preserved the original meaning, to sing, celebrate in song.

Although the literal meaning of RECANT, to sing again, is obsolete, a third of adult readers still interpret RECANT, in the test phrase: 'RECANT your statement', to mean REPEAT. Today RECANT means withdraw, retract, take back; but 57 per cent of adult readers fail to recognize this modern use.

849. *PROSAIC* (*prō-zā'-ĭk*, not *prō-sā'-ĭk*) *adj.* Commonplace, unimaginative, matter of fact, dull, lacking those qualities which impart animation and interest.
PROSAIC is from the Latin *prosa*, straightforward. It is the adjective which corresponds to the noun PROSE. Both of the words PROSE and POETRY have two meanings. POETRY may be used in a limited, technical sense to mean verse which scans and rhymes. In this sense, PROSE, the opposite of POETRY, is literature which is not written in the form of verse. But POETRY, which comes from the Greek word, ποιεῖν, to make, may be used in a broader sense to mean any literature which is creative, imaginative, anything which shows craftsmanship. In this sense PROSE, the opposite, is unimaginative, commonplace. The adjective PROSAIC means, like PROSE in this last use, commonplace.

To 33 per cent of college seniors PROSAIC incorrectly means

QUAINT. QUAINT is odd, singular, curious, whimsical, unusual, almost an opposite of PROSAIC, unimaginative.

850. *RAMIFY* (*răm'-ĭ-fĭ*) *v.* To branch out, divide into branches, diverge in various ways.

The corresponding noun RAMIFICATION, as: 'The RAMIFICATIONS of a subject', means branching.

In the test phrase: 'The wires RAMIFY', CROSS is the common misconception of the verb and is believed by 17 per cent of adult readers to be synonymous with RAMIFY. This probably comes from the fact that some dictionaries define RAMIFY as, to form a network, an incorrect definition. RAMIFY comes from the Latin *ramus*, branch; and *facere*, to make; and means literally to make branches. RAMUS (*rā'-mŭs*) is today a botanical word for a branch or something which branches, as a vein or artery. RAMOSE (*rā'-mōs*), the adjective, means branched.

The Latin word *ramus* came from an older Greek word, ράδιξ, branch, from which comes another Latin word *radix*, a root. RADIX (*rā'-dĭks*) is today an English word in good use meaning root. From the Latin word, *radix*, come RACE, RADISH (*răd'-ĭsh*), and RADICAL. The latter means pertaining to the root, concerned with fundamental truths, as: 'A RADICAL opinion'. This use of RADICAL does not mean branching from the conservative viewpoint, as one might suppose, but pursuing a theory to the limit, going to the roots. Those who are today called RADICALS were at one time called: 'Root and branch men'.

851. *COMMISERATE* (*kŏm-mĭz'-ĕ-rāt*, not *kŏm-mĭs'-ĕ-rāt*) *v.* To pity, be sorry for, feel compassion for, sympathize, condole (366).

To 20 per cent of preparatory-school juniors to COMMISERATE incorrectly means to AFFECT. An unusual meaning of the verb AFFECT is to be fond of, love, show a liking for; a more usual meaning is pretend to feel.

COMMISERATE is from the Latin *com*; and ultimately *miser*, wretched, the source of the English word MISERABLE, wretched; and by derivation means to be miserable with and so to sympathize. Although COMMISERATE contains the Latin *com*, with, it is followed in English by the preposition WITH, one COMMISERATES with a friend.

852. *VITUPERATE* (*vĭ-tū'-per-āt*, not *vĭ-tū'-per-āt*) *v*. To find fault with abusively, upbraid (573), rail at, berate, objurgate, vilify, curse, scold eloquently, assail with contumely (979).
To 14 per cent of college seniors VITUPERATE incorrectly means to CHEER, to salute with shouts of approval, encourage, practically an opposite of VITUPERATE, find fault with. To another 11 per cent VITUPERATE incorrectly means to PRAISE, another opposite of the correct meaning.
VITUPERATE and OBJURGATE, and the corresponding nouns, VITUPERATION and OBJURGATION, are strong words for censuring an equal. The difference between the two is in the manner of execution. One may OBJURGATE another in a single sentence. In order to VITUPERATE, one must have effective eloquence at one's command.

853. *PISCATORIAL* (*pĭs-kă-tō'-rĭ-ăl*) *adj*. Fishy, piscine (*pĭs'-sĭn*), ichthyic (*ĭk'-thĭ-ĭk*), pertaining to fishes; also pertaining to fishing.
PISCATORIAL and PISCATORY (*pĭs'-kă-tō-rĭ*) are two forms of the same adjective. Both words come from the Latin noun *piscator*. This word PISCATOR (*pĭs'-kă-tŏr*) was used as an English word by Izaak Walton to mean a fisherman, angler.
To 22 per cent of adult readers PISCATORIAL incorrectly means PICTURESQUE, graphic, quaint, suitable to be drawn, having the qualities of a picture.
To 10 per cent of preparatory-school juniors PISCATORIAL incorrectly means UNPLEASANT, disagreeable.

854. *ACCOUTREMENTS* (*ăk-koot'-rĕ-mĕnts*) *n*. Equipment, apparel, trappings, garb, any outfit carried about one's person.
In the test phrase: 'Well-chosen ACCOUTREMENTS', the word is thought by 24 per cent of adult readers to mean SURROUNDINGS, the popular misconception. Ordinarily, the plural SURROUNDINGS, means environs, objects making up an environment distinct from the body, external conditions.

ACCOUTREMENTS are personal articles worn, carried, about the body.

The three words ACCOUTREMENTS, EQUIPAGE (ĕk'-wĭ-pāj), and VESTMENT, all designate personal equipment. Of the three, a VESTMENT, or the more unusual word an INVEST-MENT, is a garment, article of clothing, explicitly a cere-monial robe, an official garment. An EQUIPAGE was originally the equipment of a ship or of an army. In the 18th century the word was used for the collection of implements, tooth-pick, nail cleaner, and private seal, carried by every person of quality. Later, the meaning of the word changed again and an EQUIPAGE meant a carriage, including its horses and servants in liveries; and the word is used most frequently today in this last sense. The word ACCOUTREMENT, in the singular, may mean clothing alone; but in the plural, AC-COUTREMENTS, it is not limited to garments, clothing; nor, on the other hand, does it ordinarily include such things as carriages, horses, or servants. ACCOUTREMENTS are those things which might be carried about one's person.

855. *STIPEND* (stī'-pĕnd) *n.* Fixed salary, allowance, wages, periodical pay; technically the salary paid a Scottish clergyman, income of an ecclesiastic living.

STIPEND is from the Latin *stips*, a gift; and *pendere*, to weigh; and, as the word is ordinarily used in English, STIPEND means a salary as small as a gift carefully weighed before it is given.

There are several terms for money paid in return for work. PAY is the simple, generic word. WAGES and HIRE both imply employment for short periods, by the day or week. WAGES are paid to mechanical workers, although the word is variously used. HIRE is limited to farm hands and country help. SALARY and STIPEND imply payment at greater intervals, for mental effort as contrasted with physical labor. SALARY is general. STIPEND, although used loosely for any small sal-ary, is technically a Scottish or English church salary.

STIPEND is believed by 29 per cent of adult readers to mean PROFIT. A STIPEND is a fixed sum paid regularly to a person, one which does not vary directly with his efforts. PROFIT is the amount by which income exceeds expenses, and varies directly with the success of a business and the personal effort of the owner.

STIPEND is believed by another 10 per cent to mean STALK, stem, support. This is perhaps a confusion of STIPEND, salary, with STIPE (*stīp*), a botanical and anatomical word which means stalk, support. STIPEND can mean support only indirectly, in the figurative sense, as support for a family, the provision of necessities; it cannot mean stalk, stem.

856. *IMMOLATE* (*ĭm'-mō-lāt*) *v.* To sacrifice, offer in sacrifice (359), kill as a sacrificial victim.

IMMOLATE, to sacrifice, should not be confused with the more usual EMULATE, try to equal, hope to excel, copy. IMMOLATE is from the Latin *im;* and *mola*, meal; and by derivation means to sprinkle a sacrificial victim with meal.

In the test phrase: 'IMMOLATE the traitor', the word is thought by 27 per cent of preparatory-school juniors to mean PROSECUTE. This may be due to a confusion between the four words, PROSECUTE, PERSECUTE, EXECUTE, and IMMOLATE. To PROSECUTE, to PERSECUTE, and to EXECUTE, all come from the same Latin word, *sequi*, to follow; and all suggest following up in various ways. To PROSECUTE an inquiry is to continue it, follow it up to the end. To PERSECUTE is to harass (*hăr'-ăs*), run down. To EXECUTE is literally to follow out, carry out. The verb, to EXECUTE, has come to be used legally to mean to perform a sentence, carry out the judgment of the court, explicitly, to inflict capital punishment, and so to put to death, kill. In this last sense, to EXECUTE is not far in meaning from the verb, to IMMOLATE, which means to kill as a sacrifice.

To IMMOLATE and to SACRIFICE are practically synonymous. SACRIFICE applies to any offering; IMMOLATE can be used only for the sacrifice of a life.

857. *BANEFUL* (*bān'-fŭl*) *adj.* Poisonous, toxic (542), noxious, venomous, deadly, destructive, pernicious (786), virulent (1097).

In the test phrase: 'BANEFUL herbs', the word is thought by 18 per cent of adult readers to mean BITTER. This may be due to a confusion of BANEFUL, poisonous, with BALE-

FUL (992), a word which may mean either injurious, destructive, calamitous; or wretched, woeful. BANEFUL and BALEFUL are so close in sound, spelling, and meaning, that they are confused even by dictionaries. BALE comes from Anglo-Saxon words for evil; and the adjective BALEFUL means evil, destructive. BANE, from an Anglo-Saxon word meaning murderer, is a deadly poison. BANE appears today with its correct meaning in the word RATSBANE, rat poison, white arsenic; and also in the names of the two poisonous plants DOGBANE and HENBANE. BANEFUL is the adjective and should be reserved for the meaning poisonous.

To another 16 per cent BANEFUL incorrectly means HARMLESS, an opposite of the correct meaning.

858. *FOIBLE* (*foi'-bl*) *n.* Weakness on which one prides one's self, moral failing, frailty, defect in character, peccadillo, minor infirmity (622).

FOIBLE, from the Latin *flere*, to weep, is from the same source as the English adjective, FEEBLE, weak.

A FOIBLE and an IDIOSYNCRASY are both personal peculiarities. An IDIOSYNCRASY may be either good or bad, it is merely a distinctive characteristic. A FOIBLE is always a minor weakness, a slight defect.

859. *PALPABLE* (*păl'-pā-bl*) *adj.* Perceptible to the touch, tangible, capable of being touched; figuratively, readily perceived, perceptible, manifest, obvious, plain.

PALPABLE is from the Latin *palpare*, to feel. When used figuratively to mean obvious, clear, apparent, conspicuous, as in the phrase: 'A PALPABLE truth', it is unknown to 58 per cent of adult readers.

To 10 per cent of preparatory-school juniors PALPABLE incorrectly means THROBBING, pulsating, vibrating. To another 10 per cent it incorrectly means QUAKING, shaking, shivering, trembling. These are probably both confusions of PALPABLE, tangible, with some form of the verb to PALPITATE. PALPITATE comes from the same Latin source as PALPABLE, but means to throb, beat, pulsate. PALPITATING, the participial adjective, is generally used in this sense, but there is an unusual adjective, PALPITANT, throbbing. PALPABLE never has this meaning but always denotes tangible, visible, perceptible.

PALPABLE and TANGIBLE, when used literally to mean capable of being touched, are interchangeable. When used figuratively they differ. TANGIBLE keeps nearly its literal sense. Thus, TANGIBLE property is that on which one can lay one's hands. TANGIBLE is rarely used of that which can be grasped by the mind. PALPABLE, in its figurative use, means plain, clear, obvious, characterizing that which can be grasped mentally.

860. PLIGHT (*plīt*) *v.* To pledge (363), give as security, promise earnestly, engage one's self to do something.
In the test phrase: 'I PLIGHT my faith', the verb is thought by 13 per cent of adult readers to mean STATE, say; and by another 13 per cent to mean TEST, to try.

861. COMITY (*kŏm'-ĭ-tĭ*) *n.* Mutual agreeableness, civility, courtly politeness, amenity, urbanity, complaisance, courtesy between nations with friendly recognition of one another's customs.
To 24 per cent of adult readers, COMITY incorrectly means UNION, unity, combination. This may be due to a confusion of COMITY, politeness, with one of the words from the Latin *communis*, common, such as COMMUNITY, a body of persons united for a common purpose, and COMMUNISM, united ownership. COMITY is from the Latin *comis*, friendly, loving, courteous; but the word is now used most frequently for courtesy between nations.

862. BLUFF (*blŭf*) *adj.* Abrupt, blunt, frank, outspoken, brusquely sincere, unceremoniously hearty.
In the test phrase: 'A stout, loud, red, BLUFF man', the word is thought by 21 per cent of preparatory-school juniors to mean DECEIVING. This confusion may come from the verb, to BLUFF, which may mean to deceive, impose upon, hoodwink. There is also a noun, a BLUFF, the act of deceiving; and another noun, a BLUFFER, one who deceives; but the adjective, BLUFF, cannot mean deceiving. It comes apparently from a different source, and embraces within itself two

distinct meanings: FRANK, the opposite of which is DECEIVING; and ABRUPT, blunt, opposites of which are SUAVE (*swahv*) and BLAND. BLUFF means blunt and frank.

863. *IMMEW* (*ĭm-mū'*) *v.* To imprison, confine, coop up, incarcerate, hold in duress (*dū'-rĕs*) or durance. To 17 per cent of adult readers, IMMEW incorrectly means to PUNISH, chastise. IMPRISONMENT, the condition of being IMMEWED, is a form of punishment; otherwise there is no connection between the words PUNISH and IMMEW.

To another 17 per cent, IMMEW incorrectly means SET FREE, an exact opposite of the correct meaning.

To IMMEW and to IMMURE are, in present usage, practically synonymous, although the two words come from different sources. To IMMURE is from the Latin *murus*, wall, and by derivation means to place within walls. To IMMEW is from the Latin *mutare*, to change; from the same source as MUTABLE, changeable; and MUTATION, a change. Only by a circuitous route has it come to mean imprison, coop up.

Originally a MEW was a cage used for hawks while they MEWED, changed, molted, shed their feathers. The MEWS, in London, was originally the place where the king's falcons MEWED, molted. In 1537, the MEWS were rebuilt by Henry VIII into the royal stables; and today MEWS means any alley, any enclosed place, where stables are located. From MEW, a cage, the word came to mean any place of confinement; and the verb, to IMMEW, means to place in confinement.

864. *ADAMANT* (*ăd'-ă-mănt*) *n.* A hard stone, impervious mineral, impenetrable substance.
The corresponding adjective ADAMANTINE means hard, impenetrable, unyielding (392).

ADAMANT is from the Greek *ὰ*, not; and *δαμᾶν*, to conquer; and by derivation means unconquerable. The Greek verb, to conquer, became in Latin, *domare*, to conquer, tame; from which in turn comes the English adjective INDOMITABLE, not conquerable.

The word ADAMANT has been used in the past as the name of various hard substances. At one time it was the name of the metal from which armor was made; at another, it was the name of the diamond itself. Parallel with this physical use, has gone the figurative application which dates back as far as Homer who used the word with reference to: 'A person of ADAMANT', one of stone.

The words ADAMANT and DIAMOND both come from the same original source, and have often been used interchangeably. Milton, for instance, describes a man armed in DIAMOND, meaning an impenetrable metal.

The word DIAMOND is, today, the name of a precious stone of great hardness; while ADAMANT refers to no actual metal, but is used only in a figurative sense referring to an imaginary substance of great hardness.

When used in the test phrase: 'Her heart is ADAMANT', the word is thought by 26 per cent of adult readers to mean TOUCHED. TOUCHED when used in this way means softened, in connotation an opposite of ADAMANT.

865. OFFAL (ŏf'-făl) n. Rubbish, refuse of any kind, waste stuff, garbage, waste meats, scraps discarded by the butcher.

OFFAL, waste, and AWFUL, awe-inspiring, dreadful, terrible, despite their similarity of sound, have no connection. OFFAL is a combination of OFF and FALL and means by derivation that which falls off. It was first used for the chips which fell from wood as it was being chopped or from stone which was being cut. AWFUL is a combination of AWE, veneration, fear combined with admiration, dread mingled with reverence; and FULL; and means fearful, dread-arousing.

In the test phrase: 'No OFFAL in the streets', the word is thought by 18 per cent of preparatory-school juniors to mean NOISE, loud sound, clamor, din. This confusion can perhaps be traced to an obsolete meaning of the word NOISE; for, although the origin of NOISE is unknown, it is said by some to come from the Latin *nausea*, disgust, loathing, the source of the English word NAUSEA (naw'-shă). An obsolete meaning of the English word, NOISE, is an offensive taste, an offense of any kind. Furthermore, NOISOME (noi'-sŭm), although of different origin, means disgusting, offensive, obnoxious. OFFAL is usually thought of as offensive, although the real meaning of the word is refuse, rubbish, waste.

866. *DELETERIOUS (dĕl-ĕ-tē'-rĭ-ŭs) adj.* Destructive, hurtful, injurious, pernicious (786), baneful (857), unwholesome, noxious.

To 28 per cent of adult readers, DELETERIOUS incorrectly means ELIMINATING. This is perhaps a confusion of DELETERIOUS, injurious, with the verb to DELETE, to blot out, erase, destroy. Although DELETE (*dē-lēt'*) and DELETERIOUS come from the same Latin word *delere*, to abolish, annihilate, they differ in modern application. The word to DELETE means to remove in a colorless, innocuous fashion. One DELETES an error, a superfluous word. The adjective, DELETERIOUS, is stronger, and means destructive.

DELETERIOUS, PERNICIOUS, and NOXIOUS, are similar in meaning. NOXIOUS is the weakest of the three; and means hurtful, harmful. Both PERNICIOUS and DELETERIOUS mean destructive, annihilating.

867. *GLUTINOUS (glū'-tĭ-nŭs) adj.* Sticky, viscous, tenacious, having a semi-fluid clinging consistency.

The word is thought by 28 per cent of preparatory-school juniors to mean HUNGRY. This is no doubt a confusion of GLUTINOUS, sticky, with GLUTTONOUS, given to excessive eating. GLUTINOUS is from the Latin *gluten*, glue, and means having the characteristics of glue.

868. *RUMINATION (rū-mĭ-nā'-shŭn) n.* Reflection, meditation, cogitating (261), musing, deliberation, pondering, perpending.

To 20 per cent of college seniors, the word RUMINATION incorrectly means EXAMINATION, a word which may mean either test or careful search, inquiry, investigation. The corresponding verb, to RUMINATE, is thought by 7 per cent of preparatory-school juniors to mean to HUNT, look for. Both of these may be due to some confusion of the verb, to RUMINATE, with the verb to RUMMAGE, which means to search thoroughly but in a disorderly fashion.

RUMINATION is from the Latin *rumen*, throat, gullet; from the same source as the word RUMINANT. A RUMINANT is any animal, such as the cow, which chews its cud. By derivation RUMINATION means chewing the cud; but the word is used most frequently today to mean that kind of thinking in which one goes over and over an idea, gradually digesting it.

869. *BULLION* (*bŏŏl'-yŭn*) *n.* Ingot, gold or silver, coin valued only as metal.

To 43 per cent of adult readers, BULLION incorrectly means SOUP. This is obviously a confusion of BULLION, gold, with BOUILLON (*bool-yogn'*) (193), clear soup, broth. These two words may be related at their source. BULLION may be related to the Latin *bullire*, to boil, and so perhaps to melt down, the source of BOUILLON. BULLION may also be related to the Latin *bullare*, to stamp; perhaps ultimately from *bulla*, seal, the source of the English word BULLETIN, public notice. From *bulla* comes a French word which means a mint, the place where money is coined; and from this in turn comes the word BULLION, raw, precious metal, before it is minted, made into coins.

870. *CREDENCE* (*krē'-dĕns*, not *krĕd'-ĕns*) *n.* Belief, faith, trust, reliance, confidence, credit.

CREDENCE comes from the Latin *credere*, to believe. To 14 per cent of adult readers CREDENCE incorrectly means LOANS. This is perhaps because of the close association in business of the two words, CREDIT and LOANS. To another 14 per cent, CREDENCE incorrectly means RESPECT, honor, esteem. One has RESPECT for a person. One has CREDENCE, faith, belief, in his statements.

871. *MATRIX* (*mā'-trĭks*) *n.* A mold in which something is cast, that which gives form, anything capable of giving shape to another object embedded within it.

Matrix is the Latin word for womb and comes from the Latin *mater*, mother. From the same source come MATERNAL, motherly; MATRIMONY, marriage, wedlock; and MATRON, a married woman.

872. *SUPPLICATORY* (*sŭp'-plĭ-kǎ-tō-rĭ*) *adj.* Imploring, beseeching (324), entreating, making a humble petition to, begging for mercy, asking for a boon.

To 16 per cent of preparatory-school juniors SUPPLICATORY

incorrectly means FLEXIBLE. This is perhaps a confusion of SUPPLICATORY, imploring, with SUPPLE, flexible. Both words come from the Latin *sub*, under; and *plicare*, to fold, bend. SUPPLE is easily bent. SUPPLICATORY suggests kneeling in a humble, beseeching position.

To another 14 per cent SUPPLICATORY incorrectly means ADDITIONAL. This is probably a confusion of SUPPLICATORY with SUPPLEMENTARY, added, additional.

The two nouns, a SUPPLICANT, which comes directly from the Latin, and a SUPPLIANT which comes indirectly through the French, both mean a humble petitioner and are exactly synonymous. SUPPLICATORY is the corresponding adjective.

The verbs, to SUPPLICATE and to IMPLORE, are both to ask earnestly because of extreme distress. One IMPLORES equals; one SUPPLICATES superiors.

873. *PRAGMATIC* (*prăg-măt'-ĭk*) *adj.* Practical, not theoretical, based upon actual experience, concerned with practical consequences.

PRAGMATIC is from the Greek word πράσσειν, to do; it is from the same source as PRACTICE and PRACTICAL.

To 21 per cent of college seniors PRAGMATIC incorrectly means BLUNDERING. This may come from one of the meanings of PRAGMATICAL, ending in ICAL. PRAGMATICAL once meant skilled in business, and may now mean pertaining to business affairs. PRAGMATICAL may also mean meddlesome, dictatorial, officious, impertinent, fussily busy. The PRAGMATICAL person exaggerates the importance of what he is doing, and is spoken of as BLUNDERING IN where he does not belong. But BLUNDERING alone, as used in this sense, means floundering, stumbling, not necessarily interfering with another.

PRAGMATISM is a philosophical doctrine which states that things should be judged by their practical effects, success in practice being the final criterion. PRAGMATIC, ending in IC, is the corresponding adjective.

874. *INEXORABLE* (*ĭn-ĕks'-ō-ră-bl*) *adj.* Relentless, unyielding (392), unrelenting, implacable (673), immovable, not to be appeased.

INEXORABLE is thought by 25 per cent of preparatory-school

juniors to mean INEVITABLE, unavoidable. INEVITABLE ordinarily modifies events, as: 'An INEVITABLE occurrence'; whereas INEXORABLE modifies persons. There are rare instances where the two can modify the same word, as: 'INEVITABLE fate', 'INEXORABLE fate'. In this case both words suggest that which is bound to happen. The INEVITABLE happens because of the operation of the laws of nature. The INEXORABLE happens because of the relentlessness of human beings.

875. *ROCOCO* (*rō-kō'-kō*) *adj.* Florid, ornate, baroque, profusely decorated, excessively embellished, over-elaborate to the point of extravagance.

To 29 per cent of college seniors, ROCOCO incorrectly means MOORISH. MOORISH, as the word is used in architecture, applies to a style which was introduced into Spain by the Moors, in 710 A.D., and which continued for approximately eight hundred years. It is embellished with elaborate designs carved on flat surfaces. In this it differs from ROCOCO, a word which comes probably from the French *roche*, rock, and which consists of an assemblage of fantastic, rocklike projections, grotesque scrolls, and conventionalized shell-work.

The words ROCOCO and BAROQUE (*bă-rŏk'*) are almost synonymous. BAROQUE is often used to mean heavy, grotesque, bizarre. Correctly the word applies to the architectural style which began in Italy at the beginning of the 17th century, a reaction against the standardized Classical Renaissance of the time, and a style responsible for several buildings which show life and vitality. Later, the style became heavy and grotesque, and at about this time spread to France. It is because of this later development that the word BAROQUE suggests the grotesque and bizarre.

Rococo applies to the kind of ornamentation so freely used in the later BAROQUE style. Rococo ornamentation developed in France during the reigns of Louis XIV, 1643–1715, and Louis XV, 1715–1774. The word is not limited to architecture but may be used of any elaborate ornamentation. It does not necessarily imply heaviness, ugliness; but it is often used figuratively with reference to any elaborate, extravagant style, heavy with ornamentation.

876. *SQUALID* (*skwŏl'-ĭd*) *adj.* Foul, filthy, wretched, poverty-stricken, dirty through neglect.

SQUALID, and the corresponding noun SQUALOR (*skwŏl'-ŏr* or *skwä'-lŏr*), come from the Latin *squalere*, to be stiff, rough. To 29 per cent of college seniors SQUALID incorrectly means DEPRESSING, sad, disheartening, dispiriting. Although conditions which are SQUALID, filthy, and DEPRESSING, sad, are found together, the word SQUALID implies neglect, want of care, not necessarily DEPRESSING.

To 14 per cent of preparatory-school juniors SQUALID incorrectly means FLOWING. This is perhaps a confusion of SQUALID, dirty, with SQUALLY, gusty, stormy. Although today the noun, a SQUALL, is a sudden gust of wind, the word comes from Swedish and Norwegian words which mean a rush of water, gushing, a rapid flow. Etymologically SQUALLY might mean flowing, but there is no etymological connection between SQUALLY, gusty, and SQUALID, filthy, dirty, wretched.

877. *CONDONE* (*kŏn-dōn'*) *v.* To pardon, forgive, excuse, overlook, tacitly ignore an offense.

CONDONE is from the Latin *com*; and *donare*, to give. To 18 per cent of adult readers CONDONE incorrectly means DEPLORE, regret, lament, mourn, bemoan, bewail. This may be due to a confusion of CONDONE, forgive, with CONDOLE, lament with another, mourn over; for CONDOLE and DEPLORE differ only slightly. To CONDOLE, from the same source as DOLE, grief, and DOLOROUS, mournful, suggests another person with whom one sympathizes. To DEPLORE, from the same source as IMPLORE, is more apt to imply that one blames the other person for the act which one laments. To CONDONE is from the same source as DONATE, to give, and DONATION, and suggests generosity in forgiving.

To another 16 per cent of readers to CONDONE incorrectly means to DENOUNCE, censure, stigmatize. To DENOUNCE, accuse, stigmatize, and to CONDONE, forgive, pardon, are practically opposites.

To CONDONE, to FORGIVE, and to PARDON, are nearly synonymous. To FORGIVE and to PARDON both suggest that an offense has been recognized, excused, but not forgotten. To

CONDONE suggests that an offense will be treated as if it had not existed.

878. *DISQUISITION* (*dĭs-kwĭ-zĭ′-shŭn*) *n.* An essay, dissertation, discussion, discourse, literary composition, treatise based on systematic investigation.

To 29 per cent of college seniors DISQUISITION incorrectly means ATTAINMENT, that which is accomplished, gained, as the result of exertion. This is probably a confusion of DISQUISITION, an essay, treatise, with ACQUISITION, that which is acquired, gained, a synonym of ATTAINMENT.

Three words, DISQUISITION, INQUISITION, and ACQUISITION, all come from the Latin verb *quaerere*, to seek. An ACQUISITION, from the Latin *ad*, to, is the object attained. The word INQUISITION, spelt with a capital, was used for the tribunal which examined heretics in the twelfth and thirteenth centuries. The word, with a small letter, means today an official investigation, often a legal investigation, into the actions and opinions of human beings.

A DISQUISITION is most frequently a scholastic inquiry (*ĭn-kwĭ′-rĭ*, not *ĭn′-kwĭ-rĭ*), an investigation for the sake of gaining further knowledge. A DISQUISITION is also the name of the essay or treatise which describes such an investigation and its findings.

879. *MIEN* (*mēn*) *n.* Aspect, demeanor, bearing, manner, appearance, presence (569), expression, countenance.
In the test phrase: 'An attractive MIEN', the word is believed by 19 per cent of adult readers to mean BILL OF FARE. This is doubtless a confusion with the word MENU, bill of fare, list of dishes served at a meal. Although MENU has been adopted in English it is a French word and should be given its French pronunciation and accented on the last syllable. MIEN comes also through French, probably originally from the Latin *minere*, to project, the source of PROMINENT, projecting, jutting out; IMMINENT, by derivation jutting out too far and so about to fall, about to happen; MENACE (649), a threat; and MINATORY, threatening. MIEN may once have implied a threatening appearance, but today means merely appearance, demeanor.

FACE ordinarily means the front part of the head, the forehead, eyes, nose, mouth, and chin; it may however mean expression, countenance, outward appearance, and in this sense is an exact synonym of MIEN.

880. *INGENUE* (*ăn-zhā-nü'*) *n.* Artless girl, ingenuous young woman; technically a character on the stage who displays qualities of innocent girlishness.
INGENUE is a French word appropriated by English. It comes from the Latin *ingenuus*, free-born, noble, upright, frank. From this same source come the English words INGENUOUS, candid, frank, sincere; and its opposite DISINGENUOUS (917).
To 26 per cent of adult readers, INGENUE incorrectly means a SOPHISTICATED PERSON, one who is worldly wise, well-informed in the ways of the world, the opposite of an INGENUE, an unsophisticated girl.

881. *FOOTPAD* (*foot'-păd*) *n.* A highwayman who robs on foot, freebooter, robber, thief, ruffian, marauder.
To 24 per cent of preparatory-school juniors FOOTPAD incorrectly means NARROW WALK. This is probably a confusion of FOOTPAD, a highwayman, with FOOTPATH, a narrow path for pedestrians. PAD alone is an obsolete word for path; but a FOOTPAD is always a highwayman.

882. *SUASION* (*swā'-zhŭn*) *n.* Urging, persuasion, successful entreaty, the act of convincing through reasoning.
SUASION, and the more commonly used PERSUASION, are practically synonymous. Both come from the same Latin word, *suavis*, gracious, pleasant, sweet, the source of the English word, SUAVE, bland, soothingly agreeable, mollifying.
PERSUASION and DISSUASION both succeed in their aims. DISSUASION keeps one from acting as one had intended; PERSUASION makes one act as one had not intended. The word SUASION is now limited almost exclusively to the phrase: 'Moral SUASION'.

883. *STRIDULOUS* (*strĭd'-ū-lŭs*) *adj.* Shrill, harsh, squeaky, grating, creaking, rasping.
The adjectives STRIDULOUS and STRIDENT (1055) and the verb

to STRIDULATE are from the Latin *stridere*, to creak. To STRIDULATE is to emit a shrill, grating sound similar to that produced by a locust, cricket, katydid, or cicada (*sĭ-kă'-dă*), usually by rubbing the legs or wings against the body.

884. *IMPRESARIO* (*ĭm-prĕ-sahr'-ĭ-ō*) *n.* Manager of an opera company, producer, entrepreneur, one who is responsible for a public musical performance.

In the test phrase: 'The company's IMPRESARIO', the word is thought by 24 per cent of college seniors to mean GOOD WILL; and by another 19 per cent to mean ADVERTISING. These misunderstandings are perhaps due to some confusion of IMPRESARIO, manager, with IMPRESSION, effect produced, a word which is spelt with two s's and comes from the Latin *pressus*, the past participle of the verb *premere*, to press. IMPRESARIO, with one s, is an Italian word, accepted by English. It comes originally from the Latin *in*; and *prendere*, to take on, as in the phrase: 'To TAKE ON a new responsibility'. An IMPRESARIO is by derivation one who takes on the responsibilities of an organization, especially of an opera company.

885. *COMPUNCTION* (*kŏm-pŭngk'-shŭn*) *n.* Regret, remorse, contrition, penitence, pricking of conscience, uneasiness caused by self-reproach.

In the test phrase: 'No touch of COMPUNCTION', the word is thought by 27 per cent of preparatory-school juniors to mean SYMPATHY, literally feeling with another.

COMPUNCTION comes from the Latin *punctus*, the past participle of the verb *pungere*, to prick, sting. The verb *pungere* is also the source of the English words PUNCTURE, which needs no definition; PUNCTUATE, the verb, and PUNCTUATION, the noun; and PUNGENT, sharp, biting. COMPUNCTION is literally a pricking of the conscience.

886. *PERISTYLE* (*pĕr'-ĭ-stīl*) *n.* A row of columns around a temple; range of columns surrounding the cella in a Greek temple; also a row of columns around any inner court.

PERISTYLE comes from the two Greek words, περί, about, around; and στῦλος, column. The same PERI appears in such words as: PERIMETER, literally the measure around an object, the outer boundary of a figure; and PERISCOPE, which by derivation means a looking around, now an instrument by means of which one can look around a corner.

To 20 per cent of college seniors PERISTYLE incorrectly means SCROLL. A SCROLL, in architecture, is round; it is a sculptured ornament resembling a roll of parchment, and is used at the top of columns in both Ionic and Corinthian capitals.

PERISTYLE, COLONNADE, and CLOISTER, are architectural forms. A CLOISTER is a covered walk, often around the inner court of a monastic building. A CLOISTER is usually lined, on one side, with columns which support the roof, but primarily a CLOISTER is a walk. A COLONNADE is any line of columns placed at regular intervals, and is a more general word than PERISTYLE. A PERISTYLE is a colonnade around the outside of a building, or around an inner court.

887. *STRAGGLE* (străg'-gl) *v.* To stray from one's companions, leave the direct path, wander aimlessly, ramble. In the test phrase: 'A soldier STRAGGLED off', the word is thought by 26 per cent of adult readers to mean LIMPED, the popular misconception. To LIMP is to walk in the manner of a lame person, as a cripple. To HALT is to walk in this same way but the word is more familiar as a noun than as a verb, in the phrase: 'The HALT and the blind'; to HALT also means to hesitate, to be in doubt and in this sense is not far from STRAGGLE. LIMP and STRAGGLE are not synonymous. The nearest approach is when LIMPED is used figuratively in the phrase: 'His argument LIMPED'.

LINGER and LOITER (70), STRAY and STRAGGLE, imply time wasted on the road; the first two by inaction, the last two by indirection.

888. *VICISSITUDE* (vĭ-sĭs'-ĭ-tūd, not vĭ-sĭs'-ĭ-tūd) *n.* An irregular change, revolution, mutation, change from one thing to another. VICISSITUDES are ups and downs.

To 36 per cent of college seniors VICISSITUDE incorrectly means DANGER, peril, hazard, risk. Both words, DANGER and VICISSITUDE, imply unstable conditions; but a DANGER is a peril, risk; whereas ᷉a VICISSITUDE is any change, whether perilous or safe.

889. *SWARD* (*swawrd*) *n.* Turf, sod, greensward, smoothly cut lawn, stretch of land covered thickly with short grass.

SWARD is of Anglo-Saxon origin. To 19 per cent of adult readers it incorrectly means a GARMENT, an article of clothing. To another 15 per cent SWARD incorrectly means BAND. This is no doubt a confusion of SWARD, turf, with SWATH (*swawth*, with TH as in THIN), a band of any kind, specifically, a band cut by a mower through tall grass. A SWATH is the band, stripe, line; while SWARD is grass-covered land.

890. *HISTRIONIC* (*hĭs-trĭ-ŏn'-ĭk*) *adj.* Theatrical, dramatic, stagy, relating to the playhouse, pertaining to actors or the stage. HISTRIONIC may also be used to mean unreal, affected, feigned.

To 20 per cent of college seniors HISTRIONIC incorrectly means LATENT, unawakened, dormant, existing but not apparent.

To another 10 per cent HISTRIONIC incorrectly means HISTORICAL, pertaining to history, relating to the past. Despite the similarity of these words, they come from different sources. HISTORICAL comes from the Greek word ἵστωρ, knowing, learned; HISTRIONIC, from a Latin word *histrio*, an actor, player. HISTRIONIC, by derivation, means pertaining to an actor, dramatic.

891. *INEFFABLE* (*ĭn-ĕf'-fă-bl*) *adj.* Unutterable, indescribable, unspeakable, transcending expression.

INEFFABLE is from the Latin *in*, not; *ex*, out; and *fori*, to speak, the source of the English word FABLE, a story, myth, legend. INEFFABLE means literally incapable of being spoken out.

INEFFABLE and UNSPEAKABLE are practically synonymous. UNSPEAKABLE refers more frequently to unpleasant subjects; INEFFABLE to pleasant ones.

By 22 per cent of adult readers INEFFABLE is thought to mean HEAVENLY. HEAVENLY may mean supremely beautiful, angelic, beatific (816), excellent in every way. The confusion between HEAVENLY and INEFFABLE comes perhaps from the fact that INEFFABLE is used most frequently with reference to that which is ineffably pleasant, ineffably beautiful; but the word INEFFABLE alone means surpassing description, unutterable.

892. *TENEBROUS* (*tĕn'-ĕ-brŭs*) *adj.* Dark, gloomy, dusky, shadowy, cloudy, umbrageous, obscure, dim, tending to blackness.

In the test phrase: 'A TENEBROUS evening', the word is thought by 36 per cent of college seniors to mean STICKY. This may be due to a confusion of TENEBROUS, dark, with TENACIOUS, holding fast, apt to adhere to another surface.

TENEBROUS is from the Latin *tenebrae* (*tĕn'-ĕ-brē*), darkness, gloom, a word which is used by the Roman Catholic Church as the office for Wednesday, Thursday, and Friday, of Holy Week, commemorating the sufferings and death of Christ.

893. *MALIGNITY* (*mă-lĭg'-nĭ-tĭ*) *n.* Intense malice (391), extreme malevolence, disposition to do harm, active ill will, animosity (764), deliberate intention to injure another, chronic spitefulness.

MALIGNITY is from the Latin *malus*, bad; and *genus*, birth, race, sort. In the test phrase: 'A clear case of MALIGNITY', it is thought by 24 per cent of adult readers to mean SLANDER. The verbs, to SLANDER, and to MALIGN, a more familiar word unknown to 30 per cent of adult readers, are synonymous; but the noun, SLANDER, means untrue gossip, false report. SLANDER is uttered with the intention of doing harm. It is the act which is an indication of MALIGNITY. MALIGNITY itself is the spirit, the intention, the desire to do harm; it is not the harmful act.

MALIGNITY and MALIGNANCY are both from the same source and are almost synonymous, but differ slightly in application. MALIGNANCY need not necessarily be a human characteristic. One may speak of the MALIGNANCY of a disease to mean its destructive qualities. MALIGNANCY, when applied to a human being, is a characteristic which shows itself by acts of destruction. MALIGNITY can be only a human characteristic. It is an intention to injure, a desire to do harm.

894. *EVINCE* (*ē-vĭns'*) *v.* To make clear by convincing evidence, reveal, show, display (118), exhibit, prove beyond reasonable doubt.

To EVINCE is thought by 18 per cent of preparatory-school juniors to mean SUPPRESS, put down, overpower; and by another 10 per cent to mean to CONQUER; both exact translations of the original Latin. EVINCE is from the Latin *e*, out; and *vincere*, to conquer, overcome, prevail over. The Latin *vincere* appears with its original meaning in the English word INVINCIBLE, which means literally unconquerable. Originally in English EVINCE meant to conquer, but this meaning is now obsolete.

To EVINCE is often incorrectly used in such a phrase as: 'He EVINCED astonishment', to mean merely showed, exhibited. EVINCE cannot be used with reference to that which can be seen by the eye. The word still retains enough of its Latin background and its original English meaning, conquer, so that it can be used only in situations where there is some room for doubt which has been conquered. To EVINCE implies an inference, deduction. To EVINCE and to CONVINCE are both to conquer a doubt. To CONVINCE is to conquer as the result of an argument; the word suggests opposition which has been overcome. To EVINCE is to prove at one stroke the truth of the final conclusion. One CONVINCES someone else of the truth. An incident, a happening, EVINCES the truth itself.

To EVINCE and to EVIDENCE are often synonymous but differ in finality. That which EVIDENCES the truth is a step toward its proof; that which EVINCES the truth proves it beyond reasonable doubt.

895. *FARRIER* (*făr'-rĭ-er*) *n.* A horseshoer (1), blacksmith; occasionally one who treats the diseases of horses, veterinary surgeon, veterinarian.

FARRIER is not from any word meaning horse, as might be supposed, but from the Latin *ferrum*, iron. From *ferrum* comes also the adjective FERROUS, pertaining to iron, a word

used in modern chemistry in such compounds as FERROUS
CHLORIDE.

896. *EFFICACY* (*ĕf′-fĭ-kă-sĭ*) *n.* Force, efficiency, effective
energy, effectiveness, power of producing a result.
EFFICACY comes from the Latin *efficere*, to effect, accomplish, do; from the Latin *ex*, out; and *facere*, to do. It is
from the same source as the English word EFFECT, result,
and by derivation means the power of producing an effect.
EFFICACY and EFFICIENCY are practically synonymous.
EFFICIENCY is used most frequently of human beings and
their actions. EFFICACY is used elsewhere, as: 'The EFFICACY
of a phrase', 'The EFFICACY of a medicine'.

897. *APHRODISIACAL* (*ăf-rō-dĭ-zĭ′-ă-kl*) *adj.* Passionate,
fervent in love, ardent, amorous, libidinous (1021),
stimulating sexual desire.
By 19 per cent of college seniors APHRODISIACAL is thought
to mean FRANTIC, mad, raving, wild, maniacal, the adjective
which corresponds to the word FRENZY.
To another 13 per cent APHRODISIACAL incorrectly means
INDIFFERENT, in suggestion an opposite of the correct meaning.
APHRODISIACAL, and the shorter, preferable, form APHRO-
DISIAC (*ăf-rō-dĭz′-ĭ-ăk*), are adjectives formed from the name
of the Greek goddess, APHRODITE (*ăf-rō-dĭ′-tē*), the goddess
of love. The same goddess appears later under the name
VENUS in Roman mythology.

898. *DEIGN* (*dān*) *v.* To condescend, stoop, concede, grant,
vouchsafe, allow in a patronizing manner.
DEIGN comes from the Latin *dignus*, worthy, the direct
source of the English word DIGNITY; and the word DEIGN
suggests a dignified person condescending to comply.
By 25 per cent of adult readers DEIGN is thought to mean
REFUSE, decline. The expression: 'He did not DEIGN to answer', means he REFUSED to answer, and the phrase: 'Did not
DEIGN', is practically synonymous with REFUSED. But DEIGN
alone is almost an opposite of REFUSE.
To DISDAIN comes from the same source as DEIGN, and

was originally spelt *disdeign*. To DISDAIN is to despise, look down upon, consider unworthy of notice, scorn, contemn. In form DISDAIN is the negative of DEIGN, but in modern usage it is not an opposite in meaning. One may DISDAIN, despise, scorn a beggar, but despite the prevalence of the expression one cannot correctly DISDAIN to answer in the sense of refuse. To DEIGN originally meant think well of, consider worthy of notice, an opposite of DISDAIN, but now has the limited meaning condescend.

To DISDAIN and to WORSHIP are opposites; to DEIGN and to SCORN, as used in the phrase: 'He SCORNED to answer', are practically opposites.

899. *TEMPORIZE* (tĕm'-pō-rīz) v. To gain time, procrastinate (679), avoid committing one's self, mark time, wait for a favorable moment.

In the test phrase: 'Let us TEMPORIZE', the word is thought by 32 per cent of adult readers to mean SOFTEN. This may be due to some confusion of TEMPORIZE, gain time, with the verb to TEMPER which may indirectly mean to soften. Both TEMPORIZE and TEMPER come ultimately from the same Latin word *tempus*, time. To TEMPER, which comes more directly from the verb *temperare*, to mingle in due proportion, regulate, means in English to modify by mixing, combine, blend. The derived meaning to soothe, calm, moderate, soften, has the suggestion of soothing by blending, as: 'To TEMPER justice with mercy'. One may TEMPORIZE in order to smooth over a situation but TEMPORIZE always has the precise meaning of yielding for the moment only, of complying for the sake of gaining time.

To another 14 per cent to TEMPORIZE incorrectly means to HARDEN. This may be due to a confusion of TEMPORIZE with another use of the verb to TEMPER; for in metallurgy the first step in the TEMPERING process is a hardening operation. The metal to be TEMPERED is first hardened by heating it to a high temperature and then cooling it rapidly. The resulting hard and brittle metal is then TEMPERED or slightly softened by heating it gently. The word TEMPORIZE has no connection with this TEMPERING process; it means to gain time by putting off.

900. *MILITATE* (*mĭl'-ĭ-tāt*) *v.* Oppose, contend, offer resistance to, use force against, operate against, serve as an influence in opposition to some result.

To 28 per cent of college seniors MILITATE incorrectly means to ARBITRATE, to settle a dispute, adjust; and to another 15 per cent to BARGAIN, to agree to terms, make a contract. Although MILITATE comes from the Latin *militare*, to be a soldier, from the same source as MILITARY and MILITIA, the word is never used of physical warfare, but only in the figurative sense of an argument in opposition to some conclusion. MILITATE is almost always followed by the word AGAINST, as: 'It MILITATED AGAINST success'.

901. *SALLOW* (*săl'-lō*) *adj.* Yellowish, fallow, jaundiced in color, of a pale sickly complexion with a yellowish tinge.

SALLOW is of Anglo-Saxon origin, from the same source as the French *sale*, dirty.

SALLOW and FALLOW are practically synonymous, but differ in usage. FALLOW is used in the hyphenated word, a FALLOW-DEER to mean one yellowish in color. FALLOW is also used of a field which has been plowed but not planted, perhaps because of its color. But SALLOW is the word used for the yellowish complexion of a human being.

902. *DICHOTOMY* (*dī-kŏt'-ō-mĭ*) *n.* Division or distribution by pairs. DICHOTOMY is a term used in the sciences. In logic, it is a division into two opposed sub-classes. In astronomy, it is the phase of the moon which shows half its disc. In botany it is the subdivision of a stem into two branches. In psychiatry, it designates a divided personality. DICHOTOMY comes from the Greek words δίχα, in two; and τέμνειν, to cut. To 28 per cent of college seniors it incorrectly means SOUNDNESS. SOUNDNESS may mean the state of being unbroken, whole; and in this sense, at least in suggestion, it is an opposite of DICHOTOMY, division into two.

From the same Greek source comes TOME. Although a TOME is today any large volume, it was originally a part, section, piece, cut from a larger book. ANATOMY, from the

Greek ἀνά, up, is a cutting up. An EPITOME (ĕ-pĭt'-ō-mē) is a summary, abstract, synopsis, abridgment, something cut down from the original. DICHOTOMY is a cutting into two parts.

903. *EXCULPATE* (ĕks-kŭl'-pāt) *v.* To acquit (500), discharge, release, vindicate, excuse, absolve, exonerate, free from blame, clear from a charge of guilt.

EXCULPATE is from the Latin *ex*, out; and *culpare*, to blame, a word which in turn comes from the Latin noun *culpa*, blame. From this come the English words CULPRIT, one who is guilty, an offender; and CULPABLE, worthy of censure, blameworthy. CULPABLE and INNOCENT are opposites; EXCULPATE and CENSURE are opposites.

To 20 per cent of adult readers EXCULPATE incorrectly means SCALP, the popular misconception. The verb, to SCALP, may be used in a figurative sense to mean censure severely, rebuke savagely. In this sense it is practically an opposite of EXCULPATE which means to free of blame.

904. *CANTING* (kănt'-ĭng) *p. adj.* Affectedly pious, hypocritical, whining, addicted to the use of a singing or whining manner of insincere moral talk.

The verb, to CANT, appeared in English in about the sixteenth century. Its source is probably the Latin verb *cantare*, to sing.

To 24 per cent of college seniors CANTING incorrectly means BOLD. BOLD may signify rude, forward, impudent; or, in another sense, vigorous, clear. In both senses a BOLD manner is almost the other extreme from CANTING, whining.

905. *MARTINET* (mahr-tĭ-nĕt') *n.* A strict disciplinarian, one who enforces order, one who requires rigid obedience.

In the test phrase: 'A well-known MARTINET', the word is thought by 20 per cent of adult readers to mean SINGER.

The noun MARTINET comes from the name General Martinet, a French infantry officer in the reign of Louis XIV. The word was first used for a military or naval officer who was a stickler for discipline, but is now used more generally to mean any strict disciplinarian.

906. *PROLIX (prō-lĭks')* adj. Long-winded, wordy, tiresome, verbose (797), redundant, pleonastic (1053), tautological, long drawn out.

PROLIX is from the Latin *prolixus*, stretched out, extended. To 21 per cent of adult readers it incorrectly means INSPIRING, stimulating. An INSPIRING speech is practically the opposite of a PROLIX one.

To another 18 per cent, PROLIX incorrectly means SHORT, an exact opposite of the correct meaning.

907. *PERFORCE (per-fōrs')* adv. Necessarily, under compulsion, under obligation, by constraint.

In the test phrase: 'He allied himself PERFORCE with them', the word is thought by 20 per cent of preparatory-school juniors to mean WITHOUT INVITATION. This is practically an opposite of the correct meaning. PERFORCE is from the Latin *per*, by; and ought to mean by force. As used in English the word does not suggest that he allied himself with them by force, without invitation; but rather that he was forced by circumstances to ally himself with them; did so under compulsion of necessity.

908. *FLITCH (flĭtch)* n. A side of a pig, salted and cured. 'The FLITCH of bacon.'

To 20 per cent of adult readers FLITCH incorrectly means SAMPLE, the most popular misconception, with no apparent justification. FLITCH and RASHER are both words applied to bacon. A RASHER is a thin slice. FLITCH, from an Anglo-Saxon word, is the piece cut from the pig, salted and cured, made ready for the butcher to slice into rashers.

909. *JADED (jā'-dĕd)* adj. Fatigued by the forced repetition of the same act, tired out, wearied with long continued effort.

In English, the noun, a JADE, means an old mare, a worn-out horse; and there are similar words for mare in the Scandinavian languages. The verb, to JADE, is to tire out, drive unsparingly, weary, fatigue.

To 36 per cent of college seniors JADED incorrectly means DEPRESSED, dejected, saddened, dispirited. DEPRESSED and

JADED have in common a state of depletion, loss of energy. DEPRESSED refers to the loss of mental or spiritual energy; JADED to the loss of physical energy.

Both JADED and WEARY describe states which may result from repetition of some action. One becomes WEARY from mere repetition. One becomes JADED from forced repetition.

910. *EMULATIVE* (*ĕm'-ū-lā-tĭv*) *adj.* Rivaling, vying with, jealously combative, competitive, desirous of fame, striving for superiority by copying another, disposed to compete imitatively.

To 29 per cent of preparatory-school juniors EMULATIVE incorrectly means REMINDING. In the phrase: 'REMINDING one of him', the word REMINDING means bringing him to mind, recalling him to one's attention. EMULATION is primarily the ambition to equal or to excel another. It is a wish for a superiority as great as that already gained by someone else. 'EMULATIVE of him' means struggling to equal or excel him.

911. *COMMENSURATE* (*kŏm-mĕn'-shŭr-āt*) *adj.* Proportionate, equivalent, adequate, equal in extent; also: having a common standard or measure.

COMMENSURATE is from the Latin *con*, with; and *mensurare*, to measure. The word today has at least two distinct senses. It originally meant capable of being measured by the same standard. Thus, a foot and a yard are COMMENSURATE because both can be expressed in inches. COMMENSURATE may also mean equal in extent, of the same value. The adjective COMMENSURABLE has only the original scientific meaning, capable of being measured in the same units, of being divided by the same number.

In the test phrase: 'COMMENSURATE to the deed', the word is thought by 29 per cent of adult readers to mean PERTAINING. To PERTAIN to is to belong to, be related to, be relevant. To be COMMENSURATE to or COMMENSURATE with, in this sense, means to equal, be of the same value as.

912. *INTRINSIC* (*ĭn-trĭn'-sĭk*) *adj.* Inherent, essential, real, genuine, internal, true, not merely apparent.

INTRINSIC is from the Latin *inter*, *intra*, within; and *secus*, apart, by the side of, beside. In the test phrase: 'Of INTRINSIC value', the word is thought by 32 per cent of adult readers to mean COMMERCIAL, mercantile, of the nature of trade. The COMMERCIAL value of a commodity can often be changed artificially by manipulating the market. Its INTRINSIC value cannot be altered. In this sense COMMERCIAL and INTRINSIC are opposed to one another.

The three words INTRINSIC, INHERENT, and INHERITED, are similar in suggestion. INHERENT and INHERITED, although alike in appearance, come from different Latin words and should not be confused. INHERITED is from the Latin *in*, in; and *heres, heredis*, heirs, the source of the English words HEIR (*ār*); HERITAGE (*hĕr'-ĭ-tāj*); and HEREDITARY (*hĕ-rĕd'-ĭ-tā-rĭ*). INHERITED characteristics are handed from one generation to another, and the word INHERITED can be used only with reference to characteristics of living things. INHERENT is from the Latin *in*, in; and *haerere*, to stick, the source of the English words ADHERE, literally to stick to; and COHERE, to stick together. INHERENT characteristics may be inherited, may be handed from father to son; but the word INHERENT means essential, real, and is applied to characteristics which stick. INHERENT can be used of inanimate objects as well as of living things.

INTRINSIC and INHERENT are often used interchangeably but differ slightly in meaning. INHERENT may be used of any quality which is a true characteristic of a person or object whether or not that quality is important. INTRINSIC is used only of an important, essential, vital quality.

913. *SANGUINARY* (*săng'-gwĭn-ā-rĭ*) *adj.* Bloodthirsty, murderous, bloody, eager to spill blood, attended with much bloodshed.

The Latin *sanguis*, blood, is the source not only of SANGUINARY, bloody; and SANGUINE, confident; but also of SANGFROID (*săng-frwah'*), cold-bloodedness, calmness in difficult situations; and CONSANGUINITY (914), blood relationship.

In the test phrase: 'Their leaders were SANGUINARY', the word is thought by 22 per cent of adult readers to mean OPTIMISTIC; and by another 19 per cent to mean CONFIDENT. This is no doubt a confusion of SANGUINARY, bloody, with

SANGUINE, hopeful, optimistic, confident, assured, having good circulation. Although SANGUINE should be limited to the meaning of hopeful, confident, it is sometimes used to mean bloody and occasionally bloodthirsty, like SANGUINARY; but SANGUINARY never means optimistic, confident.

914. *CONSANGUINITY* (*kŏn-săng-gwĭn'-ĭ-tĭ*) *n.* Blood relationship, the relationship that proceeds from common ancestry.

CONSANGUINITY is unknown to practically the same percentage of adult readers as SANGUINARY (913). To 24 per cent CON-SANGUINITY incorrectly means FELLOWSHIP, companionship. This may be due to some confusion of CONSANGUINITY, blood relationship, with AFFINITY. AFFINITY is relation by marriage, and hence is used also for a natural liking or attraction; CON-SANGUINITY is limited to relation by blood. AFFINITY and CONSANGUINITY, when strictly used, are mutually exclusive.

915. *TRANSPORT* (*trăns'-pōrt*) *n.* Rapture, elation, ecstasy, exaltation, passion, vehement emotion.

TRANSPORT is from the Latin *trans*, over; and *portare*, to carry. A TRANSPORT (228) is, in its first meaning, a carriage or conveyance and the word is used technically today to mean a ship or vessel to carry troops. The meaning, rapture, ecstasy, probably comes from the verb, to TRANSPORT, which still means to convey, carry, but which has come in addition to have the derived meaning, to carry away by strong emotion. A TRANSPORT is that which carries one away. The word is used most frequently in the plural as: 'TRANSPORTS of joy'.

916. *SONOROUS* (*sō-nō'-rŭs*, not *sŏn'-ō-rŭs*) *adj.* Reso-nant, deep-toned, plangent, full-volumed, loud, having a rich powerful sound.

In the test phrase: 'A SONOROUS sermon', the word is thought by 20 per cent of preparatory-school juniors to mean SLEEP-PRODUCING. This is perhaps a confusion of SONOROUS, deep-toned, with SOPORIFIC, SOPORIFEROUS, or SOPOROUS, all three of which mean tending to produce sleep. SONOROUS comes from the Latin *sonare*, to sound, and means sounding with a rich, full-volumed tone.

917. *DISINGENUOUS* (dĭs-ĭn-jĕn'-ū-ŭs) *adj.* Insincere, crafty, deceptive, artful, cunning (320), close-mouthed, evasive, sham, pretending, not candid (272), not ingenuous (1099), as: 'A DISINGENUOUS attitude'.

To 22 per cent of college seniors DISINGENUOUS incorrectly means CANDID, frank, open, ingenuous, an exact opposite of DISINGENUOUS, insincere, crafty.

918. *PELF* (pĕlf) *n.* Money, riches, wealth, lucre, ill-gotten gains, stolen property.

The most common misinterpretation of PELF is FUR. This is obviously a confusion of PELF, lucre, with PELT, the fur from a small animal. PELF is from an Old French word meaning spoil, plunder; and, although the English word PELF always refers to money, it is used contemptuously to signify ill-gotten gains, tainted money.

919. *APPREHEND* (ăp-prē-hĕnd') *v.* To look forward to with fear, anticipate with dread, be anxious about, be apprehensive of, feel alarm.

To APPREHEND comes from the Latin *ad*, to; and *prendere*, to seize; and the word APPREHEND in English may have this literal meaning of to seize, especially in the sense of to arrest, take into custody. To APPREHEND may also mean to grasp mentally, understand. To APPREHEND has also the derived meaning of to fear, anticipate with dread, expect evil, as in the phrase: 'Nothing to APPREHEND', nothing to fear. The adjective, APPREHENSIVE (396), which is more familiar, has only this last meaning, fearful, suspicious.

920. *PROMISCUOUS* (prō-mĭs'-kū-ŭs) *adj.* Indiscriminate, mixed, unsorted, haphazard, heterogeneous (666), disorderly, confusedly mingled.

PROMISCUOUS and MISCELLANEOUS come from the same Latin verb *miscere*, to mix. A MISCELLANEOUS collection is composed of different kinds of things, a PROMISCUOUS one is without order or arrangement.

To 37 per cent of adult readers PROMISCUOUS incorrectly means BOUNTIFUL. BOUNTIFUL is ample, abundant, unlimited, unrestricted. There are situations in which BOUNTIFUL and

PROMISCUOUS may both be used to mean unrestricted, unlimited; but BOUNTIFUL means not restricted in amount, while PROMISCUOUS means not restricted in arrangement, not held to an orderly pattern.

921. *REVULSION* (*rē-vŭl'-shŭn*) *n.* Marked drawing back,
    violent pull away, sudden change of feeling, strong
reaction, vehement recoil.
By 28 per cent of preparatory-school juniors REVULSION, recoil, is thought to mean DISGUST. This may be due to a mistaken belief that REVULSION is the noun corresponding to the verb REVOLT. REVOLT, and the participial adjective REVOLTING, come from the Latin *re* and *volvere*, to turn around, roll, the source of the English verb to REVOLVE. To REVOLT is to turn against, mutiny, renounce allegiance to; or, when used in a transitive sense, cause to turn away with abhorrence, disgust. The participial adjective, REVOLTING, means disgusting, offensive, shocking. The noun REVULSION comes from the Latin *re*, and *vellere*, to pull, pluck. It is from the same source as the noun CONVULSION, a sudden pulling together of the muscles, spasm; and the verb to CONVULSE, to tense, throw into spasms of rage or mirth. The noun REVULSION does not imply disgust, loathing, abhorrence; but signifies a sudden pulling back, recoil for any reason.

922. *ARABLE* (*ăr'-ă-bl*) *adj.* Suitable for plowing, tillable,
    cultivable, fit for agricultural cultivation, capable of
being used for the growing of crops.
In the test phrase: 'ARABLE lands', the word is thought by 37 per cent of adult readers to mean DESERT, without cultivation, barren, desolate, waste, dry and sandy, an exact opposite of ARABLE. This is no doubt in part a confusion of ARABLE, tillable, with ARID, dry, parched. This same type of confusion was found among a large group of college seniors where the meaning of ARABLE was unknown to 54 per cent. By 22 per cent it was thought to mean DRY, parched, moistureless, arid. This again is a confusion, probably, of ARABLE, tillable, with ARID, dry. By another 8 per cent of this group ARABLE was thought to mean WASTE. In the phrase: 'WASTE lands', the word means uncultivated, practically an opposite of ARABLE.

ARABLE comes from the Latin *arare,* to plow, and means literally plowable, fit for cultivation.

923. *SCONE (skŏn* or *skoon) n.* Biscuit, a species of cake made of wheat or barley meal and baked on a griddle. SCONES are round, but are usually cut into quarters, giving the familiar wedge-shaped piece with a circular edge. The broad Scotch bonnet of the lowlands was called a SCONE or SCONE-CAP because of its shape.

To 20 per cent of college seniors SCONE incorrectly means JEWEL, precious stone; and to another 14 per cent, PEBBLE. The similarity in sound and spelling of SCONE and STONE may lead to these confusions. There is also a historical connection between SCONE and STONE. The STONE OF DESTINY, on which Celtic kings were crowned, was taken to SCONE, a parish of Perthshire, Scotland, in order that Scottish kings might be crowned like Celtic kings of an earlier period. As a result the stone became the STONE OF SCONE. Later when Edward the First was to be crowned it was moved again in 1296 to Westminster Abbey in London, where it now forms a part of the coronation chair.

924. *DISTRAIT (dĭs-trā') adj.* Absent-minded, preoccupied, oblivious, inattentive, unheeding, abstracted.

DISTRAIT, ABSTRACTED, and DISTRACTED, are all from the Latin, *tractus,* the past participle of *trahere,* to draw. DISTRACTED may mean that the attention has been drawn away from the matter in hand. ABSTRACTED and DISTRAIT are synonymous. ABSTRACTED is directly from the Latin. DISTRAIT is a French word so recently borrowed that when used with a feminine noun it is often given its French ending of E and its French pronunciation. Thus one says: 'He was DISTRAIT *(dĭs-trā')*'; but 'She was DISTRAITE *(dĭs-trāt')*'.

925. *DESUETUDE (dĕs'-wē-tūd,* not *dĕz'-wē-tūd) n.* Passing into disuse, oblivion (840), obsolescence, neglect, out of employment, discontinuance of practice.

DESUETUDE is from the Latin *de,* not; and *suere,* to use. Despite Grover Cleveland's well-known phrase: 'Innocuous DESUETUDE', harmless disuse, the word is thought by 22 per cent of adult readers to mean DISGRACE; and by another 22 per cent to mean RUIN. RUIN means downfall, impaired condition; and also at times that which caused the downfall, as in the phrase: 'It was their RUIN', meaning it was the cause of their downfall. DESUETUDE, disuse, may lead to impairment, ruin, but not necessarily; and there is nothing in the word DESUETUDE which implies ruin.

DESUETUDE and DISUSE are practically synonymous. DISUSE applies to material objects; a church may fall into disuse. DESUETUDE applies to customs, habits, practices. The habit of attending church may fall into desuetude.

CONSUETUDE, usage, habit, custom, is the opposite of DESUETUDE, disuse.

926. *DISCOMFIT* (*dĭs-kŭm′-fĭt*) *v.* To disconcert, perplex, rout, frustrate, defeat, baffle (189), suddenly embarrass by breaking up the plans of.

DISCOMFIT is from the Latin *dis*; and *conficere*, to finish; and by derivation means to keep from finishing.

In the test phrase: 'He was DISCOMFITED', the word is believed by 28 per cent of preparatory-school juniors to mean UNCOMFORTABLE. This is obviously a confusion of DISCOMFIT with DISCOMFORT, two words which are similar in meaning but which should be distinguished. To DISCOMFORT is to destroy the peace of, take away the happiness of. To DISCOMFIT is more specific; it is to rout, disconcert, defeat the plans of.

927. *VORACIOUS* (*vō-rā′-shŭs*) *adj.* Very hungry, gluttonous, greedy, crapulous, ravenous, ravening, rapacious.

VORACIOUS comes from the Latin *vorare*, to devour; plus ACIOUS. The suffix, ACIOUS, is a Latin termination added to express intensity of physical or mental action; thus: AUDACIOUS, from the Latin *audere*, to be bold, means actively bold; RAPACIOUS, from *rapere*, to seize, is actively grasping, seizing, plundering; VIVACIOUS, from *vivere*, to live, is actively alive; and VORACIOUS, from *vorare*, to swallow, is greedy, ravenous. The Latin verb, *vorare*, is the source also of the English verb, to DEVOUR.

To 16 per cent of adult readers VORACIOUS incorrectly

means ENERGETIC. This may perhaps be due to some confusion of VORACIOUS, gluttonous, with VIGOROUS, energetic; or it may be due to an understanding of ACIOUS but not of the verb *vorare*, devour.

To another 15 per cent VORACIOUS incorrectly means BARBAROUS. This may be a confusion of VORACIOUS, gluttonous, with FEROCIOUS, barbarous, savage, fierce, cruel.

To still another 14 per cent, VORACIOUS incorrectly means TRUTHFUL. This is no doubt a confusion of VORACIOUS, gluttonous, with VERACIOUS (*vē-rā'-shŭs*), truthful.

VORACIOUS originally applied only to food and meant greedy in eating. It is now frequently used in a figurative sense to mean greedy for other things, insatiable, omnivorous, as: 'A VORACIOUS reader'.

928. *DEBILITATE* (*dē-bĭl'-ĭ-tāt*) v. To enfeeble, exhaust, jade, weaken, enervate (1093), make languid.

In the test phrase: 'He was DEBILITATED', the word is thought by 19 per cent of adult readers to mean OUTLAWED. To OUTLAW is to place a person outside the protection of the law. DEBILITATE is from the Latin *de*, not; and *habere*, to have, hold, the source of the English words ABLE and ABILITY. To DEBILITATE is by derivation to disable, deprive of ability.

929. *EQUANIMITY* (*ē-kwă-nĭm'-ĭ-tĭ*, not *ĕk-wă-nĭm'-ĭ-tĭ*) n. Evenness of temper, serenity, imperturbability, composure of spirit, calmness amid trying circumstances.

To 46 per cent of college seniors EQUANIMITY incorrectly means FAIRNESS. This is no doubt a confusion of EQUANIMITY, calmness, serenity, with EQUITY, fairness, impartiality, a word from the same Latin source. EQUANIMITY comes from the Latin *aequus*, even, equal; and *animus*, mind, spirit. ANIMUS is now an English word and usually means hostile intention, wrath. In EQUANIMITY it returns to one of its more dispassionate Latin meanings. EQUANIMITY is literally even-mindedness.

930. *INTRANSIGENT* (*ĭn-trăns'-ĭ-jĕnt* is the American pronunciation; *ĭn-trănz'-ĭ-jĕnt*, the British) adj. Irreconcilable, uncompromising (333), implacable (673), refusing to agree.

INTRANSIGENT is from the Latin prefix *in*; and *transigere*, to come to an understanding. The verb *transigere* is in turn a combination of *trans*, through; and *agere*, to drive, do. The English verb, to TRANSACT, to carry through, settle affairs, make a compromise, is from *transactus*, the past participle of the same verb. The prefix *in*, when of Anglo-Saxon origin, conveys the idea of into, as in the word INLAND. When of Latin origin, it more often means NOT, as in this instance.

In the test phrase: 'The INTRANSIGENT person', the word is thought by 16 per cent of adult readers to mean HELPLESS. It is difficult to see why this is the most common misconception of the word INTRANSIGENT.

To another 10 per cent INTRANSIGENT, irreconcilable, means PREJUDICED, the second most common misconception. A PREJUDICED person is biased, having formed his opinion without considering the facts. He has literally pre-judged the situation. A common, though not invariable, use of PREJUDICE implies opposition. Thus, one is PREJUDICED more often against than in favor of something. INTRANSIGENT carries no suggestion of pre-judgment or prejudice or opposition, but refers solely to a person who will not compromise to gain his own ends.

931. *TENURE* (*tĕn'-ūr*) *n.* A hold upon something, title, control, authority. 'She has a life TENURE.'

TENURE is from the Latin *tenere*, to hold. TENEMENT is from the same source and originally meant the possession of something, a hold upon something, and was synonymous with TENURE. This meaning is now obsolete. TENEMENT then came to designate the thing possessed, the land or property held; and then by a natural process of generalization it was used for a house, dwelling, abode, residence. It is now used to mean a flat, apartment, a part of a building lived in as a separate dwelling-place. In American usage it differs from an APARTMENT in being of a lower grade.

TENANT comes also from the same source and meant originally the person holding or possessing a TENURE or TENEMENT. It now means one renting or holding a lease on a house or an apartment. A TENANT is the one who holds; a TENEMENT, that which is held; while the TENURE is the act or fact or process of holding.

932. *DIFFIDENCE* (dĭf'-fĭ-dĕns) *n.* Shyness (12), timidity, modest reserve, bashfulness, humility, self-distrust, lack of self-reliance.

DIFFIDENCE is from the Latin *dis*, not; and *fidere*, to trust; and means literally lack of trust in one's self.

In the test phrase: 'He spoke with DIFFIDENCE', the word is thought by 25 per cent of preparatory-school juniors to mean RELUCTANCE, unwillingness, disinclination. DIFFIDENCE and RELUCTANCE both suggest hesitation but for different reasons. One who is RELUCTANT hesitates because he has thought out the consequences and feels that it is wiser not to act. One who is DIFFIDENT hesitates through shyness, timidity.

CONFIDENCE, self-assurance, a word from the same Latin *fidere*, to trust, is an exact opposite of DIFFIDENCE, lack of self-assurance.

933. *FETID* (fĕt'-ĭd, not fē'-tĭd) *adj.* Stinking, bad-smelling, giving off an offensive odor.

FETID is from the Latin *fetere*, to stink. In the test phrase: 'FETID swamps', the word is thought by 38 per cent of adult readers to mean DISEASE-BREEDING, the only common misconception. FETID is used ordinarily in referring to putrid, rotten, decayed matter which is by its nature, disease breeding. There is therefore a close connection in thought between FETID and DISEASE-BREEDING, but the two are in no way synonymous.

934. *THRENODY* (thrĕn'-ō-dĭ) *n.* A dirge (603), elegy, requiem, placebo (plă-sē'-bō), lament, song of lamentation, ode composed for a funeral, epicedium (ĕp-ĭ-sē'-dĭ-ŭm). Coronach (kŏr'-ō-năk) is the Gaelic word for THRENODY. THRENODY comes from the Greek words θρῆνος, wailing, lamentation; and ᾠδή, song, ode. From θρῆνος comes also the unusual English word THRENETICAL (thrĕn-ĕt'-ĭ-kal), mournful, sorrowful, elegiacal (791). THRENODY was once written *threnode*, and although this spelling is today never used the word means an ode of lamentation. From the same source comes the English word MELODY.

A THRENODY, an ELEGY, a DIRGE, and a REQUIEM, are all expressions of sorrow for the dead. The last two, DIRGE and

REQUIEM, may be songs or music without words. An ELEGY is a poem, and may occasionally be sung. A THRENODY is expressed in words and is always sung.

935. *INDEMNIFY* (ĭn-dĕm'-nĭ-fī) *v.* To compensate, reimburse, requite, recompense, make good to, secure from loss, exempt from penalty, make up for that which is past. In the test phrase: 'I shall INDEMNIFY them', the word is thought by 29 per cent of adult readers to mean SLANDER, circulate false gossip about, defame, vilify. This is perhaps due to some remote confusion of INDEMNIFY with the verb to CONDEMN. Both to CONDEMN and to INDEMNIFY come from the same Latin verb, *damnare*, hurt, damage, injure, damn. To CONDEMN is to blame, pronounce sentence against, doom. To INDEMNIFY, from the Latin *in*, not; and *damnare*, to damn; may mean not to damn, that is to exempt from penalty; but more often it means to recompense, compensate, reimburse.

936. *FURTIVELY* (fer'-tĭv-lĭ) *adv.* Stealthily, slyly, secretly, surreptitiously, clandestinely, in an underhand manner. FURTIVELY is from the Latin *furtum*, theft; and the English word FURTIVE, secret (5), stealthy (367), clandestine (455), suggests the manner of a thief. 'A FURTIVE glance' is literally a stolen glance.

To 36 per cent of preparatory-school juniors FURTIVELY incorrectly means FEARFULLY, in a frightened manner, in a terrified way. The word FURTIVELY does not necessarily imply fright or fear, but means stealthily, slyly.

937. *PROMULGATE* (prō-mŭl'-gāt) *v.* To proclaim, broadcast, publish, announce, spread, disseminate, declare, circulate, utter (1109), make known.
PROMULGATE, DISSEMINATE, and PROCLAIM, are practically synonymous. PROCLAIM, from the Latin verb *clamare*, to cry out, the source of the English word CLAMOR (242), is literally to call out, cry forth, an announcement. DISSEMINATE, from the Latin *dis*; and *semen*, seed; and therefore spelt with two s's, suggests scattering news about as one sows seed.

PROMULGATE, and the corresponding noun PROMULGATION, are practically the only words from the Latin *promulgare*, to make known, the ultimate derivation of which is uncertain. To PROMULGATE and to PUBLISH are both to make known. To PUBLISH is the general word, and may be used for making something known to a few or to many. The verb to PROMULGATE can be used only of making known to a large number, of making generally known. Laws, edicts, opinions, doctrines, principles, are PROMULGATED.

In the test phrase: 'He PROMULGATED the decree', the word is thought by 20 per cent of adult readers to mean REVOKED. To REVOKE is to call back, rescind, withdraw, cancel, almost an opposite of PROMULGATE, proclaim.

938. *CAPARISON* (*că-păr'-ĭ-sŭn*) *n.* Gay rich clothing, sumptuous apparel; specifically, a cloth laid over the saddle of a horse, especially a horse equipped for a state occasion.

To 30 per cent of college seniors CAPARISON incorrectly means WIT, neat turn of speech, unexpected comparison, unlooked for association of ideas causing surprise and delight. This may perhaps be due to some confusion of CAPARISON, decorated saddle cloth, with CAPRICE, a whim, unexpected action; or with the adjective, CAPRICIOUS, whimsical, unaccountable.

Although CAPARISON, from a Spanish word meaning saddle cover, is literally trappings, equipment for a horse, the word is used generally, as in the phrase: 'His gay CAPARISON', to mean any sumptuous apparel, clothing, showy outfit.

939. *DISPENSE* (*dĭs-pĕns'*) *v.* To administer, distribute, mete out, deal out in portions. The noun, a DISPENSER, may mean a manager; and it is in this sense that the verb is applied to the administration of laws.

DISPENSE is from the Latin *dis*, apart; and *pensus*, the past participle of the verb *pendere*, to weigh. Because DISPENSE comes from the frequentative form of the Latin verb it does not mean to weigh out grudgingly, but to give in a more general way. From the same source comes the noun DISPENSARY, originally a place within a hospital where medi-

cines were weighed and given out; now an institution which
gives free medical service to the poor.

In the test phrase: 'He DISPENSED the laws', the word is
believed by 36 per cent of adult readers to mean DISREGARDED.
To DISPENSE WITH is to go without, give up, omit, almost
disregard. But the word, to DISPENSE, without the preposition WITH, means to deal out, administer.

940. *DOCILE* (*dŏs'-ĭl*) *adj.* Teachable, amenable, tractable,
     easily taught, readily managed.
DOCILE comes from the Latin *docere*, to teach. From the
same source comes DOCENT, teacher, instructor, tutor; strictly
a person licensed as a teacher but not on a regular salary.
In the United States the word DOCENT is used especially of
one who teaches in a museum.

Docile is unknown to 70 per cent of adult readers. In the
test phrase: 'The DOCILE child', the two common misconceptions are LOVABLE and DULL. The first is held by 32 per cent,
and the second by 20 per cent of adult readers. DULL, which
may mean slow to comprehend, slow-witted, is almost an
opposite of DOCILE, teachable, easily taught.

AMENABLE, TRACTABLE, and DOCILE, are close in meaning;
but accurately, AMENABLE means easily driven; TRACTABLE,
easily led; and DOCILE, easily taught.

941. *DISPARAGE* (*dĭs-păr'-āj*) *v.* To belittle, speak of
     slightingly, depreciate, undervalue, discredit, vilify.
In the test phrase: 'He DISPARAGED the food', the word is
believed by 40 per cent of adult readers to mean DEVOURED,
ate greedily, consumed ravenously. This may be due to a
confusion of DISPARAGE, to belittle, with the verb to RAVAGE,
to lay waste, destroy. Or it may be due to the idea of
diminishing which is common to both DISPARAGE and DEVOUR.
'He DISPARAGED the food' does not mean he diminished the
amount of food; but that he diminished the reputation of
the food.

The noun DISPARAGEMENT, disrepute, reproach, dishonor,
discredit, originally meant a giving in marriage to one of
inferior rank, the degradation of a person caused by an
unequal marriage. This was the exact meaning of the French

word from which DISPARAGEMENT comes; but this meaning is now obsolete in English. DISPARAGEMENT is now used only in the figurative sense to mean the act of dishonoring by comparison, the act of undervaluing, discrediting. To DISPARAGE and to DEPRECIATE both mean to diminish, decrease, in reputation. To DEPRECIATE, practically an opposite of APPRECIATE, is literally to decrease the price of, and so to undervalue, discredit. To DISPARAGE is from the same Latin *par*, equal, as PEERAGE, the nobility, or the rank of a nobleman. To DISPARAGE is to decrease the rank of.

942. *CONTRITE* (*kŏn'-trīt*, not *kŏn-trīt'*) *adj.* Penitent, repentant, remorseful, humble, broken in spirit, conscience-stricken, filled with humility.

CONTRITE, and the corresponding noun CONTRITION, come from the Latin *con*, together; and *terrere*, to rub. CONTRITE originally meant bruised, worn, rubbed. It still has the suggestion of broken in spirit by a sense of guilt.

To 31 per cent of college seniors CONTRITE incorrectly means TO THE POINT, direct, brief. This may be a confusion of CONTRITE, penitent, with CONCISE (*kŏn-sīs'*), to the point.

To another 14 per cent CONTRITE incorrectly means HACKNEYED, commonplace. This is probably a confusion of CONTRITE, penitent, conscience-stricken, with TRITE, hackneyed, commonplace. TRITE is from the same source as CONTRITE and by derivation means rubbed, worn out, frayed, but today is used only in the figurative sense of hackneyed, commonplace.

CONTRITE, REPENTANT, and REMORSEFUL, apply to sorrow for a past act. REMORSEFUL is to feel a gnawing regret. REPENTANT, although not so strong as REMORSEFUL, adds to it the desire to make amends. The REPENTANT person expresses his repentance in some form. CONTRITE is more spiritual; it is to be continuously in a state of self-condemnation, with no outlet in action.

943. *VAGARY* (*vā-gā'-rĭ*, not *vā'-gă-rĭ*) *n.* Whim, caprice, whimsicality, fanciful freak, extravagant idea, wild fancy, irresponsible dreaming.

In the test phrase: 'That is only a VAGARY', the word is

thought by 31 per cent of adult readers to mean EXCUSE, apology, justification.

VAGUE, ill-defined, obscure, hazy; VAGABOND, a wanderer; and VAGARY; all come from the same Latin word, *vagus*, wandering, rambling, strolling. VAGARY was originally a verb and meant to gad, to go about without purpose, ramble. A VAGARY is the kind of vague whimsicality which enters the head of one who likes to ramble aimlessly.

944. *ONEROUS* (ŏn'-er-ŭs, not ō'-ner-ŭs) *adj.* Burdensome, tedious (194), oppressive (427), weighty, toilsome, troublesome, irksome, heavy with responsibility.

ONEROUS is from the Latin *onus*, load, burden, a word which has come unchanged into the English language as: 'The ONUS (ō'-nŭs) of the situation', the burden, responsibility, duty, obligation.

ONEROUS and ARDUOUS are similar in suggestion. An ARDUOUS task requires continuous, persevering, active toil. An ONEROUS task need require no effort, no exertion, but must weigh upon one as a responsibility.

Two equally common misconceptions of the word are MONOTONOUS and IGNOBLE, each held by 15 per cent of adult readers. Because an ONEROUS task must be burdensome without necessarily demanding physical exertion it is apt to be either monotonous or ignoble; but neither MONOTONOUS, which means wearisome, nor IGNOBLE, base, mean, of low position, is an exact synonym of ONEROUS, which means burdensome, oppressive.

945. *ASCETICISM* (ăs-sĕt'-ĭ-sĭzm) *n.* Severe self-denial, austerity, abstinence (663), the practice of ascetics.
An ASCETIC, in the early days of the Church, was a hermit, recluse, one who retired from the customary business of life and dedicated himself to piety and devotion. ASCETICISM is the life, the practice, the character, of an ASCETIC. Both words come originally from the Greek ἀσκεῖν, to work, exercise; but more directly from ἄσκησις, the regimen undergone by an athlete while in training.

In the test phrase: 'ASCETICISM reflects cowardice', the word is thought by 18 per cent of college seniors to mean

INDULGENCE, excess, license, unrestraint, yielding to inclination, an exact opposite of ASCETICISM.

ASCETICISM and AESTHETICISM (*ĕs-thĕt'-ĭ-sĭzm*) should be differentiated both in pronunciation and in meaning. AESTHETICISM may mean devotion to beauty, appreciation of the beautiful. It may also signify the principles of good taste in the arts. ASCETICISM is abstinence, severe self-denial.

ASCETICISM was never a philosophy and should not be confused with other words ending in ISM such as STOICISM, the doctrine of freedom from passion, indifference to joy, resolute calm; and HEDONISM, the doctrine that the pleasure of the moment is the ultimate aim. ASCETICISM has played a part in many philosophies but is a characteristic rather than a philosophy.

ASCETICISM and HEDONISM are opposites in suggestion.

946. *OBFUSCATE* (*ŏb-fŭs'-kāt*) *v.* To confuse, obscure, muddle (161), darken, bewilder (185), becloud, stupefy, perplex.

OBFUSCATE comes from the Latin *ob*, to; and *fuscus*, dark, dusky, tawny. FUSCOUS is an English word and means dark brown in color or more generally of any dark color.

In the test phrase: 'To OBFUSCATE someone', the word is believed by 23 per cent of adult readers to mean DISCOURAGE; and by another 22 per cent to mean HINDER. These misconceptions may be due to the similarity in sound of OBFUSCATE and FRUSTRATE. To FRUSTRATE is to baffle (189), cause to fail, defeat, bring to nought. To OBFUSCATE is to confuse, bewilder.

HINDER and AID; DISCOURAGE and ENCOURAGE; OBFUSCATE and ENLIGHTEN; are opposites of one another.

947. *CACOPHONOUS* (*kă-kŏf'-ŏ-nŭs*) *adj.* Discordant, inharmonious, harsh-sounding, dissonant, clashing, disagreeable in sound.

In the test phrase: 'CACOPHONOUS winds', the word is believed by 23 per cent of adult readers to mean SIGHING, mournful.

CACOPHONOUS is from the Greek κακός, bad; and φωνή, voice, sound; and means literally bad-sounding. From the same Greek word for voice come also the words TELEPHONE,

literally a far-away voice; and TELEPHONY, the science of
producing voices from afar. The noun CACOPHONY (kă-kŏf'-
ō-nĭ), like the noun TELEPHONY (tĕ-lĕf'-ō-nĭ), should be
accented on the second syllable.
CACOPHONOUS and EUPHONIOUS are opposites.

948. *BEDIZEN* (bē-dĭz'-ĕn) *v.* To adorn (198), bedeck,
     dress gaudily, trick out, clothe with tawdry splendor.
In the test phrase: 'They BEDIZEN themselves', the word is
thought by 26 per cent of adult readers to mean DECEIVE,
cheat, delude, trick. This is perhaps a confusion between
two meanings of the verb TRICK. To TRICK may mean deceive, cheat; or when used with UP or OUT it may mean
to dress, bedeck, bedizen.
   The original meaning of the prefix BE was about, around,
sometimes all over. The prefix survives with this clear-cut
meaning in only a few verbs, as: BEDECK, to adorn, literally
to deck about; BEGIRD, to surround with a band, literally to
gird about or around; and BEDIZEN. In all three cases the
word without the prefix BE survives, although DIZEN, to
dress, adorn, is more unusual than BEDIZEN.

949. *SHIVE* (shīv) *n.* Splinter, sliver, shiver (shĭv'-er), frag-
     ment of wood.
SHIVE can be traced back to Middle English. To 31 per cent
of college seniors it incorrectly means BUNDLE, a number of
things fastened together. This may be due to a confusion
of SHIVE with SHEAF (shēf) or perhaps with the plural
SHEAVES (shēvz), any bundle of things, especially a bundle
of unthreshed stocks of grain.
   To another 13 per cent, SHIVE, splinter, sliver, incorrectly
means GROOVED WHEEL. This is probably a confusion of
SHIVE (shīv) with SHEAVE (shēv), colloquially pronounced
(shĭv), a word from the same original source as SHIVE, but
which now means a grooved wheel, as the wheel in a block
or pulley.

950. *CARBOY* (kahr'-boi) *n.* Large bottle usually protected
     by wickerwork or by a wooden frame.
In the test phrase: 'Do not tip the CARBOY', the word is

thought by 27 per cent of adult readers to mean CHAUFFEUR. CARBOY, DEMIJOHN, and FLAGON, are names for bottles, and all three words are related. A FLAGON is a bottle with a spout and a handle, ordinarily for table use. The Persian word, from which comes the English word CARBOY, meant a large FLAGON. A DEMIJOHN is a large bulging glass bottle protected by wickerwork or by a wooden frame. A DEMIJOHN is used for such fluids as vinegar, wines, and sometimes hard liquors. The word CARBOY was once synonymous with DEMIJOHN, but is used today more often for a protected bottle used in shipping acids and also spring water.

951. *EXPOSTULATION* (*ĕks-pŏs-tū-lā'-shŭn*) *n.* A remonstrance, argumentative protest, reasoning earnestly against, attempt at dissuasion.

EXPOSTULATION is from the Latin *ex*; and *postulare*, to ask, require. In the test phrase: 'His EXPOSTULATION continued', the word is thought by 31 per cent of preparatory-school juniors to mean NARRATION, the telling of a story. This is perhaps a confusion of EXPOSTULATION, remonstrance, with EXPOSITION, for although EXPOSITION does not mean narration, the word comes from a Latin word *exponere*, to set forth, narrate. An EXPOSITION, as the word is used in English, is an elucidation, explanation, explication, a setting forth in any form.

EXPOSTULATION and REMONSTRANCE are practically synonymous. Both are argumentative. Both are of the nature of advice, rather than of censure or reproof. Both apply to acts taking place or about to take place. They differ in that REMONSTRANCE is the milder of the two, and is more apt to be made by an equal. EXPOSTULATION is apt to be made by a superior, and therefore to be more dictatorial.

952. *PROCLIVITY* (*prō-klĭv'-ĭ-tĭ*) *n.* Propensity (709), tendency, proneness, penchant (824), inclination, natural leaning, bent, bias, predisposition, aptitude.

When given a choice between TENDENCY and SLOPE as synonyms of PROCLIVITY in the phrase: 'A noticeable PROCLIVITY', 25 per cent of adult readers choose SLOPE. PROCLIVITY is not thus used today. It comes from the Latin *clivus*, a declivity or slope; but the word PROCLIVITY in English is used figuratively to mean a leaning toward or inclination toward something and not to mean DECLIVITY, an actual physical slope, a descending surface.

The word INCLINATION, slope, bent, bias, propensity, disposition, tendency, can be used both literally and figuratively. The word PROCLIVITY can be used only figuratively.

An ACCLIVITY is an upward slope, an ascent. A DECLIVITY is a downward slope. A PROCLIVITY is a tendency.

953. *FORTUITOUS* (for-tū'-ĭ-tŭs) *adj.* Accidental, chance, random (472), casual, adventitious, contingent, occurring unexpectedly, happening without any known cause.

In the test phrase: 'A FORTUITOUS development', the word is thought by 46 per cent of college seniors to mean FORTUNATE, lucky, auspicious. FORTUITOUS, FORTUNATE, and the noun FORTUNE, all come from the Latin *fors, fortis,* chance. FORTUNE, like the word LUCK, may mean pure chance, either good or bad as: 'The FORTUNES of war'; or it may mean good luck, as: 'He had the FORTUNE to be a gainer'. The adjective FORTUNATE, like LUCKY, can mean happening only by good luck, successful, opportune. FORTUITOUS means happening by pure chance, incidental; the word conveys no suggestion of good or bad.

FORTUITOUS and ACCIDENTAL are practically synonymous. ACCIDENTAL comes from the Latin *cadere*, to happen, and often distinguishes a happening due to a combination of known causes, something which might have been anticipated, prevented. FORTUITOUS distinguishes a happening due to unknown causes.

954. *LEVITY* (lĕv'-ĭ-tĭ) *n.* Frivolity, flippancy, volatility, flightiness, inappropriate gaiety, mirth which is out of place, want of seriousness, lightness of temperament.

In the test phrase: 'The spirit of LEVITY', the word is thought by 30 per cent of adult readers to mean RIGHTEOUSNESS. This is perhaps a confusion of LEVITY, lightness of temperament, with EQUITY. EQUITY comes from the Latin *aequus*, equal, fair, just, and means justice, impartiality, rectitude, honesty, uprightness, righteousness. LEVITY is from the

Latin *levis*, light; from the same source as ALLEVIATE, to lighten. LEVITY originally meant in English lightness of weight in a purely physical sense. Although the word is now used most often figuratively it always specifies inappropriate lightness of touch. In this it differs from MIRTH and GAIETY, both of which are lightness of spirit exhibited on appropriate occasions.

To another 14 per cent LEVITY incorrectly means GRAVITY, seriousness, earnestness, sobriety, an antonym of LEVITY.

LEVITY, VOLATILITY, and FRIVOLITY, are all tendencies to trifle with important matters. FRIVOLITY, from the Latin *frivolus*, trifling, silly, suggests an inherent inability to treat matters seriously. VOLATILITY from the Latin *volare*, to fly, is a tendency to fly too quickly from one thing to another. LEVITY is a tendency to treat important matters too lightly.

955. *KISMET* (*kĭs'-mĕt*) *n*. Destiny, fate, lot, portion, fortune, chance, doom.

To 31 per cent of adult readers KISMET incorrectly means MOHAMMED. This is perhaps a confusion of KISMET, destiny, with the KORAN, the sacred book of the Mohammedans.

The word KISMET is not capitalized, and is not related to the name of any god or goddess. In this it differs from such English words as FORTUNE, and FATE, both of which are sometimes capitalized, and either of which may be thought of as a power determining future events. FORTUNE is closely related to the Roman goddess FORTUNA, the goddess of destiny; and FATE to the three FATES: CLOTHO (*klō'-thō*), who spins the thread of life; LACHESIS (*lăk'-ē-sĭs*), who measures off the thread; and ATROPOS (*ăt'-rō-pŏs*), who cuts the thread. KISMET comes directly from an Arabic word meaning to divide, apportion, and by derivation means one's lot in life. It is synonymous with the English words LOT and PORTION.

956. *PELLUCID* (*pĕl-lū'-sĭd*) *adj*. Crystal-clear, transparent (150), translucent, perfectly lucid, limpid, not roiled, not turbid (1037). When PELLUCID is used figuratively it means perspicuous, clear to the understanding.

PELLUCID is from the Latin *lucidus*, light, clear, bright, an adjective which in turn comes from *lucere*, to shine. The verb *lucere* is the direct source of the English word LUCENT, bright, lustrous, resplendent, which has almost exactly the meaning of the Latin word. The prefix PER, which before L becomes PEL, intensifies the meaning as in: PERTINACIOUS, very tenacious; and PERACUTE, very acute. PELLUCID means very lucid.

To 18 per cent of adult readers PELLUCID incorrectly means VAGUE, indistinct, hazy, practically an opposite of PELLUCID. To another 16 per cent PELLUCID incorrectly means OBSCURE, not clear, not easily understood, an exact opposite of PELLUCID. Both of these misunderstandings may be intensified by the misnomer LUCIFER. The word LUCIFER is from *lucere*, to shine; and *ferre*, to carry; and by derivation means light-bearer. LUCIFER was once the name of the morning star. Apparently through a curious misinterpretation of a passage from Isaiah this name was given to SATAN, so that today SATAN, the Prince of Darkness, bears the name of the bright and shining morning star.

PELLUCID, PERSPICUOUS, and PERSPICACIOUS, are related. The last two are from the Latin *per*, through; and *specere*, to see. PERSPICACIOUS means of clear understanding, having insight, keen, penetrating, and is applied to a clear mind. PERSPICUOUS, and PELLUCID in its figurative sense, are practically synonymous. Both mean expressed with clarity, clear to the understanding, and apply to subject matter.

957. *COGNATE* (*kŏg'-nāt*) *adj.* Kindred, allied by blood, consanguineous, proceeding from the same stock.

In the test phrase: 'COGNATE races', the word is thought by 44 per cent of college seniors to mean KNOWN. This may be a confusion of COGNATE, kindred, allied, with the noun COGNIZANCE, knowledge, notice, awareness. Both words come from Latin sources; COGNIZANCE from the verb, *cognoscere*, to know, and COGNATE from the Latin *cognatus*, related by birth, from *con*, together, and *natus*, the past participle of *nasci*, to be born, and the source of the English word NATIVE.

COGNATE and ALLIED both mean bound together. ALLIED is the general word for any union of interests; nations may be ALLIED by treaty. COGNATE means allied in origin, springing from the same source.

958. *EQUIVOCAL* (*ē-kwĭv'-ō-kăl*) *adj.* Ambiguous, doubtful, questionable, dubious, of double meaning.

EQUIVOCAL is from the Latin *aequus*, equal; and *vocare*, to call; and by derivation applies to that which is said in such a manner that it can be understood equally well in two different ways.

In the test phrase: 'EQUIVOCAL position', the word is thought by 27 per cent of adult readers to mean PRECARIOUS. Although this interpretation of the word would ordinarily be incorrect, it can be justified. A business position may be PRECARIOUS (362), uncertain, because it depends upon the will of another, and can therefore be taken away at any moment. A political position, stand, platform, may be EQUIVOCAL, uncertain, because of the manner of expression. Occasionally the two words are interchangeable although the connotation may differ slightly.

DOUBTFUL, DUBIOUS, OBSCURE, AMBIGUOUS, and EQUIVOCAL, are closely allied in meaning. DOUBTFUL is the general word for uncertain; DUBIOUS is anxiously uncertain; OBSCURE is literally covered over, and means uncertain because of lack of light; AMBIGUOUS means uncertain primarily in reference to words; EQUIVOCAL is deliberately, intentionally, ambiguous.

959. *OBSEQUIOUS* (*ŏb-sē'-kwĭ-ŭs*) *adj.* Fawning, compliant (418), servile (632), obviously ingratiating, truckling, currying favor, meanly submissive, sycophantic.

In the test phrase: 'His manner was OBSEQUIOUS', the word is thought by 25 per cent of adult readers to mean INSULTING, abusive. This is perhaps because INSULTING, at least in implication, is an opposite of OBSEQUIOUS, which may imply eager to gain favor for one's self; or it may be because of some confusion of OBSEQUIOUS, servile, with OBNOXIOUS, offensive, objectionable, a word which has many of the disagreeable suggestions of INSULTING.

To another 14 per cent OBSEQUIOUS means DIGNIFIED, self-respecting, stately, an opposite of OBSEQUIOUS, servile.

OBSEQUIOUS is from the Latin *ob*, upon, and *sequi*, to follow, and by derivation means following upon. It is today always used in the figurative sense of following submissively. OBSEQUIOUS, SUBMISSIVE, and OBEDIENT, are three ways of recognizing superiority. An OBEDIENT person obeys a recognized and legitimate authority with no hope of reward or praise for so doing. A SUBMISSIVE person obeys a superior who has no proper authority or who is not admitted to have proper authority by the one who submits. SUBMISSION may be forced upon one or may be easier than rebellion; it is a negative characteristic. An OBSEQUIOUS person obeys a superior with the hope of gaining a reward for so doing.

960. *PLATITUDINOUS* (*plăt-ĭ-tū'-dĭ-nŭs*) *adj.* Trite, dull, stale (32), hackneyed, flat, commonplace, bromidic, insipid (375), as: 'PLATITUDINOUS comments'.

The noun, a PLATITUDE, is a hackneyed sentence, commonplace remark, truism, cliché.

PLATITUDINOUS is from the French *plat*, flat. The English adjective FLAT may be used figuratively to mean dull, uninteresting, monotonous, as: 'A FLAT lecture', and it is in this sense that the French *plat* is used in the word PLATITUDE.

To 18 per cent of college seniors PLATITUDINOUS incorrectly means SUGGESTIVE, containing a hint, intimating, full of suggestion.

To another 12 per cent, it incorrectly means WITTY, brilliant, sparkling, original in expressing amusing ideas, an opposite of PLATITUDINOUS, stale, commonplace.

961. *PARSIMONIOUS* (*pahr-sĭ-mō'-nĭ-ŭs*) *adj.* Stingy, close, frugal (617) to excess, niggardly, penurious (711), miserly, immoderately sparing, economizing (204) in the expenditure of money.

In the test phrase: 'He was PARSIMONIOUS', the word is thought by 20 per cent of adult readers to mean FORMAL. This is perhaps a confusion of PARSIMONIOUS, stingy, frugal, with CEREMONIOUS, formal.

PARSIMONIOUS is thought by 16 per cent of college seniors to mean RELIGIOUS. This may be due to the word PARSON, clergyman. There is no etymological connection. PARSON comes from the Latin *persona*, a person, from the same source as the English word PERSON. PARSIMONIOUS is from the Latin *parcere*, to spare.

PARSIMONIOUS and ECONOMICAL both mean saving of money. ECONOMICAL is used only in the good sense of spending intelligently, of not being wasteful; and the word is often applied to large expenditures. It is through ECONOMY that a large organization flourishes. PARSIMONIOUS is used ordinarily in the bad sense of economical to excess, of saving in petty expenses. It is through PARSIMONY that the poor grow rich.

PARSIMONIOUS, PENURIOUS, and SPARING, all mean inordinately economical. SPARING is the mildest of the three. PENURIOUS is the strongest; it is carrying economy to the extreme of sordid want and suffering. PARSIMONIOUS is between the others; it is saving in every trivial way.

962. *CEPHALIC* (sĕ-făl'-ĭk) *adj.* Pertaining to the head in any way. CEPHALIC is used only as a scientific word, as for instance in the phrase: 'CEPHALIC index'; or as a part of another scientific word, as BRACHYCEPHALIC and DOLICHOCEPHALIC.

In the test phrase: 'The CEPHALIC index', the word is thought by 37 per cent of adult readers to mean COLOR. The CEPHALIC index is the greatest width of the skull, from side to side, divided by its length from front to back, and then multiplied usually by 100 in order to eliminate the decimal point. A skull with a CEPHALIC index of 80 or above is called BRACHYCEPHALIC (brăk-ĭ-sĕ-făl'-ĭk), literally short-headed, a skull only a little longer from front to back than it is wide from side to side. Skulls of Armenians are in general of this type. A skull with a CEPHALIC index of less than 80 is called DOLICHOCEPHALIC (dŏl-ĭ-kō-sĕ-făl'-ĭk), literally long-headed. Skulls of negroes are in general of this type.

The word CEPHALIC comes, through Latin, from Greek. The most familiar Latin word for head is *caput*, which appears in the word DECAPITATE, to cut off the head, and in many other English words. The most familiar Greek word for head is κρανίον, which respelt in Roman letters becomes the English word CRANIUM, skull. Historically, the word

CEPHALIC is probably not directly connected with either of these but of separate origin.

963. *NECROMANCY* (*nĕk'-rō-măn-sĭ*) *n.* The art of revealing future events by means of communication with the dead. From this, the word has come to have the more general meaning, magic, wizardry, sorcery, witchcraft, enchantment, conjuration.

NECROMANCY comes from the Greek words, νεκρός, dead; and μάντις, a prophet, seer, diviner. The first part of the word is from the same source as NECROPOLIS, literally a city of the dead, a large cemetery. NECROMANCY is sometimes fallaciously thought to be derived from NEGRO; and the word was, for a long time, spelt *negromancy*. This misconception is perhaps even now apparent in the popular phrase: 'The BLACK ART', magic, witchcraft, sorcery, a corrupted form of NECROMANCY, which flourished in the 17th century.

To 37 per cent of college seniors NECROMANCY incorrectly means IDOL WORSHIP, the adoration, reverence, of an image, statue. It is barely possible that this confusion is caused by the word MANTIS which is the Greek word μάντις, prophet, written in Roman letters. The PRAYING MANTIS is an insect which eats other insects and which bends its front legs as if kneeling.

964. *PROPITIATE* (*prō-pĭsh'-ĭ-āt*) *v.* To appease, conciliate, mollify, placate, pacify, gain the favor of.

In the test phrase: 'He PROPITIATED them', the word is thought by 20 per cent of adult readers to mean ASSISTED, the popular misconception.

To PROPITIATE, CONCILIATE, and APPEASE, all apply to persons. To APPEASE, by derivation at peace, is to pacify. One may APPEASE a child or an inferior. To CONCILIATE, which goes further than APPEASE, is to win over, gain the friendship of. One CONCILIATES an ill-treated equal. To PROPITIATE is from the Latin *propitius*, favorable, a word which was applied almost exclusively to the attitude of a deity. To PROPITIATE means literally to make propitious, favorable, well-disposed toward one's self. One PROPITIATES the gods; one PROPITIATES superiors who are reluctant to be pacified.

965. *PERTINACIOUS* (*per-tĭ-nā'-shŭs*) *adj.* Persistent, inflexible (241), stubborn (266), dogged, resolute, obstinate, unyielding (392).

PERTINACIOUS is from the Latin *per*, very; and *tenax, tenacis,* tenacious, originally from *tenere,* to hold. The English word TENACIOUS, from the same source, means slow to relinquish a hold, clinging tightly, holding fast, strongly adhesive. TENACIOUS can be used of substances which are sticky, not easily separable, or which cling physically, as: 'A TENACIOUS vine'. Or TENACIOUS may be used of individuals. It may be used in a complimentary sense, as: 'A TENACIOUS memory'; or in a derogatory sense to mean stubborn, obstinate, in clinging to a belief. PERTINACIOUS, which means very tenacious, is used only in this last sense. It is applied to mental attitudes and not to physical acts and is usually derogatory. A PERTINACIOUS person holds persistently to a point of view, resisting any effort of persuasion.

The Latin prefix *per*, meaning very, intensively, appears also in PELLUCID (956), very lucid; and PERACUTE (1074), very acute.

To 13 per cent of adult readers PERTINACIOUS incorrectly means REBELLIOUS, refractory, insubordinate, mutinous, contumacious. Both REBELLIOUS and PERTINACIOUS persons disregard authority; the REBELLIOUS person by overt acts, often of violence; the PERTINACIOUS person by persistently sticking to his own opinion.

966. *EXIGENCY* (*ĕk'-sĭ-jĕn-sĭ*) *n.* An emergency, urgency, pressing necessity, case demanding immediate action.

EXIGENCY is from the Latin *exigere,* to drive out, in a more figurative sense to demand, exact, a word which in turn comes from *ex*, out, and *agere*, to drive.

In the test phrase: 'A serious EXIGENCY', the word is thought by 22 per cent of adult readers to mean BLUNDER, error, mistake.

To 16 per cent of college seniors, the word EXIGENCY incorrectly means DIFFICULTY, perplexity, trouble. A DIFFICULTY and an EXIGENCY have in common the fact that both present a problem. A DIFFICULTY is any problem, whether of long standing or not; the word does not imply that a solution is imperative. An EXIGENCY is a problem which demands immediate attention.

Both an EXIGENCY and an EMERGENCY require action; an EXIGENCY is a minor emergency.

967. *PREDATORY* (*prĕd'-ă-tō-rĭ*) *adj.* Plundering, pillaging, despoiling, preying upon, living by spoil.

To 27 per cent of college seniors PREDATORY incorrectly means EXPECTED, anticipated, looked for, foreseen; and to another 26 per cent it incorrectly means PREDICTABLE, capable of being foretold. These may perhaps be due to a confusion of PREDATORY, plundering, with PREDICTORY, prophetic, predictive, that which predicts.

PREDATORY comes from the Latin *praedare*, to plunder, prey upon. From the same source come the English verb, to DEPREDATE, to prey upon, plunder; and the noun, DEPREDATION, pillaging, plundering, robbing. DEPREDATION and to DEPREDATE are used in place of the corresponding noun and verb which might be formed from PREDATORY.

968. *RETRIBUTION* (*rĕt-rĭ-bū'-shŭn*) *n.* Punishment, repayment, reward, redress, reparation, requital (1070), retaliation. RETRIBUTIVE is the corresponding adjective.

RETRIBUTION is from the Latin *re*, back; and *tribuere*, bestow, pay, assign; and is by derivation a paying back. From the same source come the English nouns TRIBUTE, originally money paid a conqueror; and CONTRIBUTION, any gift to a common fund, subscription for a common purpose.

Of the various synonyms for RETRIBUTION at least two, REVENGE and RETALIATION, are used with reference to the return for some past unkindness. REWARD and REPAYMENT specify a return for some past kindness. REQUITAL and RETRIBUTION may be used for either; although the latter is more frequently used for the return of an unkindness.

969. *NIB* (*nĭb*) *n.* The point of anything, especially the point of a pen, pen-point.

In the test phrase: 'A small NIB', the word is thought by 28 per cent of adult readers to mean BITE. This may be a confusion of NIB, point, with NIBBLE, which etymologically is probably the frequentative of NIB. A NIBBLE is a small bite, a morsel.

By another 13 per cent NIB is thought to mean PINCH. This is obviously a confusion of NIB, point, with NIP, pinch, a word probably from the same original source as NIB, point.

970. *STOLID* (*stŏl'-ĭd*) *adj.* Impassive, wooden, heavy, phlegmatic, apathetic, unemotional, sluggish, not easily moved, slow to betray feeling.

In the test phrase: 'An air of STOLID despair', the word is thought by 27 per cent of preparatory-school juniors to mean INTENSE, the popular misconception. INTENSE originally meant strong, powerful, extreme, as in the phrase: 'INTENSE pain'; but the word may also mean emotional, ardent, strenuous, as: 'An INTENSE person'. In this sense it is an exact opposite of STOLID, unemotional.

971. *AQUILINE* (*ăk'-wĭ-līn*) *adj.* Curving, hooked, resembling the beak of an eagle. AQUILINE is used most frequently in the phrase: 'An AQUILINE nose', and occasionally 'AQUILINE features'.

To 32 per cent of college seniors AQUILINE incorrectly means STRAIGHT, an exact opposite of AQUILINE.

To another 15 per cent AQUILINE incorrectly means FISH-LIKE. This is perhaps a confusion of AQUILINE, hooked, with some word from *aqua*, the Latin word for water, as, for instance, AQUARIUM, a place in which fish are exhibited.

AQUILINE comes from the Latin *aquila*, eagle, a word used today as the name of one of the constellations. AQUILA (*ăk'-wĭ-lah*), the Eagle, contains one bright star, ALTAIR, which with VEGA in Lyra and DENEB in Cygnus form a large triangle pointing more or less away from the Big Dipper. AQUILINE, by derivation, means like an eagle.

972. *ATYPICAL* (*ă-tĭp'-ĭ-kăl*) *adj.* Unrepresentative, abnormal, unusual, not showing the characteristics of its group, not typical (275).

In the test phrase: 'An ATYPICAL Scotchman', the word is thought by 29 per cent of adult readers to mean GENUINE, an exact opposite of the correct meaning. Although the prefix A has many meanings, in Greek, when used as a prefix to a word of Greek origin, it has only the negative sense, not; thus: AMORPHOUS, not morphous, without form; ACHRO-MATIC, not chromatic, without color; ASEPTIC, not septic, without putrefying poisons. In general there has been a tendency in the language to employ a prefix which comes from the same source as the word itself. Although the negative A should be used only before words of Greek origin, at least two exceptions occur in nineteenth century writings: ASEXUAL, non-sexual; and AMORAL, without morals, in distinction to IMMORAL, morally wrong, evil, dissolute. Both words, SEX and MORAL, come from Latin, not from Greek, and strictly neither should be prefixed with the Greek negative A, especially if they are to be used in a scientific disquisition.

973. *TERGIVERSATION* (*ter-jĭv-er-sā'-shŭn*) *n.* Evasion, shirking, shift, subterfuge, equivocation; specifically the desertion of one's party.

To 21 per cent of adult readers TERGIVERSATION incorrectly means CONVERSATION, a word which comes from the same ultimate Latin source.

TERGIVERSATION comes from the Latin *tergum*, back; and *vertere*, to turn. The noun TERGUM is used in English today to mean the back and is synonymous with DORSUM; the adjective TERGAL, dorsal, pertaining to the back, is an opposite of VENTRAL (1019), abdominal. A TERGIVERSATION is by derivation a turning of one's back. The word is used for the act of turning one's back upon one's professed opinions, to designate the desertion of a party. It is also used more generally of any evasion, subterfuge, shift.

974. *SENSILE* (*sĕn'-sĭl*) *adj.* Capable of affecting the senses, sensible. SENSILE is scientific in its exactness; it is limited to the one meaning, capable of affecting the senses.

TACTILE (*tăk'-tĭl*), capable of affecting the touch, tangible, perceptible by touch, pertaining to the sense of touch, is a more familiar word, related to touch much as SENSILE is to the senses.

Four closely associated words come from the Latin *sentire*, to feel. SENTIENT (*sĕn'-shĭ-ĕnt*), capable of being affected, feeling, having the faculty of sense perception, applies to that which is stimulated, much as SENSILE does to the stimulant. SENSITIVE, easily affected, keen in sensibility, feeling acutely, limited to a high degree of sensibility, applies like SENTIENT to that which is stimulated, but is quantitative, highly sentient, while both SENSILE and SENTIENT are qualitative, stating a fact without implying the extent to which it is present. SENSIBLE, the most common, is the least exact of this group of words for it may have any of the meanings of the others. Originally, it meant sensile and this use still appears in such a phrase as: 'A SENSIBLE difference', one capable of affecting the senses. SENSIBLE may also mean either sentient or sensitive, as: 'The eye is SENSIBLE to light'; and 'SENSIBLE to small changes'. In addition, SENSIBLE has recently come to mean wise, of good sense.

In the test phrase: 'A SENSILE object', the word is thought by 17 per cent of adult readers to mean RATIONAL. SENSIBLE means rational; but SENSILE means capable of affecting the senses.

975. *ANATHEMATIZE* (ă-năth'-ē-mă-tīz) v. To curse, execrate (976), denounce formally, pronounce anathema against.

To 22 per cent of college seniors the verb to ANATHEMATIZE incorrectly means to RENDER UNCONSCIOUS, to make insensible. This is no doubt a confusion of ANATHEMATIZE, to curse, with ANAESTHETIZE (ă-něs'-thē-tīz), to render insensible, make temporarily unconscious, by means of an ANAESTHETIC, such as chloroform, ether, or any gas or drug which takes away bodily feeling. The word ANAESTHETIC is a combination of the Greek AN, not; and AESTHETIC. The adjective AESTHETIC has come to mean sensitive to beauty, having a sense of the beautiful, but the word comes from the Greek αἰσθητικός, sensitive.

In classical Greek the noun, ἀνάθημα, anathema, meant a votive offering, anything offered as a sacrifice. The word is a combination of the Greek ἀνά, up; and τιθέναι, to place, put; and meant anything placed, set up, in a temple as an offering, even an ornament. It was in the New Testament that the word was first used to mean something to be sacrificed, destroyed, in the sense of an accursed thing. From this the word ANATHEMA came to mean a ban, curse pronounced by ecclesiastical authority, and accompanied by excommunication. To ANATHEMATIZE is to place such a curse upon, pronounce anathema against.

976. *EXECRATE* (*ĕks'-ē-krāt*) *v.* To curse, denounce, abhor, abominate, imprecate, call down evil upon.
EXECRATE is from the Latin *ex*, out; and *sacrare*, to consecrate. From the same source come CONSECRATE, to make sacred, devote to the service of the Deity; and DESECRATE, to profane, pollute. To 20 per cent of adult readers EXECRATE incorrectly means VENERATE, to revere, reverence, hold in exalted honor, regard as hallowed, an exact opposite of the correct meaning.
To EXECRATE, to IMPRECATE, and to ANATHEMATIZE, all mean to curse in various ways. Only the Church can ANATHEMATIZE (975), for an ANATHEMA is a formal ecclesiastical curse or condemnation. Anyone may IMPRECATE or EXECRATE. Although the last two words are so close as often to be interchangeable, they differ in implication. To IMPRECATE is to pray that evil descend upon that which is cursed; to EXECRATE is to curse primarily in order to relieve one's own feelings.

977. *RETINUE* (*rĕt'-ĭ-nū*) *n.* Suite of attendants, body of retainers, cortege (*kor-tāhz'*), train of persons.
In the test phrase: 'In sight of his RETINUE', the word is thought by 33 per cent of preparatory-school juniors to mean SERVANT. The words RETINUE and RETAINER both come from the Latin *retinere*, to retain, a combination of *re*, and *tenere*, to hold. A RETAINER is a servant, dependent, attendant; a RETINUE is always a group of servants, body of attendants, number of retainers.

978. *ANIMADVERSION* (*ăn-ĭ-măd-ver'-zhŭn*) *n.* Unfavorable criticism (152), censure, captious reproof, reprobation, stricture, adverse comment.
ANIMADVERSION comes from the Latin *animus*, mind; and *advertere*, from *ad*, to, and *vertere*, to turn; and means literally

to turn the mind to. ANIMADVERSION originally meant in English turning the mind to a subject, taking notice of. This meaning is now obsolete and ANIMADVERSION can mean only taking unfavorable notice of, carping criticism.

To 31 per cent of adult readers ANIMADVERSION incorrectly means INTERRUPTION, a break in the continuity of. It may be that this is a confusion of ANIMADVERSION, blame, with DIVERSION, amusement, pastime, a word which comes from the same Latin *vertere*, to turn.

The word CRITICISM, which is from the Greek κριτής, judge, implies an impartial judgment made after careful study. CRITICISM, in its original meaning, was neither favorable nor unfavorable, although the word is often used today to suggest unfavorable comment.

An ANIMADVERSION is always unfavorable, adverse. It is apt to be based on opinion rather than upon a careful scrutiny of the facts and to be in the nature of contradiction and reproof rather than an impartial judgment.

979. **CONTUMELY** (*kŏn'-tū-mē-lǐ*, not *kŏn-tūm'-lǐ*) *n.* Insulting rudeness in speech, scornful manner, insolence, haughty language, contemptuous behavior.

The corresponding adjective is CONTUMELIOUS, insolent, rude, sarcastic, supercilious.

CONTUMELY, from the Latin *contumelia*, reproach, abuse, is thought by 22 per cent of college seniors to mean CIVILITY, courtesy of behavior, politeness, an opposite of the correct meaning.

CONTUMELY and OBLOQUY (*ŏb'-lō-kwē*) express disparagement of another. OBLOQUY, which comes from the Latin *obloqui*, to speak against, applies to that which is spoken, either in the presence of another or behind his back. Furthermore, OBLOQUY is usually merited. CONTUMELY may apply either to speech or action; it must be shown in the presence of the other; and is usually not merited.

980. **CONDIGN** (*kŏn-dīn'*, not *kŏn'-dīn*) *adj.* Well-deserved, merited, worthy. The word is applied alike to praise, blame, and punishment.

CONDIGN comes from the Latin *dignus*, worthy, the source

of the English word DIGNITY, and means literally worthy, merited. The CON intensifies the meaning.

In the test phrase: 'CONDIGN punishment', the word is thought by 14 per cent of adult readers to mean EXTREME. Despite the attempts of dictionaries to hold the language to accurately defined meanings, the popular usage of today becomes the language of tomorrow. Although CONDIGN means well-deserved and etymologically has no suggestion of EXTREME, the word is applied so often to extreme punishment which is well-deserved, that in modern newspaper writing it often means extreme. CONDIGN cannot however be used in this sense unless well-deserved is implied. Thus, one speaks of EXTREME cold but never of CONDIGN cold.

981. *NATATION* (*nă-tā'-shŭn*) *n.* Either the art or the act of swimming.

In the test phrase: 'Skill in NATATION', the word is thought by 23 per cent of adult readers to mean SEAMANSHIP. This may be due to a confusion of NATATION, swimming, with NAVIGATION, the science of directing one's course in ships on the water or in the air, which is close to SEAMANSHIP in connotation.

Both NATATION, swimming, and the noun NATATORIUM, a place for swimming, come from the Latin verb, *natare*, to swim.

982. *TACIT* (*tăs'-ĭt*) *adj.* Unspoken, silent, understood, implied but not expressed.

TACIT comes from the Latin *tacere*, to be silent, mute. From the same source comes TACITURN, habitually silent.

In the test phrase: 'A TACIT understanding', the word is thought by 23 per cent of adult readers to mean SUBTLE. SUBTLE has many meanings. In the phrase: 'A SUBTLE understanding', it probably means quick-witted, discriminating, discerning, acute.

TACIT and IMPLICIT (733), although of different origin, have almost the same significance. Both mean implied but not expressed. IMPLICIT comes from the Latin *implicare*, to involve, from *in* and *plicare*, to fold, and signifies that something was said but that more was implied than was actually expressed. TACIT can be used even though nothing was said; it has the clear cut meaning of unspoken.

983. *UXORIOUS* (*ŭks-ō'-rĭ-ŭs*) *adj.* Excessively fond of a wife, doting, foolishly devoted to a wife.

To 16 per cent of college seniors UXORIOUS incorrectly means STINGY, close fisted, niggardly, penurious. This may be a confusion of UXORIOUS, doting, with PENURIOUS, stingy. To another 16 per cent UXORIOUS incorrectly means ROTUND, round, spherical.

UXORIOUS comes from the Latin *uxor*, wife, and does not mean fondness in general, but fondness for a wife.

984. *OBTUSE* (*ŏb-tūs'*) *adj.* Dull, blunt, stupid, insensitive, crass (734), dense, thick headed, slow of perception.

OBTUSE is from the Latin *ob*, upon; and *tundere*, to strike; but the word today has come to mean dull, blunt, probably because a sharp instrument struck on the point is blunted.

When used in the test phrase: 'An OBTUSE mind', the word is thought by 22 per cent of adult readers to mean PROFOUND. This may be a confusion of OBTUSE, dull, with ABSTRUSE, a word which may suggest deep in meaning, profound. Or the misunderstanding may be a confusion of a word with its opposite, for PROFOUND may mean penetrating, of great insight, practically an opposite of OBTUSE.

OBTUSE and its opposite ACUTE are used both in the physical sense with reference to angles and in the figurative sense with reference to mentalities. An ACUTE angle is smaller than a right angle, less than 90 degrees; it is, therefore, sharp, pointed. An ACUTE mind, in the same way, is sharp, penetrating, keen. An OBTUSE angle is greater than a right angle, exceeds 90 degrees; it is, therefore, dull, blunt. In similar manner an OBTUSE mind is dull.

985. *SAMOVAR* (*săm'-ō-vahr*) *n.* A Russian teakettle, a decorative copper or brass urn containing a vertical porcelain cylinder in which charcoal is burned in order to heat water for tea.

SAMOVAR comes from two Russian words meaning self and boiler. In the test phrase: 'We saw the SAMOVAR', the word

is thought by 28 per cent of adult readers to mean INDIAN
HOLY MAN, the common misconception, perhaps because of
SIVA (sē'-vah), a supreme god in Hindu mythology.
Other words come to the tea-table from foreign countries.
CADDY is from a Malay word meaning pound, a TEA-CADDY,
originally a box in which a pound of tea was exported, is
now a container for dry tea leaves. CANISTER is from the
Greek word κάννα, a reed. Originally a CANISTER was a
small basket made of reeds. It is now a box for tea or
coffee and is practically synonymous with CADDY. A SAMO-
VAR, unlike a CADDY or a CANISTER, does not hold tea but is
an urn in which water is heated in preparation for tea.

986. *CATHOLIC* (kăth'-ō-lĭk) *adj*. Broad, universal, liberal,
impartial, not narrow-minded, not bigoted, comprehensive in sympathies.
When the word is spelt with a small c and used in the test
phrase: 'A man of CATHOLIC tastes', it is thought by 37 per
cent of adult readers to mean RELIGIOUS. CATHOLIC may
mean pertaining to the Christian Church; specifically pertaining to the Church of Rome, the Roman Catholic Church;
or to the English Catholic Church, the Anglican Catholic
Church; or to the Greek Church, which broke away from
Rome at the end of the first great schism in 1054 A.D. But
in this sense the word must begin with a capital C. CATHOLIC
comes from the Greek word καθολικός, general, universal,
and the original meaning of the word in English was universal, with no religious connotation.
By another 17 per cent CATHOLIC is thought to mean NAR-
ROW, an exact opposite of the correct meaning.

987. *SCHISM* (sĭz'-m, not skĭz'-m) *n*. A split in a community, rent, separation, division, especially a division in
a religious denomination occasioned by diversity of opinion;
breach of unity among people of the same religious faith.
SCHISM is from the Greek word σχίσμα, division, split. To
25 per cent of college seniors SCHISM incorrectly means
THEORY, scheme, doctrine, speculative idea. This may be due
to a confusion of SCHISM with SCHEME (skēm) (149), words
similar in appearance, but not in pronunciation. A SCHEME

is a plan, design, outline, sometimes a theory. A SCHISM is a split, breach (443), division in opinion. Two great SCHISMS occurred. The first was that between the Greek and Latin Churches which began in the ninth century and lasted until 1054 A.D. The second started just after the return of the papacy from Avignon and continued from 1378 to 1417.

988. *OBVIATE* (*ŏb'-vĭ-āt*) *v.* To remove, clear away, preclude, get rid of, prevent by foresight, anticipate in such a way as to dispose of.

In the test phrase: 'He OBVIATED the difficulty', the word is thought by 24 per cent of adult readers to mean REVEALED. To REVEAL is to make obvious, expose to sight, show, divulge, make known. This is perhaps a confusion of OBVIATE with OBVIOUS. Both words come from the same Latin source *ob*, before; and *via*, way; but they have dissimilar English meanings. OBVIOUS, an adjective, means so plain as to need no explanation or comment, impossible to overlook; an OBVIOUS thing literally stands before one, in one's way. To OBVIATE, again by derivation to be in the way, originally meant to meet. This meaning is now obsolete and to OBVIATE means to remove from the way.

By another 24 per cent OBVIATE is thought to mean to EVADE. To EVADE is to avoid by dexterity, elude by artifice, escape, get out of the way of, slip away from. To EVADE and to OBVIATE both suggest not actually encountering something. To EVADE it is to go around it, avoid it; to OBVIATE it is to remove it before encountering it.

989. *REPARABLE* (*rĕp'-ă-ră-bl*, not *rē-păr'-ă-bl*) *adj.* Repairable, remediable, amendable, that can be made good.

To 42 per cent of preparatory-school juniors REPARABLE incorrectly means CHANGEABLE, variable, unstable, fickle.

REPARABLE and the noun REPARATION (*rĕp-ă-rā'-shŭn*) have the same derivation as the verb to REPAIR (245). All come from the Latin *re*; and *parare*, to prepare; and REPARABLE means literally capable of being prepared again. REPARABLE and REPAIRABLE (*rē-păr'-ă-bl*), although spelt differently as discussed under REPAIR (245), are practically the same word.

Through use REPAIRABLE and the corresponding noun, RE-
PAIR, have come to be applied to physical objects. Thus, one
speaks of the REPAIRS being made to a house. REPARABLE and
the corresponding noun, REPARATION, are applied only to
wrongs to a character, injuries to a reputation.

990. *DISCURSIVE* (dĭs-ker'-sĭv) *adj.* Digressive, rambling,
    roving, wandering away from the subject, passing from
one theme to another, not sticking to the point.
DISCURSIVE is from the Latin *dis*; and *currere*, to run. It is
from the same source as CURSORY (665). CURSORY means
hasty, slight, superficial, not thorough, as a CURSORY examination, one run through rapidly. DISCURSIVE by derivation
means running in different directions. DISCURSIVE has some
of the haste of CURSORY and yet suggests some of the fitfulness
of DESULTORY, a word which comes from the Latin *salire*, to
leap, and which means jumping from subject to subject,
changeable, casual, fitful, without coherence. CURSORY and
DELIBERATE; DESULTORY and COHERENT; DISCURSIVE and ME-
THODICAL; are opposites.

In the test phrase: 'A DISCURSIVE lecture', the word is
thought by 28 per cent of college seniors to mean DETAILED;
and by another 24 per cent to mean COMPREHENSIVE. DIS-
CURSIVE, DETAILED, and COMPREHENSIVE, all apply to a method
of writing or speaking which is long and involved. COMPRE-
HENSIVE may mean covering a wide range of subjects, inclusive, extensive in scope; in this sense it emphasizes the
breadth of the treatment. COMPREHENSIVE may also mean
dealing with a subject sympathetically and understandingly.
As opposed to this, DISCURSIVE means dealing with a subject
slightingly, fitfully. DETAILED, from the French *détailler*, to
cut up, means dealt with severally and in particular. DETAILED
emphasizes the separately considered items, the minuteness
of the treatment, and in this sense is almost an opposite of
DISCURSIVE which emphasizes the rambling character of the
treatment, its tendency to run here and there.

DISCURSIVE was once used in a favorable sense, as the
adjective corresponding to the noun DISCOURSE (dĭs-cōrs'),
dissertation, sermon, lecture, homily, to mean in the manner
of a discourse. But DISCURSIVE is now used only in an

unfavorable sense to imply the absence of method, unity, and sequence. It characterizes an unintegrated approach to a subject, one which does not estimate the logical relations of the details.

991. *COMMANDEER* (*kŏm-măn-dēr'*) *v.* To take for military purposes, impress, confiscate, seize forcibly. The word originated during the Boer War when it meant, force into military service. COMMANDEER is, today, sometimes used colloquially to mean seize for personal use.

To 37 per cent of adult readers COMMANDEER incorrectly means to CAPTAIN; and to 23 per cent to ORDER. This is probably a confusion of COMMANDEER with COMMAND. To COMMAND, to CAPTAIN, and to ORDER, all mean to manage, control, direct, regulate; while the verb to COMMANDEER has the limited technical meaning, to seize for military purposes, impress into military service.

992. *BALEFUL* (*bāl'-fŭl*) *adj.* Hurtful, injurious, destructive, malign, sinister (332), direful, bad, adverse, evil, pernicious (786), noxious.
BALEFUL is of Anglo-Saxon origin, from words meaning evil, sinister.

The corresponding noun BALE is seldom used in everyday prose. It means a malign influence, dire evil, misery, woe, that which causes sorrow. In the test phrase: 'BALEFUL looks', the word is thought by 28 per cent of adult readers to mean PUZZLED. As used in this phrase, PUZZLED means bewildered, perplexed, confused.

BALEFUL and BANEFUL (857) are confused. BANEFUL, from BANE, poison, means poisonous. BALEFUL does not mean poisonous, but destructive, evil, malign. BALE, misery, and BLISS, delight, are opposites; BALEFUL and BLISSFUL are opposites.

993. *CONTINGENCY* (*kŏn-tĭn'-jĕn-sĭ*) *n.* Chance, casualty, accident, unforeseen event, unexpected happening, fortuitous occurrence.
In the test phrase: 'Prepared to meet any CONTINGENCY', the word is thought by 27 per cent of adult readers to mean ARGUMENT. This is perhaps a confusion of CONTINGENCY,

unforeseen event, with CONTENTION, a word which may mean an argument in favor of a proposition, the main point in a controversy.

By another 20 per cent CONTINGENCY, chance happening, is thought to mean DELEGATION, a body of persons chosen to act for others. A CONTINGENT is specifically the portion of troops furnished to a group of allies by one community or by one country; and the word is sometimes used in a more general sense to mean any quota. CONTINGENCY cannot be used in this way, but always means something which may happen, a possible event.

994. *ANCILLARY* (*ăn'-sĭl-lār-ĭ*) *adj.* Subordinate, subservient, secondary, subsidiary, auxiliary.

ANCILLARY is from the Latin *ancilla*, maid servant, handmaid, a word which in turn comes from *ancus*, servant.

The word ANCILLARY is familiar to telephone engineers in the phrase: 'ANCILLARY answering jack', a part of the dial switching mechanism. In the test phrase: 'The ANCILLARY committee', the word is thought by 18 per cent of adult readers to mean TEMPORARY, lasting for a short time, not permanent, the popular misconception. A TEMPORARY committee may have great power for a short time; it need not be subordinate, ANCILLARY.

995. *ADJURATION* (*ăd-jū-rā'-shŭn*) *n.* A solemn command, earnest request, appeal, entreaty, serious charge invoking a curse in case of disobedience.

ADJURATION is from the Latin *ad*, to; and *jurare*, to swear, the source of the English words PERJURE (323), swear falsely; CONJURE (*kŏn-jūr'*), call on by a sacred name, entreat solemnly; and ABJURE, to renounce under oath.

To 20 per cent of preparatory-school juniors ADJURATION incorrectly means STATEMENT OF LAW. This is perhaps a confusion of ADJURATION with ADJUDICATION. AN ADJUDICATION is a passing of judgment, a judicial sentence, the decision of a court; or sometimes the act of a court in declaring a fact which has been determined upon. An ADJURATION is an entreaty, given in the form of a command, and with the solemnity of an oath.

996. *CABAL* (*kă-băl'*) *n.* Faction (645), political clique, secret intrigue (*ĭn-trēg'*), junto.

There are words similar to CABAL in Dutch, German, Italian, and the Scandinavian languages, but CABAL comes from the Hebrew KABALA (*kăb'-ă-lah*), a word which is in use in English today to signify a mysterious system for reading pretended meanings into the sacred Hebrew writings.

To 26 per cent of adult readers CABAL incorrectly means CELEBRATION, festival, carnival. This may be remotely due to some confusion of CABAL, political clique, faction, with CABARET (*kăb-ă-rā'*), a word which originally meant ale-house, any tavern which sold liquors, but which is now used for any restaurant providing dancing and vaudeville acts with the meals.

The word CABAL was once used in England as synonymous with CABINET, the King's advisory council. It happened that in 1671, during the reign of Charles II, the King's Cabinet consisted of five persons, Clifford, Arlington, Buckingham, Ashley, and Lauderdale. Because of the initial letters these unpopular ministers were disparagingly nicknamed the CABAL, and since that time the word has continued to be a term of contempt. A CABAL is today any small group working secretly for its own aggrandizement.

997. *DEMUR* (*dē-mer'*) *n.* An irresolute objection, hesitation, wavering, scruple, boggle, exception taken.

The corresponding verb, DEMUR (*dē-mer'*), to suggest difficulties, take exception, is spelt and pronounced like the noun.

In the test phrase: 'When questioned, he DEMURRED', the verb is believed by 28 per cent of adult readers to mean ANSWERED VAGUELY. To another 18 per cent 'He DEMURRED' means he WAS SILENT. This is probably a confusion of the verb DEMUR with the idea suggested by the adjective DEMURE (*dē-mūr'*), which may mean modest, markedly quiet.

In the phrase: 'After some DEMUR', the noun is thought by 40 per cent of preparatory-school juniors to mean CONFUSION, discomfiture, perplexity, embarrassment.

DEMUR is from the Latin *de*; and *morari*, to delay, hesitate; and originally in English, a DEMUR was a hesitation, delay.

The word now combines the ideas of hesitation and objection. A HESITATION, from the Latin *haerere*, to stick fast, stammer, is by derivation a sticking at something, holding back, indecision, vacillation. An OBJECTION, from the Latin *ob*, and *jacere*, to throw, is by derivation a throwing in front of, a definite stand in opposition to something. A DEMUR is a timid, hesitating, objection, made in order to gain time.

998. *INTEGRATE* (*ĭn'-tē-grāt*) *v.* To unify, synthesize, combine into a whole, bring together the parts of, make complete.

In English, an INTEGER is a whole number. The Latin *integer* means untouched, unhurt, whole, entire; and the English verb, to INTEGRATE, is to make whole.

To 20 per cent of adult readers INTEGRATE incorrectly means EVALUATE, to appraise, determine the value of in any way. In mathematics the mean value of a quantity may be obtained by integrating, by the mathematical process called INTEGRATION; and in this sense to EVALUATE and to INTEGRATE are not very different. To EVALUATE is, however, more general; while to INTEGRATE is specifically to bring together the parts, unify.

To another 15 per cent INTEGRATE incorrectly means DESTROY, pull down, demolish. This is probably a confusion of INTEGRATE, unify, with DISINTEGRATE, to break up, separate into parts, at least in suggestion an opposite of INTEGRATE.

999. *ERUDITE* (*ĕr'-ū-dīt*) *adj.* Learned, academic, scholarly, well-read, recondite, characterized by extensive knowledge. The adjective ERUDITE, and the corresponding noun ERUDITION (*ĕr-ū-dĭsh'-ŭn*), usually apply to knowledge of literature rather than science.

In the test phrase: 'An ERUDITE lecture', the word is thought by 23 per cent of adult readers to mean TEDIOUS, tiresome, irksome, fatiguing. An ERUDITE, learned, person is sometimes tedious, tiresome, to one with less ERUDITION, learning, but there is nothing in the word ERUDITE to suggest tedium, fatigue.

The noun, ERUDITION, learning, scholarship, knowledge, is thought by 14 per cent of college seniors to mean DECEPTION, fraud, deceit, artifice, trick. This is perhaps because of some confusion of ERUDITION with the noun ERROR, or with the verb to ERR, to stray, wander from the path, go astray, deviate from the proper course. To ERR was once used as a transitive verb and meant to lead astray, mislead, deceive; and it is perhaps this obsolete meaning which causes the confusion. There is, however, no direct etymological connection between the words ERUDITION and ERR; for the verb, to ERR, and the large group of words built upon it, such as ERROR, ERRONEOUS, ERRATIC, and ERRANT, all come from the Latin *errare*, to wander. Both ERUDITE and ERUDITION come from the Latin verb *erudire*, to instruct, educate, cultivate; which in turn is a combination of *e*, out; and *rudis*, rude; and means, literally, to free from rudeness.

ERUDITE and IGNORANT; ERUDITION and IGNORANCE; are opposites.

1000. *INDUE* (*in-dū'*) *v.* To clothe, invest, don, assume, put on as a garment.

The three words ENDOW, INDUE, and ENDUE, are inextricably confused with one another. ENDOW comes from the same source as the noun DOWRY, goods or money which a woman brings to her husband at marriage. To ENDOW is to furnish with money or with material goods, as when an alumnus ENDOWS a college. The corresponding noun, ENDOWMENT, is perhaps more familiar. INDUE is directly from the Latin *induere*, to don, put on as a garment. INDUE is used of spiritual qualities and sometimes of intangibles in general, as: 'INDUED with beauty'. ENDUE is sometimes used as a variant of ENDOW and sometimes as another form of INDUE. Although INDUE is marked archaic by some dictionaries, and ENDUE given as the modern word, INDUE is more like the Latin and is not so apt to be confused with ENDOW.

1001. *EMEND* (*ē-měnd'*) *v.* To better, amend, remedy (65), reform, correct, improve, rectify, free from faults, remove defects.

EMEND and AMEND are from the Latin *ex*, out; and *mendum*, fault; and both mean to free from faults. They differ little from the simpler, aphetic, form MEND (138), when that word is used figuratively. AMEND, and the corresponding noun AMENDMENT, apply to alterations in laws, legislative acts, and constitutions, as: 'The Fourteenth AMENDMENT'. EMEND, and the corresponding noun EMENDATION, apply to literary texts. An EMENDATION may be any correction, improvement; or the word may be used more specifically to mean a restoration to an earlier reading. In like manner to EMEND may mean to correct, improve, rectify; or it may mean to restore a text to its original form.

1002. *BETIMES* (*bē-tīmz'*) *adv.* Early, in good time, seasonably; also: soon, in a short time.

In the test phrase: 'He was up BETIMES', the word is thought by 25 per cent of preparatory-school juniors to mean REPEATEDLY, again and again, many times. By another 14 per cent it is thought to mean OCCASIONALLY, once in a while.

BETIMES and EARLY are practically synonymous but differ slightly. EARLY means merely ahead of time, and sometimes has the suggestion of needlessly ahead. BETIMES is between early and on time, and means early enough to provide an adequate margin without waste of time.

1003. *PREDILECTION* (*prē-dĭ-lĕk'-shŭn*) *n.* Preference, partiality, bias, liking, fondness, inclination toward. 'I know his PREDILECTION.'

PREDILECTION is from the Latin *prae*, before; and *diligere*, to love, the source of the English word DILIGENT, assiduous (390), a word which by derivation suggests sticking to work which one loves. The Latin verb *diligere* is in turn a combination of *di*, *dis*; and *legere*, to choose.

A LIKING, PREDILECTION, and LOVE, express increasing degrees of affection. A PREDILECTION is stronger than a LIKING, but not so strong as LOVE. A PREDILECTION is literally a feeling which comes before love. Furthermore, PREDILECTION differs from love in that it does not ordinarily exist between persons.

1004. *CONTENTIOUS* (*kŏn-tĕn'-shŭs*) *adj.* Quarrelsome, disputatious, belligerent, bellicose, wrangling, controversial, fond of strife, tiresomely persistent in dispute.
In the test phrase: 'His CONTENTIOUS disposition', the word is

thought by 31 per cent of adult readers to mean PLACID, calm, unruffled, serene, equable. This is perhaps a confusion of CONTENTIOUS, quarrelsome, with CONTENTMENT, the state of being satisfied. The two words are practically opposites of each other. CONTENTMENT, and the corresponding adjective CONTENT, come from the Latin *tenere*, to hold.

CONTENTIOUS, and the corresponding verb to CONTEND, come from the Latin *con*, with; and *tendere*. The Latin *tendere* has many meanings. When used as a transitive verb it means to stretch, as in the English verb to EXTEND, to stretch out. When used intransitively, *tendere* means to stretch one's self toward, aim at, reach for, as in the English INTEND, aim, design, plan, as: 'INTEND to go'. Finally *tendere* may mean strive for, contend, as in CONTEND and CONTENTIOUS. CONTENTIOUS, by derivation, means of a striving, reaching disposition; but the word now means quarrelsome.

1005. *TUMID* (*tū'-mĭd*) *adj.* Swollen, enlarged, distended, inflated, turgid (1088), bombastic.
In the test phrase: 'TUMID eyes', the word is thought by 21 per cent of adult readers to mean DEEP-SET.

TUMID is from the Latin *tumere*, to swell. From the same source come the nouns, TUMULT, an uproar, noisy uprising; and TUMOR, a swelling. TUMID may also be used in a figurative sense, of written style, to mean pompous, showy, vainglorious.

1006. *SURCEASE* (*ser-sēs'*) *n.* End, stop, cessation (254), intermission, respite (650), final or temporary suspension of some action. 'There is no SURCEASE.'
SURCEASE is not apparently from the verb to CEASE but from the same Latin source as SUPERSEDE, to displace.

It is not enough to know the meaning of a word; one must in addition sense its flavor. ERST, ALBEIT, and ERE, are not only poetic but of a past generation and should rarely be used, except in a dictionary, on the same page with CLAVICLE, BUCCAL, and ABDOMINAL, which are scientific in their exactness. For the past fifty years SURCEASE has been called either obsolete or archaic, but the word refuses to disappear from the language. It should ordinarily be avoided in texts which deal with everyday business life and should be used only in an otherwise carefully worked-out sentence where it is necessary to say END in an archaic manner.

1007. *KNAVERY* (nă'-ver-ĭ) *n.* Trickery, dishonesty, fraud, roguery, rascality, petty villainy.

In the test phrase: 'An indication of KNAVERY', the word is believed by 43 per cent of adult readers to mean MISCHIEF. There is historical justification for this misconception. A KNAVE was originally a boy, fellow, young servant; and KNAVERY was the naughty roguishness of a boy, mischief. This mild sense is now obsolete, and KNAVERY has the stronger suggestion of trickery, dishonesty.

1008. *PITH* (pĭth) *n.* Vigor, force, strength, energy; also: central part, essential substance, gist, essence, quintessence. PITHY (1009) is the corresponding adjective.

PITH, KERNEL, and MARROW, are all more or less scientific words for central substance. MARROW, of Anglo-Saxon origin, is the soft tissue in the center of bones. KERNEL, the diminutive of the Anglo-Saxon word CORN, is the central part of a seed or of a nut, often the edible part. PITH, also of Anglo-Saxon origin, is the central substance of a plant stem.

MEDULLA, from the Latin *medius*, middle, a word which in turn comes from the Greek μέσος, middle, is reserved for more purely scientific use. In biology it may be synonymous with MARROW; in botany, with PITH.

The three Anglo-Saxon words PITH, KERNEL, and MARROW, are also used figuratively to mean central substance. In the test phrase: 'His remarks lacked PITH', where the word is used figuratively, it is thought by 26 per cent of adult readers to mean COHERENCE, consistency, logical connection, the sticking together of the parts. The word COHERENCE presupposes a number of parts related to one another. PITH is the central point, kernel, nucleus.

1009. *PITHY* (pĭth'-ĭ) *adj.* Terse (493), forcible, pointed, laconic (629), concise, sententious, apothegmatic (ăp-ō-thĕg-măt'-ĭk), containing the heart or gist of a matter. 'Several PITHY remarks.'

PITHY is an adjective made from the noun PITH (1008), kernel, marrow, central core.

PITHY, TERSE, and SENTENTIOUS, all mean short and to the point. SENTENTIOUS is from the same source as SENTENCE; and a SENTENTIOUS style is one made up of separate sentences, one in which the sentences are striking, apart from the content of the whole. A TERSE style is one which gives the complete subject-matter with elegant conciseness. A PITHY style, like a TERSE style, gives the complete subject-matter, but does it without the necessary elegance implied by TERSE.

1010. *PROVIDENT* (*prŏv'-ĭ-dĕnt*) *adj.* Making provision
     for future needs, thrifty, frugal (617), economical.

In the test phrase: 'Her PROVIDENT mother', the word is thought by 40 per cent of adult readers to mean THOUGHTFUL. This is probably a confusion of the word PROVIDENT with PRUDENT. PRUDENT, PROVIDENT, and the verb to PROVIDE, come from the same Latin source, *pro*, forward; and *videre*, to see. PRUDENT is probably a contraction of PROVIDENT; but of the three has retained most nearly the original meaning of the Latin, seeing forward. PRUDENT means thoughtful, sagacious, wise, with an eye to the future, careful of self-interest. It does not suggest saving. PROVIDENT, like the verb to PROVIDE, implies saving for the future; it does not pass upon the wisdom of such a course, as does PRUDENT.

PRUDENT and RECKLESS; PROVIDENT and EXTRAVAGANT; are opposites.

1011. *SLEEK* (*slēk*) *adj.* Smooth, slick, glossy, oily, unctuous,
     plausible, insinuating, having an even surface, clever at
making a show.

SLEEK can be traced back to Middle English, with corresponding words in Dutch, German, and the Scandinavian languages. SLINK, to move in a smooth, oily manner, is probably from the same source.

By 56 per cent of adult readers SLEEK is thought to mean WELL-GROOMED. WELL-GROOMED, CURRIED, and SLEEK, so overlap in meaning that it is perhaps pedantic to differentiate them. WELL-GROOMED means neat, WELL-GROOMED hair is neat; and although this probably implies smoothness, WELL-

GROOMED means neat, not smooth. To CURRY and to GROOM may be synonymous; but, although the currying ·process is a smoothing, sleeking process, to CURRY is to clean, not necessarily to smooth. The verb to SLEEK means specifically to smooth.

The adjectives SLEEK and SLICK are the same word. They differ much as CREEK and CRICK. SLICK was the original form but is today regarded as provincial.

1012. *ANOMALY* (ă-nŏm'-ă-lĭ) *n.* A rare exception, peculiarity, eccentricity (321), irregularity, deviation from the normal, that which differs from an accepted classification. Both ANOMALY and the corresponding adjective ANOMALOUS, abnormal, exceptional, unusual, come from the Greek ἀν, not; and ὁμαλός, even, a word which in turn comes from ὁμός, same. This word, written in Roman letters, appears at the beginning of a number of English words, as: HOMOGENEOUS, composed all of the same kind; and HOMONYM, a word the same as another in appearance but different in meaning.

In the test phrase: 'Strange ANOMALY', the word is thought by 19 per cent of adult readers to mean CONSISTENCY, uniformity, congruity, a close opposite of ANOMALY, irregularity.

To another 17 per cent ANOMALY means NAME. This is due perhaps to some confusion of ANOMALY with ANONYMOUS which means without a name.

The adjectives ANOMALOUS and ANALOGOUS; and the nouns ANOMALY and ANALOGY; are opposites.

1013. *DISINTERESTED* (dĭs-ĭn'-ter-ĕs-tĕd, almost dĭs-ĭn'-trĕs-tĕd; not dĭs-ĭn-ter-ĕs'-ted) *adj.* Impartial, unbiased, having no personal interest or private advantage in a question, acting from unselfish motives.

The similar words DISINTERESTED and UNINTERESTED are often confused. Although both start with a negative prefix they are not synonymous. UNINTERESTED means taking no interest, unconcerned, apathetic; DISINTERESTED applies to a person with a judicial attitude, to one who has no self-interest in the outcome, who is unbiased, impartial.

The word INDIFFERENT is used in both senses. Ordinarily it means unconcerned, apathetic, uninterested; but its original meaning was unbiased, disinterested, and it can still be used in this way.

DISPROVE and DISAPPROVE are confused by grammar-school pupils. JAMB, the upright side of a door or window, and LINTEL, the horizontal top, are I believe confused by Joseph Conrad, for he twice speaks of a man leaning against the LINTEL. UNINTERESTED and DISINTERESTED are sometimes confused by dictionaries.

1014. *INSOUCIANT* (ĭn-soo'-sĭ-ănt) *adj.* Heedless, unmindful, careless, reckless, unconcerned, untroubled.

To 48 per cent of college seniors INSOUCIANT incorrectly means CUTTING. This may be due to some confusion of INSOUCIANT, careless, with INCISIVE, trenchant, cutting.

INSOUCIANT is a French word which has been anglicized in pronunciation without change of spelling. It is a combination of the privative *in*; and *souciant*, from *souci*, the French word for care. The phrase SANS SOUCI is occasionally used in English to mean without care. When spelt with capitals, SANS SOUCI, it is the name of a palace built by Frederick the Great at Potsdam in Prussia. INSOUCIANT is literally without care, careless, heedless.

1015. *VOLUPTUOUS* (vō-lŭp'-tū-ŭs, almost vō-lŭp'-chū-ŭs) *adj.* Devoted to the pleasures of the senses, luxury-loving, sensual, causing sensuous or sensual gratification, indulging to excess in sensual pleasure. In literature, Cleopatra personifies VOLUPTUOUSNESS.

VOLUPTUOUS is from the Latin *voluptas*, pleasure, enjoyment, delight. VOLUPTUOUS and APHRODISIACAL (897) both suggest excessive delight in the gratification of the senses. APHRODISIACAL refers specifically to sexual pleasures; VOLUPTUOUS is more general and applies to the gratification of all the senses.

In the phrase: 'A VOLUPTUOUS woman', the word is thought by 40 per cent of adult readers to mean LARGE. In the phrase: 'A VOLUPTUOUS room', the word is confused with LOFTY, high. These misconceptions may be due to some confusion of VOLUPTUOUS, luxury-loving, with VOLUMINOUS, ample, bulky, large. The word VOLUPTUOUS does not imply size.

Of the three words, VOLUPTUOUS, SENSUOUS, and SENSUAL,

the last means unduly indulgent, carnal, and is a discreditable adjective. SENSUOUS applies to the nicer gratification of the senses. VOLUPTUOUS is softly sensuous and borders on the sensual.

1016. *COLLUSION* (*kŏl-lū'-zhŭn*) *n.* A secret understanding between supposed opponents, conspiracy, plot, connivance, fraudulent cooperation.

In the test phrase: 'A result of COLLUSION', the word is thought by 26 per cent of adult readers to mean INTERFERENCE; and by another 16 per cent to mean BUMPING; the two popular misconceptions. These are no doubt due to the similarity in appearance of COLLUSION, fraudulent cooperation, and COLLISION, a bumping.

COLLUSION is derived from *con*, with; and *ludere*, to play together; and by derivation means to play into one another's hands. ILLUSION and DELUSION; ALLUDE, DELUDE, ELUDE, and ILLUDE; are all from the same source and are discussed under the word ELUSORY (345). COLLUDE is an unusual but similar verb meaning to conspire, have a secret understanding, play into the hands of. LUDICROUS (378) is another of the many words from this same Latin source and means playful in a grotesque manner, exciting sportive laughter.

CONSPIRACY, CONNIVANCE, and COLLUSION, are words of evil intent. A CONSPIRACY is an agreement among persons to commit an unlawful act in which all take part. CONNIVANCE is standing aside knowing that unlawful acts are going on but ignoring them. CONNIVANCE does not mean plotting, as so many think, or playing any active part. COLLUSION is more active than CONNIVANCE; it is a conspiracy between those whose interests are seemingly opposed, a secret understanding between persons acting apparently in defiance of one another.

1017. *AVOW* (*ă-vow'*) *v.* To declare openly, affirm, assert, asseverate, aver. The verb to AVOW may also mean to acknowledge frankly, confess, admit, own to.

In the test phrase: 'I AVOW to you', the word is thought by 53 per cent of preparatory-school juniors to mean PROMISE, assure. This is no doubt a confusion of AVOW, to declare, with an obsolete verb to AVOW, identical in spelling but from a different source. This obsolete AVOW and the verb to vow, which is still in good standing, are from the Latin *vovere*, to promise and both mean to promise solemnly.

Avow, to declare, and AVER, although so similar in appearance and in meaning, come from different sources. AVER is from the Latin *ad*, to; and *verus*, true, the source of the English words VERITY, truth, and VERIFY, to prove to be true. To AVER originally meant declare to be true but the word is now used more generally to mean affirm with confidence and is practically synonymous with AVOW. To AVOW, and the noun AVOWAL, are from the Latin *ad*, to; and *vocare*, to call. The Latin verb *advocare* meant to call upon, to call as a witness; and the English verb AVOW suggests declaring openly as one might on the witness stand.

1018. *THERAPEUTIC* (*thĕr-ă-pū'-tĭk*) *adj.* Having healing qualities, restorative, curative, remedial, alleviative.

To 48 per cent of college seniors THERAPEUTIC incorrectly means HEAT-RADIATING. This may be due to a confusion of THERAPEUTIC with some word formed from THERM, a unit of heat. A THERMOMETER is a heat-measuring device; a THERMO-STAT, a heat-controlling device; a THERMOPILE, an instrument for measuring radiant heat.

THERAPEUTIC comes from the Greek verb θεραπεύειν, to nurse, cure; and means literally curative, healing.

1019. *VENTRAL* (*vĕn'-trăl*) *adj.* Abdominal (180), of or on the belly, pertaining to the stomach.

In the test phrase: 'The VENTRAL cavity', the word is thought by 16 per cent of adult readers to mean CHEST. The CHEST is between the abdomen and the head and contains the lungs, man's breathing organs. By another 15 per cent of adult readers VENTRAL is thought to mean WINDY; and by still another 14 per cent to mean MOUTH. These are all perhaps confusions of VENTRAL, abdominal, with the many English words which come from the Latin word *ventus*, wind. Thus, a VENT is a small hole through which air may pass. To VENTILATE is to admit air. VENTRAL is not from *ventus*, wind, but from the Latin *venter*, a word still used in English as a scientific term for belly, abdomen. VENTRAL means pertaining to the abdomen.

VENTRAL, pertaining to the belly, and DORSAL, pertaining to the back, as: 'A DORSAL fin', are opposites.

1020. *PROSCRIBE* (*prō-skrīb'*) *v.* To condemn, outlaw, banish, doom, punish by declaring to be outside the protection of the law.

To 57 per cent of preparatory-school juniors PROSCRIBE incorrectly means RECORD, to make note of, put down in writing. This may be a confusion of PROSCRIBE, condemn, with INSCRIBE, to imprint, a word applied specifically to the engraving of an inscription on a tablet. INSCRIBE, PRESCRIBE, to lay down with authority, order, dictate, and PROSCRIBE, all come from the Latin verb *scribere*, to write. The Latin word *proscribere* meant to publish, and more especially to publish the name of one whose property had been forfeited. PROSCRIBE in English originally meant to publish the name of one condemned to death; but the word is now used more generally to mean condemn as dangerous.

1021. *LIBIDINOUS* (*lĭ-bĭd'-ĭ-nŭs*) *adj.* Lewd (662), lustful, lascivious, aphrodisiacal (897), licentious, lecherous, salacious, prurient.

In the test phrase: 'Books catering to the LIBIDINOUS', the word is thought by 20 per cent of adult readers to mean GREEDY, covetous, impatiently desirous, gluttonous. LIBIDINOUS comes from the Latin noun, *libido*, desire; and by derivation means full of desire; but is used in English with the special meaning of greedy for sexual indulgence.

1022. *CUBICLE* (*kū'-bĭ-kl*) *n.* Private bedroom, cubiculum, small sleeping apartment. In modern usage CUBICLES are often small sleeping rooms made by subdividing a large room.

To 21 per cent of college seniors CUBICLE incorrectly means BUILDING. CUBICLE and CUBICAL are HOMONYMS, that is they are pronounced alike but have different meanings. Despite the similarity between the two words there is no etymological connection. CUBICAL, ending in AL, is from the Greek word κύβος, a die, cube, and means like a cube in shape. CUBICLE, ending in LE, is from the Latin *cubare*, to lie down. From the same Latin source come a number of words in which an M has been inserted; as, RECUMBENT (591), lying down, reclining; INCUMBENT (807), office holder; PROCUMBENT, lying face downward, prone. From *cubare* also come two words without the M, and hence more like CUBICLE in appearance and sound, INCUBATE and ACCUBATION. INCUBATE, by derivation, lying on, is now used to mean sit on for the purpose of hatching, or, still more figuratively, to aid hatching, by any mechanical means. ACCUBATION is an unusual word which means lying down at meals after the manner of the ancients, either resting on the left elbow or lying flat on the stomach.

CUBICULAR, literally belonging to the bedchamber, hence private, is the adjective corresponding to the noun CUBICLE, a small bedroom.

1023. *FRUGIVOROUS* (*frū-jĭv'-ŏ-rŭs*) *adj.* Fruit-eating, feeding on fruits, especially soft fruits.

FRUGIVOROUS is a combination of *frux, frugis*, fruit; and *vorare*, to devour; and means literally fruit-devouring.

In the test phrase: 'The FRUGIVOROUS animal', the word is thought by 22 per cent of adult readers to mean FOOD-STORING. This may be due to some confusion of FRUGIVOROUS, fruit-eating, with FRUGAL, sparing, economical, provident. Both FRUGAL and FRUGIVOROUS come from the same Latin source *frux, frugis*, fruit, in general fruits of the soil, food.

By another 15 per cent FRUGIVOROUS is thought to mean VORACIOUS, greedy for food, ravenous. Both VORACIOUS and FRUGIVOROUS come from the Latin verb *vorare*, to devour. VORACIOUS (927) is a combination of *vorare*, and the ending ACIOUS which adds intensity to the action.

GRANIVOROUS means feeding on hard fruits, seeds, and grains. FRUGIVOROUS means feeding on soft fruits.

1024. *ALLUSION* (*ăl-lū'-zhŭn*) *n.* Hint, intimation, implication, insinuation (239), covert suggestion, indirect reference. To ALLUDE to is the corresponding verb.

To 60 per cent of preparatory-school juniors ALLUSION

incorrectly means FALSE-VISION. This is no doubt a confusion of ALLUSION, hint, indirect reference, with ILLUSION (495), an unreal vision, deceptive appearance. ILLUSION and ALLUSION both come from the Latin *ludere*, to play. To ALLUDE to something is to play at referring to it, to touch upon it lightly. An ALLUSION is the corresponding noun and means indirect reference.

1025. BUCCAL (*bŭk′-kăl*, not *būk′-kăl*) *adj.* Cheek, oral, maxillary, of or pertaining to the cheek, pertaining to the cavity of the mouth.

In the test phrase: 'The BUCCAL cavity', the word is thought by 26 per cent of adult readers to mean YAWNING, the common misconception.

BUCCAL is from the Latin *bucca*, cheek, a word which is used in anatomy today. From *bucca* came the Latin diminutive *buccula*, little cheek, at one time that part of a helmet which covered the chin and lower face, now technically the BEAVER, a word which may have contributed to the modern slang BEAVER to mean beard. The adjective, BUCCAL, means of or pertaining to the cheek.

1026. REFECTION (*rē-fĕk′-shŭn*) *n.* A slight meal, light repast, refreshment, bever, collation (1118).

In the test phrase: 'After that REFECTION', the word is thought by 34 per cent of preparatory-school juniors to mean ATTITUDE, posture, pose, doubtless a confusion of REFECTION, meal, with REFLECTION.

REFECTION comes from the Latin *re*, again; and *facere*, to make; and by derivation means a remaking, refreshment. The word REFECTORY is probably more familiar. It was originally the room in a monastery or religious institution in which meals, REFECTIONS, were taken. The word is now used more generally for the dining-hall in any institution.

1027. APPURTENANT (*ăp-per′-tē-nănt*) *adj.* Belonging, incident, related, adjoining, pertaining, appertaining, pertinent, annexed to some more important thing.

To 27 per cent of adult readers APPURTENANT incorrectly means APPROPRIATED, taken possession of. APPURTENANT is from the Latin *ad*, to; and *pertinare*, to belong; and means literally belonging to.

The adjectives APPURTENANT, spelt with a U and ending in ANT; and PERTINENT, spelt with an E and ending in ENT; are practically synonymous. The latter is more familiar and should ordinarily be used. The corresponding nouns differ. PERTINENCE is the quality of being to the point, suitability, appositeness. APPURTENANCE is the appendage, the adjunct, the subordinate part added to the principal thing.

1028. *ANCIPITAL* (*ăn-sĭp'-ĭ-tăl*) *adj.* Two-edged, double-faced, doubtful, dubious, ambiguous.

In the test phrase: 'His ANCIPITAL remarks', the word is thought by 29 per cent of college seniors to mean THOUGHT-LESS, heedless, careless. This is perhaps a confusion of AN-CIPITAL, two-edged, doubtful, with PRECIPITATE, headlong, over-hasty, thoughtless. ANCIPITAL and PRECIPITATE are both from the Latin *caput*, head. The adjective PRECIPITATE by derivation means head foremost, and is used in English to mean headlong, hasty, rash, without due deliberation. AN-CIPITAL is from the Latin *an*; and *caput*, head; and were the word of Greek origin would mean without a head and therefore perhaps thoughtless; for the Greek AN means without, as in ANHYDROUS, without water; ANEMIA, without blood; ANARCHY, without a ruler. But ANCIPITAL is of Latin origin, where AN stands for *ambi*, around, about, in this case probably on both sides, and means literally with a head on both sides, double-headed, two-faced.

ANCIPITAL is used in botany with its literal meaning, as: 'An ANCIPITAL stem', one with two sharp edges opposite one another. The word is also used figuratively in literature to mean dubious, ambiguous, equivocal, two-faced.

1029. *GRISLY* (*grĭz'-lĭ*) *adj.* Frightful, horrible, terrible, gruesome, ghastly, grim, wild, hideous.

GRISLY comes indirectly from the Danish word *gru*, terror. To 42 per cent of preparatory-school juniors GRISLY incorrectly means DIRTY, soiled. This may be a confusion of the homonyms GRISLY and GRIZZLY; for GRISLY, horrible, and GRIZZLY, grayish, are pronounced alike. GRIZZLY means grayish, somewhat gray, a mixture of black and white. The GRIZZLY BEAR is a grayish bear. GRISLY means terrible, horrible, gruesome.

1030. *REDOLENT* (*rĕd'-ō-lĕnt*) *adj.* Smelling, fragrant, odorous, scented. When used figuratively, REDOLENT means strongly suggestive, reminiscent.

There is an unusual English word OLENT which means having an odor, scented, which comes directly from the Latin *olere*, to smell. REDOLENT, more frequently used, is a combination of the prefix, RE, again, and OLENT.

REDOLENT can be used as an adjective, like FRAGRANT and AROMATIC. FRAGRANT describes that which is sweet-smelling and agreeable; AROMATIC, that which is spicy, pungent, and agreeable; REDOLENT, that which has a strong odor, either pleasant or unpleasant. REDOLENT OF can also be used like SMELLING OF, in the sense of having the odor of, but differs from SMELLING OF in that it can be used figuratively to mean suggestive of, reminiscent of.

1031. *RISIBLE* (*rĭz'-ĭ-bl*, not *rī'-zĭ-bl*) *adj.* Laughter-provoking, funny, amusing, comic, ludicrous (378), ridiculous. In the test phrase: 'RISIBLE stories', the word is thought by 48 per cent of adult readers to mean QUESTIONABLE, doubtful, not of good repute. This is perhaps a confusion of RISIBLE, laughable, with RISQUÉ (*rēs-kā'*), of questionable propriety, not of good repute.

RISIBLE is from the Latin *risus*, the past participle of *ridere*, to laugh. From *ridere* come also the English words, to RIDICULE, to make fun of, to mock, jeer at contemptuously; and the corresponding adjective, RIDICULOUS. Of the three words, RISIBLE, RIDICULOUS, and LAUGHABLE, the last is the simplest. RIDICULOUS adds to LAUGHABLE a trace of contempt. RISIBLE is synonymous with LAUGHABLE; but the word is so rare that when used it suggests inordinately laughable.

1032. *POLYGLOT* (*pŏl'-ĭ-glŏt*) *n.* A linguist, one who writes or speaks several languages. In the test phrase: 'A great POLYGLOT', the word is thought by 29 per cent of adult readers to mean GLUTTON, a voracious eater, gormandizer, the popular misconception. This may be due to the verb GLUT which means to stuff, gorge, and which comes from the Latin *gluttire*, to swallow.

POLYGLOT is from the Greek word πολύς, many; and γλῶττα, tongue. POLY, many, appears in a number of English words, as: POLYGAMIST, a man with several wives; POLYGON, a geometric figure with many angles; and POLYNESIA, by derivation, many islands, the name of a group of islands east of the Malay archipelago. GLOT, tongue, appears in the medical terms, GLOTTIS, mouth of the windpipe; and EPIGLOTTIS, by derivation, upon the glottis, a valve-like organ which prevents the entrance of food and drink into the windpipe.

POLYGLOT and MULTILINGUAL, one from the Greek, the other from the Latin, are exactly synonymous.

1033. *RATIOCINATION* (răsh-ĭ-ŏs-ĭ-nā'-shŭn) *n.* Logical thinking, process of deducing consequences from premises, abstract and severe reasoning.

To 33 per cent of college seniors RATIOCINATION incorrectly means COMPARISON, the act of considering the relation between things to discover their differences or similarities. This confusion is perhaps due to the fact that RATIO and RATIOCINATION are both from the Latin *ratio*, a reckoning, calculation, reasoning, a word which in turn comes from *ratus*, the past participle of *reri*, to think, deem, estimate. The word RATIO as ordinarily used in English has departed furthest from its original meaning, for it is now used to mean the relation between two quantities, and in this sense is a comparison. RATIOCINATION has retained the original Latin meaning and is literally the act of thinking. Because of its length, and because REASONING conveys almost the same impression, RATIOCINATION should seldom be used except for an elaborate but accurate process of drawing a conclusion from abstract premises.

1034. *CESSION* (sĕsh'-ŭn) *n.* Surrender, ceding, yielding, resignation.

CESSION is from the Latin *cessus*, the past participle of the verb *cedere*, to go, retreat, yield, give way, the source also of the verb, to CEDE, to give up, yield, submit, surrender.

In the test phrase: 'The CESSION of these territories', the word is thought by 40 per cent of adult readers to mean FUSION, uniting, coalition. This misconception is probably due to the word SECESSION (134), from the Latin *se*, apart; and the same *cedere*, to go. Since a SECESSION is a withdrawal, one might easily reason that a CESSION should be the opposite, a fusion, uniting.

SECESSION (134), RECESSION (580), CONCESSION, and CESSION, all come from the Latin *cedere* and all mean withdrawal in various senses. The four words have in the past often been used in place of one another and their meanings still overlap. There are situations where their meanings can, however, be distinguished. SECESSION is the formal withdrawal of a small group from a larger organization. RECESSION is a physical retreat. CONCESSION is yielding a point in an argument, granting a fact to an opponent. CESSION applies to yielding or surrendering rights or privileges. The CESSION of a territory is surrendering it, giving up all right to it.

1035. *FLAY (flā) v.* To skin, strip off the skin or surface of.

To FLAY is also used figuratively to mean censure harshly.

FLAY is of Anglo-Saxon origin. To 72 per cent of preparatory-school juniors FLAY incorrectly means WHIP. It is difficult to detect the cause of this misconception. An old Middle English past tense of FLAY was spelt *flog* and this may in some remote way contribute to the present misunderstanding. The word to FLOG, to whip, did not appear until the end of the 17th century and the previous history of the word is unknown.

The Latin word for whip was *flagellum;* and there is today an English verb, to FLAGELLATE, which means to whip, scourge. Or it may be the verb to FLAIL, which comes from the Latin *flagellum*, whip, and which means to thresh, beat with a flail, an instrument for threshing grain, which leads to this confusion. Whatever the cause, FLAY does not mean to beat, whip, scourge, lash, flog; but to skin, peel off the hide, strip off the fell, remove the pelt. The word may be used literally, as: 'To FLAY an ox'; or figuratively to mean criticize severely.

1036. *CELIBATE* (*sĕl'-ĭ-bāt*) *n.* An unmarried man, single man, one who lives a bachelor's existence.

CELIBATE is from the Latin word *caelebs*, a bachelor. In the test phrase: 'The life of the CELIBATE', the word is thought by 25 per cent of adult readers to mean HERMIT. A HERMIT is one who lives alone, apart from society, a recluse. A HERMIT may or may not have bound himself by religious vows. Although it is true that the word CELIBATE may be used for one who has bound himself by religious vows not to marry, it is also true that a CELIBATE may be a bachelor, a society man playing an active part in life. This phase of the word is emphasized by the second common misconception, PLEASURE-LOVER, held by 16 per cent.

1037. *TURBID* (*ter'-bĭd*) *adj.* Muddy, roiled, disturbed, thick, not clear, cloudy with sediment which has been stirred up.

In the test phrase: 'TURBID water', the word is thought by 46 per cent of preparatory-school juniors to mean SURGING. A SURGE is a large wave, billow, swell; and SURGING means swelling, rising like a wave. This may be due to the word TURGID (1088), swollen, which is confused with TURBID by renowned writers. Or the confusion of TURBID, muddy, with SURGING may be caused by the adjective TURBULENT, from the Latin *turbare*, to disturb, the source also of TURBID. TURBULENT means in violent commotion, agitated, as: 'A TURBULENT sea', 'A TURBULENT mob'. That which is TURBID is muddy because it has been stirred up, disturbed; but TURBID, despite its derivation, suggests primarily the muddy, thick, condition, rather than the motion.

1038. *PELAGIC* (*pĕ-lăj'-ĭk*) *adj.* Oceanic (80), marine, pertaining to the open sea.

To 21 per cent of adult readers PELAGIC incorrectly means CATLIKE, feline.

PELAGIC comes from the Greek word πέλαγος, the sea. From the same source comes the more familiar English word ARCHIPELAGO (*ahr-kĭ-pĕl'-ă-gō*, not *ahr-chĭ-pĕl'-ă-gō*). ARCH begins a score of English words and means chief, principal, as: ARCHBISHOP (*ahrch-bĭsh'-ŏp*), the chief bishop; ARCHDEA-

CON, the chief deacon; and ARCHITECT (ahr'-kĭ-tĕkt), by derivation the chief builder. ARCHIPELAGO is, by derivation, the
chief sea, principal ocean. The ARCHIPELAGO, spelt with a
capital, originally was the sea between Greece and Asia Minor, now called the AEGEAN Sea. Because this sea is dotted
with small islands the word ARCHIPELAGO has come to mean
any sea containing many islands; and may even designate the
islands rather than the sea. But the adjective PELAGIC has retained the original Greek meaning, pertaining to the open sea.

1039. *SCORE* (skōr) *n.* A line drawn, long scratch, one of
        a series of parallel lines cut in stone work to give tex-
ture, sometimes a taw, a mark used as a starting line or goal.
A SCORE, meaning a line, is thought by 50 per cent of adult
readers to mean a DIFFERENCE. The noun SCORE is used in
nearly a dozen senses. It comes from an Anglo-Saxon word
meaning twenty; and today a SCORE of objects is twenty objects. A SCORE is also a notch cut in a stick for the purpose
of keeping an account. Today the word is used in one of its
senses for the number of points made in a game, a tally, as
in the familiar phrase: 'A baseball SCORE'.

One of the unusual meanings of the noun, a SCORE, is a line
drawn. This meaning is familiar in the verb, to UNDERSCORE,
to draw a line under; and in the noun SCORING, the primary
meaning of which is scratch, line, groove, cut.

1040. *PANEGYRICAL* (păn-ē-jĭr'-ĭ-kăl) *adj.* In praise, laud-
        atory, eulogistic, encomiastic, extolling, plauditory, glo-
rifying, exalting. There are two adjectives, PANEGYRIC and
PANEGYRICAL; the shorter is preferable.

The PANEGYRIS, from the two Greek words, πᾶς, παντός,
all, a word which appears also in Pan-American; and ἄγυρις,
assembly; was a public meeting, an assembly of all the people.
A PANEGYRIC was originally a formal and elaborate speech
addressed to the Greek PANEGYRIS. Today a PANEGYRIC may
be either spoken or written, but it must be in praise of someone or of some event, a eulogy, encomium.

To 23 per cent of college seniors PANEGYRICAL incorrectly
means SARDONIC. SARDONIC, also of Greek origin, means bitterly ironical, sarcastic, derisive, sneering, malignant, in con-

notation an opposite of the correct meaning of PANEGYRICAL, laudatory.

1041. *APLOMB* (*ă-plogn'*) *n.* Assurance, poise, equanimity, self-possession, unabashed behavior, perfect confidence in one's self.

APLOMB is a French word which has been adopted by English without change. According to most dictionaries it still retains its French pronunciation; but in conversation it is usually anglicized and pronounced either (*ă-plŏm'* or *ă-plŭm'*).

In the test phrase: 'He received it with APLOMB', the word is thought by 25 per cent of adult readers to mean GRATITUDE, thankfulness.

APLOMB and POISE are synonymous in their figurative senses and are similar metaphorically. A POISE is a weight of any kind, specifically a weight suspended as a counterweight, one which creates a balance. A man of POISE is one who is well-balanced, a man of equanimity. POISE is almost a physical balance which reacts mentally.

A PLUMB (*plŭm*), a word which comes from the Latin *plumbum*, lead, the source of the chemical symbol PB and of the English word PLUMBER, is a lead weight attached to the end of a line which is allowed to hang free in order to indicate the perpendicular. APLOMB means by derivation perpendicularity; but the word is always used in its figurative sense to mean self-possession.

1042. *PROPRIETY* (*prō-prī'-ĕ-tĭ*) *n.* Correct conduct, decorum, seemliness, fitness, appropriateness, circumspection, suitability.

PROPER, PROPERTY, and PROPRIETY, come from the same Latin source, *proprius*, one's own, personal, particular, special; but the three words developed so far before reaching modern English that it is difficult to trace their logical sequences.

PROPRIETY means suitability to an acknowledged standard or rule, the rule of MRS. GRUNDY, an invisible character in the comedy SPEED THE PLOUGH, written in 1798 by THOMAS MORTON, an English dramatist. 'What will Mrs. Grundy say!' was at one time a current exclamation.

In the test phrase: 'He acted with PROPRIETY', the word is

thought by 29 per cent of adult readers to mean DIGNITY, nobleness of manner, excellence of character, special inherent worthiness; and by another 20 per cent to mean WISDOM. DIGNITY and WISDOM may show themselves externally but only as manifestations of inner characteristics. PROPRIETY is mere external conformity to rule.

1043. *PERIPATETIC* (*pĕr-ĭ-pă-tĕt'-ĭk*) *adj.* Itinerant, pedestrian, ambulatory, walking about, accustomed to move from place to place, not stationary.

In the test phrase: 'PERIPATETIC occupations', the word is thought by 25 per cent of adult readers to mean ROUTINE, unvarying, habitual.

The two words, PERIPATETIC and NOMADIC, both mean moving about and are both of Greek origin. NOMADIC, wandering, roving, is from the Greek νέμειν, to pasture, and by derivation means roving, wandering, like a herd of cattle in search of food. PERIPATETIC is from two Greek words περί, about; and πετεῖν, to walk; and means literally walking about.

When spelt with a capital, PERIPATETIC, the word refers to a follower of ARISTOTLE, 384 to 320 B.C., who taught as he wandered about the walks of the Lyceum at Athens; and the adjective, PERIPATETIC, spelt with a small letter, means walking about.

1044. *RETUND* (*rē-tŭnd'*) *v.* To dull, blunt, turn back the edge of a weapon. To RETUND is also used in the figurative sense of refute.

In the test phrase: 'RETUND the rumor', the word is thought by 24 per cent of adult readers to mean INVESTIGATE, examine, search into, inquire into.

RETUND comes from the Latin *re*, back; and *tundere*, to beat, strike; and means literally to beat back. From *tusus*, the past participle of *tundere*, come the English noun, a CONTUSION (*kŏn-tū'-zhŭn*, not *kŏn-tŭsh'-ŭn*), a bruise, an injury received from a blunt instrument which does not break the skin; and the adjective OBTUSE (984), blunt, referring to an angle greater than 90 degrees, a word used figuratively to mean dull, not sharp, stupid.

To RETUND and to REFUTE are practically synonymous. The

word REFUTE, from the Latin *re*, back; and *futare*, to pour; calls attention to the process which has been used in rendering an assertion invalid, to the arguments which have poured forth in opposition. The word RETUND stresses the invalid state of the original assertion, its blunted edge.

1045. *CONCATENATE* (*kŏn-kăt'-ĕ-nāt*) *v.* To link together, join, connect, combine, unite in a successive series as in a chain.

In the test phrase: 'CONCATENATE the attempts', the word is thought by 29 per cent of college seniors to mean DISCOURAGE, dissuade from, attempt to repress. To another 21 per cent it incorrectly means CUT OFF.

CONCATENATE is from the Latin *con*, together; and *catenare*, to link; and means literally to link together. From *catenare* comes also the English word CATENARY, like a chain, a word used as a noun to designate the curve formed by a chain hung from its two ends.

1046. *OPPROBRIOUS* (*ŏp-prō'-brĭ-ŭs*) *adj.* Reproachful, abusive, offensive, infamous, insulting, contumelious, scurrilous (1071).

In the test phrase: 'An OPPROBRIOUS name', the word is thought by 26 per cent of adult readers to mean ASSUMED, affected, feigned, fictitious, appropriated. This is perhaps a confusion of OPPROBRIOUS with APPROPRIATED, assumed, adopted, taken to one's self.

OPPROBRIOUS, from the Latin *ob*, upon; and *probrum*, disgrace; characterizes a more articulate dislike than does the word ODIOUS, but is not so abhorrent or evil as INFAMOUS.

1047. *INANE* (*ĭn-ān'*) *adj.* Empty, silly, senseless, characterless, pointless, fatuous, frivolous, trifling, puerile, jejune (1108), void of sense.

To 36 per cent of adult readers INANE incorrectly means CRAZY. This is probably a confusion of INANE with INSANE. INSANE is from the Latin *in*, not; and *sanus*, sound; and means literally of unsound mind, deranged, crazy. INANE, although its complete history is unknown, is considerably milder and means silly, pointless.

INANITY, emptiness, vacuity, also more figuratively mental vacuity, silliness, senselessness, is the corresponding noun.

1048. *CAPTIOUS* (*kăp'-shŭs*) *adj.* Faultfinding, cross, fretful (441), petulant, carping, caviling, hypercritical, given to raising objections.

CAPTIOUS, if traced back far enough, is found to come from the Latin *capere*, to take, seize; and the word today suggests seizing on small points, grasping at minute details.

In the test phrase: 'CAPTIOUS criticism', the word is thought by 30 per cent of adult readers to mean POINTED. POINTED, used in the phrase: 'POINTED criticism', may have either of two meanings. It may mean aimed at some particular person; or it may mean piquant, keen, sharp, acute, epigrammatical, as for instance: 'POINTED wit'. In neither case does POINTED imply faultfinding.

CAPTIOUS, CARPING, and CAVILING, are so close in meaning as often to be used interchangeably. All three mean faultfinding. CARPING is faultfinding with a boasting attitude; CAVILING is faultfinding jeeringly, tauntingly; CAPTIOUS is hypercritical, faultfinding about trifles.

1049. *PERVERSE* (*per-vers'*) *adj.* Wilfully wrong, wrongheaded, wayward, contrary, stubborn (266), unreasonable, self-willed. PERVERSE may also mean peevish, petulant, cross, fretful.

PERVERSE is from the Latin *vertere*, to turn. From the same source come not only the corresponding nouns, PERVERSITY, PERVERSENESS, and PERVERSION; the adjectives, PERVERSIVE, PERVERTED, and PERVERTIBLE; the adverb, PERVERSELY; and the verb, to PERVERT; but also a large family of words all of which mean to turn in various ways. ADVERSE (*ăd'-vers*), literally turned against, means opposed, as: 'ADVERSE criticism'; AVERSE (*ă-vers'*), also literally turned against, means unwilling, opposed, as: 'AVERSE to going'; CONVERSE, reciprocal; DIVERSE, different, various, unlike; INVERSE, turned end for end; and REVERSE, turned backward.

In the test phrase: 'Her PERVERSE attitude', the word is thought by 32 per cent of adult readers to mean CHANGING, the common misconception. This may be due to some confusion of PERVERSE with DIVERSE, by derivation, turned apart, and therefore various, different, as: 'DIVERSE opinions'. The word PERVERSE embodies the notion of continuing stubbornly, obstinately, in a wrong direction. In this sense, CHANGING is an opposite of the correct meaning.

By another group PERVERSE is thought to mean TRUCULENT, ferocious, savage, destructive, ruthless, the second most common misconception. Both TRUCULENT and PERVERSE describe an anti-social attitude; but TRUCULENT is destructive, savage; whereas PERVERSE is merely wrongheaded.

PERVERSE and FROWARD, from an Old English word meaning fromward, turned from, have today practically the same meaning but differ slightly. FROWARD means disobedient and applies to children; PERVERSE refers to a settled disposition to be contrary and is used of adults. STUBBORN, OBSTINATE, and PERTINACIOUS, also imply sticking to one's course, to one's opinion, but do not suggest that it is wrong, as does PERVERSE.

1050. *KIOSK* (*kĭ-ŏsk'*) *n.* An open pavilion, summerhouse such as is common in Turkey and Persia and which has been reproduced in the gardens and parks of other countries. A KIOSK has a roof often supported on columns, no walls, but an open balustrade.

KIOSK is from a Persian word meaning palace. To 28 per cent of college seniors KIOSK incorrectly means EGYPTIAN MONUMENT. This may be a confusion of KIOSK with OBELISK, a tall, square, Egyptian monument of stone, carved with hieroglyphics.

To another 20 per cent KIOSK incorrectly means ESKIMO CANOE. This is evidently a confusion of KIOSK with KAYAK (*kĭ'-ăk*), a light, canoe-shaped boat, usually made of seal-skin stretched over a wood frame.

The word, KIOSK, is perhaps best known with its French spelling, *kiosque*, the name of the newspaper stands in Paris, which are similar in shape to the original KIOSK.

1051. *UBIQUITOUS* (*ū-bĭk'-wĭ-tŭs*) *adj.* Omnipresent, existing everywhere at the same time, present in an indefinite number of places at once. UBIQUITOUS is often applied humorously to that which turns up unexpectedly in many places. UBIQUITOUS is from the Latin *ubique*, everywhere. In the test phrase: 'Said to be UBIQUITOUS', the word is thought by 27 per cent of adult readers to mean DISAGREEABLE. By 5 per cent of preparatory-school juniors UBIQUITOUS is thought to mean DIABOLIC, fiendish, devilish. Both of these are probably confusions of UBIQUITOUS, present everywhere, with INIQUI-TOUS, wicked, unjust.

UBIQUITOUS, OMNIPRESENT, and EVERYWHERE, are similar in meaning. EVERYWHERE, the native word of Anglo-Saxon origin, is an adverb, while the two more unusual words of Latin origin are adjectives. OMNIPRESENT means existing everywhere at the same time, as: 'God is OMNIPRESENT'. UBIQUI-TOUS is often used in an exaggerated, even in a disparaging sense, of someone or something encountered apparently everywhere, on every occasion.

1052. ADUST (*ă-dŭst'*) *adj.* Parched, burnt, scorched, shriveled with heat, seared by exposure to fire.

The word ADUST has no etymological connection with DUST, but comes from the Latin *ad*, to; and *ustus*, the past participle of the verb *urere*, to burn. From *ustus* come the familiar words COMBUST and COMBUSTION, and the unusual words US-TULATION, the act of burning, and USTULATE, the adjective, colored or blackened as if scorched. ADUST means sunburnt, not in the sense of tanned, but scorched, parched, seared, dried up with heat.

1053. PLEONASTIC (*plē-ō-năs'-tĭk*) *adj.* Superfluous, tau-tological, redundant, superabundant, verbose (797), pro-lix (906), using more words than are necessary.

PLEONASTIC and the corresponding noun PLEONASM are from a Greek word πλεονασμός, abundance, a word which in turn comes from πλέων, more, the comparative of πολύς, much, the source of the English word PLUS.

To 37 per cent of adult readers PLEONASTIC incorrectly means ARCHAIC, antiquated, ancient, out of use, obsolete.

Three technical terms differentiate redundant writings, PLE-ONASM, PERIPHRASIS, and TAUTOLOGY. TAUTOLOGY is the repetition of the same idea in different words. PERIPHRASIS (*pĕ-rĭf'-ră-sĭs*) is a roundabout but justified mode of expression, as for example, the use of a phrase to avoid a cliché, a trite expression. A PLEONASM is the use of more words than are needed to give the sense; a PLEONASM is justified if used for emphasis. PLEONASTIC is the corresponding adjective.

1054. *PRECEPT* (*prē'-sĕpt*) *n.* Instruction, maxim, commandment, rule guiding behavior, injunction as to moral conduct.
PRECEPT is from the Latin *prae*, before; and *capere*, to take. From *capere* come CAPTURE, to take, seize; CAPTOR; and CAPTIVE; as well as CAPABLE, by derivation able to take; now qualified, gifted, efficient. From the same source come the verb to CONCEIVE, to get a notion of, form a mental image of; and the noun CONCEPT, a notion, mental grasp.

In the test phrase: 'His PRECEPT was wise', the word is thought by 36 per cent of adult readers to mean PRECAUTION, an idea not far from correct. A CAUTION may be a word of warning, advice given by a teacher, admonishment; and in this sense a CAUTION and a PRECEPT are practically synonymous. A PRECAUTION, from the Latin *prae*, before; and *cavere*, to be on one's guard; is, however, not advice, but action taken to obviate a future difficulty. PRECAUTIONS may be taken as a result of a PRECEPT.

A PRECEPTOR (*prē-sĕp'-tŏr*) is an instructor, teacher; a PRECEPT is the advice, the rule of conduct, laid down by an instructor.

1055. *STRIDENT* (*strī'-dĕnt*) *adj.* Loud and harsh in sound, grating, disagreeably penetrating, raucous, rasping.
In the test phrase: 'Her STRIDENT voice', the word is thought by 44 per cent of adult readers to mean COMMANDING, imperious, authoritative, governing. This may be due to the word STRIDE, which is of Anglo-Saxon origin and which may be used as either a noun or a verb. A STRIDE is a long step, taken with confidence, and is often thought of as characterizing a person of commanding, authoritative, manner. STRIDENT is not the corresponding adjective, but comes from the Latin *stridere*, to creak, make a harsh sound.
STRIDENT and STRIDULOUS (883) are from the same source. STRIDULOUS describes a shriller, thinner, smaller, sound than

STRIDENT which is harsher, louder, but produced in the same grating fashion.

1056. COGENT (*kō'-jĕnt*) *adj.* Forcible, conclusive, convincing, appealing strongly to the reason, compelling belief.

COGENT is from the Latin *cogere*, to compel; and in English means literally compelling. In the test phrase: 'His COGENT remark', the word is thought by 45 per cent of college seniors to mean RELEVANT, apposite, pertinent, applicable, bearing on the matter at hand. Both words, RELEVANT and COGENT, imply forcefulness. RELEVANT denotes appropriateness, fitness; COGENT denotes forcefulness itself.

Both COGENT and FORCIBLE mean strong. FORCIBLE is applied most often to the mode of reasoning and to the manner of presentation; COGENT is applied to the nature of the reasons which are advanced. COGENT arguments can be presented in a FORCIBLE manner.

1057. FAIN (*fān*) *adj.* Glad, rejoiced, pleased. FAIN may also mean pleased under the circumstances, glad to accept the alternative. FAIN, in both senses, is used with the preposition TO, as: 'FAIN TO do it'.

To 59 per cent of preparatory-school juniors, FAIN TO incorrectly means RELUCTANT TO. RELUCTANT is unwilling, loath, or sometimes disposed to grant unwillingly. In this last sense both RELUCTANT and FAIN suggest compliance under the circumstances; RELUCTANT, unwillingly; FAIN, willingly.

1058. CONSCIENTIOUS (*kŏn-shĭ-ĕn'-shŭs*, not *kŏn-sĭ-ĕn'-shŭs*) *adj.* Upright, scrupulous (604), righteous, exact, careful, faithful, painstaking, obedient to ideals of right and wrong.

CONSCIENTIOUS is thought by 49 per cent of adult readers to mean THINKING. CONSCIENTIOUS and CONSCIOUS, and the nouns CONSCIENCE and CONSCIOUSNESS, all come from the Latin, *com*, together; and *scire*, to know; and suggest a joint knowledge, a community awareness. CONSCIENTIOUS once meant capable of thinking, feeling, conscious; and CONSCIENCE originally meant knowledge, consciousness. These meanings are obsolete; and CONSCIOUS now means aware, awake to one's environment, indued with feeling; CONSCIOUSNESS is the state of being conscious. CONSCIENTIOUS came to mean conscious of wrong and is now used in a more general sense to mean careful in conforming to one's own ideals of right and wrong, obedient to the dictates of one's conscience.

1059. *MEPHITIC* (*mĕ-fĭt'-ĭk*) *adj.* Pertaining to foul odors rising from the ground, noxious, pestilential, offensive to the sense of smell.

MEPHITIC is the adjective corresponding to the noun MEPHITIS (*mĕ-fĭ'-tĭs*), a noisome stench arising from the ground. There is a genus of skunk called MEPHITIS; and a goddess MEPHITIS who averts noxious exhalations.

1060. *HEDONIST* (*hē'-dŏn-ĭst* or *hĕd'-ŏn-ĭst*) *n.* Self-indulger, one who holds the doctrine that pleasure is the chief legitimate goal in life, one who indulges himself in pleasure in the belief that the gratification of one's desires is the highest good.

HEDONISM was a doctrine first propounded by Aristippus (*ăr-ĭs-tĭp'-pŭs*) of Cyrene (*sī-rē'-nē*), a city in northern Africa. Aristippus was a Greek philosopher who lived probably from 425 to 356 B.C., a pupil of Socrates.

To 28 per cent of college seniors HEDONIST incorrectly means FATALIST, one who believes that all things happen by inevitable necessity. FATALISM has never been a school of philosophy founded by one teacher; the word has never been spelt with a capital, but describes a belief which has played a part in many schools of thought.

To another 19 per cent HEDONIST incorrectly means STOIC. STOICISM, spelt with a capital, was a school of philosophy founded by ZENO about 308 B.C. The word comes from the Greek στωικός, pertaining to the porch, a word which in turn comes from στοά, porch, loggia, a covered walk the roof of which was supported by columns. STOICISM is so named because ZENO expounded his philosophy from the PAINTED PORCH, one of the covered walks about the AGORA, the public square of ancient Athens. A STOIC, spelt with a capital, was a follower of ZENO, one who believed that men should be free from passion, unmoved by joy or grief, and submit without complaint to the unavoidable necessity by which all things are governed. The word is used today, spelt with a small letter, to mean one who bears pain uncomplainingly, one who practices self-control. A STOIC is practically the opposite of a HEDONIST.

1061. *SAFFRON* (*săf'-frŏn*) *adj.* Orange-yellow in color, deep yellow. SAFFRON is the name of a plant, an autumnal crocus, which has purple flowers with orange stigmas. SAFFRON is also the dye made from the stigmas.
In the test phrase: 'A SAFFRON robe', the word is thought by 23 per cent of adult readers to mean RED; by another 20 per cent to mean PURPLE; and by still another 16 per cent to mean BLUE.

SAFFRON probably goes back to an Arabic word which means yellow. From the Arabic come the names of at least three colors; AZURE, sky blue; CRIMSON, deep red, a red bordering on purple; and CARMINE, a transparent crimson. From the Arabic come also the word LAKE, a word which is added to the name of a color to indicate transparency, as CRIMSON LAKE, PURPLE LAKE; and the names of many plants and products which were introduced into western Europe by traveling merchants; as: APRICOT, ARTICHOKE, COFFEE, COTTON, ENDIVE, HENNA, JASMINE, LEMON, LIME, SHRUB, SUGAR, SUMAC, all ultimately of Arabic origin.

1062. *METICULOUS* (*mē-tĭk'-ū-lŭs*) *adj.* Overcareful for fear of making mistakes, timid, fearful about unimportant details, overscrupulous.
METICULOUS is the popular word today for exactness, overniceness, of any sort. Etymologically, METICULOUS has no such meaning for it comes from the Latin *metus*, fear, and by derivation means timid, fearful, scared, shaking with fear. When METICULOUS is used to mean careful, punctilious, scrupulous, it should refer only to one who is fearful of small errors, overcareful because of timidity. METICULOUS suggests a fear of public opinion. It does not, like PUNCTILIOUS (533), suggest an interest in accuracy for its own sake; nor does it, like SCRUPULOUS (604), suggest a conscience.

1063. *PREDICATE* (*prĕd'-ĭ-kāt*) *v.* To assert, declare, affirm, proclaim, allege, maintain, state positively.

In the test phrase: 'PREDICATE the truth', the word is thought by 61 per cent of preparatory-school juniors to mean FORE-TELL. FORETELL, tell beforehand, is an exact translation of the Latin *prae*, before; and *dicere*, to say, tell; the source of PREDICATE. But in English PREDICT, from the same Latin *prae*; and *dicere*, to say; means to foretell, by derivation, to say beforehand. PREDICATE has never had this meaning. The word is perhaps best known as used by grammarians to mean that part of a sentence which asserts something about the subject. The noun, a PREDICATE, in a general sense, has come to mean that which is asserted as the basis of an argument, literally that which is said before the argument starts. The verb, to PREDI-CATE, is used most frequently to mean assert in any sense.

1064. *FACTITIOUS* (*făk-tĭsh'-ŭs*) *adj.* Elaborately arti-ficial (482), manufactured, unnatural, made-up, created by artful means as opposed to being created by nature.

To 27 per cent of college seniors FACTITIOUS incorrectly means FACTUAL, literal, exact, genuine, according to facts. Both FACTUAL and FACTITIOUS come from the same Latin word *facere*, to do; but the two words are at times practically opposites. FACTUAL may mean genuine; while FACTITIOUS means artificial, and, like artificial, may suggest not genuine.

FACTITIOUS and FICTITIOUS (212), except for one letter, are alike in spelling and pronunciation, and both mean artificial. ARTIFICIAL (482) means done by art, not by nature. FICTI-TIOUS, from the Latin *fingere*, to feign, pretend, make-believe, stresses the skill, cleverness, of the creation. FACTITIOUS, from the same word as FACTORY, stresses the labor which has been expended in the creation.

1065. *RECALCITRANT* (*rē-kăl'-sĭ-trănt*) *adj.* Rebellious, refractory, contumacious, mulish, obstinately unco-operative, stubbornly disobedient.

RECALCITRANT is from the Latin *re*, back; and *calcitrare*, to kick; *calcitrare* in turn comes from *calx*, *calcis*, the heel. There were two Latin words *calx*. One came from the Greek χάλιξ, a small stone, and meant a small stone, counter, lime-

stone. This is the source of the English mathematical word
CALCULUS, directly from the Latin *calculus*, a small stone,
pebble, the diminutive of *calx;* probably from the fact that
the first calculations were made with pebbles as counters.
The other Latin word *calx* meant heel and is used in anatomy today to mean heel. To 42 per cent of adult readers
RECALCITRANT incorrectly means REPENTANT, penitent, contrite, sorrowful for past conduct. The actions of a REPENTANT
person are directly opposed to those of a RECALCITRANT, rebellious, refractory, one.

RECALCITRANT, REBELLIOUS, and REFRACTORY, are similar in
meaning. REFRACTORY comes from the Latin *re*, back; and
fractus, the past participle of *frangere*, to break. The REFRAC-
TORY person breaks away, turns sharply aside from any prescribed course. REBELLIOUS is from the Latin *re*; and *bellum*,
war. The REBELLIOUS person wages open war against authority. The RECALCITRANT person kicks back, is mulishly unco-
operative.

1066. *SATURNINE* (*săt'-er-nīn*) *adj.* Heavy, dull, morose,
       gloomy, grave, taciturn.
The Roman deity SATURN was believed to have instructed
his people in agriculture and the SATURNALE (*săt-er-nă'-lē*)
was originally the harvest festival held in his honor. The
plural form of the word SATURNALIA, spelt with a small letter,
is now used to mean any wild revelry.

During the Middle Ages the alchemists used the word
SATURN to mean lead and it is undoubtedly from this application that the adjective SATURNINE has come to mean heavy.
Astrologers today believe that persons born under the influence of SATURN are grave, phlegmatic.

MERCURIAL is another adjective associated with the name
of a planet, Mercury. MERCURIAL means gay, light-hearted,
volatile, having the characteristics of the god MERCURY, ascribed to those born under the planet MERCURY. SATURNINE
and MERCURIAL are opposites.

1067. *ATTENUATE* (*ăt-těn'-ū-āt*) *v.* To enfeeble, lessen,
       weaken, impair, reduce in force.
ATTENUATE and the more familiar verb to EXTENUATE are both

from the Latin *tenuis*, thin, slender, from the same source as TENUOUS, thin, rarefied.

By 46 per cent of college seniors the verb to ATTENUATE is thought to mean INTENSIFY, to strengthen, make stronger, an exact opposite of the correct meaning of ATTENUATE.

To EXTENUATE is to make smaller in degree, render less blamable, mitigate, excuse, and is the opposite of AGGRAVATE. The present participle is familiar in the cliché: 'EXTENUATING circumstances'.

To ATTENUATE may mean to make slender, reduce in thickness in a physical sense; or it may mean to rarefy, make less dense, still in a physical sense; or it may be used in a figurative sense to mean weaken, reduce in force.

1068. *TEMERARIOUS* (*tĕm-ĕ-rā'-rĭ-ŭs*) *adj*. Rash, reckless, imprudent, heedless, adventurous, foolhardy, unreasonably venturous, contemptuous of danger.

In the test phrase: 'TEMERARIOUS persons', the word is thought by 24 per cent of adult readers to mean COWARDLY, the common misconception of the word and an opposite of the correct meaning. The confusion may be caused by the similarity in sound of the three words: TIMID, TIMOROUS, and TEMERARIOUS; or it may be another instance of the direct opposite being the common misconception. There is apparently no etymological relation, for TIMOROUS comes from the Latin *timere*, to fear; while TEMERARIOUS comes from *temere*, by chance, at random. The similarity in sound of TIMOROUS, fearful, shrinking, and TEMERARIOUS, rash, seems to be mere chance.

TEMERARIOUS and the corresponding noun, TEMERITY, rashness, foolhardiness, are used in the social sphere and of mental states, and not so often of physical encounters. Furthermore, they are usually derogatory as in the phrases: 'The TEMERITY to lie', 'The TEMERITY to give false evidence'. A TEMERARIOUS person ought to know better.

RECKLESS is probably the nearest to TEMERARIOUS in meaning in the physical sphere; it implies a disregard of consequences which might have been foreseen. RASH has something of the same meaning in physical situations but is more complimentary, perhaps because it implies a carefree lack of forethought; RASHNESS is often a youthful quality. FOOLHARDY implies not so much lack of forethought as lack of good sense; while HEEDLESS implies lack of attention. A VENTURE-SOME person hovers on the verge of danger, would perhaps like to be rash, but does not actually rush in. Although it is difficult to find an opposite of words distinguished from one another by fine shades of meaning, CAREFUL is perhaps the nearest opposite of RECKLESS; WATCHFUL, the opposite of RASH; CIRCUMSPECT, the opposite of FOOLHARDY; WARY, the opposite of HEEDLESS; and CAUTIOUS, the nearest opposite of TEMERARIOUS.

1069. *VITIATE* (*vĭsh'-ĭ-āt*) *v.* To defile, spoil, pollute (267), taint, corrupt, render faulty, cause to become defective. VITIATE comes from the Latin *vitium*, a fault, imperfection. From this same source come the English words, VICE, fault, depravity, corruption; and VICIOUS, evil, bad. VITIATE has at times in the past been spelt *viciate*, conforming with VICE and VICIOUS, but the modern spelling is more like the Latin.

To VITIATE and to CORRUPT are practically synonymous, but the two words differ slightly in application. One can either CORRUPT or VITIATE a man's principles or his tastes. One can CORRUPT the man himself, but not VITIATE him. One can VITIATE a reasoning process; and one can VITIATE a legal contract.

In the test phrase: 'The air was VITIATED', the word is thought by 59 per cent of college seniors to mean CLEANSED, an exact opposite of the correct meaning.

1070. *REQUITAL* (*rē-kwī'-tăl*) *n.* Something given in return, reward, repayment, recompense, retribution (968). REQUITAL comes probably from the same source as the Latin word *quietare*, to quiet. To 36 per cent of adult readers it incorrectly means DECISION, judgment, judicial determination, verdict. This is perhaps a confusion of REQUITAL, recompense, with ACQUITTAL (*ăk-kwĭt'-tăl*), a decision freeing one from a charge of guilt.

In international law, the two words RETORSION and REPRISAL express the idea of REQUITAL. RETORSION is doing unto others as they have done to you, the act of making a RETORT. RE-

PRISAL consists in seizing the property of another nation until the case is heard in the court for adjudication of such actions; and the reclamations, demands for redress, acted upon.

REQUITAL and RETRIBUTION are practically synonymous. They differ in that a RETRIBUTION is a just return for past conduct. A REQUITAL may be unfair in amount or severity, depending upon the will of the REQUITER.

1071. *SCURRILOUS* (*sker'-rĭ-lŭs*) *adj.* Coarse, abusive, vituperative, vulgar, opprobrious (1046), indecent in language.

In the test phrase: 'The SCURRILOUS rogue', the word is thought by 32 per cent of adult readers to mean DESPERATE, reckless, frantic, the popular misconception. An archaic meaning of DESPERATE is exceedingly bad, outrageous, a meaning close to SCURRILOUS.

By another 13 per cent, SCURRILOUS is thought to mean HURRIED. This is probably due to a confusion of SCURRILOUS, abusive, with SCURRY, a word which means to hurry, scuttle, scamper, and which is used in the familiar phrase: 'Hurry SCURRY'.

SCURRILOUS, which comes from the Latin *scurra*, jester, buffoon, is defined by Samuel Johnson, the English lexicographer, 1709–1784, as a tendency to use such language as only the license of a buffoon can warrant.

1072. *TRUCULENT* (*trŭk'-ū-lĕnt*) *adj.* Fierce, savage, barbarous, ruthless, ferocious, fell; also cruel, destructive. In the test phrase: 'A TRUCULENT look', the word is thought by 24 per cent of college seniors to mean QUESTIONING, inquiring, interrogating.

TRUCULENT is from the Latin *trux, trucis*, wild, fierce, savage; but the English word TRUCULENT has come to be used of a ferocity tempered by civilization, savageness of bearing, fierceness of manner.

1073. *EGREGIOUS* (*ē-grē'-jŭs*) *adj.* Remarkable, extraordinary, extreme, greatly exceeding others of the same class. EGREGIOUSLY is the corresponding adverb.

EGREGIOUS comes from the Latin *e*, out; and *grex, gregis*, a flock, herd, swarm; and by derivation means out of the herd. From *grex* comes also GREGARIOUS, inclined to gather together, disposed to live in herds.

In the test phrase: 'EGREGIOUS errors', the word is thought by 44 per cent of college seniors to mean VARIED, diverse, differing from one another. VARIED, in the phrase: 'VARIED errors', means errors of different kinds; even small errors may vary, differ, among themselves. That which is EGREGIOUS varies from the herd, is extraordinary; each EGREGIOUS error, as the word is ordinarily used today, is enormous, monstrous.

The word ENORMOUS has a parallel derivation and is not dissimilar in meaning. It comes from the same Latin *e*, out; and *norma*, rule; and by derivation means out of the rule, out of the ordinary. Today ENORMOUS usually means big, huge, gigantic, and may be applied to anything of size, as: 'An ENORMOUS city', 'An ENORMOUS bird', 'An ENORMOUS error'. ENORMOUS is also used occasionally to mean wicked, atrocious. The noun, an ENORMITY, always means an atrocity, outrage.

In the test phrase: 'EGREGIOUS folly', the word is thought by 28 per cent of adult readers to mean UNPARDONABLE, not to be forgiven. The suggestion of the two words is often similar but their meanings should be carefully differentiated. A slight error made by a diplomat, by a highly paid lawyer, or by a professional athlete, is often UNPARDONABLE, not to be forgiven; whereas an EGREGIOUS, extraordinary, error made by a novice is readily forgiven, willingly pardoned.

EGREGIOUS was once used in the good sense to mean distinguished, outstanding, preeminent. Although it is today less unpleasant than ENORMOUS in its disagreeable sense, outrageous, atrocious, it is applied almost exclusively to that which stands out in a wrong direction.

1074. *PERACUTE* (*per-ā-kūt'*) *adj.* Very acute, painful, violent, severe. PERACUTE is a pathological term, used in reference to bodily ailments.

In the test phrase: 'A PERACUTE fever', the word is thought by 25 per cent of college seniors to mean DEEP. One of the many meanings of DEEP is intense, profound, thorough, extreme, as: 'A DEEP sleep'. This is practically the meaning of the Latin prefix *per*, as used in PERACUTE; but there is nothing in the word DEEP to suggest painful, violent, as does PERACUTE.

The prefix PER may mean through, as in PERSUE, to follow through; and PERUSAL (763), using through to the end; or it may clearly mean very as in PERTINACIOUS (965), very tenacious; PELLUCID (956), very lucid; and PERACUTE, very acute.

1075. *REFULGENT* (*rē-fŭl'-jĕnt*) *adj.* Very bright, shining, splendid, radiant, gleaming, brilliant, resplendent.

REFULGENT is from the Latin *re*; and *fulgere*, to shine, gleam, a word associated with the Latin *fulgor*, lightning, a flash of lightning. From the same source comes the English verb to FULMINATE, to explode with sudden violence, thunder forth; figuratively, burst forth with denunciations, censure, threats.

In the test phrase: 'His REFULGENT smile', the word is thought by 23 per cent of adult readers to mean REPELLENT, forbidding, unfriendly, the common misconception and in suggestion an opposite of the correct meaning.

1076. *DIAPHANOUS* (*dī-ăf'-ă-nŭs*) *adj.* So thin and insubstantial as to be almost transparent, translucent, showing both light and form through.

In the test phrase: 'A DIAPHANOUS textile', the word is thought by 57 per cent of college seniors to mean TWO-SURFACED. This is probably a confusion of the Greek prefix δια, through, with δι, two, two-fold, double, a second Greek prefix which is used in such words as DIOXIDE, having two atoms of oxygen; DIARCHY, a government of two persons; DIPTEROUS, having two wings; and DICHOTOMY, division into two. The prefix *dia*, through, appears in DIAMETER, literally a measure through. Although it is often difficult, in the modern English word, to distinguish the two prefixes, DIAPHANOUS is not from δι, two, but is from δια, through; and φαίνειν, to show; and means literally showing through.

DIAPHANOUS, of Greek origin, and TRANSPARENT, of Latin origin, should by derivation be synonymous. TRANSPARENT is today the more general of the two, for DIAPHANOUS has recently been limited to transparent textiles. There is, however, nothing in the history of the word which restricts it to this specific use.

1077. *SUBVERSIVE* (*sŭb-ver'-sĭv*) *adj.* Overturning, overthrowing, corrupting, ruining, destructive, tending to
subvert.

The adjective SUBVERSIVE and the noun SUBVERSION are both from the Latin *sub*, under; and *vertere*, to turn; and both imply literally turning under, hence figuratively corrupting, destructive.

The noun SUBVERSION, utter ruin, overthrow, destruction, is thought by 49 per cent of college seniors to mean SUB-
ORDINATION. SUBORDINATION may mean either reduction in rank, being placed in a lower position; or it may mean the state of being under control, subjection to rule. SUBORDINA-
TION is from the Latin *sub*, under; and the verb *ordinare*, to put in order, arrange.

In the test phrase: 'SUBVERSIVE movements', the adjective is thought by 25 per cent of adult readers to mean SINKING. This is perhaps a confusion between the verbs to SUBVERT, to turn upside down, and to SUBMERGE, to dip, sink, place under water.

By another 26 per cent SUBVERSIVE is thought to mean REBELLIOUS, resisting openly, overtly defiant of authority. The word REBELLIOUS does not imply either success or failure; SUBVERSIVE, on the other hand, and the word REVOLU-
TIONARY, both imply success in resisting authority. REVOLU-
TIONARY involves a change by the substitution of something different; SUBVERSIVE is destructive only.

1078. *PHILANDER* (*fĭ-lăn'-der*) *v.* To flirt, trifle amorously,
  coquet, make love to women as a pastime.
In the test phrase: 'Always PHILANDERING', the word is thought by 29 per cent of college seniors to mean SQUANDER-
ING, wasting, dissipating, spending lavishly. By another 26 per cent PHILANDERING is thought to mean IDLING, wasting time. These misunderstandings are perhaps due to some confusion between PHILANDER, to flirt, and MEANDER, a word which, like PHILANDER, comes from a proper name. MEANDER is derived from the river MEANDER, a winding stream which

flows into the Aegean Sea near Miletus. To MEANDER is to proceed by winding and turning.

PHILANDER comes directly from the name of a youth, PHILANDER, in ORLANDO FURIOSO, a poem by Ariosto, written in 1516, in which PHILANDER flirts with a married lady. The name PHILANDER comes in turn from two Greek words φιλεῖν, to love; and ἀνήρ, ἄνδρος, man; the source of the modern English word PHILANTHROPIST, literally one who loves mankind. From the same source come PHILOSOPHY, love of wisdom; and PHILOLOGY, love of learning and literature. Although the word PHILOLOGY is often used to mean a study of language, even specifically a study of words, the meaning is broader than this; PHILOLOGY is a study of language and literature to gain an insight into man's activities.

1079. *RESCISSION* (*rē-sĭ'-zhŭn*) *n.* Cutting off, cancellation, abolition, annulment, abrogation, revoking, vacating, quashing.

In the test phrase: 'The RESCISSION of the treaty', the word is thought by 28 per cent of adult readers to mean RECONSIDERATION, the thinking over again, bringing up for further deliberation.

The nouns, RESCISSION, RECESSION (580), and SECESSION (134); and the corresponding verbs, to RESCIND, RECEDE, and SECEDE, should be differentiated. The nouns RECESSION, withdrawal, the act of receding, retiring; SECESSION, formal withdrawal of a group from an organization; and the corresponding verbs to RECEDE, to withdraw, retreat, retire; and SECEDE to withdraw from an organization; all come from the Latin *cedere*, to go, move.

RESCISSION and the corresponding verb to RESCIND are from a different source; they come from the Latin *scindere*, to cut. Correctly used, to RESCIND is to cut off, cancel, annul; it is not to withdraw. The noun RESCISSION is not the withdrawal of an act but its cutting off, its annulment, cancellation.

1080. *LARGESSE* (*lahr'-jĕs*) *n.* Gifts, bounty, lavishness, prodigality, free giving, excessive liberality, generous alms. This word is also spelt LARGESS.

In the test phrase: 'LARGESSE, gallant knight!', the word is thought by 22 per cent of adult readers to mean FORWARD, the common misconception.

Several words similar to LARGESSE have been taken from the French and gradually anglicized. Thus, RICHES, which is not the plural form of RICH as is often supposed, was originally RICHESSE. LARGESSE has not been popularly adopted to the same extent. The pronunciation has been anglicized, almost like RICHES, and the word should probably be spelt without the final E as one further step in its naturalization.

1081. *DEPRECATE* (*dĕp'-rē-kāt*) *v.* To disapprove of, urge strong reasons against, protest against, remonstrate, plead against, advise the avoidance of.

DEPRECATE comes from the Latin, *de*, from; and *precare*, to pray; and means literally to pray against, entreat the prevention of. The word is still used in English with exactly this significance; but its more frequent use is not so strong as pray, but rather argue against, plead against.

To 72 per cent of college seniors to DEPRECATE incorrectly means to RIDICULE, treat with contemptuous merriment, deride, make sport of. H. W. Fowler, in his invaluable Dictionary of Modern English Usage, gives instances of this same confusion taken from British newspapers. It is perhaps due to the similarity of DEPRECATE, disapprove, with DEPRECIATE (*dē-prē'-shĭ-āt*), to belittle, underrate, undervalue; a word which is not so strong, not so contemptuous, as RIDICULE, but with the same suggestion of belittling.

In the test phrase: 'They DEPRECATE such conditions', the word is thought by 19 per cent of adult readers to mean DENY, to say no, refuse to believe.

By another 18 per cent to DEPRECATE is thought to mean to CURSE. This is probably a confusion of DEPRECATE, to disapprove, with IMPRECATE, to curse, execrate.

In the test phrase: 'He DEPRECATED any attempt', the word is thought by 11 per cent of preparatory-school juniors to mean PREVENTED, hindered, forestalled, frustrated. DEPRECATE does not imply success in preventing, but means to try to prevent, urge reasons against.

The corresponding adjective DEPRECATORY, which means disapproving, protesting, is today most frequently employed in its developed sense to mean apologetic. APOLOGETIC is from the Greek words ἀπό, from, away; and λέγειν, to speak; and by derivation means to speak in defense. An APOLOGY may be offered in defense, in vindication, or in excuse. To DEPRECATE is always to pray against, to attempt to avoid, and the adjective should be used in this way. DEPRECATORY can be used to mean apologetic only in those instances where an apology is offered to avoid a graver issue.

1082. *TRAVESTY* (trăv'-ĕs-tĭ) *n.* Caricature, burlesque treatment, ludicrous imitation, grotesque resemblance. In the phrase: 'The TRAVESTY of justice', the word is thought by 27 per cent of adult readers to mean CONSEQUENCE, result, effect, that which follows, conclusion.

TRAVESTY comes from the Latin *trans*, over; and *vestire*, to clothe, the source of the English nouns, a VEST; a VESTMENT, an official robe, ceremonial garment; and the verb, to INVEST, to clothe. A TRAVESTY is by derivation a re-clothing in a different manner.

A TRAVESTY and a PARODY are both burlesque imitations, caricatures. A PARODY makes almost no change in the original language; but, by using it under different circumstances and putting it in the mouth of a different character, gives it an altered and ridiculous significance. A TRAVESTY keeps the characters and incidents of the original, but gains its absurd effects by putting ridiculous language in the mouths of the original characters. The TRAVESTY of justice means its grotesque imitation.

1083. *LOUT* (lowt) *n.* A lubber, bumpkin, slouch, churl, clown, oaf, boor, an awkward and ungainly fellow. The origin of LOUT is not known. In the test phrase: 'A kind of LOUT', the word is thought by 44 per cent of adult readers to mean BRAGGART. This may be due to a confusion of BRAGGART with LAGGARD, one who is slow, who falls behind, a lazy, slack fellow. Although a LAGGARD and a LOUT are not the same, they have many characteristics in common. They differ primarily in that a LAGGARD is lazy, a LOUT, awkward. A LOUT and a BRAGGART may both be disagreeable fellows, but for different reasons. A BRAGGART is a boaster, a vain, loud-mouthed fellow. A LOUT is awkward, ungainly, but in no sense a boaster, braggart.

A BOOR, a CHURL, a CLOWN, and a LOUT, are all ill-bred. A BOOR and a CHURL are both offensive, a BOOR usually because of his habits, a CHURL more often because of his surly language. Both a CLOWN and a LOUT are less offensive. A CLOWN, unless he be a professional, is stupid, and his acts are regarded as ludicrous rather than blameworthy. A LOUT is thought of as mentally more capable and therefore more blameworthy.

1084. *ACTUARIALLY* (*ăk-tū-ā'-ri̯-ăl-li̯*) *adv.* Statistically, concerned with vital statistics, in accordance with computations based on insurance statistics, in the manner of a computer in an insurance company.

ACTUARIALLY comes from the Latin *actuarius*, clerk, but the modern English word is never used except with respect to one specific kind of clerical work. In the test phrase: 'ACTU-ARIALLY speaking', the word is thought by 38 per cent of college seniors to mean AUTHORITATIVELY, in the manner of one having the right to command, of one in authority. By another 18 per cent it is thought to mean LEGALLY, according to law, lawfully.

An ACTUARY and an ACCOUNTANT are both experts in the mathematics of business. An ACCOUNTANT deals with book-keeping, with income and expenditure. An ACTUARY deals with death rates and insurance statistics. ACTUARIAL is the adjective; and ACTUARIALLY, the adverb; formed from the noun, ACTUARY.

1085. *TRUMPERY* (*trŭmp'-ĕ-ri̯*) *adj.* Showy and worthless, trashy, tawdry, rubbishy, gaudy and cheap, ostentatious but valueless.

To 39 per cent of adult readers TRUMPERY incorrectly means BRAZEN. BRAZEN usually means impudent, shameless, hardened in effrontery; but may also mean literally made of brass. The confusion of BRAZEN and TRUMPERY may be a confusion of TRUMPERY, trashy, with TRUMPET, a metal wind instrument, one of the so-called brasses of an orchestra.

TRUMPERY is from the French verb *tromper*, literally to

play on the trumpet, but which in modern French means to deceive.

The noun and verb, TRUMP, used in card games is apparently of a different origin, probably from the same source as the English word TRIUMPH; but there is an English verb to TRUMP, which means to deceive, impose upon. Although it is practically obsolete it appears in the familiar phrase: 'To TRUMP UP', to make up, invent, fabricate, as: 'To TRUMP UP a story'. TRUMPERY is from this same source, and may be used either as a noun to mean nonsense, foolishness, false talk; or as an adjective to mean showy but worthless.

1086. *GERMANE* (*jer-mān'*) *adj.* Relevant, pertinent, akin, bearing upon, connected, significant, appropriate, allied, closely related.

GERMANE comes from the Latin *germen*, a sprig, off-shoot, sprout, the source of the English word GERM. The immediate source of GERMANE is the Latin word *germanus*, akin, closely related, literally having the same father and mother, or at least the same father.

In the test phrase: 'GERMANE to the subject', the word is thought by 27 per cent of college seniors to mean FOREIGN, remote, not belonging, unconnected, the popular misconception and an opposite of GERMANE.

1087. *MONOGRAPH* (*mŏn'-ō-grăf*) *n.* A treatise, article, essay, discussion of a single subject, account of a narrowly limited branch of study.

MONO is from the Greek word μόνος, single, and appears in a number of English words: MONOGRAM, originally a single letter, now a combination of letters intertwined to look like one; MONOPOLY, control vested in one person or group; MONOLOGUE, a discourse by one person; MONOCLE, originally a one-eyed animal, now a single eyeglass. GRAPH, from the Greek γραφή, writing, is equally common in English; AUTOGRAPH, one's own writing; and PHOTOGRAPH, by derivation a writing produced by light. Strictly GRAPH should be used for the instrument which does the writing, GRAM for that which is written. Thus: TELEGRAPH is the instrument; TELEGRAM, the record.

Despite the fact that both MONO and GRAPH are familiar as parts of everyday words, in the test phrase: 'She wrote a MONOGRAPH', the word is thought by 39 per cent of adult readers to mean SOLILOQUY, the popular misconception. SOLILOQUY is a talking to one's self; not, as is a MONOGRAPH, a writing on one subject.

1088. *TURGID* (*ter'-jĭd*) *adj.* Swollen, congested, bloated, tumid (1005), distended beyond its natural state by some internal force. TURGID is generally applied to an enlarged part of the body; but it may also be used figuratively, as: 'TURGID style', 'TURGID language', to mean inflated, bombastic, pompous, grandiose, grandiloquent.

To 34 per cent of college seniors TURGID incorrectly means FILTHY, dirty, foul, unclean. This misconception is probably due to a confusion of TURGID, swollen, with TURBID (1037), muddy, roiled, foul with extraneous matter, hence filthy. TURBID is from the Latin word *turbare*, to disturb, from the same source as the English verb, to DISTURB. TURGID, on the other hand, is from the Latin *turgere*, to swell out, and means swollen.

TURGID and FLACCID are opposites in suggestion.

1089. *HIERATIC* (*hĭ-ĕ-răt'-ĭk*) *adj.* Sacred, priestly, sacerdotal (341), consecrated to sacred uses.

Although the noun, HIERARCHY, literally sacred government, a body of ecclesiastical rulers, priestly government, is accented on the first syllable (*hĭ'-ĕr-ăr-kĭ*), the adjective, HIERATIC, is accented on the third.

To 42 per cent of adult readers HIERATIC incorrectly means ANCIENT, very old, of great age, of early origin. Several words which begin with HIERO, sacred, divine, the Greek word ἱερός, sacred, written in Roman letters, are associated with the ancient Egyptians. The word HIEROLOGY (*hĭ-ĕ-rŏl'-ō-jĭ*), which by derivation means the science of sacred writings, has departed furthest from the original and now means the science of ancient Egyptian writings. This word might justifiably be confused with ANCIENT. A HIEROGLYPH, another word from the same source, is a symbol used in the picture writing of the ancient Egyptians; but the word means by derivation sacred carving, not ancient carving. HIERATIC conveys no implication of ancient, but means literally sacred.

Three types of Egyptian writing have been distinguished, HIEROGLYPHIC, HIERATIC, and DEMOTIC (dē-mŏt'-ĭk). HIEROGLYPHIC is the formal symbol writing of the Egyptians. HIERATIC writing is an abbreviated form of HIEROGLYPHIC; it is more rapid and more nearly a running hand. The word DEMOTIC, from the same source as the English word DEMOCRACY, may be used today to mean popular, pertaining to the common people. DEMOTIC writing, still more abbreviated and more rapid than the HIERATIC, was the popular writing of the Egyptians. The famous Rosetta Stone which was cut in 195 B.C., and which was found in 1799, near the mouth of the Nile, by soldiers of Napoleon, bears the same inscription in three forms; first in HIEROGLYPHIC, then in DEMOTIC, and finally in Greek.

HIERATIC and SACERDOTAL both mean priestly. SACERDOTAL is used in the strict sense of priestly, assisting at a sacrifice; HIERATIC, in the broader sense of sacred.

1090. *MENDACIOUS* (mĕn-dā'-shŭs) *adj.* Lying, deceiving, misleading, false, untruthful, deceitful, addicted to falsehood.

In the test phrase: 'The MENDACIOUS person', the word is thought by 48 per cent of college seniors to mean BEGGARLY, poor, wretched. This is probably a confusion of MENDACIOUS, lying, with MENDICANT, a word which may be used either as a noun to mean a beggar, or as an adjective to mean begging, practicing mendicancy, asking for alms.

MENDICANT is from the Latin word *mendicus*, poor, beggarly, needy. MENDACIOUS is from the Latin *mendax, mendacis*, lying, false; and the ending ACIOUS (927), which implies intense activity; and means actively lying, addicted to deception. MENDACIOUS, deceiving, and VERACIOUS, truthful, are opposites.

1091. *UNCTUOUS* (ŭngk'-tū-ŭs, not ŭngk'-shŭs) *adj.* Smooth, bland, suave, fawning, smugly fulsome, oily in manner.

UNCTUOUS comes from the Latin *unctus*, the past participle

of the verb *unguere*, to anoint, smear with oil, the source of
the English nouns: an UNGUENT (*ŭng'-gwĕnt*), an ointment,
salve; and UNCTION, the act of anointing with oil.

UNCTUOUS, SUAVE, and FULSOME, are similar. FULSOME,
which is of Anglo-Saxon origin, suggests rather too full of
flattering phrases, almost gross, nauseous. SUAVE, from the
Latin word *suavis*, sweet, pleasant, agreeable, is from the
same source as the word SUASION, and suggests pleasantly
soothing, mollifying, agreeable. Although SUAVITY may exasperate the blunt person, SUAVE by derivation has no intimation
of the disagreeable. UNCTUOUS implies the smooth oiliness of
a salve, but the word is customarily applied to one who tries
to ingratiate himself by pretense to a spirituality which he
does not possess.

1092. *BROCHURE* (*brō-shūr'*) *n.* Brief treatise, sketch,
          essay, article, monograph (1087), usually on a sub-
ject of transitory interest and presented in pamphlet form
printed and stitched.

BROCHURE is directly from the French word *brocher*, to
stitch. From the same original source as BROCHURE are the
English words: BROACH (*brōch*), an awl, spit, sharp-pointed
tool; also an ornamental pin, now usually spelt BROOCH, but
still pronounced (*brōch*); and BROCADE, a silken fabric with
a raised pattern, often in gold and silver.

In the test phrase: 'They liked the BROCHURE', the word is
thought by 39 per cent of college seniors to mean ORNAMENT.
This is evidently a confusion of BROCHURE, pamphlet, with
BROACH or BROOCH. To another 25 per cent, BROCHURE incorrectly means TAPESTRY. This may be a confusion of BROCHURE
with BROCADE.

The three words, BROCHURE, FOLIO, and PAMPHLET, designate the physical size and method of binding printed matter.
In this they differ from such words as: ESSAY, TREATISE,
DISQUISITION, and MONOGRAPH, which specify subject matter
or literary treatment. A PAMPHLET consists ordinarily of less
than five sheets, fastened together in any way; it may have
a thin paper cover but is not bound. A FOLIO is a bound
book made up of sheets which have been folded once. A
BROCHURE ordinarily contains fewer pages than a folio but

more than a pamphlet. When correctly used the word should be applied only to a booklet made of pages which are held together by stitching.

1093. *ENERVATE* (*ĕn'-er-văt*) *v.* To weaken, enfeeble, debilitate, render languid, deprive of vigor, overcome with lassitude.

ENERVATE is thought to mean INVIGORATE by 52 per cent of adult readers and by at least some writers as is demonstrated by the exhortation: 'Come and bask in our ENERVATING sunshine', a caption which headed the announcement of the opening of a fashionable beach resort. This misunderstanding may be due to a confusion of ENERVATE, weaken, with the rarely used scientific word INNERVATE (*ĭn-ner'-văt*), to supply with nerves, stimulate. Or it may be a confusion of ENERVATE with ENERGIZE, to fill with energy, make vigorous, an opposite of the correct meaning. Or it may be another instance of the opposite being the most common misconception. ENERVATE is from the Latin *e*, out; and *nervus*, nerve; which in turn comes from the Greek νεῦρον, nerve, the source of the English words NEURON, a nerve cell; and NEUROSIS, a disease of the nervous system. To ENERVATE is to rob of nervous energy, weaken, enfeeble, debilitate.

1094. *COPPLE* (*kŏp'-pl*) *n.* A small hill, hillock, barrow, hummock (579), rounded knoll, conical elevation.

COPPLE is the diminutive of the Anglo-Saxon word COP, top, summit, hill. In the test phrase: 'A COPPLE near the house', the word is thought by 39 per cent of college seniors to mean HEDGE. This is perhaps a confusion of COPPLE, a small hill, with COPPICE or COPSE (690), a thicket, wood of small trees growing from old stumps, words from the same source as the French *couper*, to cut.

To another 19 per cent, COPPLE incorrectly means RAVINE, a long narrow deep gully, a hollow worn by a stream. COPPLE and RAVINE are opposites in the same sense as MOUNTAIN and VALLEY.

COPPLE and COBBLE are often confused. A COBBLE, sometimes incorrectly spelt *copple*, is a small stone; originally a stone rounded as by the action of water; now any small stone used for paving. A COPPLE, occasionally in New England spelt and pronounced COBBLE, is a small hill.

1095. *UNMITIGATED* (*ŭn-mĭt'-ĭ-gā-tĕd*) *adj.* Utter (328), absolute, having full force, unconscionable (1103), intolerable, unassuaged, not lessened, not softened.

The verb, to MITIGATE, comes from the Latin *mitis*, mild; and *agere*, to make; and means literally to make mild. The adjective, UNMITIGATED, means not made mild.

To 36 per cent of adult readers UNMITIGATED incorrectly means CONTINUOUS. CONTINUOUS denotes unbroken in time, going on without interruption; UNMITIGATED denotes not lessened in amount, degree, intensity.

1096. *FERACIOUS* (*fē-rā'-shŭs*) *adj.* Fertile, fruitful, productive, producing abundantly.

In the test phrase: 'FERACIOUS fields', the word is thought by 41 per cent of college seniors to mean MINERAL. This may be a confusion of FERACIOUS, fruitful, with FERROUS, containing the mineral iron. FERROUS is from the Latin *ferrum*, iron, the source of the chemical symbol for iron, FE. FERACIOUS is from the Latin *ferre*, to bear; plus ACIOUS, a termination which expresses intensity of action and which is discussed under VORACIOUS (927). FERACIOUS means producing vigorously.

1097. *VIRULENT* (*vĭr'-ŭ-lĕnt*) *adj.* Malignant, poisonous, venomous, noxious, deadly.

VIRULENT comes from the Latin *virus*, a slime, poison, venom. VIRUS (*vī'-rŭs*), as the word is used in English, is a poison produced within an organism suffering from a contagious disease. VIRUS and VENOM are both poisons. VENOM is a secretion natural to certain animals such as serpents, scorpions, and bees. VIRUS is a poison produced only by a morbid, unhealthy condition. VENOMOUS and VIRULENT are the corresponding adjectives.

1098. *AVUNCULAR* (*ă-vŭn'-kū-lahr*) *adj.* Like an uncle, pertaining to an uncle.

In the test phrase: 'AVUNCULAR smile', the word is thought

by 31 per cent of college seniors to mean PERFUNCTORY, half-hearted, without zeal. By another 21 per cent it is thought to mean LINGERING, loitering, delaying.

AVUNCULAR comes directly from the Latin *avunculus*, uncle, specifically a mother's brother. The Latin word *patruus* means a father's brother. But the English word AVUNCULAR, like the English word UNCLE, is used with reference to either a father's or a mother's brother.

1099. *INGENUOUS* (ĭn-jĕn'-ū-ŭs) *adj.* Frank, candid (272), open, artless, sincere, honest, natural, unaffected, guileless, undisguised, free from reserve.

INGENUE (ăn-zhā-nū') (880), artless girl, a word which is unknown to 61 per cent of adult readers and is therefore more familiar, comes from the same Latin source but so directly through the French as to retain its French pronunciation.

To 64 per cent of adult readers INGENUOUS incorrectly means IMAGINATIVE. This is no doubt a confusion of INGENUOUS, frank, open, with INGENIOUS (ĭn-jēn'-yŭs), inventive, clever, resourceful. INGENUOUS and INGENIOUS have often been used interchangeably; even early printers did not distinguish between the two words. They should however be differentiated in modern writing. Both INGENUOUS and INGENIOUS come from the Latin *genus*, birth, race. INGENIOUS comes directly from the Latin word *ingeniosus*, born with ability, endowed with natural capacity; and the English word INGENIOUS today means inventive, clever in contriving new things, resourceful, skillful. INGENUOUS comes from the Latin *ingenuus*, free-born, noble; and the English word INGENUOUS may today mean noble, but is more often used to mean frank, open, candid.

INGENUOUS and NAIVE although today practically synonymous have quite different derivations and therefore different connotations. NAIVE, which is the feminine form of the French word NAIF, comes originally from the Latin *natus*, the past participle of *nasci*, to be born, the source of the English word NATIVE. NAIVE suggests simple in the sense of rustic, natural (26), unsophisticated (553), and may characterize a person with little cultural background. INGENUOUS by derivation has more of the intimation of honest, free from guile, and may characterize a person of social experience and culture.

1100. *CODON* (*kō'-dŏn*) *n.* Small bell; also the bell-shaped mouth of a trumpet.

CODON is the Greek word κώδων, bell, written in Roman letters. In the test phrase: 'The CODON sounded', the word is thought by 31 per cent of college seniors to mean HORN. A CODON may be the bell-shaped mouth of a trumpet or horn, and this fact may lead to the confusion of HORN with CODON, usually a small bell.

1101. *QUIXOTIC* (*kwĭks-ŏt'-ĭk*) *adj.* Extravagantly romantic, visionary, striving for an unattainable ideal, chivalrous to an absurd degree. 'A QUIXOTIC adventurer.'

The adjective QUIXOTIC comes from the proper name of DON QUIXOTE, the hero of a Spanish romance, written by CERVANTES (*ther-văn'-tās*), and printed in Madrid in 1605. DON QUIXOTE is an enthusiastically chivalrous gentleman who, with his squire, SANCHO PANZA, goes in search of knightly adventures. In pronunciation the adjective has been anglicized (*kwĭks-ŏt'-ĭk*), whereas the proper name usually has its Spanish pronunciation (*kē-hō'-tē*).

Other adjectives are derived in this same manner from literary characters. Thus: THRASONICAL, boastful, comes from the proper name THRASO, the braggart in the Latin comedy EUNUCHUS, written by TERENCE, a Roman comic poet who died about 159 B.C. STENTORIAN, loud-voiced, comes from STENTOR, a Greek herald in the Trojan War, who, according to Homer, had a voice as loud as fifty men combined.

One of DON QUIXOTE's well-known adventures is his attempt to joust with a windmill. It is performed with all of the formality of a knightly contest, but to no avail. The adjective QUIXOTIC always suggests high ideals combined with inability to obtain results.

1102. *PLETHORA* (*plĕth'-ō-ră*) *n.* Excess, overabundance, superfluity, glut, oversupply. In medicine, PLETHORA is excess of blood in the entire system or in any organ.

PLETHORA comes from the Greek πλῆθος, fullness, from the

same original source as the word PLENTY. To 63 per cent of
college seniors PLETHORA incorrectly means SCOURGE. A
SCOURGE may be a whip, lash, flagellum (*flă-jĕl'-lŭm*); or a
plague, pestilence, anything which destroys. This may be
due to some confusion of PLETHORA, overabundance, with
either PLAGUE or PESTILENCE, words sometimes used as synonymous to indicate any ravaging disease. Both a PLAGUE and
a PESTILENCE are scourges; but the word PLETHORA has no
such suggestion; it means merely an overabundance, such an
overabundance as to be a nuisance.

1103. *UNCONSCIONABLE* (*ŭn-kŏn'-shŏn-ă-bl*) *adj.* Enormous, outrageous, utter (328), unmitigated (1095), inordinate, beyond the bounds of reason.
To 38 per cent of adult readers UNCONSCIONABLE incorrectly
means IMPERCEPTIBLE, very slight, not capable of being perceived. In such a phrase as: 'An UNCONSCIONABLE error', IM-
PERCEPTIBLE is an exact opposite of the correct meaning. This
misunderstanding may be due to a confusion of UNCONSCION-
ABLE with some form of the word UNCONSCIOUS, for an
UNCONSCIOUS error is one which has not been perceived.

UNCONSCIONABLE is a combination of *un*, not; and CON-
SCIONABLE, a word formed in Queen Elizabeth's reign, 1559–
1603, from the noun CONSCIENCE. CONSCIONABLE once meant
governed by the conscience, conscientious (1058). This meaning is now obsolete and CONSCIONABLE means conforming
with what is right or wrong, proper, fitting, just. The negative
UNCONSCIONABLE is much stronger and means not merely
unfitting but outrageous, inordinate, unreasonable.

1104. *MASTIC* (*măs'-tĭk*) *adj.* Sticky, gummy, adhesive,
tenacious, cohesive, glutinous, viscid. The MASTIC tree
grows in the region of the Mediterranean and exudes a
peculiarly sticky resin, called MASTIC, which is used, among
other things, in the making of varnish, and which is also
chewed as is spruce gum.
In the test phrase: 'MASTIC substances', the word is thought
by 48 per cent of college seniors to mean EDIBLE, fit to eat,
capable of being eaten. This is perhaps a confusion of MASTIC
with MASTICATE, to chew, prepare food for swallowing by

chewing. The word MASTICATE may once have meant to chew MASTIC, and the word MASTICATE, to chew, comes perhaps from the noun MASTIC, practically the Greek word μαστίχη written in Roman letters.

To another 20 per cent of college seniors, MASTIC means PLASTIC. PLASTIC and MASTIC substances have much in common. A PLASTIC substance can however be molded like clay, can be formed into shapes; a MASTIC substance is sticky, adhesive.

1105. *ASCETIC* (ăs-sĕt'-ĭk) *adj.* Austere, severe (123), rigid (504), strict, self-disciplined, given to exacting self-denial. ASCETICISM (945) is the corresponding noun.

In the test phrase: 'An ASCETIC person', the word is thought by 44 per cent of adult readers to mean SOUR. This is no doubt a confusion of ASCETIC, with the s, and ACETIC, without the s. ACETIC, sour, having the properties of vinegar, may be correctly pronounced either (ă-sē'-tĭk or ă-sĕt'-ĭk) although the first is preferable in order to distinguish it from ASCETIC (ăs-sĕt'-ĭk), which can be pronounced in only one way. The two words, although so nearly alike, have independent derivations. ACETIC comes from the Latin *acere*, to be sour, from the same source as the English word ACID, by derivation a sour substance. ASCETIC comes from the Greek word ἀσκητής, an athlete, one who exercises; a word which was also used in an ecclesiastical sense to mean a monk, hermit.

To another 18 per cent, ASCETIC incorrectly means ARTISTIC. This is probably a confusion of ASCETIC with AESTHETIC, sensitive to beauty, possessing a cultivated taste, having artistic appreciation.

To still another 14 per cent, ASCETIC incorrectly means SELF-INDULGENT, an exact opposite of the correct meaning.

1106. *ADUMBRATION* (ăd-ŭm-brā'-shŭn) *n.* A slight sketch, outline, vague representation, faint mental image.

In the test phrase: 'Hasty ADUMBRATION', the word is thought by 30 per cent of college seniors to mean CONSIDERATION; and by another 26 per cent to mean CALCULATION. These misconceptions are doubtless caused by a confusion of ADUMBRA-

TION with CEREBRATION, any exertion of the brain, thinking, consideration, calculation.

ADUMBRATION is from the Latin *ad*, to; and *umbra*, shadow; and means literally casting a shadow. The Latin *umbra* appears in other English words as: UMBRAGE, literally shade, obscurity, and figuratively the feeling of being overshadowed, hence resentment, pique; and PENUMBRA, partial shadow. ADUMBRATION has no sharp, clear-cut meaning. The verb, to ADUMBRATE (*ăd'-ŭm-brāt*), has been used to mean cast a shadow over, overshadow, darken slightly; but if one wishes a little-known word of Latin origin one should probably use OBFUSCATE in place of ADUMBRATE in this sense. To ADUMBRATE should be used to mean make a faint resemblance of, show in vague outline, suggest by imperfect representation. To ADUMBRATE has also been used to mean foreshadow, almost to predict, but there is no more in the word to suggest predict than there is in the word SHADOW itself. The noun ADUMBRATION should be used to mean faint resemblance, vague outline, imperfect representation.

1107. *QUIZZICAL* (*kwĭz'-zĭ-kăl*) *adj.* Bantering, jesting, chaffing, teasing, making fun of, ridiculing humorously, regarding ironically, humorously questioning.

The noun, a QUIZ, was originally the name of a toy, a wheel with a deep groove, fastened at the end of a string by which the wheel was made to unwind and rewind itself. The toy was popular about 1790. From this QUIZ came to mean anything designed to puzzle one. The modern meaning of QUIZ, an examination, is still marked by most dictionaries as colloquial. The adjective QUIZZICAL comes from one of the early recognized meanings of QUIZ and means puzzling, teasing, bantering, rallying.

1108. *JEJUNE* (*jē-joon'*) *adj.* Barren, empty, dry, uninteresting, insipid (375), shallow, wanting pith, lacking quality, devoid of sense.

JEJUNE sounds as if it should come from the French *jeune*, young, and is often used as if it meant youthful; JEJUNE hats have been seen advertised. It comes in reality from the Latin *jejunus*, fasting, hungry, empty, barren, dry; and is probably related to the second part of the French *dejeuner*, breakfast, by derivation to break fast. JEJUNE means empty but is often applied in a figurative sense to mean barren, uninteresting.

1109. *UTTER* (*ŭt′-ter*) *v*. To publish, put in circulation. The familiar meaning of the verb to UTTER is to express, disclose, pronounce, speak.

In the test phrase: 'He UTTERED the document', the word is thought by 54 per cent of adult readers to mean EXPLAINED. UTTER is from an Anglo-Saxon word which means out, outside; and the original English meaning of UTTER was to put out, put forth, emit. UTTER today may mean to offer for sale, dispose of in trade. In this same sense it is often used specifically of money to mean put into circulation. The common use of the word, to speak, is only one of its applications. UTTER may correctly be used to mean emit in almost any way, speak, publish, put into circulation.

1110. *ANFRACTUOUS* (*ăn-frăk′-tū-ŭs*, almost *ăn-frăk′-chū-ŭs*) *adj*. Twisted, tortuous, sinuous, winding, full of windings and turnings.

In the test phrase: 'ANFRACTUOUS lines', the word is thought by 47 per cent of college seniors to mean DOTTED, broken, a literal translation of the Latin *frangere*, to break, the source of the English words, a FRACTURE, a break; and FRAGILE, breakable; as well as ANFRACTUOUS, winding.

To another 28 per cent of college seniors, ANFRACTUOUS incorrectly means CONTINUOUS. The Greek AN, used in such a word as ANECDOTE, literally a bit of gossip which cannot be published, means not. Were ANFRACTUOUS of Greek derivation it would mean not broken, continuous. It comes however from the Latin, where the prefix AN is a contraction of *ambi*, around, as in the word ANCIPITAL (1028). ANFRACTUOUS means literally breaking around, winding, tortuous.

1111. *POLITY* (*pŏl′-ĭ-tĭ*) *n*. Form of government of a nation or state, constitution, method of government.

In the test phrase: 'They made a POLITY', the word is thought by 66 per cent of college seniors to mean PACT. A PACT is an agreement, compact, covenant. A POLITY may be the result of pact, agreement, between persons, but is the structure of the government.

POLITY is from the Greek πόλις, city, through the Latin *politia*, state. From the same word come: POLICY, POLITICAL, POLITICS, and POLITIC. POLITICAL, although it has recently deteriorated, when properly used has the same suggestion as POLITY. POLITICAL means referring to the government of a city or country. POLITIC, judicious, expedient, diplomatic, like the word POLICY, may have the narrower suggestion of clever in management.

POLITY differs from POLICY, for POLICY applies to the management of the government, while POLITY is confined to the construction of the government.

1112. *UNWONTED* (*ŭn-wŭnt'-ĕd*) *adj.* Rare, unusual, uncommon, infrequent, unaccustomed, not habitual.

To 45 per cent of adult readers UNWONTED incorrectly means UNEXPECTED, not looked for, unforeseen, sudden, not provided against, without warning. An eclipse of the sun is UNWONTED, rare, unusual, but today is never unexpected.

To 41 per cent of adult readers UNWONTED incorrectly means UNWELCOME, not desired, not wished for. This is obviously a confusion of UNWONTED, pronounced (*ŭn-wŭnt'-ĕd*), like ONE (*wŭn*), with UNWANTED, not wanted, not welcome.

The noun, WONT (*wŭnt*), of Anglo-Saxon origin, means custom, habit, practice, and is most familiar in the phrase: 'It was his WONT to'. The adjective WONTED means customary, frequently done, usual, as: 'A WONTED occurrence'. UNWONTED is the opposite, unusual, infrequent.

1113. *LAMBENT* (*lăm'-bĕnt*) *adj.* Touching lightly, twinkling, flickering, gleaming, softly bright, running over as if licking.

LAMBENT comes from the Latin *lambere*, to lick. From this same source come the English words: to LAP, lick up, drink by licking; and LAMPOON, originally a drinking song, now a sarcastic, humorous writing, aimed at a person's character, a virulent personal satire.

In the test phrase: 'The LAMBENT movement', the word is

thought by 18 per cent of college seniors to mean CONTINU-
OUS, uninterrupted, continual, unbroken, constant. CONTINU-
OUS is almost an opposite of LAMBENT which means twinkling.
By another 25 per cent LAMBENT is thought to mean
WINDING, twisting from a direct line, bending. A LAMBENT
flame has an undulating, wavelike motion, and it is perhaps
this which suggests winding. There is however in LAMBENT
the idea of intermittent glow, not suggested by the word
WINDING.

TWINKLING, FLICKERING, and LAMBENT, may all be used to
characterize flames. TWINKLING is applied to the way in
which light is given off by a flame more often than to the
flame itself. It means intermittent, spasmodic, not continuous, shining with a tremulous, rapidly pulsating light. FLICK-
ERING means swaying, moving with an unsteady motion.
LAMBENT combines the two and suggests both the intermittent illumination of TWINKLING, and the unsteady motion of
FLICKERING.

1114. *DETRACTION* (*dē-trăk'-shŭn*) *n.* Calumny, slander,
      disparagement, defamation, aspersion, belittling, depre-
ciation. To DETRACT is the corresponding verb.
In the phrase: 'To DETRACT from the value', the verb is
doubtless more familiar than the noun DETRACTION, which is
practically unknown to adult readers. To 46 per cent of
adult readers, DETRACTION incorrectly means EVASION, a
dodging, excusing one's self, eluding, getting out of the
way. To another 40 per cent, it incorrectly means CON-
FUSION, disorder, tumult; and, when applied to the mind,
discomfiture, bewilderment, embarrassment. Both misunderstandings may be due to a failure to distinguish between
DETRACTION, slander, and DISTRACTION, utter perplexity,
frenzy, both of which come from the same Latin source
trahere, to draw.

DISTRACTION and DETRACTION differ in modern usage. A
DISTRACTION may be that which draws the attention from
one object to another. One may create a DISTRACTION in
order to draw away the attention of a questioner and
so evade answering. Or the word DISTRACTION may be
stronger and mean that which confuses, which draws the

attention in different directions, bewilders, perplexes. Or it may be even stronger, and mean madness, frenzy, insanity. It is by derivation the pulling apart, usually of the mind. DETRACTION does not refer to the mind, but, in modern usage, to the reputation, to pulling away from the reputation, belittling, defaming.

1115. *TENUOUS* (*tĕn'-ū-ŭs*) *adj*. Rarefied, thin, not dense, rare, slight, subtle.

TENUOUS comes from the Latin *tenuis*, thin, slender; and the English word, in one of its uses, means thin, slim, slender, delicate. From the same source comes the verb, to ATTENUATE (1067), to make thin, either in the sense of slender, delicate; or rare, not dense.

In the test phrase: 'The fog was TENUOUS', the word is thought by 60 per cent of college seniors to mean LONGLASTING. This is perhaps a confusion of TENUOUS, rarefied, with TENACIOUS. TENACIOUS is from the Latin *tenere*, to hold; and means holding fast for a long time, pertinacious, retentive.

By another 26 per cent TENUOUS is thought to mean HEAVY, weighty, having great weight, by connotation an opposite of TENUOUS, light in substance.

1116. *GLABROUS* (*glā'-brŭs*) *adj*. Smooth, bald, having an even surface without hairs or projections.

The meaning of GLABROUS is practically unknown to adult readers. The most common misconception of the word is STICKY. This is probably a confusion of GLABROUS, bald, with GLUTINOUS, sticky, viscid (*vĭs'-sĭd*).

GLABROUS is from the Latin *glaber*, smooth, without hair; and is related to the English word GLAD, which originally meant smooth and therefore bright, shining. Although GLAD is still used in English in a figurative sense to mean shining, bright, as in the phrase: 'A GLAD countenance', the word is today most frequently used to mean pleased, happy, gratified, joyful. GLADE, a bright open place in a woods, one without trees, is another word related to GLABROUS.

GLABROUS and CILIATED, as the words are sometimes used in botany, are opposites. CILIATED, from the Latin *cilium*, eyelid, means covered with CILIA, fine hairs; GLABROUS means smooth in the sense of lacking hair, bald.

1117. *INCHOATE* (*ĭn'-kō-āt*, not *ĭn-kō'-āt*) *adj.* Incipient, elementary, embryonic, rudimentary (370), begun but not in full existence.

In the test phrase: 'INCHOATE mass', the word is thought by 33 per cent of adult readers to mean DISORDERLY, confused, irregular, without proper order or disposition. This is probably a confusion of INCHOATE, elementary, with CHAOTIC, disorderly. CHAOTIC comes from the Greek word χάος, chaos, empty space, that confused mass in which matter is supposed to have existed before it was separated into its different kinds, and reduced to order. INCHOATE is practically the only English word from a Latin verb meaning to begin. CHAOTIC and INCHOATE may both describe similar conditions; but CHAOTIC specifies the confusion; and INCHOATE, the elementary, embryonic nature.

1118. *COLLATE* (*kŏl-lāt'*) *v.* To compare writings critically with a view to noting agreements and discrepancies; examine in order to verify and correct the arrangement.

COLLATE comes from the Latin *com*, together; and *latus*, the past participle of the irregular verb, *ferre*, to bear; and by derivation is to bring together.

The noun COLLATION may mean the act of collating, a bringing together and comparing. COLLATION is also used to designate a collection of the lives of the fathers of the church, among them BARNABAS, CLEMENT OF ROME, HERMAS, IGNATIUS, PAPIAS, and POLYCARP, the so-called APOSTOLIC FATHERS, all of whom lived between the time of Christ and 150 A.D. From this last use, COLLATION came to be applied to the light meal, refection, partaken of by the monks after a reading of such lives. As a result, a COLLATION is today any light meal, especially one at an unusual time.

In the test phrase: 'He COLLATED his data', the word is thought by 69 per cent of college seniors to mean CLASSIFIED. Although the actions described by the words COLLATE and CLASSIFY are almost inseparable, for a CLASSIFICATION, arrangement, almost necessarily depends upon a previous COLLATION, examination, the words are not synonymous. To CLASSIFY is to arrange, group in sets. To COLLATE is to compare in such a way as to pick out similarities and dissimilarities.

To COLLATE and to COMPARE are more nearly synonymous. To COMPARE may be used of matters in general; and is to note a general resemblance or dissimilarity. To COLLATE is usually limited to literary criticism; and is to note specific points of agreement and disagreement.

EXPLANATION OF INDEX

In this index 1118 words are printed in small capital letters. These are the words which have been used in the vocabulary tests administered by the Human Engineering Laboratory. They have been studied statistically, appear in this volume in order of difficulty, and are discussed at length. The other 7700 words are synonyms of these or occur in the discussions.

References are to word numbers. Wherever two or more references are given, the first is the most important and the others are, where possible, in order of importance.

accubation, *n.* 1022
accumulate, *v.* 412, 17
accumulated, *adj.* 412
accumulation, *n.* 551
accuracy, *n.* 814
accurate, *adj.* 278, 287, 518
accusation, *n.* 280
accuse, *v.* 388, 498, 476, 636, 877
acetic, *adj.* 1105
ache, *n.* 170
achieve, *v.* 769
achievement, *n.* 620
achromatic, *adj.* 972
acid, *adj.* 766
acid, *n.* 1105
acidulous, *adj.* 539
-acious, 927, 1090, 1096
acknowledge, *v.* 262, 1017, 178
acme, *n.* 398
acoustic, *adj.* 458, 542
ACOUSTICAL, *adj.* 458
acoustics, *n.* 458
acquaintance, *n.* 230, 173
acquainted, *adj.* 230
acquiescent, *adj.* 788
acquiescing, *adj.* 418
acquire, *v.* 9, 264
acquired, *adj.* 26, 200
acquisition, *n.* 878
acquisitiveness, *n.* 379
ACQUIT, *v.* 500, 516, 903
acquittal, *n.* 500, 512, 1070
acquittance, *n.* 478
acrid, *adj.* 766, 539
ACRIMONIOUS, *adj.* 766, 572
across, *prep.* or *adv.* 536
act, *n.* 462
active, *adj.* 169, 218, 531, 311, 162

actor, *n.* 242, 813
actuarial, *adj.* 1084
ACTUARIALLY, *adv.* 1084
actuary, *n.* 1084
actuate, *v.* 475
acute, *adj.* 315, 766, 984, 320, 576, 746, 1074, 522, 982, 1048
acuteness, *n.* 814
ADAMANT, *n.* 864
adamant, *adj.* 864
adamantine, *adj.* 864
ADAPT, *v.* 562, 325
add, *v.* 178, 656
added, *adj.* 872
addicted, *adj.* 648
addition, *n.* 250, 645
additional, *adj.* 872
ADDRESS, *v.* 125, 388, 458, 614
address, *n.* 458
addressing, *adj.* 458
ADEPT, *adj.* 219, 192
adequate, *adj.* 135
adhere, *v.* 351, 37, 912
adhesive, *adj.* 351, 965, 1104
adipose, *adj.* 847
adjoining, *adj.* 1027
adjourn, *v.* 305
adjudication, *n.* 995
ADJURATION, *n.* 995
adjust, *v.* 292, 325, 497, 562, 900
administer, *v.* 939
ADMIRABLE, *adj.* 104
admiral, *n.* 104
admiration, *n.* 309
admire, *v.* 104, 198, 459
admired, *adj.* 49, 198
admissible, *adj.* 416
admit, *v.* 1017, 580
ADMONISH, *v.* 670, 506, 565, 573

aid, *v.* 65, 532, 946, 637, 729
aid, *n.* 842
ailment, *n.* 374
aim, *n.* 91, 145
aim, *v.* 1004
aimless, *adj.* 472, 634
aimlessly, *adv.* 472
airy, *adj.* 548, 692
akin, *adj.* 173, 153, 1086, 371
al-, 104, 244
-al, 285
alacrity, *n.* 790
alarm, *n.* 830
alarmed, *adj.* 389, 396
ALBEIT, *conj.* 244, 1006
alchemy, *n.* 104
alcohol, *n.* 104
alcove, *n.* 104
ale-house, *n.* 996
alert, *adj.* 311
algebra, *n.* 104
alien, *adj.* 483, 732
ALIENATE, *v.* 483
alike, *adj.* 371
alkali, *n.* 104
ALLAY, *v.* 607, 575, 317, 349
allege, *v.* 607, 435, 1063
allegiance, *n.* 767
ALLEVIATE, *v.* 575, 607, 792,
 349, 954
alleviative, *adj.* 1018
alley, *n.* 863
ALLIED, *adj.* 153, 173, 371, 957,
 1086
Allies, 153
ALLOCATE, *v.* 775
allot, *v.* 775
allow, *v.* 898
allowance, *n.* 512, 855
alloy, *v.* 607

allude, *v.* 345, 1016, 1024
allure, *v.* 544, 611
ALLUSION, *n.* 1024, 239
ally, *v.* 153
ally, *n.* 153, 192, 302
almanac, *n.* 322, 104
alms, *n.* 1080
alone, *adj.* 7
aloof, *adv.* 22
aloof, *adj.* 186
Altair, 971
alteration, *n.* 254
ALTERCATION, *n.* 753
alternative, *n.* 599
although, *conj.* 244
altitude, *n.* 183
A.M., 3
amalgamate, *v.* 292
amalgamation, *n.* 393
amass, *v.* 17
ambi-, 1110
ambiguous, *adj.* 958, 1028
amble, *v.* 129, 330
ambling, *v.* 129
ambulance, *n.* 129
ambulatory, *n.* 129
ambulatory, *adj.* 1043
ameer, *n.* 104
AMELIORATE, *v.* 792, 349
amenable, *adj.* 940
amend, *v.* 138, 1001, 792
amendable, *adj.* 989
amendment, *n.* 642, 1001
AMENDS, *n.* 642, 359, 728
amenities, *n.* 570
AMENITY, *n.* 570, 861
amiability, *n.* 227
AMIABLE, *adj.* 227, 717
amicable, *adj.* 358
amir, *n.* 104

assertive, *adj.* 827
asseverate, *v.* 1017
ASSEVERATION, *n.* 758
ASSIDUOUS, *adj.* 390, 114, 255, 1003
assign, *v.* 775, 785
assist, *v.* 274, 842
assistant, *n.* 297
assisted, *v.* 964
ASSOCIATE, *n.* 302, 192
associate, *v.* 155
associated, *adj.* 153
association, *n.* 302
assuage, *v.* 317, 607
ASSUME, *v.* 47, 1000
assumed, *adj.* 1046, 212
assurance, *n.* 465, 1041, 818
assure, *v.* 238, 532, 1017
assured, *adj.* 913
aster, *n.* 357
astounded, *adj.* 819
ASTRAL, *adj.* 357
astrology, *n.* 231
astronomy, *n.* 357, 231
ASTUTE, *adj.* 746, 576, 320
astutely, *adv.* 746
astuteness, *n.* 746
asunder, *adv.* 839
atheistic, *adj.* 638
ATHEISTICAL, *adj.* 638
athirst, *adj.* 413
athwart, *adj.* 209
atlas, *n.* 226
Atlas, 226
atonement, *n.* 467, 799
atrocious, *adj.* 547, 1073
atrocity, *n.* 1073
Atropos, 452, 955
attach, *v.* 178
attached, *adj.* 648

attack, *n.* 379, 473
attack, *v.* 399, 785
attainment, *n.* 878
attempt, *n.* 285, 496
attempt, *v.* 285, 496
attend, *v.* 395
attendant, *n.* 977
attention, *n.* 395
attentively, *adv.* 836
ATTENUATE, *v.* 1067, 1115
attire, *n.* 127
attire, *v.* 739
attitude, *n.* 1026
attract, *v.* 214
attraction, *n.* 329, 709, 914
attractions, *n.* 570
attractive, *adj.* 644, 227, 320, 641
attractiveness, *n.* 570
attribute, *n.* 742
attribute, *v.* 785
attributing, *v.* 785
attrition, *n.* 310
attune, *v.* 562
ATYPICAL, *adj.* 972
AUCTION, *n.* 50
audacious, *adj.* 927, 593
AUDACITY, *n.* 208, 818
AUDIBLE, *adj.* 251
audience, *n.* 251, 458
auditor, *n.* 251
auditorium, *n.* 251, 458
auditory, *adj.* 400, 458
AUGMENT, *v.* 656, 76, 50, 615
AUGURY, *n.* 608
auspicious, *adj.* 332, 494, 953
AUSTERE, *adj.* 715, 123, 1105
austerely, *adv.* 123
austerity, *n.* 207, 945, 123
authenticate, *v.* 237

belonging, *adj.* 1027
bemoan, *v.* 877
bend, *n.* 19, 95
bend, *v.* 117 .
bending, *adj.* 397, 1113
benefit, *n.* 515, 620, 767
benevolent, *adj.* 644, 549
benign, *adj.* 598
BENIGNANT, *adj.* 717, 549, 196
bent, *adj.* 19
bent, *n.* 952, 824
berate, *v.* 852
BERSERK, *adj.* 643
berserk, *n.* 643
berserker, *n.* 643
BESEECH, *v.* 324, 59, 407
beseeching, *adj.* 872
BESTOW, *v.* 202, 238, 407
BETIMES, *adv.* 1002, 460
betoken, *v.* 395
betray, *v.* 247
betrayal, *n.* 121
betroth, *v.* 381
better, *adj.* 243
better, *v.* 792, 1001
bever, *n.* 51, 1026
BEVERAGE, *n.* 51
bevy, *n.* 24
bewail, *v.* 877
BEWILDER, *v.* 185, 161, 946
bewildered, *adj.* 185, 992
bewilderingly, *adv.* 185
bewilderment, *n.* 185, 1114
bewitch, *v.* 214
bias, *n.* 217, 709, 824, 952, 1003
bias, *v.* 770
biased, *adj.* 930
bib, *n.* 51
BICAMERAL, *adj.* 530
bid, *v.* 99

biennial, *adj.* 460
biennial, *n.* 460
big, *adj.* 63, 226, 249, 319, 745,
    822, 1073
bigot, *n.* 364
billow, *n.* 1037
bind, *v.* 273, 381
binding, *adj.* 807
Birmingham, 284
biscuit, *n.* 923
bit, *n.* 744, 756
bite, *v.* 800
bite, *n.* 969
biting, *adj.* 761, 766, 885, 572
bitter, *adj.* 313, 766, 857, 572
bizarre, *adj.* 90, 401, 875, 643
black art, 963
blacksmith, *n.* 1, 895
blame, *v.* 565, 573, 498, 463,
    388, 935
blame, *n.* 978
blameless, *adj.* 476
blameworthy, *adj.* 903
bland, *adj.* 1091, 862, 882, 715
blandish, *v.* 508
blank, *adj.* 572
blasphemous, *adj.* 341
blast, *v.* 687, 220
bleach, *v.* 100
BLEAK, *adj.* 100
blemish, *n.* 10, 220
blemish, *v.* 220, 561
BLEND, *n.* 393, 14
blend, *v.* 899
bless, *v.* 213
blessed, *adj.* 15, 752
blessing, *n.* 620
blind, *adj.* 733
bliss, *n.* 992
blissful, *adj.* 816, 992

blithe, *adj.* 793
bloated, *adj.* 1088
block, *n.* 70
blood, *n.* 404
bloodless, *adj.* 703
bloodthirsty, *adj.* 913
bloody, *adj.* 913
BLOOM, *v.* 166
bloom, *n.* 166
blooming, *adj.* 410, 846
blossom, *v.* 166
blossom, *n.* 166
blossoming, *adj.* 846
blot, *v.* 220
blot, *n.* 220
BLOTCH, *v.* 220
blotch, *n.* 386
blow, *n.* 231, 170
blowing, *adj.* 410
BLUDGEON, *n.* 404
blue, *adj.* 1061
BLUFF, *adj.* 862
bluff, *v.* 862
bluff, *n.* 862
bluffer, *n.* 862
bluish, *adj.* 840
BLUNDER, *n.* 77, 966
blundering, *adj.* 873
blunt, *adj.* 862, 984, 272
blunt, *v.* 1044
bluntness, *n.* 795
blur, *v.* 220
blusterer, *n.* 747
boast, *n.* 749
boaster, *n.* 1083, 707, 616
boastful, *adj.* 406, 428, 144, 1101
boastfulness, *n.* 812
boat, *n.* 398
bodily, *adj.* 567, 806

body, *n.* 568, 690
boggle, *n.* 997
bogus, *adj.* 683
boil, *v.* 782
boiling, *n.* 193
boisterous, *adj.* 747, 718
bold, *adj.* 534, 162, 211, 904, 927
boldness, *n.* 208, 121, 12, 818
bole, *n.* 58
bombastic, *adj.* 581, 1005, 1088
bond, *n.* 141
bondsman, *n.* 557, 214
bone, *n.* 535
boom, *n.* 70, 620
boom, *v.* 620
BOON, *n.* 620
boor, *n.* 1083
boorish, *adj.* 710
boot, *n.* 270
bootee, *n.* 270
BOOTY, *n.* 270
border, *n.* 832
bore, *v.* 163, 513
boredom, *n.* 501
boring, *adj.* 194
botanical, *adj.* 666
botany, *n.* 666
botch, *v.* 220
bottle, *n.* 950
BOUILLON, *n.* 193, 869
BOULEVARD, *n.* 58
bound, *v.* 330
boundary, *n.* 156, 886
BOUNTIFUL, *adj.* 135, 920
bounty, *n.* 1080
bowl, *n.* 58
boy, *n.* 25, 31, 1007
brachycephalic, *adj.* 962
bracing, *adj.* 542, 1093

brag, *n.* 749
braggart, *n.* 1083, 616, 707
bragging, *n.* 812
braid, *v.* 573, 169
branch, *n.* 510, 850, 587, 37
branch, *v.* 850
branched, *adj.* 850
branching, *n.* 850
brand, *v.* 687
brandish, *v.* 573
BRAVE, *v.* 203
brave, *adj.* 162
bravery, *n.* 121, 759
bravo, *n.* 520
brawl, *n.* 443, 658
brawn, *n.* 82
BRAWNY, *adj.* 82, 793
brazen, *adj.* 1085, 593
BREACH, *n.* 443, 469, 987, 258
breadth, *n.* 751
break, *v.* 174, 215, 839
break, *n.* 443, 469, 1110
breakable, *adj.* 1110
breaking, *n.* 469
breathe, *v.* 164
bred, *v.* 246
BREED, *v.* 246, 405
breezy, *adj.* 692
bribe, *v.* 544
bridle, *n.* 169
bridle, *v.* 172
brief, *adj.* 493, 629, 942
bright, *adj.* 725, 956, 1075, 740,
    1116, 410
brighten, *v.* 103
brightness, *n.* 846
brilliant, *adj.* 725, 1075, 442,
    428, 846, 960, 196
brisk, *adj.* 218, 311
bristling, *adj.* 674

brittle, *adj.* 28, 319
broach, *n.* 1092
broad, *adj.* 534, 157, 278, 409,
    986
broadcast, *v.* 937
brocade, *n.* 1092
BROCHURE, *n.* 1092
broke, *adj.* 777
broken, *adj.* 1110
brooch, *n.* 1092
broth, *n.* 193, 869
brown, *adj.* 946
brownie, *n.* 774
bruise, *v.* 116
bruise, *n.* 1044
bruised, *adj.* 942
brusque, *adj.* 641
brusqueness, *n.* 271
bubble, *v.* 782
bubbling, *n.* 782
BUCCAL, *adj.* 1025, 1006
bud, *v.* 166
BUDGE, *v.* 74
buffoon, *n.* 502
buffoonery, *n.* 809
builder, *n.* 1038
building, *n.* 1022
bulkiness, *n.* 468
bulky, *adj.* 745, 1015
bull, *n.* 154, 77
BULLETIN, *n.* 154, 869
BULLION, *n.* 869, 193
bulwark, *n.* 58
bum, *n.* 590
bummer, *n.* 590
bump, *n.* 579
BUMPER, *n.* 590
bumping, *n.* 1016
bumpkin, *n.* 1083
bunch, *n.* 24

bundle, *n.* 949
bungle, *v.* 220
burden, *n.* 319, 807, 944
burden, *v.* 724, 807
burdensome, *adj.* 194, 319,
427, 944
burgeon, *v.* 166
burial, *n.* 600
burlesque, *adj.* 378
burlesque, *v.* 394
burlesque, *n.* 1082
burn, *v.* 687, 757
burned, *v.* 689
burning, *adj.* 766, 476, 757
burnish, *v.* 103
burnt, *adj.* 1052
bury, *v.* 600
bush, *n.* 33
BUSHY, *adj.* 33
bustled, *v.* 450
BUXOM, *adj.* 438
buzz, *v.* 112
buzz, *n.* 112

CABAL, *n.* 996
cabaret, *n.* 996
cabinet, *n.* 996
CABLE, *n.* 54, 545
CACHE, *v.* 299
cache, *n.* 299
cacologistic, *adj.* 675
cacology, *n.* 675
CACOPHONOUS, *adj.* 947
cacophony, *n.* 947
cadaver, *n.* 560
cage, *n.* 508, 863
caitiff, *n.* 502, 520
CAJOLE, *v.* 508, 544
cajoler, *n.* 508
calamitous, *adj.* 857

calamity, *n.* 108, 231
calculation, *n.* 1106
calculus, *n.* 1065
calendar, *n.* 322
call, *v.* 614
callous, *adj.* 588, 519, 765
callus, *n.* 588
calm, *adj.* 186, 518, 762, 788,
105, 1004
calm, *v.* 221, 607, 423, 899
calm, *n.* 309
calming, *adj.* 390
calmness, *n.* 271, 929, 130, 913
calumniate, *v.* 598
CALUMNY, *n.* 845, 1114
CAMEO, *n.* 577
camera, *n.* 530
cancel, *v.* 761, 689, 1079, 937
canceled, *v.* 761
cancellation, *n.* 1079
cancelli, *n.* 761
CANDID, *adj.* 272, 594, 795, 917,
880, 1099
CANDIDACY, *n.* 594
candidateship, *n.* 594
candidature, *n.* 594
candidness, *n.* 594, 795
candle, *n.* 272, 594
CANDOR, *n.* 795
canoe, *n.* 1050
cant, *n.* 812
cant, *v.* 904
cantata, *n.* 848
CANTING, *adj.* 904
cap, *n.* 508
capability, *n.* 208, 677
capable, *adj.* 755
capacious, *adj.* 157, 54
capacitate, *v.* 755
capacity, *n.* 355, 562, 208, 755

CAPARISON, *n.* 938
caper, *v.* 190, 330
capillaceous, *adj.* 602
CAPILLARY, *adj.* 602
capital, *n.* 602, 726
Capitol, *n.* 602
CAPITULATE, *v.* 817
caprice, *n.* 943, 938
capricious, *adj.* 401, 531, 938
captain, *v.* 991
CAPTIOUS, *adj.* 1048
captivate, *v.* 214
captive, *n.* 54
capture, *v.* 449
CARBOY, *n.* 950
cardinal, *adj.* 372
care, *n.* 191, 204, 523
careful, *adj.* 1058, 1068, 741
carefully, *adv.* 126, 836
careless, *adj.* 1014, 191, 436,
    1028
caress, *v.* 612
caricature, *n.* 394, 1082
carmine, *adj.* 1061
carnal, *adj.* 806, 1015
carnival, *n.* 996
carnivorous, *adj.* 806
carousal, *n.* 631
carousing, *n.* 631
carping, *adj.* 1048
carriage, *n.* 228, 569, 738, 854,
    915
CARRION, *n.* 806
carry, *v.* 228, 423, 719, 486,
    915
carve, *v.* 69
CARVED, *adj.* 69
cash, *n.* 473
castigate, *v.* 787, 723
castigation, *n.* 147

casual, *adj.* 472, 953, 387, 990
casualty, *n.* 993
cataclysm, *n.* 108, 140
catacomb, *n.* 140
CATALOGUE, *v.* 140
catapult, *v.* 817
catastasis, *n.* 108
CATASTROPHE, *n.* 108, 231, 140,
    52
catch, *v.* 449
catechism, *n.* 507
CATECHIST, *n.* 507
catenary, *adj.* 1045
catenary, *n.* 1045
cathedra, *n.* 52
CATHEDRAL, *n.* 52
CATHOLIC, *adj.* 986
Catholic, *adj.* 986
catholicon, *n.* 772
CAUDAL, *adj.* 757
caught, *v.* 449
causative form, 38, 2
cause, *v.* 811, 246, 801
caustic, *adj.* 766, 539, 757, 572
cauterize, *v.* 687, 757
caution, *v.* 670
caution, *n.* 1054, 708
cautious, *adj.* 1068
cautiously, *adv.* 836
cave, *n.* 210
cavern, *n.* 210
caviling, *n.* 1048, 809
-ce, 196
cease, *v.* 201
ceasing, *n.* 254
cede, *v.* 1034
ceding, *n.* 1034
celebrated, *adj.* 647
celebration, *n.* 509, 996
celestial, *adj.* 286

CELIBATE, *n.* 1036
cemetery, *n.* 963
censorious, *adj.* 675
censure, *v.* 565, 506, 573, 670,
903, 125, 498, 877, 1035
censure, *n.* 152, 785, 978
CEPHALIC, *adj.* 962
cerebrate, *v.* 261
cerebration, *n.* 465, 1106
ceremonial, *adj.* 105
ceremonious, *adj.* 533, 961
ceremony, *n.* 509
certain, *adj.* 195, 654
Cervantes, 1101
cessant, *adj.* 201
CESSATION, *n.* 254, 156, 650,
1006, 201
CESSION, *n.* 1034
chafe, *v.* 103
chaffing, *adj.* 1107
chafing, *n.* 310
chain, *n.* 54
challenge, *v.* 203, 785, 420
chamber, *n.* 530
CHAMP, *v.* 800
chance, *n.* 955, 993, 387
chance, *adj.* 953
chandelier, *n.* 726
change, *v.* 562, 574, 486
change, *n.* 888, 863, 254, 642
changeable, *adj.* 990, 863, 989
changed, *v.* 863
changing, *adj.* 1049
chant, *v.* 848
chaotic, *adj.* 16, 1117
character, *n.* 479, 183, 365
characteristic, *adj.* 275
characteristic, *n.* 447
characterless, *adj.* 1047
Chares, 249

charge, *n.* 67, 280
charge, *v.* 388, 498, 785
charity, *n.* 601
charlatan, *n.* 820
CHARLATANIC, *adj.* 820
Charles II, 996
charm, *v.* 214, 784
charm, *n.* 570, 625
charming, *adj.* 227, 644
chase, *v.* 789, 537, 133
chased, *adj.* 789, 385
CHASTE, *adj.* 789, 385, 386, 787
chasten, *v.* 147, 723
chasteness, *n.* 385
chastening, *n.* 147
chastise, *v.* 147, 723, 294, 480,
152, 863
CHASTISEMENT, *n.* 147
CHASTITY, *n.* 385, 386, 601, 789
chat, *n.* 11
chatter, *n.* 750, 44
chatter, *v.* 633
chattering, *n.* 44, 369
chattering, *adj.* 700
chatty, *adj.* 777
chauffeur, *n.* 950
cheap, *adj.* 725
cheat, *n.* 320, 459
cheat, *v.* 345, 598, 679, 948
CHECK, *v.* 399, 172, 189, 532,
259
check, *n.* 473
cheek, *n.* 1025
cheer, *v.* 852, 88
cheer, *n.* 424
cheerless, *adj.* 100, 346
cheers, *n.* 424
cherish, *v.* 405
chess, *n.* 399
chest, *n.* 1019

climb, *v.* 351
CLING, *v.* 351, 37
clinging, *adj.* 965
clique, *n.* 645, 996
clog, *v.* 532
clog, *n.* 807
cloister, *n.* 886
close, *adj.* 32, 222, 961, 808, 335, 521
close, *n.* 254
close-mouthed, *adj.* 917
clothe, *v.* 948, 1000, 1082
clothes, *n.* 127
clothing, *n.* 854, 938, 744
Clotho, 452, 955
clouds, *n.* 412
cloudy, *adj.* 335, 831, 1037
clown, *n.* 1083
clownish, *adj.* 710
club, *n.* 404
clumsy, *adj.* 336, 444, 634
CLUSTER, *n.* 24, 551, 756
coadjutor, *n.* 192
coalition, *n.* 1034
COARSE, *adj.* 411, 64, 641, 734, 1071, 288, 605
coarsely, *adv.* 745
coast, *n.* 388
coax, *v.* 508, 544
coaxing, *n.* 508
cobble, *n.* 1094
cocktail, *n.* 590
CODON, *n.* 1100
COERCION, *n.* 571
coffee, *n.* 1061
cogency, *n.* 196
COGENT, *adj.* 1056, 196
COGITATE, *v.* 261, 771
cogitating, *n.* 868
COGNATE, *adj.* 957

cognizance, *n.* 957
cognomen, *n.* 685
cohere, *v.* 660, 912
coherence, *n.* 1008
coherent, *adj.* 990
COHERENTLY, *adv.* 660
cohesive, *adj.* 1104
coincidence, *n.* 196
coincident, *adj.* 646, 196
coiner, *n.* 778
coir, *n.* 54
cold, *adj.* 100, 485
cold-bloodedness, *n.* 913
COLLATE, *v.* 1118
collation, *n.* 1118, 1026, 51
colleague, *n.* 302
collect, *v.* 299, 446
collected, *adj.* 412, 775
collecting, *v.* 800
collection, *n.* 24, 551
collision, *n.* 1016
collude, *v.* 1016
COLLUSION, *n.* 1016
colonnade, *n.* 886
color, *n.* 242, 962
colored, *adj.* 725
colorful, *adj.* 63
colorless, *adj.* 703
COLOSSAL, *adj.* 249, 63, 226, 822
Colosseum, *n.* 249
Colossus, 249, 822
column, *n.* 726
combat, *n.* 67
combative, *adj.* 910
combination, *n.* 14, 393, 592, 645, 861
combine, *v.* 153, 234, 292, 899, 998, 1045
combust, *v.* 1052
combustion, *n.* 1052

comfort, *n.* 728
comforting, *adj.* 816
comic, *adj.* 1031, 629, 610
comical, *adj.* 378, 666
COMITY, *n.* 861
command, *n.* 995, 478
command, *v.* 991
COMMANDEER, *v.* 991
commander, *n.* 104
commanding, *adj.* 1055
commandment, *n.* 4, 1054
commencement, *n.* 73
commend, *v.* 729
commendatory, *adj.* 675
commended, *v.* 769
COMMENSURATE, *adj.* 911
commerce, *n.* 737
commercial, *adj.* 912, 605
COMMISERATE, *v.* 851, 366
commodious, *adj.* 314
common, *adj.* 315, 342, 411
commonplace, *adj.* 32, 360,
849, 960, 605, 942
commotion, *n.* 481, 509, 181
commune, *v.* 501
communicate, *v.* 501, 247
communication, *n.* 132
communism, *n.* 861
community, *n.* 861, 426
compact, *adj.* 253
compact, *n.* 1111
companion, *n.* 302
companionable, *adj.* 740
companionship, *n.* 302, 914
compare, *v.* 1118
comparison, *n.* 1033
compassion, *n.* 596
compassionate, *adj.* 196
compatible, *adj.* 348
compeer, *n.* 302

compelling, *adj.* 1056
compensate, *v.* 935
compensation, *n.* 9, 642, 728,
359, 799
competency, *n.* 677
competition, *n.* 583
COMPLACENT, *adj.* 644
complain, *v.* 598
complaint, *n.* 280, 374
complaisance, *n.* 861
complaisant, *adj.* 644, 308, 418
complement, *n.* 461
complete, *adj.* 328, 418, 733,
629, 35
complete, *v.* 769
completion, *n.* 156, 197
complex, *adj.* 559, 192, 111
complexion, *n.* 559
complexity, *n.* 559
COMPLIANT, *adj.* 418, 308, 959,
392
complicated, *adj.* 559, 111, 175
compliment, *n.* 624
complimentary, *adj.* 675
comply, *v.* 418, 392
COMPORT, *v.* 423
COMPOSE, *v.* 221, 423
composed, *adj.* 762, 390, 627
composition, *n.* 592, 878
composure, *n.* 929
compound, *n.* 14
comprehending, *adj.* 665
comprehensive, *adj.* 990, 278,
534
compress, *v.* 415, 537, 116
compromise, *v.* 152
compromise, *n.* 333
compulsion, *n.* 571
compulsory, *adj.* 55
COMPUNCTION, *n.* 885

compute, *v.* 785
comrade, *n.* 302
con-, 11, 366, 980
CONCATENATE, *v.* 1045
conceal, *v.* 256, 247, 455, 730
concealed, *adj.* 5, 455, 511
concealing, *adj.* 150
concede, *v.* 580, 238, 898
conceit, *n.* 419, 613
conceited, *adj.* 837, 749
concentrate, *v.* 415
concentration, *n.* 395
concentric, *adj.* 321
conception, *n.* 459
concern, *v.* 235
concerned, *adj.* 334
concession, *n.* 1034, 580
conciliate, *v.* 964, 497
conciliatory, *adj.* 518
concise, *adj.* 493, 629, 1009, 942
conciseness, *n.* 1009
conclave, *n.* 11
conclude, *v.* 137
conclusion, *n.* 156, 254, 1082
conclusive, *adj.* 1056
CONCOCT, *v.* 234
concoction, *n.* 743, 551
concord, *n.* 528, 408
concordance, *n.* 525, 528
concurrence, *n.* 528, 238
concurrent, *adj.* 646
condemn, v. 935, 573, 636, 1020, 512, 213
condemnation, *n.* 512
condense, *v.* 415, 537
condescend, *v.* 898
condescended, *v.* 487
condescending, *adj.* 717
CONDIGN, *adj.* 980

condiment, *n.* 188
condition, *n.* 706
CONDOLE, *v.* 366, 851, 877
CONDONE, *v.* 877
CONDUCE, *v.* 637
conducive, *adj.* 637
conduct, *v.* 423, 129
CONDUCTOR, *n.* 236
conduit, *n.* 184
confab, *n.* 11
confab, *v.* 11
confabulation, *n.* 11
confederate, *n.* 192, 302
confederated, *adj.* 153
CONFER, *v.* 155, 202, 366, 238
CONFERENCE, *n.* 11, 283, 155
confess, *v.* 1017
confidence, *n.* 932, 1041, 96, 208, 870
confident, *adj.* 913
confidential, *adj.* 5
confine, *v.* 172, 273, 463, 787, 863
confinement, *n.* 609, 600
confirm, *v.* 237, 607
confirmation, *n.* 465
confiscate, *v.* 991
conflict, *n.* 583
conflict, *v.* 781
conflicting, *adj.* 348
conformity, *n.* 1042
confound, *v.* 189, 306
confrere, *n.* 302
confront, *v.* 420
confuse, *v.* 161, 185, 189, 306, 946
confused, *adj.* 16, 992, 1117
confusion, *n.* 509, 779, 997, 1114
confute, *v.* 659

cordial, *adj.* 238
cordiality, *n.* 238
core, *n.* 1009
corn, *n.* 1008
cornice, *n.* 832
coronach, *n.* 934
corporeal, *adj.* 567
corpse, *n.* 568, 690
corpulent, *adj.* 847
correct, *v.* 65, 138, 792, 1001
correct, *adj.* 278
correction, *n.* 147, 1001
corrective, *n.* 66
correlative, *n.* 461
correspondence, *n.* 525
corresponding, *adj.* 461, 275, 196
corroborate, *v.* 237
CORROBORATION, *n.* 465
corrode, *v.* 151
corrosive, *adj.* 757
corrupt, *v.* 823, 1069, 498
corrupt, *adj.* 826, 553
corrupting, *adj.* 1077
corruption, *n.* 1069
cortège, *n.* 977
cost, *v.* 388
costal, *adj.* 388
costly, *adj.* 672, 278, 745
costume, *n.* 127
cot, *n.* 284
coterie, *n.* 645
cottage, *n.* 284
cotton, *n.* 1061
couch, *n.* 284
council, *n.* 524
counsel, *v.* 670
counsel, *n.* 751
counselor, *n.* 343, 236
countenance, *v.* 565

countenance, *n.* 879
counter-, 461
counteract, *v.* 461
counterbalance, *v.* 461
counterfeit, *adj.* 683, 457, 212
counterfeit, *v.* 461
counterfeited, *adj.* 778
COUNTERPART, *n.* 461, 46
countryman, *n.* 403
courage, *n.* 121, 130, 759, 764
courageous, *adj.* 162, 534, 830
course, *n.* 736
courteous, *adj.* 308
courtesy, *n.* 861, 979
courtly, *adj.* 227
court martial, *n.* 176
court-martial, *v.* 176
covenant, *n.* 706, 1111
cover, *v.* 256
covert, *adj.* 367, 455, 834
covet, *v.* 780
covetous, *adj.* 1021
covetousness, *n.* 448
coward, *n.* 707, 502
cowardice, *n.* 130
cowardly, *adj.* 59, 1068
cower, *v.* 383
cowering, *adj.* 389
coxcomb, *n.* 508
COY, *adj.* 611
coy, *v.* 611
coyness, *n.* 12
crabbed, *adj.* 313
crack, *n.* 803
cracked, *adj.* 803
craft, *n.* 784
CRAFTINESS, *n.* 265, 391, 746
craftsmanship, *n.* 265
crafty, *adj.* 265, 320, 746, 734, 917

cure-all, *n.* 772
curious, *adj.* 90, 382, 849
current, *adj.* 315, 342
current, *n.* 342, 665
curried, *adj.* 1011
curry, *v.* 1011
currying, *adj.* 1011
curse, *v.* 852, 975, 976, 220,
   665, 679, 1081
curse, *n.* 975
cursed, *adj.* 665
CURSORY, *adj.* 665, 990
curst, *adj.* 665
curtail, *v.* 664
curtailment, *n.* 661
curve, *n.* 19
curved, *adj.* 19
curving, *adj.* 971
custom, *n.* 4, 1112, 925
customary, *adj.* 1112
cut, *v.* 69, 116, 174, 493
cut, *adj.* 69
cut, *n.* 635, 1039
cutting, *adj.* 123, 539, 1014
-cy, 196

dab, *v.* 220, 103
dabbed, *v.* 103
dabbing, *v.* 103
dagger, *n.* 404
DAILY, *adj.* 20
daily, *n.* 20
daintiness, *n.* 814
dainty, *adj.* 382
dally, *v.* 70, 107
damage, *n.* 10, 250
damage, *v.* 770, 245
damp, *adj.* 75, 335, 808, 485
dandified, *adj.* 804
dandy, *n.* 537

danger, *n.* 84, 649, 888, 413
dangerous, *adj.* 253, 546, 552,
   362, 740, 837
Danish words, 8
dank, *adj.* 75
dapper, *adj.* 804
dare, *v.* 203
daring, *n.* 121, 208
daring, *adj.* 534
dark, *adj.* 892
darken, *v.* 946, 1106
darkness, *n.* 578, 840
DASTARD, *n.* 707, 502
date, *n.* 296
daub, *v.* 220, 103
daubed, *v.* 103
dauber, *n.* 103
daubing, *v.* 103
daunt, *v.* 162
DAUNTLESS, *adj.* 162
dawdle, *v.* 70
DAWN, *n.* 73
day, *n.* 20
daybreak, *n.* 73
daze, *n.* 60
daze, *v.* 185
dazzling, *adj.* 725, 63
deadly, *adj.* 786, 857, 1097,
   433, 448, 542, 200, 837
dealer, *n.* 737
death, *n.* 466
deathlike, *adj.* 819
debase, *v.* 498
debased, *adj.* 826, 553
DEBATABLE, *adj.* 373, 416
debate, *n.* 373, 416, 753
debate, *v.* 373, 633
DEBAUCH, *v.* 823
debauched, *adj.* 826
DEBILITATE, *v.* 928, 1093

debility, *n.* 622
decagon, *n.* 98
decapitate, *v.* 962, 755
decay, *n.* 691
decayed, *adj.* 933
decease, *n.* 466
deceit, *n.* 391, 784, 999
deceitful, *adj.* 19, 345, 1090,
 734, 239, 536, 611
deceive, *v.* 345, 784, 862, 679,
 948, 999, 1085, 720, 823
deceived, *v.* 449, 823
deceiving, *adj.* 320, 1090, 572,
 862
decency, *n.* 196
decent, *adj.* 718, 196
deception, *n.* 459, 999
deceptive, *adj.* 345, 917
decide, *v.* 137
decided, *adj.* 191, 333
decision, *n.* 1070, 995
decisive, *adj.* 827
declaim, *v.* 636
declaration, *n.* 758, 381
declare, *v.* 435, 1017, 937,
 1063, 195
decline, *v.* 114, 659, 898
decline, *n.* 431
declining, *adj.* 566, 97
declivity, *n.* 952
decoct, *v.* 782
decoction, *n.* 782
decompose, *v.* 782
decorate, *v.* 198, 537
decorated, *adj.* 198, 69, 385,
 789
decoration, *n.* 385, 789
DECOROUS, *adj.* 718
decorum, *n.* 1042
decoy, *v.* 544, 611

decrease, *v.* 76, 664
decree, *n.* 4, 154
decrement, *n.* 250
decrepit, *adj.* 435
dedicate, *v.* 213
deducible, *adj.* 416
deduct, *v.* 661
deep, *adj.* 409, 1074, 984
deep-set, *adj.* 1005
deep-toned, *adj.* 916
defalcate, *v.* 661
DEFALCATION, *n.* 661
defalk, *v.* 661
defamation, *n.* 845, 1114
defame, *v.* 598, 935
defaming, *n.* 1114
default, *v.* 661
default, *n.* 661
defeat, *v.* 53, 189, 263, 291,
 926, 946
defeat, *n.* 802
defeated, *adj.* 707
defect, *n.* 622, 858
defensible, *adj.* 416
DEFER, *v.* 305, 3, 679, 658
defiant, *adj.* 1077
deficiency, *n.* 661
defile, *v.* 267, 561, 1069, 498
define, *v.* 720
definite, *adj.* 278, 287, 518
deflect, *v.* 654
deformed, *adj.* 8
defraud, *v.* 598
DEFRAY, *v.* 658
defy, *v.* 203
degenerate, *adj.* 826
DEIGN, *v.* 898, 487
DEITY, *n.* 257
Deity, *n.* 257
dejected, *adj.* 40, 441, 909

dejection, *n.* 408
DELAY, *v.* 85, 305, 3, 70, 259,
    679, 667, 658, 660
delay, *n.* 650, 997
delayed, *adj.* 511
delaying, *adj.* 1098
delegation, *n.* 993
delete, *v.* 866
DELETERIOUS, *adj.* 866, 542, 786
deliberate, *adj.* 105, 990
deliberate, *v.* 155
deliberation, *n.* 868
delicacy, *n.* 34, 499
delicate, *adj.* 34, 1115, 28, 319
delight, *n.* 992
delightful, *adj.* 34, 682
delightfulness, *n.* 570
delinquent, *adj.* 396
delirium, *n.* 556
delude, *v.* 345, 720, 189, 784,
    508, 948, 1016, 449
deluding, *adj.* 572
deluge, *n.* 140
deluge, *v.* 702
delusion, *n.* 495, 345, 1016
delusive, *adj.* 720
demand, *v.* 99, 287, 384, 705,
    470, 517
demand, *n.* 384, 706
demanding, *adj.* 201
demean, *v.* 423
demeanor, *n.* 569, 879
demijohn, *n.* 950
DEMOCRACY, *n.* 505, 1089
demolish, *v.* 689, 724, 839, 998
demolishing, *adj.* 786
demoniac, *adj.* 536
demotic, *adj.* 1089
DEMUR, *n.* 997
demur, *v.* 997

demure, *adj.* 997
demureness, *n.* 12
den, *n.* 210
Deneb, 971
DENIAL, *n.* 285, 359, 758
denounce, *v.* 975, 976, 636,
    877, 679
denounced, *v.* 843
dense, *adj.* 734, 984, 253
dental, *adj.* 742
dentist, *n.* 742
dentistry, *n.* 742
DENUDE, *v.* 206
deny, *v.* 285, 712, 416, 1081,
    435
depart, *v.* 654
depend, *v.* 124
dependability, *n.* 96, 124
dependable, *adj.* 97
dependent, *n.* 977, 557
depict, *v.* 694
DEPILATE, *v.* 843
depilatory, *n.* 843
deplore, *v.* 877
deport, *v.* 423, 535
deportment, *n.* 569
deposit, *v.* 141, 202, 299, 363
deposition, *n.* 600
deprave, *v.* 823, 498
DEPRAVED, *adj.* 826, 566
depravity, *n.* 1069
DEPRECATE, *v.* 1081, 40, 843
deprecatory, *adj.* 1081
depreciate, *v.* 941, 101, 1081
depreciating, *adj.* 675
depreciation, *n.* 1114
depredate, *v.* 967
depredation, *n.* 967
depressed, *adj.* 909, 408
depressing, *adj.* 427, 876

depression, *n.* 798
deranged, *adj.* 1047
deride, *v.* 88, 223, 240, 573, 1081
derision, *n.* 281
derisive, *adj.* 378, 1040
descend, *v.* 680
descent, *n.* 431
describe, *v.* 694
DESCRY, *v.* 694
desecrate, *v.* 976
desert, *v.* 56
desert, *adj.* 922
deserted, *adj.* 438
deserve, *v.* 9
design, *n.* 46, 149, 987
design, *v.* 137, 1004
designate, *v.* 657
designation, *n.* 657
designing, *adj.* 175
desire, *v.* 59, 780
desire, *n.* 379
desirous, *adj.* 1021
desolate, *adj.* 100, 346, 922
desperate, *adj.* 1071
despise, *v.* 168, 152, 898
despoil, *v.* 206
despoiling, *adj.* 967
despondency, *n.* 798
destine, *v.* 755
DESTINY, *n.* 452, 955, 837
destitute, *adj.* 777
destroy, *v.* 109, 151, 439, 689, 263, 635, 839, 998, 688, 866, 941
destroying, *adj.* 786
destroys, *v.* 561
destruction, *n.* 307, 1077, 772
destructive, *adj.* 786, 857, 866, 992, 1072, 1077, 757, 1049

DESUETUDE, *n.* 925, 293
desultory, *adj.* 990
detail, *n.* 279
detailed, *adj.* 990
details, *n.* 604
detain, *v.* 85, 787
detect, *v.* 694
deter, *v.* 305
deteriorating, *adj.* 566
deterioration, *n.* 691, 566
determination, *n.* 1070
determine, *v.* 137, 195
detest, *v.* 168, 780
detestable, *adj.* 180, 647, 104, 665
DETONATION, *n.* 344
DETRACTION, *n.* 1114
DETRIMENT, *n.* 250, 10
devastate, *v.* 439
develop, *v.* 78, 405, 415
development, *n.* 73, 108
DEVIATE, *v.* 654, 269, 451, 999
deviation, *n.* 751, 1012
device, *n.* 810
devilish, *adj.* 1051
devious, *adj.* 654, 841
devise, *v.* 234, 152
devote, *v.* 213
devoted, *adj.* 648
devour, *v.* 927
devoured, *v.* 941
devout, *adj.* 105, 638
dexter, *adj.* 332, 417
dexterity, *n.* 143, 417, 192, 391
dexterous, *adj.* 332, 219
DEXTEROUSLY, *adv.* 417
dextrad, *adv.* 417
dextrally, *adv.* 417
di-, 536, 1076
dia-, 536, 1076

diabolic, *adj.* 1051
DIABOLICAL, *adj.* 536
diagram, *n.* 149
diameter, *n.* 258, 1076
diamond, *n.* 864
diapason, *n.* 626
DIAPHANOUS, *adj.* 1076, 150, 831
diarchy, *n.* 1076
dice, *n.* 298, 61
DICHOTOMY, *n.* 902, 1076
dichromatic, *adj.* 536
dictate, *v.* 1020
dictatorial, *adj.* 827, 873
dictionary, *n.* 280
DIE, *n.* 298, 61
die, *v.* 164
dies, *n.* 298
diet, *n.* 736
difference, *n.* 1039
differences, *n.* 570
different, *adj.* 356, 1049, 1073
differing, *adj.* 666, 776, 1073
difficult, *adj.* 496, 179, 180
difficulty, *n.* 556, 310, 966
DIFFIDENCE, *n.* 932, 12
diffident, *adj.* 611, 932
diffusion, *n.* 779
dignified, *adj.* 959
dignitary, *n.* 364
dignity, *n.* 1042, 898, 980
DIGRESS, *v.* 451, 654, 215
digressive, *adj.* 990
DILAPIDATION, *n.* 691
DILATE, *v.* 429, 229
dilemma, *n.* 556
diligent, *adj.* 390, 1003
dim, *v.* 102
dim, *adj.* 892, 251
diminish, *v.* 664, 561, 76, 615

diminution, *n.* 250, 661
dimness, *n.* 840
din, *n.* 242, 865
dining-hall, *n.* 1026
Dionysus, 631
dioxide, *n.* 1076
dip, *v.* 122, 256, 1077
dipterous, *adj.* 536
direct, *adj.* 942
direct, *v.* 991
director, *n.* 236
DIRGE, *n.* 603, 934, 791
dirtied, *adj.* 187
dirty, *adj.* 876, 314, 1029, 1088
dirty, *v.* 561
dirtying, *v.* 561
dis-, 16, 36
disable, *v.* 294, 755, 802, 928
disabled, *adj.* 8
disadvantage, *n.* 250
disadvantageous, *adj.* 314
disaffect, *v.* 483
disagreeable, *adj.* 333, 853, 1051
disagreeing, *adj.* 333, 776
disagreement, *n.* 753, 510, 408, 525
disappearance, *n.* 256
disappoint, *v.* 97
disapprove, *v.* 40, 659, 565, 1081
disapproving, *adj.* 675, 1081
disarranged, *adj.* 16, 187
DISASTER, *n.* 231, 108, 387
disastrous, *adj.* 13, 387, 837
disavow, *v.* 262, 848, 264
disavowal, *n.* 285
disbelief, *n.* 453
disbelieving, *adj.* 638
discard, *v.* 659

dressy, *adj.* 492
dried, *adj.* 218
dried-up, *adj.* 397
drier, *adj.* 218
driest, *adj.* 218
drift, *n.* 126
drill, *v.* 163, 480
drink, *v.* 51
drink, *n.* 51, 503
drinking, *n.* 448
drive, *v.* 475, 126, 532, 909
droll, *adj.* 378, 794
droop, *v.* 114
drooping, *adj.* 477, 114, 567
dross, *n.* 94
drown, *v.* 23
drowsy, *adj.* 433, 527
DRUDGERY, *n.* 79
dry, *adj.* 32, 485, 1108, 922,
    218, 735
dubious, *adj.* 958, 654
duck, *v.* 122, 23
duck, *n.* 300
duel, *n.* 67
dull, *v.* 102, 1044
dull, *adj.* 433, 572, 734, 765,
    849, 960, 984, 1066, 940, 60,
    266, 360, 710
dull-witted, *adj.* 847
duplicate, *n.* 46, 461
duplicate, *adj.* 111
durable, *adj.* 519
dusk, *n.* 578
dusky, *adj.* 892
dust, *n.* 1052
Dutch words, 70
duty, *n.* 445
dwarf, *n.* 63, 774
dwell, *v.* 229
dwelling, *n.* 931

dyslogistic, *adj.* 675

eager, *adj.* 476
eagerness, *n.* 430, 693
Eagle, 971
earlier, *adj.* 358, 835, 841
early, *adj.* 460
early, *adv.* 1002
earn, *v.* 9
earnest, *adj.* 105, 652
earnestness, *n.* 795, 954
EARNINGS, *n.* 9
earthly, *adj.* 286, 815
earthquake, *n.* 108
ease, *v.* 349
ease, *n.* 582
easy, *adj.* 26
eat, *v.* 151
eatable, *adj.* 124
ebullition, *n.* 782, 193
ECCENTRICITY, *n.* 321, 447,
    1012
ecclesia, *n.* 364
ECCLESIASTIC, *n.* 364
echo, *n.* 507
economical, *adj.* 961, 617,
    1010, 1023
economically, *adv.* 126
economics, *n.* 204
ECONOMIZE, *v.* 204
economizing, *adj.* 961
economy, *n.* 204, 126, 961
ecstasy, *n.* 915
ecstatic, *adj.* 816
-ed, 9, 103, 218
edge, *v.* 450
edible, *adj.* 1104
edict, *n.* 4
educate, *v.* 480
educated, *adj.* 64

exterior, *n.* 136
exterior, *adj.* 136
exterminate, *v.* 109, 839, 688
external, *adj.* 732, 136
extinguish, *v.* 38, 317
EXTIRPATE, *v.* 109, 688
extol, *v.* 101
extolling, *adj.* 675, 1040
extort, *v.* 287, 434
extract, *v.* 434
EXTRANEOUS, *adj.* 732
extraordinary, *adj.* 1073, 733, 136
extravagant, *adj.* 546, 385, 617, 789, 643, 1010
EXTREME, *n.* 136
extreme, *adj.* 328, 1073, 123, 136, 980, 1074, 970, 629
extremes, *n.* 136
EXTRICATE, *v.* 688
extrinsic, *adj.* 732
extrude, *v.* 71
exuberant, *adj.* 546
exudation, *n.* 470
EXUDE, *v.* 470
exultation, *n.* 915
eye, *n.* 585
eyeglass, *n.* 1087

fable, *n.* 891, 529, 674
fabric, *n.* 1092, 744
fabricate, *v.* 1085
fabricated, *adj.* 212, 778
fabrication, *n.* 743, 297
fabulous, *adj.* 249, 212
face, *v.* 420
face, *n.* 879
facetious, *adj.* 794, 629
facile, *adj.* 219
facility, *n.* 143, 230

FACTION, *n.* 645, 510, 996
FACTITIOUS, *adj.* 1064, 437, 482, 212
factory, *n.* 1064
factual, *adj.* 1064
faded, *adj.* 397
fading, *adj.* 846
fail, *v.* 97, 114, 383
failing, *adj.* 858, 97, 114
failure, *n.* 661
FAIN, *adj.* 1057
faint, *v.* 574
faint-hearted, *adj.* 677
fair, *adj.* 594
fairness, *n.* 596, 929
fairy, *n.* 774
faith, *n.* 870, 601
faithful, *adj.* 1058, 308, 225
faithfulness, *n.* 124, 522, 767, 381
fall, *v.* 38, 865
fallacious, *adj.* 345, 416
fallible, *adj.* 416
fallow, *adj.* 901
false, *adj.* 19, 212, 457, 1090, 553
falseness, *n.* 522
falsified, *adj.* 778
famed, *adj.* 521
familiar, *adj.* 230, 442
famous, *adj.* 647
fanatic, *n.* 364
fanaticism, *n.* 447
fancied, *adj.* 440, 831
fanciful, *adj.* 401, 440
fancy, *n.* 943
FANTASTIC, *adj.* 401, 90, 440, 822
farmer, *n.* 403, 747
farmhand, *n.* 403

flatter, *v.* 508, 272, 463, 506, 729

flattering, *adj.* 272, 715

flattery, *n.* 624

flavor, *n.* 696, 393

flavoring, *n.* 188

flavorless, *adj.* 375

FLAY, *v.* 1035

fleck, *n.* 386

fleeting, *adj.* 741, 846

fleshy, *adj.* 82, 847

FLEXIBLE, *adj.* 28, 117, 397, 111, 118, 241, 872, 504

flickering, *adj.* 1113

flightiness, *n.* 954

flimsy, *adj.* 721

flinch, *v.* 383

flippancy, *n.* 954

flirt, *n.* 31

flirt, *v.* 1078

flirtation, *n.* 624

flirtatious, *adj.* 438

FLITCH, *n.* 908

flock, *n.* 24

flock, *v.* 595

flog, *v.* 1035

flood, *v.* 702

floral, *adj.* 357

FLORID, *adj.* 410, 131, 875

floundering, *adj.* 873

flourish, *v.* 620

flout, *v.* 223, 240, 573

flow, *n.* 665, 342

flow, *v.* 681

flower, *v.* 166

flowery, *adj.* 797, 410

flowing, *adj.* 876

fluency, *n.* 750

fluent, *adj.* 700, 777

FLURRY, *n.* 481, 509

flushed, *adj.* 410

FLUSTER, *n.* 509, 481

fluster, *v.* 306

flutter, *v.* 268

flutter, *n.* 481

fodder, *n.* 697, 640

FOIBLE, *n.* 858, 622

foil, *v.* 189, 304, 564

fold, *n.* 111, 117

fold, *v.* 117

folded, *adj.* 111

folio, *n.* 1092

follow, *v.* 133, 43, 232, 148

folly, *n.* 814

fondle, *v.* 612

fondness, *n.* 1003

food, *n.* 233, 697, 640, 740, 669

food-storing, *adj.* 1023

fool, *n.* 837, 502

foolhardiness, *n.* 130, 1068

foolhardy, *adj.* 593, 1068

foolish, *adj.* 765, 837, 576, 685, 779, 348, 472, 378

foolishness, *n.* 1085, 814

FOOTPAD, *n.* 881

footpath, *n.* 881

foppish, *adj.* 722

forage, *v.* 640

forage, *n.* 640

foraging, *adj.* 640

FORAY, *n.* 640

forbearance, *n.* 760

forbearing, *adj.* 196

forbid, *v.* 81

forbidden, *adj.* 216, 434

forbidding, *adj.* 205, 674, 752, 1075

force, *n.* 896, 1008, 571, 95

force, *v.* 544, 513

forceful, *adj.* 759

forcible, *adj.* 1009, 1056
foreboding, *n.* 608
forecast, *n.* 708
foreign, *adj.* 732, 1086, 483
forerunner, *n.* 514
foresee, *v.* 679
foreseen, *adj.* 967
foreshadow, *v.* 801, 1106
forestall, *v.* 349, 679
forestalled, *v.* 1081
foretell, *v.* 801, 708, 1063
foretelling, *n.* 708, 603
forged, *adj.* 778
forget, *v.* 85
forgetful, *adj.* 436
forgive, *v.* 877
forgiveness, *n.* 478, 516
forlorn, *adj.* 438, 346
form, *n.* 298, 421
formal, *adj.* 105, 278, 961
formerly, *adv.* 668
formidable, *adj.* 674, 701
formless, *adj.* 831
formula, *n.* 298
forsake, *v.* 56
forswear, *v.* 323, 636, 848, 329
fort, *n.* 210
fortified, *adj.* 210
fortress, *n.* 210
FORTUITOUS, *adj.* 953, 472
Fortuna, 955
fortunate, *adj.* 953, 13
fortune, *n.* 452, 955, 953
fortune-telling, *n.* 175
forward, *adj.* 904
forward, *v.* 1080
foster, *v.* 405, 780
foul, *adj.* 876, 32, 1088, 808
foul, *v.* 267
found, *v.* 142

foundation, *n.* 142, 285
four-fold, *adj.* 111
fraction, *n.* 645
fractious, *adj.* 776
fracture, *n.* 469, 1110
fragile, *adj.* 1110, 28, 319
fragment, *n.* 949
FRAGRANT, *adj.* 34, 692, 1030, 811, 727
frail, *adj.* 28
frailty, *n.* 622, 858
frank, *adj.* 272, 862, 1099, 594, 795, 880, 917
frankness, *n.* 795, 594
frantic, *adj.* 897, 1071
fratch, *n.* 776
fraud, *n.* 1007, 999, 459
fraudulent, *adj.* 19, 683, 820
fray, *n.* 658, 443
frayed, *adj.* 942
free, *adj.* 169, 501, 478
free, *v.* 688, 500, 516, 903
freebooter, *n.* 881
freedom, *n.* 582, 609, 276
frenzied, *adj.* 643
frenzy, *n.* 309, 556, 1114, 897
frequentative form, 161
fresh, *adj.* 442
fret, *v.* 449
FRETFUL, *adj.* 441, 1048, 1049, 593, 776
frication, *n.* 310
FRICTION, *n.* 310
friend, *n.* 173
friendly, *adj.* 227, 302, 740, 358, 549, 552
FRIEZE, *n.* 832
frighten, *v.* 162
frightening, *adj.* 409
frightens, *v.* 235

gay, *adj.* 442, 492, 548, 793,
   725, 794, 105, 428
gem, *n.* 577, 42
general, *adj.* 342, 278
generate, *v.* 246, 316, 811
generosity, *n.* 677, 547
generous, *adj.* 547, 135, 677,
   711, 713
geniality, *n.* 570
genteel, *adj.* 548
gentility, *n.* 271
gentle, *adj.* 548, 816, 196, 549
gentleness, *n.* 596
genuine, *adj.* 912, 972, 1064
genus, *n.* 666
germ, *n.* 279, 1086
GERMANE, *adj.* 1086
germinate, *v.* 166
gesticulation, *n.* 42
gesture, *n.* 42
get, *v.* 247
gewgaw, *n.* 107
ghastly, *adj.* 703, 1029, 819
ghost, *n.* 819
ghostly, *adj.* 458, 819
giant, *n.* 63, 585, 42
gibbon, *n.* 48
gibe, *v.* 88
gift, *n.* 620, 341, 968, 709
gifted, *adj.* 230
gifts, *n.* 1080
GIGANTIC, *adj.* 63, 226, 249,
   547, 1073
GIGGLE, *n.* 44, 369
giggling, *n.* 44
ginger, *n.* 42
GIRD, *v.* 273, 420
girder, *n.* 273
girl, *n.* 25
girth, *n.* 273

gist, *n.* 1008
give, *v.* 238, 202, 775, 407
GLABROUS, *adj.* 1116
glad, *adj.* 1057, 1116
glade, *n.* 1116
glance, *n.* 763
glaring, *adj.* 745
glasses, *n.* 771
gleam, *n.* 676
gleaming, *adj.* 1075, 1113
glee, *n.* 424
gleeful, *adj.* 793
GLIB, *adj.* 700
glibness, *n.* 750
glide, *v.* 700
glimmer, *n.* 676
glimpse, *n.* 676, 763
GLINT, *n.* 676
glisten, *n.* 676
glitter, *n.* 676
glittering, *adj.* 492, 725, 846
GLOAMING, *n.* 578
globe, *n.* 551
globular, *adj.* 27
gloom, *n.* 578
gloominess, *n.* 840
gloomy, *adj.* 313, 346, 892,
   1066
glorifying, *adj.* 1040
glossy, *adj.* 1011
glot-, 1032
glottis, *n.* 1032
glowing, *adj.* 652
glut, *v.* 139, 1032
glut, *n.* 1102
GLUTINOUS, *adj.* 867, 1104,
   1116, 351
glutton, *n.* 616, 1032
gluttonous, *adj.* 927, 619,
   1021, 867

GROUCH, *n.* 45
groundless, *adj.* 142
groundwork, *n.* 142, 285
group, *n.* 24, 645, 756, 768
group, *v.* 1118
grove, *n.* 690
grow, *v.* 76
growl, *v.* 446
growth, *n.* 73
GRUDGE, *n.* 337, 693, 764
grudge, *v.* 337
gruel, *v.* 802
GRUELLING, *n.* 802
gruesome, *adj.* 1029
GRUFF, *adj.* 641
grumble, *v.* 446, 598
Grundy, Mrs., 1042
guarantee, *v.* 363
guarantee, *n.* 796
guard, *n.* 343
GUESS, *n.* 42, 608
guess, *v.* 771
guide, *n.* 236, 42
guild, *n.* 42
guile, *n.* 265, 784, 544, 795, 42
guile, *v.* 784
guileful, *adj.* 320
guileless, *adj.* 1099
guilt, *n.* 42
guilty, *adj.* 396
guise, *n.* 89
guitar, *n.* 42
gullibility, *n.* 453
gully, *n.* 1094
gummy, *adj.* 1104
gushing, *adj.* 779
gust, *n.* 481
gustatory, *adj.* 400
gusty, *adj.* 876
habiliment, *n.* 127

habit, *n.* 447, 925, 1112
habitual, *adj.* 1043
hackneyed, *adj.* 32, 960, 942
hail, *v.* 388
hairlike, *adj.* 602
hairy, *adj.* 33
half, *n.* 756
half-hearted, *adj.* 1098
hall, *n.* 251
hallow, *v.* 213, 15
hallowed, *adj.* 15, 752, 341
Hallowe'en, 15
hallucination, *n.* 495
halt, *v.* 259, 887
halt, *n.* 887
-ham, 284
HAMLET, *n.* 284
hammock, *n.* 579
hamper, *v.* 532
hampering, *adj.* 319
handicraftsman, *n.* 482
handily, *adv.* 417
handiwork, *n.* 265
handle, *n.* 169
handled, *v.* 705
handling, *n.* 802
hand-made, *adj.* 482
hanger-on, *n.* 828
hanging, *adj.* 709
hap, *v.* 387
hap, *n.* 387
haphazard, *adj.* 472, 920, 387
HAPLESS, *adj.* 387, 13
happen, *v.* 387, 470
happy, *adj.* 816, 1116
harangue, *v.* 125
harass, *v.* 513, 773, 856
harbinger, *n.* 514, 445
harbor, *n.* 224
hard, *adj.* 864, 765, 841, 179

herd, *n.* 24
herd, *v.* 595
hereditary, *adj.* 912
heritage, *n.* 912
Hermas, 1118
hermit, *n.* 1036, 945, 1105
heroism, *n.* 121
hesitate, *v.* 191, 660, 887
hesitating, *adj.* 581
hesitation, *n.* 997, 191
HETEROGENEOUS, *adj.* 666, 920
HEXAGON, *n.* 98, 589
HIBERNAL, *adj.* 731
hibernate, *v.* 731
Hibernian, *adj.* 731
hidden, *adj.* 5, 511, 455, 829
hide, *v.* 299, 5, 455, 247, 256, 730
hideous, *adj.* 1029, 819
hiemal, *adj.* 731
hierarchy, *n.* 1089
HIERATIC, *adj.* 1089
hiero-, 1089
hieroglyph, *n.* 1089
hieroglyphic, *adj.* 1089
hierology, *n.* 1089
high, *adj.* 682, 1015
high-colored, *adj.* 410
higher, *adj.* 243
highest, *adj.* 243, 277, 554
high-minded, *adj.* 547
high-mindedness, *n.* 677
high-strung, *adj.* 531
highway, *n.* 58
highwayman, *n.* 881
HILARITY, *n.* 424
hill, *n.* 579, 1094
hillock, *n.* 579, 1094
hinder, *v.* 81, 85, 399, 532, 564, 476, 946, 349, 305

hindered, *v.* 1081
hindmost, *adj.* 757
hint, *n.* 239, 1024
hire, *n.* 855
hired, *adj.* 605
HISS, *v.* 112
hiss, *n.* 112
historical, *adj.* 890
history, *n.* 322
HISTRIONIC, *adj.* 890
hitherto, *adv.* 668
hoard, *v.* 446
hoarded, *v.* 446
hoarfrost, *n.* 803
hobgoblin, *n.* 774
hold, *v.* 37, 351, 172, 399
hold, *n.* 931
holding, *adj.* 965, 402, 892
hole, *n.* 258, 327, 1019
holiness, *n.* 474, 15
hollow, *n.* 210, 1094
HOLY, *adj.* 15, 341, 752
homage, *n.* 767
home economics, *n.* 204
homestead, *n.* 224
homicide, *n.* 828
homily, *n.* 990
homogeneous, *adj.* 666, 1012
homonym, *n.* 1012
honest, *adj.* 272, 19
honesty, *n.* 704, 790, 954
honor, *n.* 704, 242, 870
honorable, *adj.* 547
honorary, *adj.* 352
hoodwink, *v.* 862
hooked, *adj.* 971
hop, *v.* 330
hope, *n.* 601
hopeful, *adj.* 913, 334
horn, *n.* 1110

ill-founded, *adj.* 416
ill-humored, *adj.* 313
illicit, *adj.* 434, 216
ill-looking, *adj.* 332
ill-made, *adj.* 336
illness, *n.* 374
ill-omened, *adj.* 336
ill-smelling, *adj.* 808
ill-sorted, *adj.* 666
ill-starred, *adj.* 387
ill-tempered, *adj.* 665
illude, *v.* 345, 1016
ILLUSION, *n.* 495, 459, 779,
   1016, 345, 1024
illusive, *adj.* 345, 401
illustrate, *v.* 415
illustration, *n.* 495
ill will, *n.* 337, 391, 693, 764,
   893, 598, 570
ill-willed, *adj.* 717
im-, 211, 253
image, *n.* 89, 297, 459, 421,
   1106, 678, 469
IMAGINARY, *adj.* 440, 212, 401,
   822, 201, 831, 249
imaginative, *adj.* 401, 1099
imbecile, *adj.* 837
imbecility, *n.* 622
imbedded, *adj.* 558
imbibe, *v.* 51
imitate, *v.* 240, 461
imitation, *n.* 46, 1082, 482
imitative, *adj.* 813
IMMACULATE, *adj.* 386, 789
immaculateness, *n.* 385, 386
immaterial, *adj.* 567
IMMEMORIAL, *adj.* 844
immense, *adj.* 63, 226
IMMERSE, *v.* 256, 2, 23, 122,
   303

immersed, *adj.* 256
immersion, *n.* 256
IMMEW, *v.* 863, 787
IMMINENT, *adj.* 521, 339
immodest, *adj.* 662, 718
immodesty, *n.* 262
IMMOLATE, *v.* 856
immolation, *n.* 359
immoral, *adj.* 972, 718
immortal, *adj.* 550
immovable, *adj.* 874, 266
IMMUNE, *adj.* 501
immunity, *n.* 767
immure, *v.* 787, 863
imp, *n.* 774
impair, *v.* 1067, 245, 770
impairment, *n.* 10, 691
impart, *v.* 202, 247, 501, 480
impartial, *adj.* 986, 1013, 594
impartiality, *n.* 596, 929, 954
impassable, *adj.* 253
impassioned, *adj.* 652
impassive, *adj.* 970
impatient, *adj.* 441, 593
impeach, *v.* 476
impeachment, *n.* 280
IMPEDE, *v.* 532, 399, 781, 476
impediment, *n.* 319, 807
impeding, *adj.* 314
IMPEL, *v.* 475, 295, 513, 532
impending, *adj.* 521, 339
IMPENETRABLE, *adj.* 253, 821,
   841, 864
impenitent, *adj.* 588
imperceptible, *adj.* 367, 1103
imperfection, *n.* 622
imperil, *v.* 84
imperious, *adj.* 827, 1055
impermeable, *adj.* 253
impertinence, *n.* 211, 818, 842

jeopardize, *v.* 84
JEOPARDY, *n.* 84, 413
jerk, *v.* 169
jerky, *adj.* 686
jester, *n.* 837
jesting, *adj.* 794, 1107
jests, *n.* 809
jewel, *n.* 923
jibe, *v.* 223
jinn, *n.* 774
JOCOSE, *adj.* 794, 793
jocular, *adj.* 794, 793
JOCUND, *adj.* 793, 794
Johnson, Samuel, 1071
join, *v.* 1045
joined, *adj.* 153
joking, *adj.* 794, 793, 629
jollity, *n.* 424
jolly, *adj.* 438, 793
jot, *n.* 744
journal, *n.* 20
journey, *n.* 836
joust, *n.* 67
Jove, 424
jovial, *adj.* 740, 793
joviality, *n.* 424
joyful, *adj.* 1116
joyousness, *n.* 424
jubilance, *n.* 424
jubilation, *n.* 424
judge, *v.* 152, 95, 512
judgment, *n.* 128, 152, 708,
    978, 704, 512, 1070
judicious, *adj.* 1111, 576
juggler, *n.* 820
jumble, *n.* 779
jump, *n.* 749
junto, *n.* 996
Jupiter, 424
jury, *n.* 323

just, *adj.* 594
justice, *n.* 704, 596, 954
justification, *n.* 943
justness, *n.* 596
jut, *v.* 71
jutting, *adj.* 521

kabala, *n.* 996
kayak, *n.* 1050
keen, *adj.* 746, 123, 956, 1048,
    984
keenness, *n.* 320
keen-witted, *adj.* 320
keep, *v.* 368
keepsake, *n.* 796
kernel, *n.* 1009, 1008
kill, *v.* 856, 540
kiln, *n.* 340
KIN, *n.* 173
kind, *adj.* 549, 196, 741
kind, *n.* 666
kind-hearted, *adj.* 227
kindle, *v.* 38
kindly, *adj.* 227, 308, 717, 644,
    598
kindred, *n.* 173
kindred, *adj.* 957
King Arthur, 27, 67
kinsfolk, *n.* 173
KIOSK, *n.* 1050
KISMET, *n.* 955, 452
kith, *n.* 173
KNACK, *n.* 143
knave, *n.* 520, 1007
KNAVERY, *n.* 1007
KNELL, *v.* 606
knell, *n.* 603
knife, *n.* 298
knoll, *n.* 579
know, *v.* 436

lecherous, *adj.* 1021
lecture, *v.* 125, 458
lecture, *n.* 990, 458
lees, *n.* 627
left, *adj.* 332
LEGAL, *adj.* 35, 4
legally, *adv.* 1084
legend, *n.* 891
legislature, *n.* 35
legitimate, *adj.* 35
lemon, *n.* 1061
lengthen, *v.* 667, 395, 801
lenience, *n.* 196
leniency, *n.* 196
LENIENT, *adj.* 196
LEPROSY, *n.* 380
-less, 121
lessen, *v.* 349, 575, 607, 664,
 1067, 76
lessens, *v.* 561
lesson, *n.* 736
lethal, *adj.* 542, 433
LETHARGIC, *adj.* 433
lethargy, *n.* 60, 433
Lethe, 433
level, *v.* 689
LEVITY, *n.* 954, 792
LEWD, *adj.* 662, 1021, 539
liberal, *adj.* 986, 547, 534, 713
liberality, *n.* 1080, 677
liberate, *v.* 688
liberty, *n.* 582, 609, 276, 767
LIBIDINOUS, *adj.* 1021, 897
license, *n.* 582, 609, 945
licentious, *adj.* 1021
licit, *adj.* 35
lick, *v.* 1113
licking, *v.* 800
lie, *v.* 323
LIEU, *n.* 699, 224

life, *n.* 164, 764
lift, *v.* 792, 842, 545
lift, *n.* 792
light, *v.* 38
light-bearer, *n.* 956
lighted, *v.* 38
lighten, *v.* 349, 575, 792, 954
likeable, *adj.* 488
likeness, *n.* 89, 297, 469
liking, *n.* 1003, 914, 709
Lilliput, 226
Lilliputian, *adj.* 226
Lilliputian, *n.* 226
limber, *adj.* 28, 117, 397
lime, *n.* 1061
limit, *n.* 136, 463, 156
limit, *v.* 463
limitless, *adj.* 346
limp, *adj.* 114
limp, *v.* 887
limpid, *adj.* 150, 956
line, *n.* 1039, 545, 889
linger, *v.* 70, 85, 887
lingerer, *n.* 477
lingering, *adj.* 1098
lingo, *n.* 812
linguist, *n.* 1032
link, *v.* 1045
liquid, *n.* 51
liquidate, *v.* 292
liquor, *n.* 51
lissom, *adj.* 28, 117, 397
list, *v.* 140
listless, *adj.* 433, 567
listlessness, *n.* 582
lit, *v.* 38
literal, *adj.* 534, 1064
literary, *adj.* 212
lithe, *adj.* 28, 117, 397
liveliness, *n.* 430, 764

lively, *adj.* 169, 181, 218, 311, 531, 793, 105, 148, 794
livid, *adj.* 840
lizard, *n.* 716
loafer, *n.* 590
loans, *n.* 870
loath, *adj.* 168, 1057
LOATHE, *v.* 168
loathsome, *adj.* 205, 252, 783
lob, *v.* 103
lobbed, *v.* 103
local, *adj.* 315
locate, *v.* 775
lofty, *adj.* 454, 581, 682, 1015
logically, *adv.* 660
LOITER, *v.* 70, 85, 330, 887
loiterer, *n.* 477
loitering, *adj.* 1098
lonely, *adj.* 346
long, *v.* 59
LONGEVITY, *n.* 471
long-headed, *adj.* 962
longitude, *n.* 751
long-lasting, *adj.* 1115
long-winded, *adj.* 906
long-windedly, *adv.* 746
look, *n.* 763
look, *v.* 771
loose, *adj.* 317, 477
loosen, *v.* 478, 317
loot, *n.* 270
loquacious, *adj.* 700, 777
loquacity, *n.* 750
loss, *n.* 10, 250, 359
lost, *v.* 656
lot, *n.* 955
loth, *adj.* 168
loud, *adj.* 916, 1055
loud-voiced, *adj.* 1101
LOUT, *n.* 1083

lovable, *adj.* 227, 940
lovableness, *n.* 227
love, *v.* 171, 851
love, *n.* 1003
lovely, *adj.* 34
low-spirited, *adj.* 677
loyal, *adj.* 225, 308
loyalty, *n.* 124, 767, 522
lubber, *n.* 1083
LUBRICATE, *v.* 248
lucent, *adj.* 956
lucid, *adj.* 956, 415
Lucifer, 956
luck, *n.* 387
lucky, *adj.* 953, 332
LUCRATIVE, *adj.* 610
lucre, *n.* 918, 610, 376
LUDICROUS, *adj.* 378, 1031, 1016, 610
luff, *v.* 70
luke, *adj.* 18
LUKEWARM, *adj.* 18, 422
lumbering, *adj.* 336
lump, *v.* 17
lunar, *adj.* 815
lunch, *n.* 143
lure, *n.* 544
LURK, *v.* 618
lust, *n.* 448
luster, *n.* 726
lustful, *adj.* 662, 1021
lustrous, *adj.* 725, 956, 846
lusty, *adj.* 72, 560
luxurious, *adj.* 672
luxury-loving, *adj.* 1015
-ly, 20
lying, *adj.* 1090, 431, 591, 724, 807

macerate, *v.* 303

moiety, *n.* 756
moist, *adj.* 75, 808, 335, 222, 485
moisture, *n.* 75
moistureless, *adj.* 922
mold, *n.* 871, 222, 726
moldy, *adj.* 222, 808
mole, *n.* 716
mollify, *v.* 575, 964
mollifying, *adj.* 518, 882
molted, *v.* 863
momentary, *adj.* 741
momentous, *adj.* 748, 372, 822
monarch, *n.* 353, 277
monetary, *adj.* 347
money, *n.* 918, 473, 9, 376, 610
monitor, *n.* 670
monk, *n.* 1105
monkey, *n.* 48
mono-, 1087
monocle, *n.* 1087
monogram, *n.* 1087
MONOGRAPH, *n.* 1087, 1092
monologue, *n.* 1087
monopolize, *v.* 312
monopoly, *n.* 1087
monotonous, *adj.* 194, 346, 960, 944
monster, *n.* 822, 585
monstrous, *adj.* 249, 1073
monthly, *adj.* 20
monument, *n.* 462, 678
mood, *n.* 479
moodiness, *n.* 301
Moorish, *adj.* 875
Moors, 875
moot, *adj.* 373
moral, *adj.* 972
mordant, *adj.* 766
MOROSE, *adj.* 313, 1066

moroseness, *n.* 301, 45
morsel, *n.* 969
mortal, *adj.* 448
mortgage, *n.* 141
mortgage, *v.* 363
motherly, *adj.* 871
motion, *n.* 42
motionless, *adj.* 788, 225
motive, *n.* 669
mound, *v.* 17
mound, *n.* 579, 58
mountain, *n.* 1094
mountebank, *n.* 820
mourn, *v.* 877
mournful, *adj.* 791, 366, 934, 947
mouth, *n.* 1019
movement, *n.* 481, 42
moving, *adj.* 68, 727
mud, *v.* 161
MUDDLE, *v.* 161, 185, 946
muddy, *adj.* 1037, 1088
MUGGY, *adj.* 808
mulish, *adj.* 1065
multiform, *adj.* 559
multilingual, *adj.* 1032
multiplication, *n.* 510
multiply, *v.* 76
multitude, *n.* 768, 595
munch, *v.* 800
MUNDANE, *adj.* 815, 286
murkiness, *n.* 840
muscular, *adj.* 82, 560, 793
muse, *v.* 261
musing, *n.* 868
musk, *n.* 222
musky, *adj.* 222
mussed, *adj.* 187
must, *n.* 222
mustard, *n.* 222

MUSTY, *adj.* 222, 808

mutable, *adj.* 863

mutation, *n.* 888, 863

mute, *adj.* 788

mutilate, *v.* 294

mutinous, *adj.* 965

mutiny, *n.* 764, 921

MYRIAD, *n.* 768

myriad, *adj.* 768

mysterious, *adj.* 821, 786, 829

mystic, *adj.* 821

mystify, *v.* 185

myth, *n.* 891

mythical, *adj.* 249

nag, *v.* 95

naive, *adj.* 553, 1099

naïveté, *n.* 795

naked, *adj.* 206

name, *n.* 657, 1012

namely, *adv.* 436

narration, *n.* 951

narrative, *n.* 297

narrow, *adj.* 986

NATATION, *n.* 981

natatorium, *n.* 981

native, *adj.* 26, 957, 1099

NATTY, *adj.* 804, 548

NATURAL, *adj.* 26, 200, 553,
   482, 1099

nature, *n.* 479, 600

nausea, *n.* 865

nauseous, *adj.* 1091

nautical terms, 70

naval, *adj.* 104, 226

nave, *n.* 52

navigation, *n.* 981

NEAT, *adj.* 282, 493, 6, 804,
   1011

NEBULOUS, *adj.* 831

necessarily, *adv.* 907

necessity, *n.* 384, 966

necrological, *adj.* 466

necrology, *n.* 786

NECROMANCY, *n.* 963

necropolis, *n.* 963

need, *v.* 384, 680

NEFARIOUS, *adj.* 783

negation, *n.* 285

negative, *adj.* 285, 282

neglect, *v.* 168, 526

neglect, *n.* 293, 925

negligent, *adj.* 533

negotiator, *n.* 737

negro, *n.* 963

negromancy, *n.* 963

neighborhood, *n.* 568

nemesis, *n.* 772

Nemesis, 772

Neptune, 742

nervous, *adj.* 531

-ness, 12, 96, 121

net, *adj.* 282

net, *v.* 449

NETTLE, *v.* 449, 754

nettle, *n.* 449

network, *n.* 559

neutrality, *n.* 663

nevertheless, *adv.* and *conj.*
   555

new, *adj.* 442

newspaper, *n.* 20

NIB, *n.* 969

nibble, *n.* 969

nice, *adj.* 282, 533

niceness, *n.* 499

NICETY, *n.* 814, 499

nidor, *n.* 696

niggard, *n.* 711

niggardly, *adj.* 711, 961, 983

opalescent, *adj.* 432
OPAQUE, *adj.* 432, 150
open, *adj.* 272, 1099, 795, 594, 917
opening, *n.* 258, 443
opinion, *n.* 42, 152, 402
opportune, *adj.* 953, 646
opportunity, *n.* 515, 233
oppose, *v.* 40, 350, 712, 781, 900, 221, 416, 427, 420
opposed, *adj.* 252, 1049
opposed, *v.* 427
opposing, *adj.* 461
opposite, *adj.* 252, 461
opposition, *n.* 805, 781, 930
oppress, *v.* 427, 724
oppression, *n.* 207
OPPRESSIVE, *adj.* 427, 808, 944
oppressor, *n.* 496
OPPROBRIOUS, *adj.* 1046, 685, 675, 1071
optimistic, *adj.* 913
OPTION, *n.* 599, 43
optional, *adj.* 599, 43
opulence, *n.* 777
OPULENT, *adj.* 777
-or, 242
oral, *adj.* 1025, 171
orang, *n.* 48
orange-yellow, *adj.* 1061
orang-utan, *n.* 48
oration, *n.* 458
oratorio, *n.* 848
orbit, *n.* 466
ordeal, *n.* 496
order, *n.* 4, 384, 528
order, *v.* 1020, 991
orderly, *adj.* 718, 6, 804
ordinance, *n.* 4, 462
ordinary, *adj.* 360, 605

organize, *v.* 152
orgies, *n.* 631
ORGY, *n.* 631
orifice, *n.* 258
origin, *n.* 73
original, *adj.* 358, 960
originate, *v.* 681
Orlando Furioso, 1078
ornament, *v.* 198, 537
ornament, *n.* 385, 1092
ornamentation, *n.* 789
ornamented, *adj.* 410, 198
ornate, *adj.* 875, 410, 198, 797
os, *n.* 535
oscillate, *v.* 606
OSTENSIBLE, *adj.* 825, 416
ostentation, *n.* 144
OSTENTATIOUS, *adj.* 428, 406, 442, 144, 825
ostracism, *n.* 535
OSTRACIZE, *v.* 535
-our, 242
OUST, *v.* 86, 274
out, *adv.* 179
outburst, *n.* 309
outcome, *n.* 156, 452, 649
outdo, *v.* 232
outer, *adj.* 136
outfit, *n.* 854, 938, 127
outlandish, *adj.* 710
outlaw, *n.* 4
outlaw, *v.* 1020
outlawed, *v.* 928
outline, *n.* 421, 1106, 149, 987
outlive, *v.* 148
outlook, *n.* 355
outpouring, *n.* 779
outrage, *n.* 818, 1073
outrageous, *adj.* 1103, 1071
outside, *adj.* 136

outskirts, *n.* 115
outspoken, *adj.* 272, 862, 733
outspokenness, *n.* 795
OUTSTANDING, *adj.* 179, 339,
    494, 1073, 521
outstrip, *v.* 680
outward, *adj.* 732
outworn, *adj.* 413
over-, 263
overabundance, *n.* 1102
overbearing, *adj.* 338, 827, 593
overburden, *v.* 427
overcareful, *adj.* 1062
overcome, *v.* 263, 291, 53
overconfidence, *n.* 613
over-elaborate, *adj.* 875
overexact, *adj.* 278
overflow, *v.* 702
overgrown, *adj.* 33
overhasty, *adj.* 1028
overload, *v.* 807
overlook, *v.* 877, 526
overnice, *adj.* 604, 722, 278,
    493
overpower, *v.* 263, 894
overpowering, *n.* 307
overpowering, *adj.* 427
overpraise, *v.* 463
overprecise, *adj.* 722
overscrupulous, *adj.* 1062
oversee, *v.* 29
overshadow, *v.* 1106
OVERSIGHT, *n.* 526
overstep, *v.* 215, 451
oversupply, *n.* 1102
OVERT, *adj.* 834
overthrow, *v.* 53, 724
overthrow, *n.* 1077
overthrowing, *adj.* 1077
overtrained, *adj.* 32

overturning, *adj.* 1077
OVERWHELM, *v.* 263, 702
overwhelming, *adj.* 427
overwrought, *adj.* 797
oviparous, *adj.* 716
ownership, *n.* 599
oyster, *n.* 535

pace, *v.* 129
PACIFIC, *adj.* 518
pacify, *v.* 221, 964, 673
pack, *n.* 24
pact, *n.* 1111
PAIN, *n.* 541, 159, 170, 655,
    334, 307
painful, *adj.* 1074
painstaking, *adj.* 1058
pale, *adj.* 703, 458
PALLID, *adj.* 703
PALPABLE, *adj.* 859, 745
palpitant, *adj.* 859
palpitate, *v.* 268, 859
palpitating, *adj.* 859
pamphlet, *n.* 1092
PANACEA, *n.* 772
panegyric, *n.* 1040
panegyric, *adj.* 1040
PANEGYRICAL, *adj.* 1040, 675
panegyris, *n.* 1040
panel, *n.* 489
pang, *n.* 170, 655
Papias, 1118
parable, *n.* 529
parade, *n.* 749
PARAGON, *n.* 589
paragraph, *n.* 529
parallel, *adj.* 529, 587
paralyze, *v.* 110
paramount, *adj.* 277, 494, 529,
    554

pelt, *n.* 918
pen, *n.* 398
penalty, *n.* 541
PENANCE, *n.* 467
PENCHANT, *n.* 824, 709, 952
pencil, *n.* 398
pendant, *n.* 709
pendent, *adj.* 709
pendulum, *n.* 709
penetrable, *adj.* 841, 253
penetrate, *v.* 253
penetrating, *adj.* 746, 1055,
   956, 222, 665, 984
penitence, *n.* 885, 467
penitent, *adj.* 942, 1065
penknife, *n.* 398
pen-point, *n.* 969
pentagon, *n.* 98, 589
pent-house, *n.* 709
penumbra, *n.* 1106
PENURIOUS, *adj.* 711, 961, 983
penury, *n.* 711, 467
people, *n.* 49, 505
per-, 522, 956
PERACUTE, *adj.* 1074, 522, 956
perceive, *v.* 694, 40
perceptible, *adj.* 251, 859, 440,
   416
perceptive, *adj.* 576
perchance, *adv.* 387
percussion, *n.* 93
PEREMPTORY, *adj.* 827
PERENNIAL, *adj.* 460
perennial, *n.* 460
perfect, *adj.* 328, 35
perfect, *v.* 78, 769
PERFECTION, *n.* 197
perfidious, *adj.* 536
PERFIDY, *n.* 522
PERFORATE, *v.* 163

perforation, *n.* 258, 163
PERFORCE, *adv.* 907
perfumed, *adj.* 34, 811
perfunctory, *adj.* 1098, 629
perhaps, *adv.* 555, 387
peri-, 886
peril, *n.* 84, 888
perilous, *adj.* 362, 837, 552,
   740
perimeter, *n.* 886
period, *n.* 296
PERIPATETIC, *adj.* 1043
Peripatetic, *n.* 1043
periphrasis, *n.* 1053
periscope, *n.* 886
PERISTYLE, *n.* 886
PERJURE, *v.* 323, 995, 522
permanent, *adj.* 835
permeable, *adj.* 841
permeate, *v.* 139
permission, *n.* 478
permit, *v.* 81
PERNICIOUS, *adj.* 786, 857, 866,
   992
perpendicularity, *n.* 1041
perpending, *n.* 868
PERPETUAL, *adj.* 550, 201, 460
perplex, *v.* 161, 185, 926, 946,
   807, 762
perplexed, *adj.* 992
perplexing, *adj.* 179
perplexity, *n.* 556, 966, 997,
   1114
persecute, *v.* 856
persevering, *adj.* 255, 390
persistent, *adj.* 255, 390, 965
person, *n.* 30, 961
personal, *adj.* 713, 347
personality, *n.* 479
perspicacious, *adj.* 576, 956

perspicuous, *adj.* 956
perspire, *v.* 470
persuasion, *n.* 882
persuasive, *adj.* 827
pert, *adj.* 211
pertain, *v.* 911
pertaining, *adj.* 1027, 911
PERTINACIOUS, *adj.* 965, 522,
1049, 1115
pertinence, *n.* 1027
pertinency, *n.* 842
pertinent, *adj.* 1027, 1086, 211,
1056
pertness, *n.* 211
perturb, *v.* 762
perturbable, *adj.* 762
perturbation, *n.* 830
perturbed, *v.* 762
PERUSAL, *n.* 763
peruse, *v.* 763
PERVERSE, *adj.* 1049, 266, 333,
392, 776
perversely, *adv.* 1049
perverseness, *n.* 1049
perversion, *n.* 1049
perversity, *n.* 1049
perversive, *adj.* 1049
pervert, *v.* 823, 1049
perverted, *adj.* 826, 1049
pervertible, *adj.* 1049
PERVIOUS, *adj.* 841, 150
pestilence, *n.* 1102
pestilential, *adj.* 1059
petalism, *n.* 535
petition, *v.* 407
petitioner, *n.* 872
PETRIFY, *v.* 110
petrography, *n.* 110
petrology, *n.* 110
pettish, *adj.* 441

PETTY, *adj.* 331
petulant, *adj.* 441, 1048, 1049,
593
PHILANDER, *v.* 1078
Philander, 1078
philanderer, *n.* 624
philandering, *n.* 624
philanthropist, *n.* 1078
philology, *n.* 1078
philosopher, *n.* 543, 553
philosophy, *n.* 1078
phlegmatic, *adj.* 970
phosphorescent, *adj.* 846
photograph, *n.* 1087
phylactery, *n.* 625
physique, *n.* 462
picture, *n.* 495
picturesque, *adj.* 853
piece, *n.* 756
pierce, *v.* 163
pierceless, *adj.* 494
piercing, *adj.* 761, 222
Piers Plowman, 265
PILASTER, *n.* 726
PILE, *v.* 17
pile, *n.* 843
piled, *adj.* 412
pilfer, *v.* 778, 376
PILFERER, *n.* 376, 778
pilfering, *adj.* 538, 376
pillage, *n.* 270
pillage, *v.* 439, 773, 618
pillaging, *adj.* 967
pillaging, *n.* 967
pillar, *n.* 225
pilot, *n.* 236
pin, *n.* 398, 1092
pinch, *n.* 170, 969
pinnace, *n.* 398
PINNACLE, *n.* 398, 91

pinnate, *adj.* 398
pious, *adj.* 904, 638
piquant, *adj.* 539, 1048
pique, *v.* 449
pique, *n.* 1106
piquing, *adj.* 175
piscator, *n.* 853
PISCATORIAL, *adj.* 853
piscatory, *adj.* 853
piscine, *adj.* 853
PITH, *n.* 1008, 1009
PITHY, *adj.* 1009, 493, 629, 1008
pitiful, *adj.* 438
pitiless, *adj.* 673, 411
pittance, *n.* 512
pity, *n.* 760
pity, *v.* 851
pixie, *n.* 774
placate, *v.* 964, 673
place, *v.* 142, 775, 202
place, *n.* 224, 699, 183
placebo, *n.* 934
placid, *adj.* 762, 788, 390, 1004
PLACIDITY, *n.* 271
plague, *v.* 120
plague, *n.* 1102
plain, *adj.* 534, 834, 859, 278, 988
plainly, *adv.* 628
plaintive, *adj.* 791
plait, *v.* 118
plaited, *adj.* 118, 111
plan, *n.* 149, 46, 594, 987
plan, *v.* 366, 234, 1004
plangent, *adj.* 916
plant, *v.* 109, 206
plaque, *n.* 489
plastic, *adj.* 1104
platform, *n.* 594

platitude, *n.* 960
PLATITUDINOUS, *adj.* 960
plauditory, *adj.* 1040
plausible, *adj.* 700, 1011, 416
play, *v.* 118, 144
plead, *v.* 324, 407
pleading, *n.* 508
pleasant, *adj.* 227, 375
pleasantness, *n.* 570
please, *v.* 612, 271
pleased, *adj.* 1057, 644, 1116
pleases, *v.* 235
pleasing, *adj.* 104, 227, 308, 34, 597, 644
pleasure-lover, *n.* 1036
pleasures, *n.* 570
pleat, *v.* 118
PLEDGE, *v.* 363, 860
pledge, *n.* 796, 363
plenteous, *adj.* 135
plentiful, *adj.* 135
plenty, *n.* 615, 1102
pleonasm, *n.* 1053
PLEONASTIC, *adj.* 1053, 797, 906
PLETHORA, *n.* 1102
PLEXIFORM, *adj.* 559
plexus, *n.* 559
PLIABLE, *adj.* 117, 28, 397, 118, 241
pliant, *adj.* 117, 28, 397, 418, 111
plicate, *adj.* 111
PLIGHT, *v.* 860, 363
plight, *n.* 556
plot, *n.* 149
plot, *v.* 175
plotting, *n.* 175
plowable, *adj.* 922
pluck, *n.* 121
plucked, *adj.* 33

power, *n.* 896, 208, 355, 365, 473, 478
powerful, *adj.* 82, 353, 793, 970
power-house, *n.* 353
PRACTICABLE, *adj.* 484, 290
practical, *adj.* 873, 484
practice, *n.* 4, 873, 1112
PRAGMATIC, *adj.* 873
pragmatical, *adj.* 873
pragmatism, *n.* 873
praise, *v.* 101, 852, 272, 506, 598, 573
pranks, *n.* 809
PRATE, *v.* 633
prattle, *n.* 633, 44
preaching, *n.* 790
PREAMBLE, *n.* 129
PRECARIOUS, *adj.* 362, 958, 837
precariously, *adv.* 362
precariousness, *n.* 362
precaution, *n.* 1054
preceding, *adj.* 835
PRECEPT, *n.* 1054, 402
preceptor, *n.* 1054
precious, *adj.* 278
precipitant, *adj.* 593
precipitate, *adj.* 534, 700, 1028
precipitate, *v.* 801
PRECISE, *adj.* 278, 282, 533, 604, 287, 518
precision, *n.* 814
preclude, *v.* 81, 988
precursor, *n.* 514
PREDATORY, *adj.* 967
predicament, *n.* 556
PREDICATE, *v.* 1063
predicate, *n.* 1063
predict, *v.* 801, 1106, 1063
predictable, *adj.* 967

prediction, *n.* 708, 608, 603
predictions, *n.* 706
predictive, *adj.* 967
predictory, *adj.* 967
PREDILECTION, *n.* 1003
predisposition, *n.* 709, 952
PREDOMINATE, *v.* 597
predominating, *adj.* 315
PREEMINENT, *adj.* 339, 179, 277, 494, 682, 1073
preface, *n.* 129, 720
prefatory, *adj.* 720
preference, *n.* 599, 1003
PREGNANT, *adj.* 714
prejudgment, *n.* 217
PREJUDICE, *n.* 217, 770, 930
PREJUDICE, *v.* 770
prejudiced, *adj.* 930
preliminary, *adj.* 720
prelude, *n.* 129, 720
prelude, *v.* 720
prelusive, *adj.* 720
PRELUSORY, *adj.* 720
preoccupied, *adj.* 924
preparatory, *adj.* 720
prepare, *v.* 245
preponderate, *v.* 597
preposterous, *adj.* 576
prerogative, *n.* 767
presage, *n.* 608
prescribe, *v.* 1020
PRESENCE, *n.* 569, 421, 879
present, *v.* 21, 202, 238, 118
presentiment, *n.* 608
press, *v.* 427
pressing, *adj.* 201
presume, *v.* 47
presumption, *n.* 613
pretend, *v.* 487, 406, 395, 297, 743

pull, *v.* 573
pulley, *n.* 70
PULSATE, *v.* 268, 859
pulsating, *adj.* 859
pulse, *n.* 268
punch, *v.* 163
punch, *n.* 170
punctilios, *n.* 604
PUNCTILIOUS, *adj.* 533, 278,
  604, 1062
punctual, *adj.* 533
puncture, *v.* 533
pungent, *adj.* 539, 761, 885,
  766, 1030
punish, *v.* 723, 480, 802, 787,
  294, 630, 863
punishment, *n.* 147, 467, 541,
  565, 968, 723, 152, 772
PUNITIVE, *adj.* 723
puny, *adj.* 63, 723
pure, *adj.* 386, 789, 385, 594,
  785, 787, 714
purgatory, *n.* 498
PURGE, *v.* 498, 785
purify, *v.* 213, 498, 147
puritan, *n.* 785
PURITY, *n.* 601, 385, 789
PURLOIN, *v.* 778
purloined, *adj.* 778
purloiner, *n.* 376, 778
purloining, *adj.* 538
purple, *adj.* 1061
purpose, *v.* 137
purse, *n.* 812
pursue, *v.* 133
pursy, *adj.* 847
push, *n.* 95
push, *v.* 190, 427
pushing, *adj.* 379
pusillanimity, *n.* 677

pusillanimous, *adj.* 677
putrid, *adj.* 933
puzzle, *v.* 185
puzzled, *adj.* 992
puzzling, *adj.* 1107
pygmean, *adj.* 63
pygmy, *n.* 63

quack, *n.* 820
quacksalver, *n.* 820
quadruple, *adj.* 111
quadruplicate, *adj.* 111
QUAIL, *v.* 383
quailing, *adj.* 389
QUAINT, *adj.* 382, 90, 849, 853
quaking, *adj.* 859
QUANDARY, *n.* 556
quantity, *n.* 768, 756
quarrel, *n.* 753, 443, 776
quarreling, *n.* 583
quarrelsome, *adj.* 1004, 530,
  776
QUARTER, *n.* 760
quashing, *n.* 1079
queer, *adj.* 90, 666, 347
quelling, *n.* 307
QUENCH, *v.* 38, 317
querulous, *adj.* 441
question, *v.* 785
questionable, *adj.* 373, 958,
  1031, 416
questioner, *n.* 507
questioning, *adj.* 1107, 1072
quibble, *v.* 653
quibbling, *adj.* 464
quibbling, *n.* 809
quick, *adj.* 218, 311, 836, 439,
  367, 700, 320
quicken, *v.* 836
quickly, *adv.* 836

quickness, *n.* 790, 836
quick-witted, *adj.* 982
QUIESCENT, *adj.* 788, 511
quiet, *adj.* 105, 367, 788, 390,
    548, 627, 997, 442
quiet, *v.* 221, 607, 500, 423
quiet, *n.* 309
quieting, *adj.* 816
quietness, *n.* 271
quill, *n.* 398
quintessence, *n.* 1008
quit, *v.* 517, 636
QUITTANCE, *n.* 512, 500
quiver, *v.* 268
QUIXOTIC, *adj.* 1101
quiz, *n.* 1107
QUIZZICAL, *adj.* 1107

race, *n.* 850
radiant, *adj.* 725, 1075, 717
radical, *adj.* 136, 850
radicals, *n.* 850
radish, *n.* 850
radix, *n.* 850
rag, *n.* 165
ragamuffin, *n.* 165
rage, *v.* 754, 76
rage, *n.* 309, 479
raid, *n.* 640
rail, *v.* 223
rail, *n.* 343
raise, *v.* 246, 792, 545
raised, *v.* 775
raising, *n.* 481
rally, *v.* 221
rallying, *adj.* 1107
ramble, *v.* 330, 887, 943, 129
rambling, *adj.* 990, 700
ramification, *n.* 850
RAMIFY, *v.* 850

ramose, *adj.* 850
ramp, *n.* 546
RAMPANT, *adj.* 546
rampart, *n.* 58
ramus, *n.* 850
rancid, *adj.* 222, 754
RANCOR, *n.* 693, 337, 391, 764,
    570
RANDOM, *adj.* 472, 953, 387
random, *n.* 472
range, *n.* 751, 355, 626
rank, *n.* 183
rank, *adj.* 222, 754
RANKLE, *v.* 754, 449
rankness, *n.* 754
rapacious, *adj.* 927
rape, *v.* 439
rapid, *adj.* 439, 367
rapidly, *adv.* 836
rapture, *n.* 915
rapturous, *adj.* 816
rare, *adj.* 1112, 1115, 682, 392,
    643, 315
rarefied, *adj.* 1115, 1067
rarefy, *v.* 1067
rascal, *n.* 520, 689
rascality, *n.* 1007
rase, *v.* 689
rash, *adj.* 1068, 593, 130, 1028,
    534, 700, 838
rasher, *n.* 908
RASHNESS, *n.* 130, 1068
rasping, *adj.* 883, 1055
rather, *adv.* 244
ratio, *n.* 1033
RATIOCINATION, *n.* 1033
rational, *adj.* 974
rats, *n.* 716
ratsbane, *n.* 857
raucous, *adj.* 1055

refectory, *n.* 1026
refer, *v.* 785
reference, *n.* 1024
refill, *v.* 615
refine, *v.* 496
refined, *adj.* 493, 548, 227, 791, 278
refinement, *n.* 499
reflect, *v.* 261
reflection, *n.* 868, 469, 1026
reflectiveness, *n.* 468
reform, *v.* 138, 792, 1001
reform, *n.* 642
reformation, *n.* 316
refraction, *n.* 469
REFRACTORY, *adj.* 776, 1065, 965
refraining, *n.* 663
refreshing, *adj.* 692
refreshment, *n.* 1026
REFULGENT, *adj.* 1075, 725, 717
refusal, *n.* 285
refuse, *n.* 94, 865, 627
refuse, *v.* 780, 898, 659, 1081
refutation, *n.* 285
refute, *v.* 659, 1044
regain, *v.* 92
regal, *adj.* 672
regenerate, *v.* 316
REGENERATION, *n.* 316
regent, *n.* 83
regime, *n.* 736
REGIMEN, *n.* 736
REGION, *n.* 83
regional, *adj.* 83
register, *n.* 322
regress, *v.* 215, 799
regret, *v.* 329, 877
regret, *n.* 885
regular, *adj.* 275

regulate, *v.* 991
regulation, *n.* 4
REHABILITATE, *v.* 490
reign, *v.* 277
reimburse, *v.* 935
reinstate, *v.* 490
reiterate, *v.* 229
reject, *v.* 636, 780, 659, 324
rejection, *n.* 285
rejoiced, *adj.* 1057
related, *adj.* 153, 1027, 1086, 371
relationship, *n.* 914
relatives, *n.* 173
relaxing, *adj.* 457
release, *n.* 512, 478
release, *v.* 688, 903, 500
relentless, *adj.* 673, 874
RELEVANCY, *n.* 842
relevant, *adj.* 1086, 842, 1056
RELIABILITY, *n.* 124, 96
reliable, *adj.* 97, 225, 762, 124
reliance, *n.* 870
relief, *n.* 66
RELIEVE, *v.* 349, 65, 317, 327, 575, 607, 842
religious, *adj.* 105, 638, 961, 986
relinquish, *v.* 29, 517, 636
relish, *n.* 696, 188, 393
reluctance, *n.* 932
reluctant, *adj.* 252, 168, 1057
rely, *v.* 35, 124
remain, *v.* 568, 37
remainder, *n.* 568
REMAINS, *n.* 568
remarkable, *adj.* 1073, 416
remediable, *adj.* 989
remedial, *adj.* 1018
REMEDY, *n.* 66, 523, 728, 772

requiring, *n.* 384
requisite, *adj.* 135
requisite, *n.* 384
REQUISITION, *n.* 384
REQUITAL, *n.* 1070, 642, 728, 968
requite, *v.* 935
requiter, *n.* 1070
RESCIND, *v.* 635, 848, 1079, 937
RESCISSION, *n.* 1079
rescuer, *n.* 696
resemblance, *n.* 89, 1106, 469
resembling, *adj.* 275
resentment, *n.* 1106
reserve, *n.* 12, 798, 932
reshape, *v.* 574
residence, *n.* 931
resign, *v.* 517
resignation, *n.* 1034, 134, 580
resigned, *adj.* 39
resigning, *n.* 134
resist, *v.* 325
resistance, *n.* 310, 764
resisting, *adj.* 392, 519, 1077
resolute, *adj.* 72, 965
RESOLVE, *v.* 137
resonant, *adj.* 916
resort, *v.* 326
resort, *n.* 563
resourceful, *adj.* 1099
resources, *n.* 473
respect, *v.* 87
respect, *n.* 870
respectable, *adj.* 718, 196
respectful, *adj.* 788
RESPIRE, *v.* 164
RESPITE, *n.* 650, 61, 254, 1006
RESPLENDENT, *adj.* 725, 1075, 956
responsibility, *n.* 124, 944, 515

RESPONSIVE, *adj.* 648
rest, *n.* 254, 201
restaurant, *n.* 996
resting, *adj.* 431, 788, 201
restitution, *n.* 642, 728, 359
restoration, *n.* 642
restorative, *n.* 523
restorative, *adj.* 1018
restore, *v.* 65, 92, 245, 490. 138, 141
restrain, *v.* 81, 172, 259, 463, 327, 405
restrained, *v.* 105
restraint, *n.* 307, 571, 463, 609
restrict, *v.* 463
restriction, *n.* 609
result, *v.* 133
result, *n.* 896, 649, 1082
results, *n.* 62
resume, *v.* 47
retain, *v.* 368
retainer, *n.* 557, 977
retaining, *n.* 368
retaliate, *v.* 630
retaliation, *n.* 968, 799
retard, *v.* 399
retarded, *adj.* 511
RETENTION, *n.* 368
retentive, *adj.* 1115
reticence, *n.* 798
RETINUE, *n.* 977
retire, *v.* 134, 580, 1079, 383
retirement, *n.* 276, 580
retorsion, *n.* 1070
retort, *n.* 1070, 586
RETRACT, *v.* 329, 848, 667
retreat, *n.* 210, 276, 580, 134, 1034
retreat, *v.* 580, 1079, 383
retrench, *v.* 204

RETRIBUTION, *n.* 968, 1070, 596, 772

retributive, *adj.* 723

RETRIEVE, *v.* 92, 245

retriever, *n.* 92

retro-, 566

retroactive, *adj.* 566

RETROGRADE, *adj.* 566

retrogressive, *adj.* 566

retrospection, *n.* 586

retrospective, *adj.* 566

RETUND, *v.* 1044

return, *v.* 304

return, *n.* 1070

returned, *v.* 563

returning, *adj.* 342

returns, *n.* 62

reveal, *v.* 247, 894, 785, 988

revel, *n.* 631

reveler, *n.* 747

revelry, *n.* 631

revenge, *v.* 630

revenge, *n.* 968, 799

revenue, *n.* 473

revere, *v.* 976

reverence, *v.* 171, 976

reverence, *n.* 767, 788

reverent, *adj.* 105, 788

reverse, *adj.* 252, 1049

reversing, *adj.* 566

review, *n.* 650

revive, *v.* 148

revoke, *v.* 329, 635, 937, 614

revoking, *n.* 1079

revolt, *v.* 921

revolting, *adj.* 104, 205, 921, 180

revolution, *n.* 888

revolutionary, *adj.* 1077

REVOLVE, *v.* 146, 921

revolving, *adj.* 146

REVULSION, *n.* 921

reward, *n.* 9, 968, 1070

rewrite, *v.* 486

Rhodes, 249

rich, *adj.* 777, 711

riches, *n.* 918, 376, 1080

richesse, *n.* 1080

rid, *v.* 988

ridge, *n.* 579

ridicule, *v.* 223, 240, 1031, 189, 1081

ridiculing, *adj.* 1107

ridiculous, *adj.* 378, 1031

rift, *n.* 443, 126

right, *adj.* 278, 332

righteous, *adj.* 1058

righteousness, *n.* 704, 790, 954

right-handed, *adj.* 332

right-handedness, *n.* 417

rightly, *adv.* 417

RIGID, *adj.* 504, 241, 715, 1105, 123, 629

rigidity, *n.* 207, 504

rigidness, *n.* 207

RIGOR, *n.* 207, 504

rigorous, *adj.* 504, 715, 123

rime, *n.* 803

RIMOSE, *adj.* 803

rimy, *adj.* 803

ring, *v.* 606

riot, *v.* 439

riot, *n.* 443

riotous, *adj.* 439, 455

ripen, *v.* 78

RISIBLE, *adj.* 1031, 378

risk, *n.* 84, 888

risky, *adj.* 362, 837

risqué, *adj.* 1031

rivaling, *adj.* 910

rivalry, *n.* 583
rive, *v.* 126
road, *n.* 58
roadstead, *n.* 224
roam, *v.* 129
roaming, *adj.* 727
roar, *n.* 242
roar, *v.* 439
roaring, *adj.* 439
rob, *v.* 618
robber, *n.* 881, 376
robbing, *n.* 967
robe, *n.* 854, 1082
ROBUST, *adj.* 560, 72, 438, 465, 548
rock, *v.* 269
ROCOCO, *adj.* 875
rodent, *n.* 716, 151
rogue, *n.* 520
roguery, *n.* 1007
roguishness, *n.* 1007
roiled, *adj.* 1037, 762, 1088
ROISTERER, *n.* 747
roll, *v.* 269
rollicking, *adj.* 793
romance, *v.* 487
romantic, *adj.* 1101
Rome, 249
romp, *n.* 31
romp, *v.* 144
room, *n.* 699, 530
roomy, *adj.* 157, 54
root, *n.* 558, 850
ROOTED, *adj.* 558
rope, *n.* 54, 545
roseate, *adj.* 131
Rosetta Stone, *n.* 1089
rosy, *adj.* 131
rotate, *v.* 146
rotten, *adj.* 933

rotund, *adj.* 983
rotundity, *n.* 27
rough, *adj.* 288, 411
rough-mannered, *adj.* 641
round, *adj.* 27, 410, 983
roundabout, *adj.* 654
rounded, *adj.* 410
ROUNDNESS, *n.* 27
round robin, *n.* 27
Round Table, 27
rouse, *v.* 295
rousing, *adj.* 181, 527
rout, *v.* 53, 719, 926
routine, *adj.* 1043
roving, *adj.* 727, 990, 1043
row, *n.* 753
RUB, *v.* 103
rubbed, *v.* 103
rubbed, *adj.* 942
rubber, *n.* 103
rubbing, *v.* 103
rubbing, *n.* 310
rubbish, *n.* 94, 865
rubbishy, *adj.* 1085
rubicund, *adj.* 131, 410
ruby, *n.* 131
ruby, *adj.* 131
RUDDY, *adj.* 131, 410
RUDE, *adj.* 64
RUDE, *adj.* 288, 211, 411, 641, 979, 533, 593, 904
rudeness, *n.* 818, 979
RUDIMENT, *n.* 279, 370
RUDIMENTARY, *adj.* 370, 288, 358, 1117, 279
ruffian, *n.* 881
rugged, *adj.* 288
ruin, *v.* 724, 263
ruin, *n.* 691, 1077, 925
ruining, *adj.* 1077

ruinous, *adj.* 786
rule, *n.* 4, 298, 456, 462, 736, 1054
rule, *v.* 597
ruler, *n.* 353, 277, 790
ruminant, *n.* 868
ruminate, *v.* 261, 771, 868
RUMINATION, *n.* 868
rummage, *v.* 719, 868
rumpled, *adj.* 187
running, *n.* 342
rural, *adj.* 115, 747
rush, *n.* 620
rushing, *n.* 472
rustic, *n.* 747, 445
rustic, *adj.* 629, 1099
ruthless, *adj.* 1072, 1049

-s, 9
SACERDOTAL, *adj.* 341, 1089
sack, *v.* 439
sacred, *adj.* 15, 752, 1089, 105, 341
sacredness, *n.* 474
SACRIFICE, *n.* 359, 341
sacrifice, *v.* 856, 359, 213
SACROSANCT, *adj.* 752, 15
sad, *adj.* 791, 433, 876
saddened, *adj.* 909
sadness, *n.* 798
safe, *adj.* 696
SAFFRON, *adj.* 1061
SAGACIOUS, *adj.* 576, 746, 1010
sagaciously, *adv.* 746
sagacity, *n.* 704
sage, *adj.* 576, 543
sailor, *n.* 545
saint, *n.* 474
saintliness, *n.* 474
salacious, *adj.* 1021

salary, *n.* 9, 855
sale, *n.* 50
salient, *adj.* 179
SALLOW, *adj.* 901
salt, *n.* 188
salute, *v.* 388
salve, *n.* 820, 1091
same, *adj.* 371
SAMOVAR, *n.* 985
sample, *n.* 908
Sancho Panza, 1101
sanctified, *v.* 213
SANCTIFY, *v.* 213
sanction, *v.* 40, 81, 565
sanction, *n.* 474
SANCTITY, *n.* 474
sandy, *adj.* 922
sangfroid, *n.* 913
SANGUINARY, *adj.* 913
sanguine, *adj.* 913
sapid, *adj.* 375, 576
sapient, *adj.* 543, 576
sarcastic, *adj.* 766, 979, 1040
sardonic, *adj.* 1040
sash, *n.* 273
Satan, 956
satanic, *adj.* 536
sate, *v.* 139
satiate, *v.* 139
satisfaction, *n.* 642, 728
satisfactory, *adj.* 167, 412
satisfied, *adj.* 39, 644
satisfy, *v.* 317, 612, 139
SATURATE, *v.* 139, 2, 23, 303
saturated, *adj.* 139
Saturn, 1066
Saturnale, *n.* 1066
saturnalia, *n.* 1066
SATURNINE, *adj.* 1066
sauce, *n.* 188

sauciness, *n.* 211
saucy, *adj.* 211, 593
SAUNTER, *v.* 330, 70
savage, *adj.* 643, 1072, 927, 1049
savannah, *n.* 579
SAVANT, *n.* 543
save, *v.* 204, 696
saver, *n.* 696
saving, *adj.* 617, 1010
savior, *n.* 696
SAVOR, *n.* 696, 393
savory, *adj.* 375, 576
sawyer, *n.* 4
say, *v.* 328, 860
scale, *n.* 626
scalp, *v.* 903
scamper, *v.* 190, 1071
scandal, *n.* 845
scandalous, *adj.* 685
scared, *adj.* 1062
scatter, *v.* 773
scavage, *n.* 445
SCAVENGER, *n.* 445
scavenger-crab, *n.* 445
scented, *adj.* 34, 1030
SCHEME, *n.* 149, 987
scheme, *v.* 175
scheming, *n.* 175
SCHISM, *n.* 987, 443, 510
scholar, *n.* 543
scholarly, *adj.* 999
scholarship, *n.* 999
school, *n.* 24
schooner, *n.* 70
science, *n.* 814
scientist, *n.* 543
scintilla, *n.* 744
scissors, *n.* 635
SCOFF, *v.* 223, 88, 240

scold, *v.* 506, 852, 95, 223
SCONE, *n.* 923
scone-cap, *n.* 923
SCOPE, *n.* 355, 751
scorch, *v.* 687
scorched, *adj.* 1052
scorching, *adj.* 485
SCORE, *n.* 1039
scoring, *n.* 1039
scorn, *n.* 281
scorn, *v.* 898
scornful, *adj.* 454, 766, 508
Scott, Sir Walter, 67
scoundrel, *n.* 520
scour, *v.* 103
scourge, *v.* 1035
scourge, *n.* 1102
scrape, *v.* 103, 573
scraps, *n.* 865
scratch, *v.* 689
scratch, *n.* 1039
screen, *v.* 730
scroll, *n.* 886
scruple, *n.* 997, 604
SCRUPULOUS, *adj.* 604, 278, 1058, 533
SCRUTINY, *n.* 281, 177, 763, 821
sculptured, *adj.* 69
scum, *n.* 627
SCURRILOUS, *adj.* 1071, 1046
scurry, *v.* 1071
scuttle, *v.* 1071
seamanship, *n.* 981
SEAR, *v.* 687, 757
search, *v.* 719, 1044
search, *n.* 868
searching, *adj.* 538
seared, *adj.* 1052
season, *v.* 188
season, *n.* 188

sinking, *adj.* 1077
sins, *n.* 448
sinuous, *adj.* 1110, 239
sit, *v.* 105
sitting, *adj.* 627
skepticism, *n.* 453
sketch, *n.* 1092, 1106, 495
sketchy, *adj.* 629
skill, *n.* 143, 265, 230, 208, 192,
    391, 479
skilled, *adj.* 219, 230, 192
skillful, *adj.* 1099
skillfully, *adv.* 417, 126
skimmings, *n.* 627
skin, *v.* 1035
skip, *v.* 330
skipper, *n.* 70
SKITTISH, *adj.* 531
skulk, *v.* 618
skull, *n.* 962
slab, *n.* 489
slack, *adj.* 317, 477
slacken, *v.* 114, 317
SLAKE, *v.* 317, 349, 38
slander, *v.* 598, 893, 935
slander, *n.* 845, 1114, **893**
slang, *n.* 812
slanting, *adj.* 666
slash, *v.* 116
slave, *n.* 557, 214, 838
slavery, *n.* 214
slavish, *adj.* 632
SLEAZY, *adj.* 721
SLEEK, *adj.* 1011, 721
sleeplessness, *n.* 527
sleep-producing, *adj.* 527, 916
sleepy, *adj.* 527
slender, *adj.* 602, 1115
slice, *n.* 908
slick, *adj.* 1011

slide, *v.* 700
slight, *v.* 818, 168
slight, *adj.* 665, 1115, 721, 990,
    745, 319, 1103
slim, *adj.* 1115
slink, *v.* 1011
slip, *v.* 700
slippery, *adj.* 700
slipshod, *adj.* 191
slit, *v.* 116
sliver, *n.* 949
sloop, *n.* 70
slope, *n.* 431, 952
SLOTH, *n.* 448
slouch, *n.* 1083
slovenly, *adj.* 6, 16, 191, 282
slow, *adj.* 984, 266, 317, 360,
    511, 940
slowness, *n.* 448
slow-witted, *adj.* 266, 940
sluggard, *n.* 502
sluggish, *adj.* 433, 970, 317,
    567
sluggishness, *n.* 448
sly, *adj.* 320, 367, 265, 239
slyly, *adv.* 936
slyness, *n.* 499
smack, *n.* 70
small, *adj.* 63, 226, 723
smart, *adj.* 804
smartness, *n.* 804
smell, *n.* 400
smelling, *adj.* 1030, 400
smooth, *adj.* 518, 1011, 1091,
    1116, 493, 700, 715, 721,
    803
smooth, *v.* 1011
smother, *v.* 38
smuggled, *adj.* 216
snack, *n.* 51, 143

stop, *v.* 81, 259, 399, 189, 664, 248, 349

stopping, *adj.* 531

stopping, *n.* 254, 201

store, *n.* 756

store, *v.* 299, 446

stormy, *adj.* 876

story, *n.* 891, 212, 529, 674

stout, *adj.* 72, 82, 847, 548

stow, *v.* 202

STRAGGLE, *v.* 887, 70

straight, *adj.* 19, 209, 971

straighten, *v.* 728, 790

straightforward, *adj.* 272, 19, 594, 654

straight-lined, *adj.* 33

straightway, *adv.* 413

strain, *n.* 395, 95, 108

strain, *v.* 95

strange, *adj.* 90, 347, 387, 392, 442

strangle, *v.* 540

stratagem, *n.* 175, 265, 809

stratum, *n.* 361, 724

stratus, *n.* 724

stray, *adj.* 666, 727

stray, *v.* 887, 999

street, *n.* 58

street-cleaner, *n.* 445

street-sweeper, *n.* 445

strength, *n.* 1008, 759, 669, 365

strengthen, *v.* 237, 664, 1067

strengthening, *adj.* 542

strenuous, *adj.* 970

STRESS, *v.* 95

stress, *n.* 95, 395, 344

stretch, *v.* 667, 395, 1004

strict, *adj.* 504, 533, 715, 1105, 123, 278

stricture, *n.* 152, 978

stride, *n.* 1055

STRIDENT, *adj.* 1055, 883

stridulate, *v.* 883

STRIDULOUS, *adj.* 883, 1055

STRIFE, *n.* 583, 395, 408

striking, *adj.* 179, 442, 448, 745, 748

string, *n.* 54

strip, *v.* 206

stripe, *n.* 889

strive, *v.* 350, 583, 395

striving, *adj.* 291

stroke, *v.* 612

stroll, *v.* 330

strong, *adj.* 72, 82, 225, 560, 1056, 210, 754, 353, 548, 793, 970, 28

stronghold, *n.* 210

strophe, *n.* 108

struggle, *n.* 583

struggle, *v.* 583, 395, 350

strut, *n.* 812

stub, *n.* 266

STUBBORN, *adj.* 266, 333, 392, 519, 776, 965, 1049

studiousness, *n.* 468

stuff, *v.* 1032

stuffy, *adj.* 222

stumble, *v.* 330

stumbling, *adj.* 873

stump, *n.* 266

stupefy, *v.* 946, 110

stupendous, *adj.* 249

stupid, *adj.* 572, 734, 765, 837, 984, 444, 60, 1044, 266, 847, 378, 472

STUPOR, *n.* 60, 433

STURDY, *adj.* 72, 438, 560, 548

style, *n.* 414, 756

summarize, *v.* 769
summary, *n.* 769
summation, *n.* 769
summerhouse, *n.* 1050
summit, *n.* 91, 398, 1094
summon, *v.* 99, 614, 181
SUMPTUOUS, *adj.* 672
sunburnt, *adj.* 1052
SUNDER, *v.* 839, 174
SUNDRY, *adj.* 735, 356
superabundant, *adj.* 1053
SUPERCILIOUS, *adj.* 338, 454,
    979
superficial, *adj.* 665, 990, 700
superfluity, *n.* 1102
superfluous, *adj.* 1053
superior, *adj.* 339, 529, 338,
    454, 243
superiority, *n.* 515
supernatural, *adj.* 263
supersede, *v.* 274
supervene, *v.* 133
supine, *adj.* 431, 591, 724
SUPPLANT, *v.* 274, 86
SUPPLE, *adj.* 397, 28, 117, 111,
    872
supplementary, *adj.* 872
suppliant, *n.* 872
supplicant, *n.* 872
supplicate, *v.* 324, 407, 872
SUPPLICATORY, *adj.* 872
supply, *n.* 756
support, *n.* 225, 842, 855
support, *v.* 233, 729
supportable, *adj.* 167
supposition, *n.* 42, 608
SUPPOSITIOUS, *adj.* 457, 683
supposititious, *adj.* 457
suppository, *n.* 457
suppress, *v.* 405, 894, 38, 664

suppressed, *v.* 405
SUPPRESSION, *n.* 307
SUPREME, *adj.* 243, 277, 339,
    554
sur-, 29
SURCEASE, *n.* 1006, 254
sure, *adj.* 97, 195
surface, *n.* 29
surfeit, *n.* 615
surfeit, *v.* 139
surfeited, *adj.* 318, 615
surge, *n.* 1037
surging, *adj.* 1037
surly, *adj.* 313, 641
surmise, *n.* 42
surmount, *v.* 680
surname, *n.* 685
surpass, *v.* 680, 597, 232
surpassing, *adj.* 339, 682
surprise, *n.* 29
surprise, *v.* 152
surrender, *n.* 1034, 580
SURRENDER, *v.* 29, 56, 517,
    1034, 817
surreptitious, *adj.* 367, 455
surreptitiously, *adv.* 936
surround, *v.* 420, 273, 948
surroundings, *n.* 420, 568, 854,
    578
survey, *n.* 763
survey, *v.* 526, 29
SURVIVE, *v.* 148
SUSPECT, *v.* 87, 36
suspecting, *adj.* 313
suspension, *n.* 1006
suspicious, *adj.* 396, 919, 313
sustain, *v.* 233
sustained, *adj.* 114
SUSTENANCE, *n.* 233, 669
swagger, *n.* 812

tautology, *n.* 1053
tavern, *n.* 996
taw, *n.* 1039
tawdry, *adj.* 1085, 725
teach, *v.* 480
teachable, *adj.* 940
teacher, *n.* 480, 1054, 940, 838
teakettle, *n.* 985
tear, *v.* 165, 787
tease, *v.* 120
teasing, *adj.* 1107, 120
TEDIOUS, *adj.* 194, 944, 513, 999, 346
tediously, *adv.* 746
tedium, *n.* 194, 999
TEEM, *v.* 318
teeming, *adj.* 714
telegram, *n.* 1087
telegraph, *n.* 1087
telephone, *n.* 947
telephony, *n.* 947
tell, *v.* 247
TEMERARIOUS, *adj.* 1068
temerity, *n.* 1068
temper, *n.* 479
temper, *v.* 899, 188
TEMPERAMENT, *n.* 479, 600
temperance, *n.* 663
temperate, *adj.* 619, 485
temperature, *n.* 188
tempering, *adj.* 899
temple, *n.* 398
temporal, *adj.* 815, 567
temporary, *adj.* 835, 994
TEMPORIZE, *v.* 899
tempt, *v.* 544
tenacious, *adj.* 867, 1104, 402, 965, 522, 892, 1115
tenant, *n.* 931
tendency, *n.* 709, 952, 743

tender, *adj.* 549
tender, *v.* 182
tenderness, *n.* 596
TENEBROUS, *adj.* 892
tenement, *n.* 931
TENET, *n.* 402
tense, *v.* 921
TENSION, *n.* 395, 108
tent, *n.* 395, 398
tentative, *adj.* 835
TENUOUS, *adj.* 1115, 1067
TENURE, *n.* 931
TEPID, *adj.* 422, 18
tepidarium, *n.* 422
Terence, 1101
tergal, *adj.* 973
TERGIVERSATION, *n.* 973
tergum, *n.* 973
terminal, *adj.* 156
terminal, *n.* 156
TERMINATION, *n.* 156, 254, 137
terminus, *n.* 156
Terminus, 156
terra, *n.* 286
terra firma, *n.* 286
terrene, *adj.* 286
TERRESTRIAL, *adj.* 286, 815
terrible, *adj.* 701, 1029, 121, 865
terrier, *n.* 286
terrified, *adj.* 819
terrifying, *adj.* 409
territory, *n.* 83
terror, *n.* 408
TERSE, *adj.* 493, 629, 1009
test, *n.* 177, 352, 868
test, *v.* 860
textbook, *n.* 507
textile, *n.* 744
texture, *n.* 744

tip, *n.* 91
tip-cart, *n.* 514
tire, *v.* 513, 255, 114
tired, *adj.* 909, 501
tired, *v.* 114
tireless, *adj.* 255
tiresome, *adj.* 194, 906, 999
tiresomely, *adv.* 746
tiring, *adj.* 346
TITANIC, *adj.* 226, 63, 249
Titanic, 226
Titans, 226
title, *n.* 657, 931, 599
TITTER, *n.* 369, 44
toga, *n.* 127
together, *adv.* 646
TOGGERY, *n.* 127
togs, *n.* 127
toil, *n.* 79
toilsome, *adj.* 944
TOKEN, *n.* 796
TOLERABLE, *adj.* 167
tolerate, *v.* 317
toll, *v.* 606
Tom, 31
tomb, *n.* 140
TOMBOY, *n.* 31
tomcat, 31
tongue, *n.* 1032
tonic, *adj.* 542
top, *n.* 91, 398, 1094
torment, *n.* 159
torment, *v.* 773, 120
tormented, *adj.* 665
tormenting, *adj.* 120
torpid, *adj.* 433
torpor, *n.* 60
TORRID, *adj.* 485, 335
torsion, *n.* 159
tortuous, *adj.* 1110, 239

TORTURE, *n.* 159
total, *adj.* 328, 312
TOUCH, *v.* 235
touch, *n.* 132, 400
touched, *v.* 864
touchstone, *n.* 456
tough, *adj.* 28
toughened, *adj.* 588
tour, *n.* 41
TOURIST, *n.* 41
TOURNAMENT, *n.* 67
tourney, *n.* 67
tousled, *adj.* 187
towline, *n.* 54
town, *n.* 284
TOXIC, *adj.* 542, 857
trace, *n.* 698, 744, 756
tract, *n.* 83
tractable, *adj.* 940
traction, *n.* 329
tractor, *n.* 329
trade, *n.* 737
trader, *n.* 199, 737
trading, *adj.* 605
traduce, *v.* 598
traffic, *n.* 737
TRAFFICKER, *n.* 737, 199
train, *v.* 405, 480
traitor, *n.* 737
tramp, *n.* 727, 477, 800
tranquil, *adj.* 186, 518, 762,
    788
tranquilize, *v.* 221, 423
tranquilizing, *adj.* 390
tranquillity, *n.* 271, 309
transact, *v.* 930
TRANSCEND, *v.* 680
TRANSCRIBE, *v.* 486
transcript, *n.* 46
transept, *n.* 52

unbelief, *n.* 453

unbending, *adj.* 241, 392, 519

unbiased, *adj.* 1013

UNBRIDLED, *adj.* 169, 546

unbroken, *adj.* 902, 1113

unceasing, *adj.* 201, 460, 346

uncertain, *adj.* 362, 827, 958, 701

uncertainty, *n.* 556, 604

unchanged, *adj.* 57

unchecked, *adj.* 169, 546

uncivil, *adj.* 64, 211, 533

uncle, *n.* 1098

unclean, *adj.* 1088

unclothed, *v.* 206

uncomfortable, *adj.* 926

uncommon, *adj.* 1112, 392, 643, 682

uncommunicativeness, *n.* 798

UNCOMPROMISING, *adj.* 333, 930

unconcealed, *adj.* 834

unconcern, *n.* 663

unconcerned, *adj.* 1014, 1013, 334

unconnected, *adj.* 1086

unconquerable, *adj.* 864, 162, 894

UNCONSCIONABLE, *adj.* 1103, 1095

unconscious, *adj.* 436, 1103

uncontrolled, *adj.* 169

uncooperative, *adj.* 1065

UNCOUTH, *adj.* 710, 336

uncover, *v.* 247

uncovered, *adj.* 206

unction, *n.* 1091

UNCTUOUS, *adj.* 1091, 1011

uncultivated, *adj.* 922

uncurbed, *adj.* 169

undaunted, *adj.* 830

underground, *adj.* 682

underlying, *adj.* 682

undermine, *v.* 574

underneath, *adv.* 682

underrate, *v.* 1081

underscore, *v.* 1039

undersized, *adj.* 63

understand, *v.* 919, 237

understanding, *adj.* 196

understood, *adj.* 982, 733, 798

understudy, *n.* 361

undertake, *v.* 47

undervalue, *v.* 941, 1081

undervaluing, *adj.* 675

undetermined, *adj.* 727

undeveloped, *adj.* 370

undisguised, *adj.* 1099

undisturbed, *adj.* 57, 186

undulate, *v.* 702

uneasiness, *n.* 453

uneasy, *adj.* 334

unemotional, *adj.* 970

unemployment, *n.* 293

unequaled, *adj.* 529

unessential, *adj.* 732

unexpected, *adj.* 1112, 442

unexplained, *adj.* 786

UNFAILING, *adj.* 97, 550

unfair, *adj.* 673

UNFALTERING, *adj.* 113, 191

unfathomable, *adj.* 253

UNFAVORABLE, *adj.* 552, 252

unfeeling, *adj.* 588, 765

unfit, *adj.* 651, 581

unfitting, *adj.* 211

UNFLAGGING, *adj.* 114, 255, 390, 113

unflinching, *adj.* 113

unfold, *v.* 118

verdigris, *n.* 639

verdure, *n.* 639

verification, *n.* 465

verifies, *v.* 237

verify, *v.* 237, 195, 1017

verity, *n.* 1017

vernal, *adj.* 731

VERSATILE, *adj.* 488, 564

verse, *n.* 849

versed, *adj.* 230

version, *n.* 488

vertex, *n.* 91

Vespasian, 249

vessel, *n.* 228, 70

vest, *n.* 1082

VESTIGE, *n.* 744, 698, 756

vestment, *n.* 854, 1082

vesture, *n.* 744

veterinarian, *n.* 895

vex, *v.* 449, 513, 120

vexed, *adj.* 441

vexing, *adj.* 120

vibrate, *v.* 268, 702

vibrating, *adj.* 859

vice, *n.* 1069

vicinity, *n.* 83

vicious, *adj.* 1069, 566

VICISSITUDE, *n.* 888

victims, *n.* 806

victual, *n.* 740

victuals, *n.* 233

view, *n.* 495, 763

view, *v.* 490, 771

vigor, *n.* 1008

vigorous, *adj.* 72, 218, 438, 560, 754, 904

vile, *adj.* 647, 783

vilify, *v.* 598, 852, 941, 935

village, *n.* 284, 520

VILLAIN, *n.* 520

villainous, *adj.* 783

villainy, *n.* 1007

vindicate, *v.* 630, 903

violate, *v.* 215, 781, 451, 799

violation, *n.* 469

violence, *n.* 123

violent, *adj.* 643, 686, 1074, 123

virginal, *adj.* 714

viridescent, *adj.* 639

VIRILE, *adj.* 759

virtue, *n.* 385, 601, 704, 759

virtuous, *adj.* 789, 385

VIRULENT, *adj.* 1097, 542, 857, 766

virus, *n.* 1097

viscid, *adj.* 1104, 1116

viscous, *adj.* 867

visible, *adj.* 859, 251, 440

vision, *n.* 779, 1024

visionary, *adj.* 401, 440, 822, 1101, 567

visual, *adj.* 400

vital, *adj.* 740

vitality, *n.* 473

VITIATE, *v.* 1069, 498

VITUPERATE, *v.* 852

vituperation, *n.* 852

vituperative, *adj.* 1071

vivacious, *adj.* 148, 927

vivacity, *n.* 430, 764

vivid, *adj.* 725, 148, 740

viviparous, *adj.* 716

VOGUE, *n.* 414

void, *v.* 635

volatile, *adj.* 531

volatility, *n.* 954

volubility, *n.* 750

voluble, *adj.* 700

voluminous, *adj.* 1015